Multicultural Education

Multicultural Education
Issues and Perspectives

SEVENTH EDITION

Edited by

JAMES A. BANKS
University of Washington, Seattle

CHERRY A. McGEE BANKS
University of Washington, Bothell

WILEY

VICE PRESIDENT AND EXECUTIVE PUBLISHER	Jay O'Callaghan
EXECUTIVE EDITOR	Christopher Johnston
ACQUISITIONS EDITOR	Robert Johnston
PRODUCTION MANAGER	Dorothy Sinclair
SENIOR PRODUCTION EDITOR	Trish McFadden
ASSISTANT EDITOR	Eileen McKeever
MARKETING MANAGER	Danielle Torio
EDITORIAL ASSISTANT	Mariah Maguire-Fong
SENIOR DESIGNER	Madelyn Lesure
SENIOR PHOTO EDITOR	Lisa Gee

This book was set in 10/12 Janson by Laserwords and printed and bound by RRD Crawfordsville. The cover was printed by Phoenix Color Corporation.

This book is printed on acid-free paper. ∞

To order books or for customer service, please call 1-800-CALL WILEY (225-5945).

ISBN 978-0-470-48328-2

Printed in the United States of America

10 9 8 7 6 5 4 3 2

Preface

Both diversity and the recognition of diversity have increased in nations around the world within the last two decades (Banks, 2004, Banks, 2009; Castles, 2009). The near zero population growth in many of the Western nations and Japan and the rapid population growth in the developing nations have created a demographic divide and a demand for immigrants to meet labor needs. The growth of the population of ethnic, racial, linguistic, and religious minorities within the Western nations is also increasing at a much faster rate than are mainstream groups. The percentage of the non-Hispanic White population in the United States is projected to decrease during the 2030s and 2040s and comprise 50 percent of the population in 2042, down from 66 percent in 2008 (U. S. Census Bureau, 2008). Ethnic minorities are projected to increase from one-third of the nation's population in 2006 to 50 percent in 2042 (cited in Roberts, 2008).

The election of Barack Obama as the 44th president of the United States in 2008 is a significant marker of important demographic changes in the United States as well as the promises and challenges of diversity. Obama received significant support from young people, many of whom worked in his election. His support among the college-educated population, Asian Americans, Hispanics, and Jewish Americans was also significant. Obama was supported by 63 percent of Asian, 67 percent of Hispanic, and 77 percent of Jewish voters (Nichols, 2008). Forty-two percent of White voters also voted for Obama, which exceeded the percentage who voted for John Kerry in 2004 (Boynton, 2009). Despite the impressive support he received from many demographic groups, Obama was the victim of veiled racial attacks that tried to depict him as an "Other" who would not be an acceptable American president. Massing (2008) states that the attacks on Obama were "perhaps the most vicious smear campaign ever mounted against an American politician" (p. 26). Consequently, the campaign and election of Obama illustrate both the promises and challenges of diversity in the United States.

Because of worldwide migration and globalization, racial, ethnic, cultural, linguistic, and religious diversity is increasing in nations around the world, including the United States (Banks, 2009; Castles, 2009). Diversity in the United States is becoming increasingly reflected in the nation's schools, colleges, and universities. In 2006, 43 percent of the students enrolled in grades one to 12 in the public schools were students of color (Planty et al., 2008). It is projected that 66 percent of the students in the United States will be African American, Asian, Latino, or Native American by 2020 (Johnson, 2008). In 2007, 20 percent of school-age youth spoke a language other than English at home (Planty et al.). Consequently, a significant percentage of students in U.S. schools are English-language learners. It is projected that by 2030 about 40 percent of the students in the United States will speak English as a second language (Peebles, 2008).

Many of the nation's students are poor. In 2007, 37.3 million people in the United States were living in poverty, including 17.4 percent of students (DeNavas-Walt, Proctor, & Smith, 2008). The gap between the rich and the poor is also widening. In 1980, the top five percent of

Americans owned 15.8 percent of the nation's wealth. The top five percent owned 21.2 percent of U.S. wealth in 2007 (DeNavas-Walt et al.).

These demographic, social, and economic trends have important implications for teaching and learning in today's schools. As U.S. students become increasingly diverse, most of the nation's teachers remain White, middle class, and female. In 2004, approximately 83 percent of the nation's teachers were White and 75 percent were female (Planty et al., 2007). Consequently, a wide gap exists between the racial, cultural, and linguistic characteristics of U.S. students and teachers.

The increasing diversity within U.S. schools provides both opportunities and challenges. Diverse classrooms and schools make it possible to teach students from many different cultures and groups how to live together cooperatively and productively. However, racial prejudice and discrimination are challenges that arise when people from diverse groups interact. Teachers need to acquire the knowledge and skills necessary to maximize the opportunities that diversity offers and to minimize its challenges. Teacher education programs should help teachers attain the knowledge, attitudes, and skills needed to work effectively with students from diverse groups as well as help students from mainstream groups develop cross-cultural knowledge, values, and competencies.

Multicultural Education: Issues and Perspectives, seventh edition, is designed to help current and future educators acquire the concepts, paradigms, and explanations needed to become effective practitioners in culturally, racially, and linguistically diverse classrooms and schools. This seventh edition has been revised to reflect current and emerging research, theories, and practices related to the education of students from both genders and from different cultural, racial, ethnic, and language groups. Exceptionality is part of our concept of diversity because there are exceptional students in each group discussed in this book.

Chapters 8 and 9 are new to this seventh edition. The coauthors added to Chapters 14 and 16 have brought new information, insights, and perspectives to the revisions of these chapters. Chapters 2, 6, 12, 13, and 14 have been significantly shortened, which enabled the authors of these chapters to focus them more tightly as well as to revise them substantially. All of the chapters from the previous edition have been revised to reflect new research, theories, census data, statistics, interpretations, and developments. The Multicultural Resources in the Appendix have been substantially revised and updated. A new section on Sexual and Gender Minorities has been added to the Appendix. The Glossary has been revised to incorporate new census data and developments in the field.

This book consists of six parts. The chapters in Part I discuss how race, gender, class, and exceptionality interact to influence student behavior. Social class and religion and their effects on education are discussed in Part II. Part III describes how educational opportunity differs for female and male students and how schools can foster gender equity. Chapter 8—which is new to this seventh edition—describes how race and gender are interacting rather than separate and discrete variables. The other new chapter to this edition—Chapter 9—examines the role of queer studies and sexual and gender minorities in multicultural education. The issues, problems, and opportunities for educating students of color and students with language differences are discussed in Part IV. Chapter 11—on the colorblind perspective—highlights the importance of race even when it is unacknowledged by teachers. Part V focuses on exceptionality, describing the issues involved in creating equal educational opportunity for students who have disabilities and for those who are gifted. The final part, Part VI, discusses multicultural education as a process of school reform and ways to increase student academic achievement and to work more effectively with parents. The Appendix consists of a list of books for further reading, and the Glossary defines many of the key concepts and terms used throughout the book.

Acknowledgments

We are grateful to a number of colleagues who helped with the preparation of this seventh edition. First, we would like to thank the authors who revised their chapters in a timely and professional way and for incorporating our editorial suggestions. We would also like to thank Annette Henry and Cris Mayo for taking time from busy schedules to write and revise new chapters for this edition. Lisa Albrecht and Mary Kay Thompson Tetreault prepared perceptive prepublication reviews of Chapter 8 that enabled the author to strengthen it. Kevin Kumashiro and Nelson Rodriguez provided insightful comments on Chapter 9 that the author used to improve it. Mollie Blackburn, Kevin Kumashiro, Cris Mayo, Erica Meiners, Nelson Rodriguez, and Mary Kay Thompson Tetreault recommended books for inclusion in the Appendix. We appreciate their recommendations. We would also like to thank Ricardo Garcia of the University of Nebraska, Raynice Jean Sigur of Kennesaw State University, Martha Lue Stewart of the University of Central Florida, and Marva Solomon of Texas State University, for their thoughtful feedback on the sixth edition.

We thank Dennis Rudnick, Kosta Kyriacopoulos, Yuhshi Lee, and Adebowale Adekile—research assistants in the Center for Multicultural Education at the Univeristy of Washington—for helping to update the statistics in this edition and for their work on the chapters to make them consistent with APA style requirements. We used a modified APA style in the previous editions of this book. In this edition, the style was changed to make it completely consistent with APA.

James A. Banks and Cherry A. McGee Banks

References

Banks, J. A. (Ed.). (2004). *Diversity and citizenship education: Global perspectives*. San Francisco: Jossey-Bass.

Banks, J. A. (Ed.). (2009). *The Routledge international companion to multicultural education*. New York and London: Routledge.

Boynton, R. S. (2009, January 18). Demographics and destiny. *New York Times Book Review*, 11.

Castles, S. (2009). World population movements, diversity, and education. In J. A. Banks (Ed.), *The Routledge international companion to multicultural* education (pp. 49–61). New York and London: Routledge.

DeNavas-Walt, C., Proctor, B. D., & Smith, J.C. (2008). *U.S. Census Bureau, current population reports: Income, poverty, and health insurance coverage in the United States: 2007*. Washington, DC: U.S. Government Printing Office. Retrieved January 8, 2009, from http://www.census.gov/prod/2008pubs/p60-235.pdf

Johnson, C. (2008). Meeting challenges in US education: Striving for success in a diverse society. In W. Guofang (Ed.), *The education of diverse student populations: A global perspective* (pp. 79–95). London: Springer.

Massing, M. (2008, December 18). Obama: In the divided heartland. *New York Review of Books, 55*(20), 26–30.

Nichols, J. (2008, November 5). Barack Obama's many majorities. *Nation*. Retrieved January 7, 2009, from http://www.thenation.com/blogs/thebeat/380552/barack_obama_s_many_majorities

Peebles, J. (2008). *The identification, assessment, and education process of special education limited English proficiency students. ESL Globe* [Online]. Retrieved January 12, 2009, from http://faculty.chass.ncsu .edu/swisher/VOL%205%20NO%202%20SPRING%202008/issue_peebles.html

Planty, M., Hussar, W., Snyder, T., Provasnik, S., Kena, G., Dinkes, R., et al. (2008). *The condition of education 2008* (NCES 2008-031). Washington, DC: National Center for Education Statistics. Retrieved January 8, 2009, from http://nces.ed.gov/pubs2008/2008031.pdf

Planty, M., Provasnik, S., Hussar, W., Snyder, T., Kena, G., Dinkes, R., Hampden-Thompson, G., et al. (2007). *The condition of education 2007* (NCES 2007-064). Washington, DC: National Center for Education Statistics. Retrieved January 8, 2009, from http://nces.ed.gov/pubs2007/2007064.pdf

Roberts, S. (2008, August 14). A generation away, minorities may become the majority in U.S. *New York Times*, A1, A18.

U.S. Census Bureau. (2008). *An older and more diverse nation by midcentury*. Retrieved October 20, 2008, from http://www.census.gov/Press-Release/www/releases/archives/population/012496.html

Contents

*A key goal of
multicultural education
is to change schools so
that all students will
have an equal
opportunity to learn.*

Issues and Concepts

The three chapters in Part I define the major concepts and issues in multicultural education, describe the diverse meanings of culture, and describe the ways in which such variables as race, class, gender, and exceptionality influence student behavior. Various aspects and definitions of culture are discussed. Culture is conceptualized as a dynamic and complex process of construction; its invisible and implicit characteristics are emphasized. The problems that result when culture is essentialized are described.

Multicultural education is an idea, an educational reform movement, and a process whose major goal is to change the structure of educational institutions so that male and female students, exceptional students, and students who are members of diverse racial, ethnic, language, and cultural groups will have an equal chance to achieve academically in school. It is necessary to conceptualize the school as a social system in order to implement multicultural education successfully. Each major variable in the school, such as—its culture, its power relationships, the curriculum and materials, and the attitudes and beliefs of the staff—must be changed in ways that will allow the school to promote educational equality for students from diverse groups.

To transform the schools, educators must be knowledgeable about the influence of particular groups on student behavior. The chapters in this part of the book describe the nature of culture and groups in the United States as well as the ways in which they interact to influence student behavior.

CHAPTER 1

Multicultural Education:
Characteristics and Goals

James A. Banks

THE NATURE OF MULTICULTURAL EDUCATION

Multicultural education is at least three things: an idea or concept, an educational reform movement, and a process. Multicultural education incorporates the idea that all students—regardless of their gender, social class, and ethnic, racial, or cultural characteristics—should have an equal opportunity to learn in school. Another important idea in multicultural education is that some students, because of these characteristics, have a better chance to learn in schools as they are currently structured than do students who belong to other groups or who have different cultural characteristics.

Some institutional characteristics of schools systematically deny some groups of students equal educational opportunities. For example, in the early grades, girls and boys achieve equally in mathematics and science. However, the achievement test scores of girls fall considerably behind those of boys as children progress through the grades (Clewell, 2002; Francis, 2000). Girls are less likely than boys to participate in class discussions and to be encouraged by teachers to participate. Girls are more likely than boys to be silent in the classroom. However, not all school practices favor males. As Sadker and Zittleman point out in Chapter 6, boys are more likely to be disciplined than are girls, even when their behavior does not differ from that of girls. They are also more likely than girls to be classified as learning disabled (Donovan & Cross, 2002). Males of color, especially African American males, experience a highly disproportionate rate of disciplinary actions and suspensions in school. Some scholars, such as Noguera (2008), have described the serious problems that African American males experience in school and in the wider society.

In the early grades, the academic achievement of students of color such as African Americans, Latinos, and American Indians is close to parity with the achievement of White mainstream students (Steele, 2003). However, the longer these students of color remain in school, the more their achievement lags behind that of White mainstream students. Social-class status is also strongly related to academic achievement. Persell, in Chapter 4, describes how educational opportunities are much greater for middle- and upper-income students than for low-income students. Knapp and Woolverton (2004), as well as Oakes, Joseph, and Muir (2004), describe the powerful ways in which social class influences students' opportunities to learn.

Exceptional students, whether they are physically or mentally disabled or gifted and talented, often find that they do not experience equal educational opportunities in the schools. The chapters in Part V describe the problems that such exceptional students experience in schools and suggest ways that teachers and other educators can increase their chances for educational success.

Multicultural education is also a reform movement that is trying to change the schools and other educational institutions so that students from all social-class, gender, racial, language, and cultural groups will have an equal opportunity to learn. Multicultural education involves changes in the total school or educational environment; it is not limited to curricular changes (Banks, 2009; Banks & Banks, 2004). The variables in the school environment that multicultural education tries to transform are discussed later in this chapter and illustrated in Figure 1.5. Multicultural education is also a process whose goals will never be fully realized.

Educational equality, like liberty and justice, is an ideal toward which human beings work but never fully attain. Racism, sexism, and discrimination against people with disabilities will exist to some extent no matter how hard we work to eliminate these problems. When prejudice and discrimination are reduced toward one group, they are usually directed toward another group or take new forms. Whenever groups are identified and labeled, categorization occurs. When categorization occurs, members of in-groups favor in-group members and discriminate against out-groups (Stephan, 1999). This process can occur without groups having a history of conflict, animosity, or competition, and without their having physical differences or any other kind of important difference. Social psychologists call this process *social identity theory* or the *minimal group paradigm* (Rothbart & John, 1993). Because the goals of multicultural education can never be fully attained, we should work continuously to increase educational equality for all students. Multicultural education must be viewed as an ongoing process, not as something that we "do" and thereby solve the problems that are the targets of multicultural educational reform (Banks, 2006).

HIGH-STAKES TESTING: A CHALLENGE FOR SOCIAL JUSTICE

The No Child Left Behind (NCLB) Act is being widely interpreted and implemented as a testing and assessment initiative. The emphasis on testing, standards, and accountability that is mandated in most states compels many teachers to focus on narrow and basic skills in reading, writing, and math (Sleeter, 2005). In too many classrooms, testing and test preparation are replacing teaching and learning. Research by Amrein and Berliner (2002) indicates that the emphasis on testing and accountability is having detrimental effects on student learning.

Because of the ways in which accountability is being conceptualized and implemented, the professional role of teachers is being fractured and minimized. However, some writers and researchers, such as Roderick, Jacob, and Bryk (2002), have provided evidence that the focus on the underachievement of targeted groups of students that is required by the NCLB Act has in some cases resulted in higher achievement among these students.

The national focus on basic skills and testing is diverting attention from the broad liberal education that students need to live and function effectively in a multicultural nation and world. It is essential that all students acquire basic literacy and numeracy skills. However, students also need the knowledge, skills, and values that will enable them to live, interact, and make decisions with fellow citizens from different racial, ethnic, cultural, language, and religious groups.

The schools need to teach about social justice issues in addition to basic skills. Teaching for social justice is very important because of the crises that the United States and the world face. An education that is narrowly defined as academic achievement and testing will not prepare students to become effective citizens who are committed to social justice. We should educate students to be reflective, moral, caring, and active citizens in a troubled world (Banks, 2008). The world's greatest problems do not result from people being unable to read and write. They result from people in the world—from different cultures, races, religions, and nations—being unable to get along and to work together to solve the world's problems, such as global warming, the HIV/AIDS epidemic, poverty, racism, sexism, terrorism, international conflict, and war. Examples are the conflicts between the Western and Arab nations, North Korea and its neighbors, and Israel and Palestine.

MULTICULTURAL EDUCATION: AN INTERNATIONAL REFORM MOVEMENT

Since World War II, many immigrants and groups have settled in the United Kingdom and in nations on the European continent, including France, the Netherlands, Germany, Sweden, and Switzerland (Banks, 2008, 2009). Some of these immigrants, such as the Asians and West Indians in England and the North Africans and Indochinese in France, have come from former colonies. Many Southern and Eastern European immigrants have settled in Western and Northern European nations in search of upward social mobility and other opportunities. Groups such as Italians, Greeks, and Turks have migrated to Northern and Western European nations in large numbers. Ethnic and immigrant populations have also increased significantly in Australia and Canada since World War II (Inglis, 2009; Joshee, 2009).

Most of the immigrant and ethnic groups in Europe, Australia, and Canada face problems similar to those experienced by ethnic groups in the United States (Banks, 2009). Groups such as the Jamaicans in England, the Algerians in France, and the Aborigines in Australia experience achievement problems in the schools and prejudice and discrimination in both the schools and society at large. These groups also experience problems attaining full citizenship rights and recognition in their nation-states (Luchtenberg, 2009).

The United Kingdom, various nations on the European continent, Australia, and Canada have implemented a variety of programs to increase the achievement of ethnic and immigrant students and to help students and teachers develop more positive attitudes toward racial, cultural, ethnic, and language diversity (Banks, 2008, 2009).

THE HISTORICAL DEVELOPMENT OF MULTICULTURAL EDUCATION

Multicultural education grew out of the ferment of the Civil Rights Movement of the 1960s. During this decade, African Americans embarked on a quest for their rights that was unprecedented in the United States. A major goal of the Civil Rights Movement of the 1960s was to eliminate discrimination in public accommodations, housing, employment, and education. The consequences of the Civil Rights Movement had a significant influence on educational institutions as ethnic groups—first African Americans and then other groups—demanded that the schools and other educational institutions reform curricula to reflect their experiences, histories, cultures, and perspectives. Ethnic groups also demanded that the schools hire more Black and Brown teachers and administrators so that their children would have more successful role models. Ethnic groups pushed for community control of schools in their neighborhoods and for the revision of textbooks to make them reflect the diversity of peoples in the United States.

The first responses of schools and educators to the ethnic movements of the 1960s were hurried (Banks, 2006). Courses and programs were developed without the thought and careful planning needed to make them educationally sound or to institutionalize them within the educational system. Holidays and other special days, ethnic celebrations, and courses that focused on one ethnic group were the dominant characteristics of school reforms related to ethnic and cultural diversity during the 1960s and early 1970s. Grant and Sleeter, in Chapter 3, call this approach "single-group studies." The ethnic studies courses developed and implemented during this period were usually electives and were taken primarily by students who were members of the group that was the subject of the course.

The visible success of the Civil Rights Movement, plus growing rage and a liberal national atmosphere, stimulated other marginalized groups to take actions to eliminate discrimination against them and to demand that the educational system respond to their needs, aspirations, cultures, and histories. The women's rights movement emerged as one of the most significant social reform movements of the 20th century (Schmitz, Butler, Rosenfelt, & Guy-Sheftal, 2004). During the 1960s and 1970s, discrimination against women in employment, income, and education was widespread and often blatant. The women's rights movement articulated and publicized how discrimination and institutionalized sexism limited the opportunities of women and adversely affected the nation. The leaders of this movement, such as Betty Friedan and Gloria Steinem, demanded that political, social, economic, and educational institutions act to eliminate sex discrimination and to provide opportunities for women to actualize their talents and realize their ambitions. Major goals of the women's rights movement included offering equal pay for equal work, eliminating laws that discriminated against women and made them second-class citizens, hiring more women in leadership positions, and increasing participation of men in household work and child rearing.

When *feminists* (people who work for the political, social, and economic equality of the sexes) looked at educational institutions, they noted problems similar to those identified by ethnic groups of color. Textbooks and curricula were dominated by men; women were largely invisible. Feminists pointed out that history textbooks were dominated by political and military history—areas in which men had been the main participants (Trecker, 1973). Social and family history and the history of labor and of ordinary people were largely ignored. Feminists pushed for the revision of textbooks to include more history about the important roles of women in the development of the nation and the world. They also demanded that more women be hired for administrative positions in the schools. Although most teachers in the elementary schools were women, most administrators were men.

Other marginalized groups, stimulated by the social ferment and the quest for human rights during the 1970s, articulated their grievances and demanded that institutions be reformed so they would face less discrimination and acquire more human rights. People with disabilities, senior citizens, and gays and lesbians formed groups that organized politically during this period and made significant inroads in changing institutions and laws. Advocates for citizens with disabilities attained significant legal victories during the 1970s. The Education for All Handicapped Children Act of 1975 (P.L. 94–142)—which required that students with disabilities be educated in the least restricted environment and institutionalized the word *mainstreaming* in education—was perhaps the most significant legal victory of the movement for the rights of students with disabilities in education (see Chapters 13 and 14).

HOW MULTICULTURAL EDUCATION DEVELOPED

Multicultural education emerged from the diverse courses, programs, and practices that educational institutions devised to respond to the demands, needs, and aspirations of the various groups. Consequently, as Grant and Sleeter point out in Chapter 3, multicultural education in actual practice is not one identifiable course or educational program. Rather, practicing educators use the term *multicultural education* to describe a wide variety of programs and practices related to educational equity, women, ethnic groups, language minorities, low-income groups, and people with disabilities. In one school district, multicultural education may mean a curriculum that incorporates the experiences of ethnic groups of color; in another, a program may include the experiences of both ethnic groups and women. In a third school district, this term may be used the way it is by me and by other authors, such as Nieto and Bode (2008) and Sleeter and Grant (2007); that is, to mean a total school reform effort designed to increase educational equity for a range of cultural, ethnic, and economic groups. This broader and more comprehensive notion of multicultural education is discussed in the last part of this chapter. It differs from the limited concept of multicultural education in which it is viewed as curriculum reform.

THE NATURE OF CULTURE IN THE UNITED STATES

The United States, like other Western nation-states such as the United Kingdom, Australia, and Canada, is a multicultural society. The United States consists of a shared core culture as well as many subcultures. In this book, we call the larger shared core culture the *macroculture;* the smaller cultures, which are a part of the core culture, are called *microcultures*. It is important to distinguish the macroculture from the various microcultures because the values, norms, and characteristics of the mainstream (macroculture) are frequently mediated by, as well as interpreted and expressed differently within, various microcultures. These differences often lead to cultural misunderstandings, conflicts, and institutionalized discrimination.

Students who are members of certain cultural, religious, and ethnic groups are sometimes socialized to act and think in certain ways at home but differently at school (Lee, 2006). In her study of African American students and families in Trackton, Heath (1983) found that the pattern of language use in school was very different from the pattern used at home. At home, most of the children's interaction with adults consisted of imperatives or commands. At school, questions were the dominant form of interactions between teachers and students. A challenge that multicultural education faces is how to help students from diverse groups mediate between their home and community cultures and the school culture. Students should acquire the knowledge, attitudes, and skills needed to function effectively in each cultural setting. They should also be competent to function within and across other microcultures in their society, within the national macroculture, and within the world community (Banks, 2004).

The Meaning of Culture

Bullivant (1993) defines *culture* as a group's program for survival in and adaptation to its environment. The cultural program consists of knowledge, concepts, and values shared by group members through systems of communication. Culture also consists of the shared beliefs, symbols, and interpretations within a human group. Most social scientists today view culture as consisting primarily of the symbolic, ideational, and intangible aspects of human societies. The essence of a culture is not its artifacts, tools, or other tangible cultural elements but how the members of the group interpret, use, and perceive them. It is the values, symbols, interpretations, and perspectives that distinguish one people from another in modernized societies; it is not material objects and other tangible aspects of human societies (Kuper, 1999). People in a culture usually interpret the meanings of symbols, artifacts, and behaviors in the same or in similar ways.

Identification and Description of the U.S. Core Culture

The United States, like other nation-states, has a shared set of values, ideations, and symbols that constitute the core or overarching culture. This culture is shared to some extent by all of the diverse cultural and ethnic groups that make up the nation-state. It is difficult to identify and describe the overarching culture in the United States because it is such a diverse and complex nation. It is easier to identify the core culture within an isolated premodern society, such as the Maoris before the Europeans came to New Zealand, than within highly pluralistic, modernized societies such as the United States, Canada, and Australia (Penetito, 2009).

When trying to identify the distinguishing characteristics of U.S. culture, one should realize that the political institutions in the United States, which reflect some of the nation's core values, were heavily influenced by the British. U.S. political ideals and institutions were also influenced by Native American political institutions and practices, especially those related to making group decisions, such as in the League of the Iroquois (Weatherford, 1988).

Equality

A key component in the U.S. core culture is the idea, expressed in the Declaration of Independence in 1776, that "all men are created equal, that they are endowed by their Creator with certain unalienable rights, that among these are life, liberty, and the pursuit of happiness." When this idea was expressed by the nation's founding fathers in 1776, it was considered radical. A common belief in the 18th century was that human beings were not born with equal rights—that some people had few rights and others, such as kings, had divine rights given by God. When considering the idea that "all men are created equal" is a key component of U.S. culture, one should remember to distinguish between a nation's ideals and its actual practices as well as between the meaning of the idea when it was expressed in 1776 and its meaning today. When the nation's founding fathers expressed this idea in 1776, their conception of men was limited to White males who owned property (Foner, 1998). White men without property, White women, and all African Americans and Indians were not included in their notion of people who were equal or who had "certain unalienable rights."

Although the idea of equality expressed by the founding fathers in 1776 had a very limited meaning at that time, it has proven to be a powerful and important idea in the quest for human rights in the United States. Throughout the nation's history since 1776, marginalized and excluded groups such as women, African Americans, Native Americans, and other cultural and ethnic groups have used this idea to justify and defend the extension of human rights to them and to end institutional discrimination, such as sexism, racism, and discrimination against people with disabilities (Branch, 2006). As a result, human rights have gradually been extended to various groups throughout U.S. history. The extension of these rights has been neither constant nor linear. Rather, periods of the extension of rights have often been followed by periods of retrenchment and conservatism. Schlesinger (1986) calls these patterns "cycles of American history." The United States is still a long way from realizing the ideals expressed in the Declaration of Independence in 1776. However, these ideals remain an important part of U.S. culture and are still used by marginalized groups to justify their struggles for human rights and equality.

Individualism and Individual Opportunity

Two other important ideas in the common overarching U.S. culture are individualism and individual social mobility (Stewart & Bennett, 1991). Individualism as an ideal is extreme in the U.S. core culture. Individual success is more important than commitment to family, community, and nation-state. An individual is expected to achieve success solely by his or her own efforts. Many people in the United States believe that a person can go from rags to riches within a generation and that every American-born boy can, but not necessarily will, become president. Individuals are expected to achieve success by hard work and to pull themselves up by their bootstraps. This idea was epitomized by fictional characters such as Ragged Dick, one of the heroes created by the popular writer Horatio Alger. Ragged Dick attained success by valiantly overcoming poverty and adversity. A related belief is that if a person does not succeed, it is because of the person's own shortcomings, such as being lazy or unambitious; failure is consequently the person's own fault. These beliefs are taught in the schools with success stories and myths about such U.S. heroes as George Washington, Thomas Jefferson, and Abraham Lincoln.

The beliefs about individualism in U.S. culture are related to the Protestant work ethic. This is the belief that hard work by the individual is morally good and that laziness is sinful. This belief is a legacy of the British Puritan settlers in colonial New England. It has had a powerful and significant influence on U.S. culture.

The belief in individual opportunity has proven tenacious in U.S. society. It remains strong in American culture despite the fact that individuals' chances for upward social, economic, and educational mobility in the United States are highly related to the social-class, ethnic, gender, and other ascribed groups to which they belong (Knapp & Woolverton, 2004). The findings of social science research, as well as the chapters in this book, document the extent of social-class stratification in the United States and the ways in which people's opportunities in life are strongly influenced by the groups to which they belong (Willis, 1977), yet the belief in individual opportunity remains strong in the United States.

Individualism and Groupism

Although the groups to which people belong have a major influence on their life chances in the United States, Americans—particularly those in the mainstream—are highly individualistic in their value orientations and behaviors. The nuclear family reinforces individualism in U.S. culture. One result of the strong individualism is that married children usually expect their older parents to live independently or in homes for senior citizens rather than with them. The strong individualism in U.S. culture contrasts sharply with the groupism and group commitment found in Asian nations, such as China and Japan (Butterfield, 1982; Reischauer, 1981). Individualism is viewed rather negatively in these societies. One is expected to be committed first to the family and group and then to oneself. Some U.S. social scientists, such as Lasch (1978) and Bellah, Madsen, Sullivan, Swidler, and Tipton (1985), lament the extent of individualism in U.S. society. They believe it is harmful to the common national culture. Some observers believe that groupism is too strong in China and Japan and that individualism should be more valued in those nations. Perhaps modernized, pluralistic nation-states can best benefit from a balance between individualism and groupism, with neither characteristic dominating.

Expansionism and Manifest Destiny

Other overarching U.S. values that social scientists have identified include the desire to conquer or exploit the natural environment, the focus on materialism and consumption, and the belief in the nation's inherent superiority. These beliefs justified Manifest Destiny and U.S. expansion to the West and into other nations and the annexation of one-third of Mexico's territory in 1848. These observations, which reveal the less positive side of U.S. national values, have been developed by social scientists interested in understanding the complex nature of U.S. society (Appleby, Hunt, & Jacob, 1994).

In his discussion of the nature of values in U.S. society, Myrdal (1944/1962) contends that a major ethical inconsistency exists in U.S. society. He calls this inconsistency "the American dilemma." He states that American creed values, such as equality and human dignity, exist in U.S. society as ideals. However, they exist alongside the institutionalized discriminatory treatment of African Americans and other ethnic and cultural groups in U.S. society. This variance creates a dilemma in the American mind because Americans try to reconcile their democratic ideals with their treatment of marginalized groups. Myrdal states that this dilemma has been an important factor that has enabled ethnic groups to fight discrimination effectively. In their efforts to resolve their dilemma when the inconsistencies between their ideals and actions are pointed out to them by human rights advocates, Americans, according to Myrdal, often support the elimination of practices that are inconsistent with their democratic ideals or the American creed. Some writers have refuted Myrdal's hypothesis and contend that most individuals in the United States do not experience such a dilemma (Ellison, 1995).

Microcultures in the United States

A nation as culturally diverse as the United States consists of a common overarching culture as well as a series of microcultures (see Figure 1.1). These microcultures share most of the core values of the nation-state, but these values are often mediated by the various microcultures and are interpreted differently within them. Microcultures sometimes have values that are somewhat alien to the national core culture. Also, some of the core national values and behaviors may seem somewhat alien in certain microcultures or may take different forms.

The strong belief in individuality and individualism that exists within the national macroculture is often much less endorsed by some ethnic communities and is somewhat alien within them. African Americans and Latinos who have not experienced high levels of cultural assimilation into the mainstream culture are much more group oriented than are mainstream Americans.

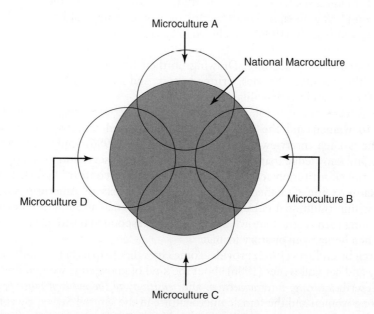

Figure 1.1   Microcultures and the National Macroculture

The shaded area represents the national macroculture. A, B, C, and D represent microcultures that consist of unique institutions, values, and cultural elements that are nonuniversalized and are shared primarily by members of specific cultural groups. A major goal of the school should be to help students acquire the knowledge, skills, and attitudes needed to function effectively within the national macroculture, their own microcultures, and within and across other microcultures.

Source: James A. Banks. (2006) *Cultural Diversity and Education: Foundations, Curriculum and Teaching,* 5th ed. (Boston: Allyn & Bacon), p. 73. Used with permission of the author.

Schools in the United States are highly individualistic in their learning and teaching styles, evaluation procedures, and norms. Many students, particularly African Americans, Latinos, and Native Americans, are group oriented (Irvine & York, 2001; Lee, 2006). These students experience problems in the school's highly individualistic learning environment. Teachers can enhance the learning opportunities of these students, who are also called *field dependent* or *field sensitive*, by using cooperative teaching strategies that have been developed and field-tested by researchers such as Slavin (2001) and Cohen and Lotan (2004).

Some theories and research indicate that female students may have preferred ways of knowing, thinking, and learning that differ to some extent from those most often preferred by males (Goldberger, Tarule, Clinchy, & Belenky, 1996; Halpern, 1986; Taylor, Gilligan, & Sullivan, 1995). Maher (1987) describes the dominant inquiry model used in social science as male constructed and dominated. She contends that the model strives for objectivity: "Personal feelings, biases, and prejudices are considered inevitable limitations" (p. 186). Feminist pedagogy is based on different assumptions about the nature of knowledge and results in a different teaching method. According to Maher and Tetreault (1994), feminist pedagogy enhances the learning of females and deepens the insight of males. In Chapter 7, Tetreault describes feminist pedagogy techniques she uses to motivate students and to enhance their understandings.

After completing a major research study on women's ways of knowing, Belenky, Clinchy, Goldberger, and Tarule (1986) concluded that conceptions of knowledge and truth in the core culture and in educational institutions "have been shaped throughout history by the male-dominated majority culture. Drawing on their own perspectives and visions, men have constructed the prevailing theories, written history, and set values that have become the guiding principles for men and women alike" (p. 5).

These researchers also found an inconsistency between the kind of knowledge most appealing to women and the kind that was emphasized in most educational institutions. Most of the women interviewed in the Belenky et al. (1986) study considered personalized knowledge and knowledge that resulted from first-hand observation most appealing. However, most educational institutions emphasize abstract, "out-of-context" knowledge (Belenky et al., p. 200). Ramírez and Castañeda (1974) found that Mexican American students who were socialized within traditional cultures also considered personalized and humanized knowledge more appealing than abstract knowledge. They also responded positively to knowledge that was presented in a humanized or story format.

Research by Gilligan (1982) provides some clues that help us better understand the findings by Belenky and her colleagues (1986) about the kind of knowledge women find most appealing. Gilligan describes *caring, interconnection,* and *sensitivity to the needs of other people* as dominant values among women and the female microculture in the United States. By contrast, she found that the values of men were more characterized by *separation* and *individualism*.

A major goal of multicultural education is to change teaching and learning approaches so that students of both genders and from diverse cultural, ethnic, and language groups will have equal opportunities to learn in educational institutions. This goal suggests that major changes ought to be made in the ways that educational programs are conceptualized, organized, and taught. Educational approaches need to be transformed.

In her research on identifying and labeling students with mental retardation, Mercer (1973) found that a disproportionate number of African American and Mexican American students were labeled mentally retarded because the testing procedures used in intelligence tests "reflect the abilities and skills valued by the American core culture" (p. 32), which Mercer describes as predominantly White, Anglo-Saxon, and middle and upper class. She also points out that measures of general intelligence consist primarily of items related to verbal skills and knowledge. Most African American and Latino students are socialized within microcultures that differ in significant ways from the U.S. core culture. These students often have not had an equal opportunity to learn the knowledge and skills that are measured in mental ability tests. Consequently, a disproportionate number of African American and Latino students are labeled mentally retarded and are placed in classes for slow learners (Donovan & Cross, 2002). Mental retardation, as Mercer points out, is a socially determined status. When students are placed in classes for the mentally retarded, the self-fulfilling prophecy develops. Students begin to act and think as though they are mentally retarded.

Groups and Group Identification

Thus far, this chapter has discussed the various microcultures that make up U.S. society. Individuals learn the values, symbols, and other components of their culture from their social group. The group is the social system that carries a culture. People belong to and live in social groups (Bullivant, 1993). A group is a collectivity of persons who share an identity, a feeling of unity. A group is also a social system that has a social structure of interrelated roles (Theodorson & Theodorson, 1969). The group's program for survival, values, ideations, and shared symbols constitutes its culture (Kuper, 1999).

The study of groups is the major focus in sociology. Sociologists believe that the group has a strong influence on the behavior of individuals, that behavior is shaped by group norms, and that the group equips individuals with the behavior patterns needed to adapt to their physical, social, and metaphysical environments. Sociologists also assume that groups have independent characteristics; they are more than aggregates of individuals. Groups possess a continuity that transcends the lives of individuals.

Sociologists also assume that knowledge about groups to which an individual belongs provides important clues to and explanations for the individual's behavior. Goodman and Marx (1982) write, "Such factors as shared religion, nationality, age, sex, marital status, and education have proved to be important determinants of what people believe, feel, and do" (p. 7). Although membership in a gender, racial, ethnic, social-class, or religious group can provide us with important clues about individuals' behavior, it cannot enable us to predict behavior. Knowing one's group affiliation can enable us to state that a certain type of behavior is probable. Membership in a particular group does not determine behavior but makes certain types of behavior more probable.

There are several important reasons that knowledge of group characteristics and modalities can enable us to predict the probability of an individual's behavior but not the precise behavior. This is, in part, because each individual belongs to several groups at the same time (see Figure 1.2). An individual may be White, Catholic, female, and middle class, all at the same time. That individual might have a strong identification with one of these groups and a very weak or almost nonexistent identification with another. A person can be a member of a particular group, such as the Catholic Church, and have a weak identification with the group and a weak commitment to the tenets of the Catholic faith. Religious identification might be another individual's strongest group identification. Identification with and attachments to

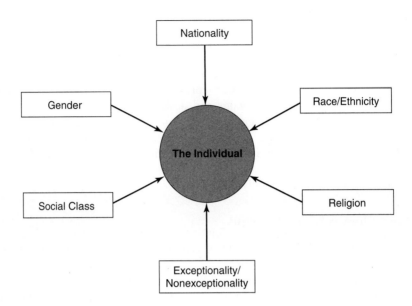

Figure 1.2   Multiple Group Memberships

An individual belongs to several different groups at the same time. This figure shows the major groups discussed in this book.

different groups may also conflict. A woman who has a strong Catholic identification but is also a feminist might find it difficult to reconcile her beliefs about equality for women with some positions of the Catholic Church, such as its prohibiting women from being ordained as priests.

The more we know about a student's level of identification with a particular group and the extent to which socialization has taken place within that group, the more accurately we can predict, explain, and understand the student's behavior in the classroom. Knowledge of the importance of a group to a student at a particular time of life and within a particular social context will also help us understand the student's behavior. Ethnic identity may become more important to a person who becomes part of an ethnic minority when he or she previously belonged to the majority. Many Whites who have moved from the U.S. mainland to Hawaii have commented on how their sense of ethnic identity increased and they began to feel marginalized. Group identity may also increase when the group feels threatened, when a social movement arises to promote its rights, or when the group attempts to revitalize its culture.

The Teaching Implications of Group Identification

What are the implications of group membership and group identity for teaching? As you read the chapters in this book that describe the characteristics of the two gender groups and of social-class, racial, ethnic, religious, language, and exceptional groups, bear in mind that individuals within these groups manifest these behaviors to various degrees. Also remember that individual students are members of several of these groups at the same time. The core U.S. culture is described earlier as having highly individualistic values and beliefs. However, research by Gilligan (1982) indicates that the values of women, as compared with those of men, are more often characterized by caring, interconnection, and sensitivity to the needs of others. This observation indicates how core values within the macroculture are often mediated by microcultures within various gender, ethnic, and cultural groups.

Also as stated previously, researchers have found that some students of color, such as African Americans and Mexican Americans, often have field-sensitive learning styles and therefore prefer more personalized learning approaches (Ramírez & Castañeda, 1974). Think about what this means. This research describes a group characteristic of these students, not the behavior of a particular African American or Mexican American student. It suggests that there is a higher probability that these students will have field-sensitive learning styles than will middle-class Anglo American students. However, students within all ethnic, racial, and social-class groups have different learning styles and characteristics (Irvine & York, 2001). Those groups influence students' behavior, such as their learning style, interactively because they are members of several groups at the same time. Knowledge of the characteristics of groups to which students belong, of the importance of each of these groups to them, and of the extent to which individuals have been socialized within each group will give the teacher important clues to students' behavior.

The Interaction of Race, Class, and Gender

When using our knowledge of groups to understand student behavior, we should also consider the ways in which such variables as class, race, and gender interact and intersect to influence student behavior. Middle-class and more highly assimilated Mexican American students tend to be more field independent than do lower-class and less assimilated Mexican American students. African American students tend to be more field-dependent (group oriented) than White students; females tend to be more field-dependent than male students.

Therefore, it can be hypothesized that African American females would be the most field dependent when compared to African American and White males and White females. This finding was made by Perney (1976).

Figure 1.3 illustrates how the major groups discussed in this book—gender, race or ethnicity, social class, religion, and exceptionality—influence student behavior, both singly and interactively. The figure also shows that other variables, such as geographic region and age, also influence an individual's behavior. The ways in which these variables influence selected student behaviors are described in Table 1.1.

The major variables of gender, race or ethnicity, social class, religion, and exceptionality influence student behavior, both singly and interactively. Other variables, such as region and age, also influence student behavior.

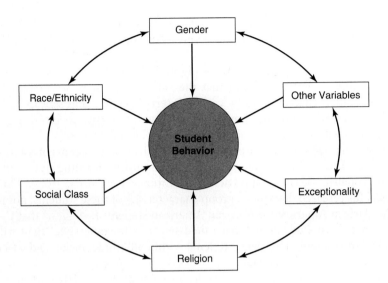

Figure 1.3   The Intersection of Variables

The major variables of gender, race or ethnicity, social class, religion, and exceptionality influence student behavior, both singly and interactively. Other variables, such as region and age, also influence student behavior.

Table 1.1   Singular and Combined Effects of Variables

Student Behavior	Gender Effects	Race/Ethnicity Effects	Social-Class Effects	Religious Effects	Combined Effects
Learning Styles (Field Independent/Field Dependent)	X[a]	X			X
Internality/Externality			X		
Fear of Success	X	X			?
Self-Esteem	X	X			?
Individual vs. Group Orientation	X	X	X		?

[a]An X indicates that the variable influences the student behavior that is described in the far-left column. An X in the far-right column means that research indicates that two or more variables combine to influence the described behavior. A question mark indicates that the research is unclear about the combined effects of the variables.

THE SOCIAL CONSTRUCTION OF CATEGORIES

The major variables and categories discussed in this book—such as gender, race, ethnicity, class, and exceptionality—are social categories (Berger & Luckman, 1967; Mannheim, 1936). The criteria for whether an individual belongs to one of these categories are determined by human beings and consequently are socially constructed. Religion is also a social category. Religious institutions, symbols, and artifacts are created by human beings to satisfy their metaphysical needs.

These categories are usually related to individuals' physical characteristics. In some cases, as when they are individuals with severe or obvious physical disabilities, the relationship between the labels given to individuals and their physical characteristics is direct and would be made in almost any culture or social system. The relationship between categories that are used to classify individuals and their physical characteristics, however, is usually indirect and complex. Even though one's sex is determined primarily by physical characteristics (genitalia, chromosome patterns, etc.), gender is a social construction created and shaped by the society in which individuals and groups function.

Gender

Gender consists of the socially and psychologically appropriate behavior for males and females sanctioned by and expected within a society. Gender-role expectations vary across cultures and at different times in a society and within microcultures in the same society. Traditionally, normative behavior for males and females has varied among mainstream Americans, African Americans, Native Americans, and Hispanic Americans. Gender-role expectations also vary somewhat across social classes within the same society. In the White mainstream society in the 1940s and 1950s, upper-middle-class women often received negative sanctions when they worked outside the home, whereas women in working-class families were frequently expected to become wage earners.

Sexual Orientation

The discussion of gender roles provides an appropriate context for the examination of issues related to sexual orientation (see Chapter 9). The quest by gays and lesbians for human and civil rights has been an important development within the United States and throughout the Western world within the last several decades. Sexual orientation deserves examination when human rights and social justice are discussed because it is an important identity for individuals and groups and because many gay youths are victims of discrimination and hate crimes ("Lesbian, Gay, Bisexual, and Transgender People," 1996; Lipkin, 1999). Sexual orientation is often a difficult issue for classroom discussion for both teachers and students. However, if done sensitively, it can help empower gay and lesbian students and enable them to experience social equality in the college and university classroom. Recognition is one important manifestation of social equality (Gutmann, 2004).

Race

Race is a socially determined category that is related to physical characteristics in a complex way (Jacobson, 1998; Roediger, 2002). Two individuals with nearly identical physical characteristics, or phenotypes, can be classified as members of different races in two different societies (Nash,

1999; Root, 2004). In the United States, where racial categories are well defined and highly inflexible, an individual with any acknowledged or publicly known African ancestry is considered Black (Davis, 1991). One who looks completely Caucasian but who acknowledges some African ancestry is classified as Black. Such an individual would be considered White in Puerto Rico, where hair texture, social status, and degree of eminence in the community are often as important as—if not more important than—physical characteristics in determining an individual's racial group or category. There is a saying in Puerto Rico that "money lightens," which means that upward social mobility considerably enhances an individual's opportunity to be classified as White. There is a strong relationship between race and social class in Puerto Rico and in most other Caribbean and Latin American nations.

Our discussion of race as a social category indicates that the criteria for determining the characteristics of a particular race vary across cultures, that an individual considered Black in one society may be considered White in another, and that racial categories reflect the social, economic, and political characteristics of a society.

Social Class

Social scientists find it difficult to agree on criteria for determining social class. The problem is complicated by the fact that societies are constantly in the throes of change. During the 1950s, social scientists often attributed characteristics to the lower class that are found in the middle class today, such as single-parent and female-headed households, high divorce rates, and substance abuse. Today, these characteristics are no longer rare among the middle class, even though their frequency is still higher among lower-class families. Variables such as income, education, occupation, lifestyle, and values are among the most frequently used indices to determine social-class status in the United States (Warner, 1949/1960). However, there is considerable disagreement among social scientists about which variables are the most important in determining the social-class status of an individual or family.

Social-class criteria also vary somewhat among various ethnic and racial groups in the United States. Teachers, preachers, and other service professionals were upper class in many rural African American communities in the South in the 1950s and 1960s but were considered middle class by mainstream White society. The systems of social stratification that exist in the mainstream society and in various microcultures are not necessarily identical.

Exceptionality

Exceptionality is also a social category. Whether a person is considered disabled or gifted is determined by criteria developed by society. As Shaver and Curtis (1981) point out, disabilities are not necessarily handicaps, and the two should be distinguished. They write, "A disability or combination of disabilities becomes a handicap only when the condition limits or impedes the person's ability to function normally" (p. 1). A person with a particular disability, such as having one arm, might have a successful college career, experience no barriers to achievements in college, and graduate with honors. However, this person may find that when trying to enter the job market, the opportunities are severely limited because potential employers view him or her as unable to perform well in some situations in which, in fact, this individual could perform effectively (Shaver & Curtis, 1981). This individual has a disability but was viewed as handicapped in one situation (the job market) but not in another (the university).

Mercer (1973) has extensively studied the social process by which individuals become labeled as persons with mental retardation. She points out that even though their physical characteristics may increase their chance of being labeled persons with mental retardation, the two are not perfectly correlated. Two people with the same biological characteristics may be considered persons with mental retardation in one social system but not in another one. An individual may be considered a person with mental retardation at school but not at home. Mercer writes, "Mental retardation is not a characteristic of the individual, nor a meaning inherent in behavior, but a socially determined status, which [people] may occupy in some social systems and not in others" (p. 31). She states that people can change their role by changing their social group.

The highly disproportionate number of African Americans, Latinos, and particularly males classified as learning disabled by the school indicates the extent to which exceptionality is a social category (Donovan & Cross, 2002). Mercer (1973) found that schools labeled more people mentally retarded than did any other institution. Many African American and Latino students who are labeled mentally retarded function normally and are considered normal in their homes and communities. Boys are more often classified as mentally retarded than are girls. Schools, as Mercer and other researchers have pointed out, use criteria to determine the mental ability of students of color that conflict with their home and community cultures. *Some students in all ethnic and cultural groups are mentally retarded and deserve special instruction, programs, and services, as the authors in Part V of this book suggest.* However, the percentage of students of color in these programs is too high. The percentage of students in each ethnic group labeled mentally retarded should be about the same as the total percentage of that group in school.

Giftedness is also a social category (Sapon-Shevin, 1994, 2007). Important results of the socially constructed nature of giftedness are the considerable disagreement among experts about how the concept should be defined and the often inconsistent views about how to identify gifted students (Ford & Harris, 1999). The highly disproportionate percentage of middle- and upper-middle-class mainstream students categorized as gifted compared to low-income students and students of color, such as African Americans, Latinos, and Native Americans, is also evidence of the social origin of the category.

Many students who are classified as gifted do have special talents and abilities and need special instruction. However, some students who are classified as gifted by school districts merely have parents with the knowledge, political skills, and power to force the school to classify their children as gifted, which will provide them with special instruction and educational enrichment (Sapon-Shevin, 1994).

Schools should try to satisfy the needs of students with special gifts and talents; however, they should also make sure that students from all social-class, cultural, language, and ethnic groups have an equal opportunity to participate in programs for academically and creatively talented students. If schools or districts do not have in their gifted programs a population that represents their various cultural, racial, language, and ethnic groups, steps should be taken to examine the criteria used to identify gifted students and to develop procedures to correct the disproportion. Both excellence and equality should be major goals of education in a pluralistic society.

THE DIMENSIONS OF MULTICULTURAL EDUCATION

When many teachers think of multicultural education, they think only or primarily of content related to ethnic, racial, and cultural groups. Conceptualizing multicultural education exclusively as content related to various ethnic and cultural groups is problematic for several reasons. Teachers who cannot easily see how their content is related to cultural issues will easily dismiss multicultural education with the argument that it is not relevant to their disciplines. This is done frequently by secondary math and science teachers.

The irrelevant-of-content argument can become a legitimized form of resistance to multicultural education when it is conceptualized primarily or exclusively as content. Math and science teachers often state that multicultural education is fine for social studies and literature teachers, but it has nothing to do with their subjects. Furthermore, they say, math and science are the same regardless of the culture or the kids. Multicultural education needs to be more broadly defined and understood so that teachers from a wide range of disciplines can respond to it in appropriate ways and resistance to it can be minimized.

Multicultural education is a broad concept with several different and important dimensions (Banks, 2004). Practicing educators can use the dimensions as a guide to school reform when trying to implement multicultural education. The dimensions are (1) content integration, (2) the knowledge construction process, (3) prejudice reduction, (4) an equity pedagogy, and (5) an empowering school culture and social structure. Each dimension is defined and illustrated next.

Content Integration

Content integration deals with the extent to which teachers use examples and content from a variety of cultures and groups to illustrate key concepts, principles, generalizations, and theories in their subject area or discipline. The infusion of ethnic and cultural content into the subject area should be logical, not contrived.

More opportunities exist for the integration of ethnic and cultural content in some subject areas than in others. In the social studies, the language arts, and music, frequent and ample opportunities exist for teachers to use ethnic and cultural content to illustrate concepts, themes, and principles. There are also opportunities to integrate multicultural content into math and science. However, the opportunities are not as ample as they are in the social studies, the language arts, and music.

The Knowledge Construction Process

The knowledge construction process relates to the extent to which teachers help students to understand, investigate, and determine how the implicit cultural assumptions, frames of reference, perspectives, and biases within a discipline influence the ways in which knowledge is constructed within it (Banks, 1996).

Students can analyze the knowledge construction process in science by studying how racism has been perpetuated in science by genetic theories of intelligence, Darwinism, and eugenics. In his important book *The Mismeasure of Man*, Gould (1996) describes how scientific racism developed and was influential in the 19th and 20th centuries. Scientific racism has had and continues to have a significant influence on the interpretations of mental ability tests in the United States.

The publication of *The Bell Curve* (Herrnstein & Murray, 1994), its widespread and enthusiastic public reception, and the social context out of which it emerged provide an excellent case study for discussion and analysis by students who are studying knowledge construction (Kincheloe, Steinberg, & Gresson, 1996). Herrnstein and Murray contend that low-income groups and African Americans have fewer intellectual abilities than do other groups and that these differences are inherited. Students can examine the arguments made by the authors, their major assumptions, and how their conclusions relate to the social and political context.

Gould (1994) contends that Herrnstein and Murray's arguments reflect the social context of the times, "a historical moment of unprecedented ungenerosity, when a mood for slashing social programs can be powerfully abetted by an argument that beneficiaries cannot be helped, owing to inborn cognitive limits expressed as low I.Q. scores" (p. 139). Students should also study counterarguments to *The Bell Curve* made by respected scientists. Two good sources are *The Bell Curve Debate: History, Documents, Opinions,* edited by Jacoby and Glauberman (1995), and *Measured Lies: The Bell Curve Examined,* edited by Kincheloe, Steinberg, and Gresson (1996).

Students can examine the knowledge construction process in the social studies when they study such units and topics as the European discovery of America and the westward movement. The teacher can ask the students the latent meanings of concepts such as the European discovery of America and the New World. The students can discuss what these concepts imply or suggest about the Native American cultures that had existed in the Americas for about 40,000 years before the Europeans arrived. When studying the westward movement, the teacher can ask students these questions: Whose point of view or perspective does this concept reflect, that of the European Americans or the Lakota Sioux? Who was moving west? How might a Lakota Sioux historian describe this period in U.S. history? What are other ways of thinking about and describing the westward movement?

Prejudice Reduction

Prejudice reduction describes lessons and activities teachers use to help students develop positive attitudes toward different racial, ethnic, and cultural groups. Research indicates that children come to school with many negative attitudes toward and misconceptions about different racial and ethnic groups (Aboud, 2009; Stephan & Vogt, 2004). Research also indicates that lessons, units, and teaching materials that include content about different racial and ethnic groups can help students to develop more positive intergroup attitudes if certain conditions exist in the teaching situation (Bigler, 1999; Stephan & Vogt). These conditions include positive images of the ethnic groups in the materials and the use of multiethnic materials in a consistent and sequential way.

Allport's (1954) contact hypothesis provides several useful guidelines for helping students to develop more positive interracial attitudes and actions in contact situations. He states that contact between groups will improve intergroup relations when the contact is characterized by these four conditions: (1) equal status, (2) cooperation rather than competition, (3) sanction by authorities such as teachers and administrators, and (4) interpersonal interactions in which students become acquainted as individuals.

An Equity Pedagogy

Teachers in each discipline can analyze their teaching procedures and styles to determine the extent to which they reflect multicultural issues and concerns. An equity pedagogy exists when teachers modify their teaching in ways that will facilitate the academic achievement of students from diverse racial, cultural, gender, and social-class groups. This includes using a variety of teaching styles and approaches that are consistent with the wide range of learning styles within various cultural and ethnic groups, being demanding but highly personalized when working with groups such as Native American and Alaskan students, and using cooperative learning techniques in math and science instruction in order to enhance the academic achievement of students of color (Cohen & Lotan, 2004; Slavin, 2001).

Several chapters in this book discuss ways in which teachers can modify their instruction in order to increase the academic achievement of students from different cultural groups and from both gender groups, including the chapters that constitute Parts III and IV.

An Empowering School Culture and Social Structure

Another important dimension of multicultural education is a school culture and organization that promote gender, racial, and social-class equity. The culture and organization of the school must be examined by all members of the school staff. They all must also participate in restructuring it. Grouping and labeling practices, sports participation, disproportionality in achievement, disproportionality in enrollment in gifted and special education programs, and the interaction of the staff and the students across ethnic and racial lines are important variables that need to be examined in order to create a school culture that empowers students from diverse racial and ethnic groups and from both gender groups.

Figure 1.4 summarizes the dimensions of multicultural education. The next section identifies the major variables of the school that must be changed in order to institutionalize a school culture that empowers students from diverse cultural, racial, ethnic, and social-class groups.

THE SCHOOL AS A SOCIAL SYSTEM

To implement multicultural education successfully, we must think of the school as a social system in which all of its major variables are closely interrelated. Thinking of the school as a social system suggests that we must formulate and initiate a change strategy that reforms the total school environment to implement multicultural education. The major school variables that must be reformed are presented in Figure 1.5.

Reforming any one of the variables in Figure 1.5, such as the formalized curriculum or curricular materials, is necessary but not sufficient. Multicultural and sensitive teaching materials are ineffective in the hands of teachers who have negative attitudes toward different racial, ethnic, and cultural groups. Such teachers are rarely likely to use multicultural materials

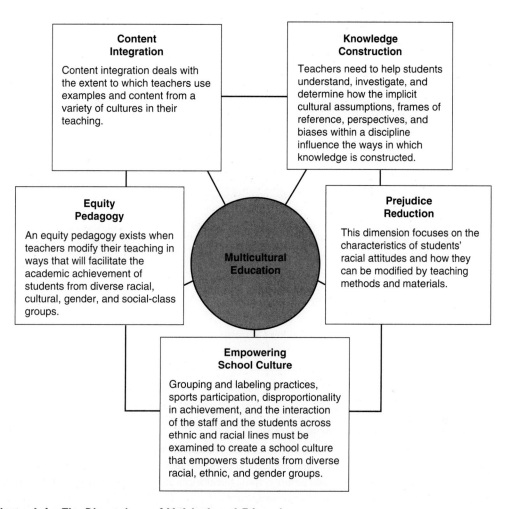

Content Integration

Content integration deals with the extent to which teachers use examples and content from a variety of cultures in their teaching.

Knowledge Construction

Teachers need to help students understand, investigate, and determine how the implicit cultural assumptions, frames of reference, perspectives, and biases within a discipline influence the ways in which knowledge is constructed.

Equity Pedagogy

An equity pedagogy exists when teachers modify their teaching in ways that will facilitate the academic achievement of students from diverse racial, cultural, gender, and social-class groups.

Prejudice Reduction

This dimension focuses on the characteristics of students' racial attitudes and how they can be modified by teaching methods and materials.

Multicultural Education

Empowering School Culture

Grouping and labeling practices, sports participation, disproportionality in achievement, and the interaction of the staff and the students across ethnic and racial lines must be examined to create a school culture that empowers students from diverse racial, ethnic, and gender groups.

Figure I.4   The Dimensions of Multicultural Education

Source: Copyright © 2009 by James A. Banks.

or are likely to use them detrimentally. Thus, helping teachers and other members of the school staff to gain knowledge about diverse groups and democratic attitudes and values is essential when implementing multicultural programs.

To implement multicultural education in a school, we must reform its power relationships, verbal interaction between teachers and students, culture, curriculum, extracurricular activities, attitudes toward minority languages (Romaine, 2009), testing program, and grouping practices. The school's institutional norms, social structures, cause–belief statements, values, and goals must be transformed and reconstructed.

Major attention should be focused on the school's hidden curriculum and its implicit norms and values. A school has both a manifest and hidden curriculum. The manifest curriculum

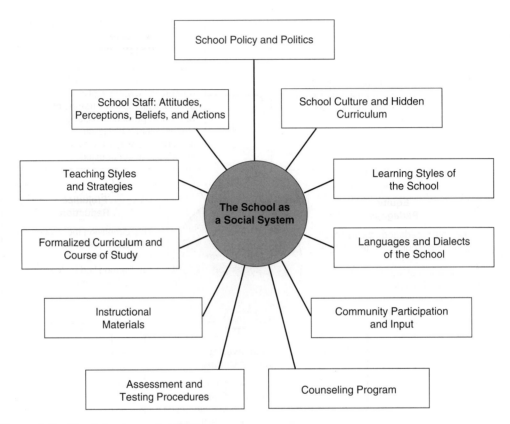

Figure 1.5   The School as a Social System

The total school environment is a system consisting of a number of major identifiable variables and factors, such as a school culture, school policy and politics, and the formalized curriculum and course of study. Any of these factors may be the focus of initial school reform, but changes must take place in each of them to create and sustain an effective multicultural school environment.

Source: Adapted with permission from James A. Banks (Ed.), *Education in the 80s: Multiethnic Education* (Washington, DC: National Education Association, 1981), Figure 2, p. 22.

consists of such factors as guides, textbooks, bulletin boards, and lesson plans. These aspects of the school environment are important and must be reformed to create a school culture that promotes positive attitudes toward diverse cultural groups and helps students from these groups experience academic success. However, the school's hidden or latent curriculum is often more important than is its manifest or overt curriculum. *The latent curriculum* has been defined as the one that no teacher explicitly teaches but that all students learn. It is that powerful part of the school culture that communicates to students the school's attitudes toward a range of issues and problems, including how the school views them as human beings and as males, females, exceptional students, and students from various religious, cultural, racial, and ethnic groups. Jackson (1992) calls the latent curriculum the "untaught lessons."

When formulating plans for multicultural education, educators should conceptualize the school as a microculture that has norms, values, statuses, and goals like other social systems. The school has a dominant culture and a variety of microcultures. Almost all classrooms in the United States are multicultural because White students as well as Black and Brown students are socialized within diverse cultures. Teachers also come from many different groups. As Erickson points out in Chapter 2, all individuals—including students and teachers—are also multicultural because components of more than one culture or group influence their behavior. Each individual belongs to an ethnic or culture group, is gay, straight, or bisexual, and is religious or nonreligious.

Many teachers were socialized in cultures other than the Anglo mainstream, although these may be forgotten and repressed. Teachers can get in touch with their own cultures and use the perspectives and insights they acquired as vehicles for helping them relate to and understand the cultures of their students.

SUMMARY

Multicultural education is an idea stating that all students, regardless of the groups to which they belong, such as those related to gender, ethnicity, race, culture, language, social class, religion, or exceptionality, should experience educational equality in the schools. Some students, because of their particular characteristics, have a better chance to succeed in school as it is currently structured than students from other groups. Multicultural education is also a reform movement designed to bring about a transformation of the school so that students from both genders and from diverse cultural, language, and ethnic groups will have an equal chance to experience school success. Multicultural education views the school as a social system that consists of highly interrelated parts and variables. Therefore, in order to transform the school to bring about educational equality, all major components of the school must be substantially changed. A focus on any one variable in the school, such as the formalized curriculum, will not implement multicultural education.

Multicultural education is a continuing process because the idealized goals it tries to actualize—such as educational equality and the eradication of all forms of discrimination—can never be fully achieved in human society. Multicultural education, which was born during the social protest of the 1960s and 1970s, is an international movement that exists in nations throughout the world (Banks, 2009). A major goal of multicultural education is to help students to develop the knowledge, attitudes, and skills needed to function within their own microcultures, the U.S. macroculture, other microcultures, and the global community.

Questions and Activities

1. What are the three components or elements of multicultural education?
2. How does Banks define multicultural education?
3. Find other definitions of multicultural education in several books listed under the category Issues and Concepts in the Appendix to this book. How are the definitions of multicultural education in these books similar to and different from the one presented in this chapter?

4. In what ways did the Civil Rights and women's rights Movements of the 1960s and 1970s influence the development of multicultural education?

5. Ask several teachers and other practicing educators to give you their views and definitions of multicultural education. What generalizations can you make about their responses?

6. Visit a local school and, by observing several classes as well as by interviewing several teachers and the principal, describe what curricular and other practices related to multicultural education have been implemented in the school. Share your report with your classmates or workshop colleagues.

7. Define *macroculture* and *microculture*.

8. How is *culture* defined? What are the most important components of culture in a modernized society?

9. List and define several core or overarching values and characteristics that make up the macroculture in the United States. To what extent are these values and characteristics consistent with practices in U.S. society? To what extent are they ideals that are inconsistent with realities in U.S. society?

10. How is individualism viewed differently in the United States and in nations such as China and Japan? Why? What are the behavioral consequences of these varying notions of individualism?

11. What is the American dilemma defined by Myrdal? To what extent is this concept an accurate description of values in U.S. society? Explain.

12. How do the preferred ways of learning and knowing among women and students of color often influence their experiences in the schools as they are currently structured? In what ways can school reform help make the school environment more consistent with the learning and cognitive styles of women and students of color?

13. In what ways does the process of identifying and labeling students with mental retardation discriminate against groups such as African Americans and Latinos?

14. In what ways can the characteristics of a group help us understand an individual's behavior? In what ways are group characteristics limited in explaining an individual's behavior?

15. How do such variables as race, class, and gender interact to influence the behavior of students? Give examples to support your response.

16. What is meant by the "social construction of categories?" In what ways are concepts such as gender, race, social class, and exceptionality social categories?

17. List and define the five dimensions of multicultural education. How can these dimensions be used to facilitate school reform?

References

Aboud, F. E. (2009). Modifying children's racial attitudes. In J. A. Banks (Ed.), *The Routledge international companion to multicultural education* (pp. 199–209). New York and London: Routledge.

Allport, G. W. (1954). *The nature of prejudice*. Reading, MA: Addison-Wesley.

Amrein, A. L., & Berliner, D. C. (2002). High-stakes testing, uncertainty, and student learning. *Education Policy Analysis Archives, 10*(8). Retrieved February 14, 2002, from http://eppa.asu.edu/eppa/v10n18/.

Appleby, J., Hunt, L., & Jacob, M. (1994). *Telling the truth about history*. New York: Norton.

Banks, J. A. (Ed.). (1996). *Multicultural education, transformative knowledge, and action*. New York: Teachers College Press.

Banks, J. A. (2004). Multicultural education: Historical development, dimensions, and practice. In J. A. Banks & C. A. M. Banks (Eds.), *Handbook of research on multicultural education* (2nd ed., pp. 3–29). San Francisco: Jossey-Bass.

Banks, J. A. (2006). *Race, culture, and education: The selected works of James A. Banks*. London & New York: Routledge.

Banks, J. A. (2008). Diversity, group identity, and citizenship education in a global age. *Educational Researcher, 37*(3), 129–139.

Banks, J. A. (Ed.). (2009). *The Routledge international companion to multicultural education*. New York and London: Routledge.

Banks, J. A., & Banks, C. A. M. (Eds.). (2004). *Handbook of research on multicultural education* (2nd ed.). San Francisco: Jossey-Bass.

Belenky, M. F., Clinchy, B. M., Goldberger, N. R., & Tarule, J. M. (1986). *Women's ways of knowing: The development of self, voice, and mind*. New York: Basic Books.

Bellah, R. N., Madsen, R., Sullivan, W. M., Swidler, A., & Tipton, S. M. (1985). *Habits of the heart: Individualism and commitment in American life*. New York: Harper & Row.

Berger, P. L., & Luckman, T. (1967). *The social construction of reality: A treatise in the sociology of knowledge*. New York: Doubleday.

Bigler, R. S. (1999). The use of multicultural curricula and materials to counter racism in children. *Journal of Social Issues, 55*, 687–705.

Branch, T. (2006). *At Canaan's edge: America in the King years, 1965–68*. New York: Simon & Schuster.

Bullivant, B. (1993). Culture: Its nature and meaning for educators. In J. A. Banks & C. A. M. Banks (Eds.), *Multicultural education: Issues and perspectives* (2nd ed., pp. 29–47). Boston: Allyn & Bacon.

Butterfield, F. (1982). *China: Alive in the bitter sea*. New York: Bantam.

Clewell, B. C. (2002). Breaking the barriers: The critical middle school years. In *The Jossey-Bass reader on gender in education* (pp. 301–313). San Francisco, CA: Jossey-Bass.

Cohen, E. G., & Lotan, R. (2004). Equity in heterogeneous classrooms. In J. A. Banks & C. A. M. Banks (Eds.), *Handbook of research on multicultural education* (2nd ed., pp. 736–750). San Francisco: Jossey-Bass.

Davis, F. J. (1991). *Who is Black? One nation's definition*. University Park: The Pennsylvania State University Press.

Donovan, M. S., & Cross, C. T. (Eds.). (2002). Minority students in special and gifted education. Washington, DC: National Academy Press.

Ellison, R. (1995). An American dilemma: A review. In J. F. Callahan (Ed.), *The collected essays of Ralph Ellison* (pp. 328–340). New York: The Modern Library.

Foner, E. (1998). *The story of American freedom*. New York: Norton.

Ford, D. Y., & Harris, J. J., III. (1999). *Multicultural gifted education*. New York: Teachers College Press.

Francis, B. (2000). *Boys, girls and achievement: Addressing the classroom issues*. London: Routledge Falmer.

Gilligan, C. (1982). *In a different voice: Psychological theory and women's development*. Cambridge, MA: Harvard University Press.

Goldberger, N., Tarule, J., Clinchy, B., & Belenky, M. (Eds.). (1996). *Knowledge, difference, and power*. New York: Basic Books.

Goodman, N., & Marx, G. T. (1982). *Society today* (4th ed.). New York: Random House.

Gould, S. J. (1994). Curveball. *The New Yorker, 70*(38), 139–149.

Gould, S. J. (1996). *The Mismeasure of Man* (Rev. & exp. ed.). New York: Norton.

Gutmann, A. (2004). Unity and diversity in democratic multicultural education: Creative and destructive tensions. In J. A. Banks (Ed.), *Diversity and citizenship education: Global perspectives* (pp. 71–98). San Francisco: Jossey-Bass.

Halpern, D. F. (1986). *Sex differences in cognitive abilities*. Hillsdale, NJ: Erlbaum.

Heath, S. B. (1983). *Ways with words: Language, life, and work in communities and classrooms*. New York: Oxford University Press.

Herrnstein, R. J., & Murray, C. (1994). *The bell curve: Intelligence and class structure in American life*. New York: Free Press.

Inglis, C. (2009). Multicultural education in Australia: Two generations of evolution. In J. A. Banks (Ed.). *The Routledge international companion to multicultural education* (pp. 109–120). New York and London: Routledge.

Irvine, J. J., & York, E. D. (2001). Learning styles and culturally diverse students: A literature review. In J. A. Banks & C. A. M. Banks (Eds.), *Handbook of research on multicultural education* (2nd ed., pp. 484–497). San Francisco: Jossey-Bass.

Jackson, P. W. (1992). *Untaught lessons*. New York: Teachers College Press.

Jacobson, M. F. (1998). *Whiteness of a different color: European immigrants and the alchemy of race*. Cambridge, MA: Harvard University Press.

Jacoby, R., & Glauberman, N. (Eds.). (1995). *The bell curve debate: History, documents, opinions*. New York: Times Books/Random House.

Joshee, R. (2009). Multicultural education in Canada: Competing ideologies, interconnected discourses. In J. A. Banks (Ed.). *The Routledge international companion to multicultural education* (pp. 96–108). New York and London: Routledge.

Kincheloe, J. L., Steinberg, S. R., & Gresson, A. D., III (Eds.). (1996). *Measured lies: The bell curve examined*. New York: St. Martin's Press.

Knapp, M. S., & Woolverton, S. (2004). Social class and schooling. In J. A. Banks & C. A. M. Banks (Eds.), *Handbook of research on multicultural education* (2nd ed., pp. 656–681). San Francisco: Jossey-Bass.

Kuper, A. (1999). *Culture: The anthropologists' account*. Cambridge, MA: Harvard University Press.

Lasch, C. (1978). *The culture of narcissism*. New York: Norton.

Lee, C. D. (2006). *Culture, literacy, and learning: Taking bloom in the midst of the whirlwind*. New York: Teachers College Press.

Lesbian, gay, bisexual, and transgender people and education. (1996). [Special issue]. *Harvard Educational Review, 66*(2).

Lipkin, A. (1999). *Understanding homosexuality: Changing schools*. Boulder, CO: Westview.

Luchtenberg, S. (2009). Migrant minority groups in Germany: Success and failure in education. In J. A. Banks (Ed.), *The Routledge international companion to multicultural education* (pp. 463–473). New York and London: Routledge.

Maher, F. A. (1987). Inquiry teaching and feminist pedagogy. *Social Education, 51*(3), 186–192.

Maher, F. A., & Tetreault, M. K. (1994). *The feminist classroom*. New York: Basic Books.

Mannheim, K. (1936). *Ideology and utopia: An introduction to the sociology of knowledge*. New York: Harcourt Brace.

Mercer, J. R. (1973). *Labeling the mentally retarded: Clinical and social system perspectives on mental retardation*. Berkeley: University of California Press.

Myrdal, G., with Sterner, R., & Rose, A. (1962). *An American dilemma: The Negro problem and modern democracy* [anniv. ed.]. New York: Harper & Row. (Original work published 1944)

Nash, G. B. (1999). *Forbidden love: The secret history of mixed-race America*. New York: Holt.

Nieto, S., & Bode, P. (2008). *Affirming diversity: The sociopolitical context of multicultural education* (5th ed.). Boston: Allyn and Bacon.

Noguera, P. A. (2008). *The trouble with Black boys, and other reflections on race, equity, and the future of public education*. San Francisco: Jossey-Bass/Wiley.

Oakes, J., Joseph, R., & Muir, K. (2004). Access and achievement in mathematics and science: Inequalities that endure and change. In J. A. Banks & C. A. M. Banks (Eds.), *Handbook of research on multicultural education* (2nd ed., pp. 69–90). San Francisco: Jossey-Bass.

Penetito, W. (2009). The struggle to educate the Maori in New Zealand. In J. A. Banks (Ed.), *The Routledge international companion to multicultural education* (pp. 288–300). New York and London: Routledge.

Perney, V. H. (1976). Effects of race and sex on field dependence–independence in children. *Perceptual and Motor Skills, 42*, 975–980.

Ramírez, M., & Castañeda, A. (1974). *Cultural democracy, bicognitive development and education*. New York: Academic Press.

Reischauer, E. O. (1981). *The Japanese*. Cambridge, MA: Harvard University Press.

Roderick, M., Jacob, B. A., & Bryk, A. S. (2002). The impact of high-stakes testing in Chicago on student achievement in promotional gate grades. *Educational Evaluation and Policy Analysis, 24*(4), 333–357.

Roediger, D. R. (2002). *Colored White: Transcending the racial past*. Berkeley: University of California Press.

Romaine, S. (2009). Language, culture, and identity across nations. In J. A. Banks (Ed.), *The Routledge international companion to multicultural education* (pp. 373–384). New York and London: Routledge.

Root, M. P. P. (2004). Multiracial families and children: Implications for educational research and practice. In J. A. Banks & C. A. M. Banks (Eds.), *Handbook of research on multicultural education* (2nd ed., pp. 110–124). San Francisco: Jossey-Bass.

Rothbart, M., & John, O. P. (1993). Intergroup relations and stereotype change: A social-cognitive analysis and some longitudinal findings. In P. M. Sniderman, P. E. Telock, & E. G. Carmines (Eds.), *Prejudice, politics, and the American dilemma* (pp. 32–59). Stanford, CA: Stanford University Press.

Sapon-Shevin, M. (1994). *Playing favorites: Gifted education and the disruption of community*. Albany: State University of New York Press.

Sapon-Shevin, M. (2007). *Widening the circle: The power of inclusive classrooms*. Boston: Beacon Press.

Schlesinger, A. M., Jr. (1986). *The cycles of American history*. Boston: Houghton Mifflin.

Schmitz, B., Butler, J., Rosenfelt, D., & Guy-Sheftal, B. (2004). Women's studies and curriculum transformation. In J. A. Banks & C. A. M. Banks (Eds.), *Handbook of research on multicultural education* (2nd ed., pp. 882–905). San Francisco: Jossey-Bass.

Shaver, J. P., & Curtis, C. K. (1981). *Handicapism and equal opportunity: Teaching about the disabled in social studies*. Reston, VA: Foundation for Exceptional Children.

Slavin, R. E. (2001). Cooperative learning and intergroup relations. In J. A. Banks & C. A. M. Banks (Eds.), *Handbook of research on multicultural education* (2nd ed., pp. 628–634). San Francisco: Jossey-Bass.

Sleeter, C. E. (2005). *Un-standardizing curriculum: Multicultural teaching in the standards-based classroom*. New York: Teachers College Press.

Sleeter, C. E., & Grant, C. A. (2007). *Making choices for multicultural education: Five approaches to race, class, and gender* (5th ed.). New York: Wiley.

Steele, C. (2003). Stereotype threat and African-American student achievement. In T. Perry, C. Steele, & A. Hilliard, III, *Young, gifted and black: Promoting high achievement among African-American students* (pp. 109–130). Boston: Beacon.

Stephan, W. G. (1999). *Reducing prejudice and stereotyping in schools*. New York: Teachers College Press.

Stephan, W. G., & Vogt, W. P. (Eds.). (2004). *Education programs for improving intergroup relations: Theory, research, and practice*. New York: Teachers College Press.

Stewart, E. C., & Bennett, M. J. (1991). *American cultural patterns: A cross-cultural perspective*. Yarmouth, ME: Intercultural Press.

Taylor, J. M., Gilligan, C., & Sullivan, A. M. (1995). *Between voice and silence: Women and girls, race and relationships*. Cambridge, MA: Harvard University Press.

Theodorson, G. A., & Theodorson, A. G. (1969). *A modern dictionary of sociology*. New York: Barnes & Noble.

Trecker, J. L. (1973). Teaching the role of women in American history. In J. A. Banks (Ed.), *Teaching ethnic studies: Concepts and strategies* (43rd Yearbook, pp. 279–297). Washington, DC: National Council for the Social Studies.

Warner, W. L., with Meeker, M., & Eells, K. (1960). *Social class in America, a manual of procedure for the measurement of social status*. New York: Harper Torchbooks. (Original work published 1949)

Weatherford, J. (1988). *Indian givers: How the Indians of the Americas transformed the world*. New York: Fawcett Columbine.

Willis, P. (1977). *Learning to labor*. New York: Columbia University Press.

CHAPTER 2

Culture in Society and in Educational Practices

Frederick Erickson

A group of first graders and their teacher are in the midst of a reading lesson in an inner-city classroom in Berkeley, California. The students are African American and their teacher is White. The children read aloud in chorus from their reading book:

1 T: All right, class, read that and remember your endings.
2 CC: Wha' did Little Duck see? (final t of "what" deleted)
3 T: What. (emphasizing final t)
4 CC: Wha'. (final t deleted as in turn 2)
5 T: I still don't hear this sad little "t."
6 CC: Wha' did—wha' did—wha'—(final t's deleted)
7 T: What.
8 T&CC: What did Little Duck see? (final t spoken)
9 T: OK, very good

(From Piestrup, 1973, pp. 96–97)

The preceding strip of talk shows a choice in instructional approach that produced confusion for students because practice in speech style was being asked of the students indirectly by the teacher. The teacher did not tell the students that she wanted them to pronounce the final *t* in *what*. These first-grade children had been asked by their teacher to read aloud a question that was printed in their reading book. The question had to do with what Little Duck was looking at. The teacher could have chosen to emphasize comprehension by teaching the students how to discover meaning in a written text. Instead, the teacher chose to use the students' reading aloud as an occasion for a short drill in correct pronunciation of speech sounds—"remember your endings." The instructional focus was on saying aloud the final *t* in the word *what*.

This chapter will argue that what happened in this sequence was "cultural." The teacher had chosen to make that moment in the reading lesson a practice session in cultural ways of speaking rather than using that moment as an opportunity for teaching children the sense of the words they were reading aloud. This put the spotlight of public attention on a subtle cultural difference, but it did so in an indirect way that was confusing for the students. The appearance of a small feature in pronunciation style (deletion of final *t*) became the occasion for the teacher's making a big thing of a small cultural difference. But the teacher did not explain that, so it was not clear to the children that what was being asked of them was to participate in a practice session in cultural style in talking. This chapter will consider that choice of focus by the teacher as an example of treating a feature of cultural difference as a *cultural border* matter rather than as a *cultural boundary* matter. Teachers have a great deal of discretion in how they frame and deal with cultural difference in the classroom—as border or as boundary. The way they choose to frame cultural difference has a profound influence on students' understanding of what is being asked of them instructionally and on their motivation to learn.

CULTURE: AN OVERVIEW

American anthropologists developed culture as a social science concept in the early 20th century. They invented it as an alternative to *race* as an explanation for why people around the world differed in their actions and beliefs. The prevailing belief was that people acted as they did because of genetic inheritance and that the "civilized" ways of Western Europeans made it evident that they were racially superior to non-Western peoples. That belief justified Western imperialism—colonial rule by those of European descent over those "others" who were not of European descent. Anthropologists argued that this view was wrong. People acted the way they did not because of race or genetic inheritance but because of learning and by following the patterned ways of being human that were experienced in everyday life, especially during childhood. Moreover, these differing learned ways of being human were not inherently superior or inferior to one another—they were just *differences*. This is called the perspective of *cultural relativism*. During the last third of the 20th century, the culturally relativist critique of racism got hijacked—distorted by a resurgence in beliefs of superiority and inferiority in ways of being human.

The notion of a *culture of poverty* developed and was then misinterpreted, especially among professional educators, on the basis of assumptions that some cultural ways of conducting family life inhibited the intellectual, linguistic, and moral development of children. Specialists in child development argued that poor people, especially poor people of color, did not know how to raise their children "right." It was the job of schools and preschools to make up for the deficiencies in family life and early childhood experience that children brought with them to school. In this way, overt expressions of cultural prejudice—with "scientific" justification from child development research—became a substitute for overt expressions of racial prejudice among educators. Such cultural prejudice could be one reason that the children in the "Little Duck" reading lesson got stopped and frisked for incorrect pronunciation of the final *t* in the word *what*. If we could interview the teacher, she might tell us, "That wasn't cultural bias. I was just trying to get the children to speak correctly." Especially in the field of education, *culture* is a term that can be easily misused and misunderstood. (For further discussions of culture see Bohannon, 1992, pp. 3-16; Gonzalez, 2004.)

One of the reasons it is hard to think about culture is that—if those who invented the idea were right—it is all around us, some of it visible and some of it transparent, much of it so familiar to us that we take it for granted. Another reason the notion of culture is elusive is that anthropologists themselves have not been able to agree on a single definition. In 1871, the anthropologist Sir Edward Burnett Tylor (1871/1970) presented this very broad definition: "Culture or Civilization . . . is that complex whole which includes knowledge, belief, art, morals, law, custom, and any other capabilities and habits acquired by man as a member of society" (p. 1). A broad-ranging review of social science literature in the mid-20th century found more than 250 different uses of the term *culture* (Kroeber & Kluckhohn, 1952). The implications of different shadings of meaning of the term *culture* continue to be argued over today without resolution (Kuper, 1999). A basic definition of culture for our purposes refers to patterns in the organization of the conduct of everyday life (Pollock, 2008). In other words, culture consists of the patterning of the practices of "doing being human"—in our routine actions, in our interpretations of meanings in those actions, and in the beliefs that underlie our meaning interpretations.

In a sense, everything in education relates to culture—to its acquisition, its transmission, and its invention. Culture is in us and all around us, just as is the air we breathe. In its scope and distribution, it is personal, familial, communal, institutional, societal, and global. Yet culture as a notion is often difficult to grasp. As we learn and use culture in daily life, it becomes habitual. Our habits become for the most part transparent to us. Thus, culture shifts inside and outside our reflective awareness. We do not think much about the structure and characteristics of culture as we use it just as we do not think reflectively about any familiar tool in the midst of its use. If we hammer things a lot, we do not think about the precise weight or chemical composition of the steel of the hammer, especially as we are actually hammering; and when we speak to someone we know well, we are unlikely to think reflectively about the sound system, grammar, vocabulary, and rhetorical conventions of our language, especially as we are doing things in the midst of our speaking.

Just as hammers and languages are tools by which we get things done, so is culture; indeed, culture can be thought of as the primary human toolkit. Culture is a product of human creativity in action; once we have it, culture enables us to extend our activity still further. In the sense that culture is entirely the product of human activity, an artifact, it is not like the air we breathe. By analogy to computers, which are information tools, culture can be considered as the software—the coding systems for doing meaning and executing sequences of work—by which our human physiological and cognitive hardware is able to operate so that we can make sense and take action with others in daily life. Culture structures the "default" conditions of the everyday practices of being human.

Another way to think of culture is as a sedimentation of the historical experience of persons and social groupings of various kinds, such as nuclear family and kin, gender, ethnicity, race, and social class, all with differing access to power in society. We have become increasingly aware that the invention and sharing of culture (in other words, its production and reproduction) happen through processes that are profoundly political in nature, having to do with access to and distribution of social power. In these processes of cultural production and reproduction, the intimate politics of immediate social relations face-to-face are combined with more public politics in the social forces and processes of economy and society writ large. How does the sedimentation of historical experience as culture take place? What are the micro- and macropolitical circumstances in which culture is learned and invented? How does culture get distributed, similarly and differently, within and across human groups and within and between human generations?

These are questions not only for social scientists or for social philosophers to address; they also are questions that raise issues that are essential for educators to consider. Culture, as it is more and less visible and invisible to its users, is profoundly involved in the processes and contents of education. Culture shapes and is shaped by the learning and teaching that happen during the practical conduct of daily life within all the educational settings we encounter as learning environments throughout the human life span—in families, in school classrooms, in community settings, and in the workplace. There is some evidence that we begin to learn culture in the womb, and we continue to learn new culture until we die. Yet people learn differing sets and subsets of culture, and they can unlearn culture—shedding it as well as adopting it. At the individual and the group levels, some aspects of culture undergo change, and other aspects stay the same within a single human life and across generations. Educators address these issues every time they teach and every time they design curricula. Educators may address these issues explicitly and with conscious awareness, or they may be addressed implicitly and without conscious awareness. But at every moment in the conduct of educational practice, cultural issues and choices are at stake. This chapter makes some of those issues and choices more explicit than they were in the "Little Duck" reading lesson.

Two final orienting assumptions are implicit in the previous discussion. First, everybody is cultural, and although there is no evidence based on which to decide that any particular cultural ways are intrinsically more valuable than others—more inherently superior or inferior—it is a plain political fact that not all cultural practices are equal in power and prestige in the United States or in any other country. Every person and social group possesses and uses culture as a tool for the conduct of human activity. This means that culture is not the possession or characteristic of an exotic other but of all of us, the dominant and the dominated alike. In other words, and to put it more bluntly, within U.S. society, White people are just as cultural as are people of color (indeed the terms *White* and *people of color* represent cultural categories that are socially constructed). Moreover, White Anglo-Saxon Protestants (WASPs) are just as cultural as are Jews or Catholics; men are just as cultural as women; adults are just as cultural as teenagers; Northerners are just as cultural as Southerners; English speakers are just as cultural as the speakers of other languages; and native-born Americans are just as cultural as immigrants or citizens who reside in other countries. This is to say that Americans of African, European, or Asian descent are just as cultural as people who live in Africa, Europe, or Asia. To reiterate, everybody in the world is cultural, even though not all cultures are equal in power or prestige.

The second orienting assumption is that everybody is multicultural. Every person and every human group possess both culture and cultural diversity. For example, Americans of Mexican descent are not culturally identical to Puerto Ricans who live on the mainland, but not all Mexican Americans or Puerto Ricans (or White Episcopalians, for that matter) are culturally identical even if they live in the same neighborhood and attend the same school or church. Members of the same family also are culturally diverse. In fact, we often encounter cultural difference as individual difference as well as encountering culture in its more institutionalized manifestations, such as school literacy, the legal system, or the broadcast media. An important way we meet culture is in the particular people with whom we interact daily. It is not possible for individuals to grow up in a complex modern society without acquiring differing subsets of culture—differing software packages that are tools that can be used in differing kinds of human activity, tools that in part enable and frame the activities in which they are used. Through the nuclear family, through early and later schooling, through peer networks, and through life at work, we encounter, learn, and to some extent help create differing microcultures and subcultures. Just as everyone learns differing variants and styles of the various languages we speak, so that everybody is multilingual (even those of us who speak only English), so, too, is everybody multicultural. No matter how culturally isolated a person's life may appear, in large-scale modern societies (and even in small-scale traditional societies), each member carries a considerable amount of that society's cultural diversity inside. This insight is very clearly stated in the article "Multiculturalism as the Normal Human Experience" by Goodenough (1976).

If it is true that every person and human group are both cultural and multicultural, then a multicultural perspective on the aims and conduct of education is of primary importance. That assumption guides this chapter. It discusses how culture is organized and distributed in society, and this raises issues that have special relevance for education. This chapter considers practices of teaching and learning in multicultural classrooms and concludes with further discussion of the diversity of culture not only within society but also within the person and the implications of that diversity for multicultural education.

Summary Discussion

Culture is generally seen as a product of human activity that is used as a tool. It is seen as being learned and transmitted from our elders and as being invented (or incrementally transformed) through recurrent improvisation within current situations of practice. How much and in what ways culture is shared within and between identifiable human groups are issues on which there is much debate currently. Power and politics seem to be involved in the processes by which culture is learned, shared, and changed. Culture, in other words, takes shape in the weight of human history. Some aspects of culture are explicit, and others are implicit, learned, and shared outside conscious awareness. Our moods and desires as well as our thoughts are culturally constructed.

Culture can be thought of as a construction—it constructs us and we construct it. That is, all thoughts, feelings, and human activity are not simply natural but are the result of historical and personal experiences that become sedimented as culture in habit. Culture varies, somehow, from one person or group to another. Because our subjective world—what we see, know, and want—is culturally constructed and because culture varies, persons really do not inhabit the same subjective worlds even though they may seem to do so. Even though some of us show up at what seems to be the same event, how we experience it is never quite the same across the various individuals who have joined together in interaction. Thus, no single or determinative human world is a fixed point of reference. Individually and collectively, we make cultural worlds, and they are multiple. This point has profound implications for educators as is discussed in the following sections of this chapter.

As human beings, not only do we live in webs of meaning, caring, and desire that we ourselves create and that create us, but also those webs hang in social gravity (Geertz, 1973). Within the webs, all of our activity is vested in the weight of history; that is, in a social world of inequality, all movement is up or down. Earlier conceptions of culture have been criticized for describing human actions that are guided or framed by it as existing in a universe without gravity. Movement in everyday life was thus unconstrained; it had no effort, no force. There was no domination or subordination, no resistance or compliance in such a cultural world. In more recent conceptions of culture, we are coming to see that, living as we do in a gravity-ridden social and cultural universe, we and our actions always have weight. We are culturally constructed and constructing beings, and in that construction, we are never effortless, never standing still.

CULTURAL ISSUES IN EDUCATION, IN SOCIETY, AND IN PERSONS

Four main issues concerning culture have special relevance for educators: (1) the notion of culture as invisible as well as visible, (2) the politics of cultural difference in school and society, (3) the inherent diversity of cultures and subcultures within human social groups, and (4) the diversity of cultures within the individual—a perspective on the self as multiculturally constructed.

Invisible Culture

The distinction between visible and invisible culture has also been called *explicit/implicit* or *overt/covert* (Hall, 1959, 1976; Philips, 1983). Much of culture not only is held outside conscious awareness but also is learned and taught outside awareness; hence, neither the cultural insiders nor the newcomers are aware that certain aspects of their culture exist. In multicultural education and in discussions of cultural diversity more generally, the focus has been on visible, explicit aspects of culture, such as language, dress, food habits, religion, and aesthetic conventions. While important, these visible aspects of culture, which are taught deliberately and learned (at least to some extent) consciously, are only the tip of the iceberg of culture. Implicit and invisible aspects of culture are also important. How long in clock time one can be late before being impolite, how one conceives or experiences emotional or physical pain, how one displays such pain behaviorally, what topics should be avoided at the beginning of a conversation, how one shows interest or attention through listening behavior, how loud is too loud or not loud enough in speaking, how one shows that one would like the speaker to move on to the next point—these are all aspects of culture that we learn and use without realizing it. When we meet other people whose invisible cultural assumptions and patterns of action differ from those we have learned and expect implicitly, we usually do not recognize what they are doing as cultural in origin. Rather, we see them as rude or uncooperative. We may apply clinical labels to the other people—passive aggressive or suffering from low self-esteem.

Differences in invisible culture can be troublesome in circumstances of intergroup conflict. The difficulty lies in our inability to recognize others' differences in ways of acting as cultural rather than personal. We tend to naturalize other people's behavior and blame them—attributing intentions, judging competence—without realizing that we are experiencing culture rather than nature.

Modern society exacerbates the difficulties that can result from differences in invisible culture. Formal organizations and institutions, such as hospitals, workplaces, the legal system, and schools, become collection sites for invisible cultural difference. If the differences were more visible, we might see less misattribution in the absence of intergroup conflict. For example, if we were to meet a woman in a hospital emergency room who was wearing exotic dress, speaking a language other than English, and carrying food that looked and smelled strange, we would not assume that we understood her thoughts and feelings or that she necessarily understood ours. Yet when such a person is dressed similarly to us, speaks English, and does not differ from us in other obvious ways, we may fail to recognize the invisible cultural orientations that differ between us, and a cycle of mutual misattribution can start.

Anthropologists with linguistic and cognitive orientations have identified aspects of invisible culture (Gumperz, 1982; Hymes, 1974). They make a helpful distinction between language community and speech community or network. People in the same language community share knowledge of the sound system, grammar, and vocabulary of a language. But within the same language community, there are diverse speech communities or networks—sets of persons who share assumptions about the purposes of speaking, modes of politeness, topics of interest, ways of responding to others. Those cultural assumptions concerning ways of speaking differ considerably, even though at a general level all are uttering the same language. That is, language community differences are visible, but speech community differences are often invisible. That may be what happened in our opening scene from a classroom, in which "What did Little Duck see?" was treated as an occasion for drill in "correct" pronunciation.

Yet cultural difference—visible and invisible—does not always lead to trouble between people. These differences become more troublesome in some circumstances than in others. That leads to a consideration of the circumstances of intercultural contact.

The Politics of Cultural Difference: Boundaries and Borders

The introductory discussion states that cultural difference demarcates lines of political difference and often of domination. By analogy to a weather map, boundaries of cultural difference can be seen as isobars of power, rank, and prestige in society. One can trace boundaries of networks of members who share cultural knowledge of various sorts, such as in language, social ideology and values, religious beliefs, technical knowledge, preferences in aesthetic tastes, in recreation and sport, in personal dress and popular music tastes, and in cultivated tastes in the fine arts, cuisine, and literature. Because these preferences have differing prestige value, they have been called *cultural capital* (Bourdieu & Passeron, 1977). Such preferences also become symbols or badges of group identity—markers of ethnicity, religion, gender, or social class.

The presence of cultural difference in society does not necessarily lead to conflict, however, nor need it lead to difficulty in education. The presence of conflict depends on whether cultural difference is being treated as a *boundary* or as a *border* (Barth, 1969; Giroux, 1991; McDermott & Gospodinoff, 1981). *Cultural boundary* refers to the simple presence of some kind of cultural difference. As noted earlier, cultural boundaries are characteristic of all human societies, traditional as well as modern. *Cultural border* is the treatment of a particular feature of cultural difference as grounds for differing rights—privilege or disprivilege, favorable or unfavorable regard. Treating a cultural difference as a border matter politicizes that difference, while treating that same cultural difference as a boundary matter depoliticizes that difference.

When a cultural boundary is treated as a cultural border, differences in privilege—in rights and obligations—are powerfully attached to the presence or absence of certain kinds of cultural knowledge. Consider, for example, the political/cultural border between the United States and Mexico. On either side of the border are people who speak English and people who speak Spanish; that is, the boundaries of language community cross over the lines demarcating national citizenship. Yet on either side of the border, fluency in Spanish—which is an aspect of cultural knowledge—is differentially rewarded or punished. On the Mexican side of the border, fluency in Spanish is an advantage legally, educationally, and in the conduct of much daily life while on the U.S. side, the same cultural knowledge is disadvantaged; indeed, in parts of south Texas, speaking Spanish is still stigmatized.

When one arrives at a cultural border, one's cultural knowledge may be held up for scrutiny—stopped and frisked as in the example from the "Little Duck" reading lesson. The same kind of stopping and frisking of cultural difference can happen when one enters the emergency room of a hospital and speaks to an admitting clerk or when one speaks to the *maitre d'* at a restaurant. Yet cultural boundaries (the objective presence of cultural difference) need not necessarily be treated as cultural borders. This is a matter of socially constructed framing.

The framing of cultural difference as boundary or as border can change over time. Sometimes that change is very rapid, as in the following example (Fanon, 1963). In Algeria shortly before France gave up colonial rule, the pronunciation of the announcers on the state radio was made a cultural border issue by the independence movement. Complaints were voiced that Radio Algiers was not employing native Algerians. The independence movement saw this practice as another symbol of colonial oppression. Radio Algiers sent out a statement that its announcers were in fact Algerians. The independence movement then asked why the radio announcers spoke cosmopolitan French rather than the Algerian dialect. The complaints about the announcers became increasingly strident in the independence-oriented press, right up to Independence Day. After that day, the announcers on Radio Algiers continued to speak cosmopolitan French, but public complaint ended instantly. The reason for the complaint was gone, and so a small feature of cultural difference, which had been framed for a time as a cultural border, was reframed as a cultural boundary.

This suggests that cultural difference, rather than being considered a cause of conflict in society (and in education), is more appropriately seen as a *resource* for conflict. If people have a reason to look for trouble, a particular feature of cultural difference—especially one that becomes a badge of social identity—can be used to start a fight. But the causes of the fight go beyond the cultural difference itself.

Cultural Differentiation as a Political Process

What happens over time when certain aspects of cultural difference are treated as border issues? Examples from language suggest that the differences become more extreme on either side. This suggests that political conflict, explicit and implicit, is a major engine of cultural change. Such conflict generates cultural resistance. The linguist William Labov (1963) found that on Martha's Vineyard, a small island off the coast of Massachusetts, certain sound features in the islanders' dialect became increasingly divergent from the more standard English spoken by summer tourists as the number of tourists staying on the island in the summer increased over time, although the islanders were not aware that this was happening. First-hand contacts with a standard model of American English had been increasing for the islanders, but across a generation, their speech was becoming more different from that of the mainlanders.

A similar process of divergence was reported as taking place across the time span of half hour interviews in experimental situations (Giles & Powesland, 1975). Speakers of differing British regional dialects were paired for two-person discussions. In some discussions, mild discomfort and conflict were experimentally introduced while in other discussions, conflict was not introduced. In the discussions with conflict and discomfort, by the end of a half hour, each person was speaking a broader form of regional dialect than before the discussion began. In other words, a person from Yorkshire talking to a person from Dorsetshire would become more distinctly Yorkshire in pronunciation, and the individual from Dorsetshire would become more Dorsetshire in pronunciation as the conversation between the two progressed. Conversely, when conflict was not introduced and the two parties spoke comfortably, pronunciation features that differed between their two dialects became less distinct—they were converging in speech style rather than diverging.

This example suggests that cultural divergence is a result rather than a cause of social conflict. Bateson, Jackson, Haley, and Weakland (1972) called the tendency of subsystems to evolve in increasingly differentiated ways *complementary schismogenesis*, which seems to be the process by which cultural resistance over time results in cultural change. It should be emphasized, however, that such change can occur entirely outside the conscious awareness of those involved in it as well as in situations of more explicit, conscious awareness in which people are deliberate regarding the change they are struggling to produce.

The classic view of culture in social science (as found in the definition of culture by Tylor [1871/1970] presented at the beginning of this chapter) was as a total system with integrated parts, the operation of which tended toward maintaining a steady state. As we have seen, culture now seems to be more labile than that—variable in the moment. This raises the question of how we conceive of cultural change—as loss, as gain, as a mixture of both, or less evaluatively as change. We must also consider how culture is shared within human groups. We usually think of ethnic and racial groups (and perhaps of gender categories as well) as necessarily identifying cultural boundaries. Such groups, we may assume, are defined by shared culture among their members. Barth (1969) contends, however, that cultural sharing is not the crucial defining attribute of ethnic group membership. Rather, the ethnic or racial group is more appropriately considered as an economic and political interest group.

Features of culture may be considered as identity badges, indicating group membership. But cultural sharing is not essential for this, according to Barth. There may be much cultural diversity within the same named social category. He used as an example the Pathans (also called Pashtun), who live as a numerical minority on one side of the border between Pakistan and Afghanistan and as a majority on the other side. Some Pathans are herders—more so on the Afghan side of the border. Other Pathans are farmers—more so on the Pakistani side. Yet both herders and farmers will identify as Pathan and are so regarded by other ethnic groups on either side of the border. Their ethnic identification is at least as strong as is their identification with the nation-state within whose border they reside; that became apparent during the war in Afghanistan in 2002.

Cultural Change as Cultural Loss—or Not

When we think of ethnic/racial groups and cultural groups as having the same boundaries—the traditional view—we sometimes think of cultural change as cultural loss. Members of an ethnic group can blame themselves for losing a language, a religion, and a household practice. Native Americans, for example, have mourned the passing of old culture and have gone beyond mourning to self-blame, considering themselves less Indian than their forebears. Yet if a Koyukon Athabaskan now uses a snowmobile rather than a dog team and sled, does that mean that person is any less Koyukon than before? Not necessarily, if we follow Barth's analysis. What is essential for the maintenance of ethnic groups and ethnic identities are not the specifics of cultural traits practiced by the members; rather, being ethnic counts economically and politically in the larger society. Even the specific ways in which it counts to be ethnic can change; yet if there continue to be economic and political consequences of being identified as ethnic, especially if that is to the advantage of the members, then the ethnic group continues. The classic view makes culture the defining attribute of ethnic identity. It becomes easy, then, to see cultural change as cultural loss. This can be thought of as the leaky bucket perspective on cultural change—as if culture were held in a human group as water is contained in a bucket. Change then becomes the holes in the bucket. As one carries such a bucket over time and space, the water gradually drains out. Alternatively, we can conceive of the bucket of culture as always full. Air may replace the water, but the bucket is never empty. The contemporary Koyukon society, with its snowmobile practices, can be considered just as full culturally as the Koyukon society in the days of sled and dog team. What is in the bucket is different now, but the bucket is still not empty. During the summer, people in an Odawa community in northern Ontario wear T-shirts as they fish from aluminum boats powered by outboard motors. They no longer wear buckskin and use birch-bark canoes. Yet they continue to fish, and they do so with differing fishing rights from those of White Canadians. Moreover, they still consider themselves Odawa, as distinct from White Canadians in neighboring villages who also fish from aluminum boats while wearing T-shirts.

Culture and Collective Identity Formation

To call something cultural has in itself political implications. Because so many aspects of culture are transparent to its users in their use, ordinarily we do not think about or notice them. Yet in complex and diverse modern societies, as ethnic, racial, religious, and gender identifications become self-aware among identification group members, they begin to notice their customary practices and to identify them as cultural. As with ethnic identification, cultural identification is always relational and comparative—with reference to another. In the early 19th century, for example, German *Kultur* began to be invoked by German intellectuals in contrast and opposition to the French and Italians, whose tastes in literature and music, architecture, and clothing had previously set the standard of what was desirable in upper-class polite society. Without the presence of French and Italian models to compete with, Germans may not have become so aware of their own Germanness. This awareness progressed beyond rediscovery to invention, with German intellectuals such as Wagner helping to create a Germanic heritage with the support of the ruling interests in German society. With this rise in in-group awareness and solidarity came a heightened awareness of boundaries with non-Teutonic others. To the extent that this perception of out-groups was invidious, the boundaries became borders.

We see a similar phenomenon today with the rise of religious nationalism and of ethnic and racial nationalism. With in-group identification, there is always the possibility for treating boundaries as borders. Especially when the heightening of cultural awareness and identification is used as a political strategy for changing power relations in society, or for legitimating territorial or colonial expansion, in-group solidarity and identification can become demonic. As Said (1978) notes in commenting on the colonial relationship between Europe and a perceived Orient that was a cultural creation of Europeans themselves, when more powerful nations or interest groups identify some "other" as exotic and different, there can be a tendency for the more powerful to project their own flaws, contradictions, and hostilities on the constructed other. Such projections are reciprocated by those who have been "othered" in a process of mutual border framing. Through this process of projective "othering," negative cultural stereotypes result, making the fostering of intercultural and multicultural awareness a tricky business indeed.

Ethnic identification need not necessarily lead to othering in the negative sense, however; the comparisons with those who differ from "Us" need not be invidious. Cultural differences can be framed as boundaries rather than as borders even though such framing takes effort to maintain. It should be noted, however, that an increase in the deliberateness and intensity of cultural awareness necessarily involves a comparative awareness. The construction of in-group identity is a relational process through which a definition of Other as well as of Self, of Them as well as of Us—and in the case of subordinated groups a specific identification of aspects of oppression—becomes more focal in conscious awareness.

MULTICULTURAL TEACHING AND LEARNING
Emphasis of Invisible as Well as Visible Culture

Schools can support or hinder the development of healthy identity and of intergroup awareness. The discussion now turns to teaching and learning in classrooms (see the review chapter by Wills, Lintz, & Mehan, 2004). This chapter emphasizes the importance of culture and criticizes our tendencies to *essentialize* it. When we essentialize culture, assuming that all persons in a given social category are culturally similar and focusing on the unitary cultures of various Others without reflecting on our own cultures and their diversity, we open a Pandora's box of opportunity for negative attribution. Sometimes social scientific notions of culture, especially of culture as a unified system and of group membership as culturally defined, have provided a justification for intergroup stereotypes. When these stereotypes come with social scientific warrant, we call them *neostereotypes*.

Teaching about the cultural practices of other people without stereotyping or misinterpreting them and teaching about one's own cultural practices without invidiously characterizing the practices of other people should be the aims of multicultural education. In situations of intergroup conflict, these aims can be ideals that are difficult to attain. Educators should face such difficulty realistically.

One problem in multicultural curriculum and pedagogy is the overemphasis on visible (explicit) culture at the expense of the invisible and implicit. Focusing mainly on explicit culture can be misleading. Even when we do this respectfully of the lifeways of others, focusing on visible culture easily slides into too comfortable a stance of cultural romance or cultural tourism.

Particular traits of visible culture, often treated in isolation, have become the basis for much of what we teach about cultural diversity in schools. Some educators speak critically of "piñata curriculum," "snowshoe curriculum," and "holidays and heroes" in characterizing this approach. By treating cultural practices as sets of static facts, we trivialize them in superficiality, and we make it seem as if culture were necessarily unchanging. What if Mexican Americans were to have a party and not break a piñata? Would they be any less Mexican? They are only if we adopt an essentialist view of culture with its accompanying leaky bucket image of cultural change.

A way to teach about explicit culture without overgeneralizing about the lifeways of other people is to emphasize the variability of culture within social groups and the continual presence of cultural change as well as cultural continuity across time (see Gutierrez & Rogoff, 2003). Unfortunately, published multicultural materials that have an essentialist emphasis may not lend themselves well to this method. Yet in every classroom there is a resource for the study of within-group cultural diversity as well as between-group diversity. That resource consists of the everyday experience and cultural practices of the students and teachers themselves. (This is most easily done in a self-contained classroom, and so this discussion may seem most relevant for elementary school teaching, but many of the issues and approaches mentioned can be undertaken by high school and college teachers as well.)

Critical Autobiography as Curriculum and as Action Research

Critically reflective autobiographies by students and oral histories of their families—a form of community action research—can become important parts of a multicultural curriculum. Even in a classroom with a student population highly segregated by race or by social class, students' reflective investigation of their own lives and of family and local community histories will reveal diversity as well as similarity (hooks, 1993; Skilton Sylvester, 1994; Torres-Guzmán, 1992; Wiggington, 1986; Witherell & Noddings, 1991). Not all Italian Americans in a classroom have had the same family experience of immigration. Not all African American students whose forebears moved from the rural South to a large city have had the same experience of urbanization. As a result of differing life experiences, there are differences in cultural funds of knowledge between families who on the surface appear to be demographically similar—differences in family microcultures (see Gonzalez, Moll, & Amanti, 2005).

Just as students can engage in critical autobiography, so their teachers need to identify the particular cultures of their individual students through observation of and dialogue with those students. An index for the individual student's distinctive cultural repertoire is that student's distinctive *daily round*—where the student shows up and what is happening there, in the specific sequences and ranges of engagement of the student in local communities of practice inside and outside school. By learning which particular communities of practice a student has had access to and the kinds of participation in those communities that a student has engaged in, a teacher can come to understand the personal culture of each student—to see each student as "cultural" without stereotyping each one simplistically as "Anglo" or "African American," as "lower class" or "upper middle class," as "boy" or "girl." (See the discussion in Gutierrez & Rogoff, 2003.) In order to develop this kind of nonstereotypical understanding of actual students, a teacher must spend time outside school in the school community(ies) from which the teacher's students come as well as pay attention to the communities of practice that are found during the school day in places beyond that teacher's own classroom. There is no substitute for this first-hand knowledge of the everyday interactional circumstances of the particular children one teaches—without it one adopts stereotypic, categorical "cultural" labels for students that are too general to be able to take accurate account of the actual lives and the personal cultures that those specific children are developing.

A close look at particular families and at the daily rounds of individuals can reveal similarity as well as distinctiveness in cultural repertoires—as in variations on a common theme of life experience such as that of the experience of racism by African Americans or of language prejudice by those who grow up speaking Spanish in the United States. But not all of the experiences, even of racism within a given racial group, are identical across individuals. Thus, diversity and similarity always accompany one another in the real stories of people in human groups. Those stories have involved struggles to change and to resist. Contemporary community issues, as students address them through local community study, also provide opportunities for students to take action to improve the circumstances of their lives and, in the process, come to see themselves and their families not simply as passive recipients of social and cultural influences but also as active agents who are making sense and making their lives.

Direct connections between the daily lives of students outside the classroom and the content of instruction in history, social studies, and literature can make the stated curriculum come alive. These connections also afford teachers an opportunity to learn the cultural backgrounds and cultural diversity they confront with each set of students. As stated earlier, formal organizations in modern societies become collection sites for cultural diversity. This is true for every school classroom. Each new set of students represents a unique sampling from the universe of local cultural diversity present in the school area. Simply knowing that one has three Haitian students and four Cambodian students—or seventeen girls and eleven boys—in a certain classroom, for example, does not tell that teacher anything (necessarily) about the specific cultural backgrounds of those students and their families and their assumptions about ethnicity, race, or gender given the cultural diversity that is possible within any social category. The teacher's tasks are to know not only about Haitians or Cambodians in general or about girls and boys in general but also about these students in particular. By making particular student culture and family history a deliberate object of study by all students in the classroom, teachers can learn much about what they need to know in order to teach the particular students in ways that are sensitive and powerfully engaging, intellectually and emotionally.

As our standards for what students need to learn change from the lower-order mastery of facts and simple skills to higher-order reasoning and the construction of knowledge that is personally distinctive and meaningful (in other words, as we move from an essentialist under-standing of curriculum, teaching, and learning to a more constructivist one), our conceptions of culture in multicultural education also need to become more constructivist and less essentialist. Teaching about culture as socially constructed and continually changing is thus consistent with contemporary definitions of good pedagogy and with recent developments in cultural theory and social theory.

Multicultural Pedagogy as Emancipatory

Some multicultural educators recommend a critical approach to cultures of domination and to the phenomenon of domination. Ladson-Billings (1994) describes African American and White teachers who were effective with African American students. They taught in a variety of styles, but one common approach was to deal directly and explicitly with issues of injustice and oppression and the privileging of mainstream knowledge and perspectives as they came up in the curriculum and in the reported daily experiences of their students. Trueba (1994), Nieto (1999), McCarthy (1993), Perry and Fraser (1993), Sleeter and Grant (1993), Apple (1996), and Giroux (1991) recommend a similar approach, sometimes called *critical pedagogy*, *counterhegemonic pedagogy*, or *emancipatory pedagogy*.

Cultural hegemony refers to the established view of things—a commonsense view of what is and why things happen that serves the interests of those people already privileged in a society. It is hegemonic when the school presents a comfortable established view of the nature of U.S. society and of the goodness and inherent rightness of school knowledge and school literacy. Students whose lives are not affirmed by the establishment seem intuitively not to accept hegemonic content and methods of instruction. They often resist, consciously or unconsciously, covertly as well as overtly.

Multicultural education has an opportunity and a challenge to be counter-hegemonic. When issues such as racism, class privilege, and sexism are left silent in the classroom, the implicit message for students of color appears to be that the teacher and the school do not acknowledge that experiences of oppression exist. If only the standard language, the standard American history, and the voices and lives of White men appear in the curriculum, then the further implicit message (by what is left in and what is left out of the knowledge presented as legitimate by the school) seems to be that the real United States and real school are only about the cultural mainstream and its establishment ideology. This approach especially marginalizes the students of color who come to school already marginalized by life experience and by the historical experience of oppression in their ethnic or racial communities. Such a hegemonic approach also marginalizes female students (Sadker & Sadker, 1994). Marginalization is alienating, and one response to alienation is resistance—the very thing that makes teaching and learning more difficult for students and their teachers.

Ironically, for teachers to name and acknowledge tough social issues, rather than turning students against school and the teachers, makes it more possible for students who have experienced oppression to affiliate with teachers and school learning. By taking the moralizing that characterizes culturally hegemonic teaching out of the picture and reframing second-culture acquisition as strategically instrumental rather than inherently right, a teacher facilitates second-culture learning by students from nonmainstream backgrounds. Through such teaching, cultural borders are reframed as boundaries, and the politics of the dominant culture and cultures are, to some extent at least, depoliticized in the classroom. The cycles of resistance and schismogenesis that are stimulated by hegemonic curriculum and teaching do not get set off.

The role of resistance to cultures of domination in student disaffiliation from school learning is a fundamental issue in public education in the United States, Canada, Australia, Britain, and the rest of Europe (Apple, 1996; Giroux, 1983; Willis, 1977). Ogbu (1987) has argued that for students of "caste-like" minority background in the United States (from groups with historic experiences of stigma and limitation of economic opportunity, such as African

Americans, Mexican Americans, Puerto Ricans, and Native Americans), resistance to school is almost inevitable because of the effects of group history. Fordham (1996) has shown that African American high school students in Washington, D.C., defined achieving in school as "acting White." Other scholars (Erickson, 1987; Foley, 1991; Trueba, 1994) have acknowledged Ogbu's insight while observing that student resistance can result not only from a group history of oppression but also from oppressive and alienating circumstances surrounding teaching and learning within the school itself. Another difficulty with Ogbu's position is that it leaves no room for the possibility of school change.

A major theme here is that when business is conducted as usual in school, student resistance results from that as well as from influences from the wider society on students. In the short run, we cannot change the wider society. But we can make school learning environments less alienating. Multicultural education, especially critical or antiracist multicultural education, is a way to change the business as usual of schools. When that happens, as Ladson-Billings (1994) and others have shown, minority students of backgrounds categorized as "caste-like" rise to the occasion. When treated with dignity and taught skillfully, such students affiliate with the school and achieve.

Process of Reframing Borders as Boundaries in the Classroom

The approach recommended in this chapter frames the cultural diversity to be found in the classroom in terms of cultural boundaries rather than cultural borders. Even when cultural difference and group identity are highly politicized in the wider society, by approaching the cultures of students forthrightly in the classroom, such differences and identities can be depoliticized to a remarkable extent (or perhaps we might think of the process as being repoliticized in a positive rather than negative frame).

A problem comes with teaching second-culture skills and knowledge as morality rather than as pragmatic skills for survival and success. Delpit (1995) observes that for students of color in the United States, the school's "second culture" often appears alien and dominating. Culturally mainstream ways of speaking and writing represent a "language and culture of power" that minority students need to master for success in the wider society. But teaching this culture of power can be unsuccessful in two ways. In the first, the teacher attempts to teach the second-culture skills in a moralizing way—the right way to act and to be. This approach is likely to stimulate student resistance and thus is a teaching strategy that risks student refusal to learn. (Consider the word *ain't*. Teachers for generations have been teaching working-class students not to say *ain't* as a moral lesson. Yet inside and outside the classroom, the students still say *ain't*.)

Another unsuccessful way to teach a second-culture skill is implicitly, according to Delpit (1995). She observes that among well-meaning middle-class White teachers, some aspects of the language of power are part of the teachers' own invisible culture. Taking it for granted themselves, they do not teach it explicitly to working-class African American students. Delpit recommends an alternative approach to teach second-culture skills explicitly and carefully but without moralizing. The school's language and culture of power can be presented as a situational dialect to be used pragmatically for special situations, such as job interviews, formal writing, and college admissions interviews.

Delpit (1995) would say that if the teacher in the "Little Duck" reading lesson wanted to teach pronunciation of "standard English" as an aspect of the language and culture of power, she could do that—and do it explicitly—explaining what was being taught and why. That would be to turn the treatment of saying aloud a final *t* in *what* from a cultural border frame to a cultural boundary frame. This demoralizes and depoliticizes the teaching of culturally different ways of speaking. It recognizes and names those differing ways without judging either way as being better or worse than the other. But what the teacher did—making a big thing of pronouncing the final *t* without explaining what she was doing as a teacher—was to treat the cultural difference in pronunciation as a border matter rather than as a boundary matter.

Gonzalez, Moll, and Amanti (2005) show that minority students' families maintain *funds of knowledge* in their cultural practices that can be used in curriculum as teachers learn what those practices are and the kinds of knowledge and skill they entail. Gutierrez, in a series of compelling studies of classroom teaching (Gutierrez, Baquedano-López, Alvarez, & Chiu, 1999; Gutierrez, Baquedano-López, & Tejeda, 1999; Gutierrez, Rymes, & Larson, 1995), shows that learning is enhanced (as is student morale—the will to learn) when teachers in classroom discourse use language and speech styles from students' homes and from popular culture. This bridging pedagogy between official school knowledge and unofficial knowledge creates an intermediate "third space"—a hybrid discourse that allows students to use the voices they bring to the classroom as they begin to affiliate with school voices and discourses and to appropriate them as their own. In such classrooms, the price of school success is not that one gives up one's own self and voice to adopt a new and alien one. Rather, the student adds new voices and discourses to those already possessed, and the teacher through his or her own language use respects both the voices that are familiar to the student and those that are new. An analogous pedagogical approach is taken by Lee (2001, 2007), in what she calls "cultural modeling"—using students' knowledge of and fluency in street language, in particular of "signifying" and hip-hop, to support students' critical discussion of literature in high school English classes. "Third space" pedagogy acknowledges cultural difference explicitly, and treating it as a boundary matter rather than as a border matter makes an instructional resource of that difference rather than a ground for conflict between teacher and student. It is a way of enacting mutual respect and trust between teachers and students.

A group history of oppression no doubt makes students and parents wary of school and its claims that the standard ways of teaching are good for students. That is, trust of a school's good intentions, especially by students and parents of color, is not automatic. But relationships of mutual trust and respect can be established between teachers and students in the classroom within which students assent to learn what teachers are trying to teach them. Sensitive multicultural pedagogy is one foundation for such trust. (On the notions of face threat in learning and on student learning as political assent, see Erickson, 1987 and Erickson et al., 2007.)

To summarize, when combined with reflective self-study of the student's own language use in the family, among peers, and in the neighborhood—study by which the student explores his or her own repertoire of differing speech styles used in differing situations—explicit teaching and learning of the language of power can be framed as a matter not of cultural borders but of cultural boundaries. This approach takes a critical and strategic view of multiculturalism for survival reasons. It does not moralize about culture difference, and it does not set up resistance to learning new cultural ways—so long as the new ways are not being presented as inherently better than the ways the students already know.

Conventional Teaching as Cultural Border Wars

When teachers treat the dominant culture in the curriculum as a matter of cultural borders rather than of boundaries, the classroom can become an unsafe place for students. Educators often use aspects of invisible culture as diagnostic indicators with clinical significance, especially in the early grades. For example, if children come from homes in which adults do not routinely ask them teacherlike questions to which the adults already know the answer, such questions by a teacher can initially seem confusing or intimidating (Heath, 1983). "What color is this?" the kindergarten teacher says on the first day of school, holding up a red piece of construction paper in front of an African American child whose mother is on welfare. "Aonh-oh' (I don't know)," the child replies, thinking there must be some trick because anybody can see that the paper is red. "Lacking in reading readiness," the teacher thinks, writes in the child's permanent record, and assigns the child to the bottom reading group.

Because we do not recognize knowing about teacherlike questions as a distinct cultural skill, we may not see the teacher's informal readiness test as cultural or as culturally biased. Such framing of cultural difference as a border can be done inadvertently by teachers who are themselves members of the student's ethnic group and speech community as well as by teachers who are of majority background.

The cultural responsiveness or relevance of a classroom learning environment can differ in contradictory ways between the visible and the invisible aspects of culture. For example, in the same multiracial kindergarten or first-grade classroom in which a teacher uses informal tests of reading readiness that treat invisible cultural knowledge and skill as a cultural border (such as recognition of teacher questions and how to answer them), the teacher may have put a picture of Frederick Douglass on the wall, read a book about his life, presented information of West Africa in a positive light, and taught basic vocabulary in Yoruba or Swahili. Yet hanging a picture of Douglass, the African American abolitionist, on the wall next to a picture of George Washington, the White slaveholder, or introducing students to an African language does not make that classroom fully multicultural if invisible aspects of the communicative cultural practices of African American students are still being treated in invidious ways.

Such contradictions between formal and informal culture must be confusing and alienating for students, even though they may experience that alienation without conscious awareness. This is why attention to issues of invisible informal culture as well as those of visible formal culture seems so important for the success of attempts at multicultural education. And in all of this work, we must critically investigate our notions of failure and success itself, for "school failure" and "school success" are themselves cultural constructions, generally within society and locally within each classroom (see Varenne & McDermott, 1998).

CONCLUSION: ON DIVERSITY OF TONGUES AND THEIR EDUCATIONAL POTENTIAL

The Russian literary critic Bakhtin (1981) provides us with a final way to consider culture in its continuity and in its diversity as transmitted across generations and as invented in the present moment. He studied the novel as it emerged in the 16th and 18th centuries in Spain, France, and England, respectively, and as it developed in England, France, and Russia in the 19th century. Bakhtin noted that the classic novelists depicted a variety of ways of speaking across their various characters who differed in social class, gender, and region. That diversity he called *heteroglossia*, from the Greek, meaning "differing tongues." He believed that a fine novel encapsulated key aspects of the total diversity in speech styles found in the society at the historical moment in which that novel was written. To produce such a text convincingly, the author must have incorporated the diversity of tongues present in the society.

Bakhtin (1981) also observed a personal heteroglossia within the characters of the novel akin to that in its author. For example, in de Cervantes's *Don Quixote* (2005), Bakhtin noticed that the good Don, of bourgeois background, usually spoke in an imitation of the literary romance. Thus, his speech style sounded like the Spanish of the nobility. Sancho Panza, the peasant, usually spoke in the speech style of the lower classes. Yet once in a while, when engaged with the Don, or when reflecting to himself on what he had been experiencing, Sancho's speech drifted slightly toward the more prestigious style of Spanish. This tendency, apparent from the beginning of the modern novel, was more pronounced in 19th-century French and Russian novels. Russian serfs, for example, were depicted as speaking in a variety of speech styles, what Bakhtin called "social languages"—some more elevated and agentive, some more subordinated and passive. Worldview, personal status, and agency seemed to shift, as did the characters' language style.

Bakhtin's (1981) insights suggest ways of understanding how cultural diversity is organized and distributed within a society and within persons. There is heteroglossia within a society. Members of distinct social categories and social networks speak more often than not in differing ways (reminiscent of the "speech community" notion discussed earlier). Men do tend to speak differently from women, African Americans from Whites, working-class people from upper-middle-class people, gay from straight, fundamentalist Christians from Unitarians, physicians from lawyers (and physicians from nurses). These ways of speaking are relatively continuously distributed within the various social groupings; they become badges of identity of such groupings; and for the most major social categories such as class, gender, race and ethnicity, and religion, these social languages tend to persist across generations. In other words, social divisions and cultural and linguistic diversity appear to be consistently reproduced in society across time.

Moreover, the differing ways of speaking carry with them differing points of view that are the result of the differing life experiences of the speakers and, as the feminist slogan puts it, "The personal is political." Thus, the historical experience of a group and its particular political interests in assuming that things are really one way rather than some other—its ideology—come with the social language of the group as uttered by a particular member of that group. Ways of speaking, then, are discourses—whole sets of assumptions about the world and roles for being in the world that are entailed in certain ways of creating oral and written texts (Foucault, 1979; Gee, 1990). Much more is involved than language style alone. To the extent that various group interests and their discourses are involved with the distribution of power in society, there can be conflict and contradiction between ways of speaking and thinking as well as between social groupings. A discourse is in a sense a social institution or a subculture.

Yet the consistency of cultural reproduction is not unitary or absolute. There is also heteroglossia within persons. Each person's life experiences differ somewhat from those of other people, and every person lives in a variety of social situations each day. Differing social situations provide differing ecologies of relationship with other people. They evoke differing aspects of the individual's overall repertoire of ways of speaking. One speaks differently to one's mother than to one's siblings, and to one's teacher than to one's mother. Sometimes in complex relationships, such as that between an employee and supervisor who are also friends or between spouses who are simultaneously lovers, parents, and administrators of household resources, varieties of interrelated voices are evoked from moment to moment in what appears to be the same social situation. The utterances of persons in dialogue lean on one another in mutual influence, Bakhtin (1981) claimed. Thus, the phenomenon of ways of speaking (and of discourses) is inherently labile as well as stable. Culture at the group level varies in part because individuals differ among one another and within themselves as they find themselves in differing social circumstances. In other words, there is an inherent hybridity in cultural practices (see Arteaga, 1994; Gutierrez, Baquedano-López, & Tejeda, 1999; Valle & Torres, 1995)—a blending of sources and voices in which new combinations and recombinations of old elements with new ones are continually being made.

As diverse persons show up in the scenes of daily life, they bring their heteroglossia with them. There can be affiliation as well as conflict across those cultural differences. And discourses can be contested; they can be interrupted or interrogated. When that happens, the assumptions of the discourse become visible and available for criticism. If a person or a group were to change discourses in a conflict, that would be to take a different stance in the world. One may feel as if that is not permitted or as if that is one's right.

Because the discourses vary within persons as well as between groups, whatever conflict or affiliation there may be between the discourses in society is experienced within the personality. This means that the diversity of tongues and of voices within the person has profound emotional content and profound significance for personal identity and wholeness. Schools are collection sites for a diversity of voices and identities. Schools ask students to try on new discourses, new ways of speaking and thinking, new ways of being a self, and to appropriate them as their own. At their best, schools ask this of teachers as well in order that they may come into closer awareness of and engagement with the voices of their students and develop intellectually within their careers, appropriating within themselves more of the various discourses and literacies of their society. That is personally risky business for both students and teachers. When discourses, or cultures, are in conflict in society, then conflict can be experienced within the self over which discourses are being tried.

As we have seen, students and teachers come to school already having appropriated multiple voices and cultures. One task of education can be reflection on the voices one already has. Multicultural education, especially that which considers invisible as well as visible culture, can assist in that process of personal and group reflection. Teachers and students, by looking within themselves, can come to see that everybody is cultural and multicultural, including themselves. By listening to the discourses around and within them and by testing how those discourses feel—more like self, more like other, owned, or alienated—students and their teachers can valorize many discourses, treating them as inherently of equivalent worth, even though not all of the discourses and cultures are treated as equal in power and prestige in the world outside the classroom. If school is a secure place to try on new cultures and voices, if cultural diversity is treated as boundaries rather than as borders, then students and their teachers can establish safe "third spaces" in which to explore growing relationships with new cultures and old ones.

Ultimately, for persons in complex multicultural societies, growth into maturity involves coming to terms with the diversity of voices and cultures within. This is especially the case when the cultures and voices have been in conflict in the wider society and when the person is a member of a dominated group. Then, coming to terms with one's own diversity means making some kind of just peace with the voices within. For example, in every man there are the voices of women, and in every woman there are the voices of men. Are these voices alien and in conflict within the person, or have they been appropriated within the self? Can a woman come to terms with the male voices within without acquiescing to male hegemony and adopting an alienated self? In every White person in the United States, because of our historical experience, there are not only White voices but also Black ones. What do those voices sound more like—Amos and Andy or Frederick Douglass? Aunt Jemima or Alice Walker? How have those voices been appropriated within the person, and what role has the school played in facilitating that process? In every African American in the United States, there are not only Black voices but also White ones. How can the African American come to terms with the White voices within, forgiving and making peace with them, coming to own them while at the same time affirming and owning the Black voices, holding a continuing sense of the injustice of continuing racism? Doing all of that is necessary to mature into full adulthood as an African American (Cross, 1991; Helms, 1990).

To come to terms with the diversity of voices within is an educative task for society, for the individual, and for the school. It is what growing up means in a multicultural society and in a multicultural world. When the voices of the school curriculum and of its teaching and learning are fully multicultural, then the appropriation of multiple voices—in dignity and without coercion, keeping a critical stance without despair—becomes possible for all students. This is a noble aim for multicultural education—how difficult it is to achieve yet how necessary. This becomes more apparent to educators as we become able to think more deeply about culture, its nuances, and its diversity in school and in society.

AFTERWORD

> What we are talking about is creating a new tradition, telling "new stories" that are fundamentally different by virtue of the role that the lives of the historically oppressed have assumed in their construction. This is a matter of redefining American culture, not once and for all, but in the negotiated meanings that are always emerging out of a curricular process. It is in the day-to-day interactions of teachers and students, dealing with a transformed curriculum and attempting to create a transformed, democratic classroom, that the new common culture will be created and continually re-created. (Perry & Fraser, 1993, pp. 19–20)

Questions and Activities

1. What does the author mean by "implicit and invisible aspects of culture?" In what ways are these aspects of culture important? Give some examples of invisible aspects of culture. What are some non-examples of the concept?

2. In what ways might differences in invisible culture cause conflict? Give specific examples.

3. According to the author, what problems result when teachers focus on visible (explicit) culture at the expense of invisible (implicit) culture? What kinds of educational practices result when teachers focus on visible and tangible aspects of culture?

4. How does the author distinguish between a cultural boundary and a cultural border? Why is this distinction important?

5. According to the author, does cultural change necessarily mean cultural loss? Explain why or why not.

6. The author states that we sometime "essentialize" culture. What does he mean? What problems result, in his view, when culture is essentialized?

7. The author states that "our conceptions of culture in multicultural education need to become more constructivist and less essentialist." Explain what he means by this statement and its implications for educational practice.

8. The author states that "multicultural education has an opportunity and a challenge to be counterhegemonic." Explain the meaning of this statement and give examples of how this might be done by classroom teachers.

References

Apple, M. W. (1996). *Cultural politics and education*. Buckingham, UK: Open University Press.

Arteaga, A. (1994). *An other tongue: Nation and ethnicity in the linguistic borderlands*. Durham, NC: Duke University Press.

Bakhtin, M. M. (1981). (M. Holquist, Ed.; C. Emerson & M. Holquist, Trans.). *The dialogic imagination* Austin, TX: University of Texas Press.

Barth, F. (1969). *Ethnic groups and boundaries: The social organization of culture difference*. Boston: Little, Brown.

Bateson, G., Jackson, D., Haley, J., & Weakland, J. (1972). Toward a theory of schizophrenia. Reprinted in G. Bateson, *Steps toward an ecology of mind* (pp. 201–227). New York: Ballantine.

Bohannon, P. (1992). *We the alien: An introduction to cultural anthropology*. Prospect Heights, IL: Waveland Press.

Bourdieu, P., & Passeron, J. C. (1977). *Reproduction: In education, society and culture*. Beverly Hills, CA: Sage.

Cross, W. E. (1991). *Shades of Black: Diversity in African American identity*. Philadelphia: Temple University Press.

de Cervantes, M. (2005). *Don Quixote*. New York: Harper Perennial.

Delpit, L. (1995). *Other people's children: Cultural conflict in the classroom*. New York: New Press.

Erickson, F. (1987). Transformation and school success: The politics and culture of educational achievement. *Anthropology and Education Quarterly, 18*(4), 335–356.

Erickson, F., Bagrodia, R., Cook-Sather, A., Espinoza, M., Jurow, S., Shultz, J., et al. (2007). Students' experience of school curriculum: The everyday circumstances of granting and withholding assent to learn. In M. Connelly, F. H. Ming, & J. Phillion (Eds.), *The Sage handbook of curriculum and instruction* (pp. 198–218). Thousand Oaks, CA: Sage.

Fanon, F. (1963). *The wretched of the earth* (C. Farrington, Trans.). New York: Grove.

Foley, D. E. (1991). Reconsidering anthropological explanations of ethnic school failure. *Anthropology & Education Quarterly, 22*(1), 60–86.

Fordham, S. (1996). *Blacked out: Dilemmas of race, identity, and success at Capital High*. Chicago: University of Chicago Press.

Foucault, M. (1979). *Discipline and punish: The birth of the prison*. New York: Random House/Vintage.

Gee, J. (1990). *Social linguistics and literacies: Ideology in discourses*. Philadelphia: Falmer.

Geertz, C. (1973). *The interpretation of cultures*. New York: Basic Books.

Giles, H., & Powesland, P. F. (1975). *Speech style and social evaluation*. London: Academic Press.

Giroux, H. A. (1983). Theories of reproduction and resistance: A critical analysis. *Harvard Educational Review, 53*(3), 257–293.

Giroux, H. (1991). *Border crossings: Cultural workers and the politics of education*. New York: Routledge.

Gonzalez, N. (2004). Disciplining the discipline: Anthropology and the pursuit of quality education. *Educational Researcher, 32*(5), 17–25.

Gonzalez, N., Moll, L. C., & Amanti, C. (2005). *Funds of knowledge: Theorizing practices in households, communities, and classrooms*. Mahwah, NJ: Lawrence Erlbaum Associates.

Goodenough, W. (1976). Multiculturalism as the normal human experience. *Anthropology & Education Quarterly. 7*(4), 4–7.

Gumperz, J. J. (1982). *Discourse strategies*. New York: Cambridge University Press.

Gutierrez, K., Baquedano-López, P., Alvarez, H., & Chiu, M. (1999). Building a culture of collaboration through hybrid language practices. *Theory into Practice, 38*(2), 87–93.

Gutierrez, K., Baquedano-López, P., & Tejeda, C. (1999). Rethinking diversity: Hybridity and hybrid language practices in the third space. *Mind, Culture, and Activity, 6*(4) 286–303.

Gutierrez, K., & Rogoff, B. (2003). Cultural ways of learning: Individual traits or repertoires of practice. *Educational Researcher, 32*(5), 19–25.

Gutierrez, K., Rymes, B., & Larson, J. (1995). Script, counterscript, and underlife in the classroom: James Brown versus Brown vs. Board of Education. *Harvard Educational Review, 65*(3), 445–471.

Hall, E. T. (1959). *The silent language*. New York: Doubleday.

Hall, E. T. (1976). *Beyond culture*. New York: Doubleday.

Heath, S. B. (1983). *Ways with words: Language, life, and work in communities and classrooms*. New York: Cambridge University Press.

Helms, J. (1990). *Black and White racial identity*. New York: Greenwood.

hooks, B. (1993). Transformative pedagogy and multiculturalism. In T. Perry & J. W. Fraser (Eds.), *Freedom's plow: Teaching in the multicultural classroom* (pp. 91–98). New York: Routledge.

Hymes, D. H. (1974). *Foundations in sociolinguistics: An ethnographic approach*. Philadelphia: University of Pennsylvania Press.

Kroeber, A. L., & Kluckhohn, C. (1952). *Culture: A critical review of concepts and definitions*, Vol. 47(1). Cambridge, MA: Peabody Museum of American Archaeology and Ethnology, Harvard University.

Kuper, A. (1999). *Culture: The anthropologists' account*. Cambridge, MA: Harvard University Press.

Labov, W. (1963). The social motivation of a sound change. *Word, 19*, 273–309.

Ladson-Billings, G. (1994). *The dreamkeepers: Successful teachers of African-American children*. San Francisco: Jossey-Bass Publishers.

Lee, C. (2001). Is October Brown Chinese? A cultural modeling activity system for underachieving students. *American Educational Research Journal, 38*(1), 97–141.

Lee, C. (2007). *The role of culture in academic literacies: Conducting our blooming in the midst of the whirlwind*. New York: Teachers College Press.

McCarthy, C. (1993). After the canon: Knowledge and ideological representation in the multicultural discourse on curriculum reform. In C. McCarthy & W. Crichlow (Eds.), *Race, identity, and representation in education* (pp. 289–305). New York: Routledge.

McDermott, R. P., & Gospodinoff, K. (1981). Social contexts for ethnic borders and school failure. In A. Wolfgang (Ed.), *Nonverbal behavior: Applications and cultural implications* (pp. 175–195). New York: Academic Press.

Nieto, S. (Ed.). (1999). *The light in their eyes: Creating multicultural learning communities*. New York: Teachers College Press.

Ogbu, J. U. (1987). Variability in minority school performance: A problem in search of an explanation. *Anthropology and Education Quarterly, 18*(4), 312–334.

Perry, T., & Fraser, J. W. (Eds.). (1993). *Freedom's plow: Teaching in the multicultural classroom*. New York: Routledge.

Philips, S. U. (1983). *The invisible culture: Communication in school and community on the Warm Springs Indian Reservation*. New York: Longman.

Pollock, M. (2008). From shallow to deep: Toward a thorough cultural analysis of school achievement patterns. *Anthropology & Education Quarterly. 39*(4), 369–380.

Piestrup, A. (1973). Black dialect interference and accommodations of reading instruction in first grade [Monograph No. 4]. *Working papers of the language-behavior research laboratory*. University of California, Berkeley. (ERIC Document Reproduction Service No. ED119113)

Sadker, M., & Sadker, D. (1994). *Failing at fairness: How America's schools cheat girls*. New York: Scribner's.

Said, E. W. (1978). *Orientalism*. New York: Pantheon.

Skilton Sylvester, P. (1994). Elementary school curricula and urban transformation. *Harvard Educational Review, 64*(3), 309–331.

Sleeter, C. E., & Grant, C. A. (1993). *Making choices for multicultural education*. New York: Merrill/Macmillan.

Torres-Guzmán, M. (1992). Stories of hope in the midst of despair: Culturally responsive education for Latino students in an alternative high school in New York City. In M. Saravia-Shore & S. F. Arvizu (Eds.), *Cross-cultural literacy: Ethnographies of communication in multiethnic classrooms* (pp. 477–490). New York: Garland.

Trueba, H. T. (1994). Reflections on alternative visions of schooling. *Anthropology and Education Quarterly, 25*(3), 376–393.

Tylor, E. B. (1970). *Primitive culture: Researches into the development of mythology, philosophy, religion, language, art, and custom*. London: Murray. (Original work published 1871)

Valle, V., & Torres, R. (1995). The idea of Mestizaje and the "race" problematic: Racialized media discourse in a Post-Fordist landscape. In A. Darder (Ed.), *Culture and difference: Critical perspectives on the bicultural experience in the United States* (pp. 139–153). Westport, CT: Bergin & Garvey.

Varenne, H., & McDermott, R. (1998). *Successful failure: The school America builds*. Boulder, CO: Westview.

Wiggington, S. (1986). *Sometimes a shining moment: The Foxfire experience*. Garden City, NY: Anchor.

Willis, P. E. (1977). *Learning to labor: How working-class kids get working-class jobs*. New York: Columbia University Press.

Wills, J. S., Lintz, A., & Mehan, H. (2004). Ethnographic studies of multicultural education in classrooms and schools. In J. A. Banks & C. A. M. Banks (Eds.), *Handbook of research on multicultural education* (2nd ed., pp. 163–183). New York: Macmillan.

Witherell, C., & Noddings, N. (1991). *Stories lives tell: Narrative and dialogue in education*. New York: Teachers College Press.

58

CHAPTER 3

Race, Class, Gender, and Disability in the Classroom

Carl A. Grant and Christine E. Sleeter

Schools have always been a focal point of debate. What should be taught? How should students be organized for instruction? How should teachers be prepared? What constitute acceptable standards, and who should set them? Ongoing social issues continuously fuel debate about these questions. We will discuss four such current issues.

First, a rapidly growing standards and testing movement coupled with a privatization movement currently drives much of schooling. These movements began to affect schooling with the report *A Nation at Risk: The Imperative for Educational Reform* (National Commission on Excellence in Education, 1983), which warned that U.S. preeminence on the world stage was being eroded by the mediocre performance of its educational institutions. A system of setting standards and measuring student performance based on them was cemented by passage of the No Child Left Behind Act in 2001, which requires that by 2014, all students will perform at a proficient level or higher in reading and math. As a vice principal recently remarked to one of us, "Everything in our school is being driven by tests." Effects of these movements vary widely. Schools in which students had already been achieving well have continued to operate much as they had before. In schools that had not been doing well—particularly schools in low-income communities and those with large proportions of students of color and/or English learners—pressure to raise test scores has been found to turn the work of teachers into that of curriculum technician and test manager (Valli, Croninger, & Chambliss, 2008). Furthermore, distinctions between public and private schooling are becoming blurred, shifting schools in many areas toward corporate control and away from democratic community participation (Lipman & Haines, 2007). Many advocates of multicultural education quickly found attention to diversity and equity being replaced by attention to standards and student test scores, particularly in schools in which multicultural education had been seen as having to do mainly with getting along rather than improving academic teaching and learning (Sleeter, 2005, 2007).

Second, at the same time, since the 1970s universities had developed an increasingly rich intellectual foundation supportive of diversity. The amount of multicultural research and curriculum mushroomed (Banks, 2009a; Banks & Banks, 2004), advancing perspectives that differed in some cases sharply from those of most political and economic leaders. This intellectual work paralleled the tremendous growth in ethnic and racial diversity the United States has experienced. By 2006, the population was roughly 66 percent non-Latino White, 15 percent Latino, 13 percent African American, 4 percent Asian and Pacific Islander, 1 percent Native American, and 1 percent other (U.S. Census Bureau, 2006a). Whites were no longer the majority in many cities. In California, Hawaii, Louisiana, Mississippi, New Mexico, and Texas, no racial or ethnic group was a majority in the public schools. The largest portion of immigrants in the United States—about 45 percent or 1.6 million—came from Latin America and the Caribbean, contributing to a social phenomenon being called "the hispanization of America" (U.S. Department of Homeland Security, 2003). Although Christianity is by far the largest religion in the United States, one increasingly finds Islamic centers and mosques, Hindu and Buddhist temples, and Jewish temples in addition to more traditional churches (Eck, 2002). Islam is the fastest-growing religion in the United States as well as in several European nations such as the United Kingdom and France (Banks, 2009a). In 2006, the U.S. Census (2006b) reported that in U.S. households, 80 percent spoke only English at home while 20 percent spoke a language other than English.

Third, the United States has apparently become increasingly polarized along several dimensions. The September 11, 2001, attacks and then the war against Iraq led to a strong wave of patriotism and reluctance on the part of many people to criticize any aspect of U.S. culture or policy. Public sentiment about diversity rapidly became more negative, particularly toward people of Arab descent. According to a Gallup poll, 58 percent of Americans thought Arab Americans should undergo more intense security checks than the rest of the population; 49 percent favored making Arab Americans have special ID cards (Crowley, 2001). In another survey, 31 percent of respondents favored putting Arab Americans in detention camps (Sen, 2002). At the same time, antiwar protests and concern that the United States was engaging in imperialist actions in the Middle East grew. The American Council of Trustees and Alumni published a report charging university faculty with being the "weak link" in the U.S. response to terrorism because of questions many have raised about U.S. policies (Gonzalez, 2001). These tensions played out in the "red state–blue state" divide in the 2004 presidential election as did growing public disagreements about the role religion should play in public institutions. Some commentators, including some conservatives, speculated that Barack Obama may bring a needed fresh style of politics that can "bridge differences among people of different political viewpoints" (Corbin, 2008).

Fourth, by 2001 the United States had grown increasingly segregated by race and class (Orfield & Lee, 2005) with gaps between "haves" and "have-nots" continuing to widen. The gradually rising levels of educational attainment had not been accompanied by a rising quality of life. As transnational corporations exported jobs to Third World nations in order to cut wages, many middle-class and working-class people in the United States experienced an erosion of their lifestyles, and the poverty level rose, especially among women and children (Johnston, 2007; Ulrich, 2004). According to the U.S. Census Bureau (2004), while the wealthiest fifth of the U.S. population's share of income increased from 44 percent of the total in 1973 to 50 percent in 2002, everyone else's share decreased. While education is necessary for upward mobility and community uplift, education does not wipe away racial advantages. For example,

African Americans and Latinos earn consistently less than their White counterparts with the same level of education. In 2006, White high school graduates earned a median annual income of $32,931 compared to $26,368 for African Americans and $27,508 for Latinos. White professionals with advanced degrees earned a median annual income of $83,785 while African Americans with the same educational level earned $64,834, and Latinos earned $70,432 (U.S. Census Bureau, 2007).

Poverty and unemployment have hit communities of color harder than White communities (U.S. Census Bureau, 2000). Prisons have become a growth industry. Many leaders of color view the explosion of prison populations as a new form of slavery, a warehousing of unemployed young men of color. Indeed, between 1977 and 1985, "when the prison population almost tripled, 70 percent of new inmates were African American, Latino, or other nonwhite minorities," a fact that had been downplayed by classifying Latinos as White (Chanse, 2002, p. 3).

Most adults with disabilities are either unemployed or underemployed, and their earnings are often below the poverty level. In 2006, only 37 percent of disabled adults aged 16 and over were employed. About 21.5 percent of the population with disabilities was living on an income below the poverty level (U.S. Census Bureau, 2006a). Passage of the Americans with Disabilities Act was designed to protect people with disabilities from discrimination, and while it has helped, it cannot solve many issues, such as lack of enough affordable housing.

A major thread running through the debates about schooling is the relative importance of preparing students for jobs versus preparing them for active citizenship. Schools have always done both, but much discussion about what schools should do increasingly has emphasized job preparation; little has been said about citizenship. What kind of a nation do we want for ourselves and our children given the challenges and problems we have been facing? How should limited resources be distributed given our diversity and virtually everyone's desire for a good life? How can tomorrow's citizens who are in the schools now be prepared to build the kinds of institutions that support a diverse democracy in which people are truly equal? Who gets to decide the most effective ways of educating children from diverse backgrounds? Students we teach usually give one of three reasons for wanting to become teachers: (1) they love kids, (2) they want to help students, and (3) they want to make school more exciting than it was when they were students. If one of these is the reason you chose to enter the teaching profession, we hope you will see the demographic and social trends previously described as being challenging and will realize that your love and help are needed not just for some students but for all students.

This chapter discusses the importance of race, class, gender, language, and disability in classroom life and provides alternative approaches to dealing with these issues in the classroom.

RACE, CLASS, GENDER, LANGUAGE, DISABILITY, AND CLASSROOM LIFE

Ask yourself what you know about race, ethnicity, class, gender, language, and disability as they apply to classroom life. Could you write one or two good paragraphs about what these words mean? How similar or different would your meanings be from those of your classmates? How much do these dynamics of social organization influence the way you think about teaching? If you and your classmates organize into small discussion groups (try it) and listen closely to each other, you will probably notice some distinct differences in the ways you see the importance of these dynamics. The point of such an exercise is not to show that you have different ideas and interpretations but to challenge you to think clearly about what your ideas and interpretations mean for working with your students: How will you teach with excellence and equity?

Race, social class, and gender are used to construct categories of people in society. On your college application form, you were probably asked to indicate your race, ethnicity, gender, disability, and parents' place of employment. Most institutions want to know such information in order to analyze and report data related to any or all of your ascribed characteristics. Social scientists studying school practices often report results according to race, class, home language, and gender. Dynamics of race, class, language, gender, and disability can influence your knowledge and understanding of your students. It is important for you to consider these dynamics collectively, not separately. Each of your students is a member of multiple status groups, and these simultaneous memberships—in interaction with dynamics in the broader society—influence the students' perceptions and actions.

For example, a child in the classroom may be not just Asian American but also male, middle class, native English speaking, Buddhist, and not disabled. Thus, he is a member of a historically marginalized group—but also of a gender group and a social class that have historically oppressed others. Therefore, his view of reality and his actions based on that view will differ from those of a middle-class Asian American girl whose first language is Korean or a lower-class Asian American boy whose first language is Hmong and who has spina bifida. A teacher's failure to consider the integration of race, social class, and gender can lead to an oversimplified or inaccurate understanding of what occurs in schools and, therefore, to an inappropriate or simplistic prescription for educational equity and excellence. You may have noticed, for example, teachers assuming (often mistakenly) that Mexican American students identify strongly with each other and that they view issues in much the same way, or that African American male students have the same goals and views as African American female students.

We often begin working with teacher candidates by having them take a self-inventory of the sociocultural groups they have been exposed to in their own schooling and religious or work situations. The more honestly you examine your familiarity with the backgrounds of different children, the more readily you can begin to learn about people to whom you have had little exposure. It will be a much greater limitation on your ability to teach well if you assume you know more about different students than you actually know than if you recognize whose lives are unfamiliar to you so that you can learn.

APPROACHES TO MULTICULTURAL EDUCATION

Educators often work with students of color, students from low-income backgrounds, and White female students according to one of five approaches to multicultural education. As we briefly explain these approaches, ask yourself which one you are most comfortable using in your teaching. Before we begin this discussion, you should understand two important points. First, space does not allow for a complete discussion of each approach; for a thorough discussion, please refer to *Making Choices for Multicultural Education: Five Approaches to Race, Class, and Gender* (Sleeter & Grant, 2007). Second, it is fine to discover that you are a true eclectic or that none of the approaches satisfies your teaching style as long as you are not straddling the fence. Indecision, dissatisfaction, and frustration in teaching style and technique may confuse your students. Also, to be the dynamic teacher you want to be, you need a teaching philosophy that is well thought out and makes learning exciting for your students. Good teaching requires that you have a comprehensive understanding of what you are doing in the classroom, why, and how you are doing it.

Teaching of the Exceptional and the Culturally Different

If you believe that a teacher's chief responsibility is to prepare all students to fit into and achieve within the existing school and society, this approach may appeal to you. It may be especially appealing if categories of students, such as students of color, special education students, or language-minority students are behind in the main subject areas of the traditional curriculum. The goals of this approach are to equip students with the cognitive skills, concepts, information, language, and values traditionally required by U.S. society and eventually to enable them to hold a job and function within society's institutions and culture. Teachers using this approach often begin by determining the achievement levels of students, comparing their achievement to grade-level norms, and then working diligently to help those who are behind to catch up.

A good deal of research documents learning strengths of students of different sociocultural groups, suggesting that if a teacher learns to identify and build on their strengths, students will learn much more effectively than if a teacher assumes the child cannot learn very well. For example, based on a study of high-performing Hispanic schools, Reyes, Scribner, and Scribner (1999) found that these schools share four characteristics: They (1) proactively involved families and communities, (2) were organized around collaborative governance and leadership that was clearly focused on student success, (3) widely used culturally responsive pedagogy, and their teachers viewed children as capable of high levels of achievement and viewed their cultural background as a valuable resource on which to build, and (4) used advocacy-oriented assessment to support high achievement by giving information that could improve instruction and guide intervention on a day-to-day basis. Language sensitivity was part of this process.

Teachers who understand how to build on the culture and language of students will read the classroom behavior of such children more accurately and adjust their instructional processes accordingly without lowering their expectations for learning. As another example, Moses and Cobb (2001) taught algebra to inner-city middle school students by building on their experience. Students were having difficulty with numerical directionality—positive and negative numbers. The teachers sent the students to the local subway and had them diagram the subway system in terms of directionality. The teachers then helped the students represent their experience with the subway numerically in the process, helping them to translate the familiar—subway routes—into the unfamiliar—positive and negative numbers.

Starting where the students are and using instructional techniques and content familiar to them are important. For example, one teacher who used this approach helped two African American students who had moved from a large urban area to a much smaller college town to catch up on their writing skills by having them write letters to the friends they had left behind in the city. Another teacher grouped the girls in her ninth-grade class who were having problems in algebra, allowing them to work together, support one another, and not be intimidated by the boys in the class who had received the kind of socialization that produces good math students. One other teacher provided two students with learning disabilities with materials written at their reading level that covered concepts comparable to those the rest of the class was reading about. Another teacher provided intensive English language development to her two limited English-speaking Latino students. A teacher may believe that only one or two students in the classroom need this approach or that all of them do, especially if the school is located in an inner-city community or barrio.

In sum, the heart of this approach is building bridges for students to help them acquire the cognitive skills and knowledge expected of the so-called average White middle-class student. This approach accepts the concept that there is a body of knowledge all students should learn but proposes that teachers should teach that knowledge in whatever way works so students understand and learn it.

Human Relations Approach

If you believe that a major purpose of the school is to help students learn to live together harmoniously in a world that is becoming smaller and smaller and if you believe that greater social equality will result if students learn to respect one another regardless of race, class, gender, or disability, then this approach may be of special interest to you. Its goal is to promote a feeling of unity, tolerance, and acceptance among people: "I'm okay and you're okay." The human relations approach engenders positive feelings among diverse students, promotes group identity and pride for students of color, reduces stereotypes, and works to eliminate prejudice and biases. For example, a teacher of a fourth-grade multiracial, mainstreamed classroom spends considerable time during the first two weeks of each year, and some time thereafter, doing activities to promote good human relations in the class. Early in the year, he uses a sociogram to learn student friendship patterns and to make certain that every child has a buddy. He also uses this activity to discover how negative or positive the boy–girl relationships are. He uses sentence-completion activities to discover how students are feeling about themselves and their family members. Using data, he integrates into his curriculum concepts of social acceptance and humanness for all people, the reduction and elimination of stereotypes, and information to help students feel good about themselves and their people. Also, he regularly brings to his classroom speakers who represent the diversity in society to show all students that they, too, can be successful.

The curriculum for the human relations approach addresses individual differences and similarities. It includes contributions of the groups of which the students are members and provides accurate information about various ethnic, racial, disability, gender, or social-class groups about whom the students hold stereotypes. Instructional processes include a good deal of cooperative learning, role-playing, and vicarious or real experiences to help the students develop appreciation of others. Advocates of this approach suggest that it should be comprehensive, integrated into several subject areas, and schoolwide. For example, a school attempting to promote gender equality is working at cross-purposes if lessons in language arts teach students to recognize sex stereotypes while in the science class girls are not expected to perform as well as boys and thus are not pushed to do so. These contradictory practices simply reaffirm sex stereotypes. While the teaching-the-exceptional-and-the-culturally-different approach emphasizes helping students acquire cognitive skills and knowledge in the traditional curriculum, the human relations approach focuses on attitudes and feelings students have about themselves and each other.

Single-Group Studies Approach

We use the phrase *single-group studies* to refer to the study of a particular group of people, for example, disability studies or Native American studies. The single-group studies approach seeks to raise the social status of the target group by helping young people examine how the group has been oppressed historically despite its capabilities and achievements. Unlike the two previous approaches, this one (and the next two) views school knowledge as political rather than neutral and presents alternatives to the existing Eurocentric, male-dominant curriculum. It focuses on one specific group at a time so the history, perspectives, and worldview of that group can be developed coherently rather than piecemeal. It also examines the current social status of the group and actions taken historically as well as contemporarily to further the group's interests. Single-group studies are oriented toward political action and liberation. Advocates of this approach hope that students will develop more respect for the group and the knowledge and commitment to work to improve the group's status in society.

For example, women's studies was created with a "vision of a world in which all persons can develop to their fullest potential and be free from all ideologies and structures that consciously and unconsciously oppress and exploit some for the advantage of others" (National Women's Studies Association, 2005). Gay and lesbian studies develop "an intellectual community for students and faculty that is ethnically diverse and committed to gender parity" (A National Survey, 1990–1991, p. 53). Ethnic studies helps "students develop the ability to make reflective decisions on issues related to race, ethnicity, culture, and language and to take personal, social, and civic actions to help solve the racial and ethnic problems in our national and world societies" (Banks, 2009b, p. 26).

Since the late 1960s and early 1970s, scholars have generated an enormous amount of research about various oppressed groups and have mapped out new conceptual frameworks within various disciplines. For example, Afrocentric scholars redefined the starting point of African American history from slavery to ancient Africa, in the process rewriting story lines for African American history. Beginning history with a group other than European males enables one to view historical events very differently. A group's story may begin in Asia and move east, begin in South or Central America and move north, begin in Europe and move west, or begin right here on the North American continent thousands of years ago. Furthermore, the story is different if one views the group as having started from a position of strength (e.g., African civilizations [Gates, 1999]), having then been subjugated, and now attempting to rebuild that strength rather than starting from a position of weakness (such as slavery) and to rise.

A single-group studies curriculum includes units or courses about the history and culture of a group (e.g., African American history, Chicano literature, disability studies). It teaches how the group has been victimized and has struggled to gain respect as well as current social issues facing the group. It is essential that such curricula be based on scholarship by people who have studied the group in depth rather than on your own ideas about what you think might be important. For example, *Pinoy Teach* (http://www.pinoyteach.com/) is a social studies curriculum from a Filipino studies perspective. Halagao (2004), one of its authors, explains that *Pinoy Teach* "is my insider's attempt to write our people's perspective into social studies. It reflects the experiences of brown people who are not passive bystanders, but rather active figures who construct historical and important moments" (p. 464).

In 2003, Tucson Unified School District's Mexican American/Raza Studies Department offered assistance to schools that were interested in incorporating Mexican American/Raza Studies into the curriculum and developed the Social Justice Education Project for high school Chicano students who were failing and considering dropping out. The social studies curriculum, which meets state standards, is taught from a Chicano/a perspective and involves students in reading college-level material and doing community research in which they develop "advanced, graduate-level skills in research, writing, and critical thinking" (VisionMark, 2005). Four cohorts have completed the Social Justice Education Project, and their graduation rates exceed those of Anglo students in the same schools. Many students have gone on to college, and they credit the project for motivating them to do so (Cammarota & Romero, 2008; Romero, 2008).

Although single-group studies focus mainly on the curriculum, they also give some attention to instructional processes that benefit the target group. Women's studies programs, for example, have developed what is known as "feminist pedagogy" (see Chapter 7 of this volume), a teaching approach that attempts to empower students. The main idea is that in the traditional classroom, women are socialized to accept other people's ideas. By reading text materials that were written mainly by men and provide a male interpretation of the world, women learn not to interpret the world for themselves. In the feminist classroom, women learn to trust and develop their own insights. The feminist teacher may assign material to read and may encourage students to generate discussion and reflections about it. The discussion and personal reflection are important parts of the process during which "control shifts from me, the teacher, the arbiter of knowing, to the interactions of students and myself with the subject matter" (Tetreault, 1989, p. 137).

In summary, the single-group studies approach works toward social change. It challenges the knowledge normally taught in schools, arguing that knowledge reinforces control by wealthy White men over everyone else. This approach offers an in-depth study of oppressed groups for the purpose of empowering group members, developing in them a sense of pride and group consciousness, and helping members of dominant groups understand where others are coming from.

Multicultural Education Approach

Multicultural education has become the most popular term used by educators to describe education for pluralism. We apply this term to a particular approach that multicultural education theorists discuss most often. As you will notice, this approach synthesizes many ideas from the previous three approaches. Its goals are to reduce prejudice and discrimination against oppressed groups, to work toward equal opportunity and social justice for all groups, and to effect an equitable distribution of power among members of the different cultural groups. These goals are actualized by attempting to reform the total schooling process for all children, regardless of whether the school is an all-White suburban school or a multiracial urban school. Schools that are reformed around principles of pluralism and equality would then contribute to broader social reform.

Various practices and processes in the school are reconstructed so that the school models equality and pluralism. For example, the curriculum is organized around concepts basic to each discipline, but content elaborating on those concepts is drawn from the experiences and perspectives of several different U.S. groups. If you are teaching literature, you select literature written by members of different groups. This not only teaches students that groups other than Whites have produced literature but also enriches the concept of literature because it enables students to experience different literature forms that are common to all writing. For example, the universal struggle for self-discovery and cultural connection within a White-dominant society can be examined by reading about a Puerto Rican girl in *Felita* (Mohr, 1990), a Chinese girl in *Dragonwings* (Yep, 1975), an African American boy in *Scorpions* (Myers, 1990), a European American girl in *The Great Gilly Hopkins* (Paterson, 1987), and Iranian youth in *Teenage Refugees from Iran Speak Out* (Strazzabosco, 1995).

It is also important that the contributions and perspectives you select depict each group as the group would depict itself and show the group as active and dynamic. This requires that you learn about various groups and become aware of what is important and meaningful to them. For example, Arab peoples are highly diverse; in contrast to popular stereotypes, they have a long history of feminism (Darraj, 2002), and in some Arab countries, women work as well-educated professionals. As another example, teachers wishing to teach about famous Native Americans would ask members of different Native American tribes whom they would like to see celebrated instead of holding up to their students Pocahantas, Kateri Tekakwitha, or Sacajawea. These Native Americans are often thought among their people to have served White interests more than those of Native Americans. Additionally, African Americans are concerned when an African American athlete or entertainer is so often held up as the hero and heroine for the group instead of African Americans who have done well in other areas of life, such as science or literature.

In this approach, instruction starts by assuming that students are capable of learning complex material and performing at a high level of skill. Each student has a personal, unique learning style that teachers discover and build on when teaching. The teacher draws on and uses the conceptual schemes (ways of thinking, knowledge about the world) that students bring to school. Cooperative learning is fostered, and both boys and girls are treated equally in a nonsexist manner. A staff as diverse as possible is hired and assigned responsibilities nonstereotypically. Ideally, more than one language is taught, enabling all students to become bilingual. The multicultural education approach, more than the previous three, advocates total school reform to make the school reflect diversity. It also advocates giving equal attention to a variety of cultural groups regardless of whether specific groups are represented in the school's student population.

Multicultural Social Justice Education

Reflect back on the various forms of social inequality mentioned at the opening of this chapter. Multicultural social justice education deals more directly than the other approaches with oppression and social structural inequality based on race, social class, gender, and disability. Its purpose is to prepare future citizens to take action to make society better serve the interests of all groups of people, especially those who are of color, poor, female, or have disabilities. The approach is rooted in social reconstructionism, which seeks to reconstruct society toward greater equity in race, class, gender, and disability. This approach also questions ethics and power relations embedded in the new global economy. It draws on the penetrating vision of George Bernard Shaw (1921/2004), who exclaimed, "You see things, and you say, 'Why?' But I dream things that never were, and I say, 'Why not?'"

This approach extends the multicultural education approach in that the curriculum and instruction of both are very similar, but four practices are unique to multicultural social justice education. First, democracy is actively practiced in the schools (Banks, 2007; Parker, 2003). Reading the U.S. Constitution and hearing lectures on the three branches of government is a passive way to learn about democracy. For students to understand democracy, they must live it. They must practice politics, debate, social action, and the use of power (Osler & Starkey, 2005). In the classroom, this means that students are given the opportunity to direct a good deal of their learning and to learn how to be responsible for that direction. This does not mean that teachers abdicate the running of their classroom to the students but that they guide and direct students so they learn how to learn and develop skills for wise decision making. Shor (1980) describes this as helping students become subjects rather than objects in the classroom, and Freire (1985) says it produces individuals "who organize themselves reflectively for action rather than men [and women] who are organized for passivity" (p. 82).

Second, students learn how to analyze institutional inequality within their own life circumstances. Freire (1973) distinguished among critical consciousness, naïve consciousness, and magical consciousness:

> Critical consciousness represents things and facts as they exist empirically, in their causal and circumstantial correlations, naïve consciousness considers itself superior to facts, in control of facts, and thus free to understand them as it pleases. Magic consciousness, in contrast, simply apprehends facts and attributes them to a superior power by which it is controlled and to which it must therefore submit (p. 44).

To put it another way, a person with *critical consciousness* wants to know how the world actually works and is willing to analyze the world carefully for him- or herself. A person with naïve or magic consciousness does not do that. If one sees the world through magic, one assumes that one cannot understand or affect the world; things just happen. If one sees the world naïvely, one assumes cause–effect relationships that one wants to assume or that one has been told exist without investigating them or thinking critically for oneself. In a stratified society, Freire (1973) argued, most ordinary people see the world naïvely or magically as the elite would wish them to see it. Ordinary people believe either that they have no power to change the way the world works for them or that their problems have no relationship to their position in the power hierarchy.

For example, students are taught that education is the doorway to success and that if they obey the teacher and do their work, they will succeed. However, in reality, education pays off better for Whites than for people of color because of institutionalized racism that can be challenged but only when people recognize it and work collectively to dismantle it. Education also pays off better for men than women due to institutional sexism. Average annual earnings of full-time working women are only about 77 percent of the earnings of full-time working men (Institute for Women's Policy Research, 2008), a gap that has remained constant since 2001 and that contributes heavily to the pauperization of women and children in female-headed households. This approach teaches students to question what they hear about how society works from other sources and to analyze experiences of people like themselves in order to understand more fully what the problems actually are.

Third, students learn to engage in social action so they can change unfair social processes. Parker (2003) explained that teaching for democracy should mean preparing young people for enlightened political engagement: "the action or participatory domain of citizenship" (p. 33), such as voting, contacting officials, deliberating, and engaging in boycotts, based on the "knowledge, norms, values, and principles that shape this engagement" (p. 34). In other words, democracy is not a spectator sport. For example, some stories that elementary school children read could deal with issues involving discrimination and oppression and could suggest ways to deal with such problems. Students of all ages can be taught to identify sexist advertising of products sold in their community and how to take action to encourage advertisers to stop these types of practices. Advocates of this approach do not expect children to reconstruct the world, but they do expect the schools to teach students how to do their part in helping the nation achieve excellence and equity in all areas of life.

Fourth, bridges are built across various oppressed groups (e.g., people who are poor, people of color, and White women) so they can work together to advance their common interests. This is important because it can energize and strengthen struggles against oppression. However, getting groups to work together is difficult because members often believe that they would have to place some of their goals second to those of other groups. Furthermore, racial groups find themselves divided along gender and class lines to the extent that middle-class males of all colors fail to take seriously the concerns of women and of lower-class members of their own groups. Childs (1994) describes "transcommunal" organizations, such as the African American/Korean alliance in Los Angeles, that bring different groups together to identify and work on common concerns.

You now have an idea of the approaches used to teach multicultural education. Which one best suits your teaching philosophy and style? An equally important question is: Which approach will best help to bring excellence and equity to education? The next section of this chapter provides an example of how one teacher brings both excellence and equity to her classroom.

MS. JULIE WILSON AND HER APPROACH TO TEACHING

The following example describes a few days in the teaching life of Ms. Julie Wilson, a first-year teacher in a medium-large city. Which approach to multicultural education do you think Ms. Wilson is using? With which of her teaching actions do you agree or disagree? What would you do if assigned to her class?

May 23

Julie Wilson was both elated and sad that she had just completed her last exam at State U. As she walked back to her apartment, she wondered where she would be at this time next year. She had applied for 10 teaching positions and had been interviewed three times. As Julie entered her apartment building, she stopped to check the mail. A large, fat, white envelope addressed to her was stuffed into the small mailbox. She hurriedly tore it open and quickly read the first sentence. "We are pleased to offer you a teaching position." Julie leaped up the stairs three at a time. She burst into the apartment, waving the letter at her two roommates. "I've got a job! I got the job at Hoover Elementary. My first teaching job, a fifth-grade class!"

Hoover Elementary had been a part of a desegregation plan that brought together students from several different neighborhoods in the city. Hoover was situated in an urban renewal area to which city officials were giving a lot of time and attention and on which they were spending a considerable amount of money. City officials wanted to bring the Whites back into the city from suburbs and to encourage middle-class people of color to remain in the city. They also wanted to improve the life chances for the poor. Julie had been hired because the principal was looking for teachers who had some record of success in working with diverse students. So far, students were doing well enough on annual testing that the school was not on the list of schools needing improvement.

Julie had a 3.5 grade point average and had worked with a diverse student population in her practicum and student-teaching experience. She had strong letters of recommendation from her cooperating teacher and university supervisor. Julie also had spent her last two summers working as a counselor in a camp that enrolled a wide diversity of students.

August 25

Julie was very pleased with the way her classroom looked. She had spent the last three days getting it ready for the first day of school. Plants, posters, goldfish, and an old rocking chair added to the warmth of an attractive classroom. There was also a big sign across the room that said "Welcome Fifth Graders." Tomorrow was the big day.

She had also studied the state curriculum standards for her grade level and had sketched out some thematic units that addressed the standards creatively. She checked with her principal to make sure he would support her ideas, which he agreed to do as long as she did not stray away from the expected curriculum standards.

August 26

Twenty-eight students entered Julie's classroom: fifteen girls and thirteen boys. There were ten White students, two Hmong students, six Latino students, nine African American students, and one Bosnian student. Three of the students were learning disabled, and one was in a wheelchair. Eleven of the students were from middle-class homes, nine were from working-class homes, and the remaining eight were from very poor homes. Julie greeted each student with a big smile and a friendly hello as each entered the room. She asked students their names and told them hers. She then asked them to take the seat with their name on the desk.

After the school bell rang, Julie introduced herself to the whole class. She told them that she had spent most of her summer in England and that while she was there, she had often thought about this day—her first day as a teacher. She talked briefly about some of the places she had visited in England as she pointed to them on a map. She concluded her introduction by telling them a few things about her family. Her mother and father owned a dairy farm in Wisconsin, and she had one older brother, Wayne, and two younger sisters, Mary and Patricia.

Julie asked if there were any students new to the school. Lester, an African American male, raised his hand, along with a female Hmong student, Mai-ka, the Bosnian female student, Dijana, and two Latino students, Maria and Jesus. Julie asked Mai-ka if she would like to tell the class her complete name, how she had spent her summer, and one favorite thing she liked to do. Then she asked the same of the other four. After all five had finished introducing themselves, Julie invited the other students to do the same. Julie then asked Lourdes, a returning student, to tell Mai-ka, Maria, Dijana, Jesus, and Lester about Hoover Elementary. As she listened to the students, she realized that Dijana and Jesus were both newcomers to the United States and neither spoke English fluently. To assist them, she asked two other students to buddy with them for the day. She realized that she would need to figure out a good buddy system, and she would also need help in making her teaching accessible to these students while they learned English.

Once the opening greetings were completed, Julie began a discussion about the importance of the fifth grade and how special this grade was. She explained that this was a grade and class where a lot of learning would take place along with a lot of fun. As Julie spoke, the students were listening intently. Julie radiated warmth and authority. Some of the students glanced at each other unsmilingly as she spoke of the hard work; however, when she mentioned "a lot of fun," the entire class perked up and looked at each other with big grins on their faces. Julie had begun working on her educational philosophy in the Introduction to Education course at State U. Although she was continually modifying the way she thought about teaching, her basic philosophical beliefs had remained much the same. One of her major beliefs was that the students should actively participate in planning and shaping their own educational experiences. This, she believed, was as important for fifth graders as twelfth graders.

Julie asked the students if they were ready to take care of their classroom governance—deciding on rules, helpers, a discipline code, and time for classroom meetings. The class responded enthusiastically. The first thing the students wanted to do was to decide on the class rules. Several began to volunteer rules:

"No stealing."
"No rock throwing on the playground."
"No sharpening pencils after the bell rings."
"No fighting."

As the students offered suggestions, Julie wrote them on the whiteboard. After giving about sixteen suggestions, the class concluded. Julie commented, "All the rules seem very important"; she then asked the class what they should do with the rules. One student, Richard, suggested that they be written on poster board and placed in the upper corner of the room for all to see. Other class members said, "Yes, this is what we did last year in fourth grade."

William, however, said, "Yes, we did do this, but we rarely followed the rules after the first day we made them." Julie assured the class this would not be the case this year and that they would have a weekly classroom meeting run by an elected official of the class. She then asked if they thought it would be helpful if they wrote their rules using positive statements, instead of "no" or negative statements. The class said yes and began to change statements such as "no stealing" to "always ask before borrowing" and "no rock throwing" to "rock throwing can severely hurt a friend." Once the rules were completed, the class elected its officers.

After the classroom governance was taken care of, Julie asked the students if they would like her to read them a story. An enthusiastic "yes" followed her question. Julie glanced at the clock as she picked up *To Break the Silence* (Barrett, 1986) from the desk. The book is a varied collection of short stories, especially for young readers, written by authors of different racial backgrounds. It was 11:35. She could hardly believe the morning had gone by so quickly. She read for twenty minutes. All of the students seemed to be enjoying the story except Lester and Ben, two African American male students. Lester and Ben were drawing pictures, communicating nonverbally between themselves, and ignoring the rest of the class members. Julie decided that because they were quiet and not creating a disturbance, she would leave them alone.

After lunch, Julie had the class do two activities designed to help her learn about each student both socially and academically. She had the students do a self-concept activity, in which they did sentence completions that asked them to express how they felt about themselves. Then she had them play math and reading games to assess informally their math and reading skills. These activities took the entire afternoon, and Julie was as pleased as the students when the school day came to an end.

When Julie arrived at her apartment, she felt exhausted. She had a quick dinner and shower and then crawled into bed. She set the alarm for 7:00 PM and quickly fell asleep. By 10:30 that night, she had examined the students' self-concept activity and compared the information she had collected from the informal math and reading assessment with the official information from the students' cumulative records. She thought about each student's achievement record, social background, race, gender, and exceptionality. She said aloud, "I need to make plans soon to meet every parent. I need to find out about the students' lives at home, the parents' expectations, and whether I can get some of them to volunteer."

Julie turned off her desk lamp at 11:45 to retire for the evening. She read a few pages from Anne Fadiman's (1997) *The Spirit Catches You and You Fall Down*, which tells the story of a Hmong child and the culture clash she experienced with American doctors. Then she turned out the light. Tonight she was going to sleep with less tension and nervousness than she had the night before. She felt good about the way things had gone today and was looking forward to tomorrow. As Julie slept, she dreamed of her class. Their faces and most of their names and backgrounds floated through her mind.

Eight of the ten White students were from Briar Creek, a middle-class single-unit housing community; these students were performing at grade level or above in all scholastic areas, and each of them was at least a year ahead in some core-area subject. Charles, who had used a wheelchair since being in an automobile accident three years ago, was three years ahead in both reading and math. However, Elaine and Bob had chosen a mixture of positive and negative adjectives when doing the self-concept activity, and this concerned Julie. She would keep her eye on them to try to determine the cause of their problems.

Estelle and Todd, the other two White students, were between six months and a year behind in most academic areas. Estelle had been diagnosed as learning disabled (LD), but the information in her personal cumulative folder seemed ambiguous about the cause of her problem. Julie wondered whether Estelle was classified as LD based on uncertain reasons. She recalled an article that discussed the LD label as being a social construction rather than a medical condition.

Both of the Hmong students were at grade level or very close in their subjects. However, both of them, Mai-ka and Chee, were having some difficulty speaking English. Chee's family owned a restaurant in the neighborhood. The rumor mill reported that they were doing very well financially, so well that they had recently opened a restaurant in the downtown area of the city. Five of the six Latino students were Mexican Americans born in the United States. Maria, José, and Lourdes were bilingual; Richard and Carmen were monolingual with English as their primary language; and Jesus spoke mainly Spanish. Maria, José, and Lourdes were from working-class homes, and Richard, Jesus, and Carmen were from very poor homes. The achievement scores of Lourdes, Carmen, and Richard were at least two years ahead of their grade level. José was working at grade level, and Maria and Jesus were one to two years behind. Jesus had immigrated to the U.S. only a year ago.

Five of the African American students—Lester, Ben, Gloria, Sharon, and Susan—were all performing two years behind grade level in all core-area subjects. All five lived in the Wendell Phillips low-rent projects. Two African American students—Shelly and Ernestine—lived in Briar Creek and were performing above grade level in all academic areas. Dolores and Gerard lived in Chatham, a working-class, predominantly African American neighborhood. Dolores was performing above grade level in all subjects; Gerard was behind in math. Gerard had also chosen several negative words when doing the self-concept activity.

Finally, Dijana, who had immigrated recently from Bosnia, did not know enough English to participate very well in any of the day's activities. Julie was glad that Shelley seemed to be taking an interest in helping her. Julie realized that she would need to think regularly about how to make sure Dijana was following along and would need to make sure both Dijana and Jesus were being tested for the English as a Second Language program. All students in Julie's class were obedient and came from families that encouraged getting a good education.

May 25, 7:30 AM

Julie liked arriving early at school. The engineer, Mike, usually had a pot of coffee made when she arrived. This was her time to get everything ready for the day. She had been teaching for almost one school year and was proud and pleased with how everything was going. The school principal, Mr. Griffin, had been in her class three times for formal visits and had told others, "Julie is an excellent teacher." He usually offered her one or two minor suggestions, such as "Don't call the roll every day; learn to take your attendance silently" and "The museum has an excellent exhibit on food and the human body your class may enjoy."

Julie had also been surprised by several things. She was surprised at how quickly most of the teachers left school at the end of the day. Out of a staff of twenty classroom teachers, only about five or six came early or stayed late. Even more surprising to her was how she and the other teachers who either came early or stayed late were chided about this behavior. She was surprised at the large number of worksheets used and at how closely many teachers followed the outline in the books regardless of the needs of students. Also, she noticed, there was a common belief among the staff that her instructional style would not work. Julie had made several changes in the curriculum. She studied the content standards she was expected to follow so that she would be sure to teach material that would be included on tests.

But she carefully wove the standards into a project-based curriculum. She had incorporated trade books into reading and language arts, using them along with the language arts package her school had adopted. She made available to the students a wide assortment of books that featured different races, exceptionalities, and socioeconomic classes. In some stories, both males and females were featured doing traditional as well as nontraditional activities. Stories were set in urban and rural settings, and some featured children with disabilities. It had taken Julie several months to acquire such a diverse collection of books for her students, and she had even spent some of her own money to buy the books, but the excitement the students had shown about the materials made the expense worthwhile. She made sure she was teaching the kinds of reading and language arts skills her students would be tested on but refused to sacrifice the richness of a literature-based curriculum for "test prep." Thankfully, her principal supported her.

Julie also had several computers in her class. A computer lab was down the hall, but she wanted her students to use the computer on a regular basis. When she discovered that Richard's father owned a computer store, she convinced him to lend the class two iMacs, and she convinced Mr. Griffin to purchase six more at cost. Several of the students from Briar Creek had computers at home. Charles and Elaine, Julie discovered, were wizards at the computer. Julie encouraged them to help the other students (and herself—because she had taken only one computer course at State U). The two students enjoyed this assignment and often had a small group of students remain after school to receive their help. Julie was pleased at how well Charles and Elaine handled this responsibility. Lester and Ben were Charles's favorite classmates; they liked the computer, but Julie believed they liked Charles and his electric wheelchair even more. Julie had heard them say on several occasions that Charles was "cool." Lester's and Ben's work was showing a steady improvement, and Charles enjoyed having two good friends. This friendship, Julie believed, had excellent mutual benefits for all concerned, including herself.

Julie's mathematics pedagogy was built on two principles. First, she built on the thinking and life experiences of the students. Second, she sought to provide students with insights into the role of mathematics in the various contexts of society. These two principles of mathematics pedagogy guided her daily teaching. Julie often took her class to the supermarket, to the bank, and to engineering firms—usually by way of on-line "field trips." She made certain that she selected firms that employed men and women of color and White women in positions of leadership. During face-to-face field trips, she requested that a representative from these groups spend a few minutes with the students, explaining their roles and duties. On one occasion, Julie's students questioned a federal government official about the purpose and intent of the U.S. Census. One biracial student asked, "How are racial categories constructed?"

Julie took the students on a field trip to supermarkets in different areas of town so the students could compare the prices and quality of products (e.g., fruit, meat, and vegetables) between the suburban area and the inner-city area. This led to a letter-writing campaign to the owner of the food chain to explain their findings. The students also wondered why the cost of gas was cheaper in the suburban areas than in the inner-city area. This became a math, social studies, and language arts lesson. Students wrote letters and conducted interviews to ascertain the cost of delivering the gas to the inner city as compared to the suburban area of the city and to ascertain the rental fee for service station property in the inner city in comparison to the suburban areas. Math skills were used to determine whether there needed to be a difference in gas prices between the areas after rental fees and delivery charges were taken into consideration.

Julie used advertisements and editorials from newspapers and magazines to help students see the real-life use of such concepts as sexism, justice, and equity. She supplemented her social studies curriculum on a regular basis. She found the text biased in several areas. She integrated into the assigned curriculum information from the history and culture of different racial and ethnic groups. For example, when teaching about the settling of the local community years ago, Julie invited a Native American historian and a White historian to give views on how the settling took place and on problems and issues associated with it. She invited an African American historian and a Latino historian to discuss what was presently happening in the area. She had her students identify toys that had been made in Third World countries, and she explored with them the child labor and low-wage work that many transnational corporations had put in place in order to maximize corporate profits. Students were usually encouraged to undertake different projects in an effort to provide a comprehensive perspective on the social studies unit under study. Choices were up to the student, but Julie maintained high expectations and insisted that excellence in every phase of the work was always necessary for each student. She made certain that during the semester each student was a project leader. She also made certain that boys and girls worked together. For example, Julie knew that Ben, Lester, and Charles usually stayed close together and did not have a girl as a member of their project team. She also knew that Carmen was assertive and had useful knowledge about the project on which they were working. She put Carmen on the project team.

By the end of the year, Julie's students were scoring well on the district-mandated achievement tests; on average, they compared with other fifth-grade students. She was especially pleased to see how well her new immigrant students, Jesus and Dijana, had learned to work with the curriculum and the rest of the class. Where they had been quiet and timid at the beginning of the semester, they were now talkative and inquisitive.

Julie did have two problems with her class that she could not figure out. Shelly and Ernestine did not get along well with any of the other African American students, especially Ben and Lester. George and Hank, two White boys from Briar Creek, had considerable difficulty getting along with José and went out of their way to be mean to Lourdes and Maria. Julie was puzzled by George's and Hank's behavior; she did not think it was racially motivated because both of the boys got along pretty well with Shelly. She labored over this problem and discussed it with the school counselor. She wondered whether she had a problem related to a combination of race, class, and gender in George's and Hank's relationship with José, Lourdes, and Maria. She also concluded that she might have a social-class problem among the African American students.

Julie decided to discuss her concerns with the students individually. After some discussion, she discovered that the problem Shelly and Ernestine had with Ben and Lester was related to social class and color. Both Shelly and Ernestine had very fair skin color. They had grown up in a predominantly White middle-class community and had spent very little time around other African American students. Ben and Lester were dark-skinned male students who lived in a very poor neighborhood. Julie felt that if her assumptions were true, she would need help with this problem. She was successful in getting an African American child psychiatrist to talk to her class. She did this in relationship to an art unit that examined "color, attitude, and feelings." His discussion enabled Julie to continue her discussion with Shelly and Ernestine and get them to examine their prejudice.

George and Hank admitted to Julie, after several discussions, that they did not care too much for any girls. But Hispanic girls who wore funny clothes and ate non-American foods were a big bore. It took Julie several months of talking with George and Hank, using different reading materials and having them all work on a group project under her direction, to get George and Hank to reduce some of their prejudices. At the end of the semester, Julie still believed this problem had not been completely resolved. Thus, she shared it with the sixth-grade teacher.

At the end of the school year, Julie felt very good about her first year. She knew she had grown as a teacher. She believed her professors at State U, her cooperating teacher, and her university supervisor would give her very high marks. They had encouraged her to become a reflective teacher—committed, responsible, and wholehearted in her teaching effort. Julie believed she was well on her way to becoming a reflective teacher, and she looked forward to her second year with enthusiasm.

She also realized that her sensitivity to things she did not know had grown, and she planned to engage in some learning over the summer. As she had become aware of resentments that students from low-income families felt toward students from upper-income families, she began to wonder what the city was doing to address poverty. She heard that the National Association for the Advancement of Colored People (NAACP), some Latino community leaders, and heads of homeless shelters were trying to work with the city council, and she wanted to find out more about how these groups viewed poverty in the city. She decided to join the NAACP so she could become more familiar with its activities. She also wanted to spend time with some Latino families because before her teaching experience she had never talked directly with Latino adults; her principal suggested she should meet Luis Reyes, who directed a local community center and could help her do this. In addition, Julie felt somewhat overwhelmed by the amount of background information she had never learned about different groups in the United States and decided to start reading; because she enjoyed novels, she would start with some by Toni Morrison, Louise Erdrich, James Baldwin, and Maxine Hong Kingston. She would also read the novel *Reading Lolita in Tehran* by Azar Nafisi (2003).

From what you know of Julie, what is her approach to multicultural education? Would you be comfortable doing as Julie did? Discuss Julie's teaching with your classmates. How would you change it?

CONCLUSION

In Julie's classroom, as in yours, race, class, gender, and disability are ascribed characteristics students bring to school that cannot be ignored. To teach with excellence, Julie had to affirm her students' diversity. Why do we say this?

For one thing, Julie needed to pay attention to her students' identities in order to help them achieve. She needed to acknowledge the importance of African American males to American life to hold the interest of Lester and Ben; she needed to acknowledge the prior learning of Mai-ka, Chee, Jesus, and Dijana to help them learn English and school material; she needed to become familiar with her students' learning styles so her teaching would be most effective.

For another thing, Julie needed to pay attention to her students' personal and social needs to help them perceive school as a positive experience. Some of her students disliked other students because of prejudices and stereotypes. Some of her students did not know how to relate to people in wheelchairs or to people who looked or talked differently. Some of her students felt negative about their own abilities. These attitudes interfere not only with achievement but also with their quality of life both today as students and later as adults in a pluralistic society.

Julie realized over the year the extent to which schools are connected with their social context. She remembered having to take a course called School and Society and had not understood why it was required. She remembered reading about societal pressures on schools; during the year, she had come to see how societal pressures translated into funding, programs, and local debates that directly affected resources and guidelines in her classroom. Furthermore, she realized the extent to which students are connected with their own cultural context. The African American students, for example, emphasized their African American identity and did not want to be regarded as White; teachers who tried to be colorblind regarded this as a problem, but teachers who found the community's diversity to be interesting saw it as a strength. On the other hand, immigrant students tried hard to fit in; Julie would not have understood why without considering why their families had immigrated and the pressures the children experienced.

Julie also knew that the future of the United States depends on its diverse children. Her students will all be U.S. adults one day regardless of the quality of their education. But what kind of adults will they become? Julie wanted them all to be skilled in a variety of areas, to be clear and critical thinkers, and to have a sense of social justice and caring for others. Julie had some personal selfish motives for this: She knew her own well-being in old age would depend directly on the ability of today's children to care for older people when they become adults. She also knew her students of today would be shaping the society in which her own children would one day grow up. She wanted to make sure they were as well prepared as possible to be productive citizens who had a vision of a better society. She drew from all of the approaches at one time or another to address specific problems and needs she saw in the classroom. But the approach she emphasized—the one that guided her planning—was multicultural social justice education.

How will you approach excellence and equity in your own classroom? We can guarantee that all of your students will have their identities shaped partly by their race, social class, and gender; all of them will notice and respond in one way or another to people who differ from themselves; and all of them will grow up in a society that is still in many ways racist, sexist, and classist. You are the only one who can decide what you will do about that.

Questions and Activities

1. Why is it important for teachers to strive to attain both excellence and equity for their students? What can you do to try to achieve both goals in your teaching?

2. What does each of these terms mean to you in relationship to classroom life: *race, ethnicity, language, class, gender,* and *disability?* How are your notions of these concepts similar to and different from those of your classmates?

3. Give an example of how such variables as race, language, class, and gender interact to influence the behavior of a particular student.

4. Name the five approaches to multicultural education identified by Grant and Sleeter. What are the assumptions and instructional goals of each approach?

5. In what significant ways does the multicultural social justice education approach differ from the other four approaches? What problems might a teacher experience when trying to implement this approach in the classroom? How might these problems be reduced or solved?

6. Visit a school in your community and interview several teachers and the principal about how the school has responded to diversity and equity both within the school and in the larger society. Using the typology of multicultural education described by the authors, determine what approach or combination of approaches to multicultural education are being used within the school. Share your findings with your classmates or fellow workshop participants.

7. Which approach to multicultural education is Julie using? Which aspects of her teaching do you especially like? Which aspects would you change?

8. Which approach to multicultural education described by the authors would you be the most comfortable using? Why?

References

A national survey of lesbian and gay college programs. (1990–1991). *Empathy, 2*(2), 53–56.

Banks, J. A. (2007). *Educating citizens in a multicultural society* (2nd ed.). New York: Teachers College Press.

Banks, J. A. (Ed.) (2009a). *The Routledge international companion to multicultural education*. New York & London: Routledge.

Banks, J. A. (2009b). *Teaching strategies for ethnic studies* (8th ed.). Boston: Allyn & Bacon.

Banks, J. A., & Banks, C. A. M. (Eds.). (2004). *Handbook of research on multicultural education* (2nd ed.). San Francisco: Jossey-Bass.

Barrett, P. A. (Ed.). (1986). *To break the silence: Thirteen short stories for young readers*. New York: Dell.

Cammarota, J., & Romero, A. (2008). The social justice education project: A critically compassionate intellectualism for Chicana/o students. In W. Ayers, T. Quinn, & D. Stovall (Eds.), *Handbook for social justice in education* (pp. 465–476). New York: Routledge.

Chanse, S. (2002). Racefile. *Colorlines, 5*(1), 3.

Childs, J. B. (1994). The value of transcommunal identity politics. *Z Magazine, 7*(7/8), 48–51.

Corbin, C. (2008, July 18). McCain, Obama seek to pick off marginal voters from opposite party. *FoxNews.com*. Retrieved August 4, 2008, from http://elections.foxnews.com/2008/07/17/mccain-obama-seek-to-pick-off-marginal-voters-from-opposite-party/

Crowley, C. (2001, October 25, 2001). Arab-Americans concerned about treatment. CNN.Com. Retrieved April 21, 2009 at http://archives.cnn.com/2001/US/10/24/rec.arab.americans/

Darraj, S. M. (2002, March). Understanding the other sister: The case of Arab feminism. *Monthly Review*, 15–25.

Eck, D. L. (2002). *A new religious America: How a "Christian country" has become the world's most religiously diverse nation*. San Francisco: Harper Collins.

Fadiman, A. (1997). *The spirit catches you and you fall down*. New York: Noonday.

Freire, P. (1973). *Education for critical consciousness*. New York: Seaburg.

Freire, P. (1985). *The politics of education: Culture, power, and liberation* (D. Macedo, Trans.). Boston: Bergin & Garvey.

Gates, H. L., Jr. (1999). *Wonders of the African world*. New York: Knopf.

Gonzalez, R. J. (2001, December 13). Lynne Cheney–Joe Lieberman group puts out a blacklist. *San Jose Mercury News*. Retrieved May 29, 2003, from http://www.commondreams.org/views01/1213-05.htm

Halagao, P. S. (2004). Holding up the mirror: The complexity of seeing your ethnic self in history. *Theory and Research in Social Education, 32*(4), 459–483.

Institute for Women's Policy Research. (2008). *The gender wage ratio: Women's and men's earnings*. Retrieved August 5, 2008, from http://www.iwpr.org/pdf/C350.pdf

Johnston, D. C. (2007, March 29). Income gap is widening, data shows. *New York Times*. Retrieved August 4, 2008, from http://www.nytimes.com/2007/03/29/business/29tax.html?ref=business

Lipman, P., & Haines, N. (2007). From accountability to privatization and African American exclusion: Chicago's "Renaissance 2010." *Educational Policy, 21*(3), 471–502.

Mohr, N. (1990). *Felita*. New York: Bantam.

Moses, R. P., & Cobb, C. E., Jr. (2001). *Radical equations: Civil rights from Mississippi to the Algebra Project*. Boston: Beacon Press.

Myers, W. D. (1990). *Scorpions*. New York: Harper Trophy.

Nafisi, A. (2003) *Reading Lolita in Tehran*. New York: Random House.

National Commission on Excellence in Education. (1983). *A Nation at risk: The imperative for educational reform*. Washington, DC: U.S. Department of Education.

National Women's Studies Association. (2005). *NWSA mission*. Retrieved May 11, 2005, from http://www.nwsa.org/about.html

Orfield, G., & Lee, C. (2005). *Why segregation matters: Poverty and educational inequality*. Cambridge, MA: Harvard University Civil Rights Project.

Osler, A., & Starkey, H. (2005). *Changing citizenship: Democracy and inclusion in education*. New York: McGraw-Hill Education.

Parker, W. C. (2003). *Teaching democracy: Unity and diversity in public life*. New York: Teachers College Press.

Paterson, K. (1987). *The great Gilly Hopkins*. New York: Harper Trophy.

Reyes, P., Scribner, J. D., & Scribner, A. P. (Eds.). (1999). *Lessons from high-performing Hispanic schools: Creating learning communities*. New York: Teachers College Press.

Romero, A. (2008). *Towards a critical compassionate intellectualism model of transformative urban education*. Unpublished doctoral dissertation, University of Arizona, Tucson.

Sen, R. (2002). Durban and the war. *Colorlines, 5*(1), 7–9.

Shaw, G. B. (2004). *Back to Methuselah* [eBook]. Salt Lake City, UT: Project Gutenberg Literary Archive Foundation. Retrieved November 3, 2008, from http://www.gutenberg.org/etext/13084 (Original work published 1921)

Shor, I. (1980). *Critical teaching and everyday life*. Boston: South End Press.

Sleeter, C. E. (2005). *Un-standardizing curriculum: Multicultural teaching in the standards-based curriculum*. New York: Teachers College Press.

Sleeter, C. E. (Ed.). (2007). *Facing accountability in education: Democracy and equity at risk*. New York: Teachers College Press.

Sleeter, C. E., & Grant, C. A. (2007). *Making choices for multicultural education: Five approaches to race, class, and gender* (5th ed.). New York: Wiley.

Strazzabosco, G. (1995). *Teenage refugees from Iran speak out*. New York: Rosen.

Tetreault, M. K. T. (1989). Integrating content about women and gender into the curriculum. In J. A. Banks & C. A. M. Banks (Eds.), *Multicultural education: Issues and perspectives* (pp. 124–144). Boston: Allyn & Bacon.

Ulrich, R. (2004). Taxing proposals. TomPaine.commonsense. Retrieved June 3, 2005, from http://www.tompaine.com/articles

U.S. Census Bureau. (2000). *Statistical abstract of the United States, 2000*. Washington, DC: U.S. Government Printing Office.

U.S. Census Bureau. (2004). *Statistical abstract of the United States, 2004–2005*. Washington, DC: U.S. Government Printing Office.

U.S. Census Bureau. (2006a). *2006 American Community Survey*. Retrieved August 5, 2008, from http://www.census.gov/hhes/www/disability/2006acs.html

U.S. Census Bureau. (2006b). *Language spoken at home*. Retrieved August 4, 2008, from http://factfinder.census.gov/servlet/STTable?_bm=y&-geo_id=01000US&-qr_name = ACS_2006_EST_G00_S1601&-ds_name = ACS_2006_EST_G00

U.S. Census Bureau. (2007). *Current population survey*. Retrieved August 5, 2008, from http://www.census.gov/hhes/www/income/incomestats.html#cps

U.S. Department of Homeland Security. (2003). *Yearbook of immigration statistics 2003*. Retrieved June 2, 2005, from http://uscis.gov/graphics/shared/statistics/yearbook/YrBk03Im.htm

Valli, L., Croninger, R. G., & Chambliss, M. J. (2008). *Test driven: High-stakes accountability in elementary schools*. New York: Teachers College Press.

VisionMark. (2005). *Students speak out on educational inequalities*. Retrieved July 28, 2005, from http://www.visionmark.org/feature.php

Yep, L. (1975). *Dragonwings*. New York: Harper & Row.

In effective multicultural classrooms, students from diverse social class and religious groups experience cultural recognition and equality.

Social Class and Religion

T he two chapters in Part II discuss the effects of two powerful variables on student behavior, beliefs, and achievement: social class and religion. Social class is a powerful variable in U.S. society despite entrenched beliefs about individual opportunity in the United States. As Persell points out in Chapter 4 and as Jonathon Kozol (2005) notes in his disturbing book *The Shame of the Nation: The Restoration of Apartheid Schooling in America*, students who attend affluent middle- and upper-class schools have more resources, better teachers, and better educational opportunities than do students who attend low-income, inner-city schools. Students from the lower, middle, and upper classes usually attend different kinds of schools and have teachers who have different beliefs and expectations about their academic achievement. The structure of educational institutions also favors middle- and upper-class students. Structures such as tracking, IQ tests, and programs for gifted and mentally retarded students are highly biased in favor of middle- and upper-class students.

Students who are socialized within religious families and communities often have beliefs and behaviors that conflict with those of the school. Religious fundamentalists often challenge the scientific theories taught by schools about the origin of human beings. The controversy that occurred over intelligent design during the 2005–2006 school year epitomizes this phenomenon. Religious fundamentalists also attack textbooks and fictional books assigned by teachers that they believe violate or contradict their doctrines. Conflicts about the right to pray in the school sometimes divide communities. The school should help students mediate between their home culture and the school culture. Lippy, in Chapter 5, describes the religious diversity within the United States and some of its educational implications.

References

Kozol, J. (2005). *The shame of the nation: The restoration of Apartheid Schooling in America*. New York: Random House.

CHAPTER 4

Social Class
and Educational Equality

Caroline Hodges Persell

Picture three babies born at the same time but to parents of different social-class backgrounds. The first baby is born into a wealthy, well-educated business or professional family. The second is born into a middle-class family in which both parents attended college and have middle-level managerial or social service jobs. The third is born into a poor family in which neither parent finished high school or has a steady job. Will these children receive the same education? Although the United States is based on the promise of equal opportunity for all people, the educational experiences of these three children are likely to be quite different.

Education in the United States is not a single, uniform system that is available to every child in the same way. Children of different social classes are likely to attend different types of schools, to receive different types of instruction, to study different curricula, and to leave school at different rates and times. As a result, when children end their schooling, they differ more than when they entered, and society may use these differences to legitimate adult inequalities. If we understand better how schools can help construct inequalities, we may be in a better position to try to change them.

Social scientists often debate the nature and meaning of social class. U.S. researchers often measure social class by asking survey questions about a person's or a family's educational level, occupation, rank in an organization, and earnings. A few have tried to include measures of wealth such as home ownership or other assets. Several features of social class in the United States are worth special mention. Social-class inequality is greater in the United States than in any other industrial or postindustrial society in the world. Germany, Japan, Italy, France, Switzerland, England, Sweden, the Netherlands, you name it—all have considerably less social-class inequality than the United States. The countries with the least amount of class-based educational inequality are Sweden and the Netherlands, and they are also the countries where a family's social-class background is less related to their children's school achievement (Blossfeld & Shavit, 1993). Furthermore, both income and wealth inequality have widened in the United States during the last 20 years, increasing inequality among children as well (Lichter & Eggebeen, 1993; Mayer, 2001).

The growing economic inequality in the United States affects how much education people receive. In states with bigger gaps between high- and low-income families (i.e., more income inequality), young people who grow up in high-income families obtain more education. Children in low-income families obtain less education compared to states with smaller gaps between high- and low-income families, where family income is not so strongly related to the amount of education children obtain (Mayer, 2001). The explanation for these differences seems to be more state spending for schooling and higher economic returns to schooling in states with greater income inequality (Mayer). At the same time, the United States has a historical belief in opportunity for all, regardless of their social origins.

This paradox of great and growing inequality and the belief in opportunity for all creates a special problem for the United States, namely, the "management of ambition" (Brint & Karabel, 1989, p. 7). Many more people aspire to high-paying careers than can actually enter them. One result has been the growth of educational credentialism, which means that more and more education is required for all jobs, especially professional and managerial occupations (Collins, 1979). Thus, education is playing an ever-increasing role in the process of sorting people into their highly unequal adult positions. This sorting does not happen randomly, however.

Social class has been consistently related to educational success through time (Coleman et al., 1966; Gamoran, 2001; Goldstein, 1967; Grissmer, Kirby, Berends, & Williamson, 1994; Hanson, 1994; Mare, 1981; Mayeske & Wisler, 1972; Persell, 1977). Although there are a number of exceptions, students from higher social-class backgrounds tend to get better grades and to stay in school longer than do students from lower-class backgrounds. The question is why this happens. Does the educational system contribute to the widening of educational results over time? If so, what might change it—and how? I argue that three features of U.S. education affect educational inequalities:

1. The structure of schooling in the United States.
2. The beliefs held by many members of U.S. society and hence by many educators.
3. Teachers, curricula, and teaching practices in U.S. schools.

The *structure of schooling* refers to such features as differences among urban, rural, and suburban schools as well as differences between public and private schools. *Educational beliefs* include beliefs about intelligence quotient (IQ) and testing. *Teachers, curricula, and teaching practices* include teacher training and recruitment, tracking of students into certain curricula, teachers' expectations about what different children can learn, and differences in the quantity and quality of what is taught. This chapter reviews research showing differences in educational structures, beliefs, and practices; examines how these differences are related to the social-class backgrounds of students; considers the consequences they have for student achievement; and analyzes how they affect individuals' adult lives. Lest this be too depressing an account, at the end of the chapter, I suggest some ways in which teachers, other educators, and parents might work to improve education.

EDUCATIONAL STRUCTURES

The three babies described earlier are not likely to attend the same school even if they live in the same area. Most students in the United States attend schools that are relatively alike with respect to the social-class backgrounds of the other students. One reason this happens is that people in the United States tend to live in areas that are fairly similar with respect to class and race. If students attend their neighborhood school, they are with students from similar backgrounds. If children grow up in a fairly diverse area such as a large city, mixed suburb, or rural area, they are less likely to attend the same schools. The states with the most private schools, for example, are the states with the largest concentrations of urban areas (Coleman, Hoffer, & Kilgore, 1982). If, by chance, students of different backgrounds do attend the same school, they are very likely to experience different programs of study because of curricular tracking.

In older suburbs or cities, children of higher-class families are likely to attend homogeneous neighborhood schools, selective public schools, or private schools and to be in higher tracks; lower-class children are also likely to attend school together. Middle-class families try to send their children to special public, parochial, or private schools if they can afford them. Private day and boarding schools are also relatively similar with respect to social class despite the fact that some scholarships are awarded. Researchers who studied elite boarding schools, for example, found that 46 percent of the families had incomes of more than $100,000 per year in the early 1980s (Cookson & Persell, 1985).

Let's look more closely at elite private schools and exclusive suburban schools, which are overwhelmingly attended by upper- and upper-middle-class students; at parochial schools attended by middle-class and working-class students; and at large urban public schools heavily attended by lower-class pupils. Although these descriptions gloss over many distinctions within each major type of school, they do convey some of the range of differences that exist under the overly broad umbrella we call U.S. education.

Schools of the Upper and Upper-Middle Classes

At most upper- and upper-middle-class high schools, the grounds are spacious and well kept; the computer, laboratory, language, and athletic facilities are extensive; the teachers are well educated and responsive to students and parents; classes are small; nearly every student studies a college preparatory curriculum; and considerable homework is assigned. At private schools, these tendencies are often intensified. The schools are quite small, with few having more than 1,200 students and many being considerably smaller. Teachers do not have tenure or belong to unions, so they can be fired by the headmaster or headmistress if they are considered unresponsive to students or parents. Classes are small, often having no more than 15 students. Numerous advanced placement courses offer the possibility of college credit. Students remark that it is "not cool to be dumb around here" (Cookson & Persell, 1985, p. 95). Most students watch very little television during the school week but do a great deal of homework (Cookson & Persell). They have many opportunities for extracurricular activities, such as debate and drama clubs, publications, and music and the chance to learn sports that selective colleges value, such as crew, ice hockey, squash, and lacrosse (Stevens, 2007). Research suggests that participating in one or more extracurricular activities increases students' desire to attend school. Private school students have both academic and personal advisers who monitor their progress, help them solve problems, and try to help them have a successful school experience.

Affluent suburban communities have a robust tax base to support annual costs, which in the 2000s often exceed $15,000 per pupil. School board members are elected by members of the community who are likely to know them. Private schools are run by self-perpetuating boards of trustees, many of whom are graduates of the school. The board of trustees chooses the school head and may replace that person if they are not satisfied.

Private Parochial Schools

Many differences exist among parochial schools, but in general these schools are also relatively small. High school students in them study an academic program and do more homework than do their public school peers. They are also subjected to somewhat stricter discipline (Coleman et al., 1982). The classes, however, are often larger than elite private, suburban, or urban school classes with sometimes as many as 40 or 50 pupils per class. Some non-Catholic middle- and working-class parents, especially those in urban areas, send their children to parochial schools (Coleman et al.).

The costs at parochial schools are relatively low, especially compared to private schools, because they are subsidized by religious groups. These schools have relatively low teacher salaries and usually have no teachers' unions. Currently, they have more lay teachers and fewer nuns, priests, and brothers as teachers. The schools are governed by the religious authority that runs them.

Urban Schools

Urban schools are usually quite large and are part of an even larger school system that is generally highly bureaucratic. They offer varied courses of study. The school systems of large cities and older, larger suburbs tend to lack both political and economic resources. These systems generally are highly centralized with school board members elected on a citywide basis. School board members are often concerned members of the community who may send their own children to private schools, and they may have little knowledge about or power over the daily operations of the public system. The authority of professional educators is often buttressed by bureaucratic procedures and by unionization of teachers and administrators (Persell, 2000). Some observers (Rogers, 1968; Rogers & Chung, 1983) have described the system as one of organizational paralysis rather than governance.

Economically, the large city school systems are also relatively powerless. Because schools are supported by local property taxes and because there is a great deal of housing segregation by social class as well as race in the United States, students who live in low-income areas are very likely to attend schools with lower per pupil expenditures. In contrast, some schools with very high per pupil spending even raise additional private funds to supplement the generous tax monies used to support the school. Thus, they are able to provide additional educational enrichments to their students. Unequal educational expenditures have serious consequences for the condition of school buildings, libraries, laboratories, computer equipment, the richness of curricular offerings, the ability to hire experienced and certified teachers, class size, and the variety of extracurricular offerings. Such disparities in educational opportunities affect how much children learn, how long they stay in school, their graduation rates, and the rates at which they successfully pursue additional education after high school.

While the question of whether money makes a difference in educational achievement has long been debated (Coleman et al., 1966; Hanushek, 1989, 1996), more recent research has refined the question to see money as a threshold condition that is necessary but not always sufficient for achievement. How the money is spent certainly matters (Elliott, 1998; Gamoran, Secada, & Marrett, 2000; Wenglinsky, 1997). Expenditures need to be connected to opportunities to learn effectively (Gamoran et al.), to have good teachers (Darling-Hammond, 2004), to use inquiry-based teaching methods (Elliott), and to have good equipment, especially in the case of science (Elliott).

Because of the importance of funding equity, 20 states have faced court challenges resulting in court decisions requiring them to provide all students with equal access to quality schools (Dively & Hickrod, 1992; Truce in New Jersey's School War, 2002). Perhaps the most extensive and bitterly contested of these suits is *Abbott v. Burke* in New Jersey brought in 1981. This case produced eight court rulings that ordered equal funding in urban and suburban schools, a high-quality preschool program for poor districts, and standards-based reforms to close the achievement gap between rich and poor students. This court case has been described by some as perhaps "the most significant education case since the Supreme Court's desegregation ruling nearly 50 years ago" (Truce in New Jersey's School War). It affects 30 underprivileged districts in the state and may have implications for other states facing such court challenges.

In general, then, a child's social-class background is related to the school attended and the school's size, the political and economic resources available to it, and the curricula it offers as well as the ensuing educational opportunities (Persell, Cookson, & Catsambis, 1992).

EDUCATIONAL BELIEFS

Since the last century, ideas about testing students have permeated education. For decades, the concept of measuring intelligence, or IQ testing, played a major role in education. The concept of IQ has been used to explain why some children learn more slowly than others, why African American children do less well in school than White children, and why lower-class children do less well than middle- and upper-middle-class children. IQ tests are often used to justify variations in education, achievement, and rewards. Brantlinger (2003) writes, "Because schools are thought to reward innate capacities rather than social standing, they are believed to be meritocracies in which students have equal chances to succeed" (p. 1). The justification usually is that because some people are more intelligent than others, they are entitled to more opportunities and rewards, including curricular track placement and exposure to special educational programs and resources.

Critics of IQ tests have raised a number of good points about their accuracy. For example, IQ tests do not measure such important features of intelligence as creative or divergent thinking, logic, and critical reasoning. Howard Gardner (1983) developed the idea of multiple intelligences in *Frames of Mind*. Stephen Jay Gould's (1996) *The Mismeasure of Man* may still be the single best critical analysis of IQ tests. A phenomenon called the Flynn effect notes the massive IQ gains of about 15 points from one generation to the next in some 30 countries in the world (Flynn, 1987, 2007). Flynn raises the question of how IQs could rise so fast in the absence of any visible genetic changes and suggests that the causes are rooted in the way industrialization and science liberated people's minds from the concrete. "People developed new habits of mind" that allowed them to solve more abstract problems (Flynn, 2007, pp. 173–174), which affected their scores on IQ tests.

In the last several decades, emphasis has increasingly been placed on the use of large-scale achievement tests. This so-called high-stakes testing has been used as the basis for deciding the educational track to which students are assigned, whether a student moves to the next grade in school, and whether a student graduates from high school. Such tests may also be used to hold educators, schools, and school districts accountable. The focus here is on how the use of tests affects individuals and whether they are discriminatory or unfair for students of certain social-class backgrounds.

The purposes of using such tests include setting high standards for student learning and raising student achievement. However, when some students do poorly on a test, schools and teachers can respond in several different ways. They can work harder with the students obtaining low scores, providing them with more personal attention, tutoring, and additional learning experiences in an effort to improve their achievement test scores. Such responses usually require additional resources, which many schools, especially ones that are already underfunded, may not have.

Another possible response is that schools try to get rid of students with lower scores by encouraging them to drop out or transfer or by other means. This is clearly an unintended consequence of high-stakes testing and one that affects most severely the most educationally needy and vulnerable students. Many teachers, while not opposed to high standards, say that the existence of mandatory testing leads to "teaching in ways that contradicted their own ideas of sound educational practice" (Winter, 2003, p. B9).

One study (Booher-Jennings, 2005) analyzed an urban elementary school's response to the Texas Accountability System and the Student Success Initiative (SSI) requiring third-grade students to pass a reading test to be promoted to the fourth grade. Influenced by the institutional logic created by the SSI, teachers practiced "educational triage." They diverted resources to students believed to be on the brink of passing the Texas Assessment of Knowledge and Skills test and to students whose scores were counted, and they reduced the size of the accountability group by referring more students to special education. Wondering why teachers would participate in such a system, Booher-Jennings found that the institutional environment defined a good teacher as one whose students had high pass rates. Teachers became competitors rather than partners with their colleagues, which weakened the faculty's ability to work together toward common goals. Booher-Jennings concluded that "the singular focus on increasing aggregate test scores rendered the school-wide discussion of the 'best interests of children' obsolete" (p. 260). This study raises important questions about how the No Child Left Behind (NCLB) Act of 2002 is implemented. Its ostensible goals are to reduce the achievement gap between low income and/or minority children and higher income and/or White children by holding educators accountable. Some of the key provisions of this federal law are state-level annual tests of third to eighth graders in reading, math, and science plus at least one test for students in grades 10–12. States and districts are required to report school-level data on students' test scores for various subgroups: African American, Latino, Native American, Asian American, White non-Hispanic, special education, limited English proficiency (LEP), and/or low-income students. NCLB rewards or punishes school districts, schools, and teachers for the tested achievement of their students but does not prescribe consequences for students (Dworkin, 2005).

When school districts implement the NCLB Act, schools with too many low scores are labeled failures, regardless of the reason for the low scores. But when their success is measured differently, for example, by impact or by how much their students are learning, about three-quarters of the schools are succeeding (Downey, von Hippel, & Hughes, 2008). Schools' actual impact on learning was measured by observing how much more students learned during the school year than during summer vacation. Students in 75 percent of the schools were learning at a reasonable rate and much faster during the school year than during summer vacation.

Another feature of NCLB is the requirement that schools have "highly qualified teachers" in the "core academic subjects" of English, reading or language arts, math, science, foreign languages, civics and government, economics, arts, history, and geography by 2005–2006. There are also requirements for schools, districts, and states to organize programs of parental involvement and improved communication (Epstein, 2005). However, the lack of federal resources to pay for mandated changes and the threat of losing a portion of existing state or local resources has led to a number of unintended consequences, including rising drop-out rates in some schools or systems, encouraging teachers to focus only on teaching for the test and hence narrowing the curriculum, and harming minority or low-income students (Dworkin, 2005; Heubert & Hauser, 1999; McNeil, 2000; Meier & Wood, 2004). In general, the law seems to assume that schools, teachers, and students operate in a vacuum rather than in socially structured contexts and organizations.

TEACHERS, CURRICULUM, AND TEACHING PRACTICES

The relatively recent growth of high-stakes testing may deflect attention from essential features of schools that affect learning. Educational equity requires that we examine not only the educational funding but also what that funding is used for and how it affects education. Three features of schools highlight how students' educational experiences vary depending on their social class—specifically, their teachers, curricular tracking, and teachers' expectations.

Teachers

Schools with high percentages of low-income students are more likely to have teachers who are not certified at all or who are teaching out of their area of certification (Darling-Hammond, 2004; Ingersoll, 2004). Large shortages of certified teachers in major urban areas such as New York City in recent years have led to several changes. The schools' chancellor developed an alternative, abbreviated path to temporary certification aimed at career changers and recent college graduates with no teaching experience. The alternative path to provisional certification involves a month of intensive education courses. At the end of this time, these teachers are placed in the 100 lowest-performing schools from the prior year. About 30 percent of the new certified teachers in the fall of 2002 in New York City had this alternative certification. In addition, New York and other cities received recruits from Teach for America, a nonprofit organization that recruits college graduates, provides a summer of intensive training, and places them in troubled schools. Like New York, many school districts around the country, including

Los Angeles, Atlanta, and Washington, D.C., have alternative certification programs in an effort to address the shortage of qualified teachers. However, there is considerable debate over the abbreviated training that alternative-route certification involves.

Arthur Levine, former president of Teachers College at Columbia University, points out that the definition of a certified teacher has been changed, but the net result "is that we will still have large numbers of students this fall whose teachers are unprepared to teach them" (as cited in Goodnough, 2002, p. B3). Research by Gomez and Grobe (1990, as cited in Darling-Hammond, 2001, p. 472) finds that alternative-route teacher candidates had more uneven performance ratings compared to trained beginners, particularly in the area of classroom management and in their knowledge of instructional techniques. Their students, in turn, scored significantly lower in language arts compared to students of fully prepared beginning teachers when students' initial achievement levels were held constant (as cited in Darling-Hammond, p. 472). As Darling-Hammond notes, "policy makers have nearly always answered the problem of teacher shortages by lowering standards, so that people who have had little or no preparation for teaching can be hired" (p. 471). It is notable that this issue does not surface in more affluent suburban public schools; they have very low percentages of teachers who are not certified or are teaching outside their areas of certification (Ingersoll, 2004). One reason that such areas can attract and retain certified teachers better than inner-city schools is that they pay higher salaries on the average. Teachers, however, work within educational structures that contribute to unequal learning opportunities. This is especially true of the educational practice of tracking.

Tracking

The first recorded instance of tracking was the Harris Plan in St. Louis, begun in 1867. Since then, tracking in the United States has followed a curious pattern of alternate popularity and disuse. In the 1920s and 1930s, when many immigrants came to the United States, tracking increased greatly. Thereafter, it fell into decline until the late 1950s when it was revived, apparently in response to the USSR's launching of *Sputnik* and the U.S. competitive concern with identifying and educating the gifted (Conant, 1961; Oakes, 1985). That period was also marked by large migrations of rural southern African Americans to northern cities and by an influx of Puerto Rican and Mexican American migrants into the United States. Darling-Hammond (2001) points out that "tracking is much more extensive in U.S. schools than in most other countries" (p. 474). This observation prompts us to ask why this is the case. Two differences between the United States and European countries might account for the difference. The United States has more racial and economic inequality than do European countries, and educational achievement and attainment are more important for a person's (more unequal) occupation, earnings, and other life chances in the United States than in European countries.

To understand tracking in elementary schools, we need to examine the distinction between ability grouping and curriculum differentiation. Proponents of ability grouping stress flexible subject-area assignments. By this, they mean that students are assigned to learning groups on the basis of their background and achievement in a subject area at any given moment and that skills and knowledge are evaluated at relatively frequent intervals. Students showing gains can be shifted readily into another group. They might also be in different ability groups in different subjects according to their own rate of growth in each one. This practice suggests a common curriculum shared by all students with only the mix of student abilities being varied. It also assumes that, within that curriculum, all groups are taught the same material.

In fact, it seems that group placement becomes self-perpetuating, that students are often grouped at the same level in all subjects, and that even a shared curriculum may be taught differently to different groups. This is especially likely to happen in large, bureaucratic, urban public schools. Quite often, different ability groups are assigned to different courses of study, resulting in simultaneous grouping by curriculum and ability. Rosenbaum (1976) notes that although ability grouping and curriculum grouping may appear different to educators, in fact they share several social similarities: (1) students are placed with those defined as similar to themselves and are segregated from those deemed different, and (2) group placement is made on the basis of criteria such as ability or postgraduate plans that are unequally esteemed. Thus, group membership immediately ranks students in a status hierarchy, formally stating that some students are better than others (Rosenbaum, 1976). Following Rosenbaum's usage, the general term *tracking* is applied here to both types of grouping.

Tracking by academic level is widespread today, particularly in large, diverse school systems and in schools serving primarily lower-class students (Lucas & Berends, 2002). It is less prevalent and less rigid when it occurs in upper-middle-class suburban and private schools and in parochial schools (Jones, Vanfossen, & Spade, 1985). In recent years, tracking has become more subtle, and school officials do not call it "tracking." High school courses now tend to be classified as regular, college prep, honors, and advanced placement (AP) or something similar. Low-income students and parents, in particular, may be unaware of what the distinctions mean or realize that decisions made in seventh or eighth grade or earlier may affect what is possible in high school. They may be unaware that grades received in AP or honors courses may be given more weight when their grade point averages are computed and thus may differentially affect their chances for college admission or scholarships (Oakes, Joseph, & Muir, 2004). They also may not realize the importance of taking certain courses (e.g., calculus) for how they do on college entrance examinations. Many inner-city and/or low-income schools do not offer even a single AP course, while many affluent suburban schools offer a dozen or more. Differences in the courses students take, especially in such areas as mathematics, science, and foreign language, go a long way toward explaining differences in achievement test scores (Darling-Hammond, 2001).

The social-class background of students is related to the prevalence of tracking in the schools, to the nature of the available tracks, and to the ways track assignments are made. Furthermore, while there is a relationship between tested ability and track placement, it is highly imperfect (Dreeben & Barr, 1988; Pallas, Entwisle, Alexander, & Stluka, 1994). Once students are assigned to different tracks, what happens to them? Researchers suggest that tracking has effects through at least three mechanisms. These are instructional, social, and institutional in nature, and all three may operate together. The major *instructional processes* that have been observed to vary according to track placement include the unequal allocation of educational resources, the instruction offered, student-teacher interactions, and student-student interactions. Dreeben and Barr found variations in the content, pacing, and quantity of instruction in different tracks. Higher-ranked reading groups were taught more (and learned more) words than lower-ranked reading groups, according to Gamoran (1984, 1986).

Hallinan (1987) studied within-class ability grouping in 34 elementary school classes. She found that ability grouping affects the learning of students in higher and lower groups because it influences their opportunities for learning, the instructional climate, and the aptitudes clustered in the different groups. High-ability groups spend more time on task during class; that is, more class time is devoted to actual teaching activities. Also, teachers use more interesting teaching methods and materials. Finally, teachers hold higher expectations and the other students support learning more in the higher-ability groups. As a result, the aptitude of students in the higher groups tends to develop more than does the aptitude of students in the lower group.

In a national sample of 20,000 students, Gamoran (1987) found that the effects of student socioeconomic status on achievement disappeared when their track placements were comparable. In the United States, 80 percent of schools track students in math, but in mathematics, average U.S. eighth graders are below their peers in Singapore, Japan, Korea, and the Netherlands. Unlike the U.S. practice, ability tracking in Japan is prohibited through middle school. In contrast to math, only 20 percent of U.S. schools practice tracking in science classes. In science, American eighth graders were comparable to their peers in the Netherlands, Sweden, and Australia and close to the world's best students in Japan, Hong Kong, and Korea. Such evidence suggests that tracking inhibits achievement. How and why does it happen? In secondary schools, college-track students consistently have better teachers, class materials, laboratory facilities, field trips, and visitors than their lower-track counterparts (Findley & Bryan, 1975; Oakes, 1985; Rosenbaum, 1976; Schafer, Olexa, & Polk, 1973).

Oakes (1985) observed that teachers of high-track students set aside more time for student learning and devoted more class time to learning activities. Fewer students in these classes engaged in "off-task" activities (p. 111). Oakes (1985) also found that:

> Students are being exposed to knowledge and taught behaviors that
> differ not only educationally but also in socially important ways.
> Students at the top are exposed to the knowledge that is highly valued
> in our culture, knowledge that identifies its possessors as "educated"
> (pp. 91–92).

Similarly, those students are taught critical thinking, creativity, and independence. Students at the bottom are denied access to these educationally and socially important experiences (Oakes).

Oakes (1985) observed that teachers spent more time in low-track classes on discipline and that students in those classes perceived their teachers as more punitive than did students in high-track classes. Freiberg (1970) found that higher-track students received more empathy, praise, and use of their ideas as well as less direction and criticism than did lower-track students. Socially, tracks may create settings that shape students' self-esteem and expectations about academic performance.

Students have been observed to pick up on the negative evaluations associated with lower track placement. They may make fun of lower-track students, call them unflattering names, or stop associating with them (Rosenbaum, 1976). Hence, a major result of tracking is differential respect from peers and teachers with implications for both instruction and esteem. Institutionally, tracking creates groups of students who are understood by teachers and parents as having certain qualities and capacities above and beyond the actual skills they possess.

Ability groups limit teachers' perceptions of what grades are appropriate for students in different tracks (Reuman, 1989). Both parents and teachers rated children in higher reading groups as more competent and likely to do better in the future than children in low reading groups, even when children's initial performance levels and parents' prior beliefs about their children's abilities were comparable (Pallas et al., 1994, p. 41). Additional consequences of tracking include segregation of students by social class and ethnicity (Esposito, 1973; Heck, Price, & Thomas, 2004; *Hobson v. Hansen*, 1967; Oakes, 1985; University of the State of New York, 1969), unequal learning by students in different tracks (Findley & Bryan, 1970; Oakes; Rosenbaum, 1976; Schafer et al., 1973), and unequal chances to attend college (Alexander, Cook, & McDill, 1978; Alexander & Eckland, 1975; Jaffe & Adams, 1970; Jones, Spade, & Vanfossen, 1987; Rosenbaum, 1976, 1980). The percentage of students in an academic curriculum may be the single most significant structural difference between different types of schools.

Darling-Hammond (2001) suggests that tracking persists because few teachers "are prepared to manage heterogeneous classrooms effectively" (p. 474). In the 1980s, tracking came under considerable attack, and a movement toward "detracking" gained support (Braddock & McPartland, 1990; Oakes, 1985, 1992; Wheelock, 1992). But even when teachers have a strong ideology of detracking and have succeeded in ending tracking in some communities, they have encountered serious resistance and opposition from parents. In their three-year longitudinal case studies of ten racially and socioeconomically mixed secondary schools that were participating in detracking reform, Oakes, Wells, Jones, and Datnow (1997) found that detracking is a "highly normative and political endeavor that confronts deeply held cultural beliefs, ideologies, and fiercely protected arrangements of material and political advantage in local communities" (p. 507). For example, being in an honors course confers advantages in the competition for college admissions. Detracking was able to occur when politically savvy teachers were able to involve powerful parents in meaningful ways in the process of implementing it (Oakes et al., 1997).

Teachers' Expectations

Educational structures such as schools that are socioeconomically homogeneous, the growing use of standardized tests, and practices such as tracking go a long way toward shaping the expectations teachers hold about students. Teacher training and textbooks have tended to attribute educational failures to deficiencies in the children. Often, such deficiencies are assumed to reside in the social characteristics of the pupils, such as their social-class background, ethnicity, language, or behavior rather than in social structure.

In a review of relevant research, Persell (1977) found that student social class was related to teacher expectations when other factors such as race were not more salient, when expectations were engendered by real children, and when teachers had a chance to draw inferences about a student's social class rather than simply being told the student's background. Sometimes social class was related to teacher expectations even when the children's current IQ and achievement were comparable. That is, teachers held lower expectations for lower-class children than for middle-class children even when those children had similar IQ scores and achievement.

Teachers' expectations may also be influenced by the behavior and physical appearance of the children (Ritts, Patterson, & Tubbs, 1992). Social class may influence teacher expectations directly or indirectly through test scores, appearance, language style, speed of task performance, and behavior. All of these traits are themselves culturally defined and are related to class position. Moreover, teacher expectations are influenced more by negative information about pupil characteristics than by positive data. It is important to know this because much of the information teachers gain about low-income children seems to be negative.

Another factor that may influence teacher expectations and pupil performance is the operation of the cultural capital possessed by families of higher social classes. As used here, the term *cultural capital* refers to the cultural resources and assets that families bring to their interactions with school personnel. By virtue of their own educational credentials and knowledge of educational institutions, parents, especially mothers, are able to help their children get the right teachers and courses and do extra work at home if necessary (Baker & Stevenson, 1986; Grissmer et al., 1994; Lareau, 1989; Useem, 1990). If teacher expectations are often influenced by the social class of students, do those expectations have significant consequences for students? Research on this question has produced seemingly contradictory results. The controversy began with the publication of *Pygmalion in the Classroom* (Rosenthal & Jacobson, 1968). That book suggested that the expectations of classroom teachers might powerfully influence the achievement of students. Hundreds of studies on the possibility of "expectancy effects" have been conducted since then (see Cooper & Good, 1983). One thing is clear: Only expectations that teachers truly believe are likely to affect their behaviors.

When teachers hold higher expectations for pupils, how does this affect their behavior? Their expectations seem to affect the frequency of interaction they have with their pupils and the kinds of behaviors they show toward different children. Teachers spend more time interacting with pupils for whom they have higher expectations (Persell, 1977). For example, Brophy and Good (1970) found that students for whom teachers held high expectations were praised more frequently when correct and were criticized less frequently when wrong or unresponsive than were pupils for whom teachers had low expectations.

Rosenthal (1974) believes that teachers convey their expectations in at least four related ways. He bases this judgment on his review of 285 studies of interpersonal influence, including at least 80 in classrooms or other settings. First, he sees a general climate factor consisting of the overall warmth a teacher shows to children, with more shown to high-expectancy students. Second, he sees students for whom high expectations are held as receiving more praise for doing something right than do students for whom low expectations are held. Third, Rosenthal notes that high-expectancy students are taught more than are low-expectancy students. This is consistent with research by others and summarized by Persell (1977). Fourth, Rosenthal indicates that expectancy may be affected by a response-opportunity factor. That is, students for whom the teacher has higher expectations are called on more often and are given more chances to reply as well as more frequent and more difficult questions. A fifth way teachers convey their expectations, which Rosenthal does not mention but which has been observed by others, is the different type of curricula teachers may present to children for whom they have different expectations. Clearly, there is evidence that at least some teachers behave differently toward students for whom they hold different expectations.

The critical question remains: Do these expectations and behaviors actually affect students? Do the students think differently about themselves or learn more as a result of the expectations teachers hold? Therein lies the heart of the Pygmalion effect controversy. Students report being aware of the different expectations teachers have for them, and they notice differences in the way teachers treat them. For example, students studied by Ferguson (2001) reported that when they asked the teacher a question, they received only a brief one-sentence reply, but when other students (for whom the teacher had higher expectations) asked the same question, the teacher spoke at length in response.

When teachers hold definite expectations and when those expectations are reflected in their behavior toward children, these expectations are related to student cognitive changes even when pupil IQ and achievement are controlled. Moreover, negative expectations, which can be observed only in natural settings because it is unethical to induce negative expectations experimentally, appear to have even more powerful consequences than do positive expectations. Moreover, socially vulnerable children (i.e., younger, lower-class, and minority children) seem to be more susceptible to lower teacher expectations (Rosenthal & Jacobson, 1968).

CONSEQUENCES OF SOCIAL CLASS AND EDUCATIONAL INEQUALITY

This profile of social-class differences in education in the United States is oversimplified, but considerable evidence suggests that the general patterns described here do exist. Social-class backgrounds affect where students go to school and what happens to them once they are there. As a result, lower-class students tend to encounter less prepared teachers, are less likely to be exposed to valued curricula, are taught less of whatever curricula they do study, and are expected to do less work in the classroom and outside of it. Hence, they learn less and are less prepared for the next level of education.

Although students have many reasons for dropping out of school or for failing to continue, their experiences in school may contribute to their desire to continue or to quit. Coleman et al. (1982) found that 24 percent of public high school students dropped out, compared to 12 percent of Catholic and 13 percent of other private school students. Social class is a more important cause of lost talent among U.S. youth in the late high school and posthigh school years than gender or race, according to Hanson (1994). Similarly, college attendance depends on a number of factors, including access to the necessary financial resources. Nevertheless, it is striking how differently students at different schools fare. Graduation from a private rather than a public high school is related to attending a four-year (rather than a two-year) college (Falsey & Heyns, 1984), attending a highly selective college (Persell et al., 1992), and earning higher income in adult life (Lewis & Wanner, 1979). Even within the same school, track placement is related to college attendance (Alexander et al., 1978; Alexander & McDill, 1976; Jaffe & Adams, 1970; Rosenbaum, 1976, 1980). College attendance, in turn, is related to the adult positions and earnings one attains (Kamens, 1974; Tinto, 1980; Useem, 1984; Useem & Karabel, 1986). In 2005, the median income of women with bachelor's degrees was $36,500 on average, compared to women with high school degrees, who earned about $21,000; men with bachelor's degrees earned $52,000, compared to men with high school degrees, who earned about $32,000 (U.S. Census Bureau, 2005). Thus, educational inequalities help create and legitimate economic and social inequalities. However, most educators do not want to enhance and legitimate social inequalities. Therefore, it seems reasonable to ask: What can they do to try to change these patterns?

RECOMMENDATIONS FOR ACTION

Teachers, educators, and concerned citizens might consider the following actions:

1. *Working politically and legally to increase the educational resources available to all children, not just those in wealthy school districts and not just the gifted and talented.* Those concerned might do this by joining a political party that works to advance the interests of the less advantaged members of society, by attending political meetings, by holding candidates accountable for their positions on education, and by supporting class action lawsuits for educational equity. We can join other people interested in scrutinizing candidates' records of support for education and contribute time, money, or both to the campaigns of candidates seeking to defeat incumbents who have not supported quality education for all children.

2. *Working to reduce economic inequalities in society.* This can be done by supporting income tax reforms at the national level that benefit hardworking low- and middle-income families, by opposing tax cuts for the rich, by supporting job programs at reasonable wages and health care programs for those who can work, and by providing aid for poor parents who are unable to work.

3. *Working to build economically and racially integrated communities.* This can be done by choosing to live in such a community, by supporting federal subsidies for low-income housing in mixed-income areas, and by opposing efforts to restrict access to certain communities by members of particular ethnic or income groups. Such restrictions might take the form of zoning that prohibits the construction of high-rise housing for low-income groups or limits housing lots to a large size, such as two acres, or of redlining by banks that refuse to provide mortgages in certain neighborhoods.

4. *Working to support prenatal care for all pregnant women.* In 2004, 16 percent of women received no prenatal care during the first trimester (National Center for Health Statistics, 2007). Prenatal care significantly reduces the potential for behavioral and learning disabilities (Blackburn, 2007).

5. *Working to support Head Start programs for all eligible children.* In 2008, due to poor funding and in spite of their proven track record toward the development of young children, 49 percent of Head Start programs reported an increase in waiting lists of eligible children coupled with a decrease in enrollment slots to serve them (National Head Start Association, 2008). Investing in quality preschool education makes sound economic sense as well, creating lower costs later on for special education, public assistance, and the incarceration of people who commit crimes (Children's Defense Fund, 2007).

6. *Using tests for diagnosing rather than dismissing students.* For example, instead of taking a low test score as evidence that a child cannot learn, we can examine what parts of a particular test were difficult for that child. If necessary, we can obtain further individual testing to identify and analyze what skills the child needs to develop and devise strategies for teaching those specific skills. We can try alternative teaching strategies with each child until we find one that works. If a child has difficulty learning to read phonetically, for example, we might try teaching that child

a different way, perhaps visually. We can help children with various kinds of learning disabilities learn ways to compensate for their difficulties. For example, planning their work in advance, organizing it so that they have enough time to complete the necessary steps, and allowing time for someone else to check their spelling are all compensatory strategies that can be adopted to good effect for children trying to overcome various learning disabilities.

7. *Working on finding the abilities students do have rather than deciding that they do not have any.* For example, we can help students who have strong artistic, musical, athletic, or auditory talents but are weaker in the verbal or mathematical areas to find ways into the difficult subjects through their strengths.

8. *Supporting efforts at detracking.*

9. *Learning about and using collaborative teaching techniques,* such as those developed by Elizabeth Cohen and her colleagues at Stanford University that work effectively in heterogeneous classes (Cohen, 1994a, 1994b, 2000; Cohen & Lotan, 1997; Sharan, 1980).

10. *Committing to the use of a variety of pedagogical techniques, curricular assignments, and projects that address the learning needs of individual children.*

11. *Expecting and demanding a lot from students in the way of effort, thought, and work.* We can help students take pride in themselves and their work by teaching them what first-rate work should look like. The written materials students receive from teachers and schools and the appearance of the classrooms and hallways should all convey a sense of care, quality, and value. We can carefully check the work students do, suggest constructive ways they might improve it, and expect them to do better the next time.

12. *Teaching students content and subject matter.* We can show students that we value them and their learning by devoting class time to pedagogically useful tasks, by refusing to waste class time on frivolous activities, and by trying to stick to an annual schedule of curricular coverage.

13. *Helping students see how education is relevant and useful for their lives,* perhaps by bringing back graduates who have used school as a springboard to better themselves and their worlds. Schools might keep a roster of successful graduates and post pictures and stories about them for current students to see. We can bring in examples that link learning with life accomplishments so students can begin to see connections between school and life. For example, we might invite people who run their own business to talk about how they use math or bring in people who work in social service organizations to show how they use writing in their daily work.

SUMMARY

This chapter has explored how educational structures, beliefs, and practices contribute to unequal educational outcomes. To achieve greater educational equality, educators must understand what social-class differences presently exist in those structures, beliefs, and practices.

If these differences are understood, then the educational experiences of students of all social classes might be made more similar. The higher one's social-class background, the more likely one is to attend a smaller school with more resources, including better teachers, smaller classes, and richer curricula. Achievement of greater educational equality means making such school experiences available to all students regardless of their social-class backgrounds.

Widespread confidence in educational testing and the growing use of high-stakes testing runs the risk of blaming students for their failure and diverting attention from how the social organization of schools may help to create failures. Instead, we should be examining how teachers, curricula, and educational policies of schools attended by children of different social classes influence their learning.

The educational process of tracking refers to the segregation of students into different learning or curriculum groups that are unequally ranked in a prestige hierarchy. Whether based on ability grouping or curricular grouping, such tracking tends to reduce learning opportunities for students in the lower groups while increasing such opportunities for students in higher groups. As a result, this educational practice contributes to educational inequalities. The detracking movement represents an important effort toward achieving greater educational equality, but it has encountered some resistance from certain parents.

Teachers may unconsciously form different expectations about students of different social-class backgrounds. When teachers hold higher expectations for students, they tend to spend more time interacting with those students, praise them more, teach them more, call on them more often, and offer them a more socially valued curriculum. When teachers hold higher expectations and when those expectations are evident in their behavior, they increase student learning. Thus, achieving greater educational equality means that teachers' expectations for lower-class students need to be raised.

Because the educational structures, beliefs, and practices examined here are related to unequal educational attainment and because educational success is related to lifetime occupations and earnings, it is important that educational inequalities be reduced. This chapter has recommended a number of steps that concerned educators and citizens can take to promote educational and social equality.

Questions and Activities

1. According to Persell, in what ways do schools contribute to inequality? What evidence does the author give to support her position?
2. Give examples of how each of the following factors contributes to educational inequality: (a) educational structures, (b) funding inequities, (c) testing practices, (d) teachers, and (e) curriculum.
3. What are the major characteristics of each of the following types of schools: (a) elite private schools and exclusive suburban schools, (b) parochial schools, and (c) large urban public school systems?
4. Why do students from different social-class backgrounds often attend different schools or assigned to different tracks when they attend the same schools? How does the social-class background of students influence the kind of education they often receive?

5. Visit and observe in (a) a local elite private school, (b) a school in an upper-middle-class suburb, and (c) an inner-city school. How are these schools alike? How are they different? Based on your visits and observations, what tentative generalizations can you make about education, social class, and inequality? To what extent are your generalizations similar to and different from those of Persell?

6. What cautions should teachers, principals, policy makers, and parents keep in mind when interpreting standardized achievement tests?

7. What is tracking? Why do you think it is more widespread in large, diverse school systems than in upper-middle-class suburban, private, and parochial schools?

8. How do the school experiences of students in lower and higher tracks differ? How does tracking contribute to educational inequality? What is detracking?

9. Why does tracking persist?

10. How do factors related to social class influence teacher expectations of students?

11. How do teacher expectations influence how teachers and pupils interact, what students are taught, and what students achieve?

References

Alexander, K. L., Cook, M., & McDill, E. L. (1978). Curriculum tracking and educational stratification: Some further evidence. *American Sociological Review, 43*(1), 47–66.

Alexander, K. L., & Eckland, B. K. (1975). Contextual effects in the high school attainment process. *American Sociological Review, 40*(3), 402–416.

Alexander, K. L., & McDill, E. L. (1976). Selection and allocation within schools: Some causes and consequences of curriculum placement. *American Sociological Review, 41*(6), 963–980.

Baker, D. P., & Stevenson, D. L. (1986). Mothers' strategies for children's school achievement: Managing the transition to high school. *Sociology of Education, 59*(3), 156–166.

Blackburn, S. T. (2007). *Maternal, fetal, & neonatal physiology: A clinical perspective* (3rd ed.). St. Louis, MO: Saunders Elsevier.

Blossfeld, H. P., & Shavit, Y. (1993). Persisting barriers: Changes in educational opportunities in thirteen countries. In Y. Shavit & H. P. Blossfeld (Eds.), *Persistent inequality: Changing educational attainment in thirteen countries* (pp. 1–23). Boulder, CO: Westview.

Booher-Jennings, J. (2005). Below the bubble: "Educational triage" and the Texas accountability system. *American Educational Research Journal, 42*(2), 231–268.

Braddock, J. H., II, & McPartland, J. M. (1990). Alternatives to tracking. *Educational Leadership, 47*(7), 76–79.

Brantlinger, E. A. (2003). *Dividing classes: How the middle class negotiates and rationalizes school advantage.* New York: Routledge-Falmer.

Brint, S., & Karabel, J. (1989). *The diverted dream: Community colleges and the promise of educational opportunity in America, 1900–1985.* New York: Oxford University Press.

Brophy, J. E., & Good, T. L. (1970). Teachers' communication of differential expectations for children's classroom performance: Some behavioral data. *Journal of Educational Psychology, 61*(5), 365–374.

Children's Defense Fund. (2007). *America's cradle to prison pipeline: A Children's Defense Fund report.* Washington, DC: Author.

Cohen, E. G. (1994a). *Designing groupwork: Strategies for the heterogeneous classroom* (2nd ed.). New York: Teachers College Press.

Cohen, E. G. (1994b). Restructuring the classroom: Conditions for productive small groups. *Review of Educational Research, 64*(1), 1–35.

Cohen, E. G. (2000). Equitable classrooms in a changing society. In M. T. Hallinan (Ed.), *Handbook of the sociology of education* (pp. 265–283). New York: Kluwer Academic/Plenum.

Cohen, E. G., & Lotan, R. A. (Eds.). (1997). *Working for equity in heterogeneous classrooms: Sociological theory in practice.* New York: Teachers College Press.

Coleman, J. S., Campbell, E. Q., Hobson, C. J., McPartland, J., Alexander, M., Mood, A. M., Weinfeld, F. D., & York, R. L. (1966). *Equality of educational opportunity (Coleman) study (EEOS).* Washington, DC: U.S. Government Printing Office.

Coleman, J. S., Hoffer, T., & Kilgore, S. (1982). *High school achievement: Public, Catholic, and private schools compared.* New York: Basic Books.

Collins, R. (1979). *The credential society: A historical sociology of education and stratification.* New York: Academic Press.

Conant, J. B. (1961). *Slums and suburbs: A commentary on schools in metropolitan areas.* New York: McGraw Hill.

Cookson, P. W., Jr., & Persell, C. H. (1985). *Preparing for power: America's elite boarding schools.* New York: Basic Books.

Cooper, H. M., & Good, T. L. (1983). *Pygmalion grows up: Studies in the expectation communication process.* New York: Longman.

Darling-Hammond, L. (2001). Inequality and access to knowledge. In J. A. Banks & C. A. M. Banks (Eds.), *Handbook of research on multicultural education* (pp. 465–483). San Francisco: Jossey-Bass.

Darling-Hammond, L. (2004). What happens to a dream deferred? The continuing quest for equal educational opportunity. In J. A. Banks & C. A. M. Banks (Eds.), *Handbook of research on multicultural education* (2nd ed., pp. 607–630). San Francisco: Jossey-Bass.

Dively, J. A., & Hickrod, G. A. (1992). Update of selected states' school equity funding litigation and the "boxscore." *Journal of Education Finance, 17*(3), 352–363.

Downey, D. B., von Hippel, P. T., & Hughes, M. (2008). Are "failing" schools really failing? Using seasonal comparison to evaluate school effectiveness. *Sociology of Education, 81*(3), 242–270.

Dreeben, R., & Barr, R. (1988). Classroom composition and the design of instruction. *Sociology of Education, 61*(3), 129–142.

Dworkin, A. G. (2005). The No Child Left Behind Act: Accountability, high-stakes testing, and roles for sociologists. *Sociology of Education, 78*(2), 170–174.

Elliott, M. (1998). School finance and opportunities to learn: Does money well spent enhance students' achievement? *Sociology of Education, 71*(3), 223–245.

Epstein, J. L. (2005). Attainable goals? The spirit and letter of the No Child Left Behind Act on parental involvement. *Sociology of Education, 78*(2), 179–182.

Esposito, D. (1973). Homogeneous and heterogeneous ability grouping: Principal findings and implications for evaluating and designing more effective educational environments. *Review of Educational Research, 43*(2), 163–179.

Falsey, B., & Heyns, B. (1984). The college channel: Private and public schools reconsidered. *Sociology of Education, 57*(2), 111–122.

Ferguson, R. F. (2001, December). Closing the achievement gap: What schools can do. Symposium conducted at New York University, New York.

Findley, W. G., & Bryan, M. M. (1970). *Ability grouping: 1970–1. The impact of ability grouping on school achievement, affective development, ethnic separation and socioeconomic separation.* Athens: University of Georgia Center for Educational Improvement. (ERIC Document Reproduction Service No. ED 048382)

Findley, W. G., & Bryan, M. M. (1975). *The pros and cons of ability grouping.* Bloomington, IN: Phi Delta Kappa Educational Foundation.

Flynn, J. R. (1987). Massive IQ gains in 14 nations: What IQ tests really measure. *Psychological Bulletin, 101,* 171–191.

Flynn, J. R. (2007). *What is intelligence? Beyond the Flynn effect.* New York: Cambridge University Press.

Freiberg, J. (1970). *The effects of ability grouping on interactions in the classroom.* (ERIC Document Reproduction Service No. ED 053194)

Gamoran, A. (1984). *Teaching, grouping, and learning: A study of the consequences of educational stratification.* Unpublished doctoral dissertation, University of Chicago.

Gamoran, A. (1986). Instructional and institutional effects of ability grouping. *Sociology of Education, 59*(4), 185–198.

Gamoran, A. (1987). The stratification of high school learning opportunities. *Sociology of Education, 60*(3), 135–155.

Gamoran, A. (2001). American schooling and educational inequality: A forecast for the 21st century. *Sociology of Education, 74*(Extra Issue), 135–153.

Gamoran, A., Secada, W. G., & Marrett, C. B. (2000). The organizational context of teaching and learning: Changing theoretical perspectives. In M. T. Hallinan (Ed.), *Handbook of the sociology of education* (pp. 37–63). New York: Kluwer Academic/Plenum.

Gardner, H. (1983). *Frames of mind: The theory of multiple intelligences.* New York: Basic Books.

Goldstein, B. (1967). *Low income youth in urban areas: A critical review of the literature.* New York: Holt, Rinehart & Winston.

Goodnough, A. (2002, August 23). Shortage ends as city lures new teachers. *New York Times,* pp. A1, B3.

Gould, S. J. (1996). *The mismeasure of man* (Rev. & expanded). New York: Norton.

Grissmer, D. W., Kirby, S. N., Berends, M., & Williamson, S. (1994). *Student achievement and the changing American family.* Santa Monica, CA: RAND.

Hallinan, M. T. (1987). Ability grouping and student learning. In M. T. Hallinan (Ed.), *The social organization of schools: New conceptualizations of the learning process* (pp. 41–69). New York: Plenum.

Hanson, S. L. (1994). Lost talent: Unrealized educational aspirations and expectations among U.S. youths. *Sociology of Education, 67*(3), 159–183.

Hanushek, E. A. (1989). The impact of differential expenditures on school performance. *Educational Researcher, 18*(4), 45–51.

Hanushek, E. A. (1996). School resources and student performance. In G. T. Burtless (Ed.), *Does money matter? The effect of school resources on student achievement and adult success* (pp. 43–73). Washington, DC: Brookings Institution Press.

Heck, R. H., Price, C. L., & Thomas, S. L. (2004). Tracks as emergent structures: A network analysis of student differentiation in a high school. *American Journal of Education, 110*(4), 321–353.

Heubert, J. P., & Hauser, R. M. (Eds.). (1999). *High stakes: Testing for tracking, promotion, and graduation.* Washington, DC: National Academy Press.

Hobson v. Hansen, Cong. Rec. 16721–16766 (1967).

Ingersoll, R. M. (2004). Why some schools have more underqualified teachers than others. In D. Ravitch (Ed.), *Brookings papers on education policy* (pp. 45–88). Washington, DC: Brookings Institution Press.

Jaffe, A., & Adams, W. (1970). *Academic and socio-economic factors related to entrance and retention at two- and four-year colleges in the late 1960's.* New York: Columbia University, Bureau of Applied Social Research.

Jones, J. D., Spade, J. N., & Vanfossen, B. E. (1987). Curriculum tracking and status maintenance. *Sociology of Education, 60*(2), 104–122.

Jones, J. D., Vanfossen, B. E., & Spade, J. Z. (1985, August). *Curriculum placement: Individual and school effects using the high school and beyond data.* Paper presented at the annual meeting of the American Sociological Association, Washington, DC.

Kamens, D. (1974). Colleges and elite formation: The case of prestigious American colleges. *Sociology of Education, 47*(3), 354–378.

Lareau, A. (1989). *Home advantage: Social class and parental intervention in elementary education.* Philadelphia: Falmer.

Lewis, L. S., & Wanner, R. A. (1979). Private schooling and the status attainment process. *Sociology of Education, 52*(2), 99–112.

Lichter, D. T., & Eggebeen, D. J. (1993). Rich kids, poor kids: Changing income inequality among American children. *Social Forces, 71*(3), 761–780.

Lucas, S. R., & Berends, M. (2002). Sociodemographic diversity, correlated achievement, and de facto tracking. *Sociology of Education, 75*(3), 328–348.

Mare, R. D. (1981). Change and stability in educational stratification. *American Sociological Review, 46*(1), 72–87.

Mayer, S. E. (2001). How did the increase in economic inequality between 1970 and 1990 affect children's educational attainment? *American Journal of Sociology, 107*(1), 1–32.

Mayeske, G. W., & Wisler, C. E. (1972). *A study of our nation's schools.* Washington, DC: U.S. Government Printing Office.

McNeil, L. M. (2000). *Contradictions of school reform: Educational costs of standardized testing.* New York: Routledge.

Meier, D., & Wood, G. (2004). *Many children left behind: How the No Child Left Behind Act is damaging our children and our schools.* Boston: Beacon.

National Center for Health Statistics. (2007). *Health, United States, 2007: With chartbook on trends in the health of Americans.* Hyattsville, MD: Author.

National Head Start Association. (2008). *Special report: Reduced funding cripples Head Start from reaching its potential.* Alexandria, VA: Author.

Oakes, J. (1985). *Keeping track: How schools structure inequality.* New Haven, CT: Yale University Press.

Oakes, J. (1992). Can tracking research inform practice? Technical, normative, and political considerations. *Educational Researcher, 21*(4), 12–21.

Oakes, J., Joseph, R., & Muir, K. (2004). Access and achievement in mathematics and science: Inequalities that endure and change. In J. A. Banks & C. A. M. Banks, *Handbook of research on multicultural education* (2nd ed., pp. 69–90). San Francisco: Jossey-Bass.

Oakes, J., Wells, A. S., Jones, M., & Datnow, A. (1997). Detracking: The social construction of ability, cultural politics, and resistance to reform. *Teachers College Record*, *98*(3), 482–510.

Pallas, A. M., Entwisle, D. R., Alexander, K. L., & Stluka, M. F. (1994). Ability-group effects: Instructional, social, or institutional? *Sociology of Education*, *67*(1), 27–46.

Persell, C. H. (1977). *Education and inequality: The roots and results of stratification in America's schools*. New York: Free Press.

Persell, C. H. (2000). Values, control, and outcomes in public and private schools. In M. T. Hallinan (Ed.), *Handbook of sociology of education* (pp. 387–407). New York: Kluwer Academic/Plenum.

Persell, C. H., Cookson, P. W., Jr., & Catsambis, S. (1992). Family background, high school type, and college attendance: A conjoint system of cultural capital transmission. *Journal of Research on Adolescence*, *2*(1), 1–23.

Reuman, D. A. (1989). How social comparison mediates the relation between ability-grouping practices and students' achievement expectancies in mathematics. *Journal of Educational Psychology*, *81*(2), 178–189.

Ritts, V., Patterson, M. L., & Tubbs, M. E. (1992). Expectations, impressions, and judgments of physically attractive students: A review. *Review of Educational Research*, *62*(4), 413–426.

Rogers, D. (1968). *110 Livingston Street: Politics and bureaucracy in the New York City school system*. New York: Random House.

Rogers, D., & Chung, N. H. (1983). *110 Livingston Street revisited: Decentralization in action*. New York: New York University Press.

Rosenbaum, J. E. (1976). *Making inequality: The hidden curriculum of high school tracking*. New York: Wiley.

Rosenbaum, J. E. (1980). Track misperceptions and frustrated college plans: An analysis of the effects of tracks and track perceptions in the national longitudinal survey. *Sociology of Education*, *53*(2), 74–88.

Rosenthal, R. (1974). The Pygmalion effect: What you expect is what you get. *Psychology Today Library Cassette, #12*. New York: Ziff-Davis.

Rosenthal, R., & Jacobson, L. (1968). *Pygmalion in the classroom: Teacher expectation and pupils' intellectual development*. New York: Holt, Rinehart & Winston.

Schafer, W. E., Olexa, C., & Polk, K. (1973). Programmed for social class: Tracking in American high schools. In N. K. Denzin (Ed.), *Children and their caretakers* (pp. 220–226). New Brunswick, NJ: Transaction Books.

Sharan, S. (1980). Cooperative learning in small groups: Recent methods and effects on achievement, attitudes, and ethnic relations. *Review of Educational Research*, *50*(2), 241–271.

Stevens, M. L. (2007). *Creating a class: College admissions and the education of elites*. Cambridge, MA: Harvard University Press.

Tinto, V. (1980). College origin and patterns of status attainment. *Sociology of Work and Occupations*, *7*(4), 457–486.

Truce in New Jersey's school war. (2002, February 9). *New York Times*, p. A18.

U.S. Census Bureau. (2005). *Housing statistics*. Retrieved November 3, 2008, from http://www
.census.gov/

University of the State of New York. (1969). *Racial and social class isolation in the schools: A report to the Board of Regents of the University of the State of New York*. Albany, NY: Author.

Useem, E. L. (1990, April). *Social class and ability group placement in mathematics in the transition to seventh grade: The role of parental involvement*. Paper presented at the annual meeting of the American Educational Research Association, Boston.

Useem, M. (1984). *The inner circle: Large corporations and the rise of business political activity in the U.S. and U.K.* New York: Oxford University Press.

Useem, M., & Karabel, J. (1986). Pathways to top corporate management. *American Sociological Review, 51*(2), 184–200.

Wenglinsky, H. (1997). How money matters: The effect of school district spending on academic achievement. *Sociology of Education, 70*(3), 221–237.

Wheelock, A. (1992). *Crossing the tracks: How "untracking" can save America's schools*. New York: New Press.

Winter, G. (2003, April 23). New ammunition for backers of do-or-die exams. *New York Times*, p. B9.

CHAPTER 5

Christian Nation or Pluralistic Culture: Religion in American Life

Charles H. Lippy

Two seemingly paradoxical themes run through American religious history:

1. The United States is a Christian nation founded on biblical principles still informing the laws under which we live. Other religious communities are tolerated, but Christianity in its many forms is the dominant religious influence in common life.
2. Religious diversity flourishes in the United States with no one group of belief system dominating. Thanks to the principle of separation of church and state, "religious freedom prevails" in the United States and Americans are free to believe whatever they want and to worship however they want.

Both perceptions have long histories; both are vital to understanding the religious dynamics of American culture in the early 21st century.

EUROPEANS PLANT CHRISTIANITY IN NORTH AMERICA

European settlement in the thirteen British colonies that became the United States in 1776 had a history of less than 175 years. Most who came from England shared a religious consciousness shaped by Protestant Christianity (Lippy, Choquette, & Poole, 1992). In southern areas such as Virginia, although some variations of belief existed, colonial arrangements included legal establishment of the Church of England. Establishment meant that public tax money supported Church of England parishes and their clergy and that all who lived there were theoretically expected to be part of a parish.

To the north, first to Plymouth and then to other areas of Massachusetts, came settlers with deep ties to the Church of England but dissatisfied with what they saw as compromises it had made with Roman Catholic ways in trying to craft a religious establishment with broad appeal. These dissenters set up churches reflecting their own understanding of religious truth. Generally, we label them all Puritans, for all sought a purer form of Protestantism than they found in the Church of England. But there were important differences. The Pilgrims who settled Plymouth in 1620 believed religious falsehood so engulfed the Church of England that only by separating from it, moving away, and forming their own religious institutions could they ensure their own salvation. The Puritans who settled much of the rest of New England still identified with the Church of England but thought that abandoning a structure that vested authority in bishops and having simpler worship rendered them a purer form of that church.

Regardless, both thought that relocating to North America would give them religious freedom, giving birth to the idea that the United States was founded on the principle of religious freedom. In actuality, neither Plymouth Pilgrims nor other Puritans believed that those who disagreed with them should have religious freedom, because they thought alternative points of view were dangerous. For example, Massachusetts authorities banished Roger Williams in the 1630s because he was too much a religious seeker. Later acclaimed a beacon of religious liberty who influenced Baptist developments, Williams then was regarded as a dangerous heretic. But all he needed to do was move a few miles away to what is now Rhode Island, where Massachusetts authorities had no power, and he could set up a church reflecting his own views.

By the end of the 17th century, political changes in Britain mandated in the colonies a broader toleration of variant forms of Protestantism so long as they did not disrupt public order. Roman Catholics, however, were still not formally recognized, although they had a place for themselves when Maryland was established. They later flourished, especially in Pennsylvania where the Quaker-dominated government supported what the state's founder William Penn called a "holy experiment" of allowing persons of all religious persuasions to settle if they supported the commonweal.

EARLY SIGNS OF DIVERSITY

Patterns of immigration generated more diversity in the English colonies than public policy recognized. From the arrival of the first slave ships in 1619, an African tribal substratum made southern Christian life diverse because many congregations in time became biracial. White Christians were at first reluctant to proselytize among the slaves, fearing that conversion would automatically result in their freedom. More sustained efforts to preach Christianity to African Americans after the middle of the 18th century resulted in a vibrant fusion of African ways with evangelical Protestantism. The chant, song, and dance central to tribal religiosity joined with the enthusiastic, often emotional style of evangelicalism to give African American Christianity a distinctive expression that flourished alongside the churches with European roots. Those whose forced migration from Africa brought them first to the Caribbean added other twists, including practices popularly associated with voodoo, once they planted new rituals on American soil. Both Europeans and African Americans were drawn to slaves with a gift for preaching. However, few Whites recognized ways the power of slave preachers echoed that of tribal conjurers, a blending that shaped many African American clergy even after the abolition of slavery and the emergence of independent African American denominations. Also, some of the first slaves were

Muslims, although the conditions of slavery made it impossible for Muslim practice to endure long among the African population in North America.

Ethnicity contributed to other manifestations of diversity. The Dutch who originally settled in New York (New Netherlands) generally espoused a Calvinistic Reformed faith; even after the English took control, they remained a strong presence there. In what became New Jersey, Scandinavian immigrants brought strands of the Lutheran tradition. Clusters of German immigrants coming to Pennsylvania carried many religious labels, most some variant of Protestant Christianity. Almost from the inception of the colonies came Jewish immigrants; they remained on the margins of colonial religious life but established synagogues and communities in places such as Charleston, South Carolina; Savannah, Georgia; New York; and Newport, Rhode Island. Often unrecognized because even well-intentioned Christian colonists did not understand them as religious, were practices of Native American tribes on whose lands the Europeans settled. They, too, added to the larger picture of diversity.

By the middle of the 18th century, Scots-Irish immigrants planted their brand of Presbyterianism especially in the middle colonies and then farther south as they moved along the eastern slopes of the Appalachian mountain chain. By mid-century, too, Methodism, then a "new religion" in England, had made its way to North America. Even with so many sects, the first national census in 1790 showed that only around 10 percent of the population were formal members of religious groups. But that figure is misleading; it underestimates the influence of the churches in colonial and early national life and ignores the conviction prevailing then that joining a church (actually becoming a member) was a serious step not to be taken lightly. Many who regularly attended worship and who tried to live by the moral codes of the churches never took that step.

English control did not extend to all areas of North America that eventually became part of the United States. Spanish settlements in areas from Florida through Texas and the Southwest to California added another layer to the tale of diversity. The last of the Spanish missions (San Francisco) was founded in 1776, the year that the English colonies proclaimed their independence from Britain. In addition, a Catholicism reflecting the French experience flourished in areas along the Gulf of Mexico from Mobile to New Orleans and along the southern Mississippi River. When these areas became part of the United States, they intensified the story of diversity because both Spanish and French Catholicism had sustained adjoining colonial empires.

COMMON THEMES

Presbyterians, Methodists, Lutherans, Dutch Reformed, Congregationalist Puritans, and Baptists were all part of the larger European Protestant heritage grounded in the Reformation of the 16th century. Although there were differences among them, common features became more evident in the first half century or so after independence. The United States struggled then with what it meant to be a republic, a representative democracy. Perhaps most widely shared was some sense that personal experience informed vital religion even if there was considerable disagreement over whether one had such experience of one's own volition or whether God alone determined whether one would experience salvation. Congregationalists, Presbyterians, and Dutch Reformed who looked back to the 16th-century reformer John Calvin tended to attribute all to the work of God, while Methodists were convinced that people had to accept God's gift of salvation of their own free will. Among Baptists, some emphasized free will, and some believed that God alone determined who would be saved. Anglicans (those who were part of the Church of England) and Lutherans also showed some diversity, but for many, the work of God in salvation was a mystery gradually apparent to those who faithfully attended worship and accepted church doctrine.

In the middle of the 18th century, emphasis on personal religious experience got a big boost when waves of revivals that historians call the Great Awakening swept through the colonies, although there is some debate as to whether historians invented both the phenomenon and the label. For about a decade after 1740, folks seemed to exhibit intensified interest in religion. Many talked about being converted, some convinced that God had given them signs that they were chosen for salvation and some believing they had willingly accepted God's gracious offer of salvation. The revival enriched the biracial character of Christianity in the southern colonies, for some evangelical preachers, as mentioned, actively sought converts among enslaved African Americans.

Although church members remained a minority of the population, the influence of Protestant denominations emphasizing personal decision and free will in religious experience grew immensely in the first half of the 19th century, and those who stressed election by God in salvation slowly shed that idea. Free will and choice seemed consistent with the democratic ideas informing American political life. In this approach, all persons were equal whether as sinners or as those who chose salvation. Just as wealth and rank were not supposed to matter in a democratic society, they likewise had no clout in evangelical denominations, such as the Methodists and Baptists, that offered salvation to all. These groups (along with Presbyterians, who gradually jettisoned the idea that God predestined some to salvation) more aggressively presented their message to ordinary folk.

As the American population grew and began to move westward, evangelicals became major proponents of the camp meeting, which brought together people living in relative isolation on the frontier for times of preaching and fellowship. As factory towns developed along the rivers and canals in the North (the Erie Canal in New York is a prime example), urban evangelists transformed frontier camp meeting techniques to make revivalism a major device for spreading the influence of Protestant Christianity. Revivalists and itinerant evangelists earned their reputations because of their preaching that moved the minds and emotions of audiences, not because of their erudite theological education once favored by New England Puritans. Denominations that still expected their clergy to have formal training saw their influence dwindle; few had the time or the money to prepare for ministry this way. Table 5.1 shows the relative growth of Christian groups from 1650 to 1996.

THE SPREAD OF EVANGELICAL PROTESTANTISM

These currents helped make a broad evangelical Protestantism the dominant style of Christianity in the United States by the time of the Civil War. Even the arrival of thousands of Roman Catholics from Ireland in the 1830s and 1840s did not diminish that influence, for Protestants were generally the ones who ran the developing businesses and industries and the ones elected or appointed to political office. This Protestant Christian character became subtly but

Table 5.1   Number of Places of Worship

	1650	1750	1850	1950	1996
Baptist	2	132	9,375	77,000	98,228
Congregationalist	62	465	1,706	5,679	6,748
Episcopal	31	289	1,459	7,784	7,517
Presbyterian	4	233	4,824	13,200	14,214
Methodist	0	0	13,328	54,000	51,311
Roman Catholic	6	30	1,221	15,533	22,728
Jewish	0	5	30	2,000	3,975
Holiness/Pentecostal	0	0	0	21,705	52,868
Lutheran	4	138	1,217	16,403	19,077

Source: Adapted from *New historical atlas of religion in America*, by E. S. Gaustad and P. L. Barlow, 2001. San Francisco: Harper, p. 390.

deeply etched into American culture as public education began to develop in the 1830s. The well-known *McGuffey Readers* (Westerhoff, 1978; Williams, 1980), standard fare in primary education for generations, presumed that pupils shared an evangelical Protestant background in their lessons, making the public schools almost arms of the Protestant denominations in their fusion of Protestant beliefs, moral values, and sound learning. Even though other groups (Irish Catholics, German Catholics, Jews, and more) were present, this broad evangelical Protestantism pervaded common life, reinforcing the image of the United States as a Christian nation.

As European immigration peaked in the decades between the Civil War and World War I, challenges came to that hegemony. Most of those millions of immigrants came not only from Protestant or even Catholic areas of Northern and Western Europe but also from Southern, Central, and Eastern Europe. The majority were not Protestants but Roman Catholics, Eastern Orthodox Christians, and Jews. Many Catholic parishes established parochial (parish) schools, in part because Protestant assumptions informed public school curricula. Some in positions of social, economic, and political power recoiled not only at the religious orientation of these immigrants but also at their cultural and ethnic folkways. Calls to Americanize the immigrants were often ill-disguised calls to protestantize them, to force them into the dominant religious style to perpetuate the image of the nation as a (Protestant) Christian country.

The Congregationalist Josiah Strong, who worked for the interdenominational Evangelical Alliance, in his *Our Country* (1886/1964), identified the religions of the immigrants along with their concentration in the nation's cities and the rapid industrialization enabled by their presence in the workforce as major threats to American identity. But they were threats only if one assumed that America's identity was wedded to evangelical Protestant Christianity.

Another layer of diversity came with the steady growth of African American Protestant denominations, most of them Methodist or Baptist. Never mirror images of their White counterparts, these groups became crucibles in forging an indigenous leadership that realized much of its potential in the Civil Rights Movement of the 20th century. In much of the South where legal discrimination replaced slavery, churches were frequently the only property owned

Table 5.2   Percentage of Americans Claiming Religious Affiliation

	1830	1890	1990	2007
Baptist	25.0%	18.0%	20.0%	17.2%
Congregationalist	12.3	2.5	1.5	0.8
Episcopal	5.0	2.6	1.8	1.5
Presbyterian	17.0	6.2	2.7	2.7
Methodist	23.4	22.3	11.8	6.2
Roman Catholic	4.2	30.2	38.9	23.9
Jewish	*	*	4.4	1.7
Holiness/Pentecostal	*	*	4.4	4.4
Lutheran	3.4	6.0	6.0	4.6
Muslim	N/A	N/A	N/A	0.6

*Less than 1 percent

Sources: Adapted from *New historical atlas of religion in America,* by E. S. Gaustad and P. L. Barlow, 2001. San Francisco: Harper, p. 389; and *U.S. religious landscape survey,* by The Pew Forum on Religion and Public Life, 2008. Retrieved January 20, 2009, from http://www.census.gov/compendia/statab/tables/09s0074.pdf

by African Americans, and the preachers serving them often the only ones with advanced education. More than mere religious centers especially in the rural South, churches became broad social institutions, centers of community life offering numerous social welfare programs that remained essential as long as legal racism penetrated the larger society.

Nonetheless, mainline Protestants continued to exert an influence in the business and political affairs that was increasingly out of proportion to their numbers in the whole population. Hence, after World War I, Congress enacted the first laws limiting immigration overall, expanding earlier restrictions on Asian immigration that affected primarily California and other areas of the West. Quotas then ensured that the bulk of those allowed to enter the United States each year would have at least nominal associations with Protestantism and thus perpetuate the image that the United States was a Christian nation. Table 5.2 presents data on religious affiliation from 1830 to 2007. Trends since 1990 suggest a steady decline in the proportion of Christians in the population, thanks largely to changes in immigration policy made in 1965.

RELIGIOUS FREEDOM AND THE SEPARATION OF CHURCH AND STATE

Countervailing forces always challenged the reality of the image of the United States as a Christian nation, sustaining the conviction that religious diversity and pluralism always flourished. In this view, the United States was never a Christian nation per se but one where religious freedom prevailed and no one religious group or tradition, such as Christianity, dominated. Those who stress religious freedom look to the First Amendment to the Constitution with its declaration that "Congress shall make no law respecting an establishment of religion, or prohibiting the free exercise thereof." Ever since the adoption of the Bill of Rights, courts and pundits have debated precisely what those words mean.

In the early U.S. Republic, one reason not to have a nationally established religion was pragmatic. If most citizens of the new nation identified with one of the numerous Christian bodies, primarily Protestant ones, no one denomination or sect had a majority as adherents, much less as members. Already Baptists, Methodists, Presbyterians, Quakers, Lutherans of many ethnic varieties, Episcopalians, and a host of others had learned to live in relative peace and harmony. This diversity, celebrated by some as leading to pluralism, made it unfair (undemocratic) to single out one group to receive governmental support. Another assumption lay behind this nod to diversity: the conviction that all religious groups inculcated the values and morals to make their followers good citizens. Differences of theological doctrine paled in importance to this ethical bent.

As well, many leading political thinkers of the age embraced ideas of rationalism and freedom of thought associated with the Enlightenment. The Age of the Revolution was also the Age of Reason. Thomas Jefferson, Benjamin Franklin, George Washington, and a host of others subscribed to Enlightenment ideas. Contrary to later lore, they were not 21st-century fundamentalists disguised as 18th-century politicians, nor were they what a later age labeled secular humanists. Most believed that an overarching Providence whom the more orthodox called God worked through human affairs. All thought that religious doctrines, even if they did not subscribe to them, helped mold people into moral citizens and therefore supported peace and social order. All were suspicious of what could not be demonstrated on the basis of logic. Yet logic and reason also decreed that one had a right to think as one wished, to follow the truth given by one's own mind, without interference.

This rationalist emphasis on what the 18th-century Boston pastor Jonathan Mayhew (1749) called the "right of private judgment" and the evangelical Protestant emphasis on a personal experience of conversion or election were actually complementary. In different ways, both made the individual (not churches, ministers, priests, or even scripture) the final authority in matters of belief and practice. Just as no one could have an experience of conversion for another, so only the individual could determine what the mind deemed right and true. Most accepting reason as a guide were confident (if not naively optimistic) that what was true would look pretty much the same to everyone. Because there was no guarantee, a democratic social order had to allow for latitude of belief among its citizens. If different minds arrived at different truths, so be it, so long as difference did not disrupt civil order.

From the point of view of reason, the danger of government's endorsing a particular belief system, no matter how worthy, or of giving official status to any one religious group or tradition, no matter how pervasive its influence, was the potential tyranny such a belief or group could exert over others. If a religious community could call on the coercive power of the state to force conformity to its beliefs and practices, the state lost its legitimacy. The religious community no longer had to persuade people of its truth rationally or move people to experience for themselves the reality of the salvation it offered.

Before ratification of the Bill of Rights, the state of Virginia had adopted a statute providing for nearly total religious freedom. Inspired by Thomas Jefferson, the Virginia statute became something of a model for other states because the Constitution restricted only the Congress from establishing a religion. When the Bill of Rights was adopted, a few New England states still provided for the payment of salaries of teachers of religion and morals from public funds. The last to drop such a provision was Massachusetts in 1833.

The phrase *separation of church and state* is not strictly speaking part of the constitutional heritage of the nation. It comes from a letter written in 1802 by President Thomas Jefferson to a group of Connecticut Baptists in which he referred to a "wall of separation between church and state." Jefferson noted that, like the Baptists who had written to him, he believed that "religion is a matter which lies solely between man and his God, that he owes account to none other for his faith or his worship" and "that the legislative powers of government reach actions only, and not opinions"(cited in Wilson, 1965, pp. 75–76). Jefferson acknowledged the reality of God; what he wanted to avoid was government involvement in determining what individuals should believe and how they should worship and live that belief.

The legal provisions for religious freedom did not mean, however, that all sorts of fanatics suddenly came to the United States, although numerous individuals tried to gain a following for their own points of view. One result paralleled other Enlightenment-era shifts in Europe, namely, ensuring that there were no political disabilities attached to Jewish identity. For centuries in much of Europe, Jews were forced into ghettoes, prohibited from practicing certain occupations in the larger community, denied access to political life, and restricted in their educational opportunities. The idea of separation of church and state, although using a Christian term (*church*) as a symbol for all religions, would make that impossible in the United States but did not eradicate either overt or covert anti-Semitism that ran through American culture.

This legal arrangement did mean that the United States became a nation where extraordinary religious experimentation and diversity prevailed just beneath the surface, even if a broad evangelical Protestantism dominated public life. In the 1830s in upstate New York, for example, Joseph Smith reported having a vision that led to the founding of the church of Jesus Christ of Latter-Day Saints, popularly called the Mormons. Hostility toward them because their teachings seemed to undermine orthodox Protestant doctrine forced them to move from one location to another. They garnered more followers as they went, finally winding up around the Great Salt Lake, just before the Utah area was transferred from Mexican to U.S. control. The Saints represent what some historians regard as the first genuinely "new" religion to emerge in the American context.

Around the same time, John Humphrey Noyes relocated from Vermont to Oneida in upstate New York, where he preached his version of the gospel that drew scores to his communitarian enterprise with its practice of complex marriage. The Shakers, although planted on North American soil by Ann Lee and a handful of adherents just before the American Revolution, also reached their peak in the 1830s. About 6,000 men and women were leading the simple, celibate life in hopes of salvation in nearly two dozen different communities, several of them in upstate New York and in New England. Countless other groups followed the lead of inspired teachers who carved a niche for themselves because government would not interfere in matters of personal belief and practice. Many experimented with communal living. As in a marketplace, each group competed to gain a following; those best able to convince men and women of their truth reaped the largest number of adherents.

Immigration in the first decades of the 19th century ensured that the United States would be home to a significant Jewish population. Although several small Jewish communities existed in the English colonies—with the earliest synagogues organized in places such as Newport, Rhode Island, and Charleston, South Carolina—the immigration of Jews from German cultures in Europe brought diversity to the Hebrew tradition itself. Eager to seize the opportunities for fuller participation in public life that followed the Enlightenment and ended centuries of forced exclusion from society, many Jews were drawn to Reform Judaism. The Reform movement sought to abandon nonessential features of Jewish practice thought inextricably wedded to ancient Near Eastern culture in order to take on a more modern appearance.

Later generations of Jewish immigrants pondered whether Reform was too radical, willing to yield too much. Those resisting most strongly became known as Orthodox Jews, while in time the largest body became known as Conservative Jews. Conservative Jews willingly made some modifications to traditional practice to accommodate life in a modern, religiously pluralistic culture but thought that Reform had jettisoned too much. Despite Christian domination of American religious life, by the middle of the 19th century, it was clear that a vibrant Jewish culture would remain a dynamic alternative.

In the first half of the 19th century, other religious teachers preached their own under-standing of the truth at frontier camp meetings or working the lecture circuit, a form of popular entertainment, in the larger cities. Along the frontier, for example, several sought to restore what they believed to be the actual practice of first-century New Testament Christianity. That meant shedding denominational structure and, in some cases, even religious professionals such as clergy. This restorationist impulse gave birth to groups that later coalesced into the Disciples of Christ and the Churches of Christ.

In cities such as New York, individuals such as William Miller drew crowds to their presentations on biblical prophecy. Miller, eagerly expecting the imminent return of Christ to usher in the millennial age, even fixed a date when the second advent would transpire, more than once revising his calculations when Christ did not return on schedule. Most of his followers scattered because of the "great disappointment" that ensued, but this teaching found new life in the Seventh-day Adventists and the doctrines advocated by their early leader, Ellen G. Harmon White.

By the end of the 19th century, many other groups had emerged, some reflecting the religious styles of the continuing streams of immigrants and others arising from ideas offered by dynamic speakers and writers. Among the better known are the Amish and their religious cousins, the Mennonites, who sought to live their version of a simple life without involvement in a larger society that they believed hopelessly corrupted by modernity. Their major immigration to the United States and Canada came in the decades after the Civil War. During that epoch also, interest in science and in applying scientific techniques to religious expression increased. Mary Baker Eddy, for example, named her approach to using mental power to effect healing Christian Science. Her influence grew rapidly as she published her views and as practitioners of her way fanned out across the country, promoting her ideas.

These examples illustrate the diversity and pluralism beginning to shape American religious life, the diversity and pluralism made possible in part because of the First Amendment. Other factors aided this religious experimentation. The seemingly vast expanse of land in the nation literally provided room for various religious teachers and groups to go about their business without really interrupting or interfering with the lives of those around them. Consequently, the American experience helped demolish a myth that had buttressed Western civilization since the days of the Roman Empire, namely, that some sort of religious uniformity (or at least tacit conformity to one religious tradition) was a necessary precondition for political stability and social harmony.

DIVERSITY, RELIGIOUS FREEDOM, AND THE COURTS

At the same time, some religious groups seemed to many Americans, primarily those identified with Protestant denominations, to overstep the limits of freedom. After all, they were minority groups on the margins of the larger religious culture. If their beliefs and practices diverged too much from those of the majority, should they be restrained or curtailed before they undermined the dominant religious style? How much diversity in free exercise should be allowed before it became dangerous, and how much control could government wield to protect the majority before it became tyrannical?

One example emerged when the Latter-day Saints founder Joseph Smith advocated plural marriage. A revelation he believed divine convinced him that the ancient biblical practice of men having more than one wife was mandated for his followers. However, most Americans were aghast at the idea of polygamy, and most states forbade the practice when the Utah Territory sought admission to the Union. The situation was convoluted, and historians are not of a single mind about how subsequent Mormon teaching came to prohibit polygamy. Although the Saints once insisted polygamy was part of their free exercise of religion, restrictions on the practice became a condition for the admission of Utah as a state. In the process, the U.S. Supreme Court heard two cases dealing with plural marriage, *Reynolds v. United States* in 1878 and *Davis v. Beason* in 1890 (Miller & Flowers, 1987). Even after the official position changed and Utah became a state whose constitution prohibited plural marriage, some individuals who claimed Mormon identity continued the practice. In 2008, one such example in Texas attracted wide attention in the media and the courts, although most cases are ignored because practitioners tend to live in remote rural areas where other residents often overlook what does not upset public order.

Laws protecting Sabbath observance go back to the colonial period. Among the earliest was a provision in Virginia, part of "Dale's Laws" in 1610. They required attendance at Christian worship and also prohibited "any gaming" in public or private on Sunday. As the American Jewish population grew, those identified with Orthodox Judaism with its strict observance of the Sabbath from sundown Friday until sundown Saturday found laws favoring Sunday as the Sabbath discriminatory. However, because the number of Jews was small and the Jewish population fairly scattered, few challenged the status quo.

Sunday laws also affected Seventh-day Adventists, who, as their name indicates, hold the Hebrew practice of the Sabbath, the seventh day or Saturday, as sacred. Most Christian groups, whether Protestant, Catholic, or Orthodox, that represented the majority of Americans believed that their practice of keeping Sunday, the first day, as sacred superseded seventh-day Sabbath observance. Well into the 20th century, many states and local communities legally restricted what kinds of work could be done on Sunday, whether and what products could be sold, and the access to certain recreational activities. Popularly known as *blue laws*, such regulations aroused little concern when the overwhelming majority of citizens in a town or area were Christians for whom Sunday was holy. They tended to keep the day sacred even without such legal restraint. But what about those for whom the seventh day was holy?

Most legal challenges involving Seventh-day Adventists and Orthodox Jews were brought in local and state courts. Early challenges to blue laws reaching the U.S. Supreme Court did not directly involve religious groups, although the issues at stake did. For example, the arrest of discount store employees for selling on Sunday products restricted by law propelled *McGowan v. Maryland* (1961); *Two Guys from Harrison-Allentown, Inc. v. McGinley* (1961) offered a similar situation but with a difference sufficient to require a separate decision. In both, the Court upheld Sunday blue laws using an "argument from history" and insisted that even if blue laws originally supported exclusively Christian observance, they promoted the general welfare by mandating a day of rest once in seven. Bringing such cases to the Supreme Court unwittingly set in motion moves to repeal most blue laws.

In times of war, most court cases have concerned those who refused to engage in military combat and sometimes in any activity that supported combat. Although hundreds have been imprisoned, generally the courts concluded that members of religious groups, such as the Quakers, the Mennonites, the Church of the Brethren, and other historic "peace churches," could refuse to serve, but most were required to perform alternative service. One consequence of protest against the U.S. military presence in Vietnam was extending conscientious objector classification to individuals who opposed all war on grounds of personal belief even if they were not formal members of any religious group.

Over the years, issues of free exercise have also involved groups that reject certain medical procedures (e.g., blood transfusions), such as the Jehovah's Witnesses and the Church of Christ, Scientist. Generally, the courts have upheld the right of persons of legal age to refuse medical treatment on religious grounds, but the situation has been much more complex when parents refuse to authorize medical procedures for their minor children on religious grounds. Here the issue has been whether the responsibility of government to promote the welfare of minors could require treatments that the faith communities nurturing them oppose.

Drawing the line between the government's duty to promote the general welfare and the right of free exercise also informed many of the cases, mostly on a state level, that concerned the ritual handling of serpents and ingesting of poisonous liquids such as strychnine. Serpent handlers claimed a biblical basis for the practice in the Gospel of Mark, Chapter 16, insisting that they did only what Scripture required. Did the possibility of death from snake bite make serpent handling a practice that undermined the general welfare, forcing the government to prohibit it? Because serpent-handling groups are concentrated in the mountains of central Appalachia, most laws making serpent handling illegal were passed by states in that region. Few were regularly enforced, however, and most had been rescinded by the end of the 20th century.

Numerous cases wrestled with whether practices sanctioned by law resulted in a *de facto* establishment of religion. Many involved public school education. Some of the earliest concerned children who were Jehovah's Witnesses. Witnesses refuse to salute the flag, insisting that reciting the Pledge of Allegiance places a blasphemous loyalty to the state before their allegiance to God. Most cases brought by Witnesses came decades before the recent controversy over whether the phrase *under God*, inserted into the Pledge of Allegiance by Congress in 1954, represented unconstitutional support for religion. Until the rights of the Witnesses received legal protection, several episodes resulted in children who were Witnesses being expelled from school and their parents being prosecuted. At first, the Supreme Court was reluctant to see refusal to recite the Pledge of Allegiance as an exercise of religious freedom. In *Minersville School District v. Gobitis* (1940), the Court decreed that the social cohesion resulting from requiring students to recite the pledge superseded free exercise. But in *West Virginia State Board of Education v. Barnette* just three years later, the Court reversed its position, setting a precedent that has prevailed since.

The more recent debates center on the words *under God*, not on issues of free exercise. In June 2004, the Supreme Court dismissed one such case from California where a lower court had ruled that the phrase was indeed unconstitutional; the Court's ruling was based on the grounds that the parent who initiated the case, an avowed atheist, lacked standing because he did not have legal custody of his daughter, so the student was required to recite the pledge. When California courts again ruled in a subsequent case involving different parties that the phrase was unconstitutional, the matter seemed more likely to come before the Supreme Court for a final ruling, but no decision has yet been issued.

As noted earlier, when public education began to become the norm in the United States in the 19th century, most students came from families identified with mainline Protestant denominations, and curriculum materials often reflected their beliefs and practices. Christian holidays, such as Christmas and Holy Week before Easter, were times when classes were suspended; Jewish holy days did not as a rule receive such preferential treatment, although Jewish children were not penalized for absences on religious holidays. In some school districts, religious groups—usually Protestants—used educational facilities for religious instruction, sometimes during the regular class day. In *McCollum v. Board of Education* (1948), the Supreme Court prohibited using school facilities and class time for instruction in a particular faith tradition, even when participation was voluntary.

Some accommodation was reached in 1952 in *Zorach v. Clauson*, when the Court sanctioned dismissing children early from regular classes to attend voluntary off-site religious instruction. For several decades, a host of cooperative endeavors among Protestant churches as well as programs set up for Roman Catholic children not enrolled in parochial schools served children dismissed from school an hour early one day a week. By the end of the 20th century, when recruiting volunteers to staff such programs became difficult and other extracurricular options expanded, most of these endeavors were dismantled.

The greatest controversy has revolved around Bible reading and prayer in the public schools and whether such activities create a tacit establishment or favor a particular religious tradition. In some communities, there have been questions about prayers at ceremonies preceding athletic events or at commencement exercises. The most famous Supreme Court cases regarding this came in the early 1960s. In 1962, the decision in *Engel v. Vitale* struck down a practice mandated by the New York State Board of Regents that required public school students to recite a presumably nonsectarian prayer at the start of each school day. Before the furor over that judgment abated, the Court announced its verdict in *Abington v. Schempp* (1963) that declared unconstitutional the devotional reading of any portion of the Bible and recitation of the Lord's Prayer, even if those for whom the prayer was not an act of worship were not required to participate.

Nearly five decades later, school districts and state legislatures still wrangle with ways to get around these decisions. Subsequent cases, mostly in lower courts, have whittled away at the absolute prohibitions, allowing in some cases student-initiated prayers at specified events and use of facilities for voluntary student religious groups outside normal class hours on the same basis that they are available for other extracurricular programs. Frequently overlooked in the heat of controversy is the Supreme Court's insistence that prohibiting devotional practices associated with particular religions did not ban the academic study of religion in public schools, something rather different from teaching that the beliefs of any faith tradition are ultimate truth. The courts never banned study of sacred texts such as the Bible from literary and historical perspectives because such study did not necessarily use any such texts to promote personal belief and commitment. Yet public school systems have been reluctant to offer the academic study of religion lest it be misconstrued as endorsing one religion over another. Curriculum materials developed for religion courses continue to increase, but few teachers have the formal background to teach religion as an academic subject.

In the early 21st century, debates continued over what separation of church and state involved and how to ensure the free exercise of religion. Some, such as a case involving whether Santeria was a religion and therefore its ritual of sacrificing chickens a protected religious practice, echoed earlier themes. Other cases concerned ways to link religion and education legally, such as whether states or communities could provide vouchers that citizens could use to defray the cost of religiously sponsored education. Several focused on whether biology textbooks should include creationism as a scientific perspective if theories of evolution were also presented. Because many saw creation science as a way to introduce a single religious perspective into public education, courts consistently rejected claims to include it in school curricula.

When others advocated intelligent design as an explanation for the origins of the universe, a new round of court battles got underway because intelligent design seemed merely a new designation for creation science. Across the country, moves to introduce intelligent design challenged traditional teaching of science and appeared poised to open doors to introduce other matters of faith into public school curricula. The first cases that made their way through the courts generally refused to require teaching theories of intelligent design because they were construed as promoting religion, although in some instances, steps taken ensured that evolution would be presented as speculative theory, not as accepted scientific fact. The most critical case came in Dover, Pennsylvania, in 2005. The local school board required teaching intelligent design in its biology curriculum along with statements that evolution was merely a theory, not a universally accepted scientific fact. Opponents soundly defeated for reelection school board candidates who had supported this position that had outraged many conservative evangelicals. Shortly thereafter, Judge John E. Jones III overturned the board's policy, declaring that "Intelligent design is not science" (Teepen, 2005). Even though this ruling seemed likely to become a precedent for similar cases elsewhere, efforts to promulgate supernatural explanations of origins did not disappear.

In retrospect, it seems that early legal cases concerned how to protect the rights of religious minorities, but some believe that later cases impose minority rule on the majority. Regardless, the array of legal cases concerning religion reveal that a deep and abiding diversity marks American life, even if in an earlier epoch a broadly based evangelical Protestantism exercised dominant influence.

PLURALISM BECOMES THE NORM

The controversial court cases of the 1960s concerning prayer and Bible reading came at a time when the image of the United States as a Christian nation was already unraveling. As early as 1955, Will Herberg, one-time labor union organizer and Jewish professor of the sociology of religion at a Methodist seminary, in his *Protestant, Catholic, Jew* (1960) argued that the vast majority of Americans regarded the many forms of Protestantism, Roman Catholicism, and

Judaism as equally valid in molding adherents into responsible citizens. Having some religious label was a badge of social worth; it mattered not what it was. For Herberg, equally important, although disturbing, was the emergence of a cultural religion, what he called the "religion of the American Way of Life." It emphasized materialism and conspicuous consumption instead of the commitment and discipleship permeating biblical faith. That unconscious push to a common ground minimizing denominational particularities and even distinctions among faith traditions echoes in the statement attributed to President Eisenhower: The government of the United States "makes no sense unless it is founded on a deeply felt religious faith—and I don't care what it is" (cited in Herberg, p. 95).

Service in the military during World War II introduced thousands of Americans to persons of other religious persuasions; shared experiences in battle minimized faith differences. As veterans reentered civilian life after the war, employment opportunities frequently entailed relocation. The long-standing model of Americans going through childhood, coming to maturity, and ultimately dying in communities where they had been born or at least near their places of birth quickly disappeared. Relocation for many meant finding a new church with which to affiliate, often chosen for reasons other than its denominational label. If the denomination of one's birth had no congregation nearby, it was easy to affiliate with another one.

The suburban sprawl accompanying increased mobility also helped erode denominational loyalty. Mainline Protestant denominations raced to build new churches in rapidly growing suburban communities, often cooperating with each other so as not to "overchurch" a particular area. Church bureaucrats knew that families tended to identify with a church, regardless of denomination, with programs oriented toward young families. Denominational switching became the norm. Denominations could no longer assume that those raised within the fold would retain a lifelong identification with a particular tradition. Deep linkage to a particular heritage disappeared; people became tied only to the specific local congregation where they worshiped or held membership. Those not steeped in a certain tradition rarely reared their own children with a firm bond to that heritage.

The rush to the nation's colleges and universities in the immediate postwar years, spurred by the famous G.I. Bill, undermined denominational loyalty in a different way. The collegiate environment, like military experience, introduced many to a variety of ways of being religious. It was not, as some feared, that college education destroyed religious faith, but it did bring an exposure to persons from other faiths or even from other Protestant denominations, which removed much of the apprehension of alternative religions. As a result, the experience of higher education led people to see faith communities as functionally equivalent; none had an exclusive claim to ultimate truth. Some Protestants demurred, believing this sort of exposure dangerous because it led to compromise with falsehood and contamination of authentic faith.

Mobility, military service, and collegiate experience were all catalysts stimulating the sharp increase in interreligious marriage as the nation moved into the Cold War era. Marriage across Protestant denominational lines had long been common. Now there came a dramatic increase in marriages between Protestants and Roman Catholics and between Christians and Jews; the boundaries separating these larger faith traditions had previously proved far more unyielding than those between Protestant denominations. Then, too, hundreds of Protestant Americans who served in the Pacific during the war brought home spouses from various Asian or Pacific cultures who, like other immigrants, sought to retain their religions of origin. Individual families carved out their own religious identities from those brought together in a single household.

Some compromised by identifying with yet another religious group; sometimes husbands and wives went their separate ways in terms of religious affiliation with children exposed to both, sometimes just to one, often to none. Many quietly dropped out of organized religion.

No matter how families resolved having multiple religious heritages, new dimensions of pluralism were taking on increasing importance. The ecumenical movement, primarily among Protestants, also contributed to this diversity. Cooperative endeavors through various councils of churches, mergers of denominations even within the same religious family such as the reunion of northern and southern Presbyterians in 1983, and talks of church union spearheaded by the Consultation on Church Union formed in the early 1960s created the impression that all Protestant bodies were pretty much alike and that denominations really made little difference and had no distinctive ways of expressing what Christian faith was. If labels made no difference, then loyalty to a particular denomination made no difference. In promoting unity among Protestants, the ecumenical movement unwittingly undermined denominational loyalty.

In addition, social forces unleashed by the Civil Rights Movement and then the antiwar efforts associated with U.S. military involvement in Vietnam challenged all forms of authority within American life, including the authority of religious groups and their leaders. The baby boom generation, reaching adulthood during that turbulent epoch of the 1960s, more than earlier generations shunned commitment to all social institutions, including religious ones. Reared when denominational loyalty was no longer paramount, they had no abiding identification with organized religion. Although earlier generations had drifted away from religious communities in late adolescence and early young adulthood, they generally had returned when they began to raise their own families, if only to provide some moral anchor for their children. Boomers did not return in the same proportion. Many, however, identified themselves as spiritual, even if they resisted being called religious.

Robert Wuthnow (1998) has argued that in the second half of the 20th century, Americans exchanged the idea of a religious "home" or center, usually fixed around a tradition or group, for a religious "quest," something more individualistic and idiosyncratic. The subtitle of an article in a popular journal captured the mood: "Design Your Own God" (Creedon, 1998). Women from the boomer generation, for example, probed resources that took them well beyond the standard denominations to forge a spirituality that speaks to the female experience. Some draw on pagan and pre-Christian forms of religious expression, sparking panic in some Christian circles that feminist spirituality threatens the integrity of the churches. All of the following signal a dynamic spirituality that exists alongside and frequently outside organized religion:

1. Those who gather in forest groves to celebrate rituals marking passages unique to women from childbirth to menopause.
2. Those who rarely attend worship but claim to be very spiritual because they occasionally read the Bible along with practicing Zen meditation techniques.
3. Those who fashion altars in their homes that may juxtapose a cross with New Age crystals.
4. Those who sport What Would Jesus Do? (WWJD) bracelets or other religious objects the way a previous generation took the cross and made it a piece of jewelry.
5. Those who walk the universal mandala, the labyrinth, in silence because organized religion has become too noisy.

At the same time, the Christian groups that have been growing have tended to resist this privatization of spirituality. At the peak of the civil rights and antiwar movements, analysts recognized that among Protestants, those denominations and independent congregations that were more orthodox in their religious teaching, more inclined to variations of fundamentalist and Pentecostal expression, were growing (Kelley, 1977). For generations, it had been easy to consign such forms of Christianity to the periphery. Scholars mistakenly assumed that fundamentalism and Pentecostalism drew only from the economically disadvantaged and politically powerless.

Fundamentalists, Pentecostals, and other evangelicals had developed networks of association that forged enduring bonds and provided resources to sustain institutions during their time on the margins (Carpenter, 1997). They gathered strength from their conviction that truth could not be questioned, thereby protecting their belief and practice from the cultural attacks on authority marking the larger culture in the later 20th century. If mainline Protestants and Catholics were torn apart by debates over civil rights, Vietnam, and feminism, Fundamentalist and Pentecostal expressions of Christianity offered a refuge, a sense of direction, and a secure way of looking at the world, one not battered by social controversy but buttressed by a certainty that they still had a corner on the truth. The presence of Fundamentalists and Pentecostals also complicates efforts to discern any common religious base to American culture, and their leaders are often in the forefront of debates about public education, such as teaching intelligent design.

Some talk about a "Judeo-Christian tradition," an artificial construct at best, as reflecting the dominant religious mood in the United States. In the opening years of the 21st century, particularly in the wake of the terrorist attacks of September 2001, many who called for posting the Ten Commandments in courthouses, schools, and other public buildings reflected a hope that this amorphous amalgamation of traditions with roots in the biblical text could still provide a base for social cohesion. But undercutting their efforts was another facet of the religious pluralism now characteristic of American society, namely, the dramatic increase in the number of Americans who identified with religious traditions such as Islam, Buddhism, and Hinduism.

NEW FACES OF PLURALISM

Changes in immigration laws in 1965 spurred a rise in immigration from Latin America, Africa, and Asia. With them has come a burgeoning interest in the religions indigenous to those areas and fresh awareness of the links between ethnicity and religious style. In the last decade of the 20th century, the greatest proportional growth in immigration from Latin America, the Near East, and Asia came in the Sun Belt. From 1990 to 2000, the percentage of those foreign born in North Carolina and Georgia (as well as in Nevada) increased by more than 200 percent, and in 2000, more than one-quarter of the population of California was foreign born (Malone, Baluja, Costanzo, & Davis, 2003). In Whitfield County, Georgia, the heart of the state's carpet industry, Hispanic Americans now constitute almost 50 percent of the population, and more than 50 percent of students in the lower grades of the public schools are Hispanic (Mahoney, 2002). Figures reported in the 2000 census indicate that 4.2 percent of the U.S. population was born in Asia (Reeves & Bennett, 2004) a figure that is increasing rapidly, a percentage roughly equivalent to the number of residents and citizens in the U.S. born in Mexico, Cuba, and El Salvador. By the early 21st century, census estimates indicated that those of Hispanic stock

(38.8 million) outnumbered African Americans (38.3 million) to constitute the largest single ethnic minority cluster in the nation (U.S. Census Bureau, 2003). Indeed, more than 10 million persons of Hispanic origin have entered the U.S. legally or illegally since 2000 (Camarota, 2007).

In most urban areas, Roman Catholic parishes have added services in Spanish, recognizing that Hispanic Catholicism brings a rich blend of traditions to Catholic life, many reflecting the cultures of Central and South America. Cuban immigrants in the Miami area, for example, have erected a shrine to Our Lady of Charity that signals both a particular religious sensibility and a Cuban nationalism (Tweed, 1997). In a sense, these immigrants are simply doing what Italian and Irish Catholics and others did more than a century before, namely bringing with them the festivals, patron saints, and fusion of religious and ethnic ways that give them a sense of identity and cultural cohesion.

Some Protestant denominations have launched special ministries to Spanish-speaking Americans, while many Pentecostal congregations, like their Roman Catholic counterparts, now provide services and programs designed to reflect the spirituality and concerns of Hispanic followers. Theologically, Hispanic Americans (both Protestant and Catholic) tend to be more traditional and conservative in their thinking even as their practice reveals considerable syncretism in its expression. Even within the Christian tradition, it has become impossible to look at Anglo-American styles as normative.

Immigration from Asia swelled the ranks of Hindus, Buddhists, and Muslims in the United States. American interest in Asian religious cultures has a long history. In the 19th century, transcendentalist writers such as Ralph Waldo Emerson were drawn to Asian religious philosophy, and thousands devoured reports of seemingly exotic religious practices in Asia through letters from missionaries published in scores of popular religious magazines. But, except for a relatively small number of immigrants from China and Japan on the West Coast, few Americans had firsthand experience with these religions; even fewer were inclined to practice them.

A more direct exposure came with the World's Parliament of Religions, held in Chicago in 1893 in conjunction with the Columbian Exposition marking the 400th anniversary of Columbus's first voyage to America. Representatives from a number of religions, including Hindus and Buddhists, were invited to Chicago; some, like the Hindu philosopher Vivekananda, remained in the United States for an extended period, speaking in the nation's larger cities and attracting some interest, primarily among intellectuals, in the philosophy behind these religious approaches. With American involvement in military endeavors in Asia in World War II, the Korean War, and the Vietnam War, thousands had more direct exposure to Asian ways of being religious. Some brought spouses back to the United States who sought to continue the religious ways in which they had been nurtured.

The 1960s also witnessed the arrival of several Asian religious figures intent on gaining American converts, particularly from among those disenchanted with traditional American religious life and who saw the dominant religious institutions as mired in racism and torn apart over government policy in Vietnam. The International Society of Krishna Consciousness, more popularly known as Hare Krishna, became a familiar presence in cities and college towns; thousands were drawn to practices such as transcendental meditation, promoted by the Maharishi Mahesh Yogi and made fashionable by celebrities such as the Beatles. A generation later, the Dalai Lama became a symbol of American interest in Tibetan Buddhism, aided by the devotion of celebrities such as Richard Gere.

While some forms of Buddhism, such as that promoted by the Dalai Lama, and some popular forms of Hinduism, such as Krishna Consciousness, have attracted primarily American devotees, the majority of American Buddhists, Hindus, and Muslims come from families who are doing what Americans have done for centuries—practicing the religion that the first generation of immigrants brought with them, albeit adapting it to the American context. What is changing the face of pluralism in the first decade of the 21st century is the steadily growing presence of immigrants for whom these traditions represent the heritages they bring with them when they come to the United States. Table 5.3 illustrates their relative growth.

Estimates suggest that the United States was home to only 30,000 Buddhists in 1900, but to two million a century later; to a mere 1,000 Hindus in 1900, but 950,000 at century's end; to just 10,000 Muslims in 1900, but perhaps (and the estimates vary widely here) between two and one-half to four million a century later, not counting those affiliated with the Nation of Islam (U.S. Census Bureau, 2000). Some believe that by 2008, the Muslim population exceeded six million, although estimates are plagued by problems ranging from the relatively small proportion of Muslims in the United States who are able to affiliate with mosques, fears of prejudice in the wake of the 9/11 terrorist attacks associated with Muslims, and the willingness of some Muslims to give up religious practice in the American context. The Hindu tradition has never been inclined to proselytize; in other cultural contexts, Buddhists and Muslims have been more active in seeking converts. However, in the U.S. context, there is relatively little association among the various immigrant Buddhist communities and the centers that cater primarily to American converts to the various stands of Buddhism. American Muslims report that they are reticent to proselytize because of popular negative perceptions of Islam and assumptions that all Muslims advocate international terrorism. Those Americans who have converted to Islam are more likely to be persons of African descent; they join a small but growing number of African immigrants who are also Muslim.

A closer look at American Hindus, Buddhists, and Muslims suggests that these traditions will grow much more rapidly from internal propagation than any Christian or Jewish group will. In 2008, the Pew Forum (2008) released a detailed study profiling adherents of all major religious communities in the nation. That survey indicated that around three-quarters of all American Muslims, Buddhists, and Hindus were under 50 years of age, an indication that many were in their peak childbearing years and a much larger proportion were children and adolescents than was true for the population as a whole. By contrast, just half of mainline Protestants were under age fifty. This internal growth made Islam one of the fastest-growing religions in the nation. There is little wonder then that historian of religion Diana Eck titled

Table 5.3   Estimates of Adherents of Asian Religions

	1900	1970	2000
Buddhists	30,000	200,000	2,000,000
Hindus	1,000	100,000	950,000
Muslims*	10,000	800,000	3,950,000

*Not including the Nation of Islam.

Source: Figures based on data from the U.S. Census Bureau.

her study of these trends *A New Religious America: How a "Christian Country" Has Become the World's Most Religiously Diverse Nation* (1997). With practices and holy days that diverge from those prevalent in a "Judeo-Christian" culture, schools and other public institutions face fresh challenges in accommodating diversity in order to protect the right to free exercise of religion. One example must suffice: Traditional Muslim practice calls for the devout to pray five times daily facing in the direction of Mecca. Stated times for prayer clash with the standard work day and school day in the United States.

The growth of these groups signals the pluralism that marks American religious life and the impossibility of regarding a single tradition as normative or perhaps even culturally dominant in the 21st century. Alongside the mushrooming pluralism linked to immigration is the slow but steady increase in the number of Americans who eschew formal religious identity altogether and do not identify themselves as members of any religious body. Recent studies suggest that the proportion of those unaffiliated grew from one of five Americans in 1991 to at least one of every three by 2004 (Ratio, 2004). Add to that cluster the millions who called themselves "spiritual, but not religious" (Fuller, 2001), and it is clear that the very character of pluralism has expanded in such a way as to undermine any assumption that the U.S. now shares a common religious base.

SUMMARY AND EDUCATIONAL IMPLICATIONS

From the colonial period to the 21st century, the American landscape became ever more religiously diverse. If the first European invaders brought with them a range of Protestant sensibilities, their efforts to plant a Christian culture in America always faced challenges. These challenges came from the Native Americans whose tribal religions once flourished in the same places where Europeans settled as well as from enslaved Africans who managed to sustain an African religious consciousness despite the horrors of slavery. They also came from a variety of other groups who promoted alternative ways of being religious. Diversity was part of the American religious experience from the outset.

That diversity received acknowledgment when the Bill of Rights added an amendment to the U.S. Constitution guaranteeing the free exercise of religion. But the questions of what free exercise means and how to balance the religious sensibilities of the majority with those of many minorities have challenged the courts ever since. In the 20th century, many of those challenges concerned the role of religion in public education.

Immigration has been a major force enhancing religious diversity over the centuries. Immigration helped cement a Roman Catholic and Jewish presence in American life in the 19th century. By the dawn of the 21st century, immigration was swelling the ranks of Buddhists, Hindus, Muslims, and a variety of others who called the United States home. At the same time, the number of Americans claiming no religious identity or formal affiliation was rising slowly but steadily.

If public education in its early years in the middle third of the 19th century could assume that the bulk of students shared a broadly based evangelical Protestant background, by the end of that century, those assumptions were no longer viable, although they had by no means vanished. At the dawn of the 21st century, however, it was clear that religious pluralism rendered it impossible for education or any other dimension of the public sector to presume that a majority shared common beliefs and values—or even a common religious sensibility. As federal policy moved more and more in the direction of funding "faith-based initiatives" on a local level to deal with ongoing social problems, it was increasingly difficult to determine how to distribute such funds without favoring any one group, how to ensure that recipients were not using funds to coerce those being helped into aligning with the religious group, and even how to ascertain which groups represented legitimate "faith-based" entities. Even more challenging is deciding how to study the religious mosaic that is the United States without either presuming allegiance to a particular faith tradition or granting any one faith community a privileged position.

RESOURCES

Jon Butler and Harry S. Stout (1998) have edited a seventeen-volume series of texts on religion in American life suitable for classroom use at the secondary level. Published by Oxford University Press, some are chronological in focus (colonial America, the 19th century, the 20th century), some treat particular groups (Catholics, Jews, Mormons, Protestants, Muslims, Buddhists, Hindus, Sikhs), and others deal with specific topics (African American religion, church and state, immigration, women, Native American religion, alternative religions). The concluding volume is a biographical supplement and index. All are by leading scholars.

Also helpful is the nine-volume *Religion by Region* series (2004–2006) produced under the auspices of the Greenberg Center for the Study of Religion in Public Life at Trinity College, Hartford, Connecticut, and edited by Mark Silk and Andrew Walsh. All are published by AltaMira Press. Eight focus on distinctive geographic regions of the country, examining how the particular religious cultures and history of a region have implications for the public policy, including education. The final volume examines the role of region more generally in determining the interplay of religion and public policy.

Numerous materials appropriate for classroom use are identified in the several sections of the Web site for the Religion and Public Education Resource Center based at the California State University at Chico: www.csuchico.edu/rs/rperc

Also specializing in teaching resources about American religious culture is the Wabash Center: www.wabashcenter.wabash.edu

The Pluralism Project at Harvard University has focused primarily on the new diversity represented by the growth of Buddhism, Hinduism, and Islam in the last half century. Its Web site includes not only state-by-state maps but also a directory of religious centers, news summaries, profiles of groups, and teaching resources: http://www.pluralism.org

The most recent demographic profiles appear in the U.S. Religious Landscape Survey conducted by the Pew Forum on Religion and Public Life. See http://religions.pewforum.org for a wealth of data on the texture of American religious life released in 2008. In a similar vein, researchers at Hartford Theological Seminary produced the study *Faith Communities Today* that provides helpful information. The results are accessible at www.fact.hartsem.edu

There are also helpful Web sites on particular groups or topics that illustrate the diversity within American religious life. On African American religious history, for example, see http://northstar.vassar.edu

The Cushwa Center at Notre Dame University offers many resources on facets of U.S. Roman Catholic life and history: www.nd.edu/~cushwa

Similarly, the American Jewish Historical Society identifies much that is useful to tracking the American Jewish experience: www.ajhs.org

Questions and Activities

1. The principle of separation of church and state is a keystone of religious freedom in the United States. Investigate how closely church and state are tied together in the United States today. For example, can churches receive federal funding? If so, under what conditions? Can parochial and other religious schools receive support from public school districts? If so, what kind of support can they receive, and what conditions do they need to meet in order to qualify for support?

2. Large numbers of African Americans and European Americans are members of Protestant churches and share religious traditions. However, services in African American and European American churches can be very different. Visit a Methodist church service and an African Methodist Episcopal (AME) church service. Compare the services at the two churches by identifying factors such as the length of service, the music, and the enthusiasm of the minister. Discuss your findings with your classmates. An informative reference for this activity is *The Black Church in the African American Experience* (Lincoln & Mamiya, 1990).

3. The media have become a powerful force for disseminating religious messages that are tied to political positions. Form a group of approximately five students and identify five different religious television programs to watch over a one-month period. Record key themes that are embedded in the programs. Analyze the themes and ideas to determine whether they include political messages. Discuss the extent to which the paradox that Lippy discusses at the beginning of the chapter is being exacerbated by the media.

4. Most racial and ethnic groups in the United States are members of the major faith communities. However, most faith communities in the United States are segregated. Investigate churches, mosques, and temples in your community to find out the extent to which faith communities are segregated. Interview heads of religious communities. Ask them why they think faith communities tend to be made up predominately of one racial or ethnic group. Also ask them whether they have made efforts to desegregate their faith communities.

5. Revivals continue to play an important role in evangelical Protestant churches. Go to the Internet and investigate the types of revivals that are being held today, where they are being held, their goals, and their intended audience. To what extent do modern revivals reflect Lippy's discussion about the new faces of pluralism?

6. Religion in the United States is frequently associated with the roles that men have played in formulating religious ideas and institutions. However, women have made significant contributions to religious life in the United States. Read the biographies of women religious leaders such as Mary Baker Eddy and Ellen G. Harmon White. Also read *Righteous*

Discontent: The Women's Movement in the Black Church, 1880–1920 (Higginbotham, 1993). Discuss how gender has influenced the lives of women in the church.

7. How does social class intersect with religion? Are religious congregations primarily composed of people from the same social-class background? How do different religious organizations respond to low-income people? How do low-income people in your community feel about religious organizations? Study these questions by dividing the class into groups.

References

Butler, J., & Stout, H. S. (Eds.). (1998). *Religion in America: A reader*. New York: Oxford University Press.

Camarota, S. A. (2007). *Immigration to the United States, 2007.* Retrieved September 11, 2008, from www.cis.org/articles/2007/back1007/html/

Carpenter, J. A. (1997). *Revive us again: The reawakening of American fundamentalism*. New York: Oxford University Press.

Creedon, J. (1998, July/August). God with a million faces: Design your own god. *Utne Reader*, 42–48.

Eck, D. (1997). *A new religious America: How a "Christian country" has become the world's most religiously diverse nation*. San Francisco: Harper.

Fuller, R. C. (2001). *Spiritual but not religious: Understanding unchurched America*. New York: Oxford University Press.

Herberg, W. (1960). *Protestant, Catholic, Jew: An essay in American religious sociology* (rev. ed.). Garden City, NY: Doubleday.

Higginbotham, E. B. (1993). *Righteous discontent: The women's movement in the Black church, 1880–1920.* Cambridge, MA: Harvard University Press.

Kelley, D. M. (1977). *Why conservative churches are growing* (2nd ed.). New York: Harper.

Lincoln, C. E., & Mamiya, L. M. (1990). *The Black church in the African American experience*. Durham, NC: Duke University Press.

Lippy, C. H., Choquette, R., & Poole, S. (1992). *Christianity comes to the Americas, 1492–1776*. New York: Paragon House.

Mahoney, P. (2002, July 26). Study says Hispanic buying power rising. *Chattanooga Times Free Press.* Retrieved May 16, 2003 from www.timesfreepress.com/2002/july/26jul/disposableincomehispanic._html.

Malone, N., Baluja, K. F., Costanzo, J. M., and Davis, C. J. (2003). The foreign-born population: 2000. *Census 2000 Brief* C2KBR-34. Washington, DC: U.S. Department of Commerce, Economics and Statistics Administration, U.S. Census Bureau.

Mayhew, J. (1749). *Seven sermons*. Boston: Rogers & Fowle.

Miller, R. T., & Flowers, R. B. (Eds.). (1987). *Toward benevolent neutrality: Church, state, and the Supreme Court* (3rd ed.). Waco, TX: Baylor University Press.

Pew Forum on Religion and Public Life (2008). *U.S. religious landscape survey.* Retrieved September 9, 2008, from http://religions.pewforum.org/

Ratio of "unchurched" up sharply since 1991. (2004, June 1). *Christian Century*, p. 15.

Reeves, T. J., and Bennett, C. E. (2004). We the people: Asians in the United States. *Census 2000 Special Reports* CENSR-17. Washington DC: U.S. Department of Commerce, Economics and Statistics Administration, U.S. Census Bureau.

Strong, J. (1964). *Our country* (J. Herbst, Ed.). Cambridge, MA: Harvard University Press. (Original work published 1886)

Teepen, T. (2005). Intelligent design lives on. *Chattanooga Times Free Press*, p. B6.

Tweed, T. A. (1997). *Our lady of the exile: Diasporic religion at a Cuban Catholic shrine in Miami.* New York: Oxford University Press.

U.S. Census Bureau. (2000). *Statistical abstract of the United States.* Retrieved May 1, 2003, from www.census.gov/statab/www/

U.S. Census Bureau. (2003). *U.S. Census Bureau guidance on the presentation and comparison of race and Hispanic origin data.* Retrieved September 11, 2008, from www.census/gov/population/www/socdemo/compraceho.html/

U.S. Census Bureau. (2006). *Population estimates.* Retrieved September 11, 2008, from www.census/gov/popest/National/

Westerhoff, J. H. (1978). *McGuffey and his readers: Piety, morality, and education in nineteenth-century America.* Nashville, TN: Abingdon.

Williams, P. W. (1980). *Popular religion in America: Symbolic change and the modernization process in historical perspective.* Englewood Cliffs, NJ: Prentice-Hall.

Wilson, J. F. (Ed.). (1965). *Church and state in American history.* Boston: Heath.

Wuthnow, R. (1998). *After Heaven: Spirituality in America since the 1950s.* Berkeley: University of California Press.

Eliminating sex bias in schools will improve educational opportunities for both female and male students.

Gender

Social, economic, and political conditions for women have improved substantially since the women's rights movement emerged as part of the Civil Rights Movement of the 1960s and 1970s. However, gender discrimination and inequality still exist in schools and in society at large. In 2007, the median earnings for women who were full-time workers were 77.8 percent of those for men, up from 76.9 percent in 2006 (Institute for Women's Policy Research, 2008). The status of women in the United States within the last three decades has changed substantially. More women are now working outside the home than ever before, and more women are heads of households. In 2006, 59 percent of women worked outside the home (U.S. Department of Labor/Bureau of Labor Statistics, 2007). In 2007, 24.1 percent of U.S. households were headed by women (U.S. Census Bureau, 2007). An increasing percentage of women and their dependents constitute the nation's poor. Some writers use the term *feminization of poverty* to describe this development. In 2007, 58.9 percent of poor families in the United States were headed by women (U.S. Census Bureau).

The first three chapters in Part III of this book describe the status of women in the United States, the ways in which schools perpetuate gender discrimination, and strategies that educators can use to create equal educational opportunities for both female and male students. As Sadker and Zittleman point out in Chapter 6, both males and females are harmed by sex stereotypes and gender discrimination. Tetreault, in Chapter 7, describes how male perspectives dominate school knowledge and how teachers can infuse their curricula with perspectives from both genders and thereby expand their students' thinking and insights. Henry, in Chapter 8, describes how race and gender are interlocking dimensions that need to be understood together rather than as separate and discrete categories. She argues that it is essential for teachers to comprehend the ways in which race and gender interact in order to avoid reproducing in schools the oppressions that exist within the larger society.

Mayo, in Chapter 9, examines the role of queer studies and sexual and gender minorities in multicultural education. She asks classroom teachers to grapple with issues such as the privileging of heterosexism within schools and society, the invisibility of gay students and their families in the curriculum, and the reason it is essential for students to study the positive aspects of lesbian, gay, bisexual, and transgender/transsexual (LGBTQ) communities and cultures. Mayo believes that to fully implement multicultural education, LGBTQ students must experience civic equality, social justice, and recognition (Gutmann, 2004) in the classroom and on the schoolyard.

References

Gutmann, A. (2004). Unity and diversity in democratic multicultural education: Creative and destructive tensions. In J. A. Banks (Ed.), *Diversity and citizenship education: Global perspectives* (pp. 71–98). San Francisco: Jossey-Bass/Wiley.

Institute for Women's Policy Research. (2008). *Gender wage ratio: Women's and men's earnings.* Retrieved October 20, 2008, from http://www.iwpr.org/pdf/C350.pdf

U. S. Census Bureau. (2007). People in families by relationship to householder, age of householder, number of children present, and family structure: 2007. Retrieved January 14, 2009, from http://pubdb3.census.gov/macro/032008/pov/new05_100_01.htm

U. S. Department of Labor, U.S. Bureau of Labor Statistics. (2007). *Women in the labor force: A databook.* Retrieved October 20, 2008, from http://www.bls.gov/cps/wlf-databook-2007.pdf

136

CHAPTER 6

Gender Bias: From Colonial America to Today's Classroom

David Sadker and Karen Zittleman*

A sage once remarked that if fish were anthropologists, the last thing they would discover would be the water. We are all like those fish, swimming in a sea of sexism, but few of us see the water, the gender bias that engulfs us. Sexism in schools is a major influence on children in urban, suburban, and rural America, in wealthy and poor communities, and in communities that are diverse as well as those that are homogeneous. In short, gender is a demographic that binds all schools and challenges all educators. Yet a cultural shortsightedness, coined "gender blindness," makes it difficult for educators to see how sexism influences virtually every aspect of how we teach and learn (Bailey, Scantlebury, & Letts, 1997).

Students, on the other hand, view a very different world, a school filled with gender challenges. In a study by Zittleman (2007) of more than 400 middle schoolers, fighting, discipline, poor grades, fear of homophobia, and difficulty with friendships and emotions were readily identified as gender issues confronting males. For females, relational aggression (gossiping, spreading rumors, and inability to trust friends) topped the list. Students also noted girls' deliberate efforts to take easier courses, do poorly on tests and assignments, and "act dumb" in school to gain popularity or have a boyfriend. Unfortunately, many of today's boys and girls are unaware of the historical struggle to gain even rudimentary educational rights for females. As a result, they—as well as their teachers—lack the perspective and tools necessary to challenge sexism in school.

This chapter provides a context for understanding gender bias in school. It includes (1) a brief historical overview of women's struggle for educational opportunity, (2) an update of the progress made and yet to be made in ensuring gender equity in schools, (3) an analysis of gender bias in curriculum, (4) insights into gender bias in instruction, (5) a view of today's trends and

---

* Myra Sadker co-authored earlier versions of this chapter. Myra died in 1995 while undergoing treatment for breast cancer. To learn more about her work, visit www.sadker.org. Some of the information in this chapter is adapted from *Still Failing at Fairness*, by Sadker and Zittleman (Scribner 2009).

challenges concerning gender issues in school, and (6) some practical suggestions for creating gender-equitable classrooms.

THE HIDDEN CIVIL RIGHTS STRUGGLE

For centuries, women fought to open the schoolhouse door. The education of America's girls was so limited that less than one-third of the women in colonial America could even sign their names. Although a woman gave the first plot of ground for a free school in New England, female children were not allowed to attend the school. In fact, women were commonly viewed as being mentally and morally inferior to men, relegated to learning only domestic skills. Not until the 1970s and 1980s did they win the right to be admitted to previously all-male Ivy League colleges and universities, and not until the 1990s did they breach the walls of the Citadel and the Virginia Military Institute. It is rare indeed that such a monumental civil rights struggle—so long, so recent, and influencing so many—has remained so invisible. Let's take a brief look at this hidden civil rights struggle.

During the colonial period, dame schools educated very young boys and girls (with few exceptions, *White* boys and girls) in the homes of women who had the time and desire to teach. Girls lucky enough to attend such schools would learn domestic skills along with reading (so that they could one day read the Bible to their children). Such schools also taught the boys how to write and prepared them for more formal education. Girls graduated to the kitchen and the sewing area, focusing on their futures as wives and mothers.

With a new democracy came new ideas and the promise of more educational opportunities for females. Elementary schools gradually opened their doors to females, and for the families financially able, secondary schools in the form of female seminaries became possible. Seminaries provided a protected and supervised climate melding religious and academic lessons. In New York, Emma Hart Willard battled to establish the Troy Female Seminary, and in Massachusetts, Mary Lyon created Mount Holyoke, a seminary that eventually became a noted women's college. Seminaries often emphasized self-denial and strict discipline, considered important elements in molding devout wives and Christian mothers. By the 1850s, with help from Quakers such as Harriet Beecher Stowe, Myrtilla Miner established the Miner Normal School for Colored Girls in the nation's capital, providing new educational opportunities for African American women. While these seminaries sometimes offered a superior education, they were also trapped in a paradox they could never fully resolve: They were educating girls for a world not ready to accept educated women. Seminaries sometimes went to extraordinary lengths to reconcile this conflict. Emma Willard's Troy Female Seminary was devoted to "professionalizing motherhood." (Who could not support motherhood?) But en route to reshaping motherhood, seminaries reshaped teaching.

For the teaching profession, seminaries became the source of new ideas and new recruits. Seminary leaders such as Emma Hart Willard and Catherine Beecher wrote textbooks on how to teach and how to teach more humanely than was the practice at the time. They denounced corporal punishment and promoted more cooperative educational practices. Because school was seen as an extension of the home and another arena for raising children, seminary graduates were allowed to become teachers—at least until they decided to marry. More than 80 percent of the graduates of Troy Female Seminary and Mount Holyoke became teachers. Female teachers were particularly attractive to school districts—not only because of their teaching effectiveness but also because they were typically paid one-third to one-half the salary of male teachers. By the end of the Civil War, a number of colleges and universities, especially tax-supported ones, were desperate for dollars. Institutions of higher learning experienced a serious student shortage due to Civil War casualties, and women became the source of much needed tuition dollars. But female wallets did not buy on-campus equality. Women often faced separate courses and hostility from male students and professors. At state universities, such as the University of Michigan, male students would stamp their feet in protest when a woman entered a classroom, a gesture some professors appreciated.

While an economic necessity for many colleges, educating women was not a popular idea, and some people even considered it dangerous. In *Sex in Education,* Dr. Edward Clarke (1873), a member of Harvard's medical faculty, argued that women attending high school and college were at medical risk. According to Dr. Clarke, the blood destined for the development and health of their ovaries would be redirected to their brains by the stress of study. Too much education would leave women with "monstrous brains and puny bodies ... flowing thought and constipated bowels" (pp. 120–128). Clarke recommended that females be provided with a less demanding education, easier courses, no competition, and rest periods so that their reproductive organs could develop. The female brain was too small and the female body too vulnerable for such mental challenges. He maintained that allowing girls to attend places such as Harvard would pose a serious health threat to the women themselves, with sterility and hysteria potential outcomes. It would take another century before Harvard and other prestigious men's colleges would finally admit women.

Clarke's ideas constructed some powerful fears in women. M. Carey Thomas, future president of Bryn Mawr and one of the first women to earn a Ph.D. in the United States, wrote of the fears created by writers like Clarke. "I remember often praying about it, and begging God that if it were true that because I was a girl, I could not successfully master Greek and go to college, and understand things, to kill me for it" (cited in Sadker, Sadker, & Zittleman, 2008, p. 298). In 1895, the faculty of the University of Virginia concluded that "women were often physically unsexed by the strains of study" (cited in Sadker, Sadker, & Zittleman, p. 298). Parents, fearing for the health of their daughters, would often place them in less demanding programs reserved for females or would keep them out of advanced education entirely. Even today, the echoes of Clarke's warnings resonate—some people still see well-educated women as less attractive, view advanced education as "too stressful" for females, or believe that education is more important for males than for females.

There were clear racist overtones in Clarke's writing. The women attending college were overwhelmingly White, and education delayed marriage and decreased childbearing. As a result, while women of color were reproducing at "alarming" rates, wealthy White women were choosing college rather than motherhood. The dangers to the White establishment were clear.

By the 20th century, women were winning more access to educational programs at all levels, although well into the 1970s, gender-segregated programs were still the rule. Although they attended the same schools as males, females often received a segregated and less valuable education. Commercial courses prepared girls to become secretaries, and vocational programs channeled them into cosmetology and other low-paying occupations. With the passage of Title IX of the Education Amendments of 1972, females saw significant progress toward gaining access to educational programs, but not equality.

Title IX of the 1972 Education Amendments Act became law as the women's movement gained momentum. The opening section of Title IX states:

> No person in the United States shall, on the basis of sex, be excluded from participation in, be denied the benefits of, or be subjected to discrimination under any education program or activity receiving federal financial assistance.

While most people have heard of Title IX in relation to sports, it reaches far beyond the athletic field. Every public school and most of the nation's colleges and universities are covered under Title IX, which prohibits discrimination in school admissions, in counseling and guidance, in competitive athletics, in student rules and regulations, and in access to programs and courses, including vocational education and physical education. Title IX also applies to sex discrimination in employment practices, including interviewing and recruitment, hiring and promotion, compensation, job assignments, and fringe benefits. Access to courses and programs were curtailed somewhat in 2007 when the second Bush administration changed Title IX to allow for gender segregation, that is, the creation of single-sex schools and classes. In recent years, Title IX enforcement has been sporadic, and the future and strength of this critical law is by no means ensured. Some even believe that Title IX is no longer needed and that gender bias has been solved. Statistics tell us otherwise.

REPORT CARD: THE COST OF SEXISM IN SCHOOLS

The following is a report card you will not find in any school, yet these statistics document how gender inequities continue to permeate schools and society and shortchange students.

- *Boys and Schools*: Poor school achievement; overdiagnosis and referral to special educational services; and excessive athletics, bullying, peer harassment, disciplinary problems, and violence remain common school problems plaguing boys. While many lump all boys into a single category, this is misleading. White and middle-class boys are performing relatively well, but low-income and racial minority boys are not. Many believe that the socialization of boys into tough and competitive roles sets the stage for such school clashes and that class and race can exacerbate academic problems (Kimmel, 2006a; Reichert & Hawley, 2006).
- *Girls and Schools*: Gender socialization may explain in part why girls appear to do so well in school. Girls receive higher report card grades, have fewer disciplinary problems, and are more likely than boys to become valedictorians and go on to college, although the value of their education is less clear. More than a third of students in grades 3–12 hold the view that "people think that the most important thing for girls is to get married and have children" (Girls, Inc., 2006).
- *Academic Courses*: Girls are the majority in biology, chemistry, algebra, and precalculus courses, while far more males enroll in calculus, physics, and computer science. Males take fewer English, sociology, psychology, foreign language, and fine arts courses than do females. Yet across all subject areas, males enroll in and score

higher on the advanced placement tests (Dalton, 2007; National Center for Education Statistics [NCES], 2004).

- *Test Scores*:   In the early years, along with their superior grades, girls are ahead of or equal to boys on most standardized measures of achievement. By the time they graduate from high school or college, they have fallen behind boys on high-stakes tests such as the SAT, ACT, MCAT, LSAT, and GRE, all key exams needed to gain entrance (and scholarships) to the most prestigious colleges and graduate schools (American Association of University Women [AAUW], 2008b; National Coalition for Women and Girls in Education [NCWGE], 2007).

- *Antiachievement Attitudes*:   Boys often view reading and writing as "feminine" subjects that threaten their masculinity. Many boys, especially minority and low-income boys, view school as irrelevant to their futures. College men have fewer intellectual interests and poorer study habits than college women. They enjoy reading books less, take fewer notes, study less, and play more. Despite their lower effort, lower grades, and lower likelihood of completing a college degree, men evaluate their academic abilities higher than those of women (Lederman, 2006; NCWGE, 2007).

- *Dropouts*:   More than a million students drop out each year, a problem most associated with boys. In fact, one in three boys—often African American, Hispanic, and Native American—will fail to graduate from high school in four years. While media attention focuses on such boys, almost half of all dropouts are girls. Girls of color are most at risk; half of Native American girls and about 40 percent of African American and Hispanic girls fail to graduate each year. When girls leave, they are less likely than boys to return to earn their high school diploma or general education degree (National Women's Law Center [NWLC], 2007).

- *Athletics*:   Participation in school athletics is at record levels for boys and girls. More than 4.3 million boys engage in a high school sport. Before Title IX, fewer than 300,000 high school girls played competitive sports; today, 3 million girls compete, but they are only about 40% of all high school athletes (Gillis, 2007; NWLC, 2007a).

- *Sexual Harassment*:   Nearly nine in ten students (85%) report that students harass other students at their school, and almost 40% of students report that school employees sexually harass as well. Some are surprised to learn that boys are the targets of such harassment almost as frequently as girls (AAUW, 2004; Zittleman, 2007).

- *Bullying*:   At least 30 percent of students are victims of bullying, and 60 percent of students witness bullying at school every day. Males are more likely to bully others and be victims of physical bullying, while females frequently experience verbal and psychological bullying (through sexual comments or rumors) (KidsHealth, 2007; Milson & Gallo, 2006).

- *Self-Esteem*:   As girls go through school, their self-esteem plummets, and the danger of depression increases. In middle school, girls rate popularity as more important than academic competence or independence. Eating disorders among females in schools and colleges are rampant and increasing. Some boys are now also displaying body image issues, including dieting and steroid abuse. Interestingly, female and male African American students report a stronger sense of self and do not suffer as much from depression, eating disorders, and body issues as do other groups (Bisaga, et al. 2005; Greenfield & Brumberg, 2006; Tolman, Impett, Tracy, & Michael, 2006; Zittleman, 2007).

- *College Enrollments*:   Men had been the majority of college students from the colonial period to the early 1980s. Today, women are the majority. Yet it is not White men who are missing from the college ranks, but minority and low-income men. In fact, more women and men attend college today than ever before (NCES, 2008).
- *College Majors*:   Women earn the majority of degrees in education, psychology, biological sciences, and accounting. Women earn more degrees in pharmacy and veterinary medicine than do males. And in law, women and men have reached parity in degree attainment. Males dominate areas such as business, computer science, and engineering. Women lag behind men in attaining medical and dental degrees (NCES, 2008).
- *Earnings*:   Women also earn less at every level of education. The median annual earnings of a female high school graduate are at least one-third less than that of her male counterpart. One year after college graduation, a female of any racial, ethnic, or socioeconomic group earns less than a White male with the same college degree. Female physicians and surgeons earn 38 percent less than their male counterparts, female college and university teachers earn 25 percent less than men, and female lawyers earn 30 percent less than male lawyers (AAUW, 2008a; NWLC, 2007b).

In the past decades, great progress has been made by males and females in battling sexism. Women are now the majority of college students, the presidents of several prestigious Ivy League colleges, and successful athletes. Today, more boys are scoring higher on standardized tests, enrolling in college more than ever before, and entering prestigious, well-paying careers. (Although for poorer and minority boys and girls, the situation is less encouraging.) But as the preceding statistics remind us, progress can be slow, and gender inequities are still a very real part of school life.

For the typical classroom teacher, gender equity emerges as a continuing challenge on at least two levels. To help you tease out the subtle biases that persist in classrooms, we focus on two central areas of classroom life: the curriculum and student–teacher interaction.

GENDER BIAS IN TODAY'S CLASSROOM: THE CURRICULUM

Few things stir up more controversy than the content of the curriculum. Teachers, parents, and students seem to be intuitively aware that schoolbooks shape what the next generation knows and how it behaves. In this case, research supports intuition. Students spend as much as 80 to 95 percent of classroom time using textbooks, and teachers make a majority of their instructional decisions based on these texts (Fan & Kaeley, 2000; Starnes, 2004). When children read about people in nontraditional gender roles, they are less likely to limit themselves to stereotypes. When children read about women and minorities in history, they are more likely to believe that these groups have made important contributions to the country. As one sixth grader told us, "I love to read biographies about women. When I learn about what they've done, I feel like a door is opening. If they can do great things, maybe I can, too." But what if your identity is misrepresented, misremembered, or just plain missing from the school curriculum?

In the 1970s and 1980s, textbook companies and professional associations, such as the American Psychological Association and the National Council of Teachers of English, issued guidelines for nonracist and nonsexist books, suggesting how to include and fairly portray different groups in the curriculum. As a result, textbooks became more balanced in their description of underrepresented groups. While yesterday's stark sexist texts are thankfully gone, subtle bias persists. No matter the subject, the names and experiences of males continue to dominate the pages of school books. Men are seen as the movers and shakers of history, scientists of achievement, and political leaders.

Studying history is a journey through time, but a journey with few women. Current elementary and high school social studies texts include five times more males than females when telling the stories of our national history (Chick, 2006). Beyond women's invisibility, selective adjectives also perpetuate linguistic bias. The 19th-century diplomat Klemens von Metternich is described in the popular high school history book *World History: Patterns of Interaction* as a man whose "charm" worked well with "elegant ladies"—words and facts of dubious historical import, but not without prurient interest (Beck, Black, Naylor, & Shabaka, 2005). Such gender and linguistic insights are frequently left unexplained in texts.

A review of 13 current elementary basal readers found that male characters outnumbered females two to one. But this male dominance comes with a price: males are still strikingly bound by traditional standards. For example, in a story from a fifth-grade book, the display of male aggressiveness is noteworthy: A boy wants to be in charge of the fair project; he is the biggest and looks at his raised fist while glancing at the other children to signify no one was to argue. No one did. In other stories, the adult males are shaking their fists and shouting at other males, often chasing them (Evans & Davies, 2000). Unfortunately, it is often little boys causing the trouble, a double impact of out-of-control youths and angry men.

These lessons in gender bias extend beyond the pages of academic texts; they are reinforced by award-winning, popular children's books read daily in classrooms and nightly at home. A study of 200 distinguished children's books—American Library Association award winners, Caldecott selections, and top-selling children's picture books—revealed that these children's tales tell twice as many male-centered tales than female, and illustrations depict 50 percent more males. Although female characters appear in roles such as doctors, lawyers, and scientists, they are given traditional jobs ten times more often than nontraditional ones. For example, the lead adult female character in *Alligator Tales* is a stewardess and a maid in *Mr. Willowby's Christmas Tree*. Males in children's books remain unlikely to stray from traditional careers as well. Boys tend to have roles as fighters, adventurers, and rescuers. They are also overwhelming shown to be aggressive, argumentative, and competitive. A passage in *Johnny and Susie's Mountain Quest* highlights the rigid roles of a brave boy and a helpless girl: "'Oh, please help me, Johnny!' cried Susie. 'We're up so high! I'm afraid I'm going to fall'" (Hamilton, Anderson, Braoddus, & Young, 2006).

How can teachers and students detect gender bias in books? The following are descriptions of seven forms of bias that emerge in today's texts. These forms of bias can also help identify prejudice related to gender as well as race, ethnicity, the elderly, people with disabilities, non-English speakers, gays and lesbians, and limited-English speakers. Learning these forms of bias develops a useful critical reading skill.

Invisibility: *What You Don't See Makes a Lasting Impression*

When groups or events are not taught in schools, they become part of the *null curriculum*. Textbooks published prior to the 1960s largely omitted African Americans, Hispanics, and Asian Americans. Many of today's textbooks continue to give minimal treatment to women, depriving students of information about half of the nation's population. When we ask students to name ten famous women from American history, most cannot do it (Sadker & Zittleman, 2009). A similar case of invisibility can be made for those with disabilities, gays and lesbians, and males in parenting and other roles nontraditional to their gender.

Stereotyping: *Glib Shortcuts*

When rigid roles or traits are assigned to all members of a group, a stereotype that denies individual attributes and differences is born. Examples include portraying all African Americans as athletes, Mexican Americans as laborers, and women only in terms of their family roles.

Imbalance and Selectivity: *A Tale Half Told*

Curriculum sometimes presents only one interpretation of an issue, situation, or group of people, simplifying and distorting complex issues by omitting different perspectives. A description of suffragettes being *given* the vote omits the work, sacrifices, and physical abuse suffered by women who *won* the right to vote.

Unreality: *Rose-Colored Glasses*

Curricular materials often paint a Pollyanna picture of the nation (and this goes for any nation!). Our history texts often ignore class differences, the lack of basic health care for tens of millions, and ongoing sexism. For example, when the nuclear family is described only as a father, mother, and children, students are being treated to romanticized and sanitized narratives, an *unreality* that omits the information they will need to confront and resolve real social challenges.

Fragmentation: *An Interesting Sideshow*

Did you ever read a textbook that separates the discussion of women in a separate section or insert? For example, many of today's texts include special inserts highlighting certain gender topics, such as "What If He Has Two Mommies?" or "Ten Women Achievers in Science." Such isolation presents women and gender issues as interesting diversions but suggests that their contributions do not constitute the mainstream of history, literature, or the sciences.

Linguistic Bias: *Words Count*

Language can be a powerful conveyor of bias in both blatant and subtle forms. The exclusive use of masculine terms and pronouns, ranging from *our forefathers, mankind*, and *businessman* to the generic *he*, denies the full participation and recognition of women. More subtle examples include word orders and choices that place males in a primary role, such as "men and their wives."

Cosmetic Bias: *Pretty Wrapping*

Cosmetic bias offers an "illusion of equity." Beyond the attractive covers, photos, or posters that prominently feature diversity, bias persists. For example, a science textbook might feature a glossy pullout of female scientists or a cover with photos of scientists from different races but provide precious little narrative on the scientific contributions of women or people of color.

Until publishers and authors eliminate gender bias, it will be up to the creativity and commitment of teachers and parents to fill in the missing pages. Children enjoy exciting, well-written books, and such books can include characters from different races, ethnic groups, religions, social classes, and both genders. But equitable materials are not enough to create a nonsexist educational environment. Attention must also be given to instruction.

GENDER BIAS IN TODAY'S CLASSROOMS: STUDENT-TEACHER INTERACTION

You probably remember an unspoken rule from your own school days. If you wanted to speak, you knew just what to do to get called on. Raising a hand might be your first move, but waving your hand would signal that you *really* wanted to talk. Eye contact with the teacher was always a good idea, but a few strategically placed grunts could work miracles in getting attention. Once called on—assuming you had the right answer (not always a sure thing)—you got to speak, your needs were met, and the teacher's needs were met as well. By calling on the eager and willing students, the teacher moves the lesson along at a good pace, the main points are all "covered," and there are smiles all around. Most teachers call on students who want to talk, leave the others alone, and everybody is comfortable. So what's the problem?

Although it *sounds* awfully good, the purpose of school is not to make everyone comfortable. Schools are for education, for learning new and sometimes uncomfortable skills. Talented teachers know that if they select only students who quickly volunteer, reticent students will be relegated to the sidelines. In this topsy-turvy world, the students who need a little more time to think—because they are by nature thoughtful, because English is a new language, because their cultural background encourages a slower response, or because they are shy—become spectators to rapid classroom exchanges. Females lose out, children of color lose out, English language learners are left behind, and shy boys are silenced.

The gendered nature of classroom interactions can be subtle and is often ignored. Watch how boys dominate the discussion in this upper elementary class about presidents.

The fifth-grade class is almost out of control. "Just a minute," the teacher admonishes. "There are too many of us here to all shout out at once. I want you to raise your hands, and then I'll call on you. If you shout out, I'll pick somebody else."

Order is restored. Then Stephen, enthusiastic to make his point, calls out.

> STEPHEN: I think Lincoln was the best president. He held the country together during the war.
> TEACHER: A lot of historians would agree with you.
> KELVIN (seeing that nothing happened to Stephen, calls out): I don't. Lincoln was okay, but my Dad liked Reagan. He always said Reagan was a great president.
> JACK (calling out): Reagan? Are you kidding?
> TEACHER: Who do you think our best president was, Jack?
> JACK: FDR. He saved us from the Depression.
> MAX (calling out): I don't think it's right to pick one best president. There were a lot of good ones.
> TEACHER: That's a terrific insight.
> REBECCA (calling out): I don't think the presidents today are as good as the ones we used to have.
> TEACHER: Okay, Rebecca. But you forgot the rule. You're supposed to raise your hand.

Most teachers try to manage their classroom with conventions such as "Raise your hand if you want to talk." Yet even a fraction of a second is too long for some students to wait to be heard. Very active and animated students challenge the rule and simply shout out the answer.

Intellectually, teachers know they should apply rules consistently, but when the discussion becomes fast paced and furious, rules are often swept aside. When this happens, it is an open invitation for male dominance. Studies show that male students frequently control classroom conversation. They call out and answer more questions more often than girls. They receive more praise for the intellectual quality of their ideas. They are criticized more publicly and harshly. They get help when they are confused. They are the heart and center of interaction (Beaman, Wheldall, & Kemp, 2006; Duffy, Warren, & Walsh, 2001; Francis, 2000; Jones & Gerig, 1994; Sadker & Zittleman, 2009). Some researchers emphasize that low-achieving males get most of the negative attention while high-achieving boys get more positive and constructive academic contacts (Babad, 1998; Spencer, Porche, & Tolman, 2003). However, no matter whether they are high or low achievers, female students are more likely to receive less instructional time, less help, and less positive and negative attention.

In the social studies class about presidents, we saw boys as a group grabbing attention while girls as a group were left out of the action. Not being allowed to call out like her male classmates during the brief conversation about presidents will not psychologically scar Rebecca; however, the system of silencing operates covertly and repeatedly. It occurs several times a day during each school week for twelve years, and even longer if Rebecca goes to college, and, most insidious of all, it happens subliminally. This microinequity eventually has a powerful cumulative impact.

Reinforced for passivity, independence and self-esteem suffer. Researchers observed hundreds of classes and watched as girls typically raised their hands, often at a right angle, arms bent at the elbow, a cautious, tentative, almost passive gesture. At other times, they raise their arms straight and high, but they signal silently (Sadker & Zittleman, 2009). Educator Diana Meehan calls this phenomenon the "girl pause": If a teacher asks a question, a girl likely pauses, doubting her knowledge or worse, her right to speak out loud. She wonders, *"Do I know this?"* Meanwhile, a boy blurts out an answer, and the class moves on (Meehan, 2007).

An important factor allowing boys to dominate interaction is the widespread gender segregation that characterizes classrooms. Occasionally, teachers divide their classrooms along gender-segregated lines in groups, work and play areas, and seating; more frequently, students gender-segregate themselves. Drawn to the sections of the classroom where the more assertive boys are clustered, the teacher is positioned to keep interacting with male students.

The gender difference in classroom communications is more than a mere counting game of who gets the teacher's attention and who does not. Teacher attention is a vote of high expectations of and commitment to a student.

Classroom management issues, steeped in gendered expectations, also contribute to male-dominated classrooms. Picture a disruptive classroom and you are likely to envision a few boys as troublemakers. Why boys? Many link male aggression with the male stereotype, the role boys are expected to play in society (Fang, 1996; Pollack, 1998; Kimmel, 2008). For the teacher, the management lesson seems clear: Control the boys and all problems will be resolved. Because boys are usually more physically aggressive than girls and more difficult to control, the teacher is advised to closely monitor males in the classroom to ensure that things do not get out of control.

While male misbehavior captures teacher attention, girls' gendered behavioral problems typically fly below the radar screen of teachers. Relational aggression—spreading rumors or forming cliques—is harder to see than the physical male aggression and can be delivered in a whisper. Research suggests that children find relational aggression as painful as physical aggression. Relational aggression harms healthy friendships and threatens adolescents' tender self-esteem (Brown, 2003; Merten, 1997). While teachers rarely react to relational aggression, they may overreact to even the potential of male misbehavior. Such disparities are readily detected by students who report that innocent boys are often targeted unfairly by teachers, and girls are able "to get away" with inappropriate and hurtful behavior (Zittleman, 2007). Such inequities detract from learning and a sense of security for all students.

TRENDS AND CHALLENGES

The Boy Crisis

So just when you think you are getting a handle on this sexism problem, we have to tell you that not everyone agrees that girls are at such great risk. Some argue that boys are the gender at risk. A 2006 *Newsweek* story quoted a psychologist who lamented that: "girl behavior becomes the gold standard. Boys are treated like defective girls" (Tyre, 2006). *The Atlantic Monthly* offered a cover story, *The War Against Boys*, declaring that teachers were feminizing males in school (Sommers, 2000). An article in the *New Republic* attacked schools for their "verbally drenched curriculum" that leaves "boys in the dust" (Rivers & Barnett, 2007). Psychologists described schools as "pathologizing what is simply normal for boys." Even the prestigious *New York Times*, in an article entitled "At Colleges, Women Are Leaving Men in the Dust," described how men were falling behind in academics and college attendance and asked what should be done about "the new gender divide" (Lewin, 2006). A 2006 *Newsweek* cover headline summed it up: "The Boy Crises. At Every Level of Education They Are Falling Behind. What to Do?" (Tyre, 2006).

The media picture of boys that has emerged is as familiar as it is one-dimensional: antsy and unable to sit for long; often learning disabled or injected with too much Ritalin; hardwired differently than girls; unable to read and disliking books; unhappy taking orders from women in school; able to focus on sports, computers, and video games but never on academics; a constant source of discipline problems in class; a potential grade repeater; perhaps one day a dropout; certainly someone less and less likely to enter a college classroom. Other boys—quiet boys, unathletic boys, thoughtful boys, caring boys, gay boys, and middle- and upper-class boys acing their school work and going on to the Ivy Leagues—all disappeared overnight.

There are legitimate concerns about some boys' achievement. But there are also legitimate concerns about the way the current discussion is being framed. The boy crisis is a tasty news story, but it is misleading. If there is a boy crisis today, boys' school grades, college attendance, and test scores would be tumbling. But none of this is happening. In fact, according to the nonpartisan Education Sector, most boys are doing better today than they were a decade or two ago (Mead, 2006; American Association of University Women, 2008b).

Boys do quite well on most tests. They outperform girls on the SATs and GREs, and their performance on other tests such as the National Assessment of Educational Progress (NAEP)—the nation's "report card"—has actually improved in recent years. Girls do test better in reading and writing, and boys often test better in math and science, but many of these gaps are narrowing. More boys are now taking advanced high school classes in calculus, chemistry, and physics than ever before, and about four times as many boys now enroll in advanced placement courses than did 20 years ago. Crime and substance abuse rates are down among boys. Although more boys than girls (36 percent to 28 percent) drop out of high school, more African American, Hispanic, and American Indian girls drop out than either White or Asian boys. When girls drop out, they are more likely to be unemployed, earn lower wages, and be on public support than male dropouts.

While females are now the majority in college, and more men are attending than ever before. One statistic often missed in the "boy crisis" stories is that men still constitute the majority of students at a number of celebrated colleges and in prestigious academic programs while women are the majority at the less prestigious two-year community colleges. These female college students are typically older with children and studying in programs in order to increase their income. When men and women graduate with the same credential (high school diploma, college degree, or graduate degree), men continue to earn significantly higher incomes. A woman with a college degree earns about the same as a man without a college degree. For women, education has more economic consequences than it does for men. Some have interpreted girls' progress in school to mean that boys are in crisis, as though life is a zero sum game and if one group advances, another must topple.

While the boy crisis is a myth, there are boys not doing well in school. Let's take a moment to focus on the difference between males in general and at-risk males. White and Asian males are not struggling on tests; they are scoring much higher than other males. In fact, the scoring gap between Asian and White males versus males of color is several times higher than the scoring gap between males and females in general. Black, Hispanic, Native American, and poor boys are the ones at risk and are far more likely to be grade repeaters than White or Asian boys (or than girls from any group) (Kimmel, 2006b; Mead, 2006; Perie, Grigg, & Donahue,

2005; NWLC, 2007). The Urban Institute reports that 76 percent of middle- to higher-income students typically graduate from high school while only 56 percent of low-income students do (Rivers & Barnett, 2006). According to UCLA researcher Gary Orfield (2004), more than 70 percent of White and Asian boys graduate from high school, but slightly more than half (51 to 58 percent) of boys of color graduate.

Let's zero in on a few states to better understand why African American students are at risk. In New Jersey, for example, African American students, mostly boys, are almost 60 times as likely as White students to be expelled for serious school violations (Witt, 2007). In Minnesota, African American students are suspended six times more often than Whites. Although they make up just 5 percent of the public school students in Iowa, African Americans account for 22 percent of the suspensions (Witt). Does African American school behavior warrant such punishments? Not according to Russell Skiba (as cited in Witt), a professor of educational psychology at Indiana University. His school discipline research shows that African American students from the same social and economic class are no more likely to misbehave than other students (Witt). "In fact, the data indicate that African-American students are punished more severely for the same offense, so clearly something else is going on. We can call it structural inequity or we can call it institutional racism." While most school districts are acutely aware of these racial disparities in discipline, they continue unabated.

Perhaps the worst thing about the "boy crisis" is that it has distracted us from boys like these, boys (and girls) who are really in need. It is not only African American boys, but boys and girls who are African American, Hispanic, Native American, and poor who are struggling. Convincing Americans that the most entitled citizens in the nation, White and Asian males in the United States, are in some sort of educational calamity is way off the mark. Perhaps a better title for this challenge is "the some boys (and girls) crisis."

But those decrying the "boy crisis" are persistent and offer a reason for the boy problem: feminized schools. Unsympathetic women teachers are promoting a "biologically disrespectful model of education" that is harming boys (Tyre, 2006). To fix this problem, these critics say, we need to abandon coeducation and reestablish all-boys' classes and schools. In fact, many public school educators have heeded their call and done just that.

The Rebirth of Single-Sex Education

At the beginning of both the 20th and 21st centuries, gender in school was center stage (Sadker & Zittleman, 2009). In the early 1900s, doctors argued that girls' fragile anatomy was endangered by too much education and that too much learning could lead to insanity and sterility. At the beginning of the 20th century, girls were routinely kept out of school "for their own good" (Sadker & Sadker, 1994; Sadker and Zittleman, 2009). Today biology once again is an issue. This time voices proclaim that biology created two different learners, girls and boys, and that trying to educate the two sexes in the same classroom is a disservice to both. By 2009, hundreds of single-sex classrooms had been created in public schools across the nation (National Association for Single Sex Education, 2008). Coeducation, once seen as a beacon of democracy and equality, is now accused of being a barrier to effective teaching and learning.

Is single-sex education a good idea? If you look to research for your answer, you will be disappointed, for the research is contradictory (Arms, 2007; AAUW, 1998; Mael, 1998; Jackson, 2002). A decade or two ago, there was some excitement when studies suggested that females in single-sex schools demonstrated strong academic achievement and self-esteem, high career goals, and less sex role stereotyping (Tyack & Hansot, 1990; Cairns, 1990). But the excitement proved premature. Many believed that these single-sex schools did not create these results but simply attracted girls with high academic goals and strong self-esteem. Others interpreted the studies to mean that these schools were excellent schools that just happened to be single-sex. Was single-sex schooling responsible for this strong female performance, or were the small class sizes, skilled teachers, strong academics, involved parents, and a selective admission process the real reasons for their success (Datnow & Hubbard, 2002)?

The research on boys' performance in single-sex education is even less convincing. Fewer studies on boys have been done, and the results conflict. On the positive side, some studies indicate that in single-sex environments, more boys enroll in nontraditional courses such as poetry or art and that poorer boys may develop better work habits in single-sex environments (Riordan, 2002; Reisman, 1990). But studies also report that all-male educational environments fan the flames of misogyny and sexism, producing boys and men who look down on girls and women. Moreover, the research does not offer any strong evidence that academic learning is any better in all-male schools (Bracey, 2006; Campbell & Sanders, 2002; Lee, Marks, & Byrd, 1993). Given such ambiguous results, the jury is still out on the success of all-male or all-female education.

So how different are boys and girls, and should they be taught separately? Janet Hyde (2005) at the University of Wisconsin used a sophisticated meta-analysis technique to investigate the underpinnings of single-sex education. She reviewed studies on how boys and girls are similar and different. Are boys more aggressive than girls? Are they better at math and science? Do girls have stronger verbal and fine motor skills? Are girls more nurturing than boys? She did what few people do: She investigated our assumptions about gender.

In some cases, her findings were counterconventional: males exhibited slightly more helping behaviors than females, while self-esteem levels for adult men and women were quite similar. Hyde (2005) did find a few educationally relevant differences: Males demonstrated more aggression and higher activity level and had a stronger ability to rotate objects mentally. Are these relatively few differences due to biology, to culture, or to a combination of the two? We don't know. But Hyde's bottom line is clear: "The evidence, often based on meta-analysis, indicates generally small gender differences for most abilities and behaviors, even those commonly said to show large differences."(Hyde & Lindberg, 2007, p. 25) After her exhaustive review, Hyde settled on a "gender similarities hypothesis": Males and females are more alike than different. Her research suggests that there are few educational reasons to separate the sexes. Several researchers in the United Kingdom agree with her conclusions. After studying single-sex schooling for years, Warrington and Younger (2003) concluded that there is no such thing as a gender-specific pedagogy. Yet many U.S. public schools pay little heed to such research and continue to create single-sex classrooms and even single-sex schools. Why?

Given the lack of research on and the destructive history of race segregation in our country, we can only conjecture why schools are so quick to segregate by gender. One possible reason is the persistent gap between research and popular culture. Trendy books and media pundits pronounce that boys and girls have different brains and different hardwiring and need to be taught differently and separately. This feeds into society's conventional view that "men are from Mars and women are from Venus." Parents and educators are told that boys learn best through physical games, tough competition, harsh discipline, and shorter lessons. On the other hand, girls, they are told, are genetically more placid and conforming, relational, and collaborative in nature and prefer a calmer learning atmosphere. Teachers are encouraged to discipline boys by yelling because boys need very clear direction and boundaries (and boys do not hear as well as girls) (Sax, 2005). On the other hand, teachers are advised not to give girls time limits on tests and to encourage them to take their shoes off in class to reduce stress (Gurian, Henley, & Trueman, 2001; Sax, 2005). Gurian, Henley and Trueman state that boys are deductive thinkers, prefer to work silently, enjoy jargon, and are easily bored, so teachers must keep stimulating them. Girls, on the other hand, are inductive and concrete thinkers, actually enjoy details, and are more group oriented. Such notions fit easily into traditional belief systems but are not supported by the research.

Some educators believe that the No Child Left Behind Act and the testing culture have pressured principals and stressed-out teachers to look for easy answers to difficult challenges (Darling-Hammond, 1997; Meier et al., 2004). Educators working in underresourced schools with failing test scores are endanger of losing their jobs and their schools. For them, single-sex classrooms could be a magic bullet, a chance to reestablish discipline and improve test scores with one simple and cheap solution: Segregate girls and boys. Public schools also face another new threat: the end of their monopoly. Many public schools are threatened by closure as their students move to newly created charter or private schools. Becoming single sex has a certain allure for schools, one that might enable a public school to compete more successfully. A few years ago, any of these single-sex classes would have been prohibited by law. In 2007, the Bush administration changed Title IX to allow public schools to separate girls and boys into different classes or different schools. Segregating students by sex is now legal.

But is segregating students by sex a good idea? We do not know. While there may be students who benefit from separate education, we do not know who they are, how they might benefit, or how to identify them. Even proponents of brain differences between the sexes concede that such differences do not apply to everyone. Generalizing a pedagogy based on sex is sure to miss many students who do not fit the gender mold. Boys differ from other boys, and girls differ from other girls, and the threat of stereotyping is very real (Arms, 2007). The single-sex supporters do not give much consideration to coeducation. What does our nation lose if coeducation is abandoned? A large and carefully crafted study that analyzed the benefits and liabilities of single-sex schools and classes would be very beneficial. Such a study would inform us about whether single-sex education is an idea whose time has come (again) or a bad idea (whose time ended decades ago).

STRATEGIES FOR CREATING GENDER-FAIR CLASSROOMS

Teachers have the power to make an enormous difference in the lives of students. The following suggestions consist of ways to make your own classroom nonsexist.

1. If the textbooks and software that you are given are biased, you may wish to confront this bias rather than ignore it. Discuss the issue directly with your students. It is entirely appropriate to acknowledge that instructional materials are not always

perfect. Teach them about the forms bias takes from stereotyping to cosmetic bias. By engaging your students in the issue, you help them to develop critical literacy skills.

2. Ask your students to list famous men and women. Do they have an equal number of women and men? More women? More men? Does the list include individuals of diverse racial and ethnic backgrounds? Discuss with them what their lists teach us. What groups are missing from their lists? How can we learn more about those "missing" Americans?

3. Analyze your seating chart to determine whether there are pockets of race, ethnic, class, or gender segregation in your classroom. Make certain that you do not teach from one area of the room, investing your time and attention on one group of students while ignoring another group sitting in another part of the room. When your students work in groups, create groups that reflect diversity. Monitor these student groups to ensure equitable participation and decision making.

4. Do not tolerate the use of harmful words, bullying, or harassment in your classroom. Do not say "boys will be boys" to excuse sexist comments or behaviors. Nor are racist or antigay comments to be ignored, laughed at, or tolerated. As a teacher, you are the model and the norm setter: If you do not tolerate hurtful prejudice, your students will learn to honor and respect each other.

5. Continue your reading and professional development in gender equity. Be discerning and remember that research publications are less susceptible to political agendas than the popular media or politically funded "think tanks." And be careful that your rights or those of your colleagues are not violated by gender discrimination.

Questions and Activities

1. The authors list seven forms of gender bias that you can use when evaluating instructional materials: (a) invisibility, (b) stereotyping, (c) linguistic bias, (d) imbalance, (e) unreality, (f) fragmentation, and (g) cosmetic bias. In your own words, define each form of bias. Examine a sample K–12 textbook or software in your teaching area and determine whether it contains any of these forms of gender bias. Are there forms of bias reflected against any other groups? Give three examples of how teachers can supplement instructional materials to eliminate the seven forms of gender bias.

2. Observe lessons being taught in several classrooms that include boys and girls and students from different racial and ethnic groups. Create a seating chart and count the interactions between the teacher and each student. Did the ways in which the teachers interacted with males and female students differ? If so, how? Did the teachers interact with students from various ethnic groups differently? If so, how? Did you notice any way in which gender, race, and socioeconomic status combined to influence how teachers interacted with particular students? If so, explain.

3. Why do you think single-sex schools are making a comeback? Do you think this trend toward single-sex schooling should be halted or supported? Why?

4. Check out the requirements of Title IX. Prepare a brief list to remind yourself of some of the ways in which the law is designed to ensure gender equity. (A good place to start is I Exercise My Rights at http://www.titleix.info/index.jsp.)

5. After reading this chapter, do you think there are some ways in which you can change your behavior to make it more gender fair? If yes, in what ways? If no, why not?

References

American Association of University Women (AAUW). (1998). *Separated by sex: A critical look at single-sex education for girls*. Washington, DC: AAUW.

American Association of University Women. (2004). *Harassment-free hallways: How to stop harassment in school*. Washington, DC: AAUW.

American Association of University Women. (2008a). *Pay gap exists as early as one year out of college, new research says*. Retrieved July 29, 2008, from http://www.aauw.org

American Association of University Women. (2008b). *Where the girls are: The facts about gender equity in education*. Washington, DC: AAUW.

Arms, E. (2007). Gender equity in coeducational and single sex environments. In S. Klein (Ed.), *Handbook for achieving gender equity through education* (pp. 171–190). Mahwah, NJ: Erlbaum Associates.

Babad, E. (1998). Preferential affect: The crux of the teacher expectancy issue. In J. Brophy (Ed.), *Advances in research on teaching: Expectations in the classroom* (pp. 183–214). Greenwich, CT: JAI Press.

Bailey, B., Scantlebury, K., & Letts, W. (1997). It's not my style: Using disclaimers to ignore issues in science. *Journal of Teacher Education, 48*(1), 29–35.

Beaman, R., Wheldall, K., & Kemp, C. (2006). Differential teacher attention to boys and girls in the classroom. *Educational Review, 58*(3), 339–366.

Beck, R., Black, L., Naylor, P., & Shabaka, D. (2005). *World history: Patterns of interaction*. Evanston, IL: McDougal Littell.

Bisaga, K., Whitaker, A., Davies, M., Chuang, S., Feldman, J., & Walsh, B. T. (2005). Eating disorders and depressive symptoms in urban high school girls from different ethnic backgrounds. *Journal of Developmental Behavioral Pediatrics, 26*(4), 257–266.

Bracey, G. (2006, November). Separate but superior? A review of issues and data bearing on single-sex education. *Educational Policy Research Unit*. Tempe: Arizona State University.

Brown, L. M. (2003). *Girlfighting: Betrayal and rejection among girls*. New York: New York University Press.

Cairns, E. (1990). The relationship between adolescent perceived self-competence and attendance at single-sex secondary school. *British Journal of Educational Psychology, 60*(3), 207–211.

Campbell, P. B., & Sanders, J. (2002). Challenging the system: Assumptions and data behind the push for single-sex schools. In A. Datnow & L. Hubbard (Eds.), *Gender in policy and practice: Perspectives on single-sex and coeducational schooling* (pp. 31–46). New York: Routledge/Falmer.

Chick, K. (2006). Gender balance in K-12 American history textbooks. *Social Studies Research and Practice, 1*(3), 2006. Available online at www.socstrp.org

Clarke, E. H. (1873). *Sex in education; or, a fair chance for the girls*. Boston: J. R. Osgood and Company.

Dalton, B. (2007). *Advanced mathematics and science course-taking in the spring high school senior classes of 1982, 1992, and 2004* (NCES 2007-312). Washington, DC: U.S. Department of Education.

Darling-Hammond, L. (1997). *The right to learn: A blueprint for creating schools that work*. San Francisco: Jossey-Bass.

Datnow, A., & Hubbard, L. (Eds.). (2002). *Gender in policy and practice: Perspectives on single-sex and coeducational schooling*. New York: Routledge/Falmer.

Duffy, J., Warren, K., & Walsh, M. (2001). Classroom interactions: Gender of teacher, gender of student, and classroom subject. *Sex Roles, 45*(9/10), 579–593.

Evans, L., & Davies, K. (2000). No sissy boys here: A content analysis of the representation of masculinity in elementary school reading textbooks. *Sex Roles, 42*, 255–270.

Fan, L., & Kaeley, G. (2000). The influence of textbooks on teaching strategies. *Mid-Western Educational Researcher, 13*(4), 2–9.

Fang, Z. (1996). A review of research on teacher beliefs and practices. *Educational Research, 38*(1), 47–65.

Francis, B. (2000). *Boys, girls, and achievement: Addressing the classroom issues*. London: Routledge/Falmer.

Gillis, J. (2007, October). 7.3 Million participants in high school sports. *High School Today*. Retrieved October 20, 2007, from http://www.nfhs.org/

Girls, Inc. (2006). *The SuperGirl dilemma: Girls feel the pressure to be perfect, accomplished, thin, and accommodating*. New York: New York.

Greenfield, L., & Brumberg, J. (2006). *Thin*. San Francisco, CA: Chronicle Books.

Gurian, M., Henley, P., and Trueman, T. (2001). *Boys and girls learn differently! A guide for teachers and parents*. San Francisco, CA: Jossey-Bass.

Hamilton, M., Anderson, D., Braoddus, M., & Young, K. (2006). Gender stereotyping and under-representation of female characters in 200 popular children's picture books: A twenty-first century update. *Sex Roles, 55*, 757–765.

Hyde, J. (2005). The gender similarities hypothesis. *American Psychologist, 60*(6), 581–592.

Hyde, J., and Lindberg, S. (2007). Facts and assumptions about the nature of gender differences and the implications for gender equity. In S. Klein (Ed.), *Handbook for achieving gender equity through education* (pp. 19–32) Mahwah, NJ: Lawrence Erlbaum Publishers.

Jackson, C. (2002). Can single-sex classes in co-educational schools enhance the learning experiences of girls and/or boys? An exploration of pupils' perceptions. *British Educational Research Journal, 28*(1), 37–48.

Jones, G., M., & Gerig, T. M. (1994). Silent sixth-grade students: Characteristics, achievement, and teacher expectations. *The Elementary School Journal, 95*(2), 169–182.

KidsHealth, (2007). *What kids say about bullying*. Retrieved July 29, 2008, from http://www.kidshealth.org/kid/feeling/school/poll_bullying.html

Kimmel, M. (2006a). What about the boys? What the current debates tell us—and don't tell us—about boys in school. In E. Disch (Ed.), *Reconstructing gender: A multicultural anthology*. (4th ed, pp. 361–375). New York: McGraw-Hill.

Kimmel, M. (Fall 2006b). A war against boys? *Dissent*. Retrieved September 29, 2007, from http://dissentmagazine.org/article/?article=700

Kimmel, M. (2008). *Guyland: The perilous world where boys become men*. New York: Harper.

Lederman, D. (2006). Clues about the gender gap. *Inside Higher Ed*. Retrieved March 30, 2008, from http://insidehighered.com/news/2007/01/15/freshmen

Lee, V., Marks, H., & Byrd, T. (1993). Sexism in single-sex and coeducational independent secondary schools. *Sociology of Education, 67*(2), 92–120.

Lewin, T. (2006, July 9). At college, women are leaving men in the dust. *New York Times*. Retrieved November 18, 2009, from http://www.nytimes.com/2006/07/09/education/09college.html?pagewanted=1&_r=1&ei=5087&en=8e11d347c097fcbf&ex=1152590400

Mael, F. (1998). A single-sex and coeducational schooling: Relationships to socioemotional and academic development. *Review of Research in Education, 68*(2), 70–85.

Mead, S. (2006). *The evidence suggests otherwise: The truth about boys and girls*. Washington, DC: The Education Sector. Retrieved September 30, 2007, from http://www.educationsector.org

Meehan, D. (2007). *Learning like a girl: Educating our daughters in schools of their own*. New York: Public Affairs.

Meier, D., Kohn, A., Darling-Hammond, L., Sizer, T. R., et al. (2004). *Many children left behind: How the No Child Left Behind Act is damaging our children and our schools*. Boston: Beacon Press.

Merten, D. (1997). The meaning of meanness: Popularity, competition, and conflict among junior high school girls. *Sociology of Education, 70*, 175–191.

Milson, A., & Gallo, G. (2006). Bullying in middle schools: Prevention and intervention. *Middle School Journal, 37*(3), 12–19.

National Association for Single Sex Education (2008). Single-sex schools/Schools with single-sex classrooms/What's the difference? Retrieved November 18, 2008, from http://www.singlesexschools.org/schools-schools.htm

National Center for Education Statistics. (2004). *Trends in educational equity for girls and women*. Washington, DC: U.S. Department of Education.

National Center for Education Statistics. (2008). *Digest of education statistics, 2007*. U.S. Department of Education: Washington, DC.

National Coalition for Women and Girls in Education. *Title IX at 35*. (2007). Washington, DC: Author.

National Women's Law Center. (2007a). *The battle for gender equity in athletics in elementary and secondary schools*. Retrieved July 28, 2008, from http://www.nwlc.org/pdf/Battle%202007.pdf

National Women's Law Center. (2007b). *When girls don't graduate we all fail: A call to improve the graduation rates of girls*. Washington, DC: National Women's Law Center. Retrieved July 29, 2008, from http://www.nwlc.org/pdf/DropoutReport.pdf

Orfield, G. (2004). *Losing our future: Being left behind by the graduation rate crises*. Urban Institute. Retrieved October 8, 2007, from www.urban.org

Perie, M., Grigg, W. S., & Donahue, P. (2005). *The nation's report card: Reading 2005*. Washington, DC: U.S. Department of Education, Institute of Education Sciences, National Center for Education Statistics. Retrieved November 18, 2008, from http://nces.ed.gov/nationsreportcard/reading/

Pollack, W. S. (1998). *Real boys: Rescuing our sons from the myths of boyhood*. New York: Holt and Company.

Reichert, M., & Hawley, R. (2006). Confronting the "boy problem": A self-study approach to deepen schools' moral stance. *Teachers College Record*. ID Number: 12813. Retrieved November 18, 2008, from www.tcrecord.org

Reisman, D. (1990). A margin of difference: The case for single-sex education. In J. R. Blau (Ed.), *Social roles and social institutions* (pp. 243–244) Boulder, CO: Westview Press.

Riordan, C. (2002). What do we know about the effects of single-sex schools in the private sector? Implications for public schools. In A. Datnow & L. Hubbard (Eds.), *Doing gender in policy and practice: Perspectives on single-sex and coeducational schooling* (pp. 10–30). New York: Routledge/Falmer.

Rivers, C., & Barnett, R. C. (2006, April 9). The myth of "the boy crisis." *Washington Post*, B01.

Rivers, C., & Barnett, R. C. (2007, October 28). The difference myth. *Boston Globe*. Retrieved November 18, 2008, from http://www.boston.com/news/globe/ideas/articles/2007/10/28/the_difference_myth/

Sadker, D., & Sadker, M., & Zittleman, K. (2008). *Teachers, schools, and society*. New York: McGraw Hill.

Sadker, M., & Sadker, D. (1994). *Failing at fairness: How America's schools cheat girls*. New York: Scribners.

Sadker, D. & Zittleman, K. (2009). *Still failing at fairness: How gender bias cheats boys and girls in school and what we can do about it* (8th ed.). New York: Scribners.

Sax, L. (2005) *Why gender matters: What parents and teachers need to know about the emerging science of sex differences*. New York: Doubleday.

Sommers, C. H. (2000, May). The war against boys. *Atlantic Monthly*, 285(5) 59–74.

Spencer, R., Porche, M., & Tolman, D. (2003). We've come a long way—maybe; New challenges for gender equity education. *Teachers College Record, 105*(9), 1774–1807.

Starnes, B. A. (2004). Textbooks, school reform, and the silver lining. *Phi Delta Kappan, 86*(2), 170–171.

Tolman, D., Impett, E., Tracy, A., Michael, A. (2006). Looking good, sounding good: Femininity ideology and adolescent girls' mental health. *Psychology of Women Quarterly, 30*, 85–95.

Tyack, D., & Hansot, E. (1990). *Learning together: A history of coeducation in American schools*. New Haven, CT: Yale University Press.

Tyre, P. (2006, January 30). The trouble with boys. *Newsweek*. Retrieved November 18, 2008, from http://www.newsweek.com/id/47522

Warrington, M., and Younger, M. (2003) "We decided to give it a twirl": Single-sex teaching in English comprehensive schools. *Gender and Education, 15*(4), 339–350.

Witt, H. (2007). School discipline tougher on African Americans. *Chicago Tribune*. Retrieved October 5, 2007, from http://www.chicagotribune.com/news/nationworld/chi-070924discipline,1,6597576.story?ctrack=1&cset=true

Zittleman, K. (2007). Gender perceptions of middle schoolers: The good and the bad. *Middle Grades Research Journal, 2*(2), 65–97.

CHAPTER 7

Classrooms For Diversity: Rethinking Curriculum and Pedagogy

Mary Kay Thompson Tetreault

> It's time to start learning about things they told you you didn't need to know ... learning about me, instead of learning about them, starting to learn about her instead of learning about him. It's a connection that makes education education.
>
> (a student of European and African American ancestry)

This student's reflection on her education signals a twin transformation that is pushing us to rethink our traditional ways of teaching. The first is that students in our classrooms are increasingly more diverse, and the second is that traditional course content has been enriched by the new scholarship in women studies, cultural studies, and multicultural studies. It is in the classroom that these transformations intersect, and it rests on the teacher to make education "education" for this student and for the majority who believe their education was not made for them—women of all backgrounds, people of color, and men who lack privilege because of their social class—by bringing the two aspects of the transformation together. The current challenges to classroom teachers are not only to incorporate multiple perspectives into the curriculum but also to engage in pedagogical practices that bring in the voices of students as a source for learning rather than managing or controlling them.

FEMINIST PHASE THEORY

One of the most effective ways I have found to set a frame for envisioning a gender-balanced, multicultural curriculum while capturing the reforms that have occurred over the past 35 years is *feminist phase theory*. Conceptually rooted in the scholarship on women, feminist phase theory is a classification system of the evolution in thought about the incorporation of women's traditions, history, and experiences into selected disciplines. The model I have developed identifies five common phases of thinking about women: *male-defined curriculum, contribution curriculum*, *bifocal curriculum*, *women's curriculum*, and *gender-balanced curriculum*. A gender-balanced perspective—one that is rooted in feminist scholarship—takes into account the experiences, perspectives, and voices of women as well as men. It examines the similarities and differences between women and men and considers how gender interacts with such factors as ethnicity, race, culture, and class.

The language of this system or schema, particularly the word *phase*, and the description of one phase and then another suggest a sequential hierarchy in which one phase supplants another. Before reviewing the schema, please refrain from thinking of these phases in a linear fashion; envision them as a series of intersecting circles, or patches on a quilt, or threads in a tapestry, that interact and undergo changes in response to one another. It is more accurate to view the phases as different emphases that coexist in feminist research. The important thing is that teachers, scholars, and curriculum developers ask and answer certain questions at each phase.

The following section identifies key concepts and questions articulated initially at each phase, using examples from history, literature, and science; it then discusses how the phases interact and undergo changes in response to one another. The final part of this chapter shows teachers grappling with the intersection of changes in the disciplines and changes in the student population and presents four themes of analysis: *mastery*, *voice*, *authority*, and *positionality*. The chapter concludes with specific objectives, practices, and teaching suggestions for incorporating content about women into the K–12 curriculum in social studies, language arts, and science.

Male-Defined Curriculum

Male-defined curriculum rests on the assumption that the male experience is universal, is representative of humanity, and constitutes a basis for generalizing about all human beings. The knowledge that is researched and taught, the substance of learning, is knowledge articulated by and about men. There is little or no consciousness that the existence of women as a group is an anomaly calling for a broader definition of knowledge. The female experience is subsumed under the male experience. For example, feminist scientists have cited methodological problems in some research about sex differences that draws conclusions about females based on experiments done only on males or that uses limited (usually White and middle-class) experimental populations from which scientists draw conclusions about all males and females.

The incorporation of women into the curriculum has not only taught us about women's lives but has also led to questions about our lopsided rendition of men's lives in which we pay attention primarily to men in the public world and conceal their lives in the private world. Historians, for example, are posing a series of interesting questions about men's history: What do we need to unlearn about men's history? What are the taken-for-granted truths about men's history that we need to rethink? How do we get at the significant masculine truths? Is man's primary sense of self defined in relation to the public sphere only? How does this sense relate to boyhood, adolescence, family life, recreation, and love? What do the answers to these questions imply about the teaching of history?

Feminist scholarship—like African American, Native American, Chicano/Latino, and Asian American scholarship—reveals the systematic and contestable exclusions in the male-defined curriculum. When we examine curriculum through the lens of this scholarship, we are forced to reconsider our understanding of the most fundamental conceptualization of knowledge and

Table 7.1   Male-Defined Curriculum

Characteristics of Phase	Questions Commonly Asked about Women in History*	Questions Commonly Asked about Women in Literature*	Questions Commonly Asked about Women in Science*
The absence of women is not noted. There is no consciousness that the male experience is a "particular knowledge" selected from a wider universe of possible knowledge and experience. It is valued, emphasized, and viewed as the knowledge most worth having.	Who is the author of a particular history? What is her or his race, ethnicity, religion, ideological orientation, social class, place of origin, and historical period? How does incorporating women's experiences lead to new understandings of the most fundamental ordering of social relations, institutions, and power arrangements? How can we define the content and methodology of history so it will be a history of us all?	How is traditional humanism, with an integrated self at its center and an authentic view of life, in effect part of patriarchal ideology? How can the objectivist illusion be dismantled? How can the idea of a literary canon of "great literature" be challenged? How are writing and reading political acts? How do race, class, and gender relate to the conflict, sufferings, and passions that attend these realities? How can we study language as specific discourse, that is, specific linguistic strategies in specific situations, rather than as universal language?	How do scientific studies reveal cultural values? What cultural, historical, and gender values are projected onto the physical and natural world? How might gender be a bias that influences choice of questions, hypotheses, subjects, experimental design, or theory formation in science? What is the underlying philosophy of an androcentric science that values objectivity, rationality, and dominance? How can the distance between the subject and the scientific observer be shortened so that the scientist has some feeling for or empathy with the organism? How can gender play a crucial role in transforming science?

*New questions generated by feminist scholars.

social relations within our society. We understand in a new way that knowledge is a social construction written by individual human beings who live and think at a particular time and within a particular social framework. All works in literature, science, and history, for example, have an author, male or female, White or ethnic or racial minority, elite or middle class or occasionally poor with motivations and beliefs. The scientist's questions and activities, for instance, are shaped, often unconsciously, by the great social issues of the day (see Table 7.1). Different perspectives on the same subject will change the patterns discerned.

Contribution Curriculum

Early efforts to reclaim women's rightful place in the curriculum were to search for missing women within a male framework. Although there was the recognition that women were missing, men continued to serve as the norm, the representative, the universal human being. Outstanding women emerged who fit this male norm of excellence or greatness or conformed to implicit assumptions about appropriate roles for women outside the home. In literature, female authors were added who performed well within the masculine tradition, internalizing its standards of art and its views on social roles. Great women of science who made it in the male scientific world, most frequently Marie Curie, for example, were added.

Examples of contribution history can be seen in U.S. history textbooks. They now include the contributions of notable American women who were outstanding in the public sphere as rulers or as contributors to wars or reform movements to a remarkable degree. Queen Liliuokalani, Hawaii's first reigning queen and a nationalist, is included in the story of the kingdom's annexation. Molly Pitcher and Deborah Sampson are depicted as contributors to the Revolutionary War, as is Clara Barton to the Civil War effort. Some authors have also included women who conform to the assumption that it is acceptable for women to engage in activities outside the home if they are an extension of women's nurturing role within the family. Examples of this are Dorothea Dix, Jane Addams, Eleanor Roosevelt, and Mary McLeod Bethune (Tetreault, 1986).

The lesson to be learned from understanding these limitations of early contribution history is not to disregard the study of notable women but to include those who worked to reshape the world according to a feminist reordering of values. This includes efforts to increase women's self-determination through a feminist transformation of the home; to increase education, political rights, and women's rights to control their bodies; and to improve their economic status. A history with women at the center moves beyond paying attention to caring for the unfortunate in the public sphere to how exceptional women influenced the lives of women in general (see Table 7.2). Just as Mary McLeod Bethune's role in the New Deal is worth teaching to our students, so is her aggressive work to project a positive image of African American women to the nation through her work in African American women's clubs and the launching of the *Afro-American Woman's Journal* (Smith, 2003).

Bifocal Curriculum

In bifocal curriculum, feminist scholars have made an important shift from a perspective that views men as the norm to one that opens up the possibility of seeing the world through women's eyes (Gornick & Moran, 1971; Millett, 1970). This dual vision, or bifocal perspective, generated global questions about women and about the differences between women and men. Historians investigated the separation between the public and the private sphere and asked, for example, how the division between them explains women's lives. Some elaborated on the construct by identifying arenas of female power in the domestic sphere. Literary critics tried to provide a new understanding of a distinctively female literary tradition and a theory of women's literary creativity. These critics sought to provide models for understanding the dynamics of female literary response to male literary assertion and coercion (Showalter, 1977). Scientists grapple with definitions of women's and men's nature by asking how the public and private, biology and culture, and personal and impersonal inform each other and affect men and women, science, and nature.

Table 7.2   Contribution Curriculum

Characteristics of Phase	Questions Commonly Asked about Women in History	Questions Commonly Asked about Women in Literature	Questions Commonly Asked about Women in Science
The absence of women is noted. There is a search for missing women according to a male norm of greatness, excellence, or humanness. Women are considered exceptional, deviant, or other. Women are added into history, but the content and notions of historical significance are not challenged.	Who are the notable women missing from history and what did they and ordinary women contribute in areas or movements traditionally dominated by men, for example, during major wars or during reform movements, such as abolitionism or the labor movement? What did notable and ordinary women contribute in areas that are an extension of women's traditional roles, for example, caring for the poor and the sick? How have major economic and political changes such as industrialization or extension of the franchise affected women in the public sphere? How did notable and ordinary women respond to their oppression, particularly through women's rights organizations? *Who were outstanding women who advocated a feminist transformation of the home, who contributed to women's greater self-determination through increased education, the right to control their bodies, an increase in their political rights, and the improvement of their economic status? *What did women contribute through the settlement house and labor movements?	Who are the missing female authors whose subject matter and use of language and form meet the male norm of "masterpiece"? What primary biological facts and interpretations are missing about major female authors?	Who are the notable women scientists who have made contributions to mainstream science? How is women's different (and supposedly inferior) nature related to hormones, brain lateralization, and sociobiology? Where are the missing females in scientific experiments? What is the current status of women within the scientific profession? *How does adding minority women into the history of science reveal patterns of exclusion and recast definitions of what it means to practice science and to be a scientist? *How is the exclusion of women from science related to the way science is done and thought? *What is the usual pattern of women working in science? How is it the same as or different from the pattern of notable women? *How do our definitions of science need to be broadened to evaluate women's contributions to science? Do institutions of science need to be reshaped to accommodate women? If so, how?

*New questions generated by feminist scholars.

Scholars have pointed out some of the problems with bifocal knowledge. Thinking about women and men is dualistic and dichotomized. Women and men are thought of as having different spheres, different notions of what is of value in life, different ways of imagining the human condition, and different associations with nature and culture. But both views are valued. In short, women are thought of as a group that is complementary but equal to men; there are some truths for men and there are some truths for women. General analyses of men's and women's experiences often come dangerously close to reiterating the sexual stereotypes scholars are trying to overcome. Because many people believe that the public sphere is more valuable than the private sphere, there is a tendency to slip back into thinking of women as inferior and subordinate (Christian, 1980; Lerner, 1979; Rosaldo & Lamphere, 1974).

The generalized view of women and men that predominates in the bifocal curriculum often does not allow for distinctions within groups as large and as complex as women and men. Important factors such as historical period, geographic location, structural barriers, race, paternity, sexual orientation, and social class, to name a few, clearly make a difference. Other common emphases in the bifocal curriculum are the oppression of women and the exploration of that oppression. Exposés of woman hating in history and literature are common. The emphasis is on the *misogyny* (the hatred of women) of the human experience, particularly the means men have used to advance their authority and to assert or imply female inferiority. The paradoxes of women's existence are sometimes overlooked with this emphasis on oppression. For example, although women have been excluded from positions of power, a few of them as wives and daughters in powerful families were often closer to actual power than were men. If some women were dissatisfied with their status and role, most adjusted and did not join efforts to improve women's status. Too much emphasis on women's oppression perpetuates a patriarchal framework presenting women as primarily passive, reacting only to the pressures of a sexist society. In the main, it emphasizes men thinking and women being thought about.

Women's scholarship from the 1970s through the present (Collins, 2000; Goldberger, Tarule, Clinchy, & Belenky, 1996; Schmitz, Butler, Guy-Sheftall, & Rosenfelt, 2004) has helped us see that understanding women's oppression is more complex than we initially thought. We do not yet have adequate concepts to explain gender systems founded on a division of labor and sexual asymmetry. To understand gender systems, it is necessary to take a structural and experiential perspective that asks from a woman's point of view where we are agents and where we are not, where our relations with men are egalitarian and where they are not. This questioning may lead to explanations of why women's experiences and interpretations of their world can differ significantly from those of men.

Furthermore, the concepts with which we approach our analysis need to be questioned. Anthropologists have pointed out that our way of seeing the world—for instance, the idea of complementary spheres for women (the private sphere) and men (the public sphere)—is a product of our experience in a Western, modern, industrial, capitalistic state with a specific history. We distort our understanding of other social systems by imposing our worldview on them (Atkinson, 1982). Feminist critics are calling for rethinking not only categories such as the domestic versus the public sphere and production and reproduction but also gender itself (Butler, 1993).

One of the most important things we have learned about a bifocal perspective is the danger of generalizing too much, of longing for women's history instead of writing histories about women. We must guard against establishing a feminist version of great literature and then resisting any modifications or additions to it. We have also learned that the traditional disciplines are limited in their ability to shed light on gender complexities, and it becomes apparent that there is a need for an interdisciplinary perspective (see Table 7.3).

Women's Curriculum

The most important idea to emerge in women's scholarship is that women's activities, not men's, are the measure of significance. What was formerly devalued—the content of women's everyday lives—assumes new value as scholars investigate female rituals, housework, childbearing, child rearing, sexuality, friendship, and studies of the life cycle. For instance, scientists investigate how research on areas of interest primarily to women—menstruation, childbirth, and menopause—challenge existing scientific theories.

Historians document women's efforts to break out of their traditional sphere of the home in a way that uses women's activities, not men's, as the measure of historical significance. These activities include women's education, paid work, and volunteer work outside the home, particularly in women's clubs and associations. Of equal importance is the development of a collective feminist consciousness, that is, of women's consciousness of their own distinct role in society. Analyses begun in the bifocal phase continue to explore what sex and gender have meant for the majority of women.

As scholars look more closely at the complex patterns of women's lives, they see the need for a pluralistic conceptualization of women. Although thinking of women as a monolithic group provides valuable information about patterns of continuity and change in the areas most central to women's lives, generalizing about a group as vast and diverse as women leads to inaccuracies. The subtle interactions among gender and other variables are investigated. Historians ask how the particulars of race, ethnicity, social class, marital status, and sexual orientation challenge the homogeneity of women's experiences. Third World feminists critique hegemonic "Western" feminisms and formulate autonomous geographically, historically, and culturally grounded feminist concerns and strategies (Mohanty, 2003).

Feminist scholars have helped us see the urgency of probing and analyzing the interactive nature of the oppressions of race, ethnicity, class, and gender (Collins, 2000; Hune & Nomura, 2003; Kesselman, McNair, & Schniedewind, 2002; Ruiz & DuBois, 2000; Saldivar-Hull, 2000). We are reminded that we can no longer take a liberal reformist approach that does not probe the needs of the system that are being satisfied by oppression (Acuña, 2004; Louie & Omatsu, 2001; Shorris, 2001; Weatherford, 1992). We have to take seriously the model of feminist scholarship that analyzes women's status within the social, cultural, historical, political, and economic contexts. Only then will issues of gender be understood in relation to the economic needs of both male dominance and capitalism that undergird such oppressions.

Questions about sex and gender are set within historical, ideological, and cultural contexts, including the culture's definition of the facts of biological development and what they mean for individuals. Researchers ask, for example, why these attitudes toward sexuality are prevalent at this time in history. What are the ways in which sexual words, categories, and ideology mirror the organization of society as a whole? What are the socioeconomic factors contributing to them? How do current conceptions of the body reflect social experiences and professional needs?

Table 7.3   Bifocal Curriculum

Characteristics of Phase	Questions Commonly Asked about Women in History	Questions Commonly Asked about Women in Literature	Questions Commonly Asked about Women in Science
Human experience is conceptualized primarily in dualist categories: male and female, private and public, agency and communion. Emphasis is on a complementary but equal conceptualization of men's and women's spheres and personal qualities. There is a focus on women's oppression and on misogyny. Women's efforts to overcome the oppression are presented. Efforts to include women lead to the insight that the traditional content, structure, and methodology of the disciplines are more appropriate to the male experience.	How does the division between the public and the private sphere explain women's lives? Who oppressed women, and how were they oppressed? *What are forms of power and value in women's world? *How have women been excluded from and deprived of power and value in men's sphere? *How do gender systems create divisions between the sexes such that experience and interpretations of their world can differ significantly from men's? *How can we rethink categories like public and private, productive and reproductive, sex and gender?	Who are the missing minor female authors whose books are unobtainable, whose lives have never been written, and whose works have been studied casually, if at all? How is literature a record of the collective consciousness of patriarchy? What myths and stereotypes about women are present in male literature? How can we critique the meritocratic pretensions of traditional literary history? How can we pair opposite-sex texts in literature as a way of understanding the differences between women's and men's experiences? How is literature one of the expressive modes of a female subculture that developed with the distinction of separate spheres for women and men? *How can feminist literary critics resist establishing their own great canon of literature and any additions to it?	How have the sciences defined (and misdefined) the nature of women? Why are there so few women scientists? What social and psychological forces have kept women in the lower ranks or out of science entirely? How do women fit into the study of history of science and health care? How do scientific findings, originally carried out on males of a species, change when carried out on the females of the same species? How do the theories and interpretations of sociobiology require constant testing and change to fit the theory for males and females with regard to competition, sexual selection, and infanticide? How does the science/gender system—the network of associations and disjunctions between public and private, personal and impersonal, and masculine and feminine—inform each other and affect men and women, science and nature? *What are the structural barriers to women in science?

*New questions generated by feminist scholars.

Life histories and autobiographies shed light on societies' perceptions of women and their perceptions of themselves. Women's individual experiences are revealed through these stories and contribute to the fashioning of the human experience from the perspective of women. Scholars find it necessary to draw on other disciplines for a clearer vision of the social structure and culture of societies as individuals encounter them in their daily life. Likewise, there are calls for new unifying frameworks and different ways to think of periods in history and literature to identify concepts that accommodate women's history and traditions. There is also a more complex conceptualization of historical time. The emphases in much history are on events, units of time too brief to afford a sense of structural change. Structural changes are changes in the way people think about their own reality and the possibilities for other realities. L'Ecole des Annales in France (a group of historians who pioneered the use of such public records as birth, marriage, and death certificates in historical analysis) has distinguished between events and what they call the *longue durée* (1982). By this, they mean the slow, glacial changes, requiring hundreds of years to complete, that represent significant shifts in the way people think.

Examples of areas of women's history that lend themselves to this concept are the structural change from a male-dominated to an egalitarian perspective and the transformation of women's traditional role in the family to their present roles as wives, mothers, and paid workers outside the home. Also important is the demographic change in the average number of children per woman of childbearing age from seven to fewer than two children between 1800 and 1990 (see Table 7.4).

Gender-Balanced Curriculum

This phase continues many of the inquiries begun in the women's curriculum phase, but it articulates questions about how women and men relate to and complement one another. Conscious of the limitations of seeing women in isolation and aware of the relational character of gender, researchers search for the nodal points at which women's and men's experiences intersect. Historians and literary critics ask whether the private, as well as the public, aspects of life are presented as a continuum in women's and men's experience.

The pluralistic and multifocal conception of women that emerged in the women's curriculum phase is extended to human beings. A central idea in this phase is *positionality* (Alcoff, 2003; Haraway, 1997; Harding, 2004), which means that important aspects of our identity (for example, our gender, race, class, and age) are markers of relational positions rather than essential qualities. Their effects and implications change according to context. Recently, feminist thinkers have seen knowledge as valid when it comes from an acknowledgment of the knower's specific position in any context always defined by gender, race, class, and other variables (Code, 1991).

Scientists ask explicit questions about the invention and reinvention of nature. For example, they ask questions about the meanings of the behavior and social lives of monkeys and apes and male–female relations in animals and inquire about how such variables as age, species, and individual variation challenge current theories. They also explore contemporary technoscience—its stories and dreams, its facts and delusions, its institutions and politics, and its scientific advances (Haraway, 1991, 1997).

Table 7.4   Women's Curriculum

Characteristics of Phase	Questions Commonly Asked about Women in History	Questions Commonly Asked about Women in Literature	Questions Commonly Asked about Women in Science
Scholarly inquiry pursues new questions, new categories, and new notions of significance that illuminate women's traditions, history, culture, values, visions, and perspectives.	What were the majority of women doing at a particular time in history? What was the significance of these activities?	What does women's sphere—for example, domesticity and family, education, marriage, sexuality, and love—reveal about our culture?	How do the cultural dualisms associated with masculinity and femininity permeate scientific thought and discourse?
A pluralistic conception of women emerges that acknowledges diversity and recognizes that variables besides gender shape women's lives—for example, race, ethnicity, and social class.	How can female friendships between kin, mothers, daughters, and friends be analyzed as one aspect of women's overall relations with others?	How can we contrast the fictional image of women in literature with the complexity and variety of the roles of individual women in real life as workers, housewives, revolutionaries, mothers, lovers, and so on?	How do women's actual experiences, as compared to the physician's analysis or scientific theory, challenge the traditional paradigms of science and of the health care systems?
Women's experience is allowed to speak for itself. Feminist history is rooted in the personal and the specific; it builds from that to the general.	What kind of productive work, paid and unpaid, did women do and under what conditions?	How do the particulars of race, ethnicity, social class, marital status, and sexual orientation, as revealed in literature, challenge the thematic homogeneity of women's experiences?	How does research on areas of primary interest to women, for instance, menopause, childbirth, and menstruation/estrus, challenge existing scientific theories?
The public and the private are seen as a continuum in women's experiences.	What were the reproductive activities of women? How did they reproduce the American family?		How do variables other than sex and gender, such as age, species, and individual variation, challenge current theories?
Women's experience is analyzed within the social, cultural, historical, political, and economic contexts.	How did the variables of race, ethnicity, social class, marital status, and sexual preference affect women's experience?	How does literature portray what binds women together and what separates them because of race, ethnicity, social class, marital status, and sexual orientation?	How do the experiences of female primates and the variation among species of primates—for example, competition among females, female agency in sexuality, and infanticide—test the traditional paradigms?
Efforts are made to reconceptualize knowledge to encompass the female experience. The conceptualization of knowledge is not characterized by disciplinary thinking but becomes multidisciplinary.	What new categories need to be added to the study of history, for instance, romance, housework, childbearing, and child rearing?	How does the social and historical context of a work of literature shed light on it?	
	How have women of different races and classes interacted throughout history?		
	What are appropriate ways of organizing or periodizing women's history? For example, how will examining women's experiences at each stage of the life span help us to understand women's experiences on their own terms?		

Accompanying this particularistic perspective is attention to the larger context, for example, the interplay among situation, meaning, economic systems, family organization, and political systems. Thus, historians ask how gender inequities are linked to economics, family organization, marriage, ritual, and politics. Research scientists probe how differences between the male and female body have been used to justify a social agenda that privileges men economically, socially, and politically. In this phase, a revolutionary relationship comes to exist between things traditionally treated as serious, primarily the activities of men in the public sphere, and those things formerly perceived as trivial, namely the activities of women in the private sphere.

This new relationship leads to a recentering of knowledge in the disciplines, a shift from a male-centered perspective to one that includes both females and males. Studying the dynamics of gender sheds light on masculinity and the implications of gender studies for men. The new field of men's studies investigates the origins, structures, and dynamics of masculinity (Kimmel, Hearn, & Connell, 2005). Men's studies investigates how men can participate in feminism as full and equal partners, respecting gender differences while sharing a common vision with women for an oppression-free future (Schacht & Ewing, 2007). This reconceptualization of knowledge from a feminist perspective works toward a more holistic view of the human experience.

Feminist scholars have cautioned against moving too quickly from women's curriculum to gender-balanced curricula. As the historian Gerda Lerner (1979) observed, our decade-and-a-half-old investigation of women's history is only a speck on the horizon compared to the centuries-old tradition of male-defined history. By turning too quickly to studies of gender, we risk short-circuiting important directions in women's studies and again having women's history and experiences subsumed under those of men. It remains politically important for feminists to defend women as women in order to counteract the male domination that continues to exist. The French philosopher Kristeva (cited in Moi, 1985) and, more recently, Butler (2004) push us to new considerations when they urge women (and men) to recognize the falsifying nature of masculinity and femininity, to explore how the fact of being born male or female determines one's position in relation to power, and to envision more fluid gender identities that have the potential to liberate both women and men to a fuller personhood (see Table 7.5). Of particular interest to teachers is the work of Thorne (1993), who draws on her daily observations in the classroom and on the playground to show how children construct gender and experience gender in the school.

Changes in Traditional Ways of Teaching

Feminist scholarship has helped us understand that all knowledge, and therefore all classroom knowledge, is a social construction. This insight affirms the evolving nature of knowledge and the role of teachers and students in its ongoing construction. For me, the term *pedagogy* applies not just to teaching techniques but also to the whole classroom production of knowledge; it encompasses the full range of relationships among course materials, teachers, and students. Such broadened conceptualizations of pedagogy challenge the commonly held assumptions of the professor as a disinterested expert, the content as inherently "objective," and the method of delivery as irrelevant to the message (hooks, 1994). To educate students for a complex, multicultural, multiracial world, we need to include the perspectives and voices of those who have not been traditionally included—women of all backgrounds, people of color, and females

Table 7.5   Gender-Balanced Curriculum

Characteristics of Phase	Questions Commonly Asked about Women in History	Questions Commonly Asked about Women in Literature	Questions Commonly Asked about Women in Science
A multifocal, gender-balanced perspective is sought that weaves together women's and men's experiences into multilayered composites of human experience. At this stage, scholars are conscious of positionality. Positionality represents the insight that all women and men are located in historical contexts, contexts defined in terms of race, class, culture, and age, as well as gender, and that they gain their knowledge and their power from the specifics of their situations. Scholars begin to define what binds together and what separates the various segments of humanity. Scholars have a deepened understanding of how the private as well as public form a continuum in individual experience. They search for the nodal points at which comparative treatment of men's and women's experience is possible. Efforts are made to reconceptualize knowledge to reflect this multilayered composite of women's and men's experience. The conceptualization of knowledge is not characterized by disciplinary thinking but becomes multidisciplinary.	What is the knower's specific position in this historical context? How is gender asymmetry linked to economic systems, family organizations, marriage, ritual, and political systems? How can we compare women and men in all aspects of their lives to reveal gender as a crucial historical determinant? Are the private, as well as the public, aspects of history presented as a continuum in women's and men's experiences? How is gender a social construction? What does the particular construction of gender in a society tell us about the society that so constructed gender? What is the intricate relation between the construction of gender and the structure of power? How can we expand our conceptualization of historical time to a pluralistic one that conceives of three levels of history: structures, trends, and events? How can we unify approaches and types of knowledge of all social sciences and history as a means of investigating specific problems in relational history?	How does the author's specific position, as defined by gender, race, and class, affect this literary work? How can we validate the full range of human expression by selecting literature according to its insight into any aspect of human experience rather than according to how it measures up to a predetermined canon? Is the private as well as the public sphere presented as a continuum in women's and men's experiences? How can we pair opposite-sex texts in literature as a way of understanding how female and male characters experience "maleness" and "femaleness" as a continuum of "humanness"? How do the variables of race, ethnicity, social class, marital status, and sexual orientation affect the experience of female and male literary characters? How can we rethink the concept of periodicity to accentuate the continuity of life and to contain the multitude of previously ignored literary works, for example, instead of Puritanism, the contexts for and consequences of sexuality? How can we deconstruct the opposition between masculinity and femininity?	What explicit questions need to be raised about the invention and reinvention of nature? What is the meaning of male–female relations in animals? How do variables such as age, species, and individual variation challenge current theories? What are the limits to generalizing beyond the data collected on limited samples to other genders, species, and conditions not sampled in the experimental protocol? How have sex differences been used to assign men and women to particular roles in the social hierarchy? How have differences between the male and female body been used to justify a social agenda that privileges men economically, socially, and politically?

and males who perceive their education as not made for them. The anthropologist Renato Rosaldo (1994) has captured well how diverse classrooms contribute to new constructions of knowledge and change relationships among teachers and students:

> The question before us now is . . . how to teach more effectively in changed classroom environments. The new classrooms are not like the old ones. . . . In diverse classrooms, the question of "The Other" begins to dissolve. Who gets to be the we and who gets to be the other rotates from one day to the next, depending on the topic of discussion. And before long the stable us/them dividing line evaporates into a larger mix of differences and solidarity. (p. 405)

Feminist teachers are demonstrating how they transform courses through their attention to cultural, ethnic, and gender diversity and give concrete form to the complexity of the struggles over knowledge, access, and power (hooks, 1994; Maher & Tetreault, 1994, 2001; Weiler, 1988). In *The Feminist Classroom*, Maher and I (Maher & Tetreault, 2001) show how all students may benefit from, and how some are even inspired by, college courses transformed by their professor's attention to cultural, ethnic, and gender diversity. We have found that the themes we used to analyze teaching and learning in 17 classrooms on six campuses across the country apply to elementary and secondary classrooms as well. The four themes—*mastery, authority, voice,* and *positionality*— all relate to issues present in today's classroom. Although all four deal with reconstituted relationships between new students and new disciplinary frameworks, the themes of mastery and authority focus on knowledge and its sources as well as on the voice and positionality of the students themselves.

Mastery has traditionally meant the goal of an individual student's rational comprehension of the material on the teacher's and expert's terms. Women (and other marginalized groups) must often give up their voices when they seek mastery on the terms of the dominant culture. We found classrooms undergoing a shift away from unidimensional sources of expertise to a multiplicity of new information and insights. Students were no longer mastering a specific body of material, nor were they emphasizing subjective experiences that risk excluding students from a wealth of knowledge. Rather, they were struggling through or integrating often widely various interpretations of texts, scientific research, and social problems. These teachers redefined mastery as interpretation, as increasingly sophisticated handling of the topics at hand, informed by but not limited to the students' links to the material from their own experience. For example, a Japanese American student reread an Emily Dickinson poem about silences and invisibilities to comment on her gender and ethnic marginality:

> I couldn't help thinking of the idea of a mute culture within a dominant culture. A "nobody" knowing she's different from the dominant culture keeps silent. . . . But to be somebody! How dreary! How public! So when you become a somebody and buy into the dominant culture, you have to live in their roles. A silly example: It's like watching a Walt

Disney movie as a child where Hayley Mills and these other girls dance and primp before a party singing "Femininity", how being a woman is all about looking pretty and smiling pretty and acting stupid to attract men. As a child I ate it up, at least it seemed benign. But once your eye gets put out and you realize how this vision has warped you, it would split your heart to try and believe that again, it would strike you dead. (Maher & Tetreault, 1994, pp. 104–105)

Students were stretched by such broadenings of interpretative frameworks and indeed became authorities for one another. A White male student in the same class said:

I could read Dickinson a thousand times and probably never try to relate to that because it just would never make an impression on me, but having the girls in that class interested in that particular topic, "How does that relate to me as a woman?" then I sit back and I think that's a really good question. Although I'm male I can learn how women react to women's texts as opposed to maybe the way I react to it or the teacher reacts to it. (Maher & Tetreault, 1994, p. 108)

The teachers in our study consciously used their *authority* to give students responsibility for their own learning (Finke, 1993). Students and professors became authorities for one another to the extent that they were explicit about themselves as social and political actors with respect to a text or an issue (Tetreault, 1991). The teachers also struggled with reconceptualizing the grounds for their own authority, both over the subject matter and with students, because their traditional positions as the sole representatives of expertise were called into question by these multiple new sources of knowledge. These professors shared a sense of their authority as being grounded in their own experiences and in their intellectual engagement with feminist scholarship and other relevant fields.

As important as the rethinking of the disciplines is the power of expression that these new forms of knowledge, coming from the students' questions as well as from new topics, give to women and to other previously silenced groups. We explored the effects on students through our theme of *voice*, which is frequently defined as the awakening of the students' own responses. However, we came to think of these classrooms as arenas where teachers and students fashion their voices rather than "find" them as they produce relevant experiences to shape a narrative of an emerging self.

Our fourth theme is *positionality*, which is defined in the section on gender-balanced curriculum. Positionality helps us to see the multiple ways in which the complex dynamics of difference and inequality, which come from outside society, also operate powerfully inside the classroom itself. Much of our emphasis in the past three decades has been on the consequences of sexism and racism on females and on students of color. We have learned much about how universalizing the position of maleness leads to intellectual domination.

Some educators and theorists are arguing that we need to become conscious in similar ways about the effects of universalizing the position of Whiteness (Frankenberg, 1993, 1997;

McIntosh, 1990; Morrison, 1993; Tatum, 1997). For example, how does the norm of Whiteness or maleness shape the construction of knowledge in classrooms? How do those assumptions contribute to the intellectual domination of groups? Why is it that when we think of the development of racial identity in our students, we think primarily of students of color rather than of White students? What happens in classrooms where Whiteness is marked, revealed as a position? In our culture, the presumptions of Whiteness or maleness act to constrict voice by universalizing the dominant positions, by letting them float free of "position."

Maher and I revisited data presented in *The Feminist Classroom* to examine how assumptions of Whiteness shape the construction of knowledge as it is produced and resisted in the classroom (Maher & Tetreault, 1997). We saw how the dominant voices continue to call the tune—that is, to maintain the conceptual and ideological frameworks through which suppressed voices are distorted or not fully heard. We saw more clearly the ways in which a thorough pedagogy of positionality must entail an excavation of Whiteness in its many dimensions and complexities. Understanding all of the ways in which positionality shapes learning is a long, interactive process.

The lessons that follow attempt to model teaching that is constructed to reveal the particular and the common denominators of human experience. These sample lessons are organized by the subject areas of language arts, science, and social studies, but they can be adapted to other subject areas as well.

Language Arts

Analyzing Children's Literature

Suggested Activities

Ask students to locate five of their favorite children's books, to read or reread them, and to keep a written record of their reactions to the books. Either on the chalkboard or on a sheet of newsprint, keep a record of the students' (and your) book choices. Divide the class into small groups according to the same or similar favorite books and have students share their written reactions to the books. Ask the groups to keep a record of the most noteworthy ideas that emerge from their small-group discussions. When you bring the small groups together, ask each group to present its noteworthy ideas. Ideas that emerge may be how differently they read the book now than at the time of their first reading; the differences and similarities in so-called girls' books and boys' books; the importance of multicultural or international perspectives; and what the stories reveal about the culture in which the stories are set. A follow-up activity could be to interview grandparents, parents, teachers, and other adults about characters and stories they remember from childhood. Questions to ask include these: How do they recall feeling about those stories? Have images of female and male behavior or expectations in children's stories changed? Is race or ethnicity treated similarly or differently?

Pairing Female and Male Autobiographies

Suggested Activities

Pairings of autobiographies and fiction by male and female authors can contribute greatly to students' multifocal, relational understanding of the human experience. Two pairings I have found to be particularly illuminating are *Black Boy*, by Richard Wright (1945/2000), and *Woman Warrior*, by Maxine Hong Kingston (1976). Other interesting pairings are Maya Angelou's *I Know Why the Caged Bird Sings* (1969) and Mark Twain's *The Adventures of Huckleberry Finn* (1912/1985); *The Autobiography of Frederick Douglass* (Douglass, 1855/1994) and *Incidents in the Life of a Slave Girl* (Jacobs, 1861/1988); *The Adventures of Tom Sawyer* (Twain, 1910/1996) and *Little Women* (Alcott, 1880/1995).

Dorothy Berkson, a professor we observed at Lewis and Clark College, used teaching logs to demystify the process of interpretation by linking the students' emotional connections to texts with their intellectual analysis. She asked her students to select a passage that puzzled or engaged them or triggered a strong emotional reaction. Believing that some of the best criticism starts with such reactions, she asked the students next to paraphrase the passage they had chosen, to understand what it means, or, in a sense, to master it (Maher & Tetreault, 1994, p. 249–250).

Students were then asked to look at the passage again to become conscious of what cannot be captured by paraphrase as well as any concerns or questions that escaped them before. They finally placed the passage in the context of the entire text, using the following questions: Where does it happen? Are there other passages that relate to it? That contradict it? That confirm it? That raise more questions about it? Concluding with a summary of where this procedure has taken them, they turn in these logs at the end of each class. Returned to the students with Berkson's comments, the logs then become the basis for the students' formal paper. This process forces students to reengage with the text over and over and to engage in continuous reinterpretation of the text rather than to think they have arrived at some final mastery.

Science

Fear of Science: Fact or Fantasy?

Suggested Activities

Fear of science and math and the stereotyping of scientists contribute to the limited participation of some students, most often female, in math and science classes. Their inadequate participation limits their choice of most undergraduate majors that depend on a minimum of three years of high school mathematics. In *Aptitude Revisited: Rethinking Math and Science Education for America's Next Century*, Drew (1996) argues that the people least encouraged to study mathematics and science in our society are those who have the least power—especially students from poverty, minority students, and young women. Policy makers, teachers, and even parents often steer certain students away from math and science for completely erroneous reasons. The result, Drew contends, is not simply an inadequately trained workforce: This educational discrepancy is widening the gap between the haves and the have-nots in our society. He challenges the conventional view that science and math are too boring or too hard for many students, arguing that virtually all students are capable of mastering these subjects.

The following exercise was designed by the Math and Science Education for Women Project at the Lawrence Hall of Science, University of California at Berkeley (Fraser, 1982). The purpose of the exercise is to decrease female and male students' fear of science by enabling them to function as researchers who define the problem and generate solutions to it.

Ask students to complete the following sentence by writing for about 15 minutes: "When I think about science, I. . . ." When they have finished, divide students into groups of five or six to discuss their responses to the cue. Ask each group to state the most important things it has learned. Discuss fear of science with the class and whether there is a difference in how girls and boys feel about science. What could be some reasons for these differences or similarities? When the findings from this exercise are clear, suggest to students that they broaden their research to include other students and teachers in the school. Have each group brainstorm questions that might appear on a science attitude questionnaire. Put the questions on the chalkboard. Analyze the questions and decide on the ten best.

Decide with the class what group of students and teachers you will research and how you will do it (for example, other science classes, all ninth-grade science classes, or the entire school during second period). Obtain permission to conduct the survey from the administration and other teachers or classes involved in your research project. Have the class complete the survey or questionnaire as a pilot activity. Analyze the questions for gender differences and make minor revisions before giving the survey and questionnaire to your research group.

Distribute the survey or conduct interviews. Have the students decide how to analyze the information. Let each group decide how it will display findings and information. Current statistics of male and female scientists in biology, chemistry, physics, and other sciences can be found via the National Science Foundation (n.d.). Other valuable resources are *Re-Engineering Female Friendly Science* (Rosser, 1997) and *Women, Gender and Technology* (Fox, Johnson, & Rosser, 2006).

Have each group give (1) a report to the class on what it found, using graph displays to convey the information, and (2) recommendations for decreasing science anxiety in the school. Place the entire student research project in the school library, main office, or gymnasium, where the rest of the school population can see the results. Have a student summarize the project and write an article for the school paper.

Doing Science

Suggested Activities

Keller's (1983) biography of Barbara McClintoch, *A Feeling for the Organism*, allows students to explore the conditions under which dissent in science arises, the function it serves, and the plurality of values and goals it reflects. Questions her story prompts include these: What role do interests—individual and collective—play in the evolution of scientific knowledge? Do all scientists seek the same kinds of explanations? Are the kinds of questions they ask the same? Do differences in methodology between different subdisciplines ever permit the same kinds of answers? Do female and male scientists approach their research differently? This book is difficult reading for high school and college students, but it is manageable if they read carefully and thoroughly. The best way I have found to help them manage is to ask them to read a chapter or section and to come to class with their questions about the reading and to propose some answers.

Social Studies

My Family's Work History

Suggested Activities

Women and men of different social classes, ethnic groups, and geographic locations have done various kinds of work inside and outside their homes in agricultural, industrial, and postindustrial economies. Before introducing students to the history of work, I pique their interest by asking them to complete a Family Work Chart (see Table 7.6). When their charts are complete, the students and I build a work chronology from 1890 to the present. Our work chronology contains information gleaned from the textbook and library sources about important inventions, laws, demographics, and labor history.

I then reproduce the work chronology on a chart so they can compare their family's history with key historical events. By seeing their families' histories alongside major events in our collective work history, students can see how their family was related to society. A sample of items from our chart includes: in 1890, women are 17 percent of the paid labor force; in 1915, the telephone connects New York and San Francisco; and in 1924, immigration was restricted (Chapman, 1979). Students conclude this unit by writing about a major theme in their family's work history. They might focus on how the lives of the women in the family differed from the lives of the men. They might focus on how their family's race or ethnicity shaped their work history.

Integrating the Public and Private Spheres

Suggested Activities

Human life is lived in both the public and the private spheres in wartime as well as in peacetime. By asking students consciously to examine individuals' lives as citizens, workers, family members, friends, members of social groups, and individuals, they learn more about the interaction of these roles in both spheres. War is an extraordinary time when the nation's underlying assumptions about these roles are often put to the test. By having students examine the interaction of these roles in wartime, they can see some of our underlying assumptions about the roles and how they are manipulated for the purposes of war. Through researching the histories of their families and by reading primary source accounts, viewing films, and reading their textbook, they will see the complexity and variety of human experiences in the United States during World War II.

Table 7.6   Family Work Chart

| | | Work Experience | | |
| | | | AFTER MARRIAGE | |
	YEAR OF BIRTH	BEFORE MARRIAGE	WHILE CHILDREN WERE YOUNG	WHEN CHILDREN WERE GROWN
Your maternal side				
Mother				
Grandmother				
Grandfather				
Great-grandmother				
Great-grandfather				
Great-great-grandmother				
Great-great-grandfather				
Your paternal side				
Father				
Grandmother				
Grandfather				
Great-grandmother				
Great-grandfather				
Great-great-grandmother				
Great-great-grandfather				

Source: This activity was developed by Carol Frenier. Reprinted with permission from the Education Development Center from Adeline Naiman, Project Director, *Sally Garcia and Family Resource Guide*, Unit 3 of *The Role of Women in American Society* (Newton, MA.: Education Development Center, Inc., 1978), p. 62.

Historical Events		Your Family History
1890	Women are 17 percent of the paid labor force	
1915	Telephone connects New York and San Francisco	
1924	Restriction of immigration	

Students research their family's history during World War II by gathering family documents and artifacts and by interviewing at least one relative who was an adult during World War II. Students determine questions beforehand to find out how the individual's social roles were affected by the war. During the two weeks they are researching their family's history, they spend two class periods on this project. During the first period, students give oral reports to a small group of fellow students in read-around groups.

Appropriate readings and films on World War II are widely available. Terkel's (1984) *The Good War* is particularly useful because of the variety of people the author interviewed. For instance, students can read about the internment of Japanese Americans and can role-play an account they read. Their textbook may provide good background information. A moving, personal account of internment is *Desert Exile: The Uprooting of a Japanese-American Family* (Uchida, 1982). My students answer two questions in this unit: World War II has been described as a "good war." From the materials you have examined, was it a good war for the lives of individuals as citizens, workers, family members, friends, and members of social groups? How were their experiences similar to or different from those of your relatives?

SUMMARY

This chapter has illustrated how women's studies is challenging male domination over curricular content. The evolution of that challenge is illuminated by understanding the different emphases that coexist in male-defined, contribution, bifocal, women's, and gender-balanced curricula. We now have a conceptual framework for a curriculum that interweaves issues of gender with ethnicity, culture, and class. This framework acknowledges and celebrates a multifocal, relational view of the human experience.

The idea of the phases of feminist scholarship as a series of intersecting circles, or patches on a quilt, or threads on a tapestry suggests parallel ways to think about a class of students. Each student brings to your classroom a particular positionality that shapes his or her way of knowing. Your challenge as a teacher is to interweave the individual truths with course content into complex understandings that legitimize students' voices.

With the authority of the school behind it, this relational knowledge has the potential to help students analyze their own social, cultural, historical, political, and economic contexts. The goal of relational knowledge is to build a world in which the oppressions of race, gender, and class—on which capitalism and patriarchy depend—are challenged by critical citizens in a democratic society.

Questions and Activities

1. What is a gender-balanced, multicultural curriculum?
2. What is feminist phase theory?
3. Define and give an example of each of the following phases of the feminist phase theory developed and described by the author: (a) male-defined curriculum, (b) contribution

curriculum, (c) bifocal curriculum, (d) women's curriculum, and (e) gender-balanced curriculum.

4. What problems do the contribution and bifocal phases have? How do the women's curriculum and gender-balanced curriculum phases help solve these problems?

5. The author states that "knowledge is a social construction." What does this mean? In what ways is the new scholarship on women and on ethnic groups alike? In what ways does the new scholarship on women and on ethnic groups challenge the dominant knowledge established in society and presented in textbooks? Give examples.

6. Examine the treatment of women in a sample of social studies, language arts, mathematics, or science textbooks (or a combination of two types of textbooks). Which phases or phase of the feminist phase theory presented by the author best describe(s) the treatment of women in the textbooks you examined?

7. What is the *longue durée?* Why is it important in the study of social history, particularly women's history?

8. Research your family history, paying particular attention to the roles, careers, and influence of women in your family's saga. Also describe your ethnic heritage and its influence on your family's past and present. Share your family history with a group of your classmates or workshop participants.

References

Acuña, R. (2004). *Occupied America: A history of Chicanos* (5th ed.). Upper Saddle River, NJ: Pearson Education.

Alcoff, L. (2003). *Identities: Race, class, gender and nationality*. London: Blackwell.

Alcott, L. M. (1995). *Little women*. New York: Scholastic. (Original work published 1880)

Angelou, M. (1969). *I know why the caged bird sings*. New York: Bantam.

Atkinson, J. M. (1982). Review essay, anthropology. *Signs, 8,* 250–251.

Butler, J. (1993). *Bodies that matter: On the discursive limits of "sex."* New York: Routledge.

Butler, J. (2004). *Undoing gender*. New York: Routledge.

Chapman, A. E. (Ed.). (1979). *Approaches to women's history: A resource book and teaching guide*. Washington, DC: American Historical Association.

Christian, B. (1980). *Black women novelists: The development of a tradition, 1892–1976*. Westport, CT: Greenwood Press.

Code, L. (1991). *What can she know? Feminist theory and the construction of knowledge*. Ithaca, NY: Cornell University Press.

Collins, P. H. (2000). *Black feminist thought: Knowledge, consciousness, and the politics of empowerment*. New York: Routledge.

Douglass, F. (1994). *The autobiography of Frederick Douglass*. New York: Penguin. (Original work published 1855)

Drew, D. E. (1996). *Aptitude revisited: Rethinking math and science education for America's next century*. Baltimore, MD: John Hopkins University Press.

Finke, L. (1993). Knowledge as bait: Feminism, voice, and the pedagogical unconscious. *College English*, 55(1), 7–27.

Fox, M. F., Johnson, D., & Rosser, S. (Eds.). (2006). *Women, gender and technology*. Champaign-Urbana: University of Illinois Press.

Frankenberg, R. (1993). *White women, race matters: The social construction of Whiteness*. Minneapolis: University of Minnesota Press.

Frankenberg, R. (Ed.). (1997). *Displacing Whiteness: Essays in social and cultural criticism*. Durham, NC: Duke University Press.

Fraser, S. (1982). *Spaces: Solving problems of access to careers in engineering and science*. Berkeley: University of California Press.

Goldberger, N., Tarule, J., Clinchy, B., & Belenky, M. (Eds.). (1996). *Knowledge, difference, and power: Essays inspired by women's ways of knowing*. New York: Basic Books.

Gornick, V., & Moran, B. (Eds.). (1971). *Woman in sexist society*. New York: Basic Books.

Haraway, D. J. (1991). *Simians, cyborgs, and women: The reinvention of nature*. New York: Routledge.

Haraway, D. J. (1997). *Modest-witness@ second-millennium. FemaleMan_meets_oncoMouse: Feminism and technoscience*. New York: Routledge.

Harding, S. G. (Ed.). (2004). *The feminist standpoint theory reader: Intellectual and political controversies*. New York: Routledge.

hooks, b. (1994). *Teaching to transgress: Education as the practice of freedom*. New York: Routledge.

Hune, S., & Nomura, G. (2003). *Asian/Pacific Islander American women: A historical anthology*. New York: New York University Press.

Jacobs, H. (1988). *Incidents in the life of a slave girl*. New York: Oxford University Press. (Original work published 1861)

Keller, E. (1983) *A feeling for the organism*. San Francisco: W.H. Freeman.

Kesselman, A., McNair, L., & Schniedewind, N. (2002). *Women: Images and realities, a multicultural anthology* (3rd ed.). New York: McGraw-Hill.

Kimmel, M., Hearn, J., & Connell, R. W. (2005). *Handbook of studies on men and masculinities*. Thousand Oaks, CA: Rowman & Littlefield.

Kingston, M. H. (1976). *Woman warrior*. New York: Knopf.

Lerner, G. (1979). *The majority finds its past*. New York: Oxford University Press.

L'Ecole des Annales. (1982). Letters to the editor. *Social Education*, 46(6), 378–380.

Louie, S., & Omatsu, G. (2001). *Asian Americans: The movement and the moment*. Los Angeles: Asian American Studies Center.

Maher, F., & Tetreault, M. K. (1994). *The feminist classroom*. New York: Basic Books.

Maher, F., & Tetreault, M. K. (1997). Learning in the dark: How assumptions of Whiteness shape classroom knowledge. *Harvard Educational Review*, 67(2), 321–349.

Maher, F., & Tetreault, M. K. (2001). *The feminist classroom* (2nd ed.). New York: Rowman & Littlefield.

McIntosh, P. (1990). White privilege and male privilege: A personal account of coming to see correspondences through work in women's studies. In M. L. Andersen & P. J. Collins (Eds.), *Race, class and gender: An anthology* (pp. 70–81). Boston: Wadsworth.

Millett, K. (1970). *Sexual politics*. Garden City, NY: Doubleday.

Mohanty, C. (2003). *Feminism without borders: Decolonizing theory, practicing solidarity*. Durham, NC: Duke University Press.

Moi, T. (1985). *Sexual/textual politics: Feminist literary theory*. New York: Methuen.

Morrison, T. (1993). *Playing in the dark: Whiteness and the literary imagination*. New York: Vintage.

National Science Foundation. (n.d.). Science and engineering statistics website. Retrieved on October 27, 2006, from www.nsf.gov/sbe/srs/seind98/start.htm

Rosaldo, R. (1994). Cultural citizenship and educational democracy. *Cultural Anthropology, 9*(3), 402–411.

Rosaldo, S. & Lamphere, L. (1974). *Woman, Culture and Society*. Stanford: Stanford University Press.

Rosser, S. V. (1997). *Re-engineering female friendly science*. New York: Teachers College Press.

Ruiz, V. L., & Dubois, E. (Eds.). (2000). *Unequal sisters: A multicultural reader in U.S. women's history* (3rd ed.). New York: Routledge.

Saldivar-Hull, S. (2000). *Feminism on the border: Chicana gender politics and literature*. Berkeley: University of California Press.

Schacht, S., & Ewing, D. (2007). *Feminism with men: Bridging the gender gap*. New York: Rowman & Littlefield.

Schmitz, B., Butler, J. E., Guy-Sheftall, B., & Rosenfelt, D. (2004). Women's studies and curriculum transformation in the United States. In J. A. Banks & C. A. M. Banks (Eds.), *Handbook of research on multicultural education* (2nd ed., pp. 882–905). San Francisco: Jossey-Bass.

Shorris, E. (2001). *Latinos: A biography of the people*. New York: W. W. Norton.

Showalter, E. (1977). *A literature of their own*. Princeton: Princeton University Press.

Smith, E. (2003). *Mary McLeod Bethune and the National Council of Negro Women: Pursuing a true and unfettered democracy*. Montgomery: Alabama State University.

Tatum, B. (1997). *"Why are all the black kids sitting together in the cafeteria?" and other conversations about race*. New York: Basic Books.

Terkel, S. (1984). *The good war: An oral history of World War II*. New York: Pantheon.

Tetreault, C. (1991). *Metacommunication in a women's studies classroom*. Unpublished senior honors thesis, Vassar College, Poughkeepsie, NY.

Tetreault, M. K. T. (1986). Integrating women's history: The case of United States history textbooks. *History Teacher, 19*(2), 211–262.

Thorne, B. (1993). *Gender play: Girls and boys in school*. New Brunswick, NJ: Rutgers University Press.

Twain, M. (1985). *The Adventures of Huckleberry Finn*. New York: Collier. (Original work published 1912)

Twain, M. (1996). *The Adventures of Tom Sawyer*. New York: Oxford University Press. (Original work published 1910)

Uchida, Y. (1982). *Desert exile: The uprooting of a Japanese-American family*. Seattle: University of Washington Press.

Weatherford, J. M. (1992). *Native roots: How the Indians enriched America*. New York: Fawcett Columbine.

Weiler, K. (1988). *Women teaching for change: Gender, class, and power*. South Hadley, MA: Bergin & Garvey.

Wright, R. (2000). *Black boy*. New York: Harper & Brothers. (Original work published 1945)

CHAPTER 8

Race and Gender in Classrooms: Implications for Teachers

Annette Henry

RACE AND GENDER AS INTERLOCKING VARIABLES

This chapter examines race and gender as interlocking dimensions in the lives of students. Teachers often consider race and gender distinct and unrelated categories. Teachers who view race and gender as interconnected rather than as separate can increase their understandings of diversity and develop effective strategies to promote social justice and democracy. The immediate concerns of teachers about appropriate curricula and effective instruction may be addressed by understanding how race and gender are manifested in their classrooms, schools, and in society (Applebaum, 2007; Titus, 2000). However, teachers may feel that as long as they ensure that "no group is left out" or that everyone is treated "the same" (Nieto, 2005), they are practicing an inclusive pedagogy. There is also evidence that teachers may feel overwhelmed by trying to determine how to teach students whose backgrounds and life experiences differ greatly from their own (Obidah & Howard, 2005). Their first step is to understand that race and gender are important factors that influence the identities, outlooks, experiences, and opportunities of students.

This chapter focuses on race and gender, which are only two identities in the complex and overlapping systems of marginalization. Audre Lorde (1984) introduced herself as a "forty-nine year-old Black lesbian feminist socialist mother of two, including one boy, and a member of an interracial couple," who often found herself as *part of some group defined as other, deviant, inferior, or just plain wrong*" [italics added] (p.113). As Lorde's biography indicates, we exist within many locations within a larger power system that may marginalize or oppress us but also within our own cultural groups (Hesse-Biber, 2004; Zinn & Dill, 1996). Cultures are dynamic processes, practices, exchanges of meanings, or representations between members of a society (Hall, 1997). Identities are *multidimensional, overlapping,* and *complex*. Power and oppression operate along many dimensions such as socioeconomic background, language, ethnicity, race, skin color, sex, sexuality, gender, and disability. Our lives are implicated in these systems of oppression rather than merely in isolated incidents of discrimination, bias, prejudice, or bigotry. These systems are pervasive, structural, hierarchical, and internalized in our consciousness (Adams, Bell, & Griffin, 2007). They affect students' material conditions, academic and life chances, and sense of well-being.

Scholars are often criticized for using race, class, and gender without describing how these variables are interrelated. An analysis of the lived experiences of individuals related to race and gender are incomplete without taking class into account (Apple, 2007; American Association of University Women, 2008; hooks, 2000). In a report on the academic success of boys and girls, the American Association of University Women (AAUW) reported that thirty-five years of quantitative data underscore "the importance of family income and race/ethnicity in both boys' and girls' academic achievement" (p. 3). The report stresses that African American and Latino students from low-income backgrounds score less well on standardized tests and have lower high school and college graduation rates than their White and Asian counterparts from higher income backgrounds. The AAUW report describes the ways in which socioeconomic factors matter and influence the lives of students in significant ways: the quality of education, the physical conditions of the learning environment, the expectations of teachers, and the outlooks of parents and students. While my concern in this chapter is largely with the intersection of race and gender, I am aware that class intersects with these variables. Consequently, I will reference class when appropriate.

My focus is on race and gender because these variables are rarely articulated clearly together in education. These concepts are fundamental structural or organizing factors that determine educational access, opportunity, democratic participation, and the general well-being in institutional settings. In the United States—perhaps partly because of its racial history—gender often is diminished in the presence of race. McCready (2004) noted that in examining gender in the analysis of student achievement with colleagues at an urban school, a well-respected faculty member said, "Let's just stick to our original agenda of race and class disparities in achievement and hold off on the gender issues; we don't want to make things too complicated too soon" (p. 137). McCready observed a sense of relief by others that this "complicated issue" would not be examined. However, after working with Black students at the school, he realized that blatant sexism and homophobia were related to the refusal to examine gender.

In everyday discourse, many people think that *race* refers to people of color, especially Black and Brown, and in the process ignore gender distinctions. *Gender* in discourses of gender equity usually refers to White females. If you examine the index pages of many education textbooks, you will see how authors conceptualize each of these dimensions and whether they analyze the intersections of race and gender. Similarly, in the media, as in educational research—and in society at large—there is a tendency to homogenize all people of a particular sex or race, for example "women," "Blacks," or "Native Americans." The dominant group—White people—remains the unmarked norm in these examples. This usage obscures specificities of particular groups, such as Black females who often remain invisible or become a comparative "minority group" in studies and discussions mainly about White girls and women but sometimes about men and boys of color. Gloria Steinem (2008) argued in an essay in the *New York Times* that if Barack Obama had been female, he would never have been a presidential frontrunner. Steinem did not mention the race of her hypothetical (White) female candidate. Several months later, Katie Couric (as cited in Elsworth, 2008)—a White NBC anchorwoman—said that "sexism in American society is more common than racism." Not only have race and gender been involved separately in simplistic binary logic (Black/White; male/female), but also they have been conceptualized in opposition (e.g., race is more important than gender and vice versa). What is missing from these statements by celebrities is an understanding of the complicated and interlocking relationships of race and gender that situate males and females differently.

The belief that race is more important than gender (or that gender is more important than race)—amplified in the 2008 presidential election campaign just mentioned—is dangerous and divisive both within and between racial and ethnic groups. The pressure to choose between the two is often encountered by individuals who live in multiple historically marginalized locations, most often females. This phenomenon may reflect sexism and patriarchal thinking as well as overlook the complexity of issues and situations. In communities of color, many accounts in which antiracism issues are considered more important than antisexism issues exist (Boyung, 2006; Henry, 2005). Women of color who are in female-specific struggles have been accused of dividing the race or fragmenting antiracist struggles—allegations that can dampen notions that women's and girls' concerns—both raced and gendered—can create beneficial spaces of collaboration in communities of color for males and females (Henry). Scholars of color—especially womanists and a range of feminists of color—have challenged this "either/or" thinking as reflective of Eurocentric patriarchal thought or White Western masculinist thinking (Collins, 2000; Henry).

WHAT IS RACE?

The general population believes that race consists of phenotype or physical characteristics. Race is a *sociopolitical construct* involving complex social and historical processes (Back & Solomos, 2000; Omi & Winant, 1994). It is an arbitrary and problematic term that has been used historically to classify human beings (James, 2003). Separate human races do not exist biologically (Gillborn, 2008). Although interventions (Forbes, 1990), race and racism and the oppression that operates through race are not fantasies in people's everyday lived experiences. Even though difficult to define, race and racism are present throughout U.S. society (Omi & Winant). Race functions differently in various sociopolitical contexts, but racism always benefits the dominant social group (e.g., White people in the United States). There is no one monolithic racism (Goldberg, 1994). Consequently, theorists speak of "multiple and situated racisms" (Bhavnani, Mirza, & Meetoo, 2005, p. 60) to emphasize that racism not only affects various groups of color differently but that other identities and oppressions such as disability, age, and sexuality are also at play.

Theories of race and racial identifications are constantly changing (Back & Solomos, 2000). Consequently, some theorists argue that we are living in a "postracial" moment, meaning that people are understanding race and identifying in new ways that require novel theories and practices in a world of transmigration and globalization. Moreover, many individuals are identifying as biracial or multiracial. The U.S. government attempted to capture this American racial and ethnic hybridity in the 2000 census forms by adding more categories of self-identification. Individuals were allowed to identify themselves as more than one race. However, the new census categories are insufficient and problematic (Alcoff, 2006; Dalmage, 2004; Morales, 2001). Morales describes an example of the complicated nature of race. Celia, a Black Panamanian Latina, acknowledges that others see her as Black but rejects the U.S.

categorization of her as a Black American. She did not check the Black category on the 2000 census. African American philosopher Charles Mills (2002) states that he is a "Red man" in Jamaica—his country of origin—but a Black man in the United States. "Black" or "Brown" may have different meanings in the United Kingdom, the United States, the Caribbean, and Brazil (Mills; Caldwell, 2007). More important, these examples show that contemporary citizens are reshaping U.S. understandings of racial identities.

In our globalized society, it is difficult to discuss race without mentioning *ethnicity*. Ethnicity traditionally has described people who identify as members of a group who may share a sense of identity on the basis of factors such as language, religion, culture, descent, and geographic territory (Banks, 1996; Bhavnani, Mirza, & Meetoo, 2005). Ethnicity is often confused with and conflated with race. This confusion becomes very complicated when some ethnic groups, such as Latinos, are described as racialized identity groups in the United States (Alcoff, 2006; Winant, 2004). Winant notes that the U.S. Census Bureau defines Hispanic as a racial, not an ethnic category, reflecting "the continuing incapacity of the census to grasp the complexities of the U.S. racial formation" (p. 321). All groups have different experiences with race, class, sex, age, gender, and geography. A range of geographies, languages, and cultural practices comprises people described as Asians, including Hmong, Chinese, Japanese, Malay, and Tamil. The social dimensions of power and oppression are manifested within this diverse and problematic ethnic category in multiple and intersecting ways. Asia consists of nearly four billion people and more than 50 countries (Chang & Au, 2007). Because of their dominant and unmarked position of privilege in the United States, White people often claim that they do not belong to an ethnic group even though they may identify as Irish Americans, German Americans, or Italian Americans.

WHAT IS GENDER?

Sex and *gender*, like race and ethnicity, are often conflated in everyday language. These terms are also often used interchangeably and are problematically defined, which causes confusion. The educational literature is striking for its vagueness and lack of clarity in its use of *sex* and *gender*. Traditional definitions refer to *sex* as the *biological* differences (i.e., physical, hormonal, and genetic) between males and females and *gender* as *socially* constructed identities (Adams et al., 2007; Cudd & Andreasen, 2005; Glasser & Smith, 2008). The notion of two sexes has been contested within the last several decades (Butler, 1993; Wilchins, 2004). Fausto-Sterling (1993) has argued for a continuum with at least five sexes rather than a misleading male/female dichotomy.

In education theory and practice, people tend to use *gender* when referring to distinctions and differences between males and females. Glasser and Smith (2008) and Francis (2006) argue that analyses of boys and girls (and men and women) in school classrooms should be framed in terms of gender (not sex) to underscore that social and cultural factors are more influential than biological differences. Some authors, American Indian (Allen, 1987; Cameron, 2005) as well as others, criticize Western categorizations of gender roles. American mainstream society is very intolerant of "gender transgressors" (Blount, 2005), such as transgender youth or indigenous conceptions of "two-spirited" people. The term *two-spirited*, which was suppressed by colonization and Christianity, is being reclaimed today in Native communities. It refers to people considered neither men nor women but who belong to genders of their own within cultural systems of multiple genders (Cameron).

Like racism, sexism is a historically and globally pervasive form of oppression (Cudd & Jones, 2005). Both racism and sexism function through individual beliefs and practices as well as through institutions, societal images, and systems of thought. They are enforced by economic structures and everyday actions (Adams, Bell, & Griffin, 2007). Sexism is a system of advantage that privileges biological men and maintains male hegemony, power, and control (Adams et al.). It is related to but is different from *patriarchy*, a term with various meanings, but for our purposes is a structure in which men have more social power and privilege than women. *Feminism*, a movement to end sexist exploitation and oppression, also recognizes that men are damaged by sexism. Heterosexism and transgender oppression are not the focus of this chapter, but it is important to mention that although different from sexism, both represent "overlapping manifestations of oppression" (Adams et al., p. 167). Moreover, queer theory as well as the writing and voices of gay, lesbian, bisexual, transgender, and queer (GLBTQ) individuals have challenged and advanced contemporary concepts of sex, sexuality, sexual orientation, and gender (see Chapter 9).

RACE AND GENDER AS AN INSEPARABLE PERFORMANCE

Race and gender are both socially constructed, politically contested, and pervasive in everyday life. They are produced in interactions within institutions (West & Zimmerman, 1987). We "perform" race and gender; that is, racialized and gendered meanings are produced and naturalized in everyday interactions in schools and daily life by ourselves and others (Lewis, 2003). The Latino father of a biracial (White/Latino) fifth-grade student observes how his son, Omar, performs race as he works out his racial identifications:

> I think that Omar identifies himself more with Latinos, in part because
> he lives with me. . . . At the same time, he feels part of the whole
> American culture. He speaks more English than Spanish, for example.
> But I don't even think that he has determined what he wants to be, and I
> think that it's definitely up to him [regarding] what he wants. If he wants
> to be, to determine himself as White, American or White-Latino or
> Latino-Latino, or Hispanic, I think that will come later. (Lewis, p. 289)

It is plausible that Omar, like many students, performs race differently in the Latino and the White communities. Raced and gendered identities are negotiated within insider communities—those are the communities to which we belong—as well as in the wider society. Haibinh, a Vietnamese American high school senior in the film *5 Girls* (Finitzo, 2001) describes herself as having a "dual personality":

> When I'm with Vietnamese people I act this way, and then when I'm
> American I act another way. I like being both ways though. I don't want
> to give up one or the other. I'm not gonna deny my heritage.

The gendered and raced identities of students are constantly constructed and renegotiated in different settings and by their unique personal and social histories.

Students may negotiate their identities through friends, clothing styles, speech, and skin color—all of which can easily become ways to cast them as the racialized, gendered "Other." The styles of interaction and clothing of Black and Latino boys have been perceived as oppositional and potentially dangerous and consequently undergo undue surveillance and disciplinary procedures (Brown, 2003; Morris, 2005). American society has perpetuated the image of young, dark-skinned men as problem (Lopez, 2003) or jail-bound youth (Ferguson, 2000) regardless of their socioeconomic background. These perceptions affect their academic and career paths.

Fanon's (1967) concept of *la négrophobe*—a fear of Black people—is visible in daily school life and may be extended to a fear of Black and Brown youth (Osler & Vincent, 2003). Morris (2005) found that East Asian and South Asian American male students exhibited similar behaviors, mannerisms, and dress as Latino boys. However, teachers perceived the White and Asian American boys as "harmless" (p. 37). They considered the Latinos as disruptive in class and gang affiliated because of their attire. Since the airplane attacks on September 11, 2001, in the United States and the bombings in London subway stations on July 7, 2005, both male and female students of Middle East and South Asian origin have experienced increased racial profiling and negative stereotypes in schools (Dwyer, Shah, & Sanghera, 2008; Zabel, 2006).

Research has shown how institutions regulate working-class, Black, and Latino male bodies through disciplinary procedures. Junior Reserve Office Training Corps and military recruitment are contemporary examples. They are marketed heavily in Black and Latino communities (Brown, 2003). Students in low-income communities of color experience a less rigorous academic curriculum, have inadequate material and intellectual resources, are sorted into lower academic tracks, and are overrepresented in special education and vocational programs (see Chapter 15). There has been a shift toward a criminalization approach to discipline in predominantly Black and Latino schools. Zero-tolerance policies, criminal justice paradigms, tools, and personnel have been imported into the school disciplinary process (Ayers, Dohrne, & Ayers, 2001; Hirschfield, 2008).

U.S. society's notions of the normal, "typical" student, "the good student," and "the bad student" represent racialized, gendered, and *classed* images (Fordham, 1996; Walkerdine, 1990). Lei (2003) examined the ways that South East Asian boys and African American girls constructed their gendered and racialized identities and performances. She found that their identities were constructed by others and by the prevailing images and ideologies in society. Teachers are in authoritative and powerful positions. They often perpetuate White middle-class views of male and female behavior, negatively interpret the raced and gendered behaviors of their students of color, and negatively assess their academic achievement.

East Asian boys are often characterized as quiet, curious, and mysterious (Lei, 2003). South East Asian boys are more likely to be characterized as gang affiliated. Class and race influence how males of color are perceived. The gang image of South East Asian boys is inconsistent with the stereotype of Asians as "model minorities," an erroneous notion that produces undue pressure on the social and emotional development of Asian students (Chang & Au, 2007; Kao & Hébert, 2006). The model minority myth asserts that Asians excel academically because of their cultural values (such as hard work and respect for authority) and natural aptitudes in the sciences and in mathematics. This harmful stereotype positions racialized minorities in opposition. "Why can't *YOU* people be like *THOSE* people," as Victor exclaimed in the well-known film used frequently in teacher education, *The Color of Fear* (Mun Wah, 1994). The lower scores on standardized tests of Black and Latino students are used as evidence of their inferiority. The structural and institutional causes of failure are underestimated in the model minority argument (Lee, 1996; Lew, 2006).

These raced and gendered stereotypes are frequently internalized not only by mainstream Whites but also by members of subordinated groups. Mr. Bailey, the Black principal in Lee's (1996) study, said that South Asian males are "hard to figure out" (p. 171). One of my Korean American teacher education candidates who had internalized this myth said in class, "We are model minorities; we do better than anyone else."

RACE AND GENDER IN THE LIVES OF STUDENTS

Since the 1980s, educational researchers have been studying boys as gendered and their behaviors and identities as racialized. McCready (2004) urges educators to recognize the multiple categories of difference and forms of oppression that belie male youth of color in schools and to develop multidimensional intervention frameworks for Black male students in urban schools, especially gay and "gender-nonconforming" male youth.

James (2005) explores the gendered and racialized identities of student athletes. He refutes the popularized belief that sports provide equality of opportunity for marginalized students. His interviews with youth and their families indicate how sports can legitimize and perpetuate racialized and gendered societal images of Black bodies—both male and female—and can perpetuate existing inequalities and the commodification of Black people. James's work can help educators, parents, and coaches to understand the personal, professional, and cultural aspirations of racial minority and immigrant youth of color and their families as well as how racism, classism, and sexism mediate the academic and extracurricular experiences of students.

Since the late 1980s, many best-selling books about raising and educating boys have appeared in the popular media. Many support conservative values, such as *The War Against Boys* by Sommers (2000), a backlash stance. This book, as well as others, makes the false claim that the gains of girls have come at the expense of those of boys (AAUW, 2008). The authors, who appear frequently on television talk shows, rarely identify the specificities of race/ethnicity, class, and gender (Weaver-Hightower, 2008). As Osler and Vincent (2003) state, the binary rhetoric about boys' failure and girls' success "masks the vast differences in gendered experiences and opportunities" (p. 12).

There is, however, a "war" against African American, Latino, and Native American boys and girls. They drop out, are pushed out, or lured out of school and are overrepresented in special education and nonacademic programs. They are also incarcerated at alarming rates (Nield & Balfanz, 2006). Race/ethnicity and gender work in specific ways. Black males and females have the highest suspension and expulsion rates (17.4 percent and 9.1 percent, respectively), followed by Native American males (10.5 percent) and females (4.8 percent). The suspension rates for other selected groups are Latino males (8.7 percent) and females (3.5 percent), White males (7.4 percent) and females (2.7 percent), and Asian/Pacific Islander males (4.3 percent) and females (1.4 percent) (Freeman & Fox, 2005).

Native American/Alaska Native males are less likely than Black males to be suspended or expelled but are more likely to be suspended or expelled than White, Latino, or Asian/Pacific

Islander males. Similarly, Native American/Alaska Native females are less likely than Black females to be suspended or expelled but more likely to be suspended or expelled than White, Latino, or Asian/Pacific Islander females. In 2007, there were 4,618 Black male sentenced prisoners per 100,000 Black males in the United States, compared to 1,747 Latino male sentenced prisoners per 100,000 Latino males and 773 White male sentenced prisoners per 100,000 White males (Sabol & Couture, 2008).

Eckholm (2006) described studies conducted by researchers from Harvard, Princeton, and Columbia universities. This data revealed that 60 percent of Black male school dropouts in their thirties had spent time in prison and indicated that there is a raced and gendered school-to-prison pipeline. Children's Defense Fund (2008) statistics for the state of California reveal that a Black boy born in 2001 has a 1 in 3 chance of going to prison in his lifetime, a Latino boy a 1 in 6 chance, and a White boy a 1 in 17 chance. A Black girl born in 2001 has a 1 in 17 chance of going to prison in her lifetime, a Latino girl a 1 in 45 chance, and a White girl a 1 in 111 chance. These raced and gendered realties are also related to poverty.

Incarceration rates, unemployment rates, overrepresentation in nonacademic programs, and leaving school without an adequate education are systemic realities that have perpetuated a popular discourse of "the endangered Black male" (Bowser, 1991; Gibbs, 1988). While some scholars have argued that this phrase perpetuates patriarchal thinking or privileges men over women (Gilroy, 1993; hooks & West, 1991), other scholars believe that the pressing issues in marginalized communities are not "either/or" issues. Race and gender organize and locate males and females in all racial groups differently. These differences influence educational access, opportunity, and democratic participation. In this view, the raced and gendered lives of female students of color will not remain hidden and obscured by either/or thinking in a patriarchal society.

The tendency to equate gender with girls in the mainstream has much to do with the role of patriarchy and the fact that males—especially White males—are the power elite and thus remain the unmarked, unproblematized gendered, raced norm. Patriarchy and sexism dictate that the educational issues of women and girls carry less importance. In a conversation that I had with a classroom teacher in an all-Black school, she confessed that she had not given the Black girls much thought although she had raised three daughters. She had spent 30 years as a teacher aware of how American society destroys Black male youth (Henry, 1998a). The racialized and gendered meanings and experiences of girls differ from those of boys and are specific to their race.

Some studies indicate that Black girls tend to express self-sufficient attitudes. Through their raced and gendered life experiences, they do not expect to be financially supported and consequently may pursue education goals more enthusiastically than White girls (Lopez, 2003; Fine & Weis, 1998). These attitudes do not guarantee societal success. Mirza (1992) found that even when African Caribbean girls adopted academic strategies that promoted success and performed well on examinations, they were disadvantaged when they entered the labor force. Equal education, Fine and Weis remind us, "does not translate across race/ethnicity and gender into equal income" (p. 234).

Race and gender position Black females to be negatively stereotyped regarding their physical, social, and affective traits (Caldwell, 2007). They tend to be assessed for their social skills rather than for academic achievement. Black females are usually evaluated by their physical characteristics, hair texture, and skin color. They are considered sex objects as they mature and are frequently sexually harassed by other students as well as by teachers (Evans,

1992; Grant, 1984; Okazawa-Rey, Robinson, & Ward, 1986; Robinson, 2007). They are not usually viewed as serious learners and receive less teacher encouragement and rewards. The acceptable female is White and middle class. Women and girls from other cultures have to engage in "gender passing" to be accepted (Fordham, 1993, p.14). Black girls are rarely seen as "lady-like" (Morris, 2005). Teachers often consider them loud, tough, and aggressive (Berlak & Moyenda, 2001; Evans; Fordham, 1993; Lei, 2003). Interestingly, however, Black teens hold a high self-concept and body image compared to White teens (Body of the Beholder, 1995). Various cultures espouse different constructions of beauty and femininity that may not resonate with the mainstream U.S. norms (Carter, 2006; Fordham, 1996; Mirza, 1992, 1993; Osler & Vincent, 2003).

White teachers often fear any perceived confrontation with Black girls and are apprehensive about aggressive, angry behavior (Evans, 1992). Euro-American notions of beauty cause many Black females to be seen as less desirable than girls of other racial groups (Okazawa-Rey et al., 1986). These stereotypes evoke the racialized dominant controlling images of the "angry Black woman," which is critiqued in Black feminist literature (Collins, 2000; Wallace, 1979). These descriptions also evoke societal images of Black females as aggressive matriarchs, mammies, or whores that have existed since slavery (Collins).

There may be several reasons why girls may adopt what society labels as "loud" or "aggressive" behaviors or display "traditional" female roles of passivity and silence. Although girls may learn to be silent or complacent in classrooms through institutional socialization, they have a lot to say (Henry, 1998a, 1998b). Their silence may be a kind of speech in itself, masking culturally resistant attitudes and behaviors (Fordham, 1993; Carter, 2006). In her ethnography of a secondary English classroom with two Black female teens, Carter (2001) found that the girls' performance of silence was a socially constructed space of rich, unaffirmed voices that the classroom teacher and the mainstream culture devalued.

Silence can be a deliberate academic strategy for students of color (Fordham, 1996; Pang, 1996). Schoolteacher Carol Tateishi (2007) writes that in her Asian upbringing, she was taught that silence is a sign of self-reliance and strength. She interviewed five Asian American secondary school students from various ethnic backgrounds. Even though their families spanned 100 years of immigration, some recurrent themes emerged, such as "you're not supposed to say too much" and "talk could cause disrespect and harsh feelings" (Tateishi, p. 22). The girls who entered U.S. schools as English language learners feared speaking up because they were self-conscious about their language skills. Another girl mentioned that girls "were not supposed to speak unless spoken to" (Tateishi, p. 22). Restraint in speech was valued by these students and their families, whereas speaking in class and classroom dialogue is taken as intellectual engagement and meaning-making in U.S. classrooms.

Pang (1996) maintains that mainstream U.S. culture has not understood the cultural ways of being of communities of color—especially women of color—and that the comportment of mainstream males has been the norm. She theorizes five kinds of silence: oppressive, submissive, defiant, dignified, and attentive. Most literature has focused on "oppressive silence" in which the "oppressor obstructs the voices of others" (p. 185). Communicating across cultures requires "a very special kind of listening" (p. 189). Pang states that teachers are in a privileged position to cultivate attentive listening, a necessary component for a democratic society.

Classrooms can be unpleasant for girls of all racial backgrounds because of the presence of patriarchal attitudes and behaviors including teacher perceptions that male issues are more important than those of females (Henry, 1998a; Sadker & Sadker, 1994). Early in their schooling, "boys learn to control both the girls in their class and the women who teach them by adopting a 'male' discourse which emphasizes negative aspects of female sexuality and embodies direct sexual insult" (Millard, 1997, p. 9). Girls of color often betray their voices in coeducational classrooms (Blake, 1995; Fine, 1991; Henry, 1998a, 1998b), producing schoolwork and responses that avoid ridicule from boys. Boys may not outnumber girls, but they command more teacher attention and their concerns override those of girls (AAUW, 2008). Girls of color—especially those who may experience multiple oppressions—need opportunities to read, discuss, write, and express themselves in safe contexts without gender-based intimidation (Blake; Henry 1998b; Carter, 2006; Davies, 1993). When educators consider not only the official, formal school curriculum but also the out-of-school curriculum of students' lives, students become more engaged (Moll & Gonzàlez, 2004; Schubert, 1986; Robinson, 2007). The out-of-school curriculum includes the kinds of gendered experiences and responsibilities that students may have in their homes (e.g., caretaking, housework, cultural and linguistic translators for parents).

Most curricula reflect and reproduce White middle-class values as well as Western male and female norms. Theorists and practitioners are calling for curricula and pedagogies that accurately reflect, critically examine, and build on students' historical and cultural realities (Aguirre, 2009; Calabrese & Tan, 2009; Gutierrez, Larson, Enciso, & Ryan, 2007; Moll & Gonzàlez, 2004). While educators acknowledge the need for students to understand themselves and their worlds through the curriculum and pedagogy that takes place in classrooms, most overlook the relationships between race and gender and how they may translate into transformative learning for females of color.

Interviews with girls of color often reveal a perception that the curriculum is irrelevant to their lives. They express feelings of marginality and lack of optimism regarding their futures (Robinson, 2007; Quiroz, 2001). These same students would respond positively to curricular themes that allow them to think about and reflect on their own lives, to understand the underlying causes of issues, and to state and solve problems (Freire, 1970; Henry, 1996, 1998b). This kind of pedagogy requires transgressive teaching (Davies, 1995; hooks, 1994) which, explains hooks, allows students to identify issues critical to their lives. Influenced by Freire's (1970) notion of education as the practice of freedom, transgressive teaching allows students to develop a critical voice toward social action. This *critical literacy*, both a tool and a weapon (Jongsma, 1991), is a departure from traditional forms of literacy education for many girls of color. Traditional forms of education produce silence and accommodation (Omolade, 1994).

Male and female students of color who come from working-class and low-income backgrounds—or who may not be native speakers of American English—are especially susceptible to mainstream scrutiny regarding what is considered acceptable language and speech. In the mid-1990s, invited by the classroom teacher, I conducted reading/writing/discussion groups with Caribbean American middle school girls (Henry, 1998b). The teacher wanted her Caribbean female students, who rarely spoke in class, to "open up." Fourteen-year-old Kay, who had emigrated from Jamaica at 11 and had minimal literacy skills, grappled with American English, an oppressive site of discrimination and alienation for speakers of non-American English dialects and creoles. Her teacher had described her as a "nonreader." I provided culturally and gender-relevant readings for Kay and her group. The girls and I communicated through dialogue journals in which they wrote their responses to the themes we were discussing in class. I responded in their journals. The goal of these written student–teacher conversations was to promote literacy in an affirming context (Larrotta, 2008). These classes were "problem-posing" (Freire, 1970) literacy circles, a process that draws on personal experiences to analyze social situations. This was a particularly good method for young teenage girls to raise issues about their personal experiences.

After a few weeks, the curricula themes were generated by the girls rather than by me. Their previous education had not allowed them to envision their lives as relevant curriculum or that school learning could be meaningful to their lives and that the curriculum could be negotiated. Kay explained her academic strategy: "If I'm in the mood, I'll write good, if I'm not, I'll just write anything. If the topics are good, I'll concentrate and write." Once she realized that she was able to bring in cultural storylines and questions from her own raced and gendered experiences—from her home, her church, her life as a Black female adolescent—and make sense of the world, her voice soared. Her writing blossomed with compelling ideas about race, gender, class, and power (Henry, 1998b).

Kay's story is a reminder that what teachers do in classrooms matters. It also reminds us that culturally relevant curricula include gender-specific themes and lived experiences in and outside of classrooms (Gay, 2000). Curriculum is not a book or a package from a publisher. Engaging students in what Gutierrez et al. (2007) call "deep learning" involves considering the lives that children live "horizontally" in various spaces, across boundaries—what they know and can do—across their everyday lives. When Kay could think and write in and from these "expanded spaces," the curriculum became transformative. She was not quiet and passive as described by her teacher. Literacy encompasses a range of social, cultural, and communicative practices.

The program with these young women was based on many ideas informed by bell hooks (1994), known for her notion of "coming to voice." She asks, "How can we transform consciousness if we do not have some sense of where the students are intellectually, psychically?" (p. 54). Indeed, "voice" is a key concept in the literature regarding marginalized girls of color, who are denied the right to learn about their own cultures from critical or culturally informed perspectives (Joseph, 1988) or whose education is not transformative and social action oriented (Banks, 2007).

RACE, GENDER, AND SCHOOL ALTERNATIVES
Culture-Centered Schools: What They Tell Us about Good Pedagogy

In the United States, the United Kingdom, and Canada, parents, educators, and community workers have expressed concerns about the underachievement of bright, vibrant Black boys. Some parents have sought alternatives such as culture-centered settings in which their children may be truly educated rather than merely schooled (Shujaa, 1996). In large urban areas in the United States, schools, programs, or classes for African American boys are sometimes seen as positive alternatives to regular public schools. In these alternative settings, children encounter smaller classes, more attention and affirmation, and lessons that reflect and build on their cultural heritages. These programs focus on developing healthy African American males in a society in which they are targeted as the Other.

I conducted interviews with African American mothers in Illinois (Henry, 2006). They believed—similar to parental concerns regarding boys—that the gender identities of their daughters would be developed more holistically and in culturally appropriate ways at the African-centered school they attended. There tends to be a perception that both culture-centered and single-sex schools will safeguard girls from sexual harassment and sexual activity (Henry; Jenkins, 2006). However, parents may send their sons or daughters to various kinds of culture-centered schools for a variety of reasons, including cultivating the heritage, languages, and cultural identities as well as for religious reasons.

The African American and Native American communities are two groups who have cherished a long tradition of culture-centered schooling. Some examples include historically Black colleges and universities, African-centered schools, and American Indian tribal schools and colleges. Professor James Earl Davis (2000) described his years at Morehouse College, the only all-male historically Black college in the United States. He said, "My conceptions of manhood and masculinity were challenged and reinforced in this race/gender-exclusive context. My current thinking about the dual role of being Black and male continues to be influenced by that experience" (p. 62). Davis stated that the diverse meanings in manhood are not discussed enough in educational institutions, especially for those who are gender transgressors and live outside society's normative views of masculinity.

In culture-centered schools, gendered identities and roles are usually understood in ways that resonate with cultural codes and community knowledge. An example is a poster from an African-centered school that encouraged Black fathers to participate in school activities and help foster Black male identities and model positive male behavior for boys:

> Come into the village and help us raise our watoto [Swahili: children].
> Hug a brother or sister. Wrestle. Read a story. Take our brothers to the
> Hoop. Spend a half-day with us. Have lunch in the cafeteria. Help teach
> a lesson. Show us, by example, the ways of manhood. . . . Teach us how
> to non-violently solve problems. . . . Our village needs its male
> warriors!!! (Henry, 1998a, p. 168)

Rites of passage such as coming-of-age ceremonies and mentoring programs (Warren, 2005) are also ways that both males and females are socialized into being well-adjusted raced and gendered youth of color. This socialization takes place in formal educational institutions as well as in informal settings such as homes and families. Mavis, a teacher at an African-centered school, describes how her niece's Black female identity was injured in the public school system:

> It lowered her self-esteem—and this is a reality. You know she's
> dealing with people calling her "nappy head." You know, she was
> competing with people who look different than her. Nothing is wrong
> with competing but when it's negative and your teachers make you feel
> negative, something is wrong with that. Afua was going through that
> when she was there. And her self-esteem was *very, very, damaged* [italics
> added]. (Henry, 2006, p. 337)

In contrast, Mavis describes her niece's confidence after several months at an African-centered school in which she cherished her African American female identity, noting that she no longer felt pressure to fit into the mainstream notions of female beauty. Mavis mentions her hair as an important racial signifier that distinguishes people of African descent from other racial groups in unique ways:

> It was only a couple of months ago she wouldn't dare wear her hair the way she wears it now. It had to be permed or pressed. But she wears a wrap. She gets those little twists. She wants locks, and she speaks out. (Henry, p. 337)

Culture-centered educational programs and schools help students to understand the world from their own culturally informed perspectives and to feel as proud and confident as Mavis's niece Afua. Culture-centered schools incorporate drumming and singing and cultural blessings into the curriculum. They also emphasize respect for elders, cultural traditions, rituals, and spirituality. The teaching and the curriculum are rigorous. At the same time, these schools legitimate cultural stores of knowledge and cultural ways of being as well as reinforce service to the community, nation, and world (Lee, 2007).

Chief Leschi K–12 Schools in Puyallup, Washington (http://www.leschischools.org/), is one example of a culture-centered school. New Concept Preschool in Chicago, Illinois, is another (http://www.savvysource.com/preschool/profile_sh53569_New_Concept_School), as well as its sister school for older students, the Betty Shabazz International Charter School (http://www.bsics.net). These schools for Native American (Chief Leschi) and African American students (New Concept and Betty Shabazz) share important characteristics.

Most successful schools based on cultural affirmation reinforce students' needs for caring teachers and a supportive environment in which they feel validated. These schools also help students make sense of the world and help them realize that they can become effective participants in society. Teachers in these settings try to construct meaningful pedagogies, cocreate transformative knowledge with their students, and develop critically literate citizens. This is not to say that these goals are unachievable in mainstream public and private schools. In fact, most progressive teachers work to accomplish these goals whether working in single-sex, private, or public schools. School settings with small classes, high teacher expectations, individual student attention, empowering lessons, positive classroom climates, student leadership development, and family involvement facilitate successful learning. Most important, parents who send their children to schools based on cultural themes have particular philosophies or beliefs about (1) the potential of these schools to educate their children or (2) the role of culture, race, and gender in the identity formation and spiritual well-being of their children.

SINGLE-SEX SCHOOLS: LESSONS ABOUT GOOD PEDAGOGY

Single-sex education has had a controversial history in the United States. Despite research findings and popular opinion that support and oppose single-sex schooling, schools that focus on gendered education have experienced a renaissance for both boys and girls since the mid-1990s. Title IX of the Education Amendments of 1972 was designed to promote educational equity for all students, regardless of their sex. Typically associated with women and sports, it has had slow but far-reaching implications for sex equity throughout education. More recently, the No

Child Left Behind Act (NCLB) of 2001 provided new regulations in 2006 that clarified legal confusion over the status of single-sex education in public schools and provided incentives for their creation.

Riordan (1985, 1990, 2003)—one of the foremost scholars of single-sex schooling—has argued that single-sex or single-gender (Datnow & Hubbard, 2002) education benefits most students from lower socioeconomic backgrounds, students who are historically disadvantaged, and students who are racial, ethnic, or religious minorities. Riordan's research indicates that urban school districts with a majority of low-income students of color are well suited for single-sex education, especially in settings where other reforms and experiments have had little success.

Gender and racial socialization take place in all academic institutions. However, parents may send their children to single-sex schools for a variety of reasons, many of which were discussed earlier in this chapter. Most often, parents believe that these schools offer optimal conditions for academic, social, and emotional success. Parents who send their children to single-gender schools believe that they will experience less bullying and harassment because of their gender performance. However, youth who express their gender in nonconformist ways, who do not experience their gender in conventional biological ways, or who do not fit into the all-male or all-female single-sex schooling dichotomy may feel unsafe in a single-sex school. The 2007 Gay Lesbian Straight Educators Network (GLSEN) school climate survey reported that 44.1 percent of students stated they were physically harassed (e.g., pushed or shoved) at school in the previous year because of their sexual orientation, and 30.4 percent because of their gender expression. The majority (60.1 percent) did not report these incidents to school faculty or staff. They believed that no action would be taken or that there would be negative repercussions (Kosciw, Diaz, & Greytak, 2007).

There are many models of single-sex education. Some regions have experimented with separate subject-based classes for both girls and boys. San Ysidro Secondary School, a predominantly Latino school (92 percent) of 2,400 youth in San Diego, gives students the option of all-male, all-female, or coeducational classes for mathematics and science. About one-third of the students opt for single-gender classes. The school principal, Hector Ezpinoza, describes an improved learning environment with "less disciplinary problems, less trying to show off with each other" (cited in Schemo, 2006).

The most well-known and traditional single-sex model involves separate schools for both girls and boys as has been the case, for example, in the history of Catholic and other religious-based education. More controversial have been separate classes, programs, or schools for one gender at the exclusion of other(s): for example, the Afrocentric boys' academies in Baltimore, Detroit, and Milwaukee based on the premise that African American males are disempowered in the mainstream public school system. These schools are seen as a way to increase literacy, academic achievement, and the presence of positive Black male images and role models. Another example is the Young Women's Leadership Schools of East Harlem, Philadelphia, Astoria, Brooklyn, Queens, and Chicago. These schools, predominantly African American and Latina, provide academically rigorous college preparatory education for low-income girls of color. The Young Women's Leadership Charter School (YWLCS) of Chicago is discussed later in this chapter.

These alternative educational settings have been established because educators and parents have been concerned about the raced and gendered ways that the academic and career opportunities of students are limited in mainstream schools. Educators usually have recognized that there are prejudices and stereotypes regarding female success in what are often considered male subject areas and professions. Certain academic disciplines (humanities and social sciences) and school subjects (reading and writing) are considered "female" while other domains (physical sciences and mathematics) and school subjects (calculus, physics) are considered "masculine." These societal attitudes were manifested in 1992 when Mattel released "Teen Talk Barbie" dolls that could utter "math class is tough!" (Company News, 1992). Lawrence Summers, the former president of Harvard University, suggested that innate sex differences may be responsible for the predominance of males in science and engineering careers (cited in Lewin, 2008). Education theorists have examined and criticized the Eurocentric and masculine assumptions of these disciplines and the positioning of White middle-class women vis-à-vis these fields (Bryson & de Castell, 1998). Atwater (2000) has argued that "gender has become a code word in science education that refers to White females' ideas" (p. 371).

Few educational researchers combine the complex interplay of race and gender with current cognitive, social, and psychological development theory. However, there are some examples. Black, Latina, and Native American scholars who are interested in understanding the learning of girls of color in science, technology, engineering, and mathematics (STEM) have considered the kinds of communities in which girls of color live, their intergenerational relationships and community networks, and their cultural values and conceptual systems (Deyhle & Margonis, 1995; Parsons & Moore, in press; Pinkard, 2005)

Young Women's Leadership Charter School of Chicago

I observed the unique and exciting teaching and learning at YWLCS of Chicago and its approach to teaching a predominantly Black and Latina female population from 2002 to 2006. (The student population in 2008 was 73 percent African American, 17 percent Latina, 9 percent White, and 1 percent Asian). In grades 7–12, girls are provided a rigorous academic education with a focus on mathematics, science, and technology in cooperative, collaborative classrooms.

It is significant that school subjects such as science and mathematics are raced and gendered and that racism and sexism influence the experiences and opportunities of girls and women of color in these domains (Calabrese & Tan, 2009; Parsons & Mutegi, 2007). Multiple and complex factors contribute to the academic disengagement of adolescent girls of color generally and specifically in mathematics, science, and technology. These factors include lack of essential facilities and resources, low parental and teacher expectations, negative peer interactions in coeducational learning environments, ineffective pedagogical approaches, a shortage of female role models and mentors, and a set of deeply rooted social dynamics, especially in low-income areas.

The YWLCS curriculum focuses on mathematics, science, and technology, areas in which women—especially women of color—have long been underrepresented. At YWLCS, educators from custodians to administrators are working to bring about a transformative learning environment. Teachers work in collaborative ways to support each other's instructional growth and to monitor student progress. The original goal of this public charter school of 345 girls was to address academic social inequality in schooling. The school leaders with whom I worked assumed that access is related to economic privilege (class) but also to the interconnectedness of race and gender oppression and exclusion. The school is racially and economically diverse, drawing students from more than 30 neighborhoods in Chicago.

Girls' voices are valued at YWLCS and the teachers *expect* girls to (re)claim their voices as confident, competent students. Self-advocacy and leadership skills are a major focus. Former instructional leader Dr. Camille Farrington writes,

> Recognizing the need to develop explicit self-advocacy strategies in historically disenfranchised groups seems to me to be very culturally responsive. It is recognizing the particular socio-historical position of minority students in majority-white institutions, and providing direct mechanisms to help students develop specific skills and strategies to better negotiate that position. (personal communication, December 15, 2008)

U.S. society expects and fosters academic achievement and advocacy skills among its most privileged, but for the least privileged, they are often not expected nor made accessible. Part of the YWLCS pedagogical project regarding race and gender involves what Audre Lorde (1984) writes about as "extirpating the oppressor within" so that young Black and Latina women can envision empowering possibilities rather than internalize societal stereotypes (p. 123). Dr. Margaret Small, founding director, explained:

> So our school takes in the urban population of young women who—the majority of them do not come into high school having high expectations or expecting a high level of success in their lives. This is like creating a new culture within their [cultural] framework and trying to provide the tools that are necessary to get them there. (personal interview, August, 24, 2004)

Understanding the raced and gendered lives of students has meant rethinking teaching practices that are entrenched in methods and ways of knowing from teachers' professional programs, traditions, and particular life experiences. These practices may further disempower already marginalized students.

Farrington and Small (2008) address two major barriers to secondary school graduation and postsecondary success: student deficiencies in course credits and gaps in necessary knowledge and skills. These are consequences of 100-year-old practices based on seat time and Carnegie units, an inherently punitive system for already marginalized students or students who need to make up credits. If students do not do well on tests and assignments right from the beginning, disadvantages can accumulate. Farrington, Small, and colleagues reconfigured the underlying philosophy and practice of student assessment.

The YWLCS system of assessment is more rigorous than that of most traditional schools because of its expectation for success and close monitoring so that students are kept on track and understand the consequences of their assessments. Students take responsibility to ensure authentic learning. Academic success and college admission are not only possible but also are attained. For example, 87 percent of the 2007 graduating class was enrolled in postsecondary education or college.

Student success is based on proficiency outcomes. Using evidence of student learning, teachers rate students as high performing (HP), proficient (P), or not yet proficient (NYP) for each course outcome. These outcome requirements increase incrementally each year, for example 70 percent proficiency in grade nine, 75 percent in grade ten, 80 percent in grade 11, and 85 percent to graduate. Girls are given opportunities to revisit and reach the proficiency requirements retroactively. Student work reflects the best work to date rather than snapshots. Many supports are in place to enable the girls to meet their goals. Teachers monitor and support students with supplementary Saturday classes, after school minicourses, and tailored summer instruction. One Spanish teacher throws "Not Yet parties" after school. He selects an outcome with a high number of NYP ratings, sends a personal invitation to each student with a NYP rating on that particular outcome, and then provides an afternoon workshop to help students learn that outcome and become proficient (Farrington & Small, 2008).

As Farrington and Small (2008) illustrate, a radical restructuring of curriculum, pedagogy, policy, and support is needed specific to the race- and gender-specific situations in which we teach. At YWLCS, the system rather than the students is envisioned as at risk. These cultivated sharp analyses of inequity are part of the teachers' antiracist/antisexist practice. They interrogated their own practices and streamlined them to the realities of their students to create an empowering environment.

CONCLUSION

This chapter emphasizes the interdependence of race and gender in education. The two are often seen as mutually exclusive or are frequently misunderstood concepts, sometimes because of their unclear usage. An important goal of this chapter is to increase understandings of these two concepts that have undergone radical rethinking in recent years. The awareness of race and gender in the academic lives of students can help teachers become critical observers of how power and privilege work and how students navigate and negotiate their lives and identities inside and outside school. Critical examinations of race and gender also help teachers to understand the ways in which social inequality is institutional and how it shapes our lives in real and often unconscious ways. As teachers, we can begin to understand how different groups experience structural and personal limitations and how we can challenge and transform these inequities. The focus on schooling alternatives gives a vision of what is possible rather than a sense of the impossibility for change in schools. Importantly, at YWLCS and other alternative schools described in this chapter, teachers were united around core beliefs and understandings that led them to work toward changing life chances for students of color.

Several Things You Can Do

1. Think outside of binaries (race-is-more-important-than-gender or Black/White; male/female; gay/straight, us/them)
2. Seek to understand how the interlocking dimensions of race and gender have shaped your own experiences and opportunities. Seek to understand how race and gender have shaped the academic and social outlooks, experiences, and opportunities of your students.

3. View your students' raced and gendered identities as rich curricula.

4. Help students develop analyses of race/gender intersections in age-appropriate ways.

5. Work to eradicate the unproductive racialized and gendered assumptions regarding academic success at your school. Work toward equity and access with other social justice-minded teachers at your school.

Questions and Activities

1. Power and oppression can operate through institutions. Consider how institutions structure your daily life. (Institutions can also be systems of thought, for example, the family, social relationships.) How has the raced and gendered nature of schooling played a role in your academic life?

2. Take the time to examine several education textbooks. Examine the index and then the table of contents. How are race and gender organized and discussed in the book? Are they discussed separately?

3. Can you think of examples in your own teaching in which you use configurations of race and gender together as part of your curriculum? If not, how might you begin to transform learning in this way?

4. Give several examples of how you "perform" gender and race. How do students at your school perform gender and race? How do race and gender play out in the academic lives of your students? What insights have you gained from reading this chapter that might cause you to rethink curriculum, pedagogy, and assessment?

5. Initiate discussions with your colleagues that explicitly examine race and gender together. What discussions might be needed to transform your learning environment?

6. Camille Farrington and Margaret Small built their assessment model on the notion that "success breeds success." Discuss what you found most interesting about the YWLCS assessment system. Did it provide you any new insights? Did it stimulate unanswered questions? What kinds of strategies are in place to make assessment inclusive for the most marginalized students at your school? Are other strategies needed?

Recommended Books

American Association of University Women (AAUW) (1998). *Separated by sex: A critical look at single-sex education for girls*. Washington, DC: AAUW Educational Foundation.

Ayers, W., Quinn, T., & Stovall, D. (2009). *Handbook of social justice in education*. New York: Routledge.

Bernal, D. D., Elenes, C. A., Godinez, F., & Villenas, S. (Eds.) (2006). *Chicana/Latina education in everyday life: Feminista perspectives on pedagogy and epistemology*. Albany: State University of New York Press.

Bornstein, K. (1998). *My gender workbook: How to become a real man, a real woman, the real you, or something else entirely*. New York: Routledge.

Combahee River Collective: A Black feminist statement (1977/1982). In P. Scott & B. Smith (Eds), *All the women are White, all the Blacks are men, but some of us are brave* (pp. 13–22). Old Westbury, NY: The Feminist Press.

Connell, R. (2005). *Masculinities* (2nd ed.). Berkeley: University of California Press.

Das Gupta, T., James, C., Maaka, R., Galabuzi G-E., & Andersen, C. (Eds.). (2007). *Race and racialization: Essential readings.* Toronto, ON: Canadian Scholars' Press.

De Jesus, M. (2005). *Pinay power: Theorizing the Filipina/American experience.* New York: Routledge.

Grande, S. (2004). *Red pedagogy: Native American social and political thought.* Lanham, MD: Rowman & Littlefield.

Haslanger, S. (2005). Gender and race: (What) are they? (What) do we want them to be? In A. Cudd & R. Andreasen (Eds.), *Feminist Theory: A Philosophical Inquiry.* (pp. 154–175). Malden, MA: Blackwell.

Kumashiro, K. (2001). *Troubling intersections of race and sexuality: Queer students of color and anti-oppressive education.* Lanham, MD: Rowman & Littlefield.

Kunjufu, J. (2005). *Keeping Black boys out of special education.* Chicago: African American Images.

References

Adams, M., Bell, L., & Griffin, P. (2007). *Teaching for diversity and social justice* (2nd ed.). New York: Routledge.

Aguirre, J. (2009, in preparation). Privileging mathematics and equity in teacher education: Framework, counter-resistance strategies, and reflections from a Latina mathematics educator. In B. Greer, S. Mukhodvadhyay, S. Nelson-Barber, & A. Powell (Eds.), *Culturally responsive mathematics education* (295–319). New York: Routledge.

Alcoff, L. M. (2006). *Visible identities: Race, gender, and the self.* New York: Oxford University Press.

Allen, P. G. (1987). *The sacred hoop: Recovering the feminine in American Indian traditions.* Boston: Beacon Press.

American Association of University Women (AAUW). (2008). *Where the girls are: The facts about gender equity in education.* Washington, DC: American Association of University Women Educational Foundation.

Apple, M. (2007). Foreword. In J. Van Galen & G. Noblit (Eds.), *Late to class: Social class and schooling in the new economy* (pp. vii–xi). Albany: State University of New York Press.

Applebaum, B. (2007). Engaging student disengagement: Resistance or disagreement? *Philosophy of Education Yearbook*, 333–345.

Atwater, M. M. (2000). Females in science education: White is the norm and class, language, lifestyle, and religion are nonissues. *Journal of Research in Science Teaching, 37*(4), 386–387.

Ayers, W., Dohrne, B., & Ayers, R. (2001). *Zero tolerance: Resisting the drive for punishment in our schools.* New York: W. W. Norton.

Back, L., & Solomos, J. (Eds.). (2000). *Theories of race and racism.* New York: Routledge.

Banks, M. (1996). *Ethnicity: Anthropological constructions.* London: Routledge.

Banks, J. A. (2007). Approaches to multicultural curriculum reform. In J. A. Banks & C. A. M. Banks (Eds.), *Multicultural education: Issues and perspectives* (6th ed., pp. 247–269). Hoboken, NJ: John Wiley.

Berlak, A., & Moyenda, S. (2001). *Taking it personally: Racism from kindergarten to college*. Philadelphia: Temple University Press.

Bhavnani, R., Mirza, H., & Meetoo, V. (2005). *Tackling the roots of racism*. London: Joseph Rowntree.

Blake, B. (1995). Broken silences: Writing and construction of cultural texts by urban pre-adolescent girls. *Journal of Educational Thought, 29*(2), 165–180.

Blount, J. (2005). *Fit to teach: Same-sex desire, gender, and school work in the twentieth century*. Albany: State University of New York Press.

Body of the beholder: White and African American body image differ. (1995, April 24). *Newsweek*, p. 14.

Bowser, B. (1991). *Black male adolescents: Parenting and education in community context*. Lanham, MD: University Press of America.

Boyung, L. (2006). Teaching justice and living peace: Body, sexuality, and religious education in Asian-American communities. *Religious Education, 101*(3), 402–419.

Brown, E. R. (2003). Freedom for some, discipline for "others": The structure of inequity in education. In K. J. Saltman, & D. A. Gabbard (Eds.), *Education as enforcement: The militarization and corporatization of schools* (pp. 127–152). New York: Routledge Falmer.

Bryson, M., & de Castell, S. (1998). Gender, new technologies, and the culture of primary schooling: Imagining teachers as Luddites in/deed. *Journal of Policy Studies, 12*(5), 542–67.

Butler, J. (1993). *Bodies that matter: On the discursive limits of sex*. London: Routledge.

Caldwell, K. (2007). *Negras in Brasil: Re-envisioning Black women, citizenship, and the politics of identity*. New Brunswick, NJ: Rutgers University Press.

Calabrese, A., & Tan, E. (2009). Funds of knowledge and discourses and hybrid space. *Journal of Research in Science Teaching, 46*(1) 1–26.

Cameron, M. (2005). Two-Spirited aboriginal people: Continuing cultural appropriation by non-aboriginal society. *Canadian Women's Studies, 24*(2/3), 123–127.

Carter, S. (2001). *The possibilities of silence: African American female cultural identity and secondary English classrooms*. Unpublished doctoral dissertation, Vanderbilt University, Nashville, Tennessee.

Carter, S. (2006). She would have still made that face expression: The use of multiple literacies by two African American young women. *Theory into Practice, 45*(4), 352–358.

Chang, B., & Au, W. (2007). You're Asian, how could you fail math? Unmasking the myth of the model minority. *Rethinking Schools, 22*(2), 16–19.

Children's Defense Fund (2008). *Cradle to prison pipeline campaign*. California Factsheet. Retrieved December 24, 2008, from http://www.childrensdefense.org/site/DocServer/CDF_CA_CPP_revised_fact_sheet_OCT_2008_Finalv2.pdf?docID=4364

Collins, P. H. (2000). *Black feminist thought*. Boston: Unwin Hyman.

Company News: Mattel says it erred; Teen talk Barbie turns silent on math. (1992, October 21). *New York Times online*. Retrieved December 16, 2008, from http://query.nytimes.com/gst/fullpage.html?res=9E0CE7DE103AF932A15753C1A964958260

Cudd, A., & Andreasen, R. (Eds.). (2005). *Feminist theory: A philosophical anthology*. Malden, MA: Blackwell.

Cudd, A., & Jones, L. (2005). Sexism. In A. Cudd & R. Andreasen (Eds.), *Feminist theory: A philosophical anthology* (pp. 73–83). Malden, MA: Blackwell.

Dalmage, H. (Ed.). (2004). *The politics of multiracialism: Challenging racial thinking*. Albany: State University of New York Press.

Datnow, A., & Hubbard, L. (2002). *Gender in policy and practice: Perspectives on single-sex and co-educational schooling*. New York: Routledge.

Davies, B. (1993). *Shards of glass: Children reading and writing beyond gendered identities*. Creskill, NJ: Hampton.

Davies, C. (1995). Hearing Black women's voices: Transgressing imposed boundaries. In C. B. Davies & M. Ogundipe-Leslie (Eds.), *Moving beyond boundaries*, vol.1 (pp. 3–14). New York: New York University Press.

Davis, J. E. (2000). Mothering for manhood: The (re)production of a Black son's gendered self. In C. Brown II & J. E. Davis (Eds.), *Black sons to mothers: Compliments, critiques, and challenges for cultural workers in education* (pp. 52–70). New York: Peter Lang.

Deyhle, D., & Margonis, F. (1995). Navajo mothers and daughters: Schools, jobs, and the family. *Anthropology and Education Quarterly*, *26*, 135–67.

Dwyer, C., Shah, B., & Sanghera, G. (2008). From cricket lover to terror suspect: Challenging representations of young Muslim men. *Gender, Place, and Culture*, *15*(2), 117–128.

Eckholm, E. (2006, March 20). Plight deepens for Black men. *New York Times online*. Retrieved December 23, 2008, from http://www.nytimes.com/2006/03/20/national/20blackmen.html?pagewanted=all

Elsworth, C. (2008, July 23). U.S. newsreader Katie Couric claims she is a victim of sexism. Telegraph.co.uk. Retrieved July 24, 2008, from http://www.telegraph.co.uk/news/worldnews/northamerica/usa/2450175/US-newsreader-Katie-Couric-claims-she-is-a-victim-of-sexism.html

Evans, G. (1992). Those loud Black girls. In D. Spender & E. Sarah (Eds.), *Learning to lose: Sexism and education* (2nd ed., pp. 183–190). London: Women's Press.

Fanon, F. (1967). *Black skin, White masks*. New York: Grove.

Farrington, C., & Small, M. (2008). *A new model of student assessment for the 21st century*. Washington, DC: American Youth Policy Forum.

Fausto-Sterling, A. (1993). The five sexes: Why male and female are not enough. *The Sciences*, *33*(2), 20–24.

Ferguson, A. (2000). *Bad boys: Public schools in the making of Black masculinity*. Ann Arbor: University of Michigan Press.

Fine, M. (1991). *Framing dropouts*. Albany: State University of New York Press.

Fine, M., & Weis, L. (1998). *The unknown city: Lives of poor and working-class adults*. Boston: Beacon.

Finitzo, M. (Director). (2001). *5 Girls* [Motion picture]. New York: Women Make Movies.

Forbes, J. (1990). The manipulation of race, caste and identity: Classifying Afro-Americans, Native American and Red-Black people. *Journal of Ethnic Studies*, *17*(4) 1–50.

Fordham, S. (1993). Those loud Black girls. *Anthropology and Education*, *24*(1), 3–32.

Fordham, S. (1996). *Blacked out*. New York: Routledge.

Francis, B. (2006). The nature of gender. In C. Skelton, B. Francis, & L. Smulyan (Eds.), *The Sage handbook of gender and education* (pp. 7–17). Thousand Oaks, CA: Sage.

Freeman, C., and Fox, M. (2005). *Status and trends in the education of American Indians and Alaska Natives* (NCES 2005-108). Washington, DC: U.S. Government Printing Office. Retrieved January 8, 2009, from http://nces.ed.gov/pubs2005/2005108.pdf

Freire, P. (1970). *Pedagogy of the oppressed*. New York: Herder & Herder.

Gay, G. (2000). *Culturally responsive teaching: Theory, research, and practice*. New York: Teachers College Press.

Gibbs, J. (1988). *Young, Black and male in America: An endangered species*. Dover, MA: Auburn House.

Gillborn, D. (2008). *Racism and education: Coincidence or conspiracy*. London & New York: Routledge.

Gilroy, P. (1993). *The Black Atlantic: Modernity and double consciousness*. Boston: Harvard University Press.

Glasser, H., & Smith, J. (2008). On the vague meaning of gender in educational research: The problem, its sources, and recommendations for practice. *Educational Researcher, 37*(6), 343–350.

Goldberg, T. (1994). *Multiculturalism: A critical reader*. Cambridge, MA: Blackwell.

Grant, L. (1984). Black females "place" in desegregated classrooms. *Sociology of Education, 57*(2), 98–111.

Gutierrez, C., Larson, J., Enciso, P., & Ryan, C. (2007). Discussing expanded spaces for learning. *Language Arts, 85*(1), 69–77.

Hall, S. (1997). Introduction. In S. Hall (Ed.), *Representation: Cultural representations and signifying practices* (pp. 1–17). Thousand Oaks, CA: Sage.

Henry, A. (1998a). Complacent and womanish: Girls negotiating their lives in an African centered school in the U.S. *Race, Ethnicity and Education, 1*(2), 151–170.

Henry, A. (1998b). Speaking up and speaking out: Examining voice in a reading/writing program with adolescent African Caribbean girls. *Journal of Literacy Research, 30*(2), 233–252.

Henry, A. (2005). Black feminist pedagogy: Critiques and contributions. In W. Watkins (Ed.), *Black protest thought* (pp. 89–106). New York: Peter Lang.

Henry, A. (2006). "There's salt-water in our blood": The "Middle Passage" epistemology of two black mothers regarding the spiritual education of their daughters. *International Journal of Qualitative Studies in Education, 19*(3), 329–345.

Hesse-Biber, S.N. (2004). *Feminist perspectives on social research*. New York: Oxford University Press.

Hirschfield, P. (2008). Preparing for prison? The criminalization of school discipline in the USA. *Theoretical Criminology, 12*(1), 79–101.

hooks, b. (1994). *Teaching to transgress*. New York: Routledge.

hooks, b. (2000). *Where we stand: Class matters*. New York: Routledge.

hooks, b., & West, C. (1991). *Breaking bread: Insurgent Black intellectual life*. Boston: South End.

James, C. (2003). *Seeing ourselves: Exploring race, ethnicity and culture*. Toronto, ON: Thompson Educational.

James, C. (2005). *Race and play: Understanding the socio-cultural worlds of student athletes*. Toronto, ON: Canadian Scholars' Press.

Jenkins, K. (2006). Constitutional lessons for the next generation of public single-sex elementary and secondary schools. *College of William and Mary Law Review, 47*(6), 1953–2044.

Jongsma, K. (1991). Critical literacy. *Reading Teacher, 44*(7), 518–519.

Joseph, G. (1988). Black feminist pedagogy in capitalist America. In M. Coles (Ed.), *Bowles and Gintis revisited: Correspondence and contradiction in educational theory* (pp. 174–186). London: Falmer.

Kao, C., & Hébert, T. (2006). Gifted Asian American adolescent males: Portraits of cultural dilemmas. *Journal for the Education of the Gifted*, *30*(1), 88–117.

Kosciw, J., Diaz, E., & Greytak, E. (2007). *The gay lesbian straight educators network national school climate survey*. New York: Gay Lesbian Straight Educators Network.

Larrotta, C. (2008). Written conversations with Hispanic adults developing English literacy. *Adult Basic Education and Literacy*, *2*(1), 13–23.

Lee, C. (2007). *Culture, literacy, and learning: Taking bloom in the midst of the whirlwind*. New York: Teachers College Press.

Lee, S. (1996). *Unraveling the model minority stereotype: Listening to the voices of Asian American youth*. New York: Teachers College Press.

Lee, S. (2004). Up against Whiteness: Students of color in our schools. *Anthropology and Education Quarterly*, *35*(1), 121–125.

Lei, J. (2003). Unnecessary toughness? Those "loud Black girls" and those "quiet Asian boys." *Anthropology and Education*, *34*(2), 156–181.

Lew, J. (2006). *Asian Americans in class: Charting the achievement gap among Korean American youth*. New York: Teachers College Press.

Lewin, T. (2008, July 25). Math scores show no gap for girls, study finds. *New York Times*, 16.

Lewis, A. (2003). Everyday racemaking: Navigating racial boundaries in schools. *American Behavioral Scientist*, *47*(3), 283–305.

Lopez, N. (2003). *Hopeful girls, troubled boys: Race and gender disparity in urban education*. New York: Routledge.

Lorde, A. (1984). *Sister outsider*. New York: The Crossing Press.

McCready, L. (2004). Understanding the marginalization of gay and gender-non-conforming Black male students. *Theory into Practice*, *42*(2), 146–143.

Millard, E. (1997). *Differently literate: Boys, girls and the schooling of literacy*. London: Falmer.

Mills, C. (2002). Red shifts: Embodied politics. In G. Jansen (Ed.), *The philosophical "I": Personal reflections on philosophy* (pp. 155–175). Lanham, MD: Rowman & Littlefield.

Mirza, H. (1992). *Young, female and Black*. London: Routledge.

Mirza, H. (1993). The social construction of Black womanhood in British educational research: Towards a new understanding. In M. Arnot & K. Weiler (Eds.), *Feminism and social justice in education* (pp. 32–57). London: Falmer.

Moll, L. C., & Gonzàlez, N. (2004). A funds-of-knowledge approach to multicultural education. In J. A. Banks & C. A. M. Banks (Eds.), *Handbook of research on multicultural education* (2nd ed, pp. 699–715). San Francisco: Jossey-Bass.

Morales, P. (2001). Latinos and the "Other Race" option: Transforming U.S. concepts of race. *NCLA Report*, *34*(6), 40–46.

Morris, E.W. (2005). Tuck in that shirt! Race, class and gender in an urban school. *Sociological Perspectives*, *48*(1), 25–48.

Mun Wah, L. (1994). *The color of fear* [Motion picture]. Oakland, CA: Stir Fry Productions.

Nield, R., & Balfanz, R. (2006). *Unfulfilled promise: The dimensions and characteristics of Philadelphia's dropout crisis, 2000–2005*. Baltimore, MD: Johns Hopkins University Center for Social Organization of Schools.

Nieto, S. (2005). *Affirming diversity: The sociopolitical context of multicultural education* (5th ed). New York: Allyn & Bacon.

Obidah, J., & Howard, T. (2005). Preparing teachers for "Monday morning" in the urban school classroom: Reflecting on our pedagogies and practices as effective teacher educators. *Journal of Teacher Education, 56*(3), 248–255.

Okazawa-Rey, M., Robinson, T., & Ward, J. (1986). Women and the politics of skin and hair. *Women and Therapy, 6*, 89–102.

Omolade, B. (1994). *The rising song of African American women*. New York: Routledge.

Omi, M., & Winant, H. (1994). *Racial formation in the United States: From the 1960s to the 1990s*. New York: Routledge.

Osler, A., & Vincent, K. (2003). *Girls and exclusion: Rethinking the agenda*. London: Routledge Falmer.

Pang, V. O. (1996). Intentional silence and communication in a democratic society. *High School Journal, 79*, 183–190.

Parsons, E. C., & Moore, F. (in press). Black feminist thought: The lived experiences of two Black female science educators. In K. Scantlebury (Ed.), *Re-visioning science education from feminist perspectives: Challenges, choices, and careers*. Rotterdam: Sense Publishers.

Parsons, E. C., & Mutegi, J. W. (2007). *Race matters: Implications for science education*. New Orleans, LA: National Association for Research in Science Teaching.

Pinkard, N. (2005). *Learning to read in culturally responsive computer environments*. (CIERA Report #1-004). Ann Arbor: University of Michigan Center for the Improvement of Early Reading Achievement.

Quiroz, P. (2001). The silencing of Latino student "voice": Puerto Rican and Mexican narratives in eighth grade and high school. *Anthropology and Education Quarterly, 32*(3), 326–349.

Riordan, C. (1985). Public and Catholic schooling: The effects of gender context policy. *American Journal of Education*, 518–540.

Riordan, C. (1990). *Girls and boys in school: Together or separate?* New York: Teachers College Press

Riordan, C. (2003). Failing in school? Yes; victims of war? No. *Sociology of Education, 76*, 369–372.

Robinson, C. (2007). *From the classroom to the corner: Female dropouts' reflections on their school years*. New York: Peter Lang.

Sabol, W. J., & Couture, H. (2008, June). Prison inmates at midyear 2007. *Bureau of Justice Statistics Bulletin*. Retrieved May 3, 2009, at http://www.ojp.usdoj.gov/bjs/abstract/pim07.htm

Sadker, D., & Sadker, M. (1994). *Failing at fairness: How America's schools cheat girls*. New York: Scribner.

Schemo, D. J. (2006, October 26). Single-sex classes backed. *San Diego Union Tribune*. Retrieved December 16, 2008, from http://www.signonsandiego.com/uniontrib/20061025/news_1n25titleix.html

Schubert, W. (1986). *Perspective paradigm and possibility*. New York: Macmillan.

Shujaa, M. (1996). *Beyond desegregation: The politics of African American schooling*. Thousand Oaks, CA: Sage.

Sommers, C. F. (2000). *The war against boys: How misguided feminism is harming our young men*. New York: Simon & Schuster.

Steinem, G. (2008, January 8). Women are never frontrunners. *New York Times*. Retrieved July 15, 2008, from http://www.nytimes.com/2008/01/08/opinion/08steinem.html

Tateishi, C. (2007). Why are the Asian-American kids silent in class? Taking a chance with words. *Rethinking Schools, 22*(2), 20–23.

Titus, J. (2000). Engaging student resistance to feminism: "How is this stuff going to make us better teachers?" *Gender and Education, 121*(1), 21–37.

Walkerdine, V. (1990). *Schoolgirl fictions*. London: Verso.

Wallace, M. (1979). *The Black macho and the myth of the superwoman*. New York: Dial.

Warren, S. (2005). Resilience and refusal: African-Caribbean young men's agency, school exclusions, and school-based mentoring programmes. *Race, Ethnicity and Education, 8*(3), 243–259.

Weaver-Hightower, M. (2008). Inventing the "All-American Boy": A case study of the capture of boys' issues by conservative groups. *Men and Masculinities, 10*(3), 267–295.

Winant, H. (2004). *The new politics of race: Globalism, difference, justice*. Minneapolis: University of Minnesota Press.

West, C., & Zimmerman, D. (1987). Doing gender. *Gender & Society, 1*(2), 125–151.

Wilchins, R. (2004). *Queer theory, gender theory: An instant primer*. Los Angeles: Alyson.

Zabel, D. (2006). (Ed.) *Arabs in the Americas: Interdisciplinary essays on the Arab diaspora*. New York: Peter Lang.

Zinn, M., & Dill, B. (1996). Theorizing difference from multiracial feminism. *Feminist Studies, 2*(22), 321–331.

CHAPTER 9

Queer Lessons: Sexual and Gender Minorities in Multicultural Education

Cris Mayo

Part of the project of critical multiculturalism involves examining the political and social construction of the identities that structure social, political, and educational relations. It may seem relatively unremarkable that school practices and policies are now increasingly interested in addressing some categories of difference. However, other categories of identity such as minority sexuality are often not part of the official school curriculum or of multicultural education. The excluded categories often include lesbian, gay, and bisexual identity or gender identity, including students who are gender nonconforming, transgender, or intersex. LGBTQ is an abbreviation for these identities.

Because sexuality is a potentially controversial topic, LGBTQ, queer, and gender identity issues are not always considered part of multicultural education. Perhaps the assumption that *culture* refers to a group of people who have overwhelmingly complete similarities to one another or the concern that something such as sexuality is too controversial to easily fit into a "culture" provides an obstacle to thinking about the relationship between multiculturalism and seemingly noncultural forms of bias. Or there may be the mistaken assumption that because movements for the rights of LGBTQ people are historically relatively young, sexuality is a new form of difference and has not yet reached a point of development into a distinct culture. Or it may be that sexuality challenges some common assumptions about what constitutes a culture or that in order for a group to exist and be recognized as deserving respect, it has to first be a unified culture.

Rather than arguing that sexuality creates a distinct culture—though there has been ample work making similar arguments—it may be better to think that minority sexuality and gender expression form multiple kinds of cultures, subcultures, counterpublics, and communities. As a result of the globalization of capital and representation—and the transnational movement of people—those cultures, subcultures, counterpublics, and communities are sometimes locally distinct and sometimes globally similar to one another. These same complications to the concept of culture have been discussed by many multicultural theorists (for example Erickson in Chapter 2 of this volume) and, thus, including the categories of sexual and gender identity when thinking about diversity and difference makes sense.

SEXUALITY AND GENDER IDENTITY

Indeed, sexuality and gender identity are themselves internally diverse concepts, including both diversity of sexual partners, gendered bodies and identities, and other related categories of difference increasingly organized under the general term *queer* and in their own distinct communities. For instance, transgender people—people for whom gender categories are insufficient to express their identities or people for whom their birth sex does not conform with their gender identity—may find some common cause with lesbian, gay, and bisexual (LGB) people. But because the identity of transgender people is more centrally organized around gender, gender identity may be more crucial and these people may (or may not) seek medical intervention to bring their bodies into conformity with their identity. For intersexed people, that is, people with bodies that are not easily categorized by dominant categories of male and female, medical intervention to "normalize" their bodies may be a problem. Intersexed people are increasingly organizing to demand the right to freedom from unwanted medical intervention. Intersexed activism reminds the medical establishment, parents, and the broader community that even young people deserve to be able to give informed consent free from gender biases related to their status as gender minorities. Transvestites, because of their gender nonconformity and possible sexual nonconformity, are also at risk for harassment. Because gender transgression and some forms of transvestism have long been part of LGBTQ and queer culture, transvestites have connections with other categories of identity or social movements seeking gender and sexuality-related rights. Because the processes of normalization and the pressure to conform to dominant understandings of gender and sexuality affect people of all sexual and gender identities—including heterosexual and conventionally gendered people—examining the processes of normalization provides all people with a way to critically engage cultural, political, and educational messages about gender and sexuality. *Queer* is a concept and identity that works against problematic forms of normalization.

LGBTQ Issues and the School Curriculum

Increasingly, sexual and gender minorities are working to see that their issues are represented in school curricula and extracurricular groups largely because they remember the isolation of growing up in some way queer. Some state laws forbid discussion of minority sexuality in curricula, and other policy and cultural barriers to addressing minority sexuality and gender identity remain even when legal prohibitions against representing LGBTQ issues are lifted. Still, many teachers who know that they are teaching students who are LGBTQ or who are being raised by lesbian, gay, bisexual, or transgender parents would like to be able to make those students feel part of the school community but fear that addressing minority sexuality issues will put their jobs at risk. LGBTQ parents also face barriers to their participation in schools and are concerned that their children are inadequately protected from harassment (Casper & Schultz, 1999). LGBTQ teachers may be concerned that their identity puts them at risk in their jobs, especially if they are not protected by antidiscrimination laws and policies that cover sexual and gender identity. LGBTQ school leaders face the same pressures, yet research indicates that their experience of their own minority status makes them more concerned with creating a respectful school environment for students and school community members of all identities and backgrounds (Capper, 1999).

Incorporating LGBTQ issues into multicultural education is one way to ensure that schools and multiculturalism itself continue to be aware of the educational stakes of diverse students, families, and communities. Understanding the political and social histories of minority sexualities and gender identities in conversation with more well-known social justice histories can not only help to explain the multicultural aspects of movements for LGBTQ people but also highlight work against biases of all forms that still needs to be done within LGBTQ communities and in other movements and communities. At the same time that LGBTQ and related issues need to be made part of education against bias, the story of bias and limitation is not the only story to be told about sexual minority people, communities, and cultures. Understanding the long histories and varying experiences of sexuality-based communities and identities can provide a broader and more complex view of how sexuality has been one feature in the organization of social relations and identities. While part of the story of all differences needs to examine the processes of normalization, oppression, and resistance, it is also important to remember that those pressures are not the only experience of difference. That people are resilient, creative, responsible, and innovative is as true for people who have lived lives that do not conform to norms of gender and sexuality as it is for anyone.

OVERLAPPING HISTORIES OF MULTICULTURALISM AND LGBTQ MOVEMENTS

The modern gay movement usually dates its beginning to a rebellion of mostly young people of color, often complexly gendered, gay, lesbian, bisexual, and transgender who were bar patrons at the Stonewall Inn in Greenwich Village, New York, on June 28, 1969. After years of harassment by police, LGBTQ people decided to fight back, unleashing days of unrest in New York City and providing a center for the political organizing already begun there and elsewhere. However, dating the start of any movement is problematic—the 1966 Compton Cafeteria riots protesting the exclusion of gender-nonconforming people from that establishment predate Stonewall and centralize the link between gender and gay liberation (Stryker, 2008). Other important dates and activities are also associated with the beginning of the LGBTQ Civil Rights Movement. Smaller political advocacy groups or activists starting in the early 20th century challenged the categorization of homosexuality as a psychological disorder. Multiple small sexual and/or gender minority communities developed in various racial, ethnic, gendered, and geographical locations before Stonewall. But placing the beginnings of the social movement for sexuality and gender identity rights in the diverse context of the Stonewall riot underscores the importance of understanding minority sexuality as multicultural and part of the history and future of multicultural education.

Making Stonewall the beginning, although unofficial, of the gay liberation movement also centralizes the often unstable and linked struggles for rights for minority sexualities and genders. Patrons of the Stonewall Inn included gay men, lesbians, and transgender, transsexual, and transvestite people, some of whom were gay and some not. As active as transgender people have been in struggles for gay rights, they have also been excluded by those in the gay rights movement seeking rights for only a limited, respectable-appearing segment of the LGBTQ community. Stonewall also stands as a reminder that even radical movements may begin to enact exclusions (Frye, 2002).

Indebted to the Civil Rights Movement, the gay liberation movement often modeled itself after activism aimed at improving the lives of people of color. In part, this was so because some gay liberation activists were people of color and in part because the civil rights and Black power movements set the standard for activism during the 1960s. Activists within civil rights, Black feminism, women of color feminism, and Black power groups pushed the gay, women's, and lesbian movements to be aware of racism, and leaders in various movements urged their members to be critical of their dislike of gay people (Anzaldúa, 1990; Clarke, 1981, 1983; Combahee River Collective, 1982; Lorde, 1984, 1988; Smith, 1983). This was by no means a simple process or a utopian moment; movements were also energetically split on whether addressing minority sexuality and gender identity would delegitimize their claims or open them to ridicule. For instance, Betty Friedan, leader of the National Organization for Women, characterized lesbian involvement in the women's movement as a "lavender menace" (as cited in Brownmiller, 1970, p. 140). Civil rights leaders involved in the 1963 March on Washington had wanted Bayard Rustin removed as the lead organizer of the march when his homosexuality became known. Only through the intercession of A. Phillip Randolph was Rustin kept in charge (D'Emilio, 2003). The same tendency to exclude or ignore LGBTQ members of dominant communities is also paralleled in minority communities. It continues today through informal messages about the unacceptability of sexual minority identities (Duncan, 2005; Kumashiro, 2001, 2002, 2003) as well as through political debate in minority communities about HIV/AIDS (Cohen, 1999). LGBTQ communities are often structured by White dominance and are unwilling to see how Whiteness structures ideas about who is legitimately LGBTQ or who can easily access LGBTQ community resources and social spaces. This White dominance may be expressed through overt racism or implicitly assume what gayness means and thus be unwilling to recognize the sexual and gender identities that emerge within racial and ethnic communities.

Even though there may not always be sustained attention to diversity within groups organizing for social justice, by focusing on moments and strands within movements that acknowledge their complicity in forms of bias, we can see that multiculturally influenced politics, a politics attentive to multiple forms of diversity, has been a part of almost every political movement. Indeed, historian Herbert Apetheker (1992) has asked why so many histories of social movements are framed only as interested in their own issues and represented as if they were made up of relatively homogeneously identified people. He asks us to consider how the expectation that people will work only on their own behalf has limited our contemporary ability to imagine diversely organized politics. Even at the height of what has come to be known as the heyday of identity politics, many groups were calling their own prejudices into question and making connections across struggles and identities. Black Panther founder Huey Newton (1973), for instance, argued that all movements needed to challenge their biases, including sexism and homophobia and learn to work together in common cause. He wrote:

> Whatever your personal opinions and your insecurities about homo-
> sexuality and the various liberation movements among homosexuals and
> women (and I speak of the homosexuals and women as oppressed

groups), we should try to unite with them in a revolutionary fashion.
… I do not remember our ever constituting any value that said that a
revolutionary must say offensive things towards homosexuals, or that a
revolutionary should make sure that women do not speak out about
their own particular kind of oppression. As a matter of fact, it is just the
opposite: we say that we recognize the women's right to be free. We
have not said much about the homosexual at all, but we must relate to
the homosexual movement because it is a real thing. And I know
through reading, and through my life experience and observations that
homosexuals are not given freedom and liberty by anyone in the society.
They might be the most oppressed people in the society. (p. 143)

Other groups such as the Black feminist Combahee River Collective opposed ranking oppressions. They viewed oppressions as "interlocking," including race, gender, class, and sexuality as part of a critique of unequal social relations (Combahee River Collective, 1982). By taking account of the intersections of categories of identity, it becomes clear that the identities of all people are multiple. By examining the critiques of the various rights and liberation movements, we can further understand that all communities are made up of diverse people, not all of whom are adequately served by the community norms or political groups that claim to represent them. Furthermore, forms of gender and sexual identity emerge from within different cultural, racial, and ethnic traditions and thus push us to understand the importance of place, context, and relation. Transnational immigration brings diverse understandings of sexual and gender identity into conversation with dominant versions, and racial and ethnic traditions provide particular forms of gender and sexual identities and activities that inform, challenge, and mingle with dominant forms (Manalansan, 2003).

Children of the Rainbow Guide

Situating the LGBTQ movement squarely within multiculturalism and civil rights provides a strategy for understanding the need to bring sexuality more firmly into multicultural education in order to address long-standing exclusions in education. While not common in all approaches to multiculturalism, sexual minority issues have been incorporated into multicultural curricula and have been strongly challenged. Controversy broke out in New York City in the early 1990s over the multicultural education teachers' guide *Children of the Rainbow* (New York City Board of Education, 1994). The guide included suggestions for lessons on the diversity of family structures—including gay and lesbian families. The goal was to help all students feel comfortable and valued in school. While the earlier outcry over the multicultural New York State social studies standards had mobilized social conservatives to work against inclusion of lessons on racial diversity, the controversy over the *Rainbow* curricula marked a switch in tactics with social conservatives advocating for the inclusion of so-called legitimate minorities but not minority sexual orientation or families (Mayo, 2004a/2007). *Children of the Rainbow* was not the first time sexual orientation was recognized in New York City's educational policy. The New York City Board of Education had included sexual orientation as a protected class since 1985

(New York City Board of Education), but *Children of the Rainbow* was the first concerted effort to bring sexual minority issues into the multicultural curriculum.

By suggesting that teachers infuse lessons on cultural diversity throughout traditional curricular areas, *Children of the Rainbow* attempted to have students understand multiculturalism as part of all of their school, community, and home activities, not simply as a stand-alone lesson on tolerance or respect. To highlight possible differences in family structures, the curriculum guide suggested that teachers make sure that they include lessons not only on families that were headed by grandparents or families created through adoption but also that *the Rainbow* Curriculum would help the children of lesbian- or gay-headed households feel appreciated by the school community (New York City Board of Education, 1994).

In 1985, when New York City began developing multicultural education, gay and lesbian educators tried to be included in the process. It was not until the curriculum guide was nearly ready for release, however, that one lesbian teacher was invited to contribute a lesson on respect for families that included gay families (Humm, 1994). Her addition was not put through what had been the standard review process; in a context in which references to gay relationships had already been removed from New York City's HIV/AIDS curriculum, the addition drew notice and protest. Protesters argued that the *Rainbow* curriculum was intent on making their children gay and that by focusing attention on sexual minorities, it took valuable time away from minorities that deserved representation (Myers, 1992). Drawing on stereotypes that gay people were White, protesters argued that the educational demands of relatively privileged White people were supplanting the needs of students of color (Lee, Murphy, North, & Ucelli, 2000). In the end, school board elections drew historic numbers of voters, and both the supporters and opponents of gay-inclusive multiculturalism believed they had made their points. By opening public debate about the place of sexual minority issues in multicultural education, debate over *Children of the Rainbow* highlighted both the tenuousness of the acceptance of multiculturalism itself and the tendency for those uncomfortable with diversity to draw lines about what types of people were acceptable members of the school community and thus who should be represented by school lessons.

Children of the Rainbow was also notable for structuring its challenge to homophobia in the context of lessons on the family. As a counterstrategy to the conservative contention that family values meant excluding sexual minorities from legal protections and other forms of representation, including lesbian and gay families in suggested plans stood as a reminder of the diversity of families. As LGBTQ families increasingly make their presence and the presence of their children known to schools, it is important that schools accommodate both children and parents. A recent survey of LGBTQ parents indicates that they are more involved in school activities than average parents and that they experience insults from students, other parents, and school personnel (Kosciw & Diaz, 2008). Children of LGBTQ parents also experience a high rate of harassment because of their parents' sexuality or gender identity (Kosciw & Diaz). Basing inclusion in the curriculum on the family potentially normalizes some sexual minorities—gay and lesbian people who have children—while excluding all others, including bisexuals, transgender people, and anyone who is not in a family with children (Mayo, 2006). Rather than arguing that people should be respected because they are members of the community, however broadly conceived, the curriculum guide tactically limited its lesson of respect to children of gay parents.

CHALLENGES TO HOMOPHOBIA AND HETEROSEXISM

Many of the objections to educating students about LGBTQ, queer, and related issues in multicultural education still remain, arising from the kind of cultural conflicts that sexuality issues often engender. Not everyone thinks that LGBTQ, queer, and gender-nonconforming people should exist or deserve respect. Commonplace derogation of gay people in such phrases as "that's so gay" or epithets such as "faggot" or "dyke" indicate that homosexuality is still a focus of disapproval. A study conducted by students in five Des Moines, Iowa, high schools found that the average student hears words insulting gay people 25 times a day (Ruenzel, 1999). Cultural beliefs and religious texts are often interpreted to mean that LGBTQ people are aberrant, sinful, or at the very least unacceptable. Pushing beyond what seem to be determinative statements from a given culture or faith tradition often shows a much more complex picture of the situation in which same-sex affection and partnership have long played an important role in the culture or in which various gender expressions have found support in a tradition. It may, of course, be difficult for adherents of particular religious traditions to see the intensity of same-sex love and commitment within their texts or to even begin to grapple with how those positive representations coexist with prohibitions against similar activities.

Further complicating the issue of sexual orientation and gender identity may be the sense that such forms of diversity and difference come from somewhere else, not from within a particular cultural tradition but imposed from outside. For instance, current dominant forms of homophobia may be directed at people who appear to be simply gay but are, in fact, living traditional, indigenous identities. Two-spirit people, that is, people who embody American Indian traditional practices that defy contemporary definitions of gender and sexuality, often find themselves harassed by those ignorant of the place of third genders and sexualities in indigenous cultures (Wilson, 1996). A commonplace assumption about homosexuality, not unrelated to the former example, is that all gay people are White, partially related to the White dominance in many gay communities and to the inability to see diversity as more than one aspect of identity at a time. Too often discussions of diversity seem to assume that all people have one identity, not that they might live complex lives in which their multiple differences intersect and affect one another.

When we begin to complicate what sexuality means in relation to race, class, gender, disability, region, and religion, it quickly becomes clear that we need to be thinking not only about multiple versions and variations of sexual identity but also how different communities and contexts shape the life possibilities and definitions of sexual and gender identity of LGBTQ, queer, and gender minority people (Bello, Flynn, Palmer, Rodriguez, & Vente, 2004; Blackburn, 2004, 2005; Irvine, 1994; Johnson & Henderson, 2005; Kumashiro, 2004; Leck, 2000; McCready, 2004; Ross, 2005; Sears, 1995; Sonnie, 2000; Wilson, 1996). Minority sexualities and gender identities—like other differences within communities—are themselves reminders that not all in a given culture, race, ethnicity, or other seemingly similar coherent group are the same; there are differences within communities and subcultures structured around sexual orientation and gender identity. This may seem an obvious point, but dissent by members of communities from the sexual and/or gender norms of that community can result in a feeling that community norms have been disrupted and perhaps even a sense that the nonconformist person is a traitor to community cohesion. Of course, one can easily reverse the dynamic and wonder why communities and cultures cannot be more accepting of diversity in their midst.

Indeed, that is one of the central challenges that multicultural education poses to U.S. public schooling: Can we conceive of education as a welcoming place that recognizes difference?

Challenging Assumptions about LGBTQ People

Assumptions about sexual minority students need to be carefully analyzed. Schools, like the rest of the social world, are structured by heterosexism—the assumption that everyone is heterosexual. Curricula, texts, school policies, and even mundane examples (such as illustrations of magnets showing males attracted to females but repulsed by one another) are most often constructed to reflect that heterosexuality is not only the norm but also the only possible option for students (Friend, 1995). Heterosexism is also reinforced by homophobia, overt expressions of dislike, harassment, and even assault of sexual minority people, a practice that members of the school community often ignore or dismiss as typical behavior based on the heterosexist assumption that either there are no gay people present in school communities, or, if there are, those gay people ought to learn to expect a hostile environment. While homophobia may possibly be—at least in some places—less socially acceptable today than it was previously, it is nonetheless the case that schools are not very supportive places for most LGBTQ, queer, questioning, intersex, and ally students (that is, students who are not themselves LGBTQ but who oppose homophobia and heterosexism). The pressure to conform to rigid ideas about proper gender and sexuality is also damaging to heterosexual and gender-conforming students as well.

Members of school communities may believe that sexuality is not an appropriate topic for young people. However, there are significant numbers of LGBTQ, queer, and ally students in schools (as well as significant numbers of sexually aware heterosexual students). Ignoring the issue of sexuality means neglecting to provide LGBTQ students representations of themselves that enable them to understand themselves and to provide examples of ways to counter bias and work toward respect for those who may not initially be willing to respect LGBTQ students. Many LGBTQ students report hearing insulting words on a daily basis. According to the 2005 National School Climate Survey of Gay, Lesbian, Straight Educators Network (GLSEN), 75.4 percent of students reported hearing derogatory language such as "faggot" and "dyke" (Kosciw & Diaz, 2005). In the same report, 37.8 percent of students reported physical harassment because of their sexual orientation while 26.1 percent experienced physical harassment because of their gender orientation (Kosciw & Diaz). Physical assault on the basis of sexual orientation was reported by 17.6 percent of the students, and 11.8 percent reported physical assault because of their gender identity (Kosciw & Diaz). GLSEN's 2007 National School Climate Survey of 6,209 students reports that 73.6 percent of students heard derogatory remarks such as "faggot" and "dyke" frequently and nearly two-thirds of students heard similar remarks from teachers (Kosciw, Diaz, & Greytak, 2008). Kevin Jennings, the executive director of GLSEN, expressed his frustration with the lack of action:

> I quite honestly feel a little depressed by how little things have
> improved from when we published our first report almost a decade ago.
> Why is it—when research shows so clearly that there are specific policy
> and programmatic interventions that will make our schools safer—that
> so many states and districts do nothing, allowing schools to remain an

unsafe space for so many LGBTQ students? (cited in Kosciw, Diaz, & Greytak, p. viii)

The 2007 National School Climate Survey indicates little change in the frequency of homophobic harassment, negative remarks about students' gender expression, or sexist and racist remarks. Although racist remarks were reported less frequently than other forms of biased remarks, their frequency has been on the rise since 2003 (Kosciw, Diaz, & Greytak, 2008). LGBTQ students of color report the highest level of harassment. Girls and young women also report being sexually harassed and homophobically harassed in schools. Gender and race intersect to affect homophobic harassment in schools. According to an American Association of University Women (2001) study, 83 percent of young women experience sexual harassment, and 20 percent of them avoid school or certain classes in order to stay away from their tormentors. Young lesbians, gender-nonconforming young women, and any young person who is deemed by a harasser to be acting in gender inappropriate ways—including turning down sexual interest—are all open to homophobic and sexist harassment. The intersection between sexual and gender identity structures harassment, and the scope of gender/sexuality-related harassment is quite broad for women. Because young men have a narrower range of acceptable masculine behavior, they too are targets for homophobic harassment on the basis of any gender-nonconforming behavior or are apt to have any forms of disagreement devolve into homophobic taunts. The intersections of categories of identity, then, must become central to how educators think and learn before they can begin to teach their students. As Kosciw and Diaz (2005) put it:

> It appears that students most often report being targeted for verbal harassment based on multiple characteristics (e.g., being gay and Latino) or perhaps on the intersections of these characteristics (e.g., being a gay Latino). With regard to the more extreme forms of victimization, physical harassment and assault, it appears that sexual orientation alone becomes more salient. For example, the largest number of students of color reported being verbally harassed because of both their sexual orientation and race/ethnicity, followed by sexual orientation only (44.4% and 35.7%, respectively). However, nearly twice as many students of color reported physical assault because of their sexual orientation alone than reported assault because of both race/ethnicity and sexual orientation (11.7% vs. 6.8%). (p. 62)

The 2007 survey reported by Kosciw, Diaz, and Greytak (2008) continues to find that racial minority students experience more frequent harassment and assault; this is especially true of multiracial students. Transgender students report more frequent experiences of harassment based on their sexual orientation and gender expression than do female or male students (Kosciw, Diaz, & Greytak).

While most LGBTQ youth flourish and learn to counter the homophobic challenges they face and while it is important not only to focus on the challenges but also to stress the strength and resiliency of all minority youth, it is also crucial to understand that the costs of homophobia and bias against gender-nonconforming students can be very high. In February

2008, fifteen-year-old Lawrence King was murdered by a younger White student who had been part of a group bullying him for most of the school year. Larry endured daily taunting. King's twelve-year-old friend Erin Mings said, "What he [King] did was really brave—to wear makeup and high-heeled boots." Mings hung out with King at E. O. Green. "Every corner he turned around, people were saying, 'Oh, my God, he's wearing makeup today.'" Mings said King stood his ground and was an outgoing and funny boy. "When people came up and started punking him, he just stood up for himself" (Saillant, 2008a, 2008b). Out to his friends, Larry's story underscores the strength of young gender-nonconforming gay people and the very real dangers they can face in public schools. Wearing eye shadow to school and trying to be himself, Larry was continually open to taunting and bullying and tried to keep strong by flirting with his tormentors (Saillant). Reports indicate that school officials were aware of the potential difficulties between Larry and his attacker but did not intervene (Saillant).

King's story not only demonstrates his energy and commitment to living his life but also stands as reminder that much homophobia is fueled by bias against gender nonconformity (Gender Public Advocacy Coalition, 2002). The Gender Public Advocacy Coalition (Gender PAC), an organization dedicated to educating about gender identity, also noted in its 2002 annual report that not only were gender-nonconforming students the victims of bullying but also students who engaged in school violence had experienced such bullying. Whether or not the student shooters in the Lawrence King case were sexual minorities or whether this form of bullying is simply common, "five of eight assailants in recent school shooting incidents were reportedly students who had been repeatedly gender-bashed and gender-baited in school" (Gender PAC, p. 8). An American Association of University Women (2001) study reported that more than almost anything else, students do not want to be called gay or lesbian; 74 percent said they would be very upset.

Even students who are not gay report overt homophobic and sexual harassment when they express support for sexual minorities. As one student put it, after experiencing pornographic death threats from other students while teachers did nothing to stop them, "Maybe it's because I have strong views. I've always spoken out for gays and lesbians, for Latinos, for those who get trampled on in our society. Still, I really have no idea why I was treated with such hostility" (Ruenzel, 1999, p. 24). This example may show that not supporting gay people is an integral part of indicating one's own heterosexuality. Like Sleeter's (1994) observations that White people perform their race by expressing racist attitudes, people may perform heterosexuality by indicating their dislike of or discomfort around homosexuality.

The pressure on all students to conform to a gendered or heterosexual norm is powerful, especially in the school context where public knowledge and choices about identity are closely watched (Thorne, 1995). The public context of fifteen-year-old, Black, gender-nonconforming Sakia Gunn's assertion of her lesbianism when sexually and homophobically harassed on a Newark Street was both an important assertion of her claiming space in her community and the occasion of her murder by her harasser (Lesbian Stabbing, 2003). Her space of assertion was honored by the Newark community's outcry against homophobic violence in a mass vigil commemorating Gunn's death and life (Smothers, 2004). A year after her killing, the school district that refused to have a moment of silence for her just after her murder allowed the anniversary to be acknowledged by having "No Name Calling Day" (Smothers). It is important to understand that homophobic violence and the potential for harassment do structure the lives of sexual minorities. But the understanding of their identities by Gunn and other young people, of the places to go to find communities that support their gender and sexual identities, and of their ability to express their identities—even in challenging situations—demonstrates that sexual and gender minority youth are actively and creatively involved in making their lives and communities.

Despite what sometimes seems to be an overwhelmingly hostile context in schools, the concerted efforts of students, teachers, administrators, and other members of the school community can shift school climates. In 1995, when the gay-straight alliance at one Massachusetts school put up pink triangles on everyone's locker to publicize a Gay and Lesbian Awareness Day, they were met with hostility and misunderstanding. Students thought the group had intentionally put the triangles on the lockers of outcast students and tore them off or were told by teachers to take them down (Bennett, 1997). But after a sustained effort at antihomophobia education with teacher and administrator action, when a similar project started two years later, the group ran out of pink triangles and had to make more (Bennett). However, progress can be undone without adequate institutional and teacher support. One of the first gay-straight alliances to attain the right to meet in public schools using the federal Equal Access Act disbanded years later because of continuing community hostility and lack of institutional advocacy and support. That group, however, was recently reorganized and supported by a unanimous vote by school officials who were educated about and supportive of antihomophobia projects (American Civil Liberties Union, 2006).

Each of these examples points to the need to address homophobia and sexual minority issues through multilevel approaches. Youth are capable of asserting themselves and finding community with others, but without the institutional support of schools and the interventions of respectful adults, the struggles they may have to face are all the more daunting. Ensuring that sexual minority and gender minority identity youth have space and time to meet together creates one space in school that addresses their communities. Incorporating LGBTQ and gender identity issues in curricula, teacher education, school leadership programs, and school antidiscrimination policies are all strategies that reinforce inclusion across the entire school institution.

Each of these steps requires more than just stopping harassment. It requires thinking critically about the messages in curricula, the way teachers and administrators talk to students, and the way school-based social events are organized. Do representations of famous authors that are included in the curriculum describe the marital status of heterosexuals but completely neglect to discuss the sexual identity of nonheterosexuals? What do lessons say about Walt Whitman, Willa Cather, James Baldwin, and Audre Lorde, among many others? When lessons discuss Civil Rights Movements, do they include gender and sexual identity rights? Do lessons on families create openings for even very young children to see a diversity of families represented in children's books and classroom discussions? Do representations of romance and sexuality in the school—and this includes everything from sex education to advertisements for dances and proms—reflect only heterosexuality? Do teachers reinforce heterosexism by referring only to heterosexual couples, by assuming that everyone has a parent of each gender, by assigning texts that represent only heterosexuality, or by neglecting to address comments such as "that's so gay" with more than a simple prohibition?

WHY HOMOPHOBIA

Education against homophobia and about sexual minority issues needs to grapple with the cultural and traditional objections to sexual minority people and communities. Without addressing the deep cultural, political, and historical obstacles to educating LGBTQ people and educating about them, progress toward multicultural education and justice will be only halfhearted at best. While some religious traditions may be the root of some cultural disapproval of homosexuality, most religious traditions do not require their adherents to demand doctrinal discipline from those outside their faith tradition. Given the pervasiveness of homophobia even among people who do not ground their discomfort in religious traditions, it is clear that other anxieties also motivate discomfort about minority sexualities and gender identities. Many religious denominations are very supportive of sexual and gender minorities. Consequently, the tendency to blame religion for homophobia is an oversimplification. Denominations supportive of sexual and gender minorities include the Metropolitan Community Church, Reform Judaism, United Church of Christ, Society of Friends (Quakers), and Unitarianism as well as segments of the Episcopal and Lutheran churches. Individual congregations of many faiths are also supportive of sexual and gender minorities.

As education against homophobia proceeds, then, it is necessary to find ways both to support people who experience homophobia and to ask difficult questions about the cultural, religious, and contemporary roots of or alibis for homophobia. Acknowledging the existence of multiple cultural, local, and global forms of same-sex affection and gender variety may be one starting point. Examining the variety of expressions of tolerance and value of minority identities within minority and majority cultures may give insights into the differences that make up even seemingly coherent and unified cultures and subcultures. These issues should be familiar to anyone grappling with how to study and educate about any form of identity. But there are particular features to sex and gender identity that make addressing it challenging.

How much of homophobia is a reflection of cultural attitudes about sex in general and how robust is discrimination when sex and youth are connected (Silin, 1995)? How much of homophobia is, as Gender PAC contends, bias against gender-nonconforming behavior? Does homophobia reflect a cultural disparagement of femininity, or as some would put it, is homophobia a weapon of sexism (Pharr, 1997)? We can think here of the use of "girls" to insult young men and what that says about the pervasiveness of sexism. Does homophobia indicate anxiety about the fragility of the heterosexual norm? When even slight gender-nonconforming behavior or friendship with someone of the same sex can begin rumors and harassment or when people feel compelled to assert their heterosexuality should doubt arise, we can see the process of normalization working on everyone. The ease with which such anxieties surface despite a climate of heterosexism that generally does not allow discussion of queer possibility indicates the haunting presence of queerness even in the midst of what is generally the unquestioned norm of heterosexuality.

It is important to consider diverse cultural and political roots of homophobia—to be, in other words, multiculturally aware of different forms of bias against sexual and gender nonconformity. However, there is a danger in letting homophobia define how and why lessons on sexual minorities are included in school. Institutional and legal restrictions have shaped the lives of sexual minority people, yet it would be a vast oversimplification to say that is the only reality of their lives. Sexuality, as with any other category of meaning, has a long and varied history—indeed histories of identities and subjectivities that bear little resemblance to the categories by which we currently define sexual identity. As much as those communities and identity formations were related to restrictions on their ability to live, they nonetheless formed cultures, associations, and—like other minorities living in a cultural context shaped by bias—reshaped their worlds. Tactically, it may be possible to convince people who do not initially want to include sexual minority issues in schooling that to do so would help address the risks that LGBTQ students face. However, we also need to be careful that LGBTQ issues are not framed as only risk or deficit. When antihomophobia and multicultural pedagogies—and chapters such as this one—defensively cite statistics on harassment or provide a panel of LGBTQ people to describe their difficulties with homophobia, they miss the opportunity to examine the positive aspects of LGBTQ communities and cultures and the abilities of sexual minority people to live lives beyond institutional constraints.

Uprisings such as that at Stonewall or the Compton Cafeteria riot underscore both the experience of harassment, exclusion, and the ability of people to resist. That resistance further points to the fact that communities were already organized and understood themselves to have developed the expectation of respect and legibility to one another as members. By focusing on the moments of conflict and the particular people injured by bias, do we imply that those groups and identities have meaning only because of their clash with dominant culture? Is the story of oppression and bias the only way schools are willing to even begin to address sexual and gender minorities? By focusing only on minority sexualities and their experience of bias, schools neglect to examine the relationship between the dominant sexuality's claim to normalcy and the resultant heterosexism and heteronormativity of the curricula, institutional organization, and school policies. By thinking of heterosexism and homophobia as evident only in spectacles of bias—such as homophobic injury, assault, or murder—the everyday forms of heterosexism go unremarked upon as does the everyday presence of people who do not conform to gender and sexual norms. If teachers are unwilling to acknowledge and educate about the positive aspects of sexuality, they also neglect the relationship between sexuality and identity; miss the place of sexuality in initiating and sustaining personal, cultural, and community relationships; and reinforce the unacceptability of educating about sexuality and pleasure.

DILEMMAS OF QUEER INCLUSION

In the 1990s, a group of young queer activists named Queer Nation coined a new protest chant, "We're here, we're queer, get over it, get used to it." While Queer Nation was immediately challenged for its racism, and groups of people of color such as QueerNAsian split off in protest, the chant is a reminder that queerness is a challenge to critically assess the meanings of gender and sexuality. It is also a reminder that centering gender and sexuality can easily fall into White dominance and the related neglect of the centrality of race and ethnicity to sexuality and gender. The confrontational politics of visibility spawned during this period stressed not the exclusions of heterosexism or the biases of homophobia but simply the presence of non-normative people, bodies, acts, and communities. One of the central claims of the gay liberation and lesbian feminist movements was recentered: gender and sexual non-normative people exist; indeed, the presence of non-normativity defines every sexual and gender identity. Furthermore, the larger conversation about queer and race was a reminder that destabilizations of one term, such as sexuality, without adequate thought and action can simply reinforce Whiteness. But the name "Queer Nation" underscored the tension between a collectivity such as a nation and the destabilizing function of the term queer.

To queer something means to trouble its core meaning and queer politics sought to trouble the claim to normalcy that structured heterosexuality. Queers of color, continuing to use that "queering" function, queered the Whiteness of the new term. Young people continue to engage and use the potential for critique and reconsideration offered by the term *queer*. By queering social norms and making those critiques into political projects, queer theory and the work that sexual minority youth and their allies do to improve schools provide a critique of standard attempts at inclusion—attempts that often leave key categories unexamined—and insist, as the transformative approaches to multicultural education do, on critiquing the political structure of schools. But a politics based on visibility can itself be queered: Who is excluded if we privilege visible or legible differences? How does the pressure to be out in a certain way rely on particular culturally specific forms of understanding identity or generationally specific forms of political engagement? Where do other forms of difference appear if the central term is *queer* and implies "White"?

Even in the absence of help and support from adults in school communities, young activists of all sexualities and gender identities now engaged in improving their schools are making it clear that sexuality and gender-related issues concern everyone. Student-led groups form alliances that include diverse identities and people who find labels restrictive, problematic, or insufficient. These groups work carefully to avoid replicating the same exclusions they have faced. Racial and ethnic exclusions, though, remain a core problem, even as LGBTQ students and allies work to teach their communities that homophobia and heterosexism are everyone's problem.

Gay-straight alliances and the Day of Silence each in its own way broaden out from addressing homophobia to creating an understanding of the place of sexual and gender identity in everyone's lives and communities. The Day of Silence is an annual event in which students who support education about LGBTQ issues remain silent for an entire day in school to dramatize the silencing of sexual and gender minority students and the lack of representation of sexual and gender difference in curricula. By focusing on the ties among students of all sexual orientations and gender identities, such groups and events shift the focus from the particularities of student differences to larger coalitional efforts to improve school communities.

Gay-straight alliances provide students a space for critical engagement with media and political issues, a space often not provided by the official curricula. As diverse students meet to queer and question their own self-definitions, they also need to critically engage with the racial, ethnic, gender, and sexual exclusions they may unthinkingly replicate (Mayo, 2004b; Miceli, 2005; Perrotti & Westheimer, 2001). Gay-straight alliances and the Day of Silence, two student-centered projects, underscore the place of youth in defining sexuality-related issues in schools. As youth begin to form new types of sexual and gender identity—such as queer, questioning, gender queer, and curious—they challenge adult understandings and educate all of us about new possibilities (Britzman, 1995, 1997; Leck, 2000; Rasmussen, 2004; Talburt, 2004). These critically important youth-led activities in public schools remind us that queer projects need to work to understand how the intersection of race, ethnicity, and gender must remain central in order for queerness to live up to its potential.

As with any other communities, LGBTQ communities are diversely raced, gendered, classed, and made up of people with complex and intersecting identities. And as with other diverse communities, LGBTQ communities face the challenges of internal and external homophobia, racism, sexism, transphobia, classism, and other forms of bias. Indeed, another way to look at LGBTQ communities is to do so more locally, in which case it becomes clear that LGBTQ people of color find spaces within their racial and ethnic communities because they value these home communities—and find more political and social support there than they would in White-dominated LGBTQ communities. The segregated nature of U.S. public education contributes to the White dominance of LGBTQ organizations within schools and communities (McCready, 2004). LGBTQ youth groups often reflect the racial and ethnic divisions that are crucial forms of support and belonging, but they are also influenced by bias exacerbated by how schools are organized and where they are situated. That is, even schools with diverse populations are often structured by internal racial and ethnic segregation. Sexual orientation and gender identity will not only enrich multicultural education but also benefit LGBTQ communities by enabling young people to be educated more vigorously to understand and value differences, whether long standing or emergent.

Five Things To Do to Improve Education for Students of All Sexual Orientations and Genders

1. Understand the complexity of sexuality and gender identity: Do not assume heterosexuality or enforce gender conformity. Think about your own coming out process, whatever your sexual orientation or preference. Think about your own experiences of enforced gender conformity. How can these memories and experiences help you to understand your students' experiences?

2. Think critically about how heterosexism and homophobia have structured all of our understandings of ourselves and of our relationships, communities, and education. Use gender-neutral terms for parents and gender-neutral examples and other techniques that make it clear that you understand that students, parents, school personnel, and other community members are not all heterosexual.

3. Challenge the implicit and explicit heterosexism, homophobia, and gender conformity in the curricula and other school-based practices. Interrupt homophobia, heterosexism, and gender-identity prejudice when you see it, and take the opportunity to educate about it. Do not let harassment continue unchallenged.

4. Understand the intersections among gender, race, sexual orientation, class, and other aspects of identity. Include references to and images of diverse LGBTQ people in your classrooms.

5. Try to queer your own categories of normal; interrogate them for problematic assumptions about sexuality, gender, and youth as well as other categories of diversity and difference.

6. Learn about diverse LGBTQ histories and cultures, and understand how heterosexual allies have been critical to obtaining social justice.

7. Know about community resources for LGBTQ youth, including ally faculty and staff at your own school. If you are unable to provide the kind of support that LGBTQ students, colleagues, or parents need, know who can.

Questions and Activities

1. In what ways have movements for social justice recognized sexual orientation and gender identity? How have they ignored sexual orientation and gender identity? Why do LGBTQ issues pose a challenge for social justice movements and multicultural education? What do LGBTQ issues bring to social justice movements and multicultural education?

2. What can schools do to be more welcoming places for sexual and gender diversity? What assumptions about LGBTQ students need to be challenged in order for their diversity to be recognized?

3. What is an intersectional approach? How does it help us to be more aware of the interplay of differences?

4. Why is it a problem to think about LGBTQ issues only in terms of harassment and difficulties in school?

5. What would it mean to queer the curriculum?

6. How could you as a teacher support the LGBTQ and ally activities in which your students might be interested?

References

American Civil Liberties Union. (2006, February 18). ACLU hails federal court ruling on school trainings aimed at reducing anti-gay harassment. Retrieved January 15, 2009, from http://aclu.org/lgbt/youth/24215prs20060218.html

American Association of University Women (AAUW). (2001). *Hostile hallways: Bullying, teasing, and sexual harassment in school*. New York: AAUW Foundation.

Anzaldúa, G. (1990). La conciencia de la mestiza: Towards a new consciousness. In G. Anzaldúa (Ed.), *Haciendo caras: Making face, making soul* (pp. 377–389). San Francisco: Aunt Lute.

Apetheker, H. (1992). *Antiracism in U. S. history: The first two hundred years*. New York: Greenwood.

Bello, N., Flynn, S., Palmer, H., Rodriguez, R., & Vente, A. (2004). *Hear me out: True stories of teens educating and confronting homophobia*. Toronto, ON: Second Story.

Bennett, L. (1997, Fall). Break the silence. *Teaching Tolerance, 12*, 24–29.

Blackburn, M. V. (2004, Spring). Understanding agency beyond school-sanctioned activities. *Theory into Practice, 43*, 102–110.

Blackburn, M. V. (2005, January). Agency in borderland discourses: Examining language use in a community center with black queer youth. *Teachers College Record, 107*, 89–113.

Britzman, D. P. (1995). Is there a queer pedagogy? Or, stop reading straight. *Educational Theory, 45*, 151–165.

Britzman, D. P. (1997). What is this thing called love? New discourses for understanding gay and lesbian youth. In S. de Castell & M. Bryson (Eds.) *Radical in(ter)ventions: Identity, politics, and difference/s in educational praxis* (pp. 183–207). Albany: State University of New York Press.

Brownmiller, S. (1970, March 15). "Sisterhood is powerful": A member of the women's liberation movement explains what it's all about. *New York Times Magazine*, 140.

Capper, C. A. (1999). (Homo)sexualities, organizations, and administration: Possibilities for inquiry. *Educational Researcher, 28*, 4–11.

Casper, V., & Schultz, S. B. (1999). *Gay parents/straight schools: Building communication and trust*. New York: Teachers College Press.

Clarke, C. L. (1981). Lesbianism: An act of resistance. In C. Moraga & G. Anzaldúa (Eds.), *This bridge called my back: Writings by radical women of color* (pp. 128–137). Watertown, MA: Persephone.

Clarke, C. L. (1983). The failure to transform: Homophobia in the Black community. In B. Smith (Ed.), *Home girls: A Black feminist anthology* (pp. 197–208). New York: Kitchen Table: Woman of Color Press.

Cohen, C. (1999). *Boundaries of Blackness: AIDS and the breakdown of Black politics*. Chicago: University of Chicago Press.

Combahee River Collective (1982). A Black feminist statement. In B. Smith, P. B. Scott, & G. T. Hull (Eds.), *All the women are White, all the men are Black, but some of us are brave: Black women's studies* (pp. 13–22). Old Westbury, NY: Feminist Press.

D'Emilio, J. (2003). *Lost prophet! The life and times of Bayard Rustin*. New York: Free Press.

Duncan, G. A. (2005). Black youth, identity, and ethics. *Educational Theory, 55*, 3–22.

Friend, R. A. (1995). Choices, not closets: Heterosexism and homophobia in schools. In L. Weis & M. Fine (Eds.), *Beyond silenced voices: Class, race, and gender in United States schools* (pp. 209–235). Albany: State University of New York Press.

Frye, P. R. (2002). Facing discrimination, organizing for freedom: The transgender community. In J. D'Emilio, W. B. Turner, & U. Vaid (Eds.), *Creating change: Sexuality, public policy, and civil rights* (pp. 451–468). New York: Stonewall Inn Editions.

Gender Political Advocacy Coalition (Gender PAC). (2002). *Gender PAC annual report 2002*. Washington, DC: Author.

Humm, A. (1994). *Re-building the "Rainbow": The holy war over inclusion in New York City*. Unpublished manuscript.

Irvine, J. (Ed.). (1994). *Sexual cultures and the construction of adolescent identities*. Philadelphia: Temple University Press.

Johnson, E. P., & Henderson, M. G. (Eds.). (2005). *Black queer studies: A critical anthology*. Durham, NC: Duke University Press.

Kosciw, J. G., & Diaz, E. (2005). *GLSEN 2005 national school climate survey*. New York: Gay, Lesbian, and Straight Education Network.

Kosciw, J. G., & Diaz, E. (2008). *Involved, invisible, and ignored: The experiences of lesbian, gay, bisexual, and transgender parents and their children in our nation's K-12 schools*. New York: Gay, Lesbian, and Straight Education Network.

Kosciw, J. G., Diaz, E. M., & Greytak, E. A. (2008). *2007 National school climate survey: The experiences of lesbian, gay, bisexual, and transgender youth in our nation's schools*. New York: Gay, Lesbian, and Straight Education Network.

Kumashiro, K. (2001). *Troubling intersections of race and sexuality: Queer students of color and anti-oppressive education*. Lanham, MD: Rowman and Littlefield.

Kumashiro, K. (2002). *Troubling education: Queer activism and anti-oppressive education*. New York: Routledge.

Kumashiro, K. (2003). Queer ideas in education. *Journal of Homosexuality, 45*(2/3/4), 365–367.

Kumashiro, K. (2004). Uncertain beginnings: Learning to teach paradoxically. *Theory into Practice, 43*(2), 111–115.

Leck, G. M. (2000). Heterosexual or homosexual? Reconsidering binary narratives on sexual identities in urban schools. *Education and Urban Society, 32*, 324–348.

Lee, N., Murphy, D., North, L., & Ucelli, J. (2000). Bridging race, class, and sexuality for school reform. In J. D'Emilio, W.B. Turner, & U. Vaid (Eds.), *Creating change: Sexuality, public policy, and civil rights,* (pp. 251–260). New York: St. Martin's.

Lorde, A. (1984). *Sister/outsider: Essays and speeches.* Trumansburg, NY: Crossing.

Lorde, A. (1988). *A burst of light Essays by Audre Lorde.* Ithaca, NY: Firebrand.

Lesbian stabbing coverage draws cries of bias. (2003, August 14). Retrieved September 18, 2008, from planetout.com/news/article-print.html?2003/08/14/4

Manalansan, M. (2003). *Global divas: Filipino men in the diaspora.* Durham, NC: Duke University Press.

Mayo, C. (2004a/2007). *Disputing the subject of sex: Sexuality and public school controversy.* Boulder, CO: Rowman and Littlefield.

Mayo, C. (2004b). The tolerance that dare not speak its name. In M. Boler (Ed.), *Democratic dialogue in education: Disturbing silence, troubling speech* (pp. 33–47). New York: Peter Lang.

Mayo, C. (2006). Pushing the limits of liberalism: Queerness, children, and the future. *Educational Theory, 56*(4), 469–487.

McCready, L. T. (2004). Understanding the marginalization of gay and gender non-conforming Black male students. *Theory into Practice, 43*, 136–143.

Miceli, M. (2005). *Standing out, standing together.* New York: Routledge.

Myers, S. L. (1992, December 1). School board in Queens shuns Fernandez meeting. *New York Times,* B4.

New York City Board of Education. (1994). *Comprehensive instructional program first grade teachers' resource guide review draft.* (*Children of the Rainbow*). New York: Board of Education Publications.

Newton, H. (1973). A letter from Huey. In L. Richmond and G. Noguera (Eds.), *The gay liberation book: Writings and photographs on gay (men's) liberation* (pp. 142–145). San Francisco: Ramparts.

Perrotti, J., and Westheimer, K. (2001). *When the drama club is not enough: Lessons from the safe schools program for gay and lesbian students.* Boston, MA: Beacon.

Pharr, S. (1997). *Homophobia: A weapon of sexism.* Hoboken, NJ: Chardon.

Rasmussen, M. L. (2004). The problem of coming out. *Theory into Practice, 43*, 144–150.

Ross, M. B. (2005). Beyond the closet as raceless paradigm. In E. P. Johnson & M. G. Henderson (Eds.), *Black queer studies: A critical anthology* (pp. 161–189). Durham, NC: Duke University Press.

Ruenzel, D. (1999, April). Pride and prejudice. *Teacher Magazine,* 22–27.

Saillant, C. (2008a, Feburary 17). 1,000 march in Oxnard in tribute to slain teen. *Los Angeles Times.* Retrieved June 17, 2008, from http://www.larticles.latimes.com/2008/feb/17/local/me-oxnard17

Saillant, C. (2008b, May 8). Lawyer blames school in shooting of gay Oxnard student. *Los Angeles Times.* Retrieved June 17, 2008, from http://www.latimes.com/news/printedition/california/la-me-oxnard 8-2008may08,0,6901056.story

Sears, J. T. (1995). Black-gay or gay-black? Choosing identities and identifying choices. In G. Unks (Ed.), *The gay teen* (pp. 135–157). New York: Routledge.

Silin, J. G. (1995). *Sex, death, and the education of children: Our passion for ignorance in the age of AIDS*. New York: Teachers College Press.

Sleeter, C. E. (1994). A multicultural educator views White racism. *Education Digest, 59*(9), 33–36.

Smith, B. (1983). Introduction. In B. Smith (Ed.), *Home girls: A Black feminist anthology* (pp. xix–lvi). New York: Kitchen Table: Woman of Color Press.

Smothers, R. (2004, May12). Newark preaches tolerance of gays year after killing. *New York Times*, p. B5. Retrieved July 4, 2009 from http://www.nytimes.com/2004/05/12/nyregion/newark-preaches-tolerance-of-gays-year-after-killing.html

Sonnie, A. (Ed.). (2000). *Revolutionary voices: A multicultural queer youth anthology*. Los Angeles: Alyson.

Stryker, S. (2008). Transgender history, homonormativity, and disciplinarity. *Radical History Review*, 145–157.

Talburt, S. (2004). Constructions of LGBT youth: Opening up subject positions. *Theory into Practice, 43*, 116–121.

Thorne, B. (1995). *Gender play: Girls and boys at school*. Brunswick, NJ: Rutgers University Press.

Wilson, A. (1996). How we find ourselves: Identity development and two-spirit people. *Harvard Educational Review, 66*, 303–317.

*Language and
ethnic diversity
can enrich
a classroom.*

PART IV

Race, Ethnicity, and Language

T he drastic increase in the percentage of students of color and of language minority students in U.S. schools is one of the most significant developments in education in the last two decades. The increase in the percentage of students of color and of language minority students in the U.S. schools results from several factors, including the wave of immigration that began after 1968 and the aging of the White population. U. S. classrooms are experiencing the largest influx of immigrant students since the beginning of the 20th century. The United States receives about 600,000 immigrants annually, most of whom come from nations in Asia and Latin America. However, the Immigration and Naturalization Service reported that in 2007, 13.5 percent of all legal immigrants came from Europe, many of them from nations in the Russian Federation. Between 2005 and 2007, nearly 1 million immigrants entered the United States (Yearbook of Immigration Statistics, 2007).

Demographers predict that if current trends continue, about 46 percent of the nation's school-age youths will be of color by the year 2020. In 2004, 41.2 percent of students in grades 1 to 12 in public schools were members of a minority group, an increase of about 8 percent since 1994. They were a majority of the students in the state of California as well as in many major cities, such as Seattle, San Francisco, Chicago, and Washington, D.C. Another important characteristic of today's students is the large percentage of low-income poor who live in female-headed households. Today, about one of every five students lives in a low-income family.

While the nation's students are becoming increasingly diverse, most of the nation's teachers remain White (87 percent), female (74 percent), and middle class. The percentage of teachers of color remains low; in 2004, they made up only 16 percent of the nation's teachers (School and Staffing Survey, 2004). The growing racial, cultural, and income gap between teachers and students underscores the need for all teachers to develop the knowledge, attitudes, and skills needed to work effectively with students from diverse racial, ethnic, social-class, and language groups. The four chapters in this part of the book present concepts, knowledge, and strategies that all teachers will find helpful in working with students from diverse groups.

References

School and Staffing Survey (2004). National Center for Education Statistics. Retrieved October 30, 2008, from http://nces.ed.gov/surveys/sass/tables/state_2004_02.asp

Yearbook of Immigration Statistics (2007). Department of Homeland Security. Retrieved October 30, 2008, from http://www.dhs.gov/ximgtn/statistics/publications/yearbook.shtm

CHAPTER 10

Approaches to Multicultural Curriculum Reform

James A. Banks

THE MAINSTREAM-CENTRIC CURRICULUM

The United States is made up of many different cultural, ethnic, racial, language, and religious groups. The U.S. Census Bureau (2008) projects that ethnic minorities will increase from one-third of the nation's population in 2006 to 50 percent in 2042 (cited in Roberts, 2008). Ethnic minorities made up 100 million of the total U.S. population of just over 300 million in 2006. U.S. schools are more diverse today than they have been since the early 1900s, when many immigrants entered the country from Southern, Central, and Eastern Europe. In the thirty-year period between 1973 and 2004, the percentage of ethnic minority students in U.S. public schools increased from 22 to 43 percent (Dillon, 2006). The U.S. Census Bureau projects that more than half of all children in the United States will be children of color by 2023 (cited in Dillon).

Despite the deepening ethnic texture within the United States, the U.S. school, college, and university mainstream curriculum is organized around concepts, paradigms, and events that primarily reflect the experiences of mainstream Americans (Banks, 2007, 2008). The dominant, mainstream curriculum has been challenged and fractured within the last four decades, beginning with the Civil Rights Movement of the 1960s and 1970s. Consequently, the mainstream curriculum and textbooks today are much more multicultural than they were when the Civil Rights Movement began. Progress has been made, and it should be acknowledged and appreciated.

An interesting and informative study by Wineburg and Monte-Sano (2008) about who were considered the most famous Americans in history by a national sample of high school students is a significant marker of the changes that have occurred in both the teaching of history and in the "societal" (Cortés, 2000) or "cultural" curriculum (Wineburg & Monte-Sano) since the late 1960s. Martin Luther King, Jr., Rosa Parks, and Harriet Tubman headed the

233

list. The other seven individuals on the list—in descending order—were Susan B. Anthony, Benjamin Franklin, Amelia Earhart, Oprah Winfrey, Marilyn Monroe, Thomas Edison, and Albert Einstein. Wineburg and Monte-Sano found that region had little effect of the students' responses. However, race was a powerful factor. African American students were much more likely than White students to name King, Tubman, Winfrey, and Parks. White students were significantly more likely to name White figures then were African American students.

The curriculum and societal changes suggested by the Wineburg and Monte-Sano (2008) study are encouraging and should be recognized and applauded. However, curricular and societal reforms have been neither as extensive nor as institutionalized as is needed to reflect the complex and increasing diversity in the United States and the world. Consequently, the process of curriculum transformation needs to continue. Curriculum transformation is a process that never ends because of the changes that are continuing within the United States and throughout the world (Banks, 2009a, 2009b).

A curriculum that focuses on the experiences of mainstream Americans and largely ignores the experiences, cultures, and histories of other ethnic, racial, cultural, language, and religious groups has negative consequences for both mainstream students and students of color. A mainstream-centric curriculum is one major way in which racism, ethnocentrism, and pernicious nationalism are reinforced and perpetuated in the schools, colleges, universities, and society at large.

A mainstream-centric curriculum has negative consequences for mainstream students because it reinforces their false sense of superiority, gives them a misleading conception of their relationship with other racial and ethnic groups, and denies them the opportunity to benefit from the knowledge, perspectives, and frames of reference that can be gained from studying and experiencing other cultures and groups. A mainstream-centric curriculum also denies mainstream U.S. students the opportunity to view their culture from the perspectives of other cultures and groups. When people view their culture from the point of view of another culture, they are able to understand their own culture more fully, to see how it is unique and distinct from other cultures, and to understand better how it relates to and interacts with other cultures.

A mainstream-centric curriculum negatively influences students of color such as African Americans, Latinos, and Asian Americans. It marginalizes their experiences and cultures and does not reflect their dreams, hopes, and perspectives. It does not provide them *social equality* within the school, an essential characteristic of democratic institutions (Gutmann, 2004). Students learn best and are more highly motivated when the school curriculum reflects their cultures, experiences, and perspectives. Many students of color are alienated in the school in part because they experience cultural conflict and discontinuities that result from the cultural differences between their school and community (Au, 2006; Lee, 2006). The school can help students of color mediate between their home and school cultures by implementing a curriculum that reflects the culture of their ethnic groups and communities. The school can and should make effective use of the community cultures of students of color when teaching them such subjects as writing, language arts, science, and mathematics (Lee).

The mainstream-centric curriculum views events, themes, concepts, and issues primarily from the perspective of mainstream Americans and Europeans. Events and cultural developments such as the European explorations in the Americas and the development of

American music are viewed from Anglo and European perspectives and are evaluated using mainstream-centric criteria and points of view (Bigelow & Peterson, 1998).

When the European explorations of the Americas are viewed from a Eurocentric perspective, the Americas are perceived as having been "discovered" by the European explorers such as Columbus and Cortés (Loewen, 2008; Zinn, 1999). The view that native peoples in the Americas were discovered by the Europeans subtly suggests that Indian cultures did not exist until they were "discovered" by the Europeans and that the lands occupied by the American Indians were rightfully owned by the Europeans after they settled on and claimed them.

When the formation and nature of U.S. cultural developments, such as music and dance, are viewed from mainstream-centric perspectives, these art forms become important and significant only when they are recognized or legitimized by mainstream critics and artists. The music of African American musicians such as Chuck Berry and Little Richard was not viewed as significant by the mainstream society until White singers such as the Beatles and Rod Stewart publicly acknowledged the significant ways in which their own music had been heavily influenced by these African American musicians. It often takes White artists to legitimize ethnic cultural forms and innovations created by Asian Americans, African Americans, Latinos, and Native Americans.

Public Sites and Popular History

Anglo-centric history is not only taught in U.S. schools, colleges, and universities but is also perpetuated in popular knowledge in the nation's parks, museums, and other public sites. Loewen (1999) describes the ways in which public history in the nation's historic sites is often distorted in order to present a positive image of Anglo Americans. The title of his book is *Lies across America: What Our Historic Sites Get Wrong*.

I have seen several examples of markers in public sites that perpetuate Anglo-centric views of American history. The first appears on a marker in a federal park on the site where a U.S. Army post once stood in Fort Townsend in the state of Washington. With the choice of words such as *settlers* (instead of *invaders*), *restive*, and *rebelled*, the author justifies the taking of the Indians' lands and depicts their resistance as unreasonable.

Fort Townsend

> A U.S. Army Post was established on this site in 1856. In [the] mid-nineteenth century the growth of Port Townsend caused the Indians to become *restive*. *Settlers* started a home guard, campaigned wherever called, and defeated the Indians in the Battle of Seattle. Indians *rebelled* as the government began enforcing the Indian Treaty of 1854, by which the Indians had ceded most of their territory. Port Townsend, a prosperous port of entry on Puget Sound, then asked protection of the U.S. army. (emphasis added)

The second example is in Marianna, Arkansas, my hometown, which is the city center for Lee County. The site commemorates the life and achievements of Confederate soldiers from Lee County and the life of Robert E. Lee, a general of the Confederate Army and a southern hero. The marker reads in part, "In loving memory of Lee County's Confederate soldiers. No braver bled for a brighter land. No brighter land had a cause so grand." The final example is from a marker in the Confederate Park in Memphis, Tennessee, which commemorates the life of Jefferson Davis, president of the Confederate States of America. The marker reads, in part: "Before the war between the States, he served with distinction as a United States Congressman and twice as a United States Senator. He also served as Secretary of War of the U.S. He was a true American patriot." Describing Davis as a "true American patriot" is arguable.

Another interesting and revealing book by Loewen (2005) is *Sundown Towns: A Hidden Dimension of American Racism*. In this informative book, Loewen describes communities that kept out groups such as African Americans, Chinese Americans, and Jewish Americans by force, law, or custom. These towns are called "sundown towns" because specific minorities had to be out of the towns before the sunset. Loewen found more than 440 of these towns that existed across the United States.

EFFORTS TO ESTABLISH A MULTICULTURAL CURRICULUM

Since the Civil Rights Movement of the 1960s, educators have been trying, in various ways, to better integrate the school curriculum with multicultural content and to move away from a mainstream-centric and Eurocentric curriculum (Banks, 2008, 2009a, 2009b). These have proven to be difficult goals for schools to attain for many complex reasons. The strong assimilationist ideology embraced by most U.S. educators is one major reason (Banks, 2006). The assimilationist ideology makes it difficult for educators to think differently about how U.S. society and culture developed and to acquire a commitment to make the curriculum multicultural. Individuals who have a strong assimilationist ideology believe that most important events and developments in U.S. society are related to the nation's British heritage and that the contributions of other ethnic and cultural groups are not very significant by comparison. When educators acquire a multicultural ideology and conception of U.S. culture, they are then able to view the experiences and contributions of a wide range of cultural, ethnic, language, and religious groups as significant to the development of the United States.

Ideological resistance is a major factor that has slowed and is still slowing the development of a multicultural curriculum, but other factors have also affected its growth and development. *Political resistance* to a multicultural curriculum is closely related to ideological resistance. Many people who resist a multicultural curriculum believe that knowledge is power and that a multicultural perspective on U.S. society challenges the existing power structure. They believe that the dominant mainstream-centric curriculum supports, reinforces, and justifies the existing social, economic, and political structure. Multicultural perspectives and points of view, in the opinion of many observers, legitimize and promote social change and social reconstruction.

During the 1980s and 1990s, a heated debate occurred about how much the curriculum should be Western and Eurocentric or reflect the cultural, ethnic, and racial diversity in the United States. At least three major positions in this debate can be identified. The Western traditionalists argue that the West, as defined and conceptualized in the past, should be the focus in school and college curricula because of the major influence of Western civilization and culture in the United States and throughout the world (Ravitch, 1990; Schlesinger, 1998). Afrocentric scholars contend that the contributions of Africa and of African peoples should receive major emphasis in the curriculum (Asante, 1998; Asante & Ravitch, 1991). The multiculturalists argue that although the West should receive a major emphasis in the curriculum, the West should be reconceptualized so that it reflects the contributions that people of color have made to it (Nieto, 2009). In addition to teaching about Western ideals, the gap between the ideals of the West and its realities of racism, sexism, and discrimination should be taught (Banks, 2009b). Multiculturalists also believe that in addition to learning about the West, students should study other world cultures, such as those in Africa, Asia, the Middle East, and the Americas as they were before the Europeans arrived (Gates, 1999).

Other factors that have slowed the institutionalization of a multicultural curriculum include the focus on high-stakes testing and accountability that has emerged within the last decade, the low level of knowledge about ethnic cultures that most educators have, and the heavy reliance on textbooks for teaching. Many studies have revealed that the textbook is still the main source for teaching, especially in such subjects as the social studies, reading, and language arts (Sleeter, 2005).

Teachers need in-depth knowledge about ethnic cultures and experiences to integrate ethnic content, experiences, and points of view into the curriculum. Many teachers tell their students that Columbus discovered America and that America is a "new world" because they know little about the diverse Native American cultures that existed in the Americas more than 40,000 years before the Europeans began to settle there in significant numbers in the 16th century. As Howard (2006) states in the title of his cogent and informative book, *We Can't Teach What We Don't Know.*

LEVELS OF INTEGRATION OF MULTICULTURAL CONTENT

The Contributions Approach

I have identified four approaches to the integration of multicultural content into the curriculum (see Figure 10.1). The contributions approach to integration (Level 1) is frequently used when a school or district first attempts to integrate multicultural content into the mainstream curriculum. The contributions approach is characterized by the insertion of ethnic heroes/heroines and discrete cultural artifacts into the curriculum, selected using criteria similar to those used to select mainstream heroes/heroines and cultural artifacts. Thus, individuals such as Crispus Attucks, Pocahontas, Martin Luther King, Jr., César Chávez, and Barack Obama are added to the curriculum. They are discussed when mainstream American heroes/heroines such as Patrick Henry, George Washington, Thomas Jefferson, Betsy Ross, and Eleanor Roosevelt are studied in the mainstream curriculum. Discrete cultural elements such as the foods, dances, music, and artifacts of ethnic groups are studied, but little attention is given to their meanings and importance within ethnic communities.

An important characteristic of the contributions approach is that the mainstream curriculum remains unchanged in its basic structure, goals, and salient characteristics. Prerequisites for the implementation of this approach are minimal. They include basic knowledge about U.S. society and knowledge about ethnic heroes/heroines and their roles and contributions to U.S. society and culture.

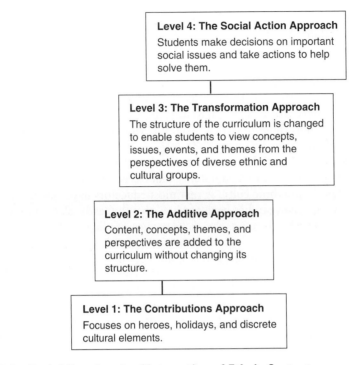

Figure 10.1   Banks' Four Levels of Integration of Ethnic Content

Copyright © 2009 by James A. Banks

Individuals who challenged the dominant society's ideologies, values, and conceptions and advocated radical social, political, and economic reform are seldom included in the contributions approach. Thus, Booker T. Washington is more likely to be chosen for study than is W. E. B. DuBois, and Pocahontas is more likely to be chosen than is Geronimo. The criteria used to select ethnic heroes/heroines for study and to judge them for success are derived from the mainstream society, not from the ethnic community. Consequently, use of the contributions approach usually results in the study of ethnic heroes/heroines who represent only one important perspective within ethnic communities. The more radical and less conformist individuals who are heroes/heroines only to the ethnic community are often invisible in textbooks, teaching materials, and activities used in the contributions approach. Paul Robeson, the singer, actor, and activist—who was a greatly admired hero in the African American community during the 1940s and 1950s—is invisible in most textbooks, in part because he was a Marxist who advocated radical social, economic, and political change (Balaji, 2007).

The heroes/heroines and holidays approach is a variant of the contributions approach. In this approach, ethnic content is limited primarily to special days, weeks, and months related to ethnic events and celebrations. Cinco de Mayo, Martin Luther King, Jr.'s birthday, and African American History Week are examples of ethnic days and weeks celebrated in the schools. During these celebrations, teachers involve students in lessons, experiences, and pageants related to the ethnic group being commemorated. When this approach is used, the class studies little or nothing about the ethnic or cultural group before or after the special event or occasion.

The contributions approach (Level 1 in Figure 10.1) provides teachers a way to integrate ethnic content into the curriculum quickly, thus giving some recognition to ethnic contributions to U.S. society and culture. Many teachers who are committed to integrating their curricula with ethnic content have little knowledge about ethnic groups and curriculum revision. Consequently, they use the contributions approach when teaching about ethnic groups. These teachers should be encouraged, supported, and given the opportunity to acquire the knowledge and skills needed to reform their curricula by using one of the more effective approaches described later in this chapter.

There are often strong political demands from ethnic communities for the school to put their heroes/heroines, contributions, and cultures into the school curriculum. These political forces may take the form of demands for heroes and contributions because mainstream heroes, such as Washington, Jefferson, and Lincoln, are highly visible in the school curriculum. Ethnic communities of color want to see their own heroes/heroines and contributions alongside those of the mainstream society. Such contributions may help give them a sense of structural inclusion, validation, and social equality. Curriculum inclusion also facilitates the quests of marginalized ethnic and cultural groups for a sense of empowerment, efficacy, and social equality. The school should help ethnic group students acquire a sense of empowerment and efficacy. These factors are positively correlated with academic achievement (Coleman et al., 1966).

The contributions approach is also the easiest approach for teachers to use to integrate the curriculum with multicultural content. However, this approach has several serious limitations. When the integration of the curriculum is accomplished primarily through the infusion of ethnic heroes/heroines and contributions, students do not attain a global view of the role of ethnic and cultural groups in U.S. society. Rather, they see ethnic issues and events primarily as additions to the curriculum and consequently as an appendage to the main story of the development of the nation and to the core curriculum in the language arts, social studies, arts, and other subject areas.

Teaching ethnic issues with the use of heroes/heroines and contributions also tends to gloss over important concepts and issues related to the victimization and oppression of ethnic groups and their struggles against racism and for power. Issues such as *racism*, *poverty*, and *oppression* tend to be avoided in the contributions approach to curriculum integration. The focus tends to be on success and the validation of the Horatio Alger myth that all Americans who are willing to work hard can go from rags to riches and "pull themselves up by their bootstraps."

The success stories of ethnic heroes such as Booker T. Washington, George Washington Carver, and Jackie Robinson are usually told with a focus on their success with little attention to racism and other barriers they encountered and how they succeeded despite the hurdles they faced. Little attention is also devoted to the *process* by which they became heroes/heroines. Students should learn about the process by which people become heroes/heroines as well as about their status and role as heroes/heroines. Only when students learn the process by which individuals become heroes/heroines will they understand fully how individuals, particularly individuals of color, achieve and maintain hero/heroine status and what the process of achieving this status means for their own lives.

When teaching about the historic election of Barack Obama as the 44th president of the United States in 2008, teachers should help students to understand both his struggles and triumphs (Obama, 2004, 2006). His successful presidential election should be discussed within the context of the racism he experienced both as a youth and as a presidential candidate. A number of events during the election had racial overtones and were designed to depict Obama as an "Outsider" who would not be an appropriate president of the United States. These events included falsely claiming that he was a Muslim, highlighting his relationship with the Reverend Jeremiah Wright, attempting to marginalize him by emphasizing that he had been a community organizer, and linking him with William Ayers—whom Sarah Palin, the Republican vice-presidential candidate called a "domestic terrorist." Michael Massing (2008) concludes about the attacks on Obama, "Amounting to a six-month-long exercise in Swift Boating, these attacks, taken together, constitute perhaps the most vicious smear campaign ever mounted against an American politician" (p. 26).

The contributions approach often results in the trivialization of ethnic cultures, the study of their strange and exotic characteristics, and the reinforcement of stereotypes and misconceptions. When the focus is on the contributions and unique aspects of ethnic cultures, students are not helped to view them as complete and dynamic wholes. The contributions approach also tends to focus on the *lifestyles* of ethnic groups rather than on the *institutional structures*, such as racism and discrimination, that significantly affect their life chances and keep them powerless and marginalized.

The contributions approach to content integration may provide students a memorable one-time experience with an ethnic hero/heroine, but it often fails to help them understand the role and influence of the hero/heroine in the total context of U.S. history and society. When ethnic heroes/heroines are studied apart from the social and political context in which they lived and worked, students attain only a partial understanding of their roles and significance in society. When Martin Luther King, Jr., and Rosa Parks are studied outside the social and political context of institutionalized racism in the U.S. South in the 1950s and 1960s and without attention to the more subtle forms of institutionalized racism in the North during this period, their full significance as social reformers and activists is neither revealed to nor understood by students.

The Additive Approach

Another important approach to the integration of ethnic content into the curriculum is the addition of content, concepts, themes, and perspectives to the curriculum without changing its basic structure, purposes, and characteristics. The additive approach (Level 2 in Figure 10.1) is often accomplished by the addition of a book, a unit, or a course to the curriculum without changing it substantially. Examples of this approach include adding a book such as *The Color Purple* to a unit on the 20th century in an English class (Walker, 1982), the use of the film *The Autobiography of Miss Jane Pittman* (Korty, 1973) during a unit on the 1960s, and the addition of a videotape on the internment of the Japanese Americans, such as *Rabbit in the Moon* (Omori, 2004), during a study of World War II in a class on U.S. history.

The additive approach allows the teacher to put ethnic content into the curriculum without restructuring it, a process that would take substantial time, effort, and training as well as a rethinking of the curriculum and its purposes, nature, and goals. The additive approach can be the first phase in a transformative curriculum reform effort designed to restructure the total curriculum and to integrate it with ethnic content, perspectives, and frames of reference.

However, this approach shares several disadvantages with the contributions approach. Its most important shortcoming is that it usually results in viewing ethnic content from the perspectives of mainstream historians, writers, artists, and scientists because it does not involve a restructuring of the curriculum. The events, concepts, issues, and problems selected for study are selected using mainstream-centric and Eurocentric criteria and perspectives. When teaching a unit entitled "The Westward Movement" in a fifth-grade U.S. history class, the teacher may integrate the unit by adding content about the Oglala Sioux Indians. However, the unit remains mainstream-centric and focused because of its perspective and point of view.

A unit called "The Westward Movement" is mainstream and Eurocentric because it focuses on the movement of European Americans from the eastern to the western part of the United States. The Oglala Sioux were already in the West and consequently were not moving westward. The unit might be called "The Invasion from the East" from the point of view of the Oglala Sioux. Black Elk, an Oglala Sioux holy man, lamented the conquering of his people, which culminated in their defeat at Wounded Knee Creek on December 29, 1890. Approximately 200 Sioux men, women, and children were killed by U.S. troops. Black Elk said, "The [Sioux] nation's hoop is broken and scattered. There is no center any longer, and the sacred tree is dead" (Black Elk & Neihardt, 1972, p. 230).

Black Elk did not consider his homeland "the West," but rather the center of the world. He viewed the cardinal directions metaphysically. The Great Spirit sent him the cup of living water and the sacred bow from the west. The daybreak star and the sacred pipe originated from the east. The Sioux nation's sacred hoop and the tree that was to bloom came from the south (Black Elk, 1964). When teaching about the movement of the Europeans across North America, teachers should help students understand that different cultural, racial, and ethnic groups often have varying and conflicting conceptions and points of view about the same historical events, concepts, issues, and developments. The victors and the vanquished, especially, often have conflicting conceptions of the same historical event (Limerick, 1987). However, it is usually the point of view of the victors that becomes institutionalized within the schools and the mainstream society. This happens because history and textbooks are usually written by the people who won the wars and gained control of the society, not by the losers—the victimized and the powerless. The perspectives of both groups are needed to help us fully understand our history, culture, and society.

The people who are conquered and the people who conquered them have histories and cultures that are intricately interwoven and interconnected. They have to learn each others' histories and cultures to understand their own fully. White Americans cannot fully understand their own history in the western United States and in America without understanding the history of the American Indians and the ways their histories and the histories of the Indians are interconnected.

James Baldwin (1985) insightfully pointed out that when White Americans distort African American history, they do not learn the truth about their own history because the histories of African Americans and Whites in the United States are tightly bound together. This is also true for African American history and Indian history. The histories of African Americans and Indians in the United States are closely interconnected, as Katz (1986) documents in *Black Indians: A Hidden Heritage.*

The histories of African Americans and Whites in the United States are tightly connected, both culturally and biologically, as Ball (1998) points out when he describes the African American ancestors in his White family and as Gordon-Reed (1997) reveals when she describes the relationship between Thomas Jefferson and Sally Hemings, his slave mistress. The additive approach fails to help students view society from diverse cultural and ethnic perspectives and to understand the ways in which the histories and cultures of the nation's diverse ethnic, racial, cultural, and religious groups are interconnected.

Multicultural history enables students and teachers to understand America's complexity and the ways in which various groups within the United States are interconnected (Takaki, 2008). Sam Hamod describes the way in which diverse ethnic perspectives enrich our understandings and lead to more accurate versions of U.S. society:

> Our dual vision of "ethnic" and American allows us to see aspects of the United States that mainstream writers often miss; thus, our perspectives often allow us a diversity of visions that, ironically, may lead us to larger truth—it's just that we were raised with different eyes. (as cited in Reed, 1997, p. xxii)

Content, materials, and issues that are added to a curriculum as appendages instead of being integral parts of a unit of instruction can become problematic. Problems might result when a book such as *The Color Purple* or a film like *Miss Jane Pittman* is added to a unit when the students lack the concepts, content background, and emotional maturity to deal with the issues and problems in these materials. The effective use of such emotion-laden and complex materials usually requires that the teacher help students acquire, in a sequential and developmental fashion, the content background and attitudinal maturity to deal with them effectively. The use of both of these materials in different classes and schools has resulted in major problems for the teachers using them. A community controversy arose in each case. The problems developed because the material was used with students who had neither the content background nor the attitudinal sophistication to respond to them appropriately. Adding ethnic content to the curriculum in a sporadic and segmented way can result in pedagogical problems, trouble for the teacher, student confusion, and community controversy.

The Transformation Approach

The transformation approach differs fundamentally from the contributions and additive approaches. In those two approaches, ethnic content is added to the mainstream core curriculum without changing its basic assumptions, nature, and structure. The fundamental goals, structure, and perspectives of the curriculum are changed in the transformation approach.

The transformation approach (Level 3 in Figure 10.1) changes the basic assumptions of the curriculum and enables students to view concepts, issues, themes, and problems from several ethnic perspectives and points of view. The mainstream-centric perspective is one of only several perspectives from which problems, concepts, and issues are viewed. Richard White (1991), a historian of the American West, indicates how viewing it from a transformative perspective can provide new insights into U.S. history. He writes, "The first Europeans to penetrate the West arrived neither as conquerors nor as explorers. Like so many others history has treated as discoverers, they were merely lost" (p. 5).

It is neither possible nor desirable to view every issue, concept, event, or problem from the point of view of every U.S. ethnic and cultural group. Rather, the goal should be to enable students to view concepts and issues from more than one perspective and from the points of view of the cultural, ethnic, and racial groups that were the most active participants in, or were most cogently influenced by, the event, issue, or concept being studied.

The key curriculum issues involved in multicultural curriculum reform is not the addition of a long list of ethnic groups, heroes, and contributions but the infusion of various perspectives, frames of references, and content from different groups that will extend students' understandings of the nature, development, and complexity of U.S. society. When students are studying the revolution in the British colonies, the perspectives of the Anglo revolutionaries, Anglo loyalists, African Americans, Indians, and British are essential for the students to attain a thorough understanding of this significant event in U.S. history (see Figure 10.2). Students must study

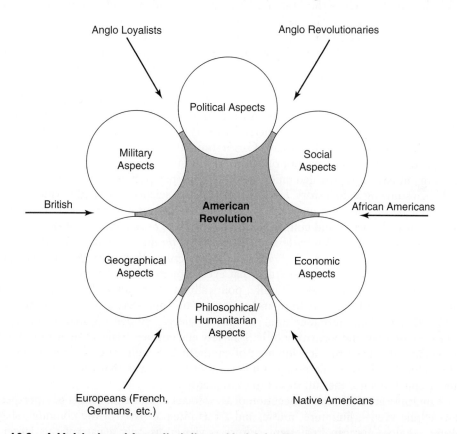

Figure 10.2   A Multicultural Interdisciplinary Model for Teaching the American Revolution

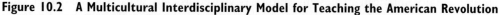

Source: James A. Banks and Geneva Gay. "Teaching the American Revolution: A Multiethnic Approach," *Social Education*, November–December 1975, 462. Used with permission of the National Council for the Social Studies.

the various and sometimes divergent meanings of the revolution to these diverse groups to understand it fully (Gay & Banks, 1975).

In the language arts, when students are studying the nature of U.S. English and proper language use, they should be helped to understand the rich linguistic and language diversity in the United States and the ways in which a wide range of regional, cultural, and ethnic groups have influenced the development of U.S. English. Students should also examine how normative language use varies with the social context, region, and situation. The use of Black English is appropriate in some social and cultural contexts and inappropriate in others. This is also true of standard U.S. English. The United States is rich in languages and dialects. The nation had 46.7 million Latino citizens in 2008; Spanish is the first language for most of them. Most of the nation's approximately 41.1 million African Americans speak both standard English as well as some form of Black English or Ebonics (Alim & Baugh, 2007). The rich language diversity in the United States includes more than 25 European languages; Asian, African, and Middle Eastern languages; and American Indian languages. Since the 1970s, languages from Indochina, spoken by groups such as the Hmong, Vietnamese, Laotians, and Cambodians, have further enriched language diversity in the United States (Ovando & McLaren, 2000).

When subjects such as music, dance, and literature are studied, the teacher should acquaint students with the ways these art forms among U.S. ethnic groups have greatly influenced and enriched the nation's artistic and literary traditions. For example, the ways in which African American musicians such as Bessie Smith, W. C. Handy, and Leontyne Price have influenced the nature and development of U.S. music should be examined when the development of U.S. music is studied (Burnim & Maultsby, 2006). African Americans and Puerto Ricans have significantly influenced the development of American dance. Writers of color, such as Langston Hughes, Toni Morrison, N. Scott Momaday, Carlos Bulosan, Maxine Hong Kingston, Rudolfo A. Anaya, and Piri Thomas, have not only significantly influenced the development of American literature but have also provided unique and revealing perspectives on U.S. society and culture.

When studying U.S. history, language, music, arts, science, and mathematics, the emphasis should not be on the ways in which various ethnic and cultural groups have contributed to mainstream U.S. society and culture. *The emphasis should be on how the common U.S. culture and society emerged from a complex synthesis and interaction of the diverse cultural elements that originated within the various cultural, racial, ethnic, and religious groups that make up U.S. society.* I call this process *multiple acculturation* and argue that even though Anglo Americans are the dominant group in the United States—culturally, politically, and economically—it is misleading and inaccurate to describe U.S. culture and society as an Anglo-Saxon Protestant culture (Banks, 2006). Other U.S. ethnic and cultural groups have deeply influenced, shaped, and participated in the development and formation of U.S. society and culture. African Americans, for example, profoundly influenced the development of southern U.S. culture even though they had very little political and economic power. One irony of conquest is that those who are conquered often deeply influence the cultures of the conquerors.

A multiple acculturation conception of U.S. society and culture leads to a perspective that views ethnic events, literature, music, and art as integral parts of the common, shared U.S. culture. Anglo American Protestant culture is viewed as only a part of this larger cultural whole. Thus, to teach American literature without including significant writers of color, such as Maxine Hong Kingston, Carlos Bulosan, and Toni Morrison, gives a partial and incomplete view of U.S. literature, culture, and society.

The Social Action Approach

The social action approach (Level 4 in Figure 10.1) includes all elements of the transformation approach but adds components that require students to make *decisions* and take *actions* related to the concept, issue, or problem studied in the unit (Banks & Banks, 1999). Major goals of instruction in this approach are to educate students for social criticism and social change and to teach them decision-making skills. To empower students and help them acquire *political efficacy*, the school must help them become reflective social critics and skilled participants in social change. The traditional goal of schooling has been to socialize students so they would accept unquestioningly the existing ideologies, institutions, and practices within society and the nation-state (Banks, 2004; Arthur, Davies, & Hahn, 2008).

Political education in the United States has traditionally fostered political passivity rather than political action. A major goal of the social action approach is to help students acquire the *knowledge, values,* and *skills* they need to participate in social change so that marginalized and excluded racial, ethnic, and cultural groups can become full participants in U.S. society and the nation will move closer to attaining its democratic ideals (Banks, 2004). To participate effectively in democratic social change, students must be taught social criticism and helped to understand the inconsistency between our ideals and social realities, the work that must be done to close this gap, and how students can, as individuals and groups, influence the social and political systems in U.S. society. In this approach, teachers are agents of social change who promote democratic values and the empowerment of students. Teaching units organized using the social action approach have the following components:

1. *A Decision Problem or Question*: An example of a question is this: What actions should we take to reduce prejudice and discrimination in our school?
2. *An Inquiry That Provides Data Related to the Decision Problem*: The inquiry might consist of questions such as these:

   a. What is prejudice?
   b. What is discrimination?
   c. What causes prejudice?
   d. What causes people to discriminate?
   e. What are examples of prejudice and discrimination in our school, community, nation, and world?
   f. How do prejudice and discrimination affect the groups listed in item *g?* How does each group view prejudice? Discrimination? To what extent is each group a victim or a perpetuator of prejudice and discrimination?
   g. How has each group dealt with prejudice and discrimination? (Groups: White mainstream Americans, African Americans, Asian Americans, Hispanic Americans, Native Americans)

   The inquiry into the nature of prejudice and discrimination would be interdisciplinary and would include readings and data sources in the various social sciences,

biography, fiction, poetry, and drama. Scientific and statistical data would be used when students investigate how discrimination affects the income, occupations, frequency of diseases, and health care within these various groups.

3. *Value Inquiry and Moral Analysis*: Students are given opportunities to examine, clarify, and reflect on their values, attitudes, beliefs, and feelings related to racial prejudice and discrimination. The teacher can provide the students with case studies from various sources, such as newspapers and magazines. The case studies can be used to involve the students in discussions and role-playing situations that enable them to express and to examine their attitudes, beliefs, and feelings about prejudice and discrimination. Poetry, biography, and powerful fiction are excellent sources for case studies that can be used for both discussion and role-playing. The powerful poem "Incident" by Countee Cullen (1993) describes the painful memories of a child who was called "nigger" on a trip to Baltimore. Langston Hughes's (1993) poem "I, too" poignantly tells how the "darker brother" is sent into the kitchen when company comes. The teacher and the students can describe verbally or write about incidents related to prejudice and discrimination they have observed or in which they have participated. The following case, based on a real-life situation, was written by the author for use with his students. After reading the case, the students discuss the questions at the end of it.

Trying to Buy a Home in Lakewood Island

About a year ago, Joan and Henry Green, a young African American couple, moved from the West Coast to a large city in the Midwest. They moved because Henry finished his Ph. D. in chemistry and took a job at a big university in Midwestern City. Since they have been in Midwestern City, the Greens have rented an apartment in the central area of the city. However, they have decided that they want to buy a house. Their apartment has become too small for the many books and other things they have accumulated during the year. In addition to wanting more space, they also want a house so that they can receive breaks on their income tax, which they do not receive living in an apartment. The Greens also think that a house will be a good financial investment.

The Greens have decided to move into a suburban community. They want a new house and most of the houses within the city limits are rather old. They also feel that they can obtain a larger house for their money in the suburbs than in the city. They have looked at several suburban communities and decided that they like Lakewood Island better than any of the others. Lakewood Island is a predominantly White community, which is composed primarily of lower-middle-class and middle-class residents.

There are a few wealthy families in Lakewood Island, but they are exceptions rather than the rule.

Joan and Henry Green have become frustrated because of the problems they have experienced trying to buy a home in Lakewood Island. Before they go out to look at a house, they carefully study the newspaper ads. When they arrived at the first house in which they were interested, the owner told them that his house had just been sold. A week later they decided to work with a realtor. When they tried to close the deal on the next house they wanted, the realtor told them that the owner had raised the price $10,000 because he had the house appraised since he put it on the market and had discovered that his selling price was much too low. When the Greens tried to buy a third house in Lakewood Island, the owner told them that he had decided not to sell because he had not received the job in another city that he was almost sure he would receive when he had put his house up for sale. He explained that the realtor had not removed the ad about his house from the newspaper even though he had told him that he had decided not to sell a week earlier. The realtor the owner had been working with had left the real estate company a few days ago. Henry is bitter and feels that he and his wife are victims of racism and discrimination. Joan believes that Henry is too sensitive and that they have been the victims of a series of events that could have happened to anyone, regardless of their race.

Questions: What should the Greens do? Why?

(Reprinted with permission from James A. Banks (2009). *Teaching Strategies for Ethnic Studies* (8th ed., p. 217). Boston: Allyn and Bacon.

4. *Decision Making and Social Action* (synthesis of knowledge and values): Students acquire knowledge about their decision problem from the activities in item 2. This interdisciplinary knowledge provides them the information they need to make reflective decisions about prejudice and discrimination in their communities and schools. The activities in item 3 enable them to identify, clarify, and analyze their values, feelings, and beliefs about prejudice and discrimination. The decision-making process enables the students to synthesize their knowledge and values to determine what actions, if any, they should take to reduce prejudice and discrimination in their school. They can develop a chart in which they list possible actions to take and their possible consequences. They can then decide on a course of action to take and implement it.

Mixing and Blending Approaches

The four approaches for the integration of multicultural content into the curriculum (see Table 10.1) are often mixed and blended in actual teaching situations. One approach, such as the contributions approach, can be used as a vehicle to move to other, more intellectually challenging approaches, such as the transformation and social action approaches. It is unrealistic to expect a teacher to move directly from a highly mainstream-centric curriculum to one that focuses on decision making and social action. Rather, the move from the first to higher levels of multicultural content integration is likely to be gradual and cumulative. A teacher who has a mainstream-centric curriculum might use the school's Martin Luther King, Jr., birthday celebration as an opportunity to integrate the curriculum with ethnic content about King as well as to think seriously about how content about African Americans and other ethnic groups can be integrated into the curriculum in an ongoing fashion. The teacher could explore with the students questions such as these during the celebration:

1. What were the conditions of other ethnic groups during the time that King was a civil rights leader?
2. How did other ethnic groups participate in and respond to the Civil Rights Movement?
3. How did these groups respond to Martin Luther King, Jr.?
4. What can we do today to improve the civil rights of groups of color?
5. What can we do to develop more positive racial and ethnic attitudes?

The students will be unable to answer all of the questions they have raised about ethnic groups during the celebration of Martin Luther King, Jr.'s birthday. Rather, the questions will enable the students to integrate content about ethnic groups throughout the year as they study such topics as the family, the school, the neighborhood, and the city. As the students study these topics, they can use the questions they have formulated to investigate ethnic families, the ethnic groups in their school and in schools in other parts of the city, ethnic neighborhoods, and various ethnic institutions in the city such as churches, temples, synagogues, mosques, schools, restaurants, and community centers.

As a culminating activity for the year, the teacher can take the students on a tour of an ethnic institution in the city, such as the Wing Luke Asian Museum (http://www.wingluke.org/home.htm) or the Northwest African American Museum (http://naamnw.org/exhibits.html) in Seattle, Washington. Similar ethnic museums are located in other major cities, such as Los Angeles, Detroit, and New York. Other ethnic institutions that the students might visit include an African American or Hispanic church, a Jewish temple, or a mosque. However, such a tour should be both preceded and followed by activities that enable the students to develop perceptive and compassionate lenses for seeing ethnic, cultural, and religious differences and for responding to them with sensitivity. A field trip to an ethnic institution might reinforce stereotypes and misconceptions if students lack the knowledge and insights needed to view ethnic and religious cultures in an understanding and caring way. Theory and research indicate that contact with an ethnic group does not necessarily lead to more positive racial and ethnic attitudes (Allport, 1979; Schofield, 2004). Rather, the conditions under which the contact occurs and the quality of the interaction in the contact situation are the important variables.

Table 10.1   Banks's Approaches for the Integration of Multicultural Content

Approach	Description	Examples	Strengths	Problems
Contributions	Heroes, cultural components, holidays, and other discrete elements related to ethnic groups are added to the curriculum on special days, occasions, and celebrations.	Famous Mexican Americans are studied only during the week of Cinco de Mayo (May 5). African Americans are studied during African American History Month in February but rarely during the rest of the year. Ethnic foods are studied in the first grade with little attention devoted to the cultures in which the foods are embedded.	Provides a quick and relatively easy way to put ethnic content into the curriculum. Gives ethnic heroes visibility in the curriculum alongside mainstream heroes. Is a popular approach among teachers and educators.	Results in a superficial understanding of ethnic cultures. Focuses on the lifestyles and artifacts of ethnic groups and reinforces stereotypes and misconceptions. Mainstream criteria are used to select heroes and cultural elements for inclusion in the curriculum.
Additive	This approach consists of the addition of content, concepts, themes, and perspectives to the curriculum without changing its structure.	Adding the book *The Color Purple* to a literature unit without reconceptualizing the unit or giving the students the background knowledge to understand the book. Adding a unit on the Japanese American internment to a U.S. history course without treating the Japanese in any other unit. Leaving the core curriculum intact but adding an ethnic studies course, as an elective, that focuses on a specific ethnic group.	Makes it possible to add ethnic content to the curriculum without changing its structure, which requires substantial curriculum changes and staff development. Can be implemented within the existing curriculum structure.	Reinforces the idea that ethnic history and culture are not integral parts of U.S. mainstream culture. Students view ethnic groups from Anglocentric and Eurocentric perspectives. Fails to help students understand how the dominant culture and ethnic cultures are interconnected and interrelated.

GUIDELINES FOR TEACHING MULTICULTURAL CONTENT

The following fourteen guidelines are designed to help you better integrate content about racial, ethnic, cultural, and language groups into the school curriculum and to teach effectively in multicultural environments.

  1. You, the teacher, are an extremely important variable in the teaching of multicultural content. If you have the necessary knowledge, attitudes, and skills,

Table 10.1   Continued

Approach	Description	Examples	Strengths	Problems
Transformation	The basic goals, structure, and nature of the curriculum are changed to enable students to view concepts, events, issues, problems, and themes from the perspectives of diverse cultural, ethnic, and racial groups.	A unit on the American Revolution describes the meaning of the revolution to Anglo revolutionaries, Anglo loyalists, African Americans, Indians, and the British. A unit on 20th-century U.S. literature includes works by William Faulkner, Joyce Carol Oates, Langston Hughes, N. Scott Momaday, Saul Bellow, Maxine Hong Kingston, Rudolfo A. Anaya, and Piri Thomas.	Enables students to understand the complex ways in which diverse racial and cultural groups participated in the formation of U.S. society and culture. Helps reduce racial and ethnic encapsulation. Enables diverse ethnic, racial, and religious groups to see their cultures, ethos, and perspectives in the school curriculum. Gives students a balanced view of the nature and development of U.S. culture and society. Helps to empower victimized racial, ethnic, and cultural groups.	The implementation of this approach requires substantial curriculum revision, inservice training, and the identification and development of materials written from the perspectives of various racial and cultural groups. Staff development for the institutionalization of this approach must be continual and ongoing.
Social Action	In this approach, students identify important social problems and issues, gather pertinent data, clarify their values on the issues, make decisions, and take reflective actions to help resolve the issue or problem.	A class studies prejudice and discrimination in their school and decides to take actions to improve race relations in the school. A class studies the treatment of ethnic groups in a local newspaper and writes a letter to the newspaper publisher suggesting ways that the treatment of ethnic groups in the newspaper should be improved.	Enables students to improve their thinking, value analysis, decision-making, and social action skills. Enables students to improve their data-gathering skills. Helps students develop a sense of political efficacy. Helps students improve their skills to work in groups.	Requires a considerable amount of curriculum planning and materials identification. May be longer in duration than more traditional teaching units. May focus on problems and issues considered controversial by some members of the school staff and citizens of the community. Students may be able to take few meaningful actions that contribute to the resolution of the social issue or problem.

when you encounter racist content in materials or observe racism in the statements and behavior of students, you can use these situations to teach important lessons about the experiences of ethnic, racial, and cultural groups in the United States. An informative source on racism is Gary Howard's (2006) *We Can't Teach What We Don't Know: White Teachers, Multiracial Schools*. Another helpful source on this topic is Chapter 11 in this book.

2. Knowledge about ethnic groups is needed to teach ethnic content effectively. Read at least one major book that surveys the histories and cultures of U.S. ethnic groups. One book that includes comprehensive historical overviews of U.S. ethnic groups is James A. Banks (2009b), *Teaching Strategies for Ethnic Studies*.

3. Be sensitive to your own racial attitudes, behaviors, and the statements you make about ethnic groups in the classroom. A statement such as "sit like an Indian" stereotypes Native Americans.

4. Make sure that your classroom conveys positive and complex images of various ethnic groups. You can do this by displaying bulletin boards, posters, and calendars that show the racial, ethnic, and religious diversity within U.S. society.

5. Be sensitive to the racial and ethnic attitudes of your students and do not accept the belief, which has been refuted by research, that "kids do not see colors." Since the pioneering research by Lasker (1929), researchers have known that very young children are aware of racial differences and that they tend to accept the evaluations of various racial groups that are normative within the wider society (Bigler & Hughes, 2009). Do not try to ignore the racial and ethnic differences that you see; try to respond to these differences positively and sensitively. Chapter 11 of this book provides thoughtful guidelines for avoiding the "colorblind" stance. Also see Walter Stephan (1999), *Reducing Prejudice and Stereotyping in Schools*.

6. Be judicious in your choice and use of teaching materials. Some materials contain both subtle and blatant stereotypes of groups. Point out to the students when an ethnic, racial, cultural, or language group is stereotyped, omitted from, or described in materials from Anglocentric and Eurocentric points of view.

7. Use trade books, films, videotapes, CDs, and recordings to supplement the textbook treatment of ethnic, cultural, and language groups and to present the perspectives of these groups to your students. Many of these sources contain rich and powerful images of the experience of being a person of color in the United States. Numerous books and videotapes are annotated in James A. Banks (2009b), *Teaching Strategies for Ethnic Studies*.

8. Get in touch with your own cultural and ethnic heritage. Sharing your ethnic and cultural story with your students will create a climate for sharing in the classroom, will help motivate students to dig into their own ethnic and cultural roots, and will result in powerful learning for your students.

9. Be sensitive to the possibly controversial nature of some ethnic studies materials. If you are clear about the teaching objectives you have in mind, you can often use a less controversial book or reading to attain the same objectives. *The Color Purple* by Alice Walker (1982), for example, can be a controversial book. A teacher, however, who

wants his or her students to gain insights about African Americans in the South can use *Roll of Thunder, Hear My Cry*, by Mildred D. Taylor (1976), instead of *The Color Purple*.

10. Be sensitive to the developmental levels of your students when you select concepts, content, and activities related to racial, ethnic, cultural, and language groups. Concepts and learning activities for students in kindergarten and the primary grades should be specific and concrete. Students in these grades should study such concepts as *similarities, differences, prejudice*, and *discrimination* rather than higher-level concepts such as *racism* and *oppression*. Fiction and biographies are excellent vehicles for introducing these concepts to students in kindergarten and the primary grades. As students progress through the grades, they can be introduced to more complex concepts, examples, and activities. (*If you teach in a racially or ethnically integrated classroom or school, you should keep the following guidelines in mind.*)

11. View your students of color as winners. Many students of color have high academic and career goals. They need teachers who believe they can be successful and are willing to help them succeed. Both research and theory indicate that students are more likely to achieve highly when their teachers have high academic expectations for them.

12. Keep in mind that most parents of color are very interested in education and want their children to be successful academically even though the parents may be alienated from the school. Do not equate education with schooling. Many parents who want their children to succeed have mixed feelings about the schools. Try to gain the support of these parents and enlist them as partners in the education of their children.

13. Use cooperative learning techniques and group work to promote racial and ethnic integration in the school and classroom. Research indicates that when learning groups are racially integrated, students develop more friends from other racial groups and race relations in the school improve. A helpful guide is Elizabeth Cohen's (1994) *Designing Groupwork: Strategies for the Heterogeneous Classroom*.

14. Make sure that school plays, pageants, cheerleading squads, publications, and other formal and informal groups are racially integrated. Also make sure that various ethnic and racial groups have equal status in school performances and presentations. In a multiracial school, if all of the leading roles in a school play are filled by White actors, an important message is sent to students and parents of color, whether such a message was intended or not.

SUMMARY

This chapter describes the nature of the mainstream-centric curriculum and the negative consequences it has for both mainstream students and students of color. This curriculum reinforces the false sense of superiority of mainstream students and fails to reflect, validate, and celebrate the cultures of students of color. Many factors have slowed the institutionalization of a multicultural curriculum in the schools, including ideological resistance, lack of teacher knowledge of ethnic groups, heavy reliance of teachers on textbooks, and focus on high-stakes testing and accountability. However, the institutionalization of ethnic content into the school, college, and university curriculum has made significant progress within the last forty years. This process needs to continue because curriculum transformation is a development that never ends.

Four approaches to the integration of ethnic content into the curriculum are identified in this chapter. In the *contributions approach*, heroes/heroines, cultural components, holidays, and other discrete elements related to ethnic groups are added to the curriculum without changing its structure. The *additive approach* consists of the addition of content, concepts, themes, and perspectives to the curriculum with its structure remaining unchanged. In the *transformation approach*, the structure, goals, and nature of the curriculum are changed to enable students to view concepts, issues, and problems from diverse ethnic perspectives.

The *social action approach* includes all elements of the transformation approach as well as elements that enable students to identify important social issues, gather data related to them, clarify their values, make reflective decisions, and take actions to implement their decisions. This approach seeks to make students social critics and reflective agents of change. The final part of this chapter presented guidelines to help you teach multicultural content and to function more effectively in multicultural classrooms and schools.

Questions and Activities

1. What is a mainstream-centric curriculum? What are its major assumptions and goals?
2. Examine several textbooks and find examples of the mainstream-centric approach. Share these examples with colleagues in your class or workshop.
3. How does a mainstream-centric curriculum influence mainstream students and students of color?
4. According to Banks, what factors have slowed the development of a multicultural curriculum in the schools? What is the best way to overcome these factors?
5. What are the major characteristics of the following approaches to curriculum reform: the contributions approach, the additive approach, the transformation approach, the social action approach?
6. Why do you think the contributions approach to curriculum reform is so popular and widespread within schools, especially in the primary and elementary grades?
7. In what fundamental ways do the transformation and social action approaches differ from the other two approaches identified?
8. What are the problems and promises of each of the four approaches?
9. What problems might a teacher encounter when trying to implement the transformation and social action approaches? How might these problems be overcome?
10. Assume that you are teaching a social studies lesson about the westward movement in U.S. history and a student makes a racist, stereotypic, or misleading statement about Native

Americans, such as, "The Indians were hostile to the White settlers." How would you handle this situation? Give reasons to explain why you would handle it in a particular way.

11. Since September 11, 2001, and the U.S./British–Iraq War that began in 2003, there has been an increased emphasis on patriotism in U.S. society. Some groups have called for more emphasis on teaching patriotism in the schools. What is patriotism? Describe ways in which multicultural content can be used to teach reflective patriotism. A useful reference for this exercise is *A Patriot's Handbook: Songs, Poems, Stories and Speeches Celebrating the Land We Love*, edited by Caroline Kennedy (2003). It contains selections by authors from diverse racial, ethnic, and cultural groups. Gwendolyn Brooks, Thomas Jefferson, Langston Hughes, Gloria Anzaldúa, E. B. White, and Paul Lawrence Dunbar are among the writers included in this comprehensive and useful collection.

References

Alim, H. S., & Baugh, J. (2007). *Talkin Black talk: Language, education, and social change*. New York: Teachers College Press.

Allport, G. W. (1979). *The nature of prejudice* (25th anniversary ed.). Reading, MA: Addison-Wesley.

Arthur, J., Davies, I., & Hahn, C. (Eds.). (2008). *Sage handbook of education for citizenship and democracy*. London & Los Angeles: Sage.

Asante, M. K. (1998). *The Afrocentric idea* (rev. ed.). Philadelphia: Temple University Press.

Asante, M. K., & Ravitch, D. (1991). Multiculturalism: An exchange. *The American Scholar, 60*(2), 267–276.

Au, K. H. (2006). *Multicultural issues and literacy achievement*. Mahwah, NJ: Lawrence Erlbaum Associates.

Balaji, M. (2007). *The professor and the pupil: The politics and friendship of W. E. B. Dubois and Paul Robeson*. New York: Nations Books.

Baldwin, J. (1985). *The price of the ticket: Collected nonfiction, 1948–1985*. New York: St. Martin's.

Ball, E. (1998). *Slaves in the family*. New York: Farrar, Straus & Giroux.

Banks, J. A. (Ed.). (2004). *Diversity and citizenship education: Global perspectives*. San Francisco: Jossey-Bass.

Banks, J. A. (2006). *Cultural diversity and education: Foundations, curriculum, and teaching* (5th ed.). Boston: Allyn & Bacon.

Banks, J. A. (2007). *Educating citizens in a multicultural society* (2nd ed.). New York: Teachers College Press.

Banks, J. A. (2008). *An introduction to multicultural education* (4th ed.). Boston: Allyn & Bacon.

Banks, J. A. Ed. (2009a). *The Routledge international companion to multicultural education*. New York and London: Routledge.

Banks, J. A. (2009b). *Teaching strategies for ethnic studies* (8th ed.). Boston: Allyn & Bacon.

Banks, J. A., & Banks, C. A. M. (with Clegg, A. A., Jr.). (1999). *Teaching strategies for the social studies: Decision-making and citizen action* (5th ed.). New York: Longman.

Bigelow, B., & Peterson, B. (1998). *Rethinking Columbus: The next 500 years. Resources for teaching about the impact of the arrival of Columbus in the Americas* (2nd ed.). Milwaukee, WI: Rethinking Schools.

Bigler, R. S., & Hughes, J. M. (2009). The nature and origins of children's racial attitudes. In J. A. Banks (Ed.), *The Routledge international companion to multicultural education* (pp. 186–198). New York and London: Routledge.

Black Elk. (1964). Black Elk's Prayer from a mountaintop in the Black Hills, 1931. In J. D. Forbes (Ed.), *The Indian in America's past* (p. 69). Englewood Cliffs, NJ: Prentice-Hall.

Black Elk, & Neihardt, J. G. (1972). *Black Elk speaks: Being the life story of a holy man of the Oglala Sioux* (rev. ed.). New York: Pocket Books.

Burnim, M. V., & Maultsby, P. K. (2006). *African American music: An introduction*. New York: Routledge.

Cohen, E. G. (1994). *Designing groupwork: Strategies for the heterogeneous classroom* (2nd ed.). New York: Teachers College Press.

Coleman, J. S., Campbell, E. Q., Hobson, C. J., McPartland, J., Mood, A. M., Weinfeld, F. D., & York, R. L. (1966). *Equality of educational opportunity*. Washington, DC: U.S. Department of Health, Education & Welfare, Office of Education.

Cortés, C. E. (2000). *The children are watching: How the media teach about diversity*. New York: Teachers College Press.

Cullen, C. (1993). Incident. In C. Cullen (Ed.), *Caroling dusk: An anthology of verse by Black poets of the twenties* (p. 187). New York: Citadel Press.

Dillon, S. (2006, August 27). In schools across U.S., the melting pot overflows. *New York Times*, A7, 16.

Gates, H. L., Jr. (1999). *Wonders of the African world*. New York: Knopf.

Gay, G., & Banks, J. A. (1975). Teaching the American Revolution: A multiethnic approach. *Social Education*, *39*(7), 461–466.

Gordon-Reed, A. (1997). *Thomas Jefferson and Sally Hemings: An American controversy*. Charlottesville: University Press of Virginia.

Gutmann, A. (2004). Unity and diversity in democratic multicultural education: Creative and destructive tensions. In J. A. Banks (Ed.), *Diversity and citizenship education: Global perspectives* (pp. 71–96). San Francisco: Jossey-Bass.

Howard, G. R. (2006). *We can't teach what we don't know: White teachers, multiracial schools* (2nd ed.). New York: Teachers College Press.

Hughes, L. (1993). I, too. In C. Cullen (Ed.), *Caroling dusk: An anthology of verse by Black poets of the twenties* (p. 145). New York: Citadel Press.

Katz, W. L. (1986). *Black Indians: A hidden heritage*. New York: Atheneum.

Kennedy, C. (Ed.). (2003). *A patriot's handbook: Songs, poems, stories, and speeches celebrating the land we love*. New York: Hyperion.

Korty, J. (Director). (1973). *The autobiography of Miss Jane Pittman* [Motion picture].

Lasker, B. (1929). *Race attitudes in children*. New York: Holt.

Lee, C. D. (2006). *Culture, literacy, and learning: Taking bloom in the midst of the whirlwind*. New York: Teachers College Press.

Limerick, P. N. (1987). *The legacy of conquest: The unbroken past of the American West*. New York: Norton.

Loewen, J. W. (1999). *Lies across America: What our historic sites get wrong*. New York: New Press.

Loewen, J. W. (2005). *Sundown towns: A hidden dimension of American racism*. New York: New Press.

Loewen, J. W. (2008). *Lies my teacher told me: Everything your American history textbook got wrong* (rev. ed.). New York: New Press.

Massing, M. (2008, December 18). Obama: In the divided heartland. *New York Review of Books, 55*(20), 26–30.

Nieto, S. (2009). Multicultural education in the United States: Historical realities, ongoing challenges, and transformative possibilities. In J. A. Banks (Ed.), *The Routledge international companion to multicultural education* (pp. 79–95). New York and London: Routledge.

Obama, B. (2004). *Dreams from my father: A story of race and inheritance.* New York: Crown.

Obama, B. (2006). *The audacity of hope: Thoughts on reclaiming the American dream.* New York: Vintage.

Omori, E. (Director). (2004). *Rabbit in the moon* [Motion picture]. Hohokus, NJ: New Day Films.

Ovando, C. J., & McLaren, P. (Eds.). (2000). *The politics of multiculturalism and bilingual education: Students and teachers caught in the cross fire.* Boston: McGraw-Hill.

Ravitch, D. (1990). Diversity and democracy: Multicultural education in America. *American Educator, 14*(1), 16–20, 46–48.

Reed, I. (Ed.). (1997). *MultiAmerica: Essays on cultural wars and cultural peace.* New York: Viking.

Rico, B. R., & Mano, S. (Eds.). (2001). *American mosaic: Multicultural readings in context* (3rd ed.). Boston: Houghton Mifflin.

Roberts, S. (2008, August 14). A generation away, minorities may become the majority in U.S. *New York Times,* A1, A18.

Schlesinger, A. M., Jr. (1998). *The disuniting of America: Reflections on a multicultural society* (rev. ed.). Knoxville, TN: Whittle Direct.

Schofield, J. W. (2004). Fostering positive intergroup relations in schools. In J. A. Banks & C. A. M. Banks (Eds.), *Handbook of research on multicultural education* (2nd ed., pp. 799–812). San Francisco: Jossey-Bass.

Sleeter, C. E. (2005). *Un-standardizing curriculum: Multicultural teaching in the standards-based classroom.* New York: Teachers College Press.

Stephan, W. (1999). *Reducing prejudice and stereotyping in schools.* New York: Teachers College Press.

Takaki, R. (2008). *A different mirror: A history of multicultural America* (rev. ed.). Boston: Little Brown.

Taylor, M. D. (1976). *Roll of thunder, hear my cry.* New York: Puffin.

U.S. Census Bureau. (2008). *An older and more diverse nation by midcentury.* Retrieved October 20, 2008, from http://www.census.gov/Press-Release/www/releases/archives/population/012496.html

Walker, A. (1982). *The color purple.* New York: Harcourt Brace.

White, R. (1991). *"It's your misfortune and none of my own": A new history of the American West.* Norman: University of Oklahoma Press.

Wineburg, S., & Monte-Sano, C. (2008). "Famous Americans": The changing pantheon of American heroes. *Journal of American History,* 94, 1186–1202. Retrieved December 27, 2008, from http://www.journalofamericanhistory.org/textbooks/2008/wineburg.html

Zinn, H. (1999). *A people's history of the United States: 1492-present* (20th anniversary ed.). New York: HarperCollins.

CHAPTER 11

The Colorblind Perspective in School: Causes and Consequences

Janet Ward Schofield*

INTRODUCTION

Race matters, or at least it has historically in the United States, although it is a scientifically imprecise construct, the meaning of which is heavily influenced by social context (Jones, 1997). Racial group membership is the basis on which some individuals were treated as the property of others. It is also the basis on which the basic rights of citizenship were denied to individuals even after the formal abolition of slavery. The civil rights laws passed in the middle of the 20th century were designed to do away with such group-based discrimination—to dismantle dual school systems, to ensure political rights, and to prevent discrimination in employment and housing. However, the passage of these laws created a situation that Jones (1998) has called the "New American Dilemma"—a conflict between

> the values embodied in the democratic principles of freedom and
> equality without regard to race, and ... the belief that current as well as
> cumulative racial biases persist making it necessary to take race into
> account in order to realize the principles of freedom and equality.
> (p. 645)

* The author expresses her deep appreciation to the students and staff of Wexler School. The research on which this chapter is based was funded by the author's contract with the National Institute of Education (Contract 400–76–0011). Other expenses relating to the chapter's preparation were covered by the Learning Research and Development Center, which was partly funded by the NIE when this research was conducted. However, all opinions expressed herein are solely those of the author, and no endorsement of the ideas by the NIE is implied or intended.

The first of these perspectives was given voice by Supreme Court Justice John Marshall Harlan in 1896 in his famous call for a colorblind society in his dissenting opinion in *Plessy v. Ferguson*. A colorblind society is one in which racial or ethnic group membership is irrelevant to the way individuals are treated (Rist, 1974). People in favor of colorblind approaches to policy argue that taking cognizance of group membership in decision making is illegitimate because it is likely to lead either to discrimination against minority groups or to reverse discrimination in their favor. Neither of these is viewed as desirable. The people aligned with this side of the debate argue that, because the laws that systematically disadvantaged African Americans were overturned decades ago, a fair system is now in place and this system can be truly fair only to the extent that it completely ignores group membership—treating individuals solely as individuals and striving to ignore race or ethnicity completely.

Yet others (Barrett & George, 2005; Bonilla-Silva, 2003; Brown et al., 2003; Guinier & Torres, 2002; Levin, 2003) argue that such an approach is the antithesis of fairness—that it is akin to a race between a well-nourished and well-trained athlete for whom most of the spectators are rooting and an individual who has just been released from an unjust prison term during which food was sparse and opportunities for exercise were denied. People taking this perspective agree with Justice Harry Blackmun, who wrote in the *Regents of the University of California v. Bakke* (1978) case that "in order to get beyond racism, we must first take account of race. In order to treat persons equally, we must treat them differently" (pp. 2806–2808). The reality of continuing racism (Sidanius & Pratto, 1999; Trent et al., 2003) as well as the continuing impact of prior discrimination, such as the striking difference in net worth among African Americans and Whites with similar incomes due at least in part to larger inheritances received by Whites (Jaynes & Williams, 1989), makes both just and wise policies designed specifically to promote the inclusion of African Americans in the economic and political life of the country. Thus, they tend to support affirmative action and related policies designed to do this by explicitly taking account of the relative participation rates of various groups—an approach at direct odds with the colorblind perspective. From this perspective, color blindness stands in the way of achieving fairness because it justifies moving away from race-based or ethnicity-based policies designed to promote fairness (Gotanda, 1991).

This tension between the view that sees taking cognizance of racial or ethnic group membership positively and the view that sees it negatively is strongly reflected in controversy over how our educational system should function (Wolsko, Park, Judd, & Wittenbrink, 2000). Specifically, one approach to education in our increasingly diverse society calls for redoubling efforts to teach all students core information and values in an attempt to strengthen a unified American identity (Bennett, 1987; Hirsch, 1996; Schlesinger, 1992). This approach, which typically decries bilingual and multicultural approaches to education, is quite consistent with the colorblind perspective in that it seeks to ignore or deemphasize subgroup identities and differences in an effort to create a unified citizenry. In contrast, another approach, typically endorsed by proponents of multicultural education, argues that responding to diversity by including material about many groups and using approaches to teaching that recognize cultural differences is needed to serve students well and to build harmony and respect between those from different backgrounds (Banks, 2005; Marcus, Steele, & Steele, 2002; Moses, 2002; Nieto, 2004; Takaki, 1993; Yinger, 1994).

Interestingly, this tension between ignoring or focusing on group membership is reflected in theoretical stances with sharply differing implications in social-psychological research on improving intergroup relations, as Wolsko et al. (2000) point out. Specifically, one major line of theorizing and research suggests that it is the categorization of individuals into groups that lays the basis for stereotyping and discrimination (Brewer & Gaertner, 2001; Tajfel, 1978). From this perspective, the logical solution to the problem is to minimize the salience of the group or to redefine the in-group in a more inclusive way so that old out-groups join together in assuming a new, more expansive shared identity (Gaertner, Dovidio, Anastasio, Bachman, & Rust, 1993). Another strongly contrasting and much less common perspective suggests that explicit focus on group differences can also contribute to improved intergroup relations (Lee & Duenas, 1995; Park & Judd, 2005; Triandis, 1976).

The issues raised by the New American Dilemma are complex and unlikely to be easily resolved. Full consideration of them would of necessity involve work from fields as disparate as philosophy, history, psychology, law, ethics, economics, and politics. Thus, this chapter does not try to solve this dilemma. Rather, it has a more modest but nonetheless important goal: to provide a glimpse of how the colorblind perspective works in reality in one of the most important institutions in our society—its schools.

I did not set out initially to explore this question. Rather, as a scholar deeply interested in the potential of interracial school settings for improving intergroup relations, I embarked on a longitudinal ethnographic study designed to illuminate the nature of peer relations in a desegregated school and the impact that school policies, structures, and culture have on those relations (Schofield, 1989). It just so happened that having chosen a particular school for study, as described later, I found myself in an environment that strongly endorsed the colorblind perspective. Furthermore, over time, it became apparent that the institution's endorsement of this perspective had important consequences that educators at the school did not anticipate and often did not recognize. Thus, the causes and consequences of this perspective became the focus of the part of my research reported here.

I argue that two basic factors make understanding the implications of the colorblind perspective important. First, evidence suggests that this perspective is widespread in schools both within the United States and elsewhere, either as part of official policy or as an informal but nonetheless powerful social norm that applies in many situations (Eaton, 2001; Gillborn, 1992; Goetz & Breneman, 1988; Jervis, 1996; Lewis, 2001; Pollock, 2004; Revilla, Wells, & Holme, 2004; Rist, 1978; Sagar & Schofield, 1984; Sleeter, 1993). Second, the colorblind approach is also frequently espoused as a goal to be sought in many other realms, including employment practices and judicial proceedings. This research led me to conclude that although the colorblind perspective is appealing because it is consistent with a long-standing American emphasis on the importance of the individual (Flagg, 1993), it easily leads to a misrepresentation of reality in ways that allow and even encourage discrimination against minority group members, as later parts of this chapter demonstrate.

THE RESEARCH SITE: WEXLER MIDDLE SCHOOL

In choosing a site for the research, I adopted a strategy that Cook and Campbell (1976, p. 237) call "generalizing to target instances." My aim was to study peer relations between African American and White students under conditions that theory suggests should be relatively conducive to the development of positive relations between them.

In his classic book *The Nature of Prejudice*, Allport (1954) proposed that intergroup contact may reinforce previously held stereotypes and increase intergroup hostility unless the contact situation is structured in a way that (1) provides equal status for minority and majority group members, (2) encourages cooperation toward shared, strongly desired goals, and (3) provides the support of law, authority, and customs for positive relations. These ideas, as elaborated and refined by subsequent theoretical and empirical work (Gaertner, Rust, Dovidio, Bachman, & Anastasio, 1994; Hewstone & Brown, 1986; Pettigrew, 1998, 2004; Pettigrew & Tropp, 2006; Schofield, 2001; Schofield & Eurich-Fulcer, 2001; Vonofakou et al., 2008), constitute a useful foundation for understanding the likely outcomes of interracial contact. Although equal status may be neither a necessary prerequisite nor a sufficient condition for change, it does appear to be very helpful (Brewer & Brown, 1998; Brown, 1995; Cohen, 1997; Cohen, Lockheed, & Lohman, 1976; Cook, 1985; Pettigrew, 1998; Riordan, 1978; Schofield & Eurich-Fulcer; Stephan & Stephan, 2001). In addition, a substantial body of research suggests that cooperation toward mutually desired goals is indeed generally conducive to improved intergroup relations (Aronson & Patnoe, 1997; Johnson, Johnson, & Maruyama, 1984; Schofield, 2001; Sherif, 1979; Slavin & Cooper, 1999; Stephan & Stephan, 2001).

Wexler Middle School was constructed in a large northeastern city to serve as a model of high-quality integrated education. When it first opened, Wexler had a student body almost precisely 50 percent African American and 50 percent White, mirroring closely the proportion of African American and White students in the city's public schools. This school, which served 1,200 children in sixth through eighth grades, was chosen for study because the decisions made in planning for it suggested that it would come reasonably close to meeting the conditions specified by Allport (1954) and theorists who have built on his work. The school's strong efforts to provide an environment conducive to improving intergroup relations is exemplified by the fact that the top four administrative positions at Wexler were filled by two African Americans and two Whites, clearly symbolizing the school's commitment to providing equal status for members of both groups and providing both White and African American students the advantages likely to flow from having those sharing their racial identity well represented in positions of authority in the school (Schofield, Wang, & Chew, 2007).

The extent to which Wexler met the conditions specified by Allport and his intellectual heirs as conducive to the development of improved intergroup relations has been discussed at length elsewhere (Schofield, 1989). Here, I merely report the conclusion drawn in that discussion: that Wexler came considerably closer to these criteria than did most desegregated public schools, yet it fell seriously short of meeting them completely in a number of ways, many of which were the direct result of societal conditions over which Wexler had little or no control. For example, in spite of Wexler's commitment to a staffing pattern that would provide equal formal status for African Americans and Whites, the proportion of African American teachers on its staff was only about 25 percent, considerably lower than the proportion of African American students in the school, because the school system did not want to put too high a proportion of its African American teachers in one specific school.

In addition, a large majority of Wexler's White students came from middle- or upper-middle-class homes. Although some of the African American children were middle class, the majority came from either poor or working-class families. These social class differences had implications for the status of African American and White students within the school. For example, in the eighth grade, which divided students into a "regular" and a "gifted" track, a much higher proportion of the White than African American students achieved scores on standardized tests that led to their placement in the gifted track. Even in the sixth and seventh grades, which had academically heterogeneous classes, this difference influenced students' status (Schofield, 1980), although not in a way emphasized and formalized by school tracking policy. In sum, Wexler made stronger than usual efforts to foster positive relations between African American and White students but fell markedly short of being a theoretically ideal milieu for accomplishing this goal.

DATA GATHERING

The analysis that follows is based on an intensive four-year study of peer relations at Wexler. The basic data-gathering strategy was intensive and extensive observation in Wexler's classrooms, hallways, playgrounds, and cafeteria. Observers used the full field-note method for recording the events they witnessed (Olson, 1976). A large number of events were observed because they were representative of the events that filled most of the school day at Wexler. However, an important subgroup of events was oversampled in relation to their frequency of occurrence because of their direct relevance to the study's focus. This strategy, which Strauss (1987) calls "theoretical sampling," led to oversampling certain activities, such as affective education classes, designed to help students get to know each other, and meetings of Wexler's interracial student advisory group set up to handle the special problems students might face in a desegregated school. Over the course of the study, more than 500 hours were devoted to the observation of students and staff at Wexler.

A wide variety of other data-gathering techniques ranging from sociometric questionnaires to experimental work to quantitative observational approaches were also used (Sagar & Schofield, 1980; Sagar, Schofield, & Snyder, 1983; Schofield, 1979; Schofield & Francis, 1982; Schofield & Sagar, 1977; Schofield & Whitley, 1983; Whitley, Schofield, & Snyder, 1984). Interviews were employed extensively. For example, randomly selected students participated in open-ended interviews twice a year. Teachers and administrators were also interviewed repeatedly. In addition, graffiti in the bathrooms and on the school walls were routinely recorded, school bulletins were collected, and careful note was taken of such things as wall decorations and public address system announcements.

Space does not allow full discussion of the many varied techniques used in collecting and analyzing the data on which this chapter is based. However, two general principles that guided the research must be mentioned. First, both data gathering and analysis were as rigorous and systematic as possible. For example, sampling techniques were employed when appropriate; trained coders, who were unaware of the race and sex of particular respondents, coded the open-ended interviews using reliable systems developed for this research; and field notes were carefully indexed so that all notes relevant to a given topic could be examined.

Second, because it is often impossible to achieve high levels of precision and control in field research, strong efforts were made to triangulate the data (Webb, Campbell, Schwartz, & Sechrest, 1966). Great care was taken to gather many different types of information bearing on the same issue, to minimize the potential problems with each data source, and to be sensitive in analyzing and interpreting data that might reflect biases in the data set that could not be completely eliminated. The basic approach used in the analysis of the qualitative data is outlined in works such as Bogdan and Taylor (1975), Campbell (1975), Miles and Huberman (1984), and Strauss and Corbin (1990). Fuller details on data gathering and analysis are presented elsewhere as is information on the strategies used to minimize observer reactivity and bias (Schofield, 1989; Schofield & Sagar, 1979).

THE COLORBLIND PERSPECTIVE AND ITS COROLLARIES

Wexler's faculty clearly tended to subscribe to the colorblind view of interracial schooling. Interviews with both African American and White teachers suggested that the majority of both groups tended to see Wexler as an institution that could help impart middle-class values and modes of behavior to lower-class students so that they could break out of the cycle of poverty and become middle-class persons themselves. Even though most of these lower-class students were African American, race was seen as quite incidental to the anticipated class assimilation process.

An African American administrator with perhaps more candor than many similarly oriented White administrators and teachers made her class assimilation goals explicit and, at the same time, made it clear just which students needed to be so assimilated:

> I really don't address myself to group differences when I am dealing with youngsters.... I try to treat youngsters, I don't care who they are, as youngsters and not as Black, White, green or yellow.... Many of the Black youngsters who have difficulty are the ones who ... have come from communities where they had to put up certain defenses and these defenses are the antithesis of the normal situation ... like they find in school. It is therefore [difficult] getting them to become aware that they have to follow these rules because [they] are here ... not over there in their community.... I think that many of the youngsters [from the] larger community have a more normal set of values that people generally want to see, and therefore do not have [as] much difficulty in coping with their school situation.... [The Black children] do have difficulty in adjusting because they are just not used to it. Until we can adjustively counsel them into the right types of behavior ... I think we're going to continue to have these types of problems.

The only thing atypical in the preceding remarks is the frank acknowledgment that the children perceived as lacking the "normal set of values that people generally want to see" were typically African American. More usually, this was implicit in remarks emphasizing the negative effects of growing up in a poor family or a low-income neighborhood.

As a reaction to the invidious distinctions that have traditionally been made in the United States on the basis of race, the colorblind perspective is understandable, even laudable. However, this orientation was accompanied at Wexler by a number of other logically related beliefs, which taken together with it, had some important though largely unrecognized negative consequences. These beliefs and their basis in the ongoing social reality at Wexler are discussed individually. Then the consequences of this belief system are discussed in some detail.

Race as an Invisible Characteristic

It is not a very great leap from the colorblind perspective, which says that race is a social category of no relevance to one's behaviors and decisions, to a belief that individuals should not and perhaps even do not notice each other's racial group membership. At Wexler, many people viewed acknowledging that one was aware of another's race as a possible sign of prejudice, as illustrated by the following excerpt from project field notes:

> When I was arranging the student interviews, I mentioned to Mr. Little [White] that I thought there was only one White girl in one of his classes. I asked if I was right about this and he said, "Well, just a minute. Let me check." After looking through the class roster in his roll book he said, "You know, you're right. I never noticed that.... I guess that's a good thing."

Our data suggest that teachers not only denied that they noticed children's race when the researchers were present but also did so among themselves. For example, when complying with a request to mark down the race of his students on a class roster for research purposes, a White teacher remarked, "Did you ever notice those teachers who say, 'I never notice what they are'?"

Although there was less unanimity on the issue of whether students noticed the race of others than of whether teachers did, a substantial proportion of Wexler's faculty asserted that the students rarely noticed race. This point of view is exemplified by the following excerpt from an interview with an African American science teacher:

> Ms. Monroe: You know, I hear the things the students usually fight about. As I said before, it's stupid things like someone taking a pencil. It's not because [the other person] is Black or White.... At this age level ... I don't think it's Black or White.
>
> Interviewer: There's something I'm wondering about. It is hard to believe, given the way our society is, that you can just bring kids together and they won't be very much aware.
>
> Ms. Monroe: They just go about their daily things and don't ... I don't think they think about it really.... I see them interacting with one another on an adult basis.... They are not really aware of color ... or race or whatever.
>
> Interviewer: You really don't see that as a factor ... in their relationships?
>
> Ms. Monroe: No.

Although the faculty at Wexler saw themselves, and to a lesser extent their students, as oblivious to the race of others, a wide variety of data suggest that this view was not accurate. Most removed from the specific situation at Wexler, but nonetheless pertinent, is a substantial body of data from research on stereotyping and person perception. This work suggests that individuals tend to use preexisting categories in perceiving and responding to others (Brewer & Gaertner, 2001; Brown, 1995). More specifically, research suggests that individuals spontaneously use the physical appearance of other people as a basis for categorizing them by race (Cosmides, Tooby, & Kurzban, 2003; Hamilton, Stroessner, & Driscoll, 1994; Ito & Urland, 2003). Furthermore, this categorization has an impact on how individuals are perceived and on how others respond to them (Devine, 1989; Dovidio et al., 1997; Eberhardt, 2005; Fazio, Jackson, Dunton, & Williams, 1995; Norton, Sommers, Apfelbaum, Pura, & Ariely, 2006; Sagar & Schofield, 1980).

The teachers and students at Wexler were to some extent self-selected members of an interracial institution and thus might conceivably be less prone to use race as a category for processing information about others than would the college student populations used in most studies just cited. However, given the importance of race as a social category in many aspects of life in the United States, it seems highly unlikely that the prevailing tendency at Wexler was for individuals not even to notice each other's race. Interviews with students made it clear that many of them were very conscious of their race or of the race of other students, which is hardly surprising given the fact that interracial schooling was a new and somewhat threatening experience for many of them. The following excerpt from an interview in which the interviewer had not herself previously mentioned race suggests just how salient racial categories were to the children:

> INTERVIEWER: Can you tell me who some of your friends are?
> BEVERLY [African American]: Well, Stacey and Lydia and Amy, even though she's White.

Similarly, students' awareness of racial group membership is seen in an excerpt from field notes taken in a seventh-grade class with a higher-than-average proportion of African American students because the teachers had decided to put many lower-achieving children in a class by themselves:

> Howard, a White male, leaned over to me (a White female observer) and said, "You know, it just wasn't fair the way they set up this class. There are 16 Black kids and only 9 White kids. I can't learn in here." I said, "Why is that?" Howard replied, "They copy and they pick on you. It just isn't fair."

Race as a Taboo Topic

Before discussing why the view that they and their students tended not even to notice race gained considerable popularity among Wexler's teachers in spite of everyday indications that this was often not the case, this section discusses two other phenomena closely related to the development of the colorblind perspective. The first was the development of a norm strong enough to be labeled a virtual taboo against the use of the words *White* and *Black* in a context in which they referred to racial group membership. Thus, for example, in almost 200 hours of observations in classrooms, hallways, and teachers' meetings during Wexler's first year, fewer than 25 direct references to race were made by school staff or students (Schofield, 1989). Any use of the words *Black* and *White* in a context in which they referred to an individual or group was classified as a reference to race, as were racial epithets and words and phrases used almost exclusively within one group to express solidarity (e.g., "Hey, Brother") or the like. As mentioned previously, this reluctance to talk about race has been noted in many other racially-mixed schools (Eaton, 2001; Gillborn, 1992; Goetz & Breneman, 1988; Jervis,

1996; Larson & Ovando, 2001; Rist, 1978; Sagar & Schofield, 1984; Sleeter, 1993; Wells, Holme, Atanda, & Revilla, 2005). This reluctance to speak about race has been characterized as "colormuteness" by Pollock (2004), who found it especially prevalent in situations in which certain kinds of problems are discussed.

The extremely infrequent reference to race at Wexler was all the more surprising when one considers that our observations included a wide variety of formal and informal situations, ranging from workshops funded by the Emergency School Assistance Act, federal legislation that provided funds to desegregating schools to help them handle special problems that might arise as a result of desegregation, to informal student interactions on the playgrounds and in the hallways.

Students' awareness of the taboo is shown clearly in the following field notes, which recount a conversation with a White social worker whose work at Wexler on the extracurricular program was funded by a local foundation concerned with race relations. Perhaps not surprisingly under these circumstances, she showed much less reluctance than did most staff to deal in a straightforward manner with the issue of race.

Ms. Fowler said that a short while ago she had heard from Martin [Black] that another child had done something wrong. The offense was serious enough that she wanted to track down this individual. She asked Martin to describe the child who had committed the offense. Martin said, "He has black hair and he's fairly tall." He did not give the race of the other person even though he went on to give a fairly complete description otherwise. Finally, Ms. Fowler asked, "Is he Black or White?" Martin replied, "Is it all right for me to say?" Ms. Fowler said that it was all right. Martin then said, "Well, the boy was White."

Students were well aware that making references to race displeased many of their teachers and might also offend peers.

> INTERVIEWER: You know, the other day I was walking around the school and heard a sixth grade student describing a student from the seventh grade to a teacher who needed to find this student in order to return something she had lost. The sixth grader said the seventh grader was tall and thin. She described what the girl had been wearing and said her hair was dark, but she didn't say whether the girl was Black or White.... Why do you think she didn't mention that?
>
> SYLVIA [African American]: The teacher might have got mad if she said whether she was White or Black.
>
> INTERVIEWER: Do some teachers get mad about things like that?
>
> SYLVIA: Some do ... they holler....
>
> INTERVIEWER: Now, when you talk to kids who are Black, do you ever mention that someone is White or Black?
>
> SYLVIA: No.
>
> INTERVIEWER: What about when you're talking with kids who are White?
>
> SYLVIA: Nope.
>
> INTERVIEWER: You never mention race? Why not?
>
> SYLVIA: They might think I'm prejudiced.

Social Life as a Web of Purely Interpersonal Relations

Consistent with the view that race is not—or at least should not be—a salient aspect of other individuals and with the practice of not speaking about race were tendencies to conceptualize social life as a web of interpersonal rather than intergroup relations and to assume that interpersonal relations are not much influenced by group membership. As one teacher put it:

> Peer-group identity here in middle school . . . has nothing to do with race. There's a strong tendency to group that exists independent of . . . racial boundaries. . . . We started in September with these students letting them know we weren't going to fool around with that. . . . You're a student and we don't care what color you are.

This tendency to minimize the potential importance of intergroup processes was illustrated clearly during an in-service training session, the stated purpose of which was to help teachers deal effectively with the racially mixed student body. The facilitator, a White clinical psychologist employed by a local foundation, began by making some general statements about the importance of understanding cultural differences between students. Although the facilitator kept trying to nudge and finally to push the group to discuss ways in which the racially-mixed nature of the student body influenced peer relations, appropriate curricular materials, and the like, the group ended up discussing issues such as the problems caused by individual children who act out aggressively in the classroom, the difficulty that overweight children have gaining peer acceptance, and the fact that children with disabilities were sometimes taunted by their classmates.

Contrasting sharply with the teachers' tendency to insist that they and their students reacted to each other exclusively as individuals and to deemphasize the importance of intergroup as opposed to interpersonal processes was the students' willingness to discuss with interviewers the important role race played in Wexler's social life.

> INTERVIEWER: I have noticed . . . that [in the cafeteria] very often White kids sit with White kids and Black kids sit with Black kids. Why do you think that this is?
>
> MARY [White]: 'Cause the White kids have White friends and the Black kids have Black friends. . . . I don't think integration is working. . . . Blacks still associate with Blacks and Whites still associate with Whites. . . .
>
> INTERVIEWER: Can you think of any White kids that have quite a few Black friends or of any Black kids who have quite a few White friends?
>
> MARY: Not really.

The tendency for students to group themselves by race in a variety of settings was very marked. For example, on a fairly typical day at the end of the school's second year of operation, 119 White and 90 African American students attended the seventh-grade lunch period. Of these more than 200 children, only 6 sat next to someone of the other race (Schofield & Sagar, 1977).

Of course, it is possible that race itself was not a factor in producing such interaction patterns, but something such as socioeconomic status, academic achievement, or the opportunity for previous contact with each other correlated with race. Such factors did appear to reinforce the tendency to prefer intergroup interactions and were often cited by teachers as the actual cause of the visually apparent tendency of students to cluster with those of their own race. Yet the

Table 11.1   Mean Ratings of Both White and Black Actors' Ambiguously Aggressive Behaviors by White and Black Participants

Subject Group	Actor Race	Rating Scale:Mean/Threatening
White	White	8.28
	Black	8.99
Black	White	7.38
	Black	8.40

Note. Means are based on sums of paired 7-point scales indicating how well the given adjective described the behaviors, from 1 (not at all) to 7 (exactly). N = 40 in each group. Each Participants rated two White and two Black actors (e.g., the perpetrator of the ambiguously aggressive act) and two White and Black targets. The 4 × 4 nature of the Latin square required treating the race permutations as four levels of a single factor. Significant F values on this factor provided justification for testing actor race, target race, and interaction effects with simple contrasts, using the error variance estimate generated by the ANOVA. The significant main effect of race permutations on the summed mean/threatening scales, $F(3,192) = 3.02$, $p < .05$, was found to reflect, as predicted, a tendency for subjects to rate the behaviors by Black actors more mean/threatening than identical behaviors by White actors, $t(144) = 2.90$, $p < .01$. Means are not broken down by target race because no statistically significant main effects or interactions were found for this variable.

Source: From Sagar, H. A., and Schofield, J. W.(1980). Racial and Behavioral Cues in Black and White Children's Perceptions of Ambiguously Aggressive Acts. *Journal of Personality and Social Psychology, 39*(4), 590–598. Copyright 1980 by the American Psychological Association. Adapted with permission.

results of an experiment conducted at Wexler demonstrate that race itself was a real factor in peer relations. In this study, 80 male sixth graders were presented with carefully drawn pictures of a number of ambiguously aggressive types of peer interactions that were quite common at Wexler, such as poking another student with a pencil. For each type of interaction, some students were shown pictures in which both students were African American, others saw pictures in which both students were White, and others saw mixed-race dyads with the African American student shown as either the initiator of the behavior or as the student to whom it was directed.

The results suggested that the race of the person depicted as initiating the behavior influenced how mean and threatening the behavior was interpreted as being (Sagar & Schofield, 1980) (see Table 11.1). Such a finding is, of course, inconsistent with the notion that students take no notice of others' race. It is also incompatible with the idea that intergroup processes have no influence on students' reactions to their peers because the data suggest that the perception of an individual's behavior is indeed influenced by the group membership of the person performing it.

THE FUNCTIONS AND CONSEQUENCES OF THE COLORBLIND PERSPECTIVE AND ITS COROLLARIES

Regardless of the fact that the colorblind perspective and its corollaries were not completely accurate views of the social processes occurring at Wexler, they appeared to influence the development of its social fabric in ways that had a number of important consequences, some positive and some negative. The following discussion of the functions of this set of beliefs suggests why the colorblind perspective was attractive to teachers and how it often negatively affected both the education and social experiences of Wexler's students.

Reducing the Potential for Overt Conflict

One concern that typifies many schools with diverse student bodies is a desire to avoid dissension and conflict that are or could appear to be race related (Sagar & Schofield, 1984). The adoption of colorblind policies is often seen as useful in achieving this goal because, if they are implemented fully, they can help protect the institution and people in positions of responsibility in it from charges of discrimination. Furthermore, a colorblind approach may be seen, especially by White educators, as keeping the school focused on issues of interest to all groups rather than on issues of differential interest to different stakeholders in the school (Larson & Ovando, 2001). This is not to say that such an approach leads to equal outcomes for members of all groups. Indeed, when there are initial group differences on criteria relevant to success in a given institution, such policies are likely to lead to differential outcomes, a situation that some people would characterize as institutional racism (Jones, 1997). However, as noted earlier, the colorblind perspective is consistent with notions of fairness that have long held sway in the United States and thus can be relatively easily defended. Policies that give clear preference to either minority or majority group members are much more likely to spark widespread controversy and conflict.

An example from Wexler illustrates how the operation of the colorblind perspective helps to minimize overt conflict in situations in which the outcomes for African Americans and Whites as a whole are extremely different. The suspension rate for African American students at Wexler was roughly four times that for White students. The strong correlation between race and socioeconomic background at Wexler made it predictable that the African American students' behavior would be less consistent than that of White students with the basically middle-class norms prevailing in the school. However, the colorblind perspective appeared instrumental in helping to keep Wexler's discipline policies from becoming a focus of contention. To my knowledge, the disparity in suspension rates was never treated as a serious issue that needed examination. When researchers asked faculty and administrators about it, some, perhaps not altogether candidly, denied having noticed it. Others argued that it was not a problem in the sense that individual students were generally treated fairly. In fact, teachers often emphasized strongly the effort they made to treat discipline problems with White and African American students in exactly the same way.

On the relatively rare occasions when charges of discrimination were raised by students unhappy with the way a teacher had dealt with them, teachers tended to discount the complaint by reiterating their commitment to the colorblind perspective:

> Ms. WILSON [White]: I try not to let myself listen to it [the charge of discrimination]. Maybe once in a while I ask myself, "Well, why would he make that statement?" But I know in my mind that I do not discriminate on the basis of race.... And I will not have someone create an issue like that when I know I have done my best not to create it.

Only an occasional teacher, more often than not African American, suggested that the colorblind perspective actually worked to help create the disparity in suspension rates; this issue is addressed later in this chapter. Be that as it may, the colorblind perspective clearly fostered an atmosphere that minimized the chances that the disparity itself was likely to become the focus of either overt discontent or constructive action.

Minimizing Discomfort and Embarrassment

Many of the faculty and students at Wexler had little prior experience in racially-mixed schools. Also, most of them lived in neighborhoods that were either heavily White or heavily African American. Thus, for many, there was an initial sense of awkwardness and anxiety like the intergroup anxiety Stephan and Stephan (1996) discuss. Under such circumstances, avoiding mention of race and contending that it rarely influenced relations between individuals seemed to minimize the potential for awkward or embarrassing social situations. This is related to the aforementioned conflict-avoidance function of these beliefs, but it can be distinguished conceptually because feelings of awkwardness and embarrassment can but do not always lead to conflict. Consistent with the conclusion that teachers avoided talk of race in order to avoid discomfort and personal embarrassment, Pollock (2004) noted that although teachers in the school she studied referred to race in describing conflicts between students of different backgrounds, they very rarely mentioned race when describing their own conflicts with students. This observation suggests that although teachers in that school were willing to entertain the idea that problems between students might have a racial element, they were not willing to raise the specter of race-related problems in their own interactions with students, a much more personally threatening possibility.

One way to illustrate the ways in which the colorblind perspective and the associated beliefs and norms helped smooth social relations between African Americans and Whites is to compare the situation at Wexler to another type of interaction that is often rather strained, at least initially: interaction between individuals who have visible disabilities and those who do not. In a fascinating analysis of this latter situation, Davis (1961) argues that the emotion aroused in the person without disabilities by the sight of a person with disabilities creates tension and an uncertainty about what is appropriate behavior; this tension interferes with normal interaction patterns. There is a tendency for the disability to become the focus of attention and to foster ambiguity about appropriate behavior. Davis argues that the initial reaction to this situation is often a fictional denial of the disability and of its potential effect on the relationship, that is, a tendency to pretend to ignore the existence of the disability, which at least temporarily relieves the interactants of the necessity of dealing with its implications.

Analogously, one can think of the racial group membership of individuals in an intergroup interaction, be they African American or White, as a type of visually apparent disability. Like a disability, group membership may provoke an affective response in others that predisposes them to avoidance or at least raises questions about appropriate behavior. Of course, just as some individuals will feel more awkward than will others when interacting with a person with a disability, so, too, some individuals are more likely than others to be strongly affected by interacting with someone of another race. However, to the extent that race is perceived as a potential threat to a smooth, relaxed, and pleasant interaction, one way of handling that threat is to actively avoid referring to the attribute that creates it. Consistent with this conclusion, Norton et al. (2006) demonstrate experimentally that Whites are more likely to mention race when describing someone when they are interacting with another White than when they are interacting with an African American, even though such avoidance impairs effective task completion.

Although Davis (1961) argues that initial interactions between people with disabilities and others are characterized by a fictional denial of the disability, he also suggests that, with time, this fiction is discarded because, being based on an obvious falsehood, it is inherently unstable and in the long run dysfunctional. Similarly, I argue that although the colorblind perspective and the accompanying taboo may have made the initial adjustment to Wexler easier, in the long run they tended to inhibit the development of positive relations between African American and White students. These students were vividly aware of differences and of tensions between them that were related to their group membership. Yet such issues could not be dealt with in a straightforward manner in the colorblind climate in which race functioned as a public secret, as Williams (1998) suggests it often does. Thus, anger sometimes festered and stereotypes were built when fuller discussion of the situation might have made it easier for individuals to see each other's perspectives.

This is not to suggest that schools have the responsibility to function as giant T-groups or as therapeutic institutions. Rather, it is to say that the refusal of many of Wexler's faculty to recognize the fundamental role that race played in peer relationships meant that they played a less constructive role than they might have in guiding students through a new and sometimes threatening experience. Jervis (1996) observed a similar phenomenon with similar results in her study of a multiethnic middle school, as did Lewis (2001) in a predominately White school. Furthermore, the norms discouraging discussion of race not only undercut potentially constructive teacher–student interactions related to this topic but also discouraged student discussion of this topic with peers. This minimized the potential for conflict. But it also minimized the potentially constructive impact of such discussions, suggested by research demonstrating that discussion of race between more and less prejudiced students can actually reduce prejudice in the former without increasing it in the latter (Aboud & Doyle, 1996; Aboud & Fenwick, 1999).

Increasing Educators' Freedom of Action

The colorblind perspective and its corollaries undoubtedly gained some of their appeal because they tended to simplify life for Wexler's staff and to increase their freedom of action. An example can illustrate both points. After being asked by one member of the research team about the outcome of a closely contested student council election, a White teacher said that she had purposely miscounted votes so that a "responsible child" (a White boy) was declared the winner rather than the "unstable child" (an African American girl) who had actually received a few more votes. The teacher seemed ambivalent about and somewhat embarrassed by her action, but the focus of her concern was her subversion of the democratic process. She reported that she had looked at the two children as individuals and decided that one was a more desirable student council representative than the other. As far as I could tell from an extended discussion with her, she did not consciously consider the race of the students involved. Furthermore, she did not appear to consider the fact that her action had changed the racial composition of the student council.

The failure to consider race clearly simplifies the decision-making process because there is one less item, and a potentially affect-laden one at that, to be factored into it. Related to this, the colorblind approach increases educators' freedom of action because policies or actions that sometimes appear acceptable if one thinks about them in a colorblind way often appear much less acceptable from a perspective that is not colorblind. For example, Goetz and Breneman (1988) point out how avoiding discussion of the fact that school policies will affect African American and White students in different ways made it easier to adopt policies that worked to African American students' disadvantage in two southern elementary schools. In addition, Pollock (2004) describes how "colormuteness," the avoidance of reference to race, can actually increase the role that race plays in schooling and its outcomes.

Indeed, the colorblind perspective and its corollaries foster an environment that research suggests is conducive to producing discriminatory behavior, at least on the part of certain types of individuals. For example, work by Snyder, Kleck, Strenta, and Mentzer (1979) demonstrates that people are more likely to act in accordance with feelings they prefer not to reveal when they can appear to be acting on some other basis than when no other obvious explanation for their behavior is available. Specifically, they found that individuals avoided people with physical disabilities when such avoidance could easily be attributed to preference for a certain kind of movie. However, when the situation did not provide this type of rationale for avoidance behavior, the tendency to avoid people with physical disabilities disappeared.

Thus, by analogy, one might expect that an environment that minimizes the importance of race and even forbids overt consideration or discussion of the topic would free individuals whose basic tendency is to discriminate (a normatively unacceptable orientation at Wexler) to do so. The vast majority of Wexler's faculty espoused basically egalitarian racial attitudes and would quite rightly be insulted by the idea that they would intentionally discriminate against their African American students. Yet research demonstrates that one need not be an old-fashioned racist to discriminate against African Americans when the conditions are conducive to doing so.

Specifically, Gaertner and Dovidio (1986, 2005) argue that a great many liberal Whites are highly motivated to maintain an image of themselves as egalitarian individuals who neither discriminate against others on the basis of race nor are prejudiced. However, the desire to maintain such an image is coupled with some negative effect and with certain beliefs that predispose them to react negatively to African Americans. This predisposition is expressed primarily in circumstances that do not threaten an egalitarian self-concept. One important relevant circumstance is the availability of nonrace-related rationales for the behavior in question (Dovidio & Gaertner, 1998; Gaertner & Dovidio, 1986), and recent research demonstrates just how readily Whites can explain race-based behavior with nonrace-related rationales (Sommers & Norton, 2007). It is precisely this aspect of the situation that is influenced by the colorblind perspective and its corollaries. To the extent that they help remove awareness of race from conscious consideration, they make other explanations for one's behavior relatively more salient. Thus, they free some individuals to act in a discriminatory fashion. Also, to the extent that the taboo at Wexler inhibited individuals from challenging the behavior of other people as racist in outcome or intent, it removed a potential barrier to racist behavior because it minimized the probability that such behavior would pose a threat to an egalitarian self-concept.

In addition, it is important to note that the colorblind perspective can be used to legitimize the racial status quo and may negatively affect racial attitudes. Specifically, experimental research suggests that antiequalitarian Whites endorse the colorblind perspective as a reaction to perceived threat to the status quo (Knowles, Lowery, Hogan, & Chow, 2009) and that being in an environment that advocates this approach increases both explicit and implicit bias in racial attitudes compared to being in one that advocates a multicultural approach (Richeson & Nussbaum, 2003).

Ignoring the Reality of Cultural Differences Between Students

Although the colorblind perspective and its corollaries served some useful purposes at Wexler, they also had several important unrecognized negative effects, as just indicated. One additional negative consequence of this mind-set was a predisposition to ignore or deny the possibility of cultural differences between White and African American children that influenced how they functioned in school. For example, the differential suspension rate for African American and White children may have stemmed partially from differences between these students in what Triandis and his colleagues (Triandis, Vassiliou, Vassiliou, Tanaka, & Shanmugam, 1972) call their "subjective culture." Specifically, data from the Sagar and Schofield (1980) experiment described earlier suggested that African American boys saw certain types of ambiguously aggressive acts as less mean and threatening and as more playful and friendly than did their White peers. These behaviors were ones that sometimes began conflicts between students that resulted in suspensions. Awareness of the differential meaning of such behaviors to White and African American students might at least have suggested ways of trying to reduce the disproportionate suspension of African American students.

Other research suggests that Black–White differences in culture relevant to education are not limited to this one area (Irvine, 1990; Jones, 1986, 1997; Lee & Slaughter-Defoe, 2004). For example, Kochman (1981) has argued convincingly that African American and White students use widely differing styles in classroom discussion and that misunderstanding the cultural context from which students come can lead peers and teachers to misinterpret involvement for belligerence. Heath's (1982) research suggests that the types of questions teachers typically pose in elementary school classrooms are quite similar to those asked in White middle-class homes but differ substantially from those typically addressed to young children in poor African American homes. Thus, there is reason to think that in assuming a completely colorblind perspective teachers may rule out awareness and use of information that would be helpful in deciding how best to structure classroom materials and interaction patterns in ways that work well for the full range of students they teach as well as in accurately interpreting aspects of their students' behavior.

Failing to Respond to and Capitalize on Diversity

There were numerous less subtle ways in which the colorblind perspective and the accompanying deemphasis on the biracial nature of the school worked to the disadvantage of Wexler's students—and more often to the disadvantage of African American than of White students. One of the more obvious of these concerned the extent to which efforts were made to use instructional materials and pedagogical approaches that were likely to reflect the interests and life experiences of Wexler's African American students (Carter & Goodwin, 1994; Irvine, 1991; Nieto, 2004; Ramsey, 1987), an approach that has been characterized by many labels including *culturally responsive teaching* and *culturally responsive pedagogy*. Wexler operated as part of a school system that made some effort to use multicultural texts. In addition, some teachers, a disproportionate number of whom were African American, took special care to relate class work to the concerns and interests likely to be found in their African American students as well as their White ones, a finding consistent with that of Ryan, Hunt, Weible, Peterson, and Casas (2007) that African Americans are more likely than Whites to prefer a multicultural rather than a colorblind perspective.

The prevailing tendency, however, was to abjure responsibility for making sure instructional materials reflected the diversity of the student body. Interviews with teachers suggested that many felt no need to try to locate or develop instructional materials that reflected African Americans' participation in and contributions to our society. For example, one math teacher who used a book in which all individuals in the illustrations were White contended that "math is math" and that an interview question about the use of multicultural materials was irrelevant to his subject matter. Perhaps more surprisingly, similar claims were made by other teachers, including some who taught reading, language arts, and social studies.

The colorblind perspective and its corollaries not only made it more likely that individual teachers would ignore the challenge of trying to present all students with materials that related in motivating ways to their own experiences but actually led to a constriction of the education obtained by students. For example, in a lesson on the social organization of ancient Rome, one social studies teacher discussed at length the various classes in Roman society, including the patricians and plebeians, but avoided all reference to slaves out of concern about raising the issue of slavery in a racially-mixed school. Another teacher included George Washington Carver on a list of great Americans from which students could pick individuals to learn about but specifically decided not to mention that Carver was African American for fear of raising racial issues. In the best of all worlds, there would be no need to make such mention because the students would have no preconception that famous people are generally White. However, in a school in which a White child was surprised to learn from a member of my research team that Martin Luther King, Jr., was African American, not White, highlighting the accomplishments of African Americans and encouraging students not to assume famous figures are White would have been more than reasonable practices.

Such constriction flowing from the colorblind perspective and its corollaries is not unique to Wexler. For example, Bolgatz (2005) describes how many students in a predominantly White high school avoided discussion of race for fear of appearing racist or offending others, even when race was relevant to the topic at hand. Although ignoring or avoiding certain topics is undeniably a low-risk approach, it fails to take advantage of the diversity of experiences and perspectives of a school's students as a resource for the educational process. Furthermore, in some cases at Wexler, it literally distorted the education all students received as teachers attempted to avoid potentially controversial facts or issues.

CONCLUSIONS

Since Supreme Court Justice Harlan first spoke of a colorblind society as a goal to strive for more than 100 years ago, the colorblind approach has often been held up as a needed antidote to the virulent racism in our society that traditionally consigned certain individuals to subordinate positions on the basis of their color and their color alone. However, this chapter takes the position that the colorblind perspective is not without some serious and often unrecognized dangers. It may ease initial tensions and minimize the frequency of overt conflict. Nonetheless, it can also foster such phenomena as a taboo against ever mentioning race or connected issues and a refusal to recognize and deal with the existence of intergroup tensions. Thus, it fosters an environment in which some individuals who are basically well-intentioned, but who nonetheless harbor some residual negative emotions towards African Americans, are prone to act in a discriminatory manner. In addition, it can foster lack of recognition of problems that might be dealt with constructively if they were acknowledged. Furthermore, the colorblind perspective makes it unlikely that the opportunities inherent in a pluralistic institution will be fully realized and that the challenge facing such an institution of providing all of its students with an engaging and effective education will be met.

Although the colorblind approach clearly has many disadvantages, this finding does not lead to the conclusion that it is best to constantly call students' attention to group membership. There are several reasons to be wary of an unrelenting emphasis on group membership, especially on group differences. First, there is substantial evidence that liking others is enhanced by the perception of similarity (Berscheid & Reis, 1998), so a constant emphasis on difference is likely to be unproductive. Second, research about a phenomenon called *stereotype threat* also suggests that it may be unwise to make race constantly salient (Alexander & Schofield, 2008; Aronson & Good, 2002; Aronson & Steele, 2005). For example, stereotype-threat researchers have found that merely raising the issue of race by having students indicate their group membership before completing a task can lead to markedly decreased performance by African American students on tasks relevant to existing negative stereotypes about their ability (Steele & Aronson, 1995). Furthermore, a large body of social psychological research mentioned earlier in this chapter has demonstrated that *categorization* of individuals into in-groups and out-groups often tends to promote stereotyping and biased behavior.

What, then, is likely to be the most effective stance for schools to take? A full answer to this question would be an entire chapter in itself. However, I would suggest that at least three things are highly desirable. First, the education system needs to make a concerted effort to be responsive to our society's diversity in planning curriculum, in making staffing choices, and in thinking about how best to serve students in working to create school environments that promote what Marcus et al. (2002, p. 457) have called "identity safety." Such efforts might well include antibias diversity training and other activities likely to make clear institutional support for a world view that accepts the existence of varied perspectives and promotes adaptation to them (Castro Atwater, 2008). Such evidence of institutional acceptance of diversity seems likely to help make school institutions that students from different backgrounds can feel engaged with and connected to in addition to providing them the breadth of information and perspectives necessary to function effectively in our increasingly diverse society. Second, schools need to help students and teachers see that groups are composed of individuals with their own unique characteristics who may be both similar to and different from those in their in-group and out-groups, which should help undercut the tendency to stereotype and to see group membership as defining an individual's characteristics. Finally, schools should provide students opportunities to build meaningful shared identities as members of the school, the community, and the nation that complement and supplement rather than replace or undermine their identities as members of specific social groups.

Questions and Activities

1. According to the author, how does the social context influence the expression of racism and discrimination?
2. What is the *colorblind perspective?* Give some examples of it. On what major beliefs and assumptions is it based?
3. In what ways does the colorblind perspective contribute to racial discrimination and institutionalized racism in schools? Give specific examples.
4. How does the colorblind perspective often lead to what the author calls a "misrepresentation of reality"? Which realities are often misrepresented by the colorblind perspective?
5. Why did the teachers at Wexler deny that they were aware of the race of their students? What were some consequences of their denial? How was their denial inconsistent with many realities related to race in the school?
6. What did the interviews with Wexler students reveal about their conceptions of race? How did their conceptions of race differ from those of the teachers? Why?
7. Why do teachers often embrace the colorblind perspective? According to the author, what are its benefits and costs?
8. How does the colorblind perspective make it easier for liberal White teachers to discriminate? Give specific examples from this chapter and from your own observations and experiences in schools and in other settings and contexts.
9. How does the colorblind perspective negatively affect the development of a multicultural curriculum? What are the most promising ways to counteract the colorblind perspective? Give specific examples.

References

Aboud, F. E., & Doyle, A. B. (1996). Does talk of race foster prejudice or tolerance in children? *Canadian Journal of Behavioural Science, 28*(3), 161–170.

Aboud, F. E., & Fenwick, V. (1999). Exploring and evaluating school-based interventions to reduce prejudice. *Journal of Social Issues, 55*(4), 767–786.

Alexander, K. M., & Schofield, J. W. (2008). Understanding and mitigating stereotype threat's negative influence on immigrant and minority students' academic performance. *Kölner Zeitschrift für Soziologie und Sozialpsychologie [Cologne Journal of Sociology and Social Psychology], 48*, 1–24.

Allport, G. W. (1954). *The nature of prejudice.* Cambridge, MA: Addison-Wesley.

Aronson, J. A., & Good, C. (2002). The development and consequences of stereotype vulnerability in adolescents. In F. Pajares & T. Urdan (Eds.), *Academic motivation of adolescents* (pp. 299–330). Greenwich, CT: Information Age.

Aronson, E., & Patnoe, S. (1997). *The jigsaw classroom: Building cooperation in the classroom* (2nd ed.). New York: Longman.

Aronson, J., & Steele, C. M. (2005). Stereotypes and the fragility of academic competence, motivation, and self-concept. In A. J. Elliot & C. S. Dweck (Eds.), *Handbook of competence and motivation* (pp. 436–460). New York: Guilford Press.

Banks, J. A. (2005). Multicultural education: Characteristics and goals. In J. A. Banks & C. A. M. Banks (Eds.), *Multicultural education: Issues and perspectives* (5th ed., pp. 3–30). New York: Wiley.

Barrett, K. H., & George, W. H. (2005). Judicial colorblindness, race neutrality, and modern racism: How psychologists can help the courts understand race matters. In K. H. Barrett & W. H. George (Eds.), *Race, culture, psychology and law* (pp. 31–46). Thousand Oaks, CA: Sage.

Bennett, W. (1987). *James Madison High School: A curriculum for American students*. Washington, DC: U.S. Department of Education.

Berscheid, E., & Reis, H. T. (1998). Attraction and close relationships. In D. T. Gilbert, S. T. Fiske, & G. Lindzey (Eds.), *The handbook of social psychology* (4th ed., pp. 193–281). New York: McGraw-Hill.

Bogdan, R. C., & Taylor, S. J. (1975). *Introduction to qualitative research methods: A phenomenological approach to the social sciences*. New York: Wiley.

Bolgatz, J. (2005). *Talking race in the classroom*. New York: Teachers College Press.

Bonilla-Silva, E. (2003). *Racism without racists: Color-blind racism and the persistence of racial inequality in the United States*. New York: Rowman & Littlefield.

Brewer, M. B., & Brown, R. J. (1998). Intergroup relations. In D. T. Gilbert, S. T. Fiske, & G. Lindzey (Eds.), *The handbook of social psychology* (4th ed., pp. 554–594). New York: McGraw-Hill.

Brewer, M. B., & Gaertner, S. L. (2001). Toward reduction of prejudice: Intergroup contact and social categorization. In R. Brown & S. Gaertner (Eds.), *Blackwell handbook of social psychology: Intergroup processes* (pp. 451–472). Oxford, UK: Blackwell.

Brown, R. (1995). *Prejudice: Its social psychology*. Oxford, UK: Blackwell.

Brown, M. K., Carnoy, M., Currie, E., Duster, T., Oppenheimer, D. B., Shultz, M. M., et al. (2003). *Whitewashing race: The myth of a color-blind society*. Berkeley: University of California Press.

Campbell, D. T. (1975). Degrees of freedom and the case study. *Comparative Political Studies*, *8*(2), 178–193.

Carter, R. T., & Goodwin, A. L. (1994). Racial identity and education. *Review of Research in Education*, *20*, 291–336.

Castro Atwater, S. (2008). Waking up to difference: Teachers, color-blindness, and the effects on students of color. *Journal of Instructional Psychology*, *35*(3), 1–8.

Cohen, E. G. (1997). Understanding status problems: Sources and consequences. In E. G. Cohen & R. A. Lotan (Eds.), *Working for equity in heterogeneous classrooms: Sociological theory in practice* (pp. 61–76). New York: Teachers College Press.

Cohen, E., Lockheed, M., & Lohman, M. (1976). The Center for Interracial Cooperation: A field experiment. *Sociology of Education*, *49*(1), 47–58.

Cook, S. W. (1985). Experimenting on social issues: The case of school desegregation. *American Psychologist*, *40*(4), 452–460.

Cook, T. D., & Campbell, D. T. (1976). The design and conduct of quasi-experiments and true experiments in field settings. In M. D. Dunnette (Ed.), *Handbook of industrial and organizational psychology* (pp. 223–281). Chicago: Rand McNally.

Cosmides, L., Tooby, J., & Kurzban, R. (2003). Perceptions of race. *Trends in Cognitive Sciences, 7*(4), 173–179.

Davis, F. (1961). Deviance disavowal: The management of strained interaction by the visibly handicapped. In H. S. Becker (Ed.), *The other side: Perspectives on deviance* (pp. 119–137). New York: Free Press.

Devine, P. G. (1989). Stereotyping and prejudice: Their automatic and controlled components. *Journal of Personality and Social Psychology, 56*(1), 5–18.

Dovidio, J. F., & Gaertner, S. L. (1998). On the nature of contemporary prejudice: The causes, consequences, and challenges of aversive racism. In J. L. Eberhardt & S. T. Fiske (Eds.), *Confronting racism: The problem and the response* (pp. 3–32). Thousand Oaks, CA: Sage.

Dovidio, J. F., Gaertner, S. L., Voulidzic, A., Matoka, A., Johnson, B., & Frazier, S. (1997). Extending the benefits of recategorization: Evaluations, self-disclosure, and helping. *Journal of Experimental Social Psychology, 33*(4), 401–420.

Eaton, S. E. (2001). *The other Boston busing story: What's won and lost across the boundary line.* New Haven, CT: Yale University Press.

Eberhardt, J. L. (2005). Imaging race. *American Psychologist, 60*(2), 181–190.

Fazio, R. H., Jackson, J. R., Dunton, B. C., & Williams, C. J. (1995). Variability in automatic activation as unobtrusive measure of racial attitudes: A bona fide pipeline? *Journal of Personality and Social Psychology, 69*(6), 1013–1027.

Flagg, B. J. (1993). "Was blind but now I see": White race consciousness and the requirement of discriminatory intent. *Michigan Law Review, 91*(5), 953–1017.

Gaertner, S. L., & Dovidio, J. F. (1986). The aversive form of racism. In J. F. Dovidio & S. L. Gaertner (Eds.), *Prejudice, discrimination, and racism* (pp. 61–89). Orlando, FL: Academic Press.

Gaertner, S. L., & Dovidio, J. F. (2005). Understanding and addressing contemporary racism: From aversive racism to the common ingroup identity model. *Journal of Social Issues, 61*(3), 615–639.

Gaertner, S. L., Dovidio, J. F., Anastasio, P. A., Bachman, B. A., & Rust, M. C. (1993). The common ingroup identity model: Recategorization and the reduction of intergroup bias. In W. Stroebe & M. Hewstone (Eds.), *European Review of Social Psychology* (Vol. 4, pp. 1–26). Chichester, UK: Wiley.

Gaertner, S. L., Rust, M. C., Dovidio, J. F., Bachman, B. A., & Anastasio, P. A. (1994). The contact hypothesis: The role of a common ingroup identity on reducing intergroup bias. *Small Group Research, 25*(2), 224–249.

Gillborn, D. (1992). Citizenship, "race" and the hidden curriculum. *International Studies in Sociology of Education, 2*(1), 57–73.

Goetz, J. P., & Breneman, E. (1988). Desegregation and Black students' experiences in two rural southern elementary schools. *Elementary School Journal, 88*(5), 489–502.

Gotanda, N. (1991). A critique of "our constitution is color-blind." *Stanford Law Review, 44*(1), 1–68.

Guinier, L., & Torres, G. (2002). *The miner's canary: Enlisting race, resisting power, transforming democracy.* Cambridge, MA: Harvard University Press.

Hamilton, D. L., Stroessner, S. J., & Driscoll, D. M. (1994). Social cognition and the study of stereotyping. In P. G. Devine, D. L. Hamilton, & T. M. Ostrom (Eds.), *Social cognition: Impact on social psychology* (pp. 291–321). San Diego, CA: Academic Press.

Heath, S. B. (1982). Questioning at home and at school: A comparative study. In G. D. Spindler (Ed.), *Doing the ethnography of schooling: Educational anthropology in action* (pp. 102–131). New York: Holt, Rinehart & Winston.

Hewstone, M., & Brown, R. (Eds.). (1986). *Contact and conflict in intergroup encounters*. Oxford, UK: Blackwell.

Hirsch, E. D. (1996). *The schools we need, and why we don't have them*. New York: Doubleday.

Irvine, J. J. (1990). *Black students and school failure: Policies, practices, and prescriptions*. Westport, CT: Praeger.

Irvine, J. J. (1991, January). *Culturally responsive and responsible pedagogy: The inclusion of culture, research, and reflection in the knowledge base of teacher education*. Paper presented at the annual meeting of the American Association of Colleges for Teacher Education, Atlanta, Georgia.

Ito, T. A., & Urland, G. R. (2003). Race and gender on the brain: Electrocortical measures of attention to the race and gender of multiply categorizable individuals. *Journal of Personality and Social Psychology, 85*(4), 616–626.

Jaynes, G. D., & Williams, R. M., Jr. (1989). *A common destiny: Blacks and American society*. Washington, DC: National Academy Press.

Jervis, K. (1996). "How come there are no brothers on that list?" Hearing the hard questions all children ask. *Harvard Educational Review, 66*(3), 546–575.

Johnson, D. W., Johnson, R. T., & Maruyama, G. (1984). Goal interdependence and interpersonal attraction in heterogeneous classrooms: A meta-analysis. In N. Miller & M. B. Brewer (Eds.), *Groups in contact: The psychology of desegregation* (pp. 187–212). Orlando, FL: Academic Press.

Jones, J. M. (1986). Racism: A cultural analysis of the problem. In J. F. Dovidio & S. L. Gaertner (Eds.), *Prejudice, discrimination, and racism* (pp. 279–313). Orlando, FL: Academic Press.

Jones, J. M. (1997). *Prejudice and racism* (2nd ed.). New York: McGraw-Hill.

Jones, J. M. (1998). Psychological knowledge and the new American dilemma of race. *Journal of Social Issues, 54*(4), 641–662.

Knowles, E. D., Lowery, B. S., Hogan, C. M., & Chow, R. M. (2009). On the malleability of ideology: Motivated construals of color blindness. *Journal of Personality and Social Psychology, 96*(4), 857–869.

Kochman, T. (1981). *Black and White styles in conflict*. Chicago: University of Chicago Press.

Larson, C. L., & Ovando, C. J. (2001). *The color of bureaucracy: The politics of equity in multicultural school communities*. Belmont, CA: Wadsworth/Thomson Learning.

Lee, C. D., & Slaughter-Defoe, D. T. (2004). Historical and sociocultural influences on African American education. In J. A. Banks & C. A. M. Banks (Eds.), *Handbook of research on multicultural education* (2nd ed., pp. 462–490). San Francisco: Jossey-Bass.

Lee, Y. T., & Duenas, G. (1995). Stereotype accuracy in multicultural business. In Y. T. Lee, L. J. Jussim, & C. R. McCauley (Eds.), *Stereotype accuracy: Toward appreciating group differences* (pp. 157–188). Washington, DC: American Psychological Association.

Levin, S. (2003). Social psychological evidence on race and racism. In M. J. Chang, D. Witt, J. Jones, & K. Hakuta (Eds.), *Compelling interest: Examining the evidence on racial dynamics in colleges and universities* (pp. 97–125). Stanford, CA: Stanford University Press.

Lewis, A. E. (2001). There is no "race" in the schoolyard: Color-blind ideology in an (almost) all-White school. *American Educational Research Journal, 38*(4), 781–811.

Marcus, H. R., Steele, C. M., & Steele, D. M. (2002). Colorblindness as a barrier to inclusion: Assimilation and nonimmigrant minorities. In R. Shweder, M. Minow, & H. R. Markus (Eds.), *Engaging cultural differences: The multicultural challenge in liberal democracies* (pp. 453–472). New York: Russell Sage Foundation.

Miles, M. B., & Huberman, A. M. (1984). *Qualitative data analysis: A sourcebook of new methods*. Newbury Park, CA: Sage.

Moses, M. S. (2002). *Embracing race: Why we need race-conscious education policy*. New York: Teachers College Press.

Nieto, S. (2004). *Affirming diversity: The sociopolitical context of multicultural education* (4th ed.). Boston: Allyn & Bacon.

Norton, M. I., Sommers, S. R., Apfelbaum, E. P., Pura, N., & Ariely, D. (2006). Color blindness and interracial interaction: Playing the political correctness game. *Psychological Science, 17*(11), 949–953.

Olson, S. (1976). *Ideas and data: Process and practice of social research*. Homewood, IL: Dorsey.

Park, B., & Judd, C. M. (2005). Rethinking the link between categorization and prejudice within the social cognition perspective. *Personality and Social Psychology Review, 9*(2), 108–130.

Pettigrew, T. F. (1998). Intergroup contact theory. *Annual Review of Psychology, 49*, 65–85.

Pettigrew, T. F. (2004). Intergroup contact: Theory, research, and new perspectives. In J. A. Banks & C. A. M. Banks (Eds.), *Handbook of research on multicultural education* (2nd ed., pp. 770–781). San Francisco: Jossey-Bass.

Pettigrew, T. F., & Tropp, L. R. (2006). A meta-analytic test of intergroup contact theory. *Journal of Personality and Social Psychology, 90*(5), 751–783.

Pollock, M. (2004). *Colormute: Race talk dilemmas in an American school*. Princeton, NJ: Princeton University Press.

Ramsey, P. G. (1987). *Teaching and learning in a diverse world: Multicultural education for young children*. New York: Teachers College Press.

Regents of the University of California v. Bakke, 76–811 U.S. (1978).

Revilla, A. T., Wells, A. S., & Holme, J. J. (2004). "We didn't see color . . . ": The salience of colorblindness in desegregated schools. In M. Fine, L. Weis, L. P. Pruitt, & A. Burns (Eds.), *Off White: Readings on power, privilege, and resistance* (2nd ed., pp. 284–301). New York: Routledge.

Richeson, J. A., & Nussbaum, R. J. (2003). The impact of multiculturalism versus color-blindness on racial bias. *Journal of Experimental Social Psychology, 40*(3), 417–423.

Riordan, C. (1978). Equal-status interracial contact: A review and revision of the concept. *International Journal of Intercultural Relations, 2*(2), 161–185.

Rist, R. C. (1974). Race, policy, and schooling. *Society, 12*(1), 59–64.

Rist, R. C. (1978). *The invisible children: School integration in American society*. Cambridge, MA: Harvard University Press.

Ryan, C. S., Hunt, J. S., Weible, J. A., Peterson, C. R., & Casas, J. F. (2007). Multicultural and colorblind ideology, stereotypes, and ethnocentrism among Black and White Americans. *Group Processes and Intergroup Relations, 10*(4), 617–637.

Sagar, H. A., & Schofield, J. W. (1980). Racial and behavioral cues in Black and White children's perceptions of ambiguously aggressive acts. *Journal of Personality and Social Psychology, 39*(4), 590–598.

Sagar, H. A., & Schofield, J. W. (1984). Integrating the desegregated school: Problems and possibilities. In M. Maehr & D. Bartz (Eds.), *Advances in motivation and achievement: A research manual* (pp. 203–242). Greenwich, CT: JAI Press.

Sagar, H. A., Schofield, J. W., & Snyder, H. N. (1983). Race and gender barriers: Preadolescent peer behavior in academic classrooms. *Child Development, 54*(4), 1032–1040.

Schlesinger, A. M., Jr. (1992). *The disuniting of America: Reflections on a multicultural society*. New York: Norton.

Schofield, J. W. (1979). The impact of positively structured contact on intergroup behavior: Does it last under adverse conditions? *Social Psychology Quarterly, 42*(3), 280–284.

Schofield, J. W. (1980). Cooperation as social exchange: Resource gaps and reciprocity in academic work. In S. Sharon, P. Hare, C. Webb, & R. Hertz-Lazarowitz (Eds.), *Cooperation in education* (pp. 160–181). Provo, UT: Brigham Young University Press.

Schofield, J. W. (1989). *Black and White in school: Trust, tension, or tolerance?* New York: Teachers College Press.

Schofield, J. W. (2001). Improving intergroup relations among students. In J. A. Banks & C. A. M. Banks (Eds.), *Handbook of research on multicultural education* (pp. 635–645). San Francisco: Jossey-Bass.

Schofield, J. W., & Eurich-Fulcer, R. (2001). When and how school desegregation improves intergroup relations. In R. Brown & S. Gaertner (Eds.), *Blackwell handbook of social psychology: Intergroup processes* (pp. 474–494). New York: Blackwell.

Schofield, J. W., & Francis, W. D. (1982). An observational study of peer interaction in racially-mixed "accelerated" classrooms. *Journal of Educational Psychology, 74*(5), 722–732.

Schofield, J. W., & Sagar, H. A. (1977). Peer interaction patterns in an integrated middle school. *Sociometry, 40*(2), 130–137.

Schofield, J. W., & Sagar, H. A. (1979). The social context of learning in an interracial school. In R. Rist (Ed.), *Inside desegregated schools: Appraisals of an American experiment* (pp. 155–199). San Francisco: Academic Press.

Schofield, J. W., Wang, L., & Chew, P. (2007). Culture and race in provider-client relationships. *Social Work in Public Health, 23*(2/3), 1–33.

Schofield, J. W., & Whitley, B. E. (1983). Peer nomination versus rating scale measurement of children's peer preferences. *Social Psychology Quarterly, 46*(3), 242–251.

Sherif, M. (1979). Superordinate goals in the reduction of intergroup conflict: An experimental evaluation. In W. G. Austin & S. Worchel (Eds.), *The social psychology of intergroup relations* (pp. 257–261). Monterey, CA: Brooks/Cole.

Sidanius, J., & Pratto, F. (1999). *Social dominance: An intergroup theory of social hierarchy and oppression*. Port Chester, NY: Cambridge University Press.

Slavin, R. E., & Cooper, R. (1999). Improving intergroup relations: Lessons learned from cooperative learning programs. *Journal of Social Issues, 55*(4), 647–663.

Sleeter, C. E. (1993). How White teachers construct race. In C. McCarthy & W. Crichlow (Eds.), *Race, identity, and representation in education* (pp. 157–171). New York: Routledge.

Snyder, M. L., Kleck, R. E., Strenta, A., & Mentzer, S. J. (1979). Avoidance of the handicapped: An attributional ambiguity analysis. *Journal of Personality and Social Psychology, 37*(12), 2297–2306.

Sommers, S. R., & Norton, M. I. (2007). Race-based judgments, race-neutral justifications: Experimental examination of peremptory use and the Batson challenge procedure. *Law and Human Behavior*, *31*(3), 261–273.

Steele, C. M., & Aronson, J. (1995). Stereotype threat and the intellectual test performance of African Americans. *Journal of Personality and Social Psychology*, *69*(5), 797–811.

Stephan, W. G., & Stephan, C. W. (1996). *Intergroup relations*. Boulder, CO: Westview.

Stephan, W. G., & Stephan, C. W. (2001). *Improving intergroup relations*. Thousand Oaks, CA: Sage.

Strauss, A. (1987). *Qualitative analysis for social scientists*. New York: Cambridge University Press.

Strauss, A., & Corbin, J. (1990). *Basics of qualitative research: Grounded theory procedures and techniques*. Newbury Park, CA: Sage.

Tajfel, H. (1978). *Differentiation between social groups: Studies in the social psychology of intergroup relations*. New York: Academic Press.

Takaki, R. (1993). *A different mirror: A history of multicultural America*. Boston: Little, Brown.

Trent, W., Owens-Nicholson, D., Eatman, T., Burke, M., Daugherty, J., & Norman, K. (2003). Justice, equality of educational opportunity, and affirmative action in higher education. In M. J. Chang, D. Witt, J. Jones, & K. Hakuta (Eds.), *Compelling interest: Examining the evidence on racial dynamics in colleges and universities* (pp. 22–48). Stanford, CA: Stanford University Press.

Triandis, H. C. (Ed.). (1976). *Variations in Black and White perceptions of the social environment*. Urbana: University of Illinois Press.

Triandis, H. C., Vassiliou, V., Vassiliou, G., Tanaka, Y., & Shanmugam, A. (Eds.). (1972). *The analysis of subjective culture*. Hoboken, NJ: Wiley.

Vonofakou, C., Hewstone, M., Voci, A., Paolini, S., Turner, R. N., Tausch, N. T., et al. (2008). The impact of direct and extended cross-group friendships on improving intergroup relations. In U. Wagner, L. R. Tropp, G. Finchilescu, & C. Tredoux (Eds.), *Improving intergroup relations: Building on the legacy of Thomas F. Pettigrew* (pp. 107–123). Malden, MA: Blackwell.

Webb, E. J., Campbell, D. T., Schwartz, R. D., & Sechrest, L. (1966). *Unobtrusive measures: Nonreactive research in the social sciences*. Chicago: Rand McNally.

Wells, A. S., Holme, J. J., Atanda, A. K., & Revilla, A. T. (2005). Tackling racial segregation one policy at a time: Why school desegregation only went so far. *Teachers College Record*, *107*(9), 2141–2177.

Whitley, B. E., Schofield, J. W., & Snyder, H. N. (1984). Peer preference in desegregated classrooms: A round robin analysis. *Journal of Personality and Social Psychology*, *46*(4), 799–810.

Williams, P. J. (1998). *Seeing a colorblind future: The paradox of race*. New York: Noonday Press.

Wolsko, C., Park, B., Judd, C., & Wittenbrink, B. (2000). Framing interethnic ideology: Effects of multicultural and color-blind perspectives on judgments of groups and individuals. *Journal of Personality and Social Psychology*, *78*(4), 635–654.

Yinger, J. M. (1994). *Ethnicity: Source of strength? Source of conflict?* Albany: State University of New York Press.

CHAPTER 12

Language Diversity and Schooling

Tom T. Stritikus
Manka M. Varghese

> Cuando eres un inmigrante, muchas puertas están cerradas. Pues, sí, algunas, algunas, están abiertas—pero están escondidas. Sin ayuda, no puedo encontrarlas.
>
> When you are an immigrant, many doors are closed. Well, yes, some, some are open—but they are hidden. Without help, I can't find them.
>
> Edgar
>
> (Stritikus, 2004, p. 1)

Edgar is a 15-year-old immigrant student from Mexico. He had been in the United States for five months when a researcher asked him to talk about what he hoped to accomplish by attending school in the United States (Stritikus, 2004). Rather than focus on his career goals or his educational plans after high school, Edgar highlighted the limited educational opportunities he believed characterized his new life in the United States. Although Edgar had been in the United States for only a limited time, he had already developed a keen sense of the social, cultural, and linguistic barriers to his success. Unfortunately, Edgar's reality is shared by many immigrant students for whom the doors of educational opportunity remain obscured and closed. In this chapter, we consider what schools and teachers can do to better assist linguistically diverse students like Edgar.

Recent immigration from Asia, Latin America, and Africa is dramatically altering the context of public schooling. Today, one in seven students speaks a language other than English at home (Meyer, Madden, & McGrath, 2004). Immigrants constitute the fastest growing group of students in U.S. schools, and many demographers predict that by 2025, approximately 20–25 percent of students enrolled in elementary and secondary schools will have limited proficiency in English (Suarez-Orozco, Suarez-Orozco, & Todorova, 2008). When considering linguistic diversity, it is also important to consider cultural and linguistic groups who do not immediately come to mind; these include African Americans and indigenous populations. Many African Americans are "bidialectal"—that is, they speak Ebonics and Standard English, and issues of language diversity have shaped their school experience in important ways (Alim & Baugh, 2007; Smitherman, 2000). Indigenous groups, such as American Indians, Alaskan Natives, and Native Hawaiians, contribute significantly to linguistic diversity, representing speakers of about 175 indigenous languages and numerous varieties of English (Krauss, 1998).

To understand how schools can better meet the needs of linguistically diverse students, we begin this chapter by taking a closer look at the linguistically diverse population in the United States. Then, to understand the legal obligations of schools in meeting the needs of linguistically diverse students, we examine important events in the legal, policy, and judicial history of linguistically diverse students in the United States. Next, we consider various programmatic responses to linguistic diversity and their efficacy in meeting the needs of linguistically diverse students. We conclude the chapter with a discussion of how teachers might better respond to the needs of immigrant students. We now turn to an examination of one of the primary sources of linguistic diversity—immigration—and consider how increased immigration has influenced U.S. schools.

THE IMMIGRANT POPULATION IN THE UNITED STATES

Immigration continues to be one of the primary sources of linguistic diversity in the United States. Foreign-born residents now make up a larger percentage of the U.S. population than at any other time since the great waves of immigration in the early 1900s (U.S. Census Bureau, 2001). Because of restrictive immigration laws, most immigrants who came to the United States between 1880 and 1930 were from Europe. Changes to immigration law during the 1960s resulted in a steady increase of immigrants from Latin America, Southeast Asia, the Caribbean, and Africa. While immigration has a tremendous influence on all of American life, nowhere has this impact been more keenly felt than in U.S. public schools.

Historically, immigration to the United States has played a significant role in shaping current perceptions of today's immigrants and, consequently, their reception in schools. The opinions that Americans have about the current wave of immigrants are shaped in part by their views of the earlier waves of immigrants—perceptions influenced by both fact and fiction. Several key differences and similarities exist between the experiences of the immigrants who came at the turn of the 20th century and those who are coming today. Understanding these similarities and differences is an important way for teachers working with linguistically diverse students to fully understand the reality faced by immigrant populations.

Despite the common perception to the contrary, the immigrants who came at the turn of the last century did not experience universal success in school. In major cities such as Boston, Chicago, and New York, the graduation and school continuation rates of Southern Italian, Polish, and Russian Jewish children lagged far behind those of native-born White students (Olneck & Lazerson, 1974). The mainstream population does not easily accept newcomer immigrants to the United States. Many of the same negative discourses about today's immigrants took place when earlier groups of immigrants came to the United States. The Italian, Jewish, and Irish immigrants of the early 20th century faced significant social, political, and cultural barriers (Jacobson, 1998). Despite these realities, today's immigration debates are often cast in terms of how the earlier immigrants were more easily absorbed and more beneficial to U.S. society than the Latin American, Asian, and African immigrants today. The concept of *ethnic succession*—which explains that new immigrants are rarely viewed as positively as the groups that came before them—can explain this pattern (Banks, 2005).

Despite the similarities between "earlier" and "new" immigrants, there are important differences as well. The current wave of immigration consists of people from several regions of the world who were not a major part of the last wave of immigration that occurred in the late 1800s and the early 1900s. In recent years, scholars from various disciplines have claimed that world economies and societies have become increasingly interconnected through advances in technology, media, and mass transit, all of which facilitate the movement of people, goods, services, and ideas. This new phenomena has been called *globalization, borderless economies*, and the *transnational era* (Castles, 2003). One of the characteristics of globalization is the increased flow of people across the planet. While some people voluntarily migrate in order to improve their lives, others are forced to migrate in order to survive (Suarez-Orozco & Suarez-Orozco, 2003). Social scientists have argued that the role of immigration in providing both cheap unskilled labor and highly technically skilled labor is a key component of the new transnational era that the world's societies have entered (Portes, 1996; Suarez-Orozco, 1997).

The back-and-forth movement of ideas and goods that characterizes the current transitional period also parallels the experience of many immigrant students, which has often been cast in terms of assimilation whereby immigrants eventually lose contact with their home communities and are slowly absorbed into their new locality. Departing from the traditional model of assimilation, scholars have argued that immigrants negotiate more complex patterns of social interaction in their new countries (Itzigsohn, Dore-Cabral, Hernandez-Medina, & Vazquez, 1999; Rose, 1997; Suarez-Orozco & Suarez-Orozco, 2003). In the current transnational era, some immigrant groups continue to have strong ties with their countries of origin once they reside in their receiving community. These ties influence immigrant children's socialization patterns and create social and cultural experiences that span transnational lines (Mahler, 1998; Portes, 1999; Smith & Guarnizo, 1998).

The mass movement of people and ideas has major consequences for education in the United States. The current back-and-forth movement of ideas and people replenishes social and cultural practices (Garcia, 1999). While previous generations of immigrants did have some contact with their home countries, it was limited by the difficulty of travel and the lack of efficient communication. For current immigrant communities, however, ethnic media, telecommunications, and ease of travel can significantly change the nature of the communities in which they settle. This is often very difficult for the native-born population to accept, but the impact of current immigration on host communities is undeniable (Garcia). Thus, immigration must be viewed as a dynamic social phenomenon. Immigrants are both significantly changing the social context of new communities while shaping the social realities in their home countries.

An important factor shaping the immigrant experience is related to the current nature of U.S. society. The immigrant family enters a country that is economically, socially, and culturally distinct from the one faced by early waves of immigrants. Previous waves of immigrants arrived on the eve of a great expansion of the industrial economy. The manufacturing jobs that were created during the transition to a fully industrialized economy provided a possible entree for immigrants to the middle class. However, not all immigrants had equal access to the economy and society. Gordon (1964) explains that earlier waves of immigrants who were members of racially diverse groups did not experience the same structural assimilation into U.S. society as did European immigrants.

Today's immigrants face many of the same issues related to structural assimilation as did older waves of immigrants. However, as Suarez-Orozco and Suarez-Orozco (2003) argue, today's economy—characterized by an hourglass shape—presents unique challenges for immigrant populations. At the top of the hourglass, highly skilled immigrants are moving into well-compensated, knowledge-based industries at an extremely high rate. At the bottom of the hourglass, immigrant workers accept the jobs that many U.S.-born workforce are unwilling to take. Immigrants are a large part of the low-skilled, low-paid workers in the service, labor, and agriculture sectors. Unlike the jobs that were available to previous waves of immigrants, these jobs offer limited prospects for upward mobility (Suarez-Orozco & Suarez-Orozco).

Immigrants today are more diverse than ever, exhibiting a significant range in educational level, social class, and economic capital. Present immigrants are more likely than native-born populations to have family members who have graduated from college. At the same time, immigrant populations are more likely not to have graduated from high school than are native-born populations (Suarez-Orozco et al., 2008). This pattern of potential outcomes for immigrant students is further examined in Portes and Rumbaut's (2001) discussion of *segmented assimilation*, which explains three possible outcomes for immigrant families: (1) economic success with integration into the middle class, (2) permanent poverty and integration into the underclass, and (3) economic advancement with the deliberate maintenance of community values and practices. Each outcome is an important factor in the immigrant community today. While a full discussion of the factors contributing to segmented assimilation is beyond the scope of this chapter, it is important for teachers to know that immigrant groups are demonstrating each outcome. A further discussion of segmented assimilation and the second generation is found in Zhou (1997).

Socially, immigrants find themselves in a tenuous position. Opinion polls on immigration indicate that the native-born population believes that recent immigrants are weakening the fabric of U.S. society because they refuse to become Americanized like previous waves of immigrants. Many native-born Americans believe that immigrants take jobs away from them and are a drain on social services and schools (Suarez-Orozco & Suarez-Orozco, 2003). Many scholars of immigration argue that the most important difference between today's immigrants and the earlier ones is that most of today's immigrants are people of color (Garcia, 1999; Olsen, 1997; Portes, 1996; Suarez-Orozco & Suarez-Orozco). Moreover, in the United States, an anti-immigrant ideology exists that affects the way immigrants and refugees are perceived (Behdad, 1997; Castles & Davidson, 2000). Today's culturally and ethnically diverse immigrants enter a racialized society that has historically sorted, classified, and excluded people based on the color of their skin (Omi & Winant, 1994). It is not as easy to eventually blend into White America as it was for the mostly European immigrants of the early 1900s. Racial tensions and structural exclusion in the United States make assimilation a problematic process for linguistically and ethnically diverse immigrants.

The social, political, and economic difficulties faced by immigrants make relocation to a new country a very taxing experience. The culture and worldviews of individuals are often challenged or threatened when they come in contact with U.S. culture (Portes & Rumbaut, 1996). The dislocation and upheaval caused by immigration can be especially challenging for immigrant children. Lucas (1997) describes the experiences of immigrant students in U.S. schools as characterized by a number of critical transitions. She points out that all children experience important transitions in life: childhood to adolescence, home to school, middle to high school. However, as she correctly notes, immigrant students undergo these critical issues while adapting to a new language and culture.

The social context in which immigrant students begin their new lives must be considered to understand the experience of linguistically diverse students in schools. Suarez-Orozco and Suarez-Orozco (2003) argue that the "ethos of reception"—the social and cultural climate students experience in schools—is strongly influenced by society's views about immigration. Thus, the strongly negative attitudes toward immigrant students in U.S. society influence these students' perceptions of U.S. schooling. Negative societal attitudes also significantly influence teacher and institutional expectations of immigrant students. Thus, the political, economic, and historical factors shaping immigration have a dramatic influence on the opportunities and experiences that immigrant students have in public schools.

Dramatic Increase in Linguistic Diversity in Schools

State educational statistics reveal the number of immigrants in the United States who are receiving special services to learn English and are classified as English language learners (ELL). There has been a dramatic increase in the students classified as ELL since the 1970s. In school districts throughout the United States, immigrants from most nations in the world can be found. Although linguistic diversity is a reality throughout the United States, the highest populations of ELL students are concentrated in a few states such as California, Texas, Florida, New York, Illinois, and Arizona. These states are currently and historically the most common places for immigrants to settle. However, almost all states have been affected by immigration. Since 1990, the largest increase in percentages of ELL students has been in what have been considered unlikely destinations for immigrants: South Carolina, Minnesota, Michigan, and Arkansas (Singer, 2004). Although the exact number is difficult to calculate, in 2004 ELL students accounted for about 8 percent, or 4.5 million, of the total U.S. school population (Meyer et al., 2004).

Additional Sources of Linguistic Diversity: Dialect Variation and Indigenous Languages

Immigration is not the sole contributor to linguistic diversity. Along with multiple languages in the United States, dialect variation contributes to our diverse tapestry of language use. A *dialect* is a variation of a language characterized by distinct pronunciation, grammar, and vocabulary. Many linguists have pointed out that the distinction between a *language* and a *dialect* is often more political than linguistic. The famed MIT linguist Noam Chomsky (2000) has often repeated the saying by Max Weinreich that a language is a dialect with an army and a navy. A common but less than perfect way of distinguishing a language from a dialect is the standard of mutual intelligibility.

Speakers of different dialects are said to be able to understand each other while speakers of different languages are not. However, what are considered dialects of some languages are so distinct that speakers cannot understand each other. Chinese has two major dialects, Cantonese and Mandarin, whose speakers have great difficulty in understanding each other. In contrast, speakers of the Scandinavian languages Danish, Norwegian, and Swedish are capable of understanding a great deal of each other's languages. Thus, it is important to note that the distinction between dialect and language has more to do with political, social, and cultural factors than specific linguistic distinctions between the two.

Political and social factors surrounding dialect variation play out in language use in U.S. schools. Educational practices in the United States embrace the idea that Standard English should be the dominant variety of language used in all written and oral communication. Many linguists dispute the idea that a pure or standard form of a language exists in any form but writing. Thus, *Standard English* often is a term associated with the groups within a society that possess social or political power (Wolfram, Adger, & Christian, 1998). Because dialect variation tends to be associated with race, social class, and geographic region, the dialects of groups with less social power tend to be viewed as inferior or incorrect versions of Standard English. This is the case with Black English (BE)—also referred to as African American vernacular English—and Black Dialect. Most linguists and sociolinguists recognize that no matter how BE is defined, it is a rule-governed language system linked to the identity of a specific community (Alim & Baugh, 2007; Labov, 1972; Smitherman, 2000). As Perry and Delpit (1998) write, "I can be neither for Ebonics nor against Ebonics any more than I can be for or against air. It exists" (p. 17). Speakers of BE are also most likely speakers of other varieties of English, including Standard English. Thus, speakers of BE, as are other speakers of dialects, are often *bidialectal*. The educational experiences of speakers of BE and the Oakland school district case are discussed later in this chapter.

Another major source of linguistic diversity in the United States is indigenous populations. Although a decreasing number of the 175 indigenous languages spoken by more than 550 tribes are spoken by children, the heritage language is still the primary language for a large number of indigenous students (Lomawaima & McCarty, 2006; McCarty, 2002). Indigenous students do not have another homeland from which to garner support for learning and maintaining their language. Krauss (1995) indicates that of 175 American Indian and Alaskan Native languages remaining, 155 are on their way to extinction. Therefore, bilingual/bicultural schooling is critical for indigenous language maintenance as it is for other linguistic and cultural groups. Most of the efforts in formal language maintenance for indigenous language groups have been directed at Hawaiian dialects and the languages of the Navajo and Pueblo nations in the U.S. Southwest. Attempts to use bilingual education to revitalize these languages have met with modest but important results (McCarty).

HISTORICAL AND LEGAL OVERVIEW OF LANGUAGE POLICY IN THE UNITED STATES

This section describes the legal and historical developments related to linguistic diversity and language education. Understanding the historical evolution of language policy in the United States as well as the legal milestones for language minority students will help us understand the legal protections for these students and the ambivalent stance that the United States historically has had toward language policy. Overall, language policy in the United States has leaned toward supporting transition into English. However, there has also been support of other languages and the rights of those speakers. There have been periods in U.S. history that have been more supportive of multilingualism than others.

Implementation of Federal Policy

The Bilingual Education Act (BEA), Title VII of the Elementary and Secondary Education Act of 1965—signed into law by President Lyndon B. Johnson—was legislation whose goal was to provide compensatory education for students who were both economically and linguistically disadvantaged in schools. From 1968 until 2002, Title VII provided funds for different types of programs for ELLs throughout the United States, including transitional bilingual education programs and two-way immersion programs; it also provided funding for program evaluators and researchers investigating these different types of programs. There were 30 two-way immersion programs in 1987 and 261 in 1999; most were supported by Title VII monies (Lindholm-Leary, 2001).

A large part of the BEA's inability to move toward a well-defined language policy was that the law did not recommend a particular instructional approach; rather, it provided funding for development, training, and research of innovative approaches to the education of ELL students. While native language instruction was originally recommended, the BEA did not specify that it must be used (Wiese & García, 1998). Since its inception, the primary aim of the BEA has been "providing meaningful and equitable access for English-language learners to the curriculum, rather than serving as an instrument of language policy for the nation through the development of their native languages" (August & Hakuta, 1997, p. 16). Echoing this, Wiese and García argue that the BEA has aimed to address equal educational opportunity for language minority students and has not evolved as a language policy. Therefore, the BEA neither legislated for a particular language policy or instructional approach nor guaranteed the rights of ELL students based on language.

As a result, immigrant students and families have frequently turned to the courts for redress. The U.S. Supreme Court's school desegregation decision in *Brown v. Board of Education* (1954), the 1964 Civil Rights Act (Title VI), and the 1974 Equal Educational Opportunity Act (EEOA) have been used as a base to protect these students' rights. This protection has come through a safeguard of these students' other civil rights and their right to equal educational opportunities (Del Valle, 2003). In the prominent case of *Lau v. Nichols* (1974), Kinney Kinmon Lau and 12 Chinese American students on behalf of about 1,800 Chinese-speaking students filed a class action suit against the San Francisco Unified School District stating that their children were not given equal educational opportunities because of the linguistic barriers they faced. In this landmark case, the San Francisco schools were found to be in violation of the rights of Chinese students under Title VI and EEOA. While lower courts disagreed with the parents, the Supreme Court supported the parents in *Lau v. Nichols* (1974) and found that "there is no equality of treatment merely by providing students with the same facilities, textbooks, teachers and curriculum; for students who do not understand English are effectively foreclosed from any meaningful education."

Lau's legacy has created important but vague contributions to the improvement of programs for ELL students. Policy guidelines, which were followed by the Office of Civil Rights (OCR), were put together in the *Lau* remedies in 1975 for school districts' compliance with the Title VI requirements upheld in the *Lau* decision. These guidelines have required districts to have a program in place for ELL students and for these students to be identified and assessed. While *Lau* did not specify any particular programs or polices for ELL students, it created momentum for subsequent federal policies and court rulings to protect the specific rights of linguistically diverse students. Moreover, particulars were fully fleshed out in *Castaneda v. Pickard* (1981), a federal district court case that offers a "test" to determine whether the needs of ELL students are being met by policies and programs. This case required that districts adhere to the following three areas:

1. *Theory*: The school must pursue a program based on an educational theory recognized as sound or at least as a legitimate experimental strategy.
2. *Practice*: The school must actually implement the program with instructional practices, resources, and personnel necessary to transfer theory into reality.
3. *Results*: The school must not persist in a program that fails to produce results.

The Supreme Court ruled in *Plyer vs. Doe* (1982) that states cannot deny a free public education to immigrant children because of their immigrant status, whether documented or undocumented. While these requirements may not offer as strong an articulation of ELL students' rights as some may have hoped, they do protect ELL students from negligence and mistreatment and help to ensure effective programs for them. The *Lau* remedies, the BEA, and Title VI have generally provided some protection for equal educational opportunities for linguistically diverse students at the federal level. They also provided federal funding that made possible the inception and growth of a number of bilingual programs in the United States (Hornberger, 2005; Ruiz, 2004; Wiley & Wright, 2004).

Similar to the *Lau* court case, the "Black English case" (1979) (as cited in Smitherman, 1981) mandated measures to teach Standard English to children speaking Black English. This 1979 case, *Martin Luther King Junior Elementary School Children v. Ann Arbor School District*, "was as much about educating Black children as about Black English" (Smitherman, 1998, p. 163). The parents of a group of African American children alleged that the school was not enabling their children to succeed in a variety of ways, including preventing them from learning Standard English. The judge ruled that the school had not helped its teachers and personnel to respond to the linguistic needs of its African American children. As a result of the ruling, school districts have been required to respond to the needs of African American children by providing professional development to its staff and the recognizing that Black English is a "systematic, rule-governed language system" in its own right (Perry & Delpit, 1998, p. 169). Black English has also been given legal standing in some districts, such as in Oakland, California.

Language Policy in Recent History

The mandates of bilingual and bidialectal education have been controversial. Critics have adopted different arguments from the historically prevalent charge that such education promotes social divisiveness to the more recent concerns that students will not learn English if they use their native language or dialect at school. Other critics have argued that bilingual education simply does not work (Porter, 1990). For example, when President Ronald Reagan took office in 1981, he made his views on bilingual education very clear, stating that he understood why teachers who spoke children's native languages were needed but also argued that "it is absolutely wrong and against American concepts to have a bilingual education program" (cited in Baker, 2001, p.194).

The proponents of English-only argue that to preserve the unity of the United States, English should become the official language (Crawford, 1992). There have been periods in the nation's history when administrations have leaned more toward a "language-as-a-resource" orientation, maintaining and supporting the teaching of languages other than English, such as Clinton's 1994 reauthorization of the BEA. The support or lack of support for a language-as-a resource orientation at the federal level has depended on the particular administration in office (Wiley & Wright, 2004).

As in the preceding 200 years, in the 2000s, the press, politics, and people in the U.S. have been grappling with the ambivalent rapport for language. In recent years, the debate has escalated to a new level with English-only initiatives, such as the state-level Unz Initiative in California, Proposition 227, spearheaded by the millionaire businessman Ron Unz and passed by California voters in June 1998, outlawing bilingual education in the state of California. Proposition 227 brought all of the debates on bilingual education under a magnifying lens. The English-only faction stressed that bilingual programs were not working and students were being ghettoized (although most ELLs were not in bilingual programs). Strong proponents of bilingual education such as Crawford (1999) have argued that the lack of large-scale political support has undermined its potential effectiveness. In bridging these two factions, Cummins (1999) states, "the challenge for opponents and advocates is to create an ideological space to collaborate in planning quality programs for bilingual students" (p. 223). After Proposition 227 was passed in California, similar laws were enacted in Arizona and Massachusetts. In 2008, 26 states had active official English laws.

Many linguists and educators regard the Ebonics debate in the same purview as bilingual education. The Oakland school board decision in 1996 to pass the Ebonics resolution, which recognized the legitimacy of Ebonics, was also a way for the school district to receive federal monies reserved for bilingual education and to use them for a Standard English program. The board resolution stated that the district's purpose should be to facilitate the acquisition and mastery of English language skills while respecting and embracing the legitimacy and richness of different language patterns. The rationale for the decision was that students could benefit from instruction that used their cultural and linguistic resources. In the same way as the Ann Arbor case brought two decades earlier (Smitherman, 1981), a large number of African American parents and students protested their children's poor academic performance, disproportionate placement in special education, and frequent suspensions.

Like Proposition 227, the Oakland school board decision resulted in gross misrepresentations and biases by the media, the public, educators, and academics. One of the most frequently stated misconceptions was that the Oakland school district proposed to replace the teaching of English with Ebonics (Bing & Woodward, 1998).

During the George W. Bush administration in 2002, Title III replaced Title VII (BEA) as part of a larger school reform measure in the United States known as the No Child Left Behind Act. Title III carried with it a new name, "Language Instruction for Limited English Proficient and Immigrant Students." The word "bilingual" had been deleted from all government offices and legislation, signaling a shift to the assimilationist, English-first orientation of the 2000–2008 Bush administration. Even though this new law is more supportive of programs that focus on learning English, it does not require English-only programs. Many scholars have argued that there is still space in the new law for the creation of bilingual programs (Freeman, 2004; Hornberger, 2005).

It is important for teachers to have a grasp of the legal and political trends and policies that influence the environments of their linguistically diverse students. Teachers who are aware of such political and social movements can establish historically relevant relationships with their students and influence programmatic decisions at the school and district levels.

PROGRAMMATIC RESPONSES TO LINGUISTIC DIVERSITY

In this section, we summarize different programmatic options for schools. Central to these decisions is the role that English and the home language of students will play in instruction. Should students learn to read in their first language (L1) and then learn to read in their second language (L2)? Should recent immigrants be instructed in content area classes in their L1 so they do not fall behind in the critical areas of math, science, and social studies? Or will culturally and linguistically diverse students benefit from instruction provided solely in English? Across the United States, schools and districts struggle with these questions. As we explore the different programmatic options available to districts, we also delve more deeply into the debate over bilingual education.

Instructional Programs

Various instructional programs have been devised and implemented over the last several decades to meet the educational needs of linguistically diverse students. We describe the five major program types that districts and schools have designed and implemented that were identified by August and Hakuta's (1997) comprehensive review of the research on linguistic minority students:

- *Submersion*: Students are placed in regular English-only classrooms and are given no special instructional support. This approach is illegal in the United States as a result of the Supreme Court decision in *Lau v. Nichols*. However, many ELL students find themselves in submersionlike settings.
- *English as a Second Language (ESL)*: No instruction is given in a student's primary language. ESL is either taught through pullout programs or integrated with academic content throughout the day.
- *Transitional Bilingual Education (TBE)*: Students receive some degree of instruction in their primary language for a period of time. However, the goal of the program is to transition to English-only instruction as rapidly as possible, generally within 1–3 years.
- *Maintenance Bilingual Education (MBE)*: Students receive instruction in their primary language and in English throughout the elementary school years (K–6) with the goal of developing academic proficiency in both languages.

- *Dual Language Programs*: Language majority and language minority students are instructed together in the same program with the goal of each group achieving bilingualism and biliteracy.

This list of five programs is not exhaustive. However, these programs do not exist in pure forms, and districts mix and blend aspects of various programs. Various large- and small-scale studies have examined the effectiveness of these programs. The authors of the studies have willingly and unwillingly become a part of the great debate about the effectiveness of bilingual education. It is difficult to determine the exact number of ELL students in each of these programs because of the lack of comprehensive national data. However, most ELL students are instructed through ESL approaches that use little to no native language instruction (Kindler, 2002).

The Bilingual Debate and the Research Context

As bilingual education continued to evolve throughout the 1960s and 1970s, a major split in public opinion regarding the program occurred. Baker (2001) explains that some citizens viewed bilingual education as failing to foster social integration and as a waste of public funds. Many opponents of bilingual education portrayed Latinos and supporters of bilingual education as using it for their own political gain (Baker). Critics of bilingual education have drawn from two major reviews of bilingual research (Baker & de Kanter, 1981; Rossel & Baker, 1996) to try to convince schools and districts to move away from bilingual education. Rossel and Baker reviewed 72 scientifically methodologically acceptable studies. They concluded that bilingual education was not superior to ESL instruction, particularly in reading achievement. This study is widely cited by critics of bilingual education. Several researchers have noted, however, that the review is plagued by many methodological issues. The Rossel and Baker review applied arbitrary and inconsistent criteria to establish methodologically acceptable studies and inaccurate and arbitrary labeling of programs (Cummins, 1999; Stritikus & Manyak, 2000). Baker points out that the study had

> a narrow range of expected outcomes for bilingual education in the [research] questions. Only English language and non-language subject areas were considered as the desirable outcome of schooling. Other outcomes such as self-esteem, employment, preservation of minority languages, and the value of different cultures were not considered. (p. 246)

Critics of bilingual education have drawn heavily from the work of Rossel and Baker (1996) and Baker and de Kanter (1981) to influence educational policy. Advocates of bilingual education have drawn from a body of research that has reached opposite conclusions and supports the use of students' native language in instruction. Willig (1985) conducted a meta-analysis of 23 of the 28 studies reviewed by Baker and de Kanter. *Meta-analysis* is a collection of systematic techniques for resolving apparent contradictions in research findings by translating results from different studies to a common metric and statistically explores relationships between study characteristics and findings. Employing this technique, Greene (1998) found that an unbiased reading of the scholarly literature indicates that limited-English-proficient students taught using bilingual approaches perform significantly better than do students taught using English-only approaches. In a review of methodologically acceptable research studies, Slavin and Chueng (2003) found that bilingual approaches—particularly those that include reading instruction in the native language—are more effective than English-only approaches.

Program Types That Contribute to Successful Educational Practice

Research examining the success or failure of various program types has not completely addressed the central question of how best to educate culturally and linguistically diverse students. A body of research has reported detailed studies of what has worked in actual classrooms. Rather than focus on program models, this research has concentrated on the characteristics of schools and classrooms that contribute to successful educational practice for culturally and linguistically diverse students.

August and Hakuta (1997) provide a comprehensive review of optimal learning conditions that serve linguistically and culturally diverse student populations and that lead to high academic performance. Their review of 33 studies indicates there is a set of generally agreed upon practices that foster academic success. These practices can exist across program types. August and Hakuta found that the following school and classroom characteristics were likely to lead to academic success:

> A supportive school-wide climate, school leadership, a customized
> learning environment, articulation and coordination within and
> between schools, use of native language and culture in instruction, a
> balanced curriculum that includes both basic and higher-order skills,
> explicit skill instruction, opportunities for student-directed instruction,
> use of instructional strategies that enhance understanding,
> opportunities for practice, systematic student assessment, staff
> development, and home and parent involvement. (p. 171)

These findings have been confirmed in other more recent studies, such as those by Corallo and McDonald (2002) and Marzano (2003). Thus, culturally and linguistically diverse students can benefit greatly from cognitively challenging and student-centered instruction that employs students' cultural and linguistic resources.

The Lived Reality of Today's Linguistically Diverse Students

Several studies of students' everyday experience provide a powerful but painful picture of how schools meet—or do not meet—the challenge of linguistic diversity. These studies are not meant as simple critique; they provide an understanding of how much further educators need to go in meeting the challenge. Valdés (2001) conducted an important study analyzing the manner in which recent immigrant students are served by schools. Focusing on the way that four Latino students' initial experience with U.S. schooling shaped their future possibilities, Valdés found that school curriculum for these students focused on English-language instruction at the expense of access to engaging grade-level curriculum in key subject areas such as science, social studies, and math. Valdés describes a significant relationship between the social position of cultural and linguistically diverse students and families in the broader society and the quality of education they receive. The students in Valdés's research found themselves in "ESL ghettoes," which afforded little possibility for academic advancement.

In a study similar to the Valdés (2001) research, Olsen (1997) studied the experiences of Latino and Asian immigrant students at Madison High School as they attempted to become "American." The teachers at Madison High believed that through hard work and perseverance, all students—regardless of their linguistic and cultural background—could succeed. The teachers accepted without question the idea of the U.S. meritocracy. Through careful interviews and observations, Olsen revealed the tensions and contradictions of this view. First, linguistically diverse students were segregated in the overall school context. They found themselves in low academic tracks with the most inexperienced teachers. Second, immigrant students felt extreme pressure to forgo defining elements of their own identities—their culture, language, dress, and values. School for recent immigrant students was not a wondrous opportunity but a process in which they found their place on the U.S. racial hierarchy.

Other researchers such as Toohey (2000) and Valenzuela (1999) have documented how racism, xenophobia, and pro-English attitdues are powerful factors that prevent educators from seeing linguistic diversity as an educational resource. To be sure, there are students who rise above these challenges, but school practices and policies unfortunately make this difficult. The next section of this chapter provides a synopsis of classroom-level issues. It examines what types of knowledge and skills will help teachers who have English language learners in their classrooms. The purpose of that section is to synthesize some of the important dimensions of second language acquisition for content area and second language (ESL and bilingual) teachers as well as to describe strategies to use in the classroom.

VIEWS ON LANGUAGE LEARNING AND TEACHING

This section summarizes what teachers of second language learners need to know about language, language learners, and language learning and teaching. Becoming proficient in a language or dialect can take on different meanings in various social, academic, and personal settings. In attempting to make students learning a second language or dialect successful in schools, scholars have observed that a distinction needs to be made between learning a language *socially* and *academically* (Cummins, 1981; Hakuta, Butler, & Witt, 2000–2001). Therefore, an important goal for teachers should be to enable students to successfully use academic English (Bartolomé, 1998; Gibbons, 2002; Valdés, 2004). In discussing language learning and teaching, we focus most of our discussion on teaching academic English and the language needed for content area subjects.

Language

Wong Fillmore and Snow (2000) describe the most salient aspects of language that will be helpful for teachers of second language/dialects to know. Language is a complex system of communication that includes the following major subsystems: *pragmatics* (sociolinguistic rules governing language use; e.g., apologizing in a specific language and culture); *syntax* (rules of word order in a sentence); *semantics* (meanings of words and sentences); *morphology* (rules of word formation); and *phonology* (the sound system of a language). When people are using language, they must manipulate and coordinate all of these subsystems together, as the following example illustrates. A child in a classroom who asks *What is photosynthesis?* would need to know the social convention of when and how to ask this question. The student would also need to know how to form a wh- question and to pronounce the words in a way that is intelligible to the person(s) being asked.

Language Learners

A number of learner characteristics can affect second language learning and success in an English-speaking school setting. Here, we focus on some of the most salient ones, such as age, the learner's first language, and motivation. Examples of others that can be considered are learning styles and aptitude. Although these tend to be described by researchers as individual learner characteristics, it is important to note that such characteristics are shaped by cultural and social contexts.

Age

There has been a push in the United States and in several other countries to start early schooling for children in a second/foreign language because younger learners are thought to be better language learners. Research indicates that younger children show advantages in terms of pronunciation and accent. Several researchers (Hyltenstam & Abrahamsson, 2001; Johnson & Newport, 1989; Patowski, 1980) also believe that there is a "critical period," a time when the brain is more predisposed to learn all linguistic features of a language, not just phonological ones. This belief has been challenged by others who did not find an advantage to being younger (Snow & Hoefnagel-Höhle, 1978). Snow and Hoefnagel-Höhle found that adolescents and adults learn at a faster rate, especially in the early stages of language development. Even among scholars who have found the data on the critical period convincing (Hyltenstam & Abrahamsson), the recommendation has been that programmatic decisions should not be based on the age of learners. Rather, the research indicates that more attention should be paid to the quality of the programs and the quantity and quality of exposure to the second/foreign language than to the age of students.

First Language

Research indicates that all second language learners, regardless of their first language, seem to progress through similar developmental stages of language learning in some areas. For example, researchers have found that there is a developmental sequence for learners of English as a second language in question formation, negation, and past tense formation (Lightbown & Spada, 1999). Learners go through preverbal negation (e.g., I no play) and are then able to insert the negative term with auxiliary verbs, although not necessarily correctly (e.g., "I can't play," He don't play"), and are finally able to produce negative sentences correctly (e.g., "She doesn't play"). Additionally, there are specific errors that we can now attribute to a learner's first language. For example, Spanish-speaking learners will stay in the preverbal negation stage (*I no like*) longer because of this structure's similarity to the Spanish language (*No quiero*). This example demonstrates that the popular belief that it is easier to learn a second language the more similar it is to the first language is not necessarily true. Actually, there can be a tendency to revert to the rules of the first language if they share many similarities. Thus, it is useful for teachers to learn about cross-linguistic similarities and differences in terms of different aspects of language, such as phonemes, spelling, writing systems, and sociolinguistic rules (Wong Fillmore & Snow, 2000).

Overall, whatever the learner's first language, students who are literate and have had prior formal schooling in their first language have been found to outperform students who have not had this experience (August & Hakuta, 1997; Collier, 1987; Cummins, 1984).

LANGUAGE LEARNING AND TEACHING

Theories of Second Language Learning

While many theories have been advanced to explain second language learning, three main theories have had the most influence on second language students in schools. The three major theories are:

- Input hypothesis
- Interactionist theory
- Basic interpersonal communication skills (BICS) and cognitive academic language proficiency (CALP)

We describe these theories in detail.

Input Hypothesis

The most influential set of hypotheses or single theory that has influenced teachers has been that of Stephen Krashen (1985), the *input hypothesis*. He, with others, has advanced the following hypotheses: (1) Acquisition is the unconscious process of acquiring a language through interaction while learning is the formal process of memorizing rules and structures of a language. He contends that language learning is most successful when built on the principle of acquisition through activities that are mostly communicative in nature. (2) Language learning consists of particular sequences and stages, an example of which was given earlier in the way negation develops for language learners. (3) For language acquisition to occur, learners must be offered comprehensible input, language that is just beyond the learner's current level.

This last part of Krashen's theory has been the most influential on classroom teaching. The recommendation for teachers is that input in the classroom can be made comprehensible through strategies such as creating visual cues and establishing background knowledge. Overall, Krashen's proposals suggest that language teaching be conducted in the most natural, communicative situations in which learners are relaxed and teachers are not focusing on error correction.

Interactionist Theory

The second theory discussed in this section is the *interactionist theory* (Lightbown & Spada, 1999), which has widely influenced and been influenced by research and teaching on immersion programs in Canada. The basic tenet of this theory is that both input and output are crucial for language learning. Teachers who draw on this theory create tasks for which conversational interactions between speakers are central to the process of language learning. This process has been described as the *negotiation of meaning*, which in many ways is similar to the process between caretakers and children in first-language acquisition.

BICS and CALP

The third theory that has most influenced the teaching of English in schools is one that focuses explicitly on language and content learning and pertains to the distinction made between learning a language socially and academically. Learning another language academically is known to be a lengthy process that can take from seven to ten years (Cummins, 1984), as compared to conversational proficiency in a language, which can take from one to five years. Cummins distinguished these language learning processes with the terms *basic interpersonal conversational skills (BICS)* and *cognitive academic language proficiency (CALP)*. Academic language offers few clues for learners and is therefore much more difficult to learn, while BICS occurs "when there are contextual supports and props for language delivery" (Baker, 2006, p. 174). If we think of it, many of us might know how to converse with a speaker in our second or third language but might have difficulty listening to an academic lecture in that language or writing a technical report. This is especially true for students who start this process in the later grades (Collier, 1987; Cummins & Swain, 1986), for students who are not literate or academically skilled in their first language, and for many students who come from war-torn countries.

We should also bear in mind the limitations of the BICS and CALP typologies (Wiley, 1996a). First, the strict dichotomy between the two is viewed by some scholars as overly simplistic (Edelsky et. al, 1983; Wiley, 1996b). In some cases, as with individuals who can read but not converse in a second language, CALP can be developed before BICS. There is also danger in viewing BICS as inferior to CALP. We know that oral conversation can be equally demanding in certain settings. Second, the notion of academic language is somewhat abstract. In a more recent reworking of this distinction, Cummins (2000) has attempted to define *academic proficiency* in more concrete terms, such as "the extent to which an individual has access to and command of the oral and written academic registers of schooling" (p. 67). Other attempts to make this concept more useful for teachers can be found in the national ESL standards (Teachers of English to Speakers of Other Languages [TESOL], 1997). Nonetheless, there is still considerable debate about how academic language should be defined (Valdés, 2004).

Instructional Methods and Approaches

The input hypothesis and the interactionist theories have provided a significant set of guidelines for creating optimal language learning environments. These theories have influenced teachers and methods in several ways, including (1) making teachers think through how to make verbal input comprehensible at a level that is slightly beyond the learner's level (e.g., using visuals, paraphrasing), (2) creating conversation-based activities (e.g., problem-solving activities) that are of a low-anxiety level, and (3) setting up tasks so that learners are forced to talk and listen to each other (e.g., through jigsaw activities). Krashen's work has been associated most closely with the *natural approach*, a method he and Terrell (1983) developed that integrates a number of these strategies.

The interactionist theory, as indicated, has been cited mostly in conjunction with immersion programs in Canada. In these programs, researchers have found that the most effective language learning situation is one that is content based or communicatively oriented (Lightbown & Spada, 1999). Therefore, as Cummins's work suggests, instruction offered to language minority students in schools should be where language and content are jointly taught. The research and scholarship subsequent to that of Cummins has focused on the importance of learning academic language and content (Bartolomé, 1998; Gibbons, 2002; Valdés, 2004). Much of this research has shown how instruction for these students learning a second language must concentrate on acquiring academic language and subject-specific knowledge in several ways.

Students can attain subject-specific knowledge by using their primary language or with richer and more sustained collaborations between content area teachers and English language specialists. When these strategies are used, ESL pullout classes do not focus exclusively on decontextualized skills and language. In many cases, content area teachers will need training in making language and content more accessible to ELL students. Content-based instruction (CBI), in which language is taught in conjunction with the academic subject matter, can be used (Snow, Met, & Genesee, 1989). One example of CBI is *specifically designed academic instruction (SDAIE)* in English, which has often been referred to as *sheltered instruction*.

A comprehensive program of sheltered instruction that has gained wide recognition is the *sheltered instruction observation protocol (SIOP)* (Echevarria, Vogt, & Short, 2000). Another is the *cognitive academic language learning approach*, which focuses on developing language, content, and learning strategies (Chamot & O'Malley, 1994). A more recent method that is becoming widely adopted is *guided language acquisition design* (Brechtel, 2001). Many of these methods are used in a large number of school districts across the United States. The resource list at the end of this chapter provides more information for mainstream teachers, including additional references for these methods.

Instructional Strategies and Contexts for Learning

The methods just described that recommend an integration of language and content indicate that teachers should use strategies similar to those described in the effective programs reported by August and Hakuta (1997), Corallo and McDonald (2002), and Marzano (2003). These strategies incorporate a student-centered, meaning-based, context-rich classroom and a cognitively demanding curriculum. Schleppegrell, Achugar, and Oteíza (2004) summarize these strategies:

> Typical recommendations for a CBI approach include
> a focus on disciplinary vocabulary and use of a variety of learning
> and teaching strategies, especially visual aids and graphic organizers
> to make meanings clear.... Teachers are encouraged to help students
> comprehend and use the language structures and discourse features
> found in different subjects and to facilitate students' practice with
> academic tasks such as listening to explanations, reading for information,
> participating in academic discussions, and writing reports. (p. 69)

A successful class for English language learners is one in which the following features often are present: a high level of noise; students working in groups with hands-on materials; word walls, graphic organizers, displays of student work; teachers modeling strategies; assessment being used to drive instruction; and high expectations for all students. One example of teacher modeling is to provide students with explicit instruction in different learning strategies for gaining academic competence, such as writing a summary (Chamot & O'Malley, 1994). Teachers cannot assume that students will know how to write a summary and must either model for them the necessary steps or collaborate with an English language specialist to accomplish the task. Setting up cooperative learning (Johnson, Johnson, & Holubec, 1986) or complex instruction groups (Cohen & Lotan, 1997) in which students are given different roles in completing a project are examples of effective group work. In addition, teachers need to learn tools for authentic assessment (O'Malley & Valdez Peirce, 1996) in order to evaluate students in different ways that facilitate learning.

Although many of the strategies and methods that we have described can be very helpful, we should realize that a number of scholars have challenged the assumption that they are sufficient to help second language students succeed, especially students in the higher grades and in gaining language skills equal to their native English-speaking peers. Bartolomé (1998), Gibbons (2002), and Valdés (2004) stress the need to create events in which students have to "address real or imaginary distant audiences with whom they can assume little shared knowledge" (Valdés, p. 122) in order to make them "elaborate linguistic messages explicitly and precisely to minimize audience misinterpretation" (Bartolomé, 1998, p. 66). Schleppegrell et al. (2004) discuss the need to delve deeply into disciplinary-specific linguistic challenges, such as those found in social studies textbooks.

Teachers should always remember that the education of linguistically diverse students is situated in larger issues about immigration, distribution of wealth and power, and the empowerment of students (Cahnmann & Varghese, 2006; Varghese & Stritikus, 2005). Thus, effective classroom strategies and climate must be situated in a supportive school and societal context. Along with the academic focus, teachers should work toward making the classroom a welcoming place for students and their families. The cultural and linguistic resources that students bring to school, especially with the involvement of parents and community partners, should also be integrated and celebrated in the classroom.

CONCLUSION

This chapter stresses the social, political, and historical realities that influence schooling for linguistically diverse students. It first examines linguistically diverse populations in the United States and considers how recent trends in immigration have influenced linguistic diversity in the United States. To understand the experiences of immigrant students in schools, the political and economic realities that drive and shape immigration must be examined. Immigration has changed the look and feel of schools in every state in the United States. The manner in which schools receive linguistically diverse students is directly related to the ways in which they are perceived and treated by society. In the early 21st century, immigrants provide a source of cheap labor as well as highly developed skills and abilities that fuel the U. S. economy. Immigrant communities find themselves pinched by social and economic pressures. Thus, it is important for teachers to consider how immigrant populations are viewed by their host countries.

The next section of this chapter considers important legal and political milestones in the evolution of language education policy. Past and recent developments in language policy demonstrate the contradictory position of the United States toward linguistic diversity. While we frequently celebrate our status as a nation of immigrants or as a land of equality, language policy in the United States has continually attempted to suppress and minimize linguistic diversity. Linguistically diverse students in the United States have rarely seen their languages and cultures promoted at the federal and state levels. Teacher practice both influences and is influenced by language policy. In order for teachers to support and promote linguistic diversity, they need to understand how language policy shapes education (Varghese & Stritikus, 2005).

In the third section of this chapter, we review the existing research regarding which programs best serve the needs of linguistically diverse students. Research indicates that students learn best in meaning-centered and intellectually rich environments and that linguistically diverse students have the maximum potential to succeed when their language and culture are used and developed in instruction. School practice has not always lived up to this ideal. Finally, the chapter provides practical knowledge required to meet the needs of linguistically diverse students.

In nearly every classroom, linguistic diversity shapes the nature of teachers' work. Linguistic and cultural diversity is one of the great assets of the United States, yet schooling for linguistically diverse students continues to be plagued by poor programs, limited resources, and lack of commitment from policy makers. The success of the U.S. educational system will be judged, in part, by how well we meet the needs of students from linguistically diverse groups. You and your colleagues can play a significant role in opening the doors of opportunity for linguistically diverse students.

Questions and Activities

1. What did you learn about immigrant students and their schooling in this chapter? Imagine you are asked to provide a 30-minute workshop for the mainstream teachers and staff in your school. What concepts and principles would you incorporate in this workshop?

2. In what ways are the challenges facing English language learners, African American students, and indigenous students in schools similar and different? What types of practices and activities can teachers implement in their classrooms that would help these students?

3. What support is provided for English language learners in a local school, and how are these decisions made? Interview school staff and document their responses to these questions.

4. You are in charge of designing the best possible program in your school for English language learners. What features would be part of this program? Why? What aspects of language and language learning would be useful for mainstream teachers to know? How can they incorporate this knowledge when teaching their subject matter?

5. Parents and households as well as their relationships with schools are critical influences on the achievement of immigrant students. Interview one parent and, if possible, one child who has been identified as an ELL student. Document their social and educational experiences before and since coming to the United States.

Resources

August, D., & Hakuta, K. (Eds.). (1997). *Improving schooling for language minority students: A research agenda*. Washington, DC: National Academy Press.

Baugh, J. (1999). *Out of the mouth of slaves: African American language educational malpractice*. New York: Oxford University Press.

Davies Samway, K., & McKeon, D. (1999). *Myths and realities: Best practices for language minority students*. Portsmouth, NH: Heinemann.

Echevarria, J., Vogt, M., & Short, D. J. (2000). *Making content comprehensible for English language learners: The SIOP model*. Boston: Allyn & Bacon.

Gibbons, P. (2002). *Scaffolding language, scaffolding learning: Teaching second language learners in the mainstream classroom*. Portsmouth, NH: Heinemann.

Herrera, S. G., & Murphy, K. G. (2005). *Mastering ESL and bilingual methods*. Boston: Allyn & Bacon.

Lightbown, P., & Spada, N. (1999). *How languages are learned* (2nd ed.). New York: Oxford University Press.

Peregoy, S. F., & Boyle, O. F. (2005). *Reading, writing, and learning in ESL: A resource book for K-12 teachers* (4th ed.). Boston: Pearson Education.

Suarez-Orozco, C. E., & Suarez-Orozco, M. M. (2003). *Children of immigration*. Cambridge, MA: Harvard University Press.

Teachers of English to Speakers of Other Languages (1997). *ESL standards for pre-K 12 students*. Alexandria, VA: Author.

Wong Fillmore, L., & Snow, C. (2000). *What teachers need to know about language*. Washington, DC: ERIC Clearinghouse on Languages and Linguistics.

Professional Associations

National Association for Bilingual Education (NABE)

National Association for Multicultural Education (NAME)

Teachers of English to Speakers of Other Languages (TESOL)

Websites

Center for Applied Linguistics: www.cal.org

National Association for Bilingual Education: www.nabe.org

National Clearinghouse for English Language Acquisition: www.ncbla.gwu.edu

Teachers of English to Speakers of Other Languages: www.tesol.org

References

Alim, H. S., & Baugh, J. (Eds.). (2007). *Talkin Black talk: Language, education, and social change*. New York: Teachers College Press.

August, D., & Hakuta, K. (Eds.). (1997). *Improving schooling for language minority students: A research agenda*. Washington, DC: National Academy Press.

Baker, C. (2001). *Foundations of bilingual education and bilingualism.* (3rd ed.). Clevedon, UK: Multilingual Matters.

Baker, C (2006). *Foundations of bilingual education and bilingualism.* (4th ed.). Clevedon, U.K: Multilingual Matters.

Baker, K., & de Kanter, A. (1981). *Effectiveness of bilingual education: A review of the literature.* Washington, DC: U.S. Department of Education.

Banks, C. A. M. (2005). *Improving multicultural education: Lessons from the intergroup education movement.* New York: Teachers College Press.

Bartolomé, L. (1998). *The misteaching of academic discourse: The politics in the language classroom.* Boulder, CO: Westview Press.

Behdad, A. (1997). Nationalism and immigration to the United States. *Diaspora, 6*(2), 155–176.

Brown v. Board of Education, 327 U.S. 483 (1954).

Bing, J. M., & Woodward, W. (1998). Nobody's listening: A frame analysis of the Ebonics debate. *SECOL Review, 22*(1), 1–16.

Brechtel, M. (2001). *Bringing it all together: Language and literacy in the multicultural classroom.* San Diego: Dominic Press.

Cahnmann, M., & Varghese, M. (2006). Critical advocacy and bilingual education in the United States. *Linguistics and Education, 16*(1), 59–73.

Castaneda v. Pickard, 648 F.2d 989, 1007 5th Cir. (1981).

Castles, S. (2003). Towards a sociology of forced migration and social transformation. *Sociology, 37*(1), 13–34.

Castles, S., & Davidson, A. (2000). *Citizenship and migration: Globalization and the politics of belonging.* New York: Routledge.

Chamot, A. U., & O'Malley, J. M. (1994). *The CALLA handbook: How to implement the cognitive academic language learning approach.* Reading, MA: Addison-Wesley.

Chomsky, N. (2000). *The architecture of language.* (N. Mukherji, B. N. Patnaik, & R. K. Agnihotri, Eds.). Oxford: Oxford University Press.

Cohen, E. G., & Lotan, R. A. (1997). *Working for equity in heterogeneous classrooms: Sociological theory in practice.* New York: Teachers College Press.

Collier, V. P. (1987). Age and rate of acquisition of second language for academic purposes. *TESOL Quarterly, 21,* 617–641.

Corallo, C., & McDonald, D. H. (2002). *What works with low-performing schools: A review of research.* Charleston, WV: AEL, Regional Educational Laboratory, Region IV Comprehensive Center.

Crawford, J. (1992). *Language loyalties: A source book on the official English controversy.* Chicago, IL: University of Chicago Press.

Crawford, J. (1999). *Bilingual education: History, politics, theory, and practice* (4th ed.). Los Angeles: Bilingual Education Services.

Cummins, J. (1981). The role of primary language development in promoting educational success for language minority students. In California State Department of Education (Ed.), *Schooling and language minority students: A theoretical framework* (pp. 3–50). Los Angeles: California State University Evaluation, Dissemination, and Assessment Center.

Cummins, J. (1984). *Bilingualism and special education: Issues in assessment and pedagogy*. Clevedon, UK: Multilingual Matters.

Cummins, J. (1999). Alternative paradigms in bilingual education research: Does theory have a place? *Educational Researcher*, *28*, 26–32.

Cummins, J. (2000). *Language, power, and pedagogy*. Clevedon, U.K.: Multilingual Matters.

Cummins, J., & Swain, M. (1986). *Bilingualism in education*. London: Longman.

Del Valle, S. (2003). *Language rights and the law in the United States: Finding our voices*. Clevedon, UK: Multilingual Matters.

Echevarria, J., Vogt, M., & Short, D. J. (2000). *Making content comprehensible for English language learners: The SIOP model*. Boston: Allyn & Bacon.

Edelsky, C, Hudelson, S., Altwerger, B., Flores, B., Barkin, F., & Jilbert, K. (1983). Semilingualism and language deficit. *Applied Linguistics*, *4*(1), 1–22.

Freeman, R. D. (2004). *Building on community bilingualism*. Philadelphia: Caslon.

Garcia, E. (1999). *Understanding and meeting the challenge of student cultural diversity*. Boston, MA: Houghton Mifflin.

Gibbons, P. (2002). *Scaffolding language, scaffolding learning: Teaching second language learners in the mainstream classroom*. Portsmouth, NH: Heinemann.

Gordon, M. (1964). *Assimilation in American life*. New York: Oxford University Press.

Greene, J. P. (1998). *A meta-analysis of the effectiveness of bilingual education*. Los Angeles: The Tomas Rivera Policy Institute, University of Southern California.

Hakuta, K., Butler, Y. G., & Witt, D. (2000–2001). *How long does it take English learners to attain proficiency?* Retrieved November 1, 2005, from http://www.stanford.edu/~hakuta

Hornberger, N. H. (2005). Nichols to NCLB: Local and global perspectives on U.S. language education policy. *Working Papers in Educational Linguistics*, *20*(2).

Hyltenstam, H., & Abrahamsson, N. (2001). Age and L2 learning: The hazards of matching practical "implications" with theoretical facts. *TESOL Quarterly*, *35*(1), 151–170.

Itzigsohn, J., Dore-Cabral, C. B., Hernandez-Medina, E., & Vazquez, O. (1999). Mapping Dominican transnationalism: Narrow and broad transnational practices. *Ethnic and Racial Studies*, *22*(2), 316–339.

Jacobson, M. F. (1998). *Whiteness of a different color: European immigrants and the alchemy of race*. Cambridge: Harvard University Press.

Johnson, J., Johnson, R. T., & Holubec, E. J. (1986). *Circles of learning: Cooperation in the classroom*. Edina, MN: Interaction Book.

Johnson, J., & Newport, E. (1989). Critical period effects in second language learning: The influence of maturational state on the acquisition of English as a second language. *Cognitive Psychology*, *21*, 60–99.

Kindler, A. (2002). *Survey of the states' limited English proficient students and available educational programs and services: 1999–2000 summary report*. Washington, DC: National Clearinghouse for English Language Acquisition and Language Instruction Educational Programs.

Krashen, S. (1985). *The input hypothesis: Issues and implications*. New York: Longman.

Krashen, S. D., & Terrell, D. (1983). *The natural approach: Language acquisition in the classroom*. Hayward, CA: Alemany Press.

Krauss, M. (1995, February 3). Endangered languages: Current issues and future prospects. Keynote address, Dartmouth College, Hanover, NH.

Krauss, M. (1998). The condition of native North American languages: The need for realistic assessment and action. *International Journal of the Sociology of Language, 132,* 9–21.

Labov, W. (1972). The logic of standard English. In W. Labov (Ed.), *Language in the inner city: Studies in Black English vernacular* (pp. 201–240). Philadelphia: University of Pennsylvania Press.

Lau v. Nichols, 414 U.S. 563 (1974).

Lightbown, P., & Spada, N. (1999). *How languages are learned* (2nd ed.). New York: Oxford University Press.

Lindholm-Leary, K. J. (2001). *Dual language education*. Clevedon, UK: Multilingual Matters.

Lomawaima, K. T., & McCarty, T. L. (2006). *"To remain an Indian": Lessons in democracy from a century of Native American education*. New York: Teachers College Press.

Lucas, T. (1997). *Into, through, and beyond secondary school: Critical transitions for immigrant youths*. New York: National Center for Restructuring Education, Schools, and Teaching, Teachers College, Columbia University.

Mahler, S. J. (1998). Theoretical and empirical contributions toward a research agenda for transnationalism. In M. P. Smith & L. E. Guarnizo (Eds.), *Transnationalism from below* (pp. 64–102). New Brunswick, NJ: Transaction.

Marzano, R. (2003). *What works in schools: Translating research into action*. Alexandria, VA: Association for Supervision and Curriculum Development.

McCarty, T. (2002). Comment: Bilingual/Bicultural schooling and indigenous students: A response to Eugene Garcia. *International Journal of the Sociology of Language, 155/156,* 161–174.

Meyer, D., Madden, D., & McGrath, D. J. (2004). *English language learner students in U.S. public schools 1994 and 2000*. Washington, DC: National Center for Education Statistics, U.S. Department of Education, Institute of Education Sciences. Retrieved January 19, 2009, from http://purl.access.gpo.gov.offcampus.lib.washington.edu/GPO/LPS60046

Olneck, M. R., & Lazerson, M. (1974). The school achievement of immigrant children, 1900–1930. *History of Education Quarterly, 14,* 453–482.

Olsen, L. (1997). *Made in America: Immigrant students in our public schools*. New York: The New York Press.

Omi, M., & Winant, H. (1994). *Racial formation in the United States: From the 1960s to the 1990s*. New York and London: Routledge.

O'Malley, J. M., & Valdez Peirce, L. (1996). *Authentic assessment for English language learners: Practical approaches for teachers*. New York: Addison-Wesley.

Patowski, M. (1980). The sensitive period for the acquisition of syntatx in a second language. *Language Learning, 30*(2), 449–472.

Perry, T., & Delpit, L. D. (1998). *The real Ebonics debate: Power, language, and the education of African-American children*. Boston: Beacon Press.

Plyer v. Doe, 457 U.S. 202, 210 (1982).

Porter, R. P. (1990). *Forked tongue: The politics of bilingual education*. New York: Basic Books.

Portes, A. (1996). Global villagers: The rise of transnational communities. *American Prospect, 25*, 74–77.

Portes, A. (1999). Towards a new world: The origins and effects of transnational activities. *Ethnic and Racial Studies, 22*(2), 463–477.

Portes, A., & Rumbaut, R. G. (1996). *Immigrant America: A portrait*. Berkeley: University of California Press.

Portes, A., & Rumbaut, R. G. (2001). *Legacies: The story of the immigrant second generation*. Berkeley: University of California Press.

Rose, P. I. (1997). *They and we: Racial ethnic relations in the United States*. New York: McGraw-Hill.

Rossel, C., & Baker, K. (1996). The effectiveness of bilingual education. *Research in the Teaching of English, 30*, 7–74.

Ruiz, R. (2004, April). *From language as a problem to language as an asset: The promise and limitations of Lau*. Paper presented at the Annual Conference of the American Educational Research Association, San Diego.

Schleppegrell, M. J., Achugar, M., & Oteíza, T. (2004). The grammar of history: Enhancing content-based instruction through a functional focus on language. *TESOL Quarterly, 38*(1), 67–94.

Singer, A. (2004). *The rise of new immigrant gateways. Living cities census series*. Washington, DC: Center on Urban and Metropolitan Policy, Brookings Institution.

Slavin, R. E., & Cheung, A. (2003). *Effective reading programs for English language learners: A best-evidence synthesis*. Baltimore, MD: Johns Hopkins University Center for Research on the Education of Students Placed at Risk.

Smith, M. P., & Guarnizo, L. E. (Eds.) (1998). *Transnationalism from below: Comparative urban and community research*. New Brunswick, NJ: Transaction.

Smitherman, G. (1981). What go round come round: King in perspective. *Harvard Educational Review, 51*(1), 40–56.

Smitherman, G. (1998). Black English/Ebonics: What it be like? In T. Perry & L. Delpit (Eds.), *The real ebonics debate: Power, language, and the education of African-American children* (pp. 29–37). Boston, MA: Beacon Press.

Smitherman, G. (2000). *Talkin that talk: Language, culture and education in African America*. New York: Routledge.

Snow, C., & Hoefnagel-Höhle, M. (1978). The critical period for language acquisition: Evidence from second language learning. *Child Development, 49*(4), 1114–1128.

Snow, M. A., Met, M., & Genesee, F. (1989). A conceptual framework for the integration of language and content in second/foreign language instruction. *TESOL Quarterly, 23*, 201–219.

Stritikus, T. (2004, April). *Latino immigrant students: Transitions and educational challenges*. Paper presented at the Annual Meeting of the American Educational Research Association, San Diego, CA.

Stritikus, T., & Manyak, P. (2000). Creating opportunities for the academic success of linguistically diverse students: What does the research say? In T. Bergeson (Ed.), *Educating limited English proficient students in Washington State*. Olympia, WA: Office of Superintendent of Public Instruction.

Suarez-Orozco, C. E., & Suarez-Orozco, M. M. (2003). *Children of immigration*. Cambridge, MA: Harvard University Press.

Suárez-Orozco, C., Suárez-Orozco, M. M., & Todorova, I. (2008). *Learning a new land: Immigrant students in American society*. Cambridge, MA: Belknap Press of Harvard University Press.

Suarez-Orozco, M. M. (1997). Globalization, immigration, and education: The research agenda. *Harvard Educational Review, 71*(3), 345–365.

Teachers of English to Speakers of Other Languages (TESOL) (1997). *ESL standards for pre-K-12 students*. Alexandria, VA: Author.

Toohey, K. (2000). *Learning English at school: Identity, social relations and classroom practice*. Clevedon, UK: Multilingual Matters.

U.S. Census Bureau. (2001, March). Census brief 2000. Retrieved November 15, 2004, http://www.census.gov/popest/national/

Valdés, G. (2001). *Learning and not learning English: Latino students in American schools*. New York: Teachers College Press.

Valdés, G. (2004). Between support and marginalization: The development of academic language in linguistic minority children. In J. Brutt-Griffler & M. Varghese (Eds.), *Bilingualism and language pedagogy* (pp. 102–132). Clevedon, UK: Multilingual Matters.

Valenzuela, A. (1999). *Subtractive schooling: U.S.–Mexican youth and the politics of caring*. New York: State University of New York Press.

Varghese, M., & Stritikus, T. (2005). "*Nadie me dijó* [Nobody told me]": Language policy negotiation and implications for teacher education. *Journal of Teacher Education, 56*(1).

Wiese, A., & Garcia, E. E. (1998). The Bilingual Education Act: Language minority students and equal educational opportunity. *Bilingual Research Journal, 22*(1), 1–18.

Wiley, T. G. (1996a). Language planning and policy. In S. L. McKay & N. H. Hornberger (Eds.), *Sociolinguistics and language teaching*, 103–148.

Wiley, T. G. (1996b). *Literacy and language diversity in the United States*. Washington, DC: Center for Applied Linguistics and Delta Systems.

Wiley, T. G., & Lukes, M. (1996). English-only and standard English ideologies in the US. *TESOL Quarterly, 30*(3), 511–535.

Wiley, T. G., & Wright, W. E. (2004). Against the undertow: Language-Minority education policy and politics in the "age of accountability." *Educational Policy, 18*(1), 142–168.

Willig, A. (1985). A meta-analysis of selected studies on the effectiveness of bilingual education. *Review of Educational Research, 55*(3), 269–317.

Wolfram, W., Adger, C. T., & Christian, D. (1998). *Dialects in schools and communities*. Mahwah, NJ: Lawrence Erlbaum.

Wong Fillmore, L., & Snow, C. (2000). *What teachers need to know about language*. Washington, DC: ERIC Clearinghouse on Languages and Linguistics.

Zhou, M. (1997). Segmented assimilation: Issues, controversies, and recent research on the new second generation. *International Migration Review, 31*(4), 975–1008.

Teachers should respond to the special educational needs of students who have disabilities as well as to those who are intellectually gifted and talented.

Exceptionality

E xpanded rights for students with disabilities was one major consequence of the Civil Rights Movement of the 1960s and 1970s. The Supreme Court's *Brown* decision, issued in 1954, established the principle that to segregate students solely because of their race is inherently unequal and unconstitutional. This decision—as well as other legal and social reforms of the 1960s—encouraged advocates for the rights of students with disabilities to push for expanded rights for them. If it was unconstitutional to segregate students because of their race, it was reasoned, segregating students because of their disabilities could also be challenged.

The advocates for the rights of students with disabilities experienced a major victory in 1975 when Congress enacted Public Law 94–142, the Education for All Handicapped Children Act (Twenty-fifth Annual Report, 2003). This act is unprecedented and revolutionary in its implications. It requires free public education for all children with disabilities, nondiscriminatory evaluation, and an individualized education program (IEP) for each student with a disability. The act also stipulates that each student with a disability should be educated in the least restricted environment. This last requirement has been one of the most controversial provisions of Public Law 94–142 (Dillon, 2007). Most students who are classified as having disabilities—about 80 percent—have mild disabilities.

Exceptionality intersects with factors such as race, ethnicity, language, gender, and sexual orientation in interesting and complex ways. Males and students of color are more frequently classified as special education students than are females and White mainstream students. Nearly twice as many males as females are classified as special education students. Consequently, males of color are the most likely group to be classified as mentally retarded or learning disabled (Demographic and School Characteristics, 2007). The higher proportion of males and students of color in special education programs is related to the fact that mental retardation is a socially constructed category (see Chapter 1).

Students with disabilities as well as gifted students are considered *exceptional*. Exceptional students are those who have learning or behavioral characteristics that differ substantially from most other students and that require special attention in instruction. Concern for U.S. students who are gifted and talented increased after the Soviet Union successfully launched *Sputnik* in

1957. Congress passes the Gifted and Talented Children's Education Act in 1978. However, concern for the gifted is ambivalent and controversial in the United States.

In 1982, special funding for gifted education was consolidated with twenty-nine other educational programs. The controversy over gifted education stems in part from the belief by many people that it is elitist. Others argue that gifted education is a way for powerful mainstream parents to acquire an excellent education for their children in the public schools. The fact that few students of color are classified as gifted is another source of controversy. Despite controversies that surround programs for gifted and talented youths, schools need to find creative and democratic ways to satisfy these students' needs.

The chapters in Part V describe the major issues, challenges, and promises involved in providing equal educational opportunities for exceptional students—those with disabilities and those who are intellectually gifted and talented.

References

Dillon, E. (2007). *The students behind NCLB's 'disabilities' designation*. Retrieved October 21, 2008 from http://www.educationsector.org/analysis/analysis_show.htm?doc_id = 509392

Twenty-fifth annual report to Congress on the implementation of the individuals with disabilities education act (2003). Retrieved October 21, 2008, from http://www.ed.gov/about/reports/annual/osep/25th-exec-summ.pdf

Demographic and school characteristics of students receiving special education in the elementary grades (2007). Retrieved October 21, 2008, from http://nces.ed.gov/pubs2007/2007005.pdf

CHAPTER 13

Educational Equality for Students with Disabilities

Sara C. Bicard
William L. Heward

Children differ from one another. Step in any classroom in any school and you will notice immediately differences in children's height, weight, style of dress, hair, skin color, and other physical characteristics. Look a bit closer and you will see some obvious differences in children's language and their academic and social skills. Closely observe the interactions among students, curriculum, and instruction, and you will begin to see how children respond differently to the curriculum content and to the instructional methods.

Children also differ from one another in ways that are not apparent to the casual observer. Differences in the educational opportunities children receive and the benefits they derive from their time in school are two examples. The educational implications of gender, race, social class, religion, ethnicity, and language diversity not only influence how children may respond to curriculum and instruction but also affect the structure and design of educational systems in general.

While diversity in social class, race, culture, and language differences increasingly characterizes U.S. classrooms, every classroom is also characterized by *skill diversity* among students. Some children quickly acquire new knowledge and skills that they have learned in relevant situations. Other children need repeated practice to learn a simple task and the next day may have difficulty successfully performing the same task. Some children begin a lesson with a large store of relevant experience and background knowledge; others come to the same lesson with little or no relevant prerequisite skills or knowledge. Some children are popular and enjoy the company of many friends. Others are ostracized because they have not learned how to be friendly. The skill differences among most children are relatively small, allowing these children to benefit from the general education program offered by their schools. When the physical, social, and academic skills of children differ to such an extent that typical school curricula or teaching methods are neither appropriate nor effective, however, equitable access to and benefits from educational programs are at stake.

Like the others in this book, this chapter is not about surface or educationally irrelevant differences among children. Teachers must have the knowledge and skills to recognize and to be instructionally responsive to the diversity their students represent. This chapter extends the concept of diversity to include children with disabilities, and it lays the foundation for teachers to examine educational equity for learners with diverse skills.

This chapter outlines the history of exclusion and educational inequality experienced by many students with disabilities in U.S. schools. It also examines the progress made during the past three decades, paying particular attention to the Individuals with Disabilities Education Act (IDEA), federal legislation that requires that all children, regardless of the type or severity of their disabilities, be provided a free and appropriate public education. We examine the key features of this landmark law, the outcomes of its implementation, and the major barriers that continue to impede true educational equity for students with disabilities. First, let's take a closer look at the concept of disability and examine when skill diversity necessitates special education.

IDENTIFICATION OF STUDENTS WITH DISABILITIES

Various terms are used to refer to children with special learning needs. When the term *exceptional* is used to describe students, it includes children who have difficulty learning and children whose performance is advanced. The performance of exceptional children differs from the norm (either above or below) to such an extent that individualized programs of special education are necessary to meet their diverse needs. *Exceptional* is an inclusive term that describes not only students with severe disabilities but also those who are gifted and talented. This chapter focuses on children with disabilities—students for whom learning presents a significant challenge.

The term *disability* refers to the loss or reduced function of a certain body part or organ; *impairment* is often used synonymously with *disability*. A child with a disability cannot perform certain tasks (e.g., walking, speaking, seeing) in the same way that nondisabled children do. A disability does not constitute a handicap, however, unless the disability leads to educational, personal, social, vocational, or other difficulties for the individual. For example, a child with one arm who functions successfully in and out of school without special support or accommodations is not considered handicapped. *Handicap* refers to the challenges a person with a disability experiences when interacting with the physical or social environment. Some disabilities pose a handicap in some environments but not in others. The child with one arm may be handicapped (i.e., disadvantaged) when competing with nondisabled classmates on the playground but experience no handicap in the classroom. Individuals with disabilities also experience handicaps that have nothing to do with their disabilities but instead are the result of negative attitudes and inappropriate behavior of others who needlessly restrict their access and ability to participate fully in school, work, or community activities.

Children who are not currently identified as handicapped but are considered to have a higher-than-normal chance of developing a disability are referred to as *at risk*. This term is used with infants and preschoolers who, because of difficulties experienced at birth or conditions in the home environment, may be expected to have developmental problems as they grow older. Some educators also use the term to refer to students who are having learning problems in the regular classroom and are therefore "at risk" of being identified as disabled and in need of special education services. Physicians also use the terms *at risk* or *high risk* to identify pregnancies in which there is a higher than usual probability that the babies will be born with a physical or developmental disability.

A physical, behavioral, or cognitive disability is considered a handicap when it adversely affects a student's educational performance. Students with disabilities are entitled to special education because their physical or behavioral attributes conform to one or more of the following categories of disability:

- Mental retardation (developmental disabilities) (Beirne-Smith, Patton, & Kim, 2006)
- Learning disabilities (Mercer & Pullen, 2009)
- Emotional or behavioral disorders (Kauffman & Landrum, 2009)
- Communication (speech and language) disorders (Anderson & Shames, 2006)
- Hearing impairments (Andrews, Leigh, & Weiner, 2004)
- Visual impairments (LaVenture, 2007)
- Physical and health impairments (Heller, Forney, Alberto, Best, & Schwartzman, 2009)
- Autism (Webber & Scheuermann, 2008)
- Traumatic brain injury (Heller et al., 2009)
- Multiple disabilities (Snell & Brown, 2006)

Regardless of the terms used to refer to students who exhibit diversity in academic, vocational, and social skills, it is incorrect to believe that there are two distinct kinds of students: those who are typical and those with disabilities. All children differ from one another to some extent. Students with disabilities are those whose skill diversity is significant enough to require a specially designed program of instruction in order to achieve educational equality. Students with disabilities are more like other students than they are different from them. All students are alike in that they can benefit from an appropriate education that enables them to do things they were previously unable to do and to do these things with greater independence and enjoyment.

Is Disability a Social Construct?

The proposition that some (perhaps all) disabilities are social constructs merits attention in any discussion of educational equity for exceptional children (Danforth, 1995; Elkind, 1998; Smith, 1999; Smith & Mitchell, 2001). This issue is particularly relevant to a text about multicultural education (Huebner, 1994). The establishment of membership criteria in any group is by definition socially constructed because the criteria have been created by human beings (Banks, 2006). How educational communities respond to the cultural-, ethnic-, gender-, and class-specific attributes children bring to the classroom is more important than how they perceive the establishment of membership criteria for a particular group. Education's response to the diversity that children represent will influence their achievement as well as the professional and societal judgments about that achievement. There is evidence that some children's "disabilities" are primarily the result of culture, class, or gender influences that are at odds with the culture, class, or gender that has established a given category of disability and the assessment procedures used to make those determinations (Gollnick & Chinn, 2009). As is discussed later in this chapter, a significant focus of special education litigation and legislation has been directed on these inequities. Deconstructing the traditional sociopolitical view of exceptionality, changing social group membership, or passing legislation will not, however, eliminate the real challenges students with disabilities experience in acquiring fundamental academic, self-help, personal-social, and vocational skills. While the criteria for determining the presence or absence of a disability may be hypothetical social constructions, the handicaps created by educational disabilities are not (Fuchs & Fuchs, 1995; Heward, 2009; Kauffman, 1999; Sugai, 1998).

Be wary of the conception that disabilities are merely socially constructed phenomena. School-age learners with disabilities—those who have pronounced difficulty acquiring and generalizing new knowledge and skills—are real children with real needs in real classrooms. The notion that all children who are identified as disabled would achieve success and behave well if others simply viewed them more positively is romantic ideology seldom promoted by individuals with disabilities themselves or by their parents and families.

Our discussion of students with disabilities and special education's role in addressing their needs assumes that a child's physical, behavioral, or cognitive skill diversity is influenced by, but also transcends, other variables such as ethnicity, gender, and social class. We also assume that the educational challenges students with disabilities experience represent real and significant barriers to their ability to experience independence and personal satisfaction across a wide range of life experiences and circumstances. Many factors contribute to educational equality for children with disabilities. Among the most important of these factors is carefully planned and systematically delivered instruction with meaningful curricula and future-oriented learning objectives (Heward & Dardig, 2001).

How Many Students with Disabilities Are There?

The most complete and systematic information about the number of students with disabilities in the United States is found in the U.S. Department of Education's child count data. The most recent information available is for the 2006–2007 school year (U.S. Department of Education, 2007):

- More than 6 million children with disabilities from birth to age 21 received special education services during the 2006–2007 school year.
- The number of children and youth who receive special education has increased every year since 1997.
- Children with disabilities in special education represent approximately 9.1 percent of the entire school-age population.
- About twice as many males as females receive special education.
- The vast majority—approximately 80 percent—of school-age children receiving special education have mild to moderate disabilities such as learning disabilities (44.6 percent), speech and language impairment (19.1 percent), mental retardation (8.6 percent), and emotional disturbance (7.5 percent) (see Table 13.1).

Table 13.1   Number of Students Ages 6–21 Who Received Special Education Services Under the Federal Government's Disability Categories (2006–2007 School Year)

Disability Category	Number	Percent of Total
Specific learning disabilities	2,710,476	44.6
Speech or language impairments	1,160,904	19.1
Other health impairments	599,494	9.9
Mental retardation	523,240	8.6
Emotional disturbance	458,881	7.5
Autism	224,594	3.7
Multiple disabilities	134,189	2.2
Developmental delay	83,931	1.4
Hearing impairments	72,559	1.2
Orthopedic impairments	61,866	1.0
Visual impairments	26,352	0.4
Traumatic brain injury	23,932	0.4
Deaf-blindness	1,472	<0.1
All disabilities	6,081,890	100.0

Source: U.S. Department of Education. (2007). *Individuals with Disabilities Education Act (IDEA)* (Table 1-3). Washington, DC: Author. Available at https://www.ideadata.org/PartBReport.asp

How Are Students with Disabilities Classified?

The classification and labeling of exceptional students have been widely debated for many years. Some educators believe the classification and labeling of exceptional students serve only to stigmatize and exclude them from the mainstream of educational opportunities (Danforth & Rhodes, 1997; Harry & Klingner, 2007; Kliewer & Biklen, 1996; Reschly, 1996). Others argue that a workable system of classification is necessary to obtain the special educational services and programs that are prerequisite to educational equality for exceptional students (Kauffman, 1999; Kauffman & Konold, 2007; Keogh, 2005a, 2005b). Like most complex questions, there are valid perspectives on both sides of the labeling issue, with political, ethical, and emotional concerns competing with educational, scientific, and fiscal considerations (Florian et al., 2006; McLaughlin et al., 2006). Common arguments for labeling students with exceptional learning needs are that labels aid in communication, including visibility and advocacy efforts that are needed to facilitate the structure of funding and resources for research and programs. The most common arguments against labeling students with exceptional learning needs involve the expense of labeling students and the impact of the label, such as the focus on deficits, impact on the child's self-esteem, low expectations held by others, and permanence of the label.

Research conducted to assess the effects of labeling has been of little help; most of the studies contribute inconclusive, often contradictory, evidence. Two important issues are how the use of categorical labels affects a child's access to special education services and the quality of instruction that the child receives as a result of classification.

What Determines Eligibility for Special Education?

A student must first be identified as having a disability to receive an individualized program of special educational services to meet that student's needs under current law. The student must be labeled and further classified into one of the categories, such as learning disabilities or visual impairment. So, in practice, membership in a given disability category and the corresponding exposure to the potential disadvantages associated with the label is a prerequisite to receiving the special education services necessary to achieve educational equality.

Kauffman (1999) points out the reality of labels as a necessary first step in serving students with important differences in behavior and learning: "Although universal interventions that apply equally to all, regardless of their behavioral characteristics or risks of developing disorders, can be implemented without labels and risk of stigma, no other interventions are possible without labels. Either all students are treated the same or some are treated differently. Any student who is treated differently is inevitably labeled" (p. 452).

How Does Classification Impact Instruction?

The classification of students according to the various categories of exceptionality is made largely under the presumption that students in each category share certain physical, behavioral, and learning characteristics that hold important implications for planning and delivering educational services. It is a mistake, however, to believe that once identified by a certain disability category, a child's educational needs and the manner in which those needs should be met have also been identified. Although it was written nearly four decades ago, this statement by Becker, Engelmann, and Thomas (1971) is still pertinent today: "For the most part the labels are not important. They rarely tell the teacher who can be taught in what way. One could put five or six labels on the same child and still not know what to teach him or how" (p. 436).

HISTORY OF EDUCATIONAL EQUALITY FOR STUDENTS WITH DISABILITIES

If a society can be judged by the way it treats people who are different, the U.S. educational system does not have a distinguished history. Students who are different, whether because of race, culture, language, gender, or disability, have often been denied equal access to educational opportunities. For many years, educational opportunity of any kind did not exist for many students with disabilities. Students with severe disabilities were completely excluded from public schools. Before 1970, many states had laws allowing local school districts to deny access to children whose physical or intellectual disability caused them, in the opinion of school officials, to be unable to benefit from instruction (Murdick, Gartin, & Crabtree, 2006).

Although students with disabilities were enrolled in school, perhaps half of the children with disabilities in the United States were denied an appropriate education through "functional exclusion." They were allowed to come to school but were not participating in an educational program designed to meet their special needs. Students with mild learning and behavior problems remained in the regular classroom but received no special help. If they failed to make satisfactory progress in the curriculum, they were called "slow learners"; if they acted out in class, they were called "disciplinary problems" and were suspended from school (Turnbull, Stowe, & Huerta, 2007).

For students who did receive a program of differentiated curriculum or instruction, special education usually meant a separate education in segregated classrooms and special schools isolated from the mainstream of education. Special education for those students with disabilities often meant a classroom especially reserved for students who could not measure up in the regular classroom. The following passage exemplified what was too often a common occurrence:

> I accepted my first teaching position in a special education class in a basement room next door to the furnace. Of the fifteen "educable mentally retarded" children assigned to work with me, most were simply nonreaders from poor families. One child had been banished to my room because she posed a behavior problem to her fourth-grade teacher. My class and I were assigned a recess spot on the opposite side of the play yard, far away from the "normal" children. I was the only teacher who did not have a lunch break. I was required to eat with my "retarded" children while the other teachers were permitted to leave their students. (Aiello, 1976, p. 14)

As society's concepts of equality, freedom, and justice have expanded, education's response to students with disabilities has changed slowly but considerably over the past several decades. Educational opportunity has gradually shifted from a pattern of exclusion and isolation to one of integration and participation. But change has not come easily, nor has it occurred by chance. Judiciary and legislative authority has been necessary to begin to correct educational inequities for children with disabilities. Recent efforts to ensure educational equality for students with disabilities can be viewed as an outgrowth of the Civil Rights Movement. All of the issues and events that helped shape society's attitudes during the 1950s and 1960s affected the development of special education, particularly the 1954 landmark case of *Brown* v. *Board of Education of Topeka*. This case challenged the common practice at the time of segregating schools according to the race of the children. The U.S. Supreme Court ruled that education must be available to all children on equal terms and that it is unconstitutional to operate segregated schools under the premise that they are separate but equal.

The *Brown* decision that public school education should be provided to African American and White children on equal terms initiated a period of intense questioning by parents of children with disabilities who wondered why the same principles of equal access to education did not also apply to their children. Numerous cases challenging the exclusion and isolation of children with disabilities by the schools were brought to court by parents and advocacy groups. One of the most influential court cases in the development of educational equality for exceptional students was *Pennsylvania Association for Retarded Children (PARC)* v. *Commonwealth of Pennsylvania* (1972). PARC brought the class action suit to challenge a state law that enabled public schools to deny education to children they considered unable to benefit from attending public school.

The attorneys and parents who represented PARC argued that it was neither rational nor necessary to assume that the children were uneducable. Because the state could neither prove that the children were uneducable nor demonstrate a rational basis for excluding them from public school programs, the court decided that the children were entitled to a free public education. Other court cases followed with similar rulings: Children with disabilities, like all other people in the United States, are entitled to the same rights and protection under the law as guaranteed in the Fourteenth Amendment, which declares that people may not be deprived of their equality or liberty on the basis of any classification such as race, nationality, or religion (for a summary of these court cases, see Heward, 2009).

The term *progressive integration* (Reynolds, 1989) has been used to describe the history of special education and the gradual but unrelenting progress of ensuring equal educational opportunity for all children. Of the many court cases involving education for children with disabilities, no single case resulted in sweeping educational reform. With each instance of litigation, however, the assembly of what was to become the Individuals with Disabilities Education Act became more complete. Together, all of these developments contributed to the passage of a federal law concerning educational equality for students with disabilities.

THE INDIVIDUALS WITH DISABILITIES ACT: A LEGISLATIVE MANDATE FOR EDUCATIONAL EQUALITY FOR STUDENTS WITH DISABILITIES

In 1975 Congress passed the Education for All Handicapped Children Act (P.L. 94–142). Since it became law in 1975, Congress has reauthorized and amended P.L. 94–142 five times, most recently in 2004. The 1990 amendments renamed the law the Individuals with Disabilities Education Act—often referred to by its acronym, IDEA.

IDEA is a landmark piece of legislation that has changed the face of education in the United States. IDEA has affected every school in the country and has changed the roles of regular and special educators, school administrators, parents, and many other people involved in the educational process. Its passage marked the culmination of the efforts of a great many educators, parents, and legislators to bring together in one comprehensive bill U.S. laws regarding the education of children with disabilities. The law reflects society's concern for treating people with disabilities as full citizens with the same rights and privileges that all other citizens enjoy. The purpose of IDEA is to ensure the rights of students with disabilities to a free appropriate public education, including early intervention services, and to provide the necessary supports and oversight for states, districts, schools, and educators to improve the educational results for students with disabilities (PL 108–466, Sec. 601(d)).

Major Principles of the Individuals with Disabilities Education Act

IDEA is directed primarily at the states, which are responsible for providing education to their residents. The majority of the many rules and regulations defining how IDEA operates are related to six major principles that have remained unchanged since 1975 (Smith, 2005; Turnbull et al., 2007).

Zero Reject

Schools must educate *all* children with disabilities. The zero reject principle applies regardless of the nature or severity of the disability; no child with disabilities may be excluded from a public education. This requirement of the law is based on the proposition that all children with disabilities can learn and benefit from an appropriate education and that schools, therefore, do not have the right to deny any child access to equal educational opportunity. Each state education agency is responsible for locating, identifying, and evaluating all children, from birth to age 21, residing in the state who have disabilities or are suspected of having disabilities. This requirement is called the *child find system* (PL 108–466, Sec. 303.321).

Nondiscriminatory Identification and Evaluation

IDEA requires that students with disabilities be evaluated fairly. The school or parents can request that a child be evaluated for special education. If the school initiates the evaluation, parents must be notified and consent to it, which for special education must be completed within 60 days of receiving parental consent. Assessment must be nondiscriminatory. This requirement is particularly important because of the disproportionate number of children from non-White and non-English-speaking cultural groups who are identified as having disabilities, often solely on the basis of a score from standardized intelligence tests. The intelligence tests that have been used most often in the identification of students with learning problems were developed based on the performance of White, middle-class children. Because of their Anglo-centric nature, the tests are often considered to be unfairly biased against children from diverse cultural groups who have had less opportunity to learn the knowledge sampled by the test items (Venn, 2007). In addition to nondiscriminatory assessment, testing must be multifactored to include as many tests and observational techniques as necessary to fairly and appropriately identify an individual child's strengths and weaknesses. The results of a single test cannot be used as the sole criterion for placement into a special education program.

Free, Appropriate Public Education

All children with disabilities, regardless of the type or severity of their disability, shall receive a free, appropriate public education. This education must be provided at public expense—that is, without cost to the child's parents. An *individualized education program* (IEP) must be developed and implemented for each child with a disability (PL 108–466, Sec. 614 [d][1][A]). IDEA is specific in identifying the kinds of information an IEP must include and who is to participate in its development. Each IEP must be created by an *IEP team* consisting of (at least) the child's parents (or guardians); at least one regular education teacher of the child; at least one special education teacher; a representative of the local school district who is qualified to provide or supervise specially designed instruction and is knowledgeable of the general curriculum and about the resources of the local education agencies; an individual who can interpret the instructional implications of evaluation results and other individuals who have knowledge of the child (at discretion of the parent or the school); and whenever appropriate, the child (PL 108–466, Sec. 614 [d][1][B]). Many IEP teams also include professionals from various disciplines such as school psychology, physical therapy, and medicine.

The IEP is the foundation of the special education and related services a child with a disability receives. A carefully and collaboratively prepared IEP specifies the skills the child needs to learn in relation to the present levels of performance, the procedures that will be used to bring about that learning, and the means of determining the extent to which learning has taken place (Bateman & Linden, 2006). Essentially, the IEP spells out where the child is, where he or she should be going, how he or she will get there, how long it will take, and how to tell when he or she has arrived. Although the IEP is a written document signed by both school personnel and the child's parents, it is not a legal document in the sense that parents cannot take their child's teachers or school to court if all goals and objectives stated in the IEP are not met. However, schools must be able to document that the services described in the IEP have been provided in a systematic effort to meet those goals (Bartlett, Etscheidt, & Weisentstein, 2007; Wright & Wright, 2006). IEPs must be reviewed by the IEP team at least annually.

Including all of the mandated components in an IEP is no guarantee that the document will guide the student's learning and the teacher's teaching in the classroom as intended by IDEA. Although most educators agree with the idealized concept of the IEP, inspection and evaluation of IEPs often reveal inconsistency between what is written on the document and what students experience in the classroom (e.g., Bateman & Linden, 2006; Grigal, Test, Beattie, & Wood, 1997; Smith & Brownell, 1995).

Least Restrictive Environment

IDEA mandates that students with disabilities be educated in the *least restrictive environment* (LRE). Specifically, the law states that:

> to the maximum extent appropriate, children with disabilities, including children in public or private institutions or other care facilities, [will be] educated with children who are not disabled, and that special classes, separate schooling or other removal of children with disabilities from the regular educational environment [may occur] only when the nature or severity of the disability is such that education in regular classes with the use of supplementary aids and services cannot be achieved satisfactorily. (PL 108–446, Sec. 612 [a][5][A])

The LRE requirement continues to be one of the most controversial and least understood aspects of IDEA. During the first few years after the passage of IDEA, some professionals and parents erroneously interpreted the law to mean that every child with disabilities, regardless of type or severity, had to be placed in a general education classroom. Instead, the LRE component of IDEA requires that each child with a disability be educated in a setting that most closely resembles a regular class placement in which his or her individual needs can be met. Although some people argue that any decision to place a child with a disability in a special class or school is inappropriate, most educators and parents realize that placement in a regular classroom can be overly restrictive if the child's academic and social needs are not met. LRE is a relative concept; the least restrictive environment for one student with a disability would not necessarily be appropriate for another. Therefore, two students who have the same disability should not necessarily be placed in the same setting.

Children with disabilities need a wide range of special education and related services. Today, most schools provide a *continuum of services*—that is, a range of placement and service options to meet the individual needs of students with disabilities. The continuum can be depicted symbolically as a pyramid, with placements ranging from least restrictive (regular classroom placement without special supports) at the bottom to most restrictive (special schools, residential programs, and hospital or homebound programs) at the top (see Figure 13.1). Typically, the

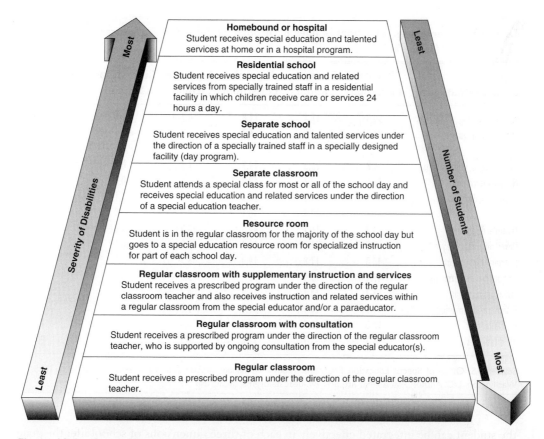

Homebound or hospital
Student receives special education and talented services at home or in a hospital program.

Residential school
Student receives special education and related services from specially trained staff in a residential facility in which children receive care or services 24 hours a day.

Separate school
Student receives special education and talented services under the direction of a specially trained staff in a specially designed facility (day program).

Separate classroom
Student attends a special class for most or all of the school day and receives special education and related services under the direction of a special education teacher.

Resource room
Student is in the regular classroom for the majority of the school day but goes to a special education resource room for specialized instruction for part of each school day.

Regular classroom with supplementary instruction and services
Student receives a prescribed program under the direction of the regular classroom teacher and also receives instruction and related services within a regular classroom from the special educator and/or a paraeducator.

Regular classroom with consultation
Student receives a prescribed program under the direction of the regular classroom teacher, who is supported by ongoing consultation from the special educator(s).

Regular classroom
Student receives a prescribed program under the direction of the regular classroom teacher.

Figure 13.1   Continuum of Educational Placements for Students with Disabilities

Source: From W. L. Heward.(2006). *Exceptional Children: An Introduction to Special Education* (8th ed., p. 78). Upper Saddle River, NJ: Merrill/Prentice-Hall. Used by permission.

more severe a child's disability, the greater is the need for more intensive and specialized services. As noted, however, the majority of students who receive special education services have mild disabilities; hence, the pyramid's progressively smaller size at the top shows that more restrictive settings are required for fewer students.

Approximately three of four students with disabilities receive at least part of their education in regular classrooms with their nondisabled peers. Many of these students, however, spend part of each school day in a resource room where they receive individualized instruction from a specially trained teacher. Approximately one of every five students with disabilities is educated in a separate classroom in a regular public school. Special schools and residential facilities provide the education for less than four percent of children with disabilities, usually students with the most severe disabilities (see Table 13.2).

Placement of a student with disabilities should not be viewed as all or nothing at any one level on the continuum or as permanent. IDEA instructs the IEP team to consider the extent to which

Table 13.2   Percentage of Students Ages 6 Through 21 Served in Six Educational Environments (2006–2007 school year)

Disability Category	Regular Classroom	Resource Room	Separate Classroom	Separate School	Residential School	Homebound or Hospital
Specific learning disabilities	54.8	31.4	11.8	0.7	0.1	0.2
Speech or language impairments	84.2	6.1	6.7	0.3	<0.1	<0.1
Other health impairments	54.8	26.5	14.9	1.6	0.2	1.0
Mental retardation	15.9	28.7	48.4	5.6	0.4	0.5
Emotional disturbance	35.1	20.8	26.6	12.3	2.1	1.2
Autism	32.3	18.4	38.7	9.0	0.7	0.3
Multiple disabilities	13.4	16.7	44.5	20.5	2.0	2.3
Developmental delay	58.9	21.2	18.4	0.8	0.1	0.2
Hearing impairments	48.8	17.8	19.8	8.2	4.2	0.2
Orthopedic impairments	47.1	19.0	26.3	5.3	0.2	1.4
Visual impairments	57.2	14.7	15.9	6.3	4.4	0.5
Traumatic brain injury	41.7	26.1	23.7	5.7	0.6	1.4
Deaf-blindness	20.8	13.4	35.4	20.5	7.5	1.8
All disabilities	53.7	23.7	17.6	2.9	0.4	0.4

Source: U.S. Office of Special Education Programs. (2007). *Individuals with Disabilities Education Act* (IDEA) (Table 2-2c). Washington, DC: Author. Available at http://www.ideadata.org/PartBdata.asp

the student can be integrated effectively in each of three dimensions of school life: the general academic curriculum, extracurricular activities (e.g., clubs), and other school activities (e.g., recess, mealtimes). The LRE "provision allows for a 'mix and match' where total integration is appropriate under one dimension and partial integration is appropriate under another dimension" (Turnbull & Cilley, 1999, p. 41). The continuum concept is intended to be flexible, with students moving from one placement to another as dictated by their individual educational needs. The IEP team should periodically review the specific goals and objectives for each child—it is required to do so at least annually—and make new placement decisions if warranted.

Neither IDEA nor the regulations that accompany it specify exactly how a school district is to determine LRE. After reviewing the rulings on litigation in four LRE suits that have reached the U.S. courts of appeals, Yell (2006) concluded that the courts have held that IDEA does not require the placement of students with disabilities in the regular classroom but fully supports the continuum of services.

Although the continuum-of-services model represents well-established practice in special education, it is not without controversy. A number of specific criticisms have been leveled at this approach to providing services to exceptional students. Some critics have argued that the continuum overly legitimizes the use of restrictive placements, implies that integration of persons with disabilities can take place only in least restrictive settings, and may infringe on the rights of people with disabilities to participate in their communities (e.g., Taylor, 1988).

The relative value of providing special education services to students with disabilities outside the regular classroom—especially in separate classrooms and schools—has been a hotly contested issue for many years (e.g., Giangreco, 2007; Kauffman & Hallahan, 2005; Mitchell, 2004a, 2004b; Schwartz, 2005; Taylor, 1988; Zigmond, 2006). Virtually all special educators, however, support the responsible inclusion of students with disabilities in which systematic modifications in curriculum and instruction enable meaningful progress toward IEP goals (Kochhar-Bryant, 2008; Schwartz, 2005; Vaughn, Schumm, & Brick, 1998).

Due Process Safeguards

IDEA acknowledges that students with disabilities are people with important legal rights. The law makes it clear that school districts do not have absolute authority over exceptional students. Schools may not make decisions about the educational programs of children with disabilities in a unilateral or arbitrary manner.

Due process is a legal concept that is implemented through a series of procedural steps designed to ensure fairness of treatment among school systems, parents, and students. Specific due process safeguards were incorporated into IDEA because of past educational abuses of children with disabilities. In the past, special education placements were often permanent, void of periodic reviews, and made solely on the basis of teacher recommendations. Furthermore, students with severe and profound disabilities were automatically excluded from public school programs and placed in residential programs where the quality of instructional programs often was very poor. The fact that children from minority cultural groups were disproportionately placed into special education programs was another factor in mandating the due process procedures.

Key elements of due process as it relates to special education are the parents' right to the following:

- Be notified in writing before the school takes any action that may alter the child's program (testing, reevaluation, change in placement)
- Give or withhold permission to have their child tested for eligibility for special education services, reevaluated, or placed in a different classroom or program
- See all school records about their child
- Have a hearing before an impartial party (not an employee of the school district) to resolve disagreements with the school system
- Receive a written decision following any hearing
- Appeal the results of a due process hearing to the state department of education (school districts may also appeal)

Parent and Student Participation and Shared Decision Making

IDEA recognizes the benefits of active parent and student participation. Parents not only have a right to be involved in their child's education but also can help professionals select appropriate instructional goals and provide information that will help teachers be more effective in working with their children. As noted, parents (and, whenever appropriate, students) are to take an active role as full members of the IEP team; their input and wishes must be considered in determining IEP goals and objectives, placement decisions, and related services needs (e.g., sign language interpreting, special transportation). Of course, parents cannot be forced to do so and may waive their right to participate.

SECTION 504 OF THE REHABILITATION ACT OF 1973

Another important law that extends civil rights to people with disabilities is Section 504 of the Rehabilitation Act of 1973 (PL 93–112). This regulation states, in part, that "no otherwise qualified handicapped individual shall, solely by reason of his handicap, be excluded from the participation in, be denied the benefits of, or be subjected to discrimination in any program or activity receiving federal financial assistance" (U.S.C. § 794(a)). This law, worded almost identically to the Civil Rights Act of 1964 (which prohibited discrimination based on race, color, or national origin), promises to expand opportunities to children and adults with disabilities in education, employment, and various other settings. It calls for the provision of "auxiliary aides for students with impaired sensory, manual, or speaking skills" (e.g., interpreters for students who are deaf) and architectural accessibility (U.S.C. § 794(a)). This requirement does not mean that schools, colleges, and employers must have *all* such aides available at *all* times or a completely barrier-free environment; it simply mandates that no person with disabilities may be excluded from a program because of the lack of an appropriate aide or accessibility to programs.

THE AMERICANS WITH DIABILITIES ACT

The Americans with Disabilities Act (PL 101–336) was signed into law on July 26, 1990. Patterned after Section 504 of the Rehabilitation Act of 1973, the Americans with Disabilities Act (ADA) extends civil rights protection to persons with disabilities in private sector employment, in all public services, and in public accommodations, transportation, and telecommunications. ADA requires that public accommodations, including school buildings, athletic stadiums, and school transportation, be accessible to students with disabilities.

THE NO CHILD LEFT BEHIND ACT

Another landmark piece of federal legislation that affects students with disabilities is the Elementary and Secondary Education Act of 2001, which was later renamed the No Child Left Behind Act (NCLB) (PL 107–110). The intended purpose of NCLB is to improve the academic achievement of all children, particularly those from low-income families (Cortiella, 2006). The ultimate goal of NCLB is for all children to be proficient in reading and math by 2014. All children are to be taught by teachers who are highly qualified in their subjects and use curriculum and instructional methods validated by rigorous scientific research. The emphasis on scientifically proven curriculum and instruction offers the promise of effective instruction in the early grades, which could reduce the number of children who require special education in particular because of reading problems. In addition, schools that do not make adequate yearly progress toward achieving state goals for test scores, including those scores of students with disabilities, are initially targeted for assistance and then subject to corrective action and ultimately restructuring.

EDUCATIONAL EQUALITY FOR STUDENTS WITH DISABILITIES: PROGRESS MADE BUT CHALLENGES REMAIN

What impact has IDEA had? The most obvious effect is that students with disabilities are receiving special education and related services that before the law's passage were not available. But access to education is what the law requires and is only one aspect of its impact. Since the passage of IDEA, there has been a dramatic increase in the number of both special education teachers and support staff. Perhaps the law has had its most dramatic effect on students with severe disabilities, many of whom had been completely denied the opportunity to benefit from an appropriate education. No longer can schools exclude students with disabilities on the premise that they are uneducable. IDEA is based on the presumption that all students can benefit from an appropriate education, and it states clearly that the local school has the responsibility to modify curriculum content and teaching methods according to the needs of each student. In essence, the law requires schools to adapt themselves to the needs of students rather than allowing schools to deny educational equality to students whose characteristics are inconsistent with traditional school norms and expectations.

IDEA has contributed positively to the education of students with disabilities, but significant barriers remain to full educational equality for exceptional students in the United States. We briefly examine five of these issues. If a truly appropriate educational opportunity is to be a reality for students with disabilities, U.S. schools must (1) bridge the research-to-practice gap with regard to effective instruction, (2) improve cooperation and collaboration between special and regular educators, (3) provide more and better early intervention programs for young children with disabilities, (4) increase the success of young adults with disabilities as they make the transition from school to adult life, and (5) ensure relevant, individualized education to students with disabilities from culturally and linguistically diverse backgrounds.

Effective Instruction

IDEA's mandates for multifactored evaluations, IEPs, due process, and placement in the least restrictive environment have enhanced the educational equality for students with disabilities. None of these mandated processes, however, teaches. True educational equality for children with disabilities can be achieved only through effective instruction (Heward & Dardig, 2001).

Properly implemented, special education is not a slowed-down, watered-down version of general education. Special education is a systematic, purposeful approach to teaching students with disabilities the academic, social, vocational, and personal skills they will need to live independent, satisfying, and productive lives, and to do it more effectively and efficiently than could be accomplished by general education alone. Effective teaching is much more than simply assigning something to be learned. An important responsibility of all teachers, especially special educators, is ensuring that the instruction they deliver is measurably effective in meeting the needs of their students. When this occurs, the education that students with disabilities receive will be truly special (Heward, 2003).

Special education can be nothing more or less than the quality of instruction provided by teachers. Teachers are ultimately responsible for providing effective instruction to exceptional students. With this responsibility come several obligations. Working collaboratively with their regular education colleagues and parents (Heron & Harris, 2001), special educators must (1) target instructional objectives that will improve the quality of students' lives in school, home, community, and workplace, (2) use research-validated methods of instruction (Lewis, Hudson, Richter, & Johnson, 2004; Lovitt, 2007), (3) continually evaluate the effectiveness of instruction with direct measures of student performance (Greenwood & Maheady, 1997), and (4) change an instructional program when it does not promote achievement and success (Bushell & Baer, 1994).

Teachers must demand effectiveness from their instructional approaches. For many years, conventional wisdom fostered the belief that it takes unending patience to teach children with disabilities. We believe this view is a disservice to students with special needs and to the educators—both special and general education teachers—whose job it is to teach them. Teachers should not wait patiently for exceptional students to learn, attributing lack of progress to some inherent attribute or faulty process within the child, such as mental retardation, learning disability, attention-deficit disorder, or emotional disturbance. Instead, the teacher should use direct and frequent measures of the student's performance as the primary guide for modifying instruction in order to improve its effectiveness. This is the real work of the educator (Heward, 2009).

To increase the likelihood that instruction is effective, special education must bridge the research-to-practice gap regarding instructional practice in the classroom (Carnine, 1997; Deshler, 2005; Gersten, 2001; Heward & Silvestri, 2005; Vaughn, Klingner, & Hughes, 2000). Contrary to the contentions of some, special education research has produced a significant and reliable knowledge base about effective teaching practices (Coyne, Kame'enui, & Carnine, 2007; Lovitt, 2007; Vaughn, Gersten, & Chard, 2000). While there is a significant gap between what is relatively well understood and what is poorly understood or not understood at all, the more distressing gap may be between what research has discovered about teaching and learning and what is practiced in many classrooms. For example, scientific research has helped us discover a great deal about the features of early reading instruction that can reduce the number of children who later develop reading problems (Kame'enui, Good, & Harn, 2005; National Reading Panel, 2000), how to enhance the success of students with learning disabilities in content-area classes (Bulgren, 2006), and the components of secondary special education programs that can increase students' success in making the transition from school to work (Test, Aspel, & Everson, 2006), but the education that many students with disabilities receive does not reflect that knowledge (Heward, 2003; Moody, Vaughn, Hughes, & Fischer, 2000; Mostert, Kavale, & Kauffman, 2008; Wehby, Symons, Canale, & Go, 1998; Zigmond, 2007).

REGULAR AND SPECIAL EDUCATION PARTNERSHIP

Traditionally, regular and special education have been viewed as separate disciplines, each serving a different student population. Today, the concepts of "your kids" and "my kids" are gradually being replaced by that of "our kids," and general and special education teachers are becoming partners in meeting the needs of all learners.

Mainstreaming has traditionally been thought of as the process of integrating students with disabilities into regular schools and classes. Today, the term *inclusive education* is changing not only the language of special education reform but also its intent (see Chapter 14, this volume). Inclusive education can be successful only with full cooperation of and collaboration among those people responsible for the educational programs of students with disabilities (Smith, Polloway, Patton, & Dowdy, 2008). Although IDEA does not specifically mention mainstreaming or inclusion, it creates a presumption in favor of regular classroom placement by requiring that educational services be provided in the least restrictive environment, which in turn necessitates cooperation between general and special educators.

The effects of IDEA on general education are neither entirely clear nor without controversy. This dissonance is further complicated by the tone and content of many discussions about how special education can or should reform while ensuring that the best interests of students with disabilities are appropriately served (Finn, Rotherham, & Hokanson, 2001; Gallagher, Heshusius, Iano, & Skrtic, 2004). What is clear, however, is that the entire educational community has the responsibility to do the best job it can in meeting the needs of children with diverse skills. In the final analysis, issues of labeling, classifying, placing, and teaching assignments are secondary to the quality of instruction that takes place in the classroom (Heward & Dardig, 2001).

Improved collaboration between special education and general education is important not only for the 9 to 12 percent of school-age children with disabilities who receive special education but also for the estimated additional 10 to 20 percent of the student population who are struggling learners. An increasingly utilized system of early intervention for students whose performance suggests they are at risk for school failure is *response to intervention* (RTI). The Individuals with Disabilities Education Improvement Act of 2004 (PL 108–446) also allows local education agencies to use RTI to identify students with learning disabilities. When implemented properly, RTI embodies scientific, research-based interventions in tiers of intensity and frequent progress monitoring to make instructional decisions and determine whether a student has learning disabilities. Most of this process occurs in general education. The authorization of this new method emphasizes the increasing importance of the collaboration between general education and special education. Both special and regular educators must develop strategies for working together and sharing their skills and resources to prevent these millions of students, who are at risk, from becoming failures of our educational system.

EARLY INTERVENTION

The years from birth to school age are critical to a child's learning and development. The typical child enters school with a large repertoire of cognitive, language, social, and physical skills on which to build. For many children with disabilities, unfortunately, the preschool years represent a long period of missed opportunities. Without systematic instruction, most young children with disabilities do not acquire many of the skills their nondisabled peers seemingly learn without effort. Parents concerned about their child's inability to reach important developmental milestones have often been told by professionals, "Don't worry. Your child will grow out of it before too long." In truth, without early intervention, many children with disabilities fall further and further behind their nondisabled peers, and minor delays in development often become major delays by the time the child reaches school age.

More than twenty-five years ago, there were very few early intervention programs for children with disabilities from birth to school age; today, early childhood special education is the fastest-growing area in the field of education. As with special education of school-age exceptional students, federal legislation has played a major role in the development of early intervention programs (Shonkoff & Meisels, 2000). By passing Public Law 99–457, the Education of the Handicapped Act Amendments of 1986, Congress reaffirmed the basic principles of the original PL 94–142 and added two major sections concerning early intervention services.

PL 99–457 required each state to show evidence of serving all three- to five-year-old children with disabilities in order to receive any preschool funds. The second major change brought about by PL 99–457 is the availability of incentive grants to states for developing systems of early identification and intervention for infants and toddlers with disabilities from birth to age two. The services must be planned by a multidisciplinary team that includes the child's parents and must be implemented according to an *individualized family services plan (IFSP)* that is similar in concept to the IEP for school-age students with disabilities (PL 108–466, Sec. 636).

Researchers realize the critical importance of early intervention for both children who are at risk and those who have been diagnosed with a disability, and most agree that the earlier intervention is begun, the better (Guralnick, 1997; Sandall, Hemmeter, McLean, & Smith, 2005). Fortunately, many educators are working to develop the programs and services so desperately needed by the increasing numbers of babies and preschoolers who have been or are at risk for developing disabilities (Cook, Klein, & Tessier, 2008). Early intervention is necessary to give these children a fighting chance to experience educational equality when they enter school.

TRANSITION FROM SCHOOL TO ADULT LIFE

If the degree of educational equality afforded to students with disabilities is to be judged, as we think it should be—by the extent to which students with disabilities can function independently in everyday environments—then special education still has a long way to go. For example, while data from the National Longitudinal Transition Study-2 (NLTS2) show that a majority of youths with disabilities have had part-time employment and completed high school, only 15 percent live independently and 32 percent have participated in postsecondary education (Wagner, Newman, Cameto, & Levine, 2005).

Education cannot be held responsible for all of the difficulties adults with disabilities face, but the results of this and other studies make it evident that many young people leave public school special education programs without the skills necessary to function in the community. Many youths with disabilities find all aspects of adult life a challenge (Flexer, Baer, Luft, & Simmons, 2008; Tymchuk, Lakin, & Luckasson, 2001). Many educators today see the development of special education programs that will effectively prepare exceptional students for adjustment and successful integration into the adult community as the ultimate measure of educational equality for students with disabilities (Ferguson & Ferguson, 2006; Test et al., 2006).

SPECIAL EDUCATION IN A DIVERSE SOCIETY

Both special and general educators face major challenges in providing relevant, individualized education to students with disabilities from culturally diverse backgrounds. Many students with disabilities experience discrimination or inadequate educational programs because their race,

Table 13.3   Racial/Ethnic Composition (Percentage) of Students Ages 6 Through 21 Served According to Disability (2006–2007 School Year)

Disability Category	American Indian/Alaskan	Asian/Pacific Islander	African American (not Hispanic)	Hispanic	White (not Hispanic)
Specific learning disabilities	1.7	1.7	20.1	22.7	53.7
Speech or language impairments	1.3	3.1	15.2	18.7	61.6
Other health impairments	1.2	1.5	17.3	10.5	69.5
Mental retardation	1.25	2.1	32.0	16.0	48.6
Emotional disturbance	1.6	1.1	28.7	11.3	57.3
Autism	0.7	5.4	14.3	12.0	67.6
Multiple disabilities	1.4	2.8	20.7	14.0	61.2
Developmental delay	3.7	2.7	22.5	9.9	61.3
Hearing impairments	1.2	5.0	16.1	23.6	54.1
Orthopedic impairments	1.0	3.6	14.7	21.6	59.2
Visual impairments	1.3	4.2	16.8	20.1	57.6
Traumatic brain injury	1.6	2.5	16.5	13.4	66.0
Deaf-blindness	1.8	4.8	13.3	21.0	59.0
All disabilities	1.5	2.2	20.3	18.5	57.5
Estimated percentage of resident population	1.0	4.2	15.0	18.5	61.3

Sums may not equal 100 percent because of rounding.
Source: U.S. Office of Special Education Programs. (2007). *Individuals with Disabilities Education Act (IDEA)* (Tables 1-19 and C-8). Washington, DC: Author. Available at http://www.ideadata.org/PartBdata.asp

ethnicity, social class, or gender is different from that of the majority. Students from culturally and linguistically diverse backgrounds are often under- or overrepresented in educational programs for exceptional children (De Valenzuela et al., 2006; Hetzner, 2007; Oswald & Coutinho, 2001).

The 1997–1998 school year was the first time the federal government required states to report the race and ethnicity of students receiving special education. These data continue to show disparities between the distribution of race/ethnicity within the general population and participation in special education, particularly for African American students. Although they constitute about 15 percent of the general school population, African American students make up 32 percent of students classified with mental retardation and 28.7 percent of students with severe emotional disturbance (U.S. Department of Education, 2007) (see Table 13.3).

The fact that culturally diverse students are identified as having disabilities is not in itself a problem. All students with a disability that adversely affects their educational performance have the right to special education services. Disproportionate representation is problematic, however, if students have been wrongly placed in special education, are segregated and stigmatized, or are denied access to needed special education because their disabilities are overlooked as a result of their membership in a racial or ethnic minority group. Although a student's ethnicity or language should never be the basis for inclusion in or exclusion from special education programs, the disproportionate numbers of students from culturally and linguistically diverse backgrounds will require that educators attend to three important issues.

First, the adequacy of assessment and placement procedures must be ensured. Multifactored assessments must be conducted in ways that will be appropriately sensitive to the student's culture and language to ensure that a special education placement is a function of the student's documented needs rather than of biased referral and assessment practices (Utley & Obiakor, 2001).

Second, providing appropriate support services that are responsive to the cultural and linguistic needs of the student may enhance the child's educational program. For example, bilingual aides, in-service training for teachers, and multicultural education for peers may be necessary to ensure that the child's education is meaningful and maximally beneficial.

Third, teachers and other school staff may need to learn about the values and standards of behavior present in the child's home. Because most teachers are White (Cochran-Smith, Feiman-Nemser, & McIntyre, 2008), learning not only to understand but also to respect and appreciate the child's culture as it is reflected in his or her home will be important to understanding the child's behavior in the classroom and in communicating with parents (Tam & Heng, 2005). Good intentions or token attempts at cultural sensitivity, of course, will do little to provide an appropriate IEP for students with disabilities from culturally diverse backgrounds. The instructional materials that educators use and the methods that they employ while teaching must be responsive to the differing cultural backgrounds of their students.

Does this mean that a teacher with students from four different cultural backgrounds needs four different methods of teaching? The answer is both "no" and "yes." For the first answer, it is our view that systematic instruction benefits children from all cultural backgrounds. When students with disabilities must also adjust to a new or different culture or language, it is especially important for the teacher to plan individualized activities, convey expectations clearly, observe and record behavior precisely, and give the child specific, immediate feedback during instruction. When coupled with a respectful attitude, these procedures will increase the motivation and achievement of most students.

Good teachers must also be responsive to changes (or lack of change) in individual students' performance. It can also be argued that the effective teacher needs as many different ways of teaching as there are students in the classroom. Cultural diversity adds another dimension to the many individual characteristics students present each day. While the basic methods of systematic instruction apply to all learners, teachers who will be most effective in helping children with disabilities from culturally diverse backgrounds achieve success in school will be those who are sensitive to and respectful of their students' heritage and values.

SUMMARY

The task of providing educational equality for students with markedly diverse skills is enormous. By embracing the challenge, U.S. schools have made a promise to exceptional students, to their parents, and to society. Progress has been made, but significant challenges must still be overcome if the promise is to be kept. The views of our society are changing and continue to be changed by people who believe that our past practice of excluding people with disabilities was primitive and unfair. As an institution, education reflects society's changing attitudes.

Common expressions of humanity and fair play dictate that all children are entitled to educational equality, but the history of exclusion and inequality for students with disabilities tells us that humanity and fair play have not driven a great deal of educational policy for children with disabilities in the absence of legislation or litigation. While much progress has been made in achieving educational equality for students with disabilities, much work remains to be done.

Educational equality for children with disabilities in the end must be assessed by the effects of the schooling those children receive. If educational equality means simply having access to curriculum and instruction in schools and classrooms attended by students without disabilities, it has largely been attained. But equal access alone does not guarantee equal outcomes. Special education must ultimately be judged by the degree to which it is effective in helping individuals with disabilities to acquire, maintain, and generalize skills that will appreciably improve their lives. New skills are needed to promote real participation and independence in the changing school, workplace, and community environments of the 21st century.

There is a limit to how much educational equality can be legislated. In many cases, it is possible to meet the letter but not necessarily the spirit of the law. Treating every student with a disability as a student first and as an individual with a disability second may be the most important factor in providing true educational equality. This approach does not diminish the student's exceptionality, but instead it might give us a more objective and positive perspective that allows us to see a disability as a set of special needs. Viewing exceptional students as individuals tells us a great deal about how to help them achieve the educational equality they deserve.

Questions and Activities

1. Why are both children who are learning disabled and those who are gifted considered exceptional?
2. In what ways are students with disabilities similar to and different from other students?
3. What are the advantages and disadvantages of labeling and classifying students with disabilities?
4. How did the Civil Rights Movement influence the movement for educational equality for students with disabilities?
5. Analyze a school district/state "report card" to determine (a) how many students in the district/state receive special education services, (b) how many of these students are English-language learners, bilingual, males, females, and/or are students of color, and (c) how many students with disabilities receive some or all of their education in the regular classroom and the portion of the school day in which they are included in the regular classroom.
6. What is an IEP, and how can it benefit students with disabling conditions?
7. How does the concept of least restrictive environment influence alternative placements for students with disabilities?

8. Do you think all students with disabilities should be educated in regular classrooms? Why or why not?

9. Why are collaboration and teaming between special educators and general classroom teachers so critical to the quality of education experienced by children with disabilities?

10. In your view, what is the most critical challenge currently facing the education of exceptional students?

References

Aiello, B. (1976, April 25). Up from the basement: A teacher's story. *New York Times*. Retrieved December 27, 2008, from http://www.nytimes.com

Anderson, N. B., & Shames, G. H. (2006). *Human communication disorders: An introduction* (7th ed.). Boston: Allyn & Bacon.

Andrews, J. F., Leigh, I. W., & Weiner, M. T. (2004). *Deaf people: Evolving perspectives from psychology, education, and sociology*. Boston: Allyn & Bacon.

Banks, J. A. (2006). *Cultural diversity and education: Foundations, curriculum, and teaching* (5th ed.). Boston: Allyn & Bacon.

Bartlett, L. D., Etscheidt, S., & Weisentstein, G. R. (2007). *Special education law and practice in public schools* (2nd ed.). Upper Saddle River, NJ: Merrill/Prentice-Hall.

Bateman, B. D., & Linden, M. L. (2006). *Better IEPs: How to develop legally correct and educationally useful programs* (4th ed.). Verona, WI: Attainment.

Becker, W. C., Engelmann, S., & Thomas, D. R. (1971). *Teaching: A course in applied psychology*. Chicago: Science Research.

Beirne-Smith, M., Patton, J. R., & Kim, S. (2006). *Mental retardation: An introduction to intellectual disability* (7th ed.). Upper Saddle River, NJ: Merrill/Prentice-Hall.

Brown v. Board of Education of Topeka. 347 U.S. 483 (1954).

Bulgren, J. A. (2006). Integrated content enhancement routines: Responding to the needs of adolescents with disabilities in rigorous inclusive secondary content classes. *Teaching Exceptional Children*, *38*(6), 54–58.

Bushell, D., Jr., & Baer, D. M. (1994). Measurably superior instruction means close, continual contact with the relevant outcome data. Revolutionary! In R. Gardner III, D. M. Sainato, J. O. Cooper, T. E. Heron, W. L. Heward, J. Eshleman, & T. A. Grossi (Eds.), *Behavior analysis in education: Focus on measurably superior instruction* (pp. 3–10). Pacific Grove, CA: Brooks/Cole.

Carnine, D. (1997). Bridging the research to practice gap. *Exceptional Children*, *63*, 513–521.

Cochran-Smith, M. Feiman-Nemser, S., & McIntyre, D. J. (Eds.) (2008). *Handbook of research on teacher education: Enduring questions in changing contexts*. New York & London: Routledge.

Cook, R. E., Klein, M. D., & Tessier, A. (2008). *Adapting early childhood curricula for children with special needs* (7th ed.). Upper Saddle River, NJ: Merrill/Prentice Hall.

Cortiella, C. (2006). *NCLB and IDEA: What parents of students with disabilities need to know and do*. Minneapolis: University of Minnesota National Center on Educational Outcomes.

Coyne, M. D., Kame'enui, E. J., & Carnine, D. W. (Eds.). (2007). *Effective teaching strategies that accommodate diverse learners* (3rd ed.). Upper Saddle River, NJ: Merrill/Prentice Hall.

Danforth, S. (1995). Toward a critical theory approach to lives considered emotionally disturbed. *Behavioral Disorders, 20*(2), 136–143.

Danforth, S., & Rhodes, W. C. (1997). On what basis hope? Modern progress and postmodern possibilities. *Remedial and Special Education, 18*, 357–366.

Deshler, D. D. (2005). *Intervention research and bridging the gap between research and practice.* ERIC clearinghouse on disabilities and gifted education. Retrieved June 25, 2007, from www.ldonline.org/article/5596

De Valenzuela, J. S., Copeland, S. R., Qi, C. H., & Park, M. (2006). Examining educational equity: Revisiting the disproportionate representation of minority students in special education. *Exceptional Children, 72*, 425–441.

Elkind, D. (1998). Behavior disorders: A postmodern perspective. *Behavioral Disorders, 23*, 153–159.

Ferguson, P. M., & Ferguson, D. L. (2006). The promise of adulthood. In M. E. Snell & E. Brown (Eds.), *Instruction of students with severe disabilities* (6th ed., pp. 610–672). Upper Saddle River, NJ: Merrill/Prentice Hall.

Finn, C. E., Rotherham, A. J., & Hokanson, C. R. (2001). *Rethinking special education for a new century.* Washington, DC: Thomas B. Fordham Foundation and the Progressive Policy Institute.

Flexer, R. W., Baer, R. M., Luft, P., & Simmons, T. J. (2008). *Transition planning for secondary students with disabilities* (3rd ed.). Upper Saddle River, NJ: Merrill/Prentice-Hall.

Florian, L., Hollenweger, J., Simeonsson, R. J., Wedell, K., Riddell, S., Terzi, L., & Holland, A. (2006). Cross-cultural perspectives on the classification of children with disabilities: Part I. Issues in the classification of children with disabilities. *Journal of Special Education, 40*, 36–45.

Fuchs, D., & Fuchs, L. S. (1995). What's "special" about special education? *Phi Delta Kappan, 76*(7), 531–540.

Gallagher, D. J., Heshusius, L., Iano, R. P., & Skrtic, T. M. (2004). *Challenging orthodoxy in special education: Dissenting voices.* Denver, CO: Love.

Gersten, R. (2001). Sorting out the roles of research in the improvement of practice. *Learning Disabilities Research and Practice, 16*, 45–50.

Giangreco, M. F. (2007). *Absurdities and realities of special education: The complete digital set.* Minnetonka, MN: Peytral.

Gollnick, D. M., & Chinn, P. G. (2009). *Multicultural education in a pluralistic society* (8th ed.). Upper Saddle River, NJ: Merrill/Prentice-Hall.

Greenwood, C. R., & Maheady, L. (1997). Measurable change in student performance: Forgotten standard in teacher preparation? *Teacher Education and Special Education, 20*, 265–275.

Grigal, M., Test, D. W., Beattie, J., & Wood, W. (1997). An evaluation of transition components of individualized education programs. *Exceptional Children, 63*, 357–372.

Guralnick, M. J. (1997). *The effectiveness of early intervention.* Baltimore, MD: Brookes.

Harry, B., & Klingner, J. (2007). Discarding the deficit model. *Educational Leadership, 64*(5), 16–21.

Heller, K. W., Forney, P. E., Alberto, P. A., Best, S. J., & Schwartzman, M. N. (2009). *Understanding physical, health, and multiple disabilities* (2nd ed.). Upper Saddle River, NJ: Merrill/Prentice-Hall.

Heron, T. E., & Harris, K. C. (2001). *The educational consultant: Helping professionals, parents, and mainstreamed students* (4th ed.). Austin, TX: PRO-ED.

Hetzner, A. (2007, March 30). Disparity shows in special ed: State deems 25 districts' minority enrollment disproportionate. *Milwaukee Journal Sentinel*. Retrieved November 21, 2008, from http://www.jsonline.com

Heward, W. L. (2009). *Exceptional children: An introduction to special education* (9th ed.). Upper Saddle River, NJ: Merrill/Prentice-Hall.

Heward, W. L. (2003). Ten faulty notions about teaching and learning that hinder the effectiveness of special education. *Journal of Special Education, 36*(4), 186–205.

Heward, W. L., & Dardig, J. C. (2001). What matters most in special education. *Education Connection*, pp. 41–44.

Heward, W. L., & Silvestri, S. M. (2005). The neutralization of special education. In J. W. Jacobson, J. A. Mulick, & R. M. Foxx (Eds.), *Fads: Dubious and improbable treatments for developmental disabilities* (pp. 193–214). Hillsdale, NJ: Erlbaum.

Huebner, T. A. (1994). Understanding multiculturalism. *Journal of Teacher Education, 45*(5), 375–377.

Kame'enui, E. J., Good, R., III, & Harn, B. A. (2005). Beginning reading failure and the quantification of risk: Reading behavior as the supreme index. In W. L. Heward, T. E. Heron, N. A. Neef, S. M. Peterson, D. M. Sainato, G. Cartledge, R. Gardner III, L. D. Peterson, S. B. Hersh, & J. C. Dardig (Eds.), *Focus on behavior analysis in education: Achievements, challenges, and opportunities* (pp. 69–89). Upper Saddle River, NJ: Merrill/Prentice Hall.

Kauffman, J. M. (1999). How we prevent the prevention of emotional and behavioral disorders. *Exceptional Children, 65*, 448–468.

Kauffman, J. M., & Hallahan, D. K. (2005). *The illusion of full inclusion: A comprehensive critique of a current special education bandwagon* (2nd ed.). Austin, TX: PRO-ED.

Kauffman, J. M., & Konold, T. R. (2007). Making sense in education: Pretense (including No Child Left Behind) and realities in rhetoric and policy about schools and schooling. *Exceptionality, 15*, 75–96.

Kauffman, J. M. & Landrum, T. J. (2009). *Characteristics of emotional and behavioral disorders of children and youth* (9th ed.). Upper Saddle River, NJ: Merrill/Prentice-Hall.

Keogh, B. K. (2005a). Revisiting classification and identification. *Learning Disability Quarterly, 28*, 115–118.

Keogh, B. K. (2005b). Revisiting classification and identification: Labeling. *Learning Disability Quarterly, 28*, 100–102.

Kliewer, C., & Biklen, D. (1996). Labeling: Who wants to be retarded? In W. Stainback & S. Stainback (Eds.), *Controversial issues confronting special education: Divergent Perspectives* (pp. 83–95). Boston: Allyn & Bacon.

Kochhar-Bryant, C. A. (2008). *Colaboration and system coordination for students with special needs: From early childhood to the postsecondary years*. Upper Saddle River, NJ: Merrill/Prentice-Hall.

LaVenture, S. (Ed.) (2007). *A parent's guide to special education for children with visual impairments*. New York: American Foundation for the Blind.

Lewis, T. J., Hudson, S., Richter, M., & Johnson, N. (2004). Scientifically supported practices in emotional and behavioral disorders: A proposed approach and brief review of current practices. *Behavioral Disorders, 29*, 247–259.

Lovitt, T. C. (2007). *Promoting school success: Tactics for teaching adolescents* (3rd ed.). Austin, TX: PRO-ED.

McLaughlin, M. J., Dyson, A., Nagle, K., Thurlow, M., Rouse, M., Hardman, M., Norwich, B., Burke, P. J., & Perlin, M. (2006). Cross-cultural perspectives on the classification of children with disabilities: Part II. Implementing classification systems in schools. *Journal of Special Education, 40,* 46–58.

Mercer, C. D., & Pullen, P. C. (2009). *Students with learning disabilities* (7th ed.). Upper Saddle River, NJ: Merrill/Prentice-Hall.

Mitchell, D. (Ed.). (2004a). *Special educational needs and inclusive education: Major themes in education.* London and New York: RoutledgeFalmer.

Mitchell, D. (Ed.). (2004b). *Contextualizing inclusive education: Evaluating old and new international paradigms.* London and New York: RoutledgeFalmer.

Moody, S. W., Vaughn, S. Hughes, M. T., & Fischer, M. (2000). Reading instruction in the resource room: Set up for failure. *Exceptional Children, 66,* 305–316.

Mostert, M. P., Kavale, K. A., & Kauffman, J. M. (2008). *Challenging the refusal of reason in special education.* Denver, CO: Love.

Murdick, N., Gartin, B., & Crabtree, T. (2006). *Special education law* (2nd ed.). Upper Saddle River, NJ: Merrill/Prentice Hall.

National Reading Panel (2000). *Teaching children to read: An evidence-based assessment of the scientific research literature on reading and its implications for reading instruction. Reports of the subgroups.* Retrived December 17, 2007, from http://www.nichd.hih.gov/publications/nrp/smallbook.htm

Oswald, D. P., & Coutinho, M. J. (2001). Trends in disproportionate representation: Implications for multicultural education. In C. Utley & F. Obiakor (Eds.), *Special education, multicultural education, and school reform: Components of quality education for learners with mild disabilities* (pp. 53–73). Springfield, IL: Thomas.

Pennsylvania Association for Retarded Children v. Commonwealth of Pennsylvania, 343 F., Supp. 279 (1972).

Reschly, D. J. (1996). Identification and assessment of students with disabilities. *Future of Children, 6*(1), 40–53.

Reynolds, M. C. (1989). An historical perspective: The delivery of special education to mildly disabled and at-risk students. *Remedial and Special Education, 10,* 6–11.

Sandall, S., Hemmeter, L., McLean, M. E., & Smith, B. J. (Eds.). (2005). *DEC recommended practices: A comprehensive guide for practical application in early intervention/early childhood special education.* Longmont, CO: Sopris West.

Schwartz, I. S. (2005). Inclusion and applied behavior analysis: Mending fences and building bridges. In W. L. Heward, T. E. Heron, N. A. Neef, S. M. Peterson, D. M. Sainato, G. Cartledge, R. Gardner, III, L. D. Peterson, S. B. Hersh, & J. C. Dardig (Eds.), *Focus on behavior analysis in education: Achievements, challenges, and opportunities* (pp. 239–251). Upper Saddle River, NJ: Merrill/Prentice Hall.

Shonkoff, J. P., & Meisels, S. J. (Eds.). (2000). *Handbook of early childhood intervention* (2nd ed.). New York: Cambridge University Press.

Smith, P. (1999). Drawing new maps: A radical cartography of developmental disabilities. *Review of Educational Research, 69,* 117–144.

Smith, T. E. C. (2005). IDEA 2004: Another round in the reauthorization process. *Remedial and Special Education, 26,* 314–319.

Smith, J. D., & Mitchell, A. L. (2001). Me? I'm not a drooler. I'm the assistant: Is it time to abandon mental retardation as a classification. *Mental Retardation, 39*(2), 144–46.

Smith, S. W., & Brownell, M. T. (1995). Individualized education programs: From intent to acquiescence. *Focus on Exceptional Children, 28*(1), 1–12.

Smith, T. E. C., Polloway, E. A., Patton, J. M., & Dowdy, C. A. (2008). *Teaching students with special needs in inclusive settings* (5th ed.). Upper Saddle River, NJ: Merrill/Prentice Hall.

Snell, M. E., & Brown, F. (Eds.). (2006). *Instruction of students with severe disabilities* (6th ed.). Upper Saddle River, NJ: Merrill/Prentice-Hall.

Sugai, G. (1998). Postmodernism and emotional and behavioral disorders: Distraction or advancement. *Behavioral Disorders, 23,* 171–177.

Tam, K. Y. B., & Heng, M. A. (2005). A case involving culturally and linguistically diverse parents in prereferral intervention. *Intervention in school and clinic, 40,* 222–230.

Taylor, S. J. (1988). Caught in the continuum: A critical analysis of the principle of least restrictive environment. *Journal of the Association for Persons with Severe Handicaps, 13,* 41–53.

Test, D. W., Aspel, N., & Everson, J. M. (2006). *Transition methods for youth with disabilities.* Upper Saddle River, NJ: Merrill/Prentice Hall.

Turnbull, H. R., & Cilley, M. (1999). *Explanations and implications of the 1997 amendments to IDEA.* Upper Saddle River, NJ: Merrill/Prentice-Hall.

Turnbull, H. R., Stowe, M. J., & Huerta, N. E. (2007). *Free appropriate public education: The law and children with disabilities* (7th ed.). Denver, CO: Love.

Tymchuk, A. J., Lakin, K. C., & Luckasson, R. (2001). *The forgotten generation: The status and challenges of adults with mild cognitive limitations.* Baltimore: Brookes.

U.S. Department of Education. (2007). *Individuals with disabilities education act (IDEA) data.* Washington, DC: Author. Retrieved November 21, 2008, from https://www.ideadata.org/PartBReport.asp

Utley, C. A., & Obiakor, F. E. (2001). Learning problems or learning disabilities of multicultural learners: Contemporary perspectives. In C. Utley & F. Obiakor (Eds.), *Special education, multicultural education, and school reform: Components of quality education for learners with mild disabilities* (pp. 90–117). Springfield, IL: Thomas.

Vaughn, S., Gersten, R. L., & Chard, D. J. (2000). The underlying message in LD intervention research: Findings from research syntheses. *Exceptional Children, 67,* 99–114.

Vaughn, S., Klingner, J., & Hughes, M. (2000). Sustainability of research-based practices. *Exceptional Children, 66,* 163–171.

Vaughn, S., Schumm, J. S., & Brick, J. B. (1998). Using a rating scale to design and evaluate inclusion programs. *Teaching Exceptional Children, 30*(4), 41–45.

Venn, J. J. (2007). *Assessing students with special needs* (4th ed.). Upper Saddle River, NJ: Merrill/Prentice-Hall.

Wagner, M., Newman, L., Cameto, R., & Levine, P. (2005). *Changes over time in the early postschool outcomes of youth with disabilities: A report of findings from the national longitudinal transition study (NTLS) and the national longitudinal transition study-2 (NLST2).* Menlo Park, CA: SRI International.

Webber, J., & Scheuermann, B. (2008). *Educating students with autism: A quick start manual.* Austin, TX: Pro-Ed.

Wehby, J. H., Symons, F. J., Canale, J. A., & Go, F. J. (1998). Teaching practices in classrooms for students with emotional and behavioral disorders. *Behavioral Disorders, 24,* 51–56.

Wright, P. W. D., & Wright, P. D. (2006). *Wrightslaw: Special education law* (2nd ed.). Hartfield, VA: Harbor House Law Press.

Yell, M. L. (2006). *The law and special education* (2nd ed.). Upper Saddle River, NJ: Merrill/Prentice-Hall.

Zigmond, N. (2006). Where should students with disabilities receive special education? Is one place better than another? In B. Cook & B. Shermer (Eds.), *What is special about special education?* (pp. 127–136). Austin, TX: Pro-Ed.

Zigmond, N. (2007). Delivering special education is a two-person job: A call for unconventional thinking. In J. B. Crockett, M. M. Gerber, & T. J. Landrum (Eds.), *Radical reform of special education: Essays in honor of James M. Kauffman* (pp. 115–138). Mahwah, NJ: Lawrence Erlbaum.

CHAPTER 14

School Inclusion and Multicultural Issues in Special Education

Luanna H. Meyer, Jill M. Bevan-Brown, Hyun-Sook Park, and Catherine Savage

Special education emerged alongside the Civil Rights Movement in the United States, representing the values of equality of educational opportunity for students who were being denied access to high-quality schooling to meet their learning needs. Throughout its history, special education has intersected with multicultural education in promoting pedagogical, curricular, and teacher education reforms that address increasingly diverse student school populations. The relationship between special and general education provides one measure of the extent to which public education is preparing students for their future adult roles. Special education represents the state's commitment to meeting diverse needs within the public school system. Yet, its very existence has enabled general educators to maintain beliefs in a mythical mainstream, a "one-size-fits-all" approach to schools, classrooms, and pedagogy.

Across the United States, culturally and linguistically diverse (CLD) students experience high rates of dropping out of school, disproportionate referrals for special education services, lower achievement on standardized tests, and harsh penalties, along with high rates of exclusion for behavior in comparison to White students who speak English as their first language (Cartledge & Kourea, 2008; Donovan & Cross, 2002). Furthermore, negative beliefs about families of children from certain non-White cultural groups have been found to be pervasive (Harry & Klingner, 2006; Harry, Klingner, & Hart, 2005). Formal inquiries into the quality and quantity of educational services and supports generally afforded to CLD learners have documented extensive inequities in curricula, pedagogy, physical facilities, and resources persisting for over 40 years (Ferri & Connor, 2005; Kozol, 1967; Rebell, 1999; Sleeter & Grant, 1987). Finally, multiple factors have resulted in limited availability of educators and teachers who are skilled in teaching diverse student populations, including inadequate teacher preparation for diversity and teacher resistance to teaching in schools populated by CLD and low-income students. There is even an absence of teachers who are themselves CLD and might thus serve as positive role models for children who are CLD (Barton, 2003; Darling-Hammond, 2004; Peske & Haycock, 2006).

This chapter focuses on the intersections between special education, general education, and multicultural education. Despite the positive language about a special education service designed to better meet student needs, special education practices in action also provide a mechanism that enables mainstream educational systems to avoid accommodating diverse learners. Troubling patterns of disproportional identification by ethnicity and failures to engage in culturally responsive educational practices seem intractable with little improvement evident despite decades of awareness of these issues. We argue that a new conceptualization for educating diverse learners is needed to shift from deficit theorizing applied to individuals (special education) and groups (race and social class). This chapter addresses how special education has operated historically and summarizes contemporary visions for shifting from monocultural mainstream practices that no longer reflect reality to acknowledging culturally situated mainstreams. We describe how the relationship between schools and families can reflect culture and power sharing that help to meet children's needs. Next, we discuss how the preparation of teachers can develop cultural competence, skills in effective teaching practices, and care for students as culturally located individuals. Finally, we describe promising practices for inclusive classrooms based on evidence regarding pedagogies and curricula incorporating communal practices and individual supports that recognize interdependencies as well as independence in learning.

SPECIAL EDUCATION AS EXCLUSION

Special education once occupied "the high ground of many contemporary educational debates" located at "the forefront of pedagogical innovation and judicial reform" (Richardson, 1994, p. 713). Following the passage of federal legislation in the 1970s guaranteeing a free and public education to children with disabilities, special education rose to the challenge of developing diverse instructional strategies and demonstrating meaningful learning even for children who had once been labeled "uneducable" (Horner, Meyer, & Fredericks, 1986). Special educators were the reformers, willing to address the complexities of children as they are rather than as they were supposed to be. This is the generous and idealistic interpretation of the history and purpose of special education.

Special Education and Segregation

Another less benign view of special education has also emerged. Dunn (1968) argued early on that special education had become the new, legally sanctioned segregation for children of color and others who were different at a time when racial segregation was otherwise illegal. His indictment of the disproportionate overrepresentation of African American and other minority groups in special classes included evidence that these classes were not so very special: children in the special education segregated programs actually did less well academically than similar children who had remained in general education without special services. Dunn questioned whether special education was being manipulated to resegregate the United States through socially acceptable strategies that once again divided children by race.

Dunn (1968) focused his critique on the diagnosis of "mild mental retardation," which at the time accounted for the largest percentage of children labeled as having a disability.

This diagnosis was always subjective and came under attack for unfairly disadvantaging children from non-White cultures, living in poverty, and who speak English as a second language: these were the students disproportionately represented in this category (Mercer, 1973). The diagnosis of mental retardation became increasingly unpopular, and by the 1980s, children with similar characteristics were more likely than in the past to be labeled as having learning disabilities and emotional/behavioral disorders. Nevertheless, the overall pattern of overrepresentation of ethnic and cultural minorities in special education has not changed. Children of color—particularly African Americans—continued to be overrepresented among those receiving services as students with mild-moderate disabilities throughout the 1980s and 1990s (Argulewicz, 1983; Finn, 1982; Oswald, Coutinho, Best, & Singh, 1999; Tucker, 1980; Webb-Johnson, 1999). There are 30 years of evidence that students who have CLD backgrounds are labeled as having disabilities at significantly higher levels and labeled as gifted and talented at significantly lower levels in comparison to their representation in the general population. Skiba et al. (2008) present overwhelming evidence that "the racial disparities in special education service remain one of the key indicators of inequity in our nation's educational system" (p. 264).

Despite overt discussion of what appear to be new forms of discrimination and exclusion, patterns remain unchanged in the 21st century (Artiles, Trent, & Palmer, 2004; Hosp & Reschly, 2004; Skiba, Poloni-Staudinger, Simmons, Feggins-Azziz, & Chung, 2005). Low-income boys who are African American or Native American are those most likely to be diagnosed as having disabilities such as mental retardation and emotional disturbance, and they are least likely to be labeled as gifted and talented (Donovan & Cross, 2002). Artiles, Rueda, Salazar, and Higareda (2005) found that Hispanic and other students whose first language is not English are particularly overrepresented in special education in California districts with diverse school populations. Klingner, Artiles, and Barletta (2006) point out that a large percentage of American students are entering school speaking a language other than English as the first language; this figure is estimated to be 20 percent of the current school population and will increase to 40 percent by 2030. Most children learning English as a second language in the United States are Hispanic, but many speak other first languages, reflecting immigration and refugee status around the world (Klingner et al.).

Furthermore, these disparities in referrals to special education cannot be attributed solely to differences in socioeconomic status—an early hypothesis that would situate the problem outside the responsibility of schools, educators, and the public education system as a whole (MacMillan & Reschly, 1998). This explanation has now largely been laid to rest by large-scale investigations of the interrelationships between race and poverty as factors influencing educational outcomes. Oswald et al. (1999) analyzed data from 4,500 U.S. school districts and reported that race contributed independently to placement in special education over and above the impact of socioeconomic status. Skiba et al. (2005) investigated this issue in depth in one state and found that poverty made a weak and inconsistent contribution to disproportionality, magnifying existing racial disparities. They concluded that where poverty had an impact, its "primary effect was to magnify existing racial disparity" (Skiba et al., p. 273). Furthermore, they reported that African American and Native American children were overrepresented in suspensions and expulsions from school.

It has now been more than 25 years since the National Research Council produced its first official report on this issue (Heller, Holtzman, & Messick, 1982) and nearly another decade since its second report (Donovan & Cross, 2002). In 2004, the reauthorization of the Individuals with Disabilities Education Improvement Act (IDEIA) included a number of changes to reinforce the accountability by state and local education agencies for addressing the disproportional representation of CLD students by ethnic/racial groups across disability categories. Significant changes included early identification of at-risk CLD students in the mainstream to prevent referral to special education and interventions to enhance culturally responsive teaching and learning in the mainstream.

Strategies to Prevent Misdiagnosis and Disproportionality

Some schools have employed a pre referral system first introduced in the 1970s that has evolved over time into a variety of models for intervening prior to attaching a formal special education label (Ortiz, 2002). With the introduction of IDEIA (2004), response to intervention (RTI) was introduced as a model for the early identification and intervention of at-risk students in general education classrooms before referral to special education services (Fuchs & Fuchs, 2006; Mellard, 2008). RTI is a multilevel prevention system (usually two to four tiers) designed to maximize student achievement and reduce behavior problems. Within each level of intervention, a teacher and/or an educational team provides high-quality interventions using evidence-based strategies and closely monitors student progress and learning outcomes. Then the intensity and the nature of interventions are adjusted depending on student responsiveness before identifying students as having learning and other disabilities (Fuchs & Fuchs).

Klingner and Edwards (2006) propose a four-tier RTI model for CLD students. At-risk students are identified applying a criterion set by the school (e.g., below 25th percentile), usually through either high-stakes or other assessments determined by the school. Tier 1 requires culturally responsive quality teaching using evidence-based strategies and close monitoring of these at-risk students in the general education classroom. Those who have not responded to the intervention in Tier 1 are provided intensive intervention (e.g., small-group tutoring after school) in Tier 2. Nonrespondents to the intervention in Tier 2 are referred to Tier 3, in which a teacher assistance team (TAT) focused on the individual child utilizes a problem-solving approach to help the teacher determine how to modify the intervention/supports being delivered to the CLD student with specific instructional objectives based on the student's performance. The TAT should consist of multiple experts on culturally responsive teaching strategies. A CLD student who does not respond to the intervention in Tier 3 is then referred to special education in Tier 4, in which more intensive and individualized instruction is provided.

The RTI is a promising approach to support the learning of CLD students in general education classrooms that would, in principle, reduce disproportional representation of CLD students in special education. Whenever schools identify at-risk students through high-stakes assessment and particular ethnic and cultural groups are overrepresented as being at risk, Tier 1 intervention in the general classroom should focus on strategies that address the needs of overrepresented groups to prevent overreferrals to special education. For example, in a school district in California, the analysis of the state standardized test revealed that a Pacific Islander group consistently scored low. The school formed a study group to find potential explanations for such a prominent pattern and develop an action plan addressing the needs of this particular group in the classroom. Reexamining assessment practices can provide direction for resolving particular equity issues for different groups. Schools must also be sensitive to issues of underrepresentation when some groups may not be noticed due to ethnic stereotypes. For example, Asian American students are sometimes overlooked despite intervention needs because of the prevalent myth of the "Asian model minority" (Chiu & Ring, 1998; Florsheim, 1997; Palmer & Jang, 2005). In contrast to this myth, Asian immigrant youth experience different types of socio-emotional and adaptive problems in schools ranging from minor socio-psychological problems to more serious ones such as juvenile delinquency, gang involvement, and suicide (Chiu & Ring; Ha, Park, & Lee, 2008; Lee & Zhan, 1998; Yeh & Inose, 2002).

The MonoCulture of Mainstream Education

RTI holds promise for refocusing on general education prior to referrals to special education, but this approach still requires that a child be failing prior to intervention and can rest on assumptions that it is the child alone who needs to change. Critics have increasingly called for shifting the focus from assumptions that patterns of disproportionality occur because of deficits in children—whether these are socioeconomic, linguistic, or developmental—and toward a reexamination of the culture of a mainstream public school system that marginalizes differences and reinforces existing disparities. Artiles and Bal (2008) are among those who challenge the present state of affairs and apparent inability or unwillingness to redress imbalances. They note that researchers, policy analysts, and educators continue to acknowledge and debate the issues, yet the imbalances persist. They theorize that the "problem of disproportionate representation" is symptomatic of the inability of public school systems to accommodate *difference*. They note the enduring assumption that the mainstream is somehow *not different*, and they critique the underlying premise that the person (e.g., a mainstream educationalist) "naming a difference does not have a cultural perspective" (Artiles & Bal, p. 5). They state:

> The issue is not that special education is bad for minority (and majority) students. Rather the challenges are greater: How are differences accounted for in systems of educational support for an increasingly diverse student population? ... Culture indexed in schools' or communities' everyday practices is not considered. (p. 6)

Unlike those who would argue that one reduces these inequities by fixing and enhancing flawed referrals, assessments, and attitudes, these authors are among those who maintain that it is the so-called mainstream that requires fixing and enhancing.

What is being increasingly emphasized is the failure of mainstream educators and systems to acknowledge that a monocultural perspective underpins and drives teacher education, approaches to pedagogy, curriculum design, classroom organization, school policy, home-school relationships, and even models of discipline in schools. This monocultural perspective is presumed to be so universal as to be invisible without acknowledgement that schools have been designed to suit a dominant culture no longer representing all children or even most children and their families. This cultural mismatch exists not only in the United States but also in many other nations as well, such as Australia, New Zealand, Britain, Germany, and Spain

(Artiles & Bal, 2008; Bishop & Berryman, 2006; Kozleski et al., 2008; Suárez-Orozco, 2001). The solution requires a major shift in mind-set: Schools are meant to add value to children's lives, not simply reestablish educational definitions for society's shortcomings. If schools cannot function without separating large numbers of children for "nonmainstream" services outside the general education classroom, we need to challenge the culture of the classroom as one that is not reflecting the culture of communities.

Harry and Klingner (2006) have called for increased attention and remediation, not of individual students or groups of students but to address "school-based risk" as a major contributing factor to student failure, exclusion, and rerouting out of general education into special education services that segregate. Skiba and his colleagues (2008) conclude that disparities in special education by race and ethnicity should not be seen as solely a special education problem but be properly attributed to general education sources of inequity including curriculum, classroom management, teacher quality, and resource distribution. The home–school relationship also contributes to the maintenance of inequities as will be discussed in the next section of this chapter.

PARENT PARTICIPATION AND WORKING WITH FAMILIES

Parent participation on behalf of children from culturally and linguistically diverse groups (CLD) is widely acknowledged as essential to effective special education services. IDEIA (2004) mandates parent-professional collaboration not only when individualized educational plans (IEP) and individualized family service plans (IFSP) are being developed but also throughout the entire special education process (Salas, Lopez, Chinn, & Menchaca-Lopez, 2005; Turnbull, Turnbull, Erwin, & Soodak, 2005). Research and practice show that such involvement is a win-win-win situation with positive academic, social, and emotional outcomes for children when parents are involved (Al-Shammari & Yawkey, 2008; Gargiulo, 2006; Howland, Anderson, Smiley, & Abbott, 2006). Parents also benefit through increased confidence, self-esteem, and understanding of the school and their child's education (Gomez & Greenough, 2002; Salas et al., 2005). Benefits for professionals include increased knowledge of the child, culture, and home circumstances; improved parent–professional relationships; and increased parental willingness to participate in school-related activities and to volunteer time (Gomez & Greenough; Salas et al.).

Nevertheless, the involvement of CLD parents in their child's special education is significantly less than their majority culture counterparts. Parents of CLD children are reported to withdraw from or be passive in school-based planning and decision making; be less involved in IEP meetings and offer fewer suggestions; have limited knowledge of the special education services entitlements; and be underrepresented in traditional schooling activities (Geenen, Powers, Lopez-Vasquez, & Bersani, 2003; Kim & Morningstar, 2005; Salas et al., 2005). Limited involvement of CLD parents is reported across the age span from early intervention (Zhang & Bennett, 2003) to transition from school (Kim & Morningstar). Many school initiatives aimed at providing child- and family-centered services and increasing parental participation have resulted in conflict, distrust, confusion, and resentment: Parents find themselves confronting an educational system that purports to seek their involvement but is unyielding and uncompromising when responding to parent and community values (Callicott, 2003).

Causes of Limited Parental Involvement

Reasons for limited parental involvement in special education are multiple, complex, and inter-related. Although CLD parents face many of the same issues and struggles as do majority-group parents of children with special needs, these barriers are often experienced by CLD parents to a greater degree. Additionally, there are obstacles that are specific to members of CLD groups. Some reasons are personal: Parents may feel that they are not valued and respected by professionals, that they are blamed for their child's difficulties, and that their requests for information are ignored (Bevan-Brown, 2002; Zhang & Bennett, 2003; Zionts, Zionts, Harrison, & Bellinger, 2003). Parents also report being discouraged from involvement because of professionals' negative attitudes and treatment of their children:

> The principal at my child's school once stood over the secretary's desk in the front office and told me that my child was lazy, disrespectful, and dumb! And she did it right there in front of all the others who were walking around in the front office and in front of my kid. I can't believe that she is called a "professional" … a professional what? (Zionts et al., p. 45)

Mistrust of professionals was frequently reported as was feeling disheartened by the ever-present focus on their child's weaknesses and labeling accompanied by low expectations (deFur, Todd-Allen & Getzel, 2001; Geenen et al., 2003; Parette & Petch-Hogan, 2000). Parents were left feeling disenfranchised by ineffective home–school communication methods and a lack of knowledge about rights, entitlements, and special education policies, procedures, and services (deFur et al.; Geenen et al.). Parents also reported being uncomfortable in the school environment due to their own negative schooling experiences (Bevan-Brown, 2002).

There can be culturally based reasons for parental noninvolvement: Parents report being reluctant to engage with professionals because of majority-culture ethnocentrism, negative cultural stereotyping, insensitivity to cultural and religious beliefs and family traditions, a propensity to lump different ethnic groups (e.g., all Polynesians) together, and discriminatory practices. In the study by Zionts et al. (2003), for example, several African American parents "believed that their children would not have been judged as severely or held to the same expectations if they had been Caucasian" (p. 47). Cultural deficit thinking can be reflected in undervaluing or ignoring children's ethnicity altogether (Bevan-Brown, 2002, 2003; Bourke et al., 2002; Murtadha-Watts & Stoughton, 2004). Salas et al. (2005) maintain that the tendency to problematize diversity instead of seeing it as a value contributes to "an eradication of the parent-special education teacher partnership" (p. 52).

Arguably, however, the greatest cause of parental noninvolvement relates to professionals' limited knowledge of diverse cultures and their failure to understand how their own cultural beliefs and attitudes influence their teaching and service provisions. Differing cultural con-cepts, values, and practices relating to disability provide fertile ground for cultural conflict and misinterpretation. Parents' reluctance to participate in their child's special education is under-standable if they do not believe the child has a special need. For example, Harry and Artiles (2007) note that majority cultural perspectives may regard conditions differing significantly from the norm to be signs of pathology to be treated by scientific and educational methods. However, many CLD families "may interpret a physical condition as a sign of a spiritual condition or may disagree that a child's difficulties in learning are important enough to be labeled as a disability" (p. 34). Similarly, Zionts et al. (2003) note that culture-based behaviors that vary from teachers' perceptions of what is "normal" can be misinterpreted, resulting in children being mislabeled as possessing behavioral or learning problems. These varying conceptions and interpretations of disability may result in professionals concluding that parents are "in denial" when they question their child's labels or when they choose not to become involved in their education.

Another area of conflict relates to the values that underpin many special education programs, interventions, and professional orientations. In their study of transition, Kim and Morningstar (2005) noted that policies and practices were dominated by Western, middle-class values of independence, autonomy, and physical and emotional separation from parents. These values conflicted with ethnic minority values of interdependence, family orientation, and extended family support, particularly in many Native American and Hispanic families. Parents from more collectivist cultures will be less likely to support IEP goals and programs that emphasize individualization and independence from the family.

Differing cultural communication styles and expectations about involvement in their child's education can contribute to parent–professional conflict. The nature and extent of parental participation in special education reflects majority culture norms and ways of operating, often assuming that all parents understand participation requirements and are comfortable interacting as expected by professionals. Some parents believe that intervention activities are the responsibility of teachers and other professionals (Huer, Parette & Saenz, 2001). This may be related to beliefs that professionals are the "experts" and that it is disrespectful for parents to interfere. Even when they disagree with professionals' opinions and recommendations, parents may refrain from speaking out because it would be culturally inappropriate to question those decisions. Salas et al. (2005) write, "Many parents may not believe that their participation is essential and that they should not interfere with professionals such as teachers, and as a result remove themselves from that process" (p. 55).

A final cluster of cultural reasons for parental noninvolvement is evidenced by recently immigrated families and those with limited English proficiency. Parental involvement is severely curtailed when professionals do not speak their language and all documentation, resources, and communications are in English. Hispanic parents, for example, reported that the lack of bilingual communication concerning their child's education was a major barrier to their participation (Kim & Morningstar, 2005). Because of an acute shortage of CLD professionals in special education, parents frequently find themselves the only minority person attending their child's IEP meetings.

Finally, there are contextual reasons for parental noninvolvement relating to poverty and its by-products (Zionts et al., 2003). The costs involved in accessing services and attending meetings is prohibitive for some parents who lack transportation and child-care support. Other barriers reported include unfriendly or intimidating meeting and service venues, heavy work commitments, fatigue, conflicting family responsibilities, lack of resources, poor health care, and inconvenient, inflexible scheduling of services and meetings (deFur et al., 2001; Geenen et al., 2003; Zionts et al.).

A Mismatch: Special Education and Families

The lack of culturally responsive service models, programs, and processes is a deterrent to parental participation. While there are good intentions behind IDEIA's requirements for parental involvement, its due process model reflects majority cultural values and processes in an IEP process based on Anglo legal traditions. Planning and assessment structures, communication methods, formal IEP meetings that cast parents in a passive role, exclusionary professional jargon and documentation, and the requirements for signatures all contribute to alienating CLD parents. Additionally, as Zionts et al. (2003) point out, a legally based system has the potential to turn the people involved into rivals. Assessment is completed and an intervention plan is formulated for many children prior to consultation with their parents, who are then expected to agree with the plan or be considered adversarial (Murtadha-Watta & Stoughton, 2004).

Furthermore, the IEP process is time consuming and work intensive. The sheer volume of paperwork produced can be confusing, overwhelming, and intimidating to parents, particularly those with limited English proficiency. It may also contribute to professional impatience that "can translate to parents as a lack of desire to include them in the process" (Murtadha-Watta & Stoughton, 2004, p. 7). This is further exacerbated by tightly scheduled meetings for which strict adherence to an agenda leaves little time for lengthy personal interaction and relationship building that typifies the communication style of some ethnic minority cultures. When working with ethnic and cultural groups with origins in the Pacific region and with immigrant groups from many other countries, it is essential that professionals take the time to get to know the family before launching into program planning (Bevan-Brown, 2002).

Salas et al. (2005) make the point that although U.S. law mandates parent involvement,

> Most districts have discretion over deciding what role they want parents
> to play, what programs are offered to parents, and what kind of
> partnership teachers want to have with parents. Unfortunately, when
> schools and teachers are the primary decision makers concerning the
> kinds of partnerships they want to have with parents—parents can
> never be truly empowered. (p. 53)

Parents are further disempowered by the medical model that underpins the special education system. This model positions professionals as experts, devalues parental knowledge and cultural capital, and locates learning and behavioral problems within the child and family (Murtadha-Watta & Stoughton, 2004). Such circumstances act as disincentives to parental involvement.

Strategies to Increase Parental Participation

The special education literature contains a variety of strategies and programs aimed at increasing parental participation and improving home–school communication. These range from minor amendments to IEP processes to large-scale home–school–community initiatives. In respect to the former, suggestions include inviting parents to bring extended family, siblings, or community members to support them at IEP meetings; holding meetings in culturally appropriate, family-friendly venues; providing bilingual documentation and translators or asking parents to nominate a suitable person to translate for them; making meetings more informal; allowing time for small talk; including food; providing transportation and child care facilities; having flexible meeting time schedules; and recording meetings for absent members for later consideration.

Strategies requiring more input and commitment include involving parents from the outset of the IEP process and including them in all decision making; employing CLD paraprofessionals or community-based workers to act as communicators, mediators, and advocates; having translators or cultural advisors work in partnership with professionals; utilizing telephone interpreter services; establishing family/community advisory councils or consultative committees from which both parents and professionals can seek help and advice or present issues; making school culturally relevant and welcoming to parents by celebrating important cultural days and festivals; and utilizing person-centered planning with its emphasis on family input into intervention plans based on parents' priorities and perceptions rather than those of the professionals (Bevan-Brown, 2003; Callicott, 2003).

School-based initiatives in North America that facilitate parental participation include Zigler's Schools for the 21st century, James Comer's school-community approach, and full-service schools (Pelletier & Corter, 2005). In these models, the school is the hub of community activity and the location of a range of services including medical, recreational, budgeting, child care, and preschool services; and parent support groups as well as language and literacy learning centers. The Toronto First Duty project integrates early childhood care, education, and community services for CLD families. An evaluation of the first stage of this program showed promising results. The model used was thought to be particularly suited to CLD families because it removed the need for them to locate scattered services—a task that often required "sophisticated knowledge of the system and its language" (Pelletier & Corter, p. 36).

Preparation of Professionals for Partnerships with Parents

There is a strong call from both parents and professionals for improved preservice, graduate, and in-service training to help professionals develop the cultural competence needed to work effectively with CLD parents and families (Bourke et al., 2002; Hains et al., 2005; Lam, 2005; Zions et al., 2003). Bevan-Brown (2002) recommends that teacher education should include (1) an examination of the teacher's own culture, biases, underlying assumptions, and the influence these have on one's teaching, (2) an investigation of how the majority culture influences a national education system and the effect this has on CLD children, and (3) a study of minority cultures and how cultural knowledge can be incorporated into all aspects of the school curriculum.

Parents in the Zions et al. (2003) study suggested that professional training should include empathetic communication, advocacy, and input from parents who had "already been through the system" (p. 48). They also recommended that teachers spend time in the neighborhoods and homes of their pupils to increase their understanding of the challenges families face. This recommendation is reflected in the Diverse Urban Interdisciplinary Teams project at the University of Wisconsin. Students are assigned to families of young children with disabilities from cultures different from their own. They spend time with the family at home and accompany them on shopping trips, visits to the park, or to special events such as family birthday parties three times during a 15-week semester (Hains et al., 2005).

Preparation of Parents for Partnerships with Educators

Parent-to-parent programs play an important role in connecting parents from similar ethnic backgrounds, emphasizing and valuing strengths of CLD families, and "teaching new ways for parents to use their strengths to overcome obstacles. Parent support programs with these characteristics have been shown to increase self-esteem and provide the skills for dealing with professionals" (Kim & Morningstar, 2005, p. 100). These programs are especially beneficial for new immigrants and others who do not have a wide circle of support. Skills to assist parental participation can also be gained through targeted training sessions. Parents have identified the need for instruction in parenting and advocacy skills, information and strategies specific to their child's disability, special education laws and services available, and ways to find assistance and support and including other family members (Zionts et al., 2003).

The need for ongoing research into effective means of increasing parental participation is critical. Investigation must move beyond measures of parental satisfaction and extent of involvement to focus on significant outcomes. What type of parental involvement leads to improved outcomes for CLD families and children with special needs? Similarly, research is required to determine what types of professional and parental training will be most effective in developing the skills and attitudes needed for these two groups to work in partnership for the benefit of all concerned.

CULTURALLY COMPETENT TEACHERS AND INCLUSIVE PEDAGOGIES

Teachers need to become culturally competent if they are to deliver culturally responsive, evidence-based high-quality teaching for students with disabilities (Cartledge & Kourea, 2008; Goldenberg, 2008) including (1) creating a nurturing classroom that honors and incorporates the cultural and linguistic heritages of all student members, (2) making connections with students as individuals and understanding how context influences their interactions with others, (3) providing structured communal learning opportunities that enhance and expand the more traditional individualistic and teacher-directed approaches characteristic of mainstream schools, (4) developing learning skills through dynamic teaching utilizing explicit, intensive, and systematic instructional techniques combined with brisk pacing, ample academic responding opportunities, and positive and corrective feedback, (5) utilizing peer-mediated and peer mentoring activities, (6) monitoring at-risk students frequently while maintaining high expectations and affirming learning for all students, and (7) providing English language and bilingual support services as needed by children for whom English is a second language or one of several languages that may be spoken by immigrant families. A tremendous gap remains between the evidence-based strategies described in the literature and those available and actually being implemented in teacher education and classrooms. Teachers may not have access to evidence-based strategies that are effective for diverse student populations either at preservice or in-service levels.

Preintervention Culturally Responsive Teaching

Beginning teacher education programs and effective professional development should equip teachers with culturally responsive, evidence-based strategies (Klingner & Edwards, 2006;

Trent, Kea, & Oh, 2008). Teachers may need access to ongoing professional development and support to implement such strategies skillfully in their classrooms with diverse learners, who will be different each year. The Te Kotahitanga professional learning program in Aotearoa, New Zealand, is designed to prepare general education teachers to teach Maori students—the indigenous population of New Zealand—in the mainstream; it has to date provided ongoing support across thirty-three secondary schools through professional facilitators (Bishop, Berryman, Cavanagh, & Teddy, 2007). These facilitators are themselves expert, consultant teachers who engage in observation and feedback sessions with their teacher colleagues. They also organize co-construction meetings with teacher teams working together to set priorities and implement practices that will better meet the educational aspirations of Māori children within mainstream classrooms.

Table 14.1 illustrates key features of the effective teaching profile (ETP) reflected in Te Kotahitanga to prepare secondary teachers to engage in culturally responsive teaching (Bishop & Berryman, 2006). The two underpinning understandings and the six reflections and interactions included in this model do not isolate delivery of culturally responsive pedagogies from good teaching. Instead, the ETP incorporates evidence-based practice for effective teaching and learning with caring for students as culturally situated individuals. Individual teachers can utilize this model to identify their own opportunities to become culturally responsive on a day-to-day basis rather than waiting for their schools or districts to provide them culturally responsive curricula or specific instructions regarding what to do for particular cultural groups.

Teachers can use a self-monitoring framework such as the ETP to reflect on their own teaching and alter their practices with CLD students as needed. Other user-friendly tools also support teachers in this way. One is Bevan-Brown's (2003) *cultural self-review*, a reflective process that enables teachers to evaluate their own practice and compare it to concrete teacher and student behaviors. This comparison will enable them to set priorities for acquiring new skills and understandings.

Culturally Responsive Interventions

Once a student labeled CLD has been referred for special education and other interventions, culturally responsive teaching diminishes further: The myth that "culture doesn't matter" becomes even more prevalent as students' disability identities take precedence. There is also a basic contradiction inherent in special education services that emphasize individualization of instruction at the expense of a child's other identities including gender, age, language, and culture. One could argue that key principles in special education are culturally biased: For example, self-determination and independent living have been regarded as ultimate goals in North America for virtually all students with disabilities. These are outcomes of value to Anglo-European cultural groups. However, CLD students from Native American, Asian, Polynesian, Hispanic, and other cultural backgrounds may value the harmony of the family and group over self-determination on certain issues such as favoring interdependence over independence. Instructional practices in special education have similarly favored adult-guided models including one-to-one teaching with a child as the most intensive form of systematic instruction.

For more than two decades, systematic instruction based on applied behavior analysis principles has been the backbone of successful teaching for students with disabilities. At the same time, multiculturalists in special education have advocated culturally responsive teaching

Table 14.1   The Effective Teaching Profile (ETP)

Relationships and Interactions	Definition	Examples of Teacher Behavior
1. Caring for students as culturally located individuals	The teacher acknowledges students' cultural identities and allows students to "be themselves" through learning interactions that are nurturing and show respect for students' language and culture.	• Incorporates terms in teacher presentations from students' first language/s • Correctly pronounces students' names • References cultural constructs and community activities
2. Caring about student performance	The teacher has high expectations for student learning and participation in classroom learning activities.	• Reinforces that all students can be effective learners • Gives all students positive and corrective feedback on how to improve • Encourages goal setting and praises effective learning behavior, including scaffolding, "You can do this: I'll help"
3. Managing the class to promote learning	The teacher has classroom management and curricular flexibility skills reflecting both individual and collective roles and responsibilities to achieve positive student outcomes.	• Has in place a classwide management system that creates a caring learning community (e.g., Tribes) • Redirects off-task or disruptive behavior in an effective, nonconfrontational way and is a "warm demander"* • After learning activity is introduced, engages personally with individual and small groups of students
4. Interacting with students discursively and co-constructing knowledge	The teacher promotes student dialogue and debate to share new knowledge and encourage problem solving and higher-order thinking.	• Incorporates co-operative learning principles and practices in group work • Promotes student-to-student problem solving rather than primarily teacher-directed knowledge • Solicits students' local stories, community experiences, and prior knowledge to develop new knowledge
5. Using a range of strategies for teaching and learning activities	The teacher uses different instructional strategies that involve teachers' and students' learning through interactions with one another.	• Facilitates student-led inquiry (e.g., students formulate questions rather than answer teacher questions) • Uses concept maps, think-pair-share, numbered heads together, jigsaw, and role-playing • Links new knowledge and concepts with students' lives through discussion of films/stories

Table 14.1   Continued

Relationships and Interactions	Definition	Examples of Teacher Behavior
6. Promoting educational aspirations within culturally responsive contexts	The teacher makes learning objectives and outcomes explicit and empowers students to make educational decisions within culturally meaningful contexts.	• Develops understandings of learning outcomes and engages students in promoting, monitoring, and reflecting on how outcomes lead to future goals • Engages students in critical examination of how knowledge reflects cultural perspectives and values • Encourages students to reflect on strengths and weaknesses as part of the assessment process including peer assessments that encourage and develop peer support networks

*For a description of "warm demander" pedagogy for diverse learners, see F. Ware (2006). Warm demander pedagogy: Culturally responsive teaching that supports a culture of achievement for African American students. *Urban Education, 41*(4), 427–456.

Source: Adapted from R. Bishop, M. Berryman, T. Cavanagh, & L. Teddy, (2007). *Te kotahitanga. Phase 3, Whānaungatanga: Establishing a culturally responsive pedagogy of relations in mainstream secondary school classrooms.* Wellington, New Zealand: Ministry of Education and Waikato University. This illustrates how teachers can ensure that their teaching is culturally responsive to diversity. Note that the ETP is also based on two major teacher understandings: (1) rejection of deficit theorizing as explanation for student failure, and (2) knowledge and commitment to enhance student success.

as essential to bridge the gap between home and school cultures for CLD students (Erickson & Mohatt, 1982; Ladson-Billings, 2007). The general education classroom assumes that students can learn in a large group, but this learning is not interdependent as much as it is teacher led with relatively inflexible expectations for group compliance, not scaffolding of learning. There have been attempts to incorporate culturally responsive practices into special education intervention, but this literature largely focuses on the home–school relationship rather than illustrating concrete practices for use by teachers (Harry, 2008; for exceptions, see Cartledge & Kourea, 2008; Goldenberg, 2008).

In contrast to both the large-group-focused general education classrooms and the intensive and individualized approaches characterizing special education, a third generation of inclusive communal and collaborative practices could provide an alternative that would empower mainstream classrooms as well as reduce referrals to special education. Clearly, such classrooms would be more responsive in reflecting collectivist cultural values such as belonging and caring for the community rather than only or even primarily individual achievement. Samoan, Maori, other Pacific Island, Asian, African American, and Native American students may be more likely to engage in school activities and enjoy learning in group activities and through peer-to-peer interactions. More work is needed for *systematic* instruction designed for interdependent student groups to guide and support one another. The integration of best practices in special education and in multicultural education is the greatest challenge facing educators.

It will not be a simple matter for teachers to provide culturally responsive assessment and instruction to CLD students. Teachers will need to acquire expanded skills so that they can incorporate visual holistic thinking skills alongside verbal analytic thinking skills for different students. They will need to create opportunities for group rewards rather than continuing to rely exclusively on individual reinforcement and recognition. Because students' learning takes place in sociocultural contexts, educators must learn to collaborate more with families and school communities toward making education more meaningful and relevant to students' cultural identities.

CULTURALLY SITUATED SCHOOLING AND INCLUSIVE PEDAGOGIES

The advancement of quality inclusive schooling began in the 1980s with the integration of students with special needs from segregated special schools into their neighborhood schools and classrooms. Unlike *mainstreaming*, which is a term describing placement in general education classrooms without special education supports, *inclusion* entails providing additional services to students in regular classrooms. Ultimately, all students—regardless of the extent of their educational needs—should be fully included and learn alongside their peers, thus "eliminating exclusionary processes from education that are a consequence of attitudes and responses to diversity in race, social class, ethnicity, religion, gender and attainment" (Vitello & Mithaug, 1998, p. 147). Booth and Ainscow (2000) describe several critical components of inclusion: (1) the presence of all students in the general education classroom without the use of withdrawal classes or other forms of integrated segregation such as ability grouping, (2) student participation in which each student can engage in meaningful educational experiences, (3) acceptance of students with special needs as full members of the classroom by teachers and peers, and (4) achievement within expectations for more academic progress, better social skills, and enhanced emotional adjustment. Descriptions such as these encourage teachers to take an active role to ensure that students are included in the learning and teaching activities of the classroom rather than assuming that inclusion happens through physical proximity alone.

Quality Inclusive Schools

Expecting our schools to accommodate all children in the general education classroom is imperative if we are to create multicultural schools to replace monocultural ones that exclude and separate children into groups of those who belong and those who do not. Inclusion therefore requires emphasis on any learners who are at risk of marginalization, exclusion, or underachievement (Harry, 2008). Inclusion requires a fundamental shift from attributing educational failure to children's characteristics toward analyzing barriers to participation and learning that are blocking student opportunity in school (Ainscow, 2007). Ultimately, the goal is to transform the mainstream in ways that increase capacity for responding to all learners (Meyer, 1997). Within inclusive educational settings, special education is reframed as additional services and supports that enhance instruction, not as a different curriculum for learners identified as having disabilities and deficits. Within inclusive classrooms, differences are seen as natural and expected, and the purpose of education is not to eliminate differences but to respond to diversity in ways that enhance all students' growth and development.

Schools that are inclusive actively challenge discrimination, create welcoming communities where everyone belongs, and value diversity (United Nations Educational, Scientific and Cultural Organization, 1994). An extensive body of international research identifies the features of quality inclusive schools (Meyer, 1997; Sapon-Shevin, 2004). Inclusive schools require a shared vision across the school community, and teachers are responsible for creating authentic learning communities in classrooms (Avramidis, Bayliss, & Burden, 2000). Ongoing analysis and appraisal are needed to focus on problem solving and power sharing that tackle new challenges as they emerge (Clarke, Dyson, Millward, & Robson, 1999).

Delivery of Special Education within the Context of General Education

Inclusive schools deliver special education services designed to meet the needs of individual students within the classroom context with meaningful participation being seen as central to learning. Students need interactions with other students and will learn through participation—from their context, their community, and the relationships they develop with others (Meyer, Park, Grenot-Scheyer, Schwartz, & Harry, 1998). Inclusive strategies and techniques that are effective with students with disabilities have been found to increase the performance of students who are low achievers, average achievers, and gifted (Baker, Gersten, & Scanlon, 2002; Montague & Applegate, 2000; Palincsar, Magnusson, Collins, & Cutter, 2001). Recent syntheses of the research on reading instruction in inclusive settings reveals that techniques such as cooperative learning and peer mediated instruction can result in substantial gains for students with and without disabilities (Doveston & Keenaghan, 2006; Schmidt, Rozendal, & Greenman, 2002). Strategies such as peer-mediated instruction and classwide peer tutoring require students to switch roles as tutor/student. These strategies individualize instruction as well as provide opportunities for all students to be actively engaged in mastering new content (Greenwood, Arreaga-Mayer, Utley, Gavin, & Terry, 2001).

These techniques are part of what has been termed *universal design for learning* (UDL) in developing strategies that are responsive to a wide range of students in heterogeneous classrooms (Cawley, Foley, & Miller, 2003; King-Sears, 2001; Rose & Meyer, 2000). King-Sears (2008) succinctly summarizes three categories of UDL techniques as (1) *representation*—new content is demonstrated and presented in auditory, visual, and/or tactile ways. Direct instruction of new and complex material incorporates strategic processes and problem solving; (2) *engagement*—students practice independently or in cooperative learning groups through a variety of activities and opportunities to acquire proficiency with new content. Feedback to students is delivered in ways that promote student self-evaluation and learning how to learn independently. Teachers monitor performance and make instructional changes based on evidence of learning, and (3) *expression*—students are allowed choices to show what they know about new content with an emphasis on relevance and real-life examples that are meaningful and motivating. For example, the teacher may allow students to demonstrate mastery of new material through projects that can be done individually, in pairs, or in small groups and that may vary in format, such as giving a presentation or designing a three-dimensional display.

These UDL techniques not only promote social interaction, cooperation, and learning from difference within the classroom but also create a context in which children can develop positive social relationships. Meyer and her colleagues (1998) describe the range of possible social relationships in children's lives that can be influenced by educational practices and the organization of schooling. Their work highlights the importance of attention to the implementation of inclusive schooling, which is much more than the physical presence of students with disabilities in the classroom or even the provision of special education services within the general education environment. They found that when teachers communicate through actions and words that did not fully include children with disabilities, children mirrored those social patterns in their peer interactions. Thus, when teachers emphasized "helping" students with disabilities rather than working together, children without disabilities were most likely to either ignore peers with disabilities or treat them "specially," much as one would interact with very young children or even playthings (Evans, Salisbury, Palombaro, Berryman, & Hollowood, 1992). When classroom practices supported full participation in the range of academic and social activities occurring in school, students with even the most severe disabilities experienced social lives that included group membership as well as enjoying friendships (Meyer et al.; Schnorr, 1997).

Inclusive Schools and Teacher Education

In a study examining teachers' attitudes toward including children with special needs, Berry (2008) reported that teachers who are positive about inclusion are less apprehensive about whether they will be seen as fair if they accommodate different student needs than teachers with negative attitudes about inclusion. Teachers who are positive about inclusion believe that students with disabilities belong in their classrooms; they have confidence in their ability to teach students with disabilities and employ teaching strategies that they believe to be effective. Berry maintained that teacher education programs should have the major responsibility for helping teachers to develop the attitudes and dispositions necessary for teaching in inclusive contexts.

King-Sears (2008) argues that these positive attitudes must also be supported by deliberate instructional actions based on well-developed lesson planning. Spooner, Baker, Harris, Ahlgrim-Delzell, and Browder (2007) found that teachers in graduate courses who received a brief introduction to UDL designed lesson plans accessible for diverse students whereas the control group of teachers who received no UDL instruction designed lesson plans with fewer modifications, alternatives for communication, and activities that involved students. Clearly, teachers working in inclusive schools must possess the beliefs, attitudes, skills, and dispositions that will enable them to be confident, effective teachers with the skills to design and implement inclusive strategic programs that increase opportunities for all students to learn.

Inclusive Discipline and Restorative Justice

As noted earlier in this chapter, children from nondominant cultures continue to be overrepresented among those diagnosed as having behavior disorders and emotional disturbance in many Western nations. Furthermore, children of color are those most likely to be suspended and expelled for behavior considered unacceptable by schools. Cavanagh (2007) and Zehr (2002) describe the essential components of a "restorative justice" approach to discipline and safety in schools that focuses on recovering from incidents in a healing way so that the dignity of the individuals involved is respected. Comprehensive, whole-school approaches to discipline that are fair and transparent for all students (such as positive behavior support; Carr et al., 2002) provide the necessary groundwork. School personnel can then be trained in restorative justice skills such as conferencing as an alternative to more punitive detentions, suspensions, and exclusions (Cameron & Thorsborne, 2001). Central to a restorative justice approach is a culture of care that builds on social relationships among members of the school community and feeling a sense of responsibility for one another rather than division and competition (Cavanagh). Furthermore, restorative justice requires mutual consideration and respect for divergent points of view as part of the process of teacher and child navigation of what has just occurred in a particular incident. How the school community addresses behavioral challenges on a day-to-day basis can both predict and shape the likelihood that diversity will be appreciated and valued as children's cultures are better understood by teachers whose own backgrounds have been culturally limited and limiting.

DIVERSITY AND CARING COMMUNITIES: OUTCOMES FOR THE SOCIAL GOOD

For more than three decades, a growing number of international scholars have argued for and presented evidence supporting the provision of quality special education services within school communities. With the introduction of IDEIA in 2004 and widespread acceptance of society's responsibility to educate all children, advocacy and research have together progressed toward the development of schools for all children (Ainscow, 2007). Inclusive education is not the sole domain of special education but instead represents a social movement opposing educational exclusion (Slee & Allan, 2005).

The existence and perpetuation of separation and segregation of students with disabilities inevitably generates (and reflects) several unintended but nonetheless very real negative outcomes:

1. *Efforts to Structure General Classrooms into Homogenous Groups of Students with Like Learning Needs Will Fail Both the Children and the Educational System:* Systems that allow narrowing of commitment and capacity to serve diverse needs, that expect children to fit curricula rather than adapting schooling to meet children's needs, and that institutionalize identification of differences through tracking and segregation—whether by ability or race—legitimize intolerance of differences and tell children that they do not belong. Such practices are dysfunctional as proportionately higher numbers of culturally and linguistically diverse students and their families join our school communities. Removing children with special needs from the mainstream turns disabilities into handicaps and drains valuable resources and expertise from general education. As long as the myth persists that general education classrooms cannot accommodate needs outside a hypothetical norm, the inevitable result will be a closed cycle of increasing referrals that continue to exceed

the resources of the various special systems, themselves marginalized and devalued by mainstream systems. When children with disabilities are segregated from their nondisabled peers, they lose access to mainstream environments that enhance their teaching and learning. They become increasingly dependent on teacher-directed, highly structured learning and on adults as the source of new knowledge and support. They also are being forced to give up their peers and the friendships that should be part of the lives of all children. If natural supports are thwarted and prevented from developing, persons with disabilities are forced to become more and more dependent on costly professional and paid services to fill the void.

2. *When Children with and without Disabilities Grow Up in Isolation from One Another, Everyone Loses. Children will "do as I do, and not as I say." If we model segregation, rejection, and stereotyping by labels in a social system as central to our democratic institutions as the public schools, we have a great deal to answer for when those exclusionary models play out in the domains of daily living.* More than half a century ago, Adorno, Frenkel-Brunswik, Levinson, and Sanford (1950) advanced their theory that one's attitudes toward persons who are viewed as different is part of a consistent pattern affecting all aspects of an individual's behavior and beliefs. Their studies of racial prejudice were premised on the theory that cultural acceptance is associated with democratic principles so that the promotion of cultural acceptance would thus have broader implications for the greater good of society. The movement to celebrate diversity in education makes this point as well while acknowledging the futility of ignoring the diversity that exists in today's schools. Learning to acknowledge and build on individual differences as strengths rather than deficits is consistent with democratic values and caring schools that support children's growth and development (Berman, 1990; Noddings, 2005; Sapon-Shevin, 2005).

The purpose of a public school system goes beyond simply meeting the needs of individual children. While this is important, it should not occur at the expense of the role of the schools in providing a pathway to a democratic community and the betterment of a nation's citizenry—*all, not just some.* Our challenge is, of course, to examine the rhetoric and practices within education with the goal of reaching a better balance between meeting unique needs and building community.

Questions and Activities

1. Why, according to the authors, are students who are culturally and linguistically diverse overrepresented in special education classes and programs, especially those for learning disabilities, mental retardation, and emotional and behavioral disorders? What kinds of solutions could change this overrepresentation?

2. Why is it important for parents of color, low-income parents, and parents of different cultures and linguistic backgrounds to be involved in special education programs for their children? How can teachers and other educators ensure that these parents will be full participants in an educational process that is culturally responsive to their values and contexts?

3. What are the characteristics of an effective teacher who is culturally responsive? Give specific examples of how a teacher can demonstrate mastery of the different interactions and relationships needed for culturally effective teaching.

4. The authors maintain that a commitment to the principles and practices of inclusive education will not only benefit special education students but also lead to classrooms and schools that reflect diversity and can thus better serve all students with and without disabilities. How might fully inclusive schools prepare our children for fully inclusive communities?

5. How can the incorporation of a schoolwide positive behavior management system and restorative justice practices assist in ensuring that the school is culturally respectful and responsive? What can individual teachers do in their classrooms to reflect fairness and justice in social and instructional interactions with students?

6. What are your own beliefs, skills, and understandings related to the role of culture in special and inclusive education? How can you become a lifelong learner in advancing your own culturally responsive practices?

References

Adorno, T. W., Frenkel-Brunswik, E., Levinson, D. J., & Sanford, R. N. (1950). *The authoritarian personality* (Vols. 1 & 2). New York: Harper.

Ainscow, M. (2007). From special education to effective schools for all: A review of progress so far. In L. Florian (Ed.), *The SAGE handbook of special education* (pp. 146–159). London: Sage.

Al-Shammari, Z., & Yawkey, T. D. (2008). Extent of parental involvement in improving the students' levels in special education programs in Kuwait. *Journal of Instructional Psychology, 35*(2), 140–150.

Argulewicz, E. N. (1983). Effects of ethnic membership, socioeconomic status, and home language on LD, EMR, and EH placements. *Learning Disabilities Quarterly, 6*(2), 195–200.

Artiles, A. J., & Bal, A. (2008). The next generation of disproportionality research: Toward a comparative model in the study of equity in ability differences. *Journal of Special Education, 42*(1), 4–14.

Artiles, A. J., Rueda, R., Salazar, J. J., & Higareda, I. (2005). Within-group diversity in minority disproportionate representation: English language learners in urban school districts. *Exceptional Children, 71*(3), 283–300.

Artiles, A. J., Trent, S. C., & Palmer, J. (2004). Culturally diverse students in special education: Legacies and prospects. In J. A. Banks & C. A. M. Banks (Eds.), *Handbook of research on multicultural education* (2nd ed., pp. 716–735). San Francisco: Jossey-Bass.

Avramidis, E., Bayliss, P., & Burden, R. (2000). Student teachers' attitudes towards the inclusion of children with special educational needs in the ordinary school. *Teaching and Teacher Education, 16*(3), 277–293.

Baker, S., Gersten, R., & Scanlon, D. (2002). Procedural facilitators and cognitive strategies: Tools for unraveling the mysteries of comprehension and the writing process, and for providing meaningful access to the general curriculum. *Learning Disabilities Research and Practice, 17*(1), 65–77.

Barton, P. E. (2003). *Parsing the achievement gap: Baselines for tracking progress. Policy information report.* Princeton, NJ: Educational Testing Services.

Berman, S. (1990). The real ropes course: The development of social consciousness. *Educating for Social Responsibility, The ESR Journal, 1*, 1–18.

Berry, R. (2008). Novice teachers' conceptions of fairness in inclusion classrooms. *Teaching and Teacher Education, 24*(5), 1149–1159.

Bevan-Brown, J. (2002). *Culturally appropriate, effective provision for Maori learners with special needs: He waka tino whakarawea.* Unpublished doctoral thesis, Massey University, Palmerston North, New Zealand.

Bevan-Brown, J. (2003). *The cultural self-review: Providing culturally effective, inclusive, education for Māori learners.* Wellington: New Zealand Council for Educational Research.

Bishop, R., & Berryman, M. (2006). *Culture speaks: Cultural relationships and classroom learning.* Wellington, NZ: Huia.

Bishop, R., Berryman, M., Cavanagh, T., & Teddy, L. (2007). *Te kotahitanga. Phase 3, Whānaungatanga: Establishing a culturally responsive pedagogy of relations in mainstream secondary school classrooms.* Wellington, NZ: Ministry of Education and Waikato University.

Booth, T., & Ainscow, M. (2000). *Index for inclusion: Developing learning and participation in schools.* Bristol, UK: Centre for Studies on Inclusive Education.

Bourke, R., Bevan-Brown, J., Carroll-Lind, J., Cullen, J., Kearney, A., McAlpine, D., Mentis, M., Poskitt, J., et al. (2002). *Special education 2000: Monitoring and evaluation of the policy. Final report phase three.* Wellington, NZ: Ministry of Education.

Callicott, K. J. (2003). Culturally sensitive collaboration within person-centered planning. *Focus on Autism and Other Developmental Disabilities, 18*(1), 60–68.

Cameron, L., & Thorsborne, M. (2001). Restorative justice and school discipline: Mutually exclusive? A practitioner's view of the impact of community conferencing in Queensland schools. In J. Braithwaite & H. Strand (Eds.), *Restorative justice and civil society* (pp. 180–194). Cambridge, UK: Cambridge University Press.

Carr, E. G., Dunlap, G., Horner, R. H., Koegel, R. L., Turnbull, A. P., Sailor, W., Anderson, J. L., et al. (2002). Positive behavior support: Evolution of an applied science. *Journal of Positive Behavior Interventions, 4*(1), 4–16, 20.

Cartledge, G., & Kourea, L. (2008). Culturally responsive classrooms for culturally diverse students with and at risk for disabilities. *Exceptional Children, 74*(3), 351–371.

Cavanagh, T. (2007). Focusing on relationships creates safety in schools. *Set: Research Information for Teachers, 1*, 31–35.

Cawley, J. F., Foley, T. E., & Miller, J. (2003). Science and students with mild disabilities: Principles of universal design. *Intervention in School and Clinic, 38*(3), 160–171.

Chiu, Y.-W., & Ring, J. M. (1998). Chinese and Vietnamese immigrant adolescents under pressure: Identifying stressors and interventions. *Professional Psychology, Research and Practice, 29*(5), 444–449.

Clarke, C., Dyson, A., Millward, A., & Robson, S. (1999). Inclusive education and schools as organizations. *International Journal of Inclusive Education, 3*(1), 37–51.

Darling-Hammond, L. (2004). Inequality and the right to learn: Access to qualified teachers in California's public schools. *Teachers College Record, 106*(10), 1936–1966.

deFur, S. H., Todd-Allen, M., & Getzel, E. E. (2001). Parent participation in the transition planning process. *Career Development for Exceptional Individuals, 24*(1), 19–36.

Donovan, S., & Cross, C. (2002). *Minority students in special and gifted education*. Washington, DC: National Academy Press.

Doveston, M., & Keenaghan, M. (2006). Improving classroom dynamics to support students' learning and social inclusion: A collaborative approach. *Support for Learning, 21*(1), 5–11.

Dunn, L. (1968). Special education for the mildly retarded: Is much of it justifiable? *Exceptional Children, 35*(1), 5–22.

Erickson, F., & Mohatt, G. (1982). Cultural organization and participation structures in two classrooms of Indian students. In G. Spindler (Ed.), *Doing the ethnography of schooling: Education anthropology in action* (pp. 131–174). New York: Holt, Rinehart, & Winston.

Evans, I. M., Salisbury, C. L., Palombaro, M. M., Berryman, J., & Hollowood, T. M. (1992). Peer interactions and social acceptance of elementary-age children with severe disabilities in an inclusive school. *Journal of the Association for Persons with Severe Handicaps, 17*(4), 205–212.

Ferri, B. A., & Connor, D. J. (2005). In the shadow of *Brown*: Special education and overrepresentation of students of color. *Remedial and Special Education, 26*(2), 93–100.

Finn, J. D. (1982). Patterns in special education placement as revealed by the OCR surveys. In K. A. Heller, W. H. Holtzman, & S. Mesrick (Eds.), *Placing children in special education: A strategy for equity* (pp. 322–381). Washington, DC: National Academy Press.

Florsheim, P. (1997). Chinese adolescent immigrants: Factors related to psychosocial adjustment. *Journal of Youth and Adolescence, 26*(2), 143–163.

Fuchs, D., & Fuchs, L. S. (2006). Introduction to response to intervention: What, why, and how valid is it? *Reading Research Quarterly, 41*(1), 95–99.

Gargiulo, R. M. (2006). *Special education in contemporary society: An introduction to exceptionality* (2nd ed.). Belmont, CA: Thomson/Wadsworth.

Geenen, S., Powers, L., Lopez-Vasquez, A., & Bersani, H. (2003). Understanding and promoting the transition of minority adolescents. *Career Development for Exceptional Individuals, 26*(1), 27–46.

Goldenberg, C. (2008). Teaching English language learners: What the research does—and does not—say. *American Educator, 33*(2), 8–44.

Gomez, R., & Greenough, R. (2002). *Parental involvement under the new Title I & Title III: From compliance to effective practice*. Portland, OR: Northwest Regional Educational Laboratory.

Greenwood, C. R., Arreaga-Mayer, C., Utley, C. A., Gavin, K. M., & Terry, B. J. (2001). Class-wide peer tutoring learning management systems: Applications with elementary-level English language learners. *Remedial and Special Education, 22*(1), 34–47.

Ha, Y., Park, H.-S., & Lee, H. (2008, March/April). Social adjustment of Korean immigrant students in secondary schools. *NABE News*, 15–18.

Hains, A. H., Rhyner, P. M., McLean, M. E., Barnekow, K., Johnson, V., & Kennedy, B. (2005). Interdisciplinary teams and diverse families: Practices in early intervention personnel preparation. *Young Exceptional Children, 8*(4), 2–10.

Harry, B. (2008). Collaboration with culturally and linguistically diverse families: Ideal versus reality. *Exceptional Children, 74*(3), 372–388.

Harry, B., & Artiles, A. J. (2007). Considerations about the cultural nature of inclusion, teaching, and learning. In M. Giangreco & M. B. Doyle (Eds.), *Quick-guides to inclusion: Ideas for educating students with disabilities* (2nd ed., pp. 31–44). Baltimore, MD: Paul H. Brookes.

Harry, B., & Klingner, J. K. (2006). *Why are so many minority students in special education? Understanding race & disability in schools*. New York: Teachers College Press.

Harry, B., Klingner, J. K., & Hart, J. (2005). African American families under fire: Ethnographic views of family strengths. *Remedial and Special Education, 26*(2), 101–112.

Heller, K. A., Holtzman, W. H., & Messick, S. (Eds.). (1982). *Placing children in special education: A strategy for equity*. Washington, DC: National Academy Press.

Horner, R. H., Meyer, L. H., & Fredericks, H. D. B. (Eds.). (1986). *Education of learners with severe handicaps: Exemplary service strategies*. Baltimore, MD: Paul H. Brookes.

Hosp, J. L., & Reschly, D. J. (2004). Disproportionate representation of minority students in special education: Academic, demographic, and economic predictors. *Exceptional Children, 70*(2), 185–199.

Howland, A., Anderson, J. A., Smiley, A. D., & Abbott, D. (2006). School liaisons: Bridging the gap between home and school. *School Community Journal, 16*(2), 47–68.

Huer, M. B., Parette, H. P., Jr., & Saenz, T. I. (2001). Conversations with Mexican Americans regarding children with disabilities and augmentative and alternative communication. *Communication Disorders Quarterly, 22*(4), 197–206.

Individuals with Disabilities Education Improvement Act (IDEIA), Public Law 108-466. (2004).

Kim, K.-H., & Morningstar, M. E. (2005). Transition planning involving culturally and linguistically diverse families. *Career Development for Exceptional Individuals, 28*(2), 92–103.

King-Sears, M. E. (2001). Three steps for gaining access to the general education curriculum for learners with disabilities. *Intervention in School and Clinic, 37*(2), 67–76.

King-Sears, M. E. (2008). Facts and fallacies: Differentiation and the general education curriculum for students with special education needs. *Support for Learning, 23*(2), 55–62.

Klingner, J. K., Artiles, A. J., & Barletta, L. M. (2006). English language learners who struggle with reading: Language acquisition or LD? *Journal of Learning Disabilities, 39*(2), 108–128.

Klingner, J. K., & Edwards, P. A. (2006). Cultural considerations with response to intervention models. *Reading Research Quarterly, 41*(1), 108–117.

Kozleski, E. B., Engelbrecht, P., Hess, R., Swart, E., Eloff, I., Oswald, M., Molina, A., & Swati, J. (2008). Where differences matter: A cross-cultural analysis of family voice in special education. *Journal of Special Education, 42*(1), 26–35.

Kozol, J. (1967). *Death at an early age: The destruction of the hearts and minds of Negro children in the Boston public schools*. Boston: Houghton-Mifflin.

Ladson-Billings, G. (2007). Culturally responsive teaching: Theory and practice. In J. A. Banks & C. A. M. Banks (Eds.), *Multicultural education: Issues and perspectives* (6th ed., pp. 221–245). Hoboken, NJ: John Wiley & Sons.

Lam, S. K.-Y. (2005). An interdisciplinary course to prepare school professionals to collaborate with families of exceptional children. *Multicultural Education, 13*(2), 38–42.

Lee, L. C., & Zhan, G. (1998). Psychosocial status of children and youths. In L. C. Lee & N. W. S. Zane (Eds.), *Handbook of Asian American psychology* (pp. 137–163). Thousand Oaks, CA: Sage.

MacMillan, D. L., & Reschly, D. J. (1998). Overrepresentation of minority students: The case for greater specificity or reconsideration of the variables examined. *Journal of Special Education, 32*(1), 15–24.

Mellard, D. (2008). *What is response to intervention (RTI)?* Webinar hosted by National Center in Response to Intervention. Retrieved September 20, 2008, from http://www.rti4success. org/index.php?option=com_content&task=view&id=732&Itemid=75

Mercer, J. R. (1973). *Labeling the mentally retarded: Clinical and social system perspectives on mental retardation.* Berkeley: University of California Press.

Meyer, L. H. (1997). Tinkering around the edges? *Journal of the Association for Persons with Severe Handicaps, 22*(2), 80–82.

Meyer, L. H., Park, H.-S., Grenot-Scheyer, M., Schwartz, I. S., & Harry, B. (Eds.). (1998). *Making friends: The influences of culture and development.* Baltimore, MD: Paul H. Brookes.

Montague, M., & Applegate, B. (2000). Middle school students' perceptions, persistence, and performance in mathematical problem solving. *Learning Disability Quarterly, 23*(3), 215–227.

Murtadha-Watts, K., & Stoughton, E. (2004). Critical cultural knowledge in special education: Reshaping the responsiveness of school leaders. *Focus on Exceptional Children, 37*(2), 1–8.

Noddings, N. (2005). *The challenge to care in schools: An alternative approach to education* (2nd ed.). New York: Teachers College Press.

Ortiz, A. A. (2002). Prevention of school failure and early intervention for English language learners. In A. J. Artiles & A. A. Ortiz (Eds.), *English language learners with special education needs: Identification, assessment, and instruction* (pp. 31–48). Washington, DC: Center for Applied Linguistics and Delta.

Oswald, D. P., Coutinho, M. J., Best, A. M., & Singh, N. N. (1999). Ethnic representation in special education: The influence of school-related economic and demographic variables. *Journal of Special Education, 32*(4), 194–206.

Palincsar, A. S., Magnusson, S. J., Collins, K. M., & Cutter, J. (2001). Making science accessible to all: Results of a design experiment in inclusive classrooms. *Learning Disability Quarterly, 24*(1), 15–32.

Palmer, J. D., & Jang, E.-Y. (2005). Korean born, Korean-American high school students' entry into understanding race and racism through social interactions and conversations. *Race, Ethnicity and Education, 8*(3), 297–317.

Parette, H. P., & Petch-Hogan, B. (2000). Approaching families: Facilitating culturally/linguistically diverse family involvement. *Teaching Exceptional Children, 33*(2), 4–10.

Pelletier, J., & Corter, C. (2005). Toronto first duty: Integrating kindergarten, childcare, and parenting support to help diverse families connect to schools. *Multicultural Education, 13*(2), 30–37.

Peske, H. G., & Haycock, K. (2006). *Teaching inequity: How poor and minority students are shortchanged on teacher quality.* Washington, DC: Education Trust.

Rebell, M. A. (1999). Fiscal equity litigation and the democratic imperative. *Equity & Excellence in Education, 32*(3), 5–18.

Richardson, J. G. (1994). Common, delinquent, and special: On the formalization of common schooling in the American states. *American Educational Research Journal, 31*(4), 695–723.

Rose, D., & Meyer, A. (2000). Universal design for individual differences. *Educational Leadership, 58*(3), 39–43.

Salas, L., Lopez, E. J., Chinn, K., & Menchaca-Lopez, E. (2005). Can special education teachers create parent partnerships with Mexican American families? Si se pueda! *Multicultural Education, 13*(2), 52–55.

Sapon-Shevin, M. (2004). Thinking inclusively about inclusive education. In K. Kesson & E. W. Ross (Eds.), *Defending public schools: Teaching for a democratic society* (Vol. 2, pp. 161–172). Westport, CT: Praeger.

Sapon-Shevin, M. (2005). Teachable moments for social justice. In B. S. Engel & A. C. Martin (Eds.), *Holding values: What we mean by progressive education* (pp. 93–97). Portsmouth, NH: Heinemann.

Schmidt, R. J., Rozendal, M. S., & Greenman, G. G. (2002). Reading instruction in the inclusive classroom: Research-based practices. *Remedial and Special Education, 23*(3), 130–140.

Schnorr, R. F. (1997). From enrollment to membership: "Belonging" in middle and high school classes. *Journal of the Association for Persons with Severe Handicaps, 22*(1), 1–15.

Skiba, R. J., Poloni-Staudinger, L., Simmons, A. B., Feggins-Azziz, L. R., & Chung, C.-G. (2005). Unproven links: Can poverty explain ethnic disproportionality in special education? *Journal of Special Education, 39*(3), 130–144.

Skiba, R. J., Simmons, A. B., Ritter, S., Gibb, A. C., Rausch, M. K., Cuadrado, J., & Chung, C.-G. (2008). Achieving equity in special education: History, status, and current challenges. *Exceptional Children, 74*(3), 264–288.

Slee, R., & Allan, J. (2005). Excluding the included: A reconsideration of inclusive education. In J. Rix, K. Simmons, M. Nind, & K. Sheehy (Eds.), *Policy and power in inclusive education: Values into practice* (pp. 13–24). London: RoutledgeFalmer.

Sleeter, C. E., & Grant, C. A. (1987). An analysis of multicultural education in the United States. *Harvard Educational Review, 57*(4), 421–444.

Spooner, F., Baker, J. N., Harris, A. A., Ahlgrim-Delzell, L., & Browder, D. M. (2007). Effects of training in universal design for learning on lesson plan development. *Remedial and Special Education, 28*(2), 108–116.

Suárez-Orozco, M. M. (2001). Globalization, immigration, and education: The research agenda. *Harvard Educational Review, 71*(3), 345–365.

Trent, S. C., Kea, C. D., & Oh, K. (2008). Preparing preservice educators for cultural diversity: How far have we come? *Exceptional Children, 74*(3), 328–350.

Tucker, J. A. (1980). Ethnic proportions in classes for the learning disabled: Issues in nonbiased assessment. *Journal of Special Education, 14*(1), 93–105.

Turnbull, A. P., Turnbull, H. R., Erwin, E. J., & Soodak, L. C. (2005). *Families, professionals and exceptionality: A special partnership* (5th ed.). Upper Saddle River, NJ: Prentice-Hall.

United Nations Educational, Scientific and Cultural Organization. (1994). *The Salamanca statement and framework for action on special education needs education: Adopted by the World Conference on Special Needs Education: Access and Quality, Salamanca, Spain.* Paris: Author.

Vitello, S. J., & Mithaug, D. E. (Eds.). (1998). *Inclusive schooling: National and international perspectives.* Mahwah, NJ: Lawrence Erlbaum.

Ware, F. (2006). Warm demander pedagogy: Culturally responsive teaching that supports a culture of achievement for African American students. *Urban Education, 41*(4), 427–456.

Webb-Johnson, G. C. (1999). Cultural contexts: Confronting the overrepresentation of African American learners in special education. In J. R. Scotti & L. H. Meyer (Eds.), *Behavioral intervention: Principles, models, and practices* (pp. 449–464). Baltimore, MD: Paul H. Brookes.

Yeh, C., & Inose, M. (2002). Difficulties and coping strategies of Chinese, Japanese, and Korean immigrant students. *Adolescence, 37*(145), 69–82.

Zehr, H. (2002). *The little book of restorative justice*. Intercourse, PA: Good Books.

Zhang, C., & Bennett, T. (2003). Facilitating the meaningful participation of culturally and linguistically diverse families in the IFSP and IEP process. *Focus on Autism and Other Developmental Disabilities, 18*(1), 51–59.

Zionts, L. T., Zionts, P., Harrison, S., & Bellinger, O. (2003). Urban African American families' perceptions of cultural sensitivity within the special education system. *Focus on Autism and Other Developmental Disabilities, 18*(1), 41–50.

CHAPTER 15

Recruiting and Retaining Gifted Students From Diverse Ethnic, Cultural, and Language Groups

Donna Y. Ford

One of the most persistent and pervasive problems in education is the underrepresentation of African American, Hispanic American, and Native American students in gifted education programs and advanced placement (AP) classes. Since at least the 1930s, reports and studies have revealed that culturally diverse students have always been inadequately represented in gifted education (Artiles, Trent, & Palmer, 2004; Donovan & Cross, 2002; Ford, 1998, 2004). Statistics show that these three groups are underrepresented by an average of 50 percent nationally (Office for Civil Rights, 1998, 2000a, 2002, 2004; U.S. Department of Education [USDE], 1993). It is equally important to note that African American students are the most underrepresented ethnic group in AP classes and among AP test takers (College Board, 2008; Ford, Grantham, & Whiting, 2008b). This point is worth highlighting for at least two reasons: (1) the heavy reliance on AP classes to serve gifted students at the high school level, and (2) the higher education opportunities afforded students who participate in AP classes.

The percentages for gifted education, shown in Table 15.1, support the notion that "a mind is a terrible thing to waste," a statement popularized by the United Negro College Fund. These data also support the reality that a mind is a terrible thing to erase. In other words, many African American, Hispanic American, and Native American students are gifted, but their gifts often go unidentified in schools. Consequently, they are neither challenged nor given the opportunity to develop their gifts and talents, which atrophy. The 2002 No Child Left Behind Act recognized that gifted students are unlikely to develop without appropriate services, as evidenced in the following definition:

> The term "gifted and talented" ... means students, children, or youth
> who give evidence of high achievement capacity in areas such as
> intellectual, creative, artistic, or leadership capacity, or in specific

academic fields, and who need services or activities not ordinarily provided by the school in order to fully develop those capabilities. (Title IX, Part A, Section 9101(22), p. 544, as cited in National Association for Gifted Children, 2002)

ASSUMPTIONS OF THE CHAPTER

This chapter explores barriers to and recommendations for recruiting and retaining racial and ethnic minority students into gifted education programs. In particular, I present data on the underrepresentation of African American students (rather than other diverse students) in gifted education for at least two reasons: (1) between 1998 and 2004, African American students were the only group of color to become *more underrepresented* in gifted education, as noted in Table 15.1, and (2) this group is more often the focus of litigation relative to inequities in gifted education (Office for Civil Rights, 2000b). I recognize that Asian Americans are also racial and ethnic minority students. However, I have yet to find a report indicating that Asian American students are underrepresented in gifted education. Furthermore, Asian Americans, unlike African American, Hispanic American, and Native American students, frequently experience positive stereotypes, and many are high achieving. Consequently, they are not discussed in this chapter. By omitting Asian American students, I am not ignoring the social injustices they have experienced and continue to experience in society and in the schools (Kitano & DiJosia, 2002; Pang, Kiang, & Pak, 2004).

Table 15.1   Gifted Education Demographics for 1998–2004

	1998		2000		2002		2004	
Race/ Ethnicity	School District %	Gifted & Talented %	School District %	Gifted & Talented %	School District %	Gifted & Talented %	School District %	Gifted & Talented %
American Indian/Alaskan Native	1.1	0.87	1.16	0.91	1.21	0.93	1.21	0.93
Black	17.0	8.40	16.99	8.23	17.16	8.43	17.16	8.43
Hispanic/ Latino	14.3	8.63	16.13	9.54	17.8	10.41	17.80	10.41
Asian/Pacific Islander	4.0	6.57	4.14	7.00	4.42	7.64	4.42	7.64
White	63.7	75.53	61.58	74.24	59.42	72.59	59.42	72.69
Total	100.00	100.00	100.00	100.00	100.00	100.00	100.00	100.00

Source: Elementary and Secondary School Civil Rights Survey, 1998, 2000, 2002, 2004, Retrieved January 26, 2009, from http://ocrdata.ed.gov/ocr2002rv30/wdsdata.html

This chapter is grounded in several assumptions and propositions. First, I propose that the majority of past and current efforts to redress the underrepresentation problem have been inadequate and misdirected, resulting in what may be the most segregated programs in our public schools. Second, gifted education is a need—not a privilege. By not being identified as gifted and receiving appropriate services and programming, gifted students from racial, ethnic, and language minorities are being denied an opportunity to reach their potential. A third assumption and proposition is that no group has a monopoly on "giftedness" or being intelligent and academically successful. Giftedness exists in every racial and ethnic group and across all economic strata (USDE, 1993). Consequently, there should be little or no underrepresentation of racial and ethnic minority students in gifted education and AP classes.

A fourth assumption and proposition is that giftedness is a social and cultural construct; subjectivity guides definitions, assessments, and perceptions of giftedness (Pfeiffer, 2003; Sternberg, 1985). This subjectivity contributes to segregated gifted education programs in numerous and insidious ways. Sapon-Shevon (1996) stated that "the ways in which gifted education is defined, constituted, and enacted lead directly to increased segregation, limited educational opportunities for the majority of students, and damage to children's social and political developments" (p. 196). Accordingly, educators must examine their views about the purposes of gifted education in particular as well as their perceptions of students from racially and ethnically diverse backgrounds.

The fifth guiding assumption is that all decisions made on behalf of students should be made with their best interests in mind. Education should be additive for students, not subtractive. We should be about the business of building on what students have when they enter our schools. Finally, I believe that efforts to recruit and retain racial and ethnic minority students in gifted education must be comprehensive, proactive, aggressive, and systematic. Educators, families, and children themselves need to work together to ensure that gifted education is desegregated (Harris, Brown, Ford, & Richardson, 2004). Gallagher's (2004) assertion seems apropos here:

> In another profession, the physician treating a patient will often start
> with the weakest treatment available and then progress to stronger
> treatments once the first attempt has seen little effect. We seem to have
> been following that approach in educating gifted students by
> prescribing a minimal treatment (one might even say a non-therapeutic
> dose) designed hopefully to do some good without upsetting other
> people . . . [A]s a profession, we need to come to some consensus that
> we need stronger treatments. (p. xxviii)

This chapter is divided into three major sections. The first section focuses on recruitment issues and barriers; the second section focuses on recruitment recommendations; and the third focuses on retention issues and recommendations. The two guiding questions of the chapter are: How can we effectively recruit and retain more racially and ethnically diverse students in gifted education? How can we ensure that gifted education programs are both excellent and equitable?

RECRUITMENT ISSUES AND BARRIERS

Most of the scholarship that explains underrepresentation focuses on some aspect of recruitment. Specifically, it is assumed that racial and ethnic minority students are underrepresented because of problems associated with screening and identification instruments, specifically tests. Little attention has been given to retention, which is discussed later in this chapter.

The first step in addressing (or redressing) the underrepresentation of racial and ethnic minority students in gifted education is to focus on recruitment. *Recruitment* refers here to screening, identifying, and placing students (or getting them into gifted education). Perceptions about racial and ethnic minority students combined with a lack of cultural understanding and competence significantly undermine the ability of educators to recruit diverse students into gifted education (and AP classes) and to retain them. Ford, Harris, Tyson, and Frazier Trotman (2002) argued, as we do here, that a "cultural deficit" perspective pervades decisions made about and on behalf of African American, Hispanic American, and Native American students. This phenomenon is described next.

Deficit Thinking

> The more we retreat from the culture and the people, the less we learn about them. The less we know about them, the more uncomfortable we feel among them. The more uncomfortable we feel among them, the more inclined we are to withdraw. The more we withdraw from the people, the more faults we find with them. The less we know about their culture, the more we seem to dislike it. And the worst of it is that, in the end, we begin to believe the very lies we've invented to console ourselves. (Storti, 1989, pp. 32–34)

As stated earlier, a major premise of this chapter is that a deficit orientation held by educators hinders access to gifted programs for diverse students as reflected in the preceding quote. This thinking hinders the ability and willingness of educators to recognize the strengths of students from diverse ethnic, racial, class, and language groups. Deficit thinking exists when educators interpret differences as deficits, dysfunctions, and/or disadvantages. Consequently, many minority students quickly acquire the "at-risk" label and the focus is on their shortcomings or weaknesses rather than their strengths. With deficit thinking, differences in someone who is culturally, racially, or ethnically diverse are interpreted negatively as if the individual and/or characteristics are abnormal, substandard, or otherwise inferior. For example, a student who speaks nonstandard English and is making good grades in school may not be referred to screening and identification if the teacher neither understands nor appreciates nonstandard English. Likewise, a student who has excellent math skills but weak writing skills may not be perceived as gifted or intelligent. Every student has strengths and weaknesses. Educators need to move beyond a deficit orientation in order to recognize the strengths and potential of racial, ethnic, and language minorities, especially those from low-income backgrounds.

Ideas about racial and ethnic groups influence the development of definitions, policies, and practices designed to understand and address differences. For instance, Gould (1996) and Menchaca (1997) noted that deficit thinking contributed to past (and, no doubt, current) beliefs about race, ethnicity, and intelligence. Gould takes readers back two centuries to demonstrate how *a priori* assumptions and fears associated with different ethnic groups, particularly African Americans, led to conscious fraud: dishonest and prejudicial research methods, deliberate miscalculations, convenient omissions, and data misinterpretation among scientists studying intelligence. These early assumptions and practices gave way to the prevailing belief that human races could be ranked in a linear scale of mental worth, as evidenced by the research of Cyril Burt, Paul Broca, and Samuel Morton on craniometry (Gould).

Later, as school districts faced increasing racial and ethnic diversity (often attributable to immigration), educators resorted to increased reliance on biased standardized tests (Armour-Thomas, 1992; Gould, 1996; Helms, 1992; Menchaca, 1997). These tests almost guaranteed low test scores for immigrants and racial and ethnic minority groups who were unfamiliar with U.S. customs, traditions, values, norms, and language (Ford, 2004). These tests measured familiarity with mainstream American culture and English proficiency, not intelligence. According to Gould, intelligence tests provide limited information about racial and ethnic minority populations. The results from these tests often limited the educational opportunities of diverse students, who tended not to score high on them. Menchaca (1997) stated:

> Racial differences in intelligence, it was contended, are most validly explained by racial differences in innate, genetically determined abilities. What emerged from these findings regarding schooling were curricular modifications ensuring that the "intellectually inferior" and the social order would best be served by providing these students concrete, low-level, segregated instruction commensurate with their alleged diminished intellectual abilities. (p. 38)

The publication of *The Bell Curve* (Herrnstein & Murray, 1994) revived deficit thinking about racially and ethnically diverse groups, specifically African Americans. Seeking to influence public and social policy, Herrnstein and Murray, like researchers of earlier centuries (such as Cyril Burt), interpreted—or misinterpreted and misrepresented—their data to confirm institutionalized prejudices. As Gould (1996) noted, the hereditarian theory of IQ is a homegrown American product that persists in current practices of testing, sorting, and discarding. Issues and barriers associated with screening support this assertion.

Screening Issues and Barriers

To be considered for placement in gifted education, students often undergo screening in which they are administered assessments with predetermined criteria (e.g., cutoff scores). If students meet the initial screening requirements, they may be given additional assessments, which are used to make final placement decisions. In most schools, entering the screening pool is based on teacher referrals (Colangelo & Davis, 2002). This practice hinders the effective screening of racial and ethnic minority students because they are seldom referred by teachers for screening

(Ford, 1996; Ford, Grantham, & Whiting, 2008b). Specifically, a Hispanic American student may meet the school district's criteria for giftedness but be overlooked because she has not been referred for screening. The teacher may not refer her because of biases and stereotypes about Hispanic Americans (deficit thinking), because the student's English skills are not strong or proficient, or because of the teacher's perceptual and attitudinal barriers. Intuitively, it makes sense that teacher referrals should be used as part of the screening and decision-making process. As the preceding example illustrates, however, this practice may negatively affect racial, ethnic, and language minority students. Furthermore, Ford et al. (2008b) reported in their review of the literature that every study on teacher referral for gifted education screening and placement revealed that teachers underrefer African American students more than any other racial or ethnic group.

Similarly, teachers and other adults (e.g., counselors, parents, administrators, and community members) may be required to complete checklists on the referred students. If the checklists ignore cultural diversity—how giftedness manifests itself differently in various cultures—then gifted diverse students may receive low ratings that do not accurately capture their strengths, abilities, and potential. A framework proposed by Frasier et al. (1995) describes how the core attributes of giftedness vary by culture. They contended that educators should define and assess giftedness with each group's cultural differences in mind. As an illustration, one core characteristic of giftedness is a keen sense of humor. A common verbal game—or match—among low-income African Americans is "playing the dozens" or "signifying" (Lee, 1993; Majors & Billson, 1992). African American students are exemplifying three characteristics of giftedness when playing the dozens—humor, creativity, and verbal skills. Teachers may be offended by the students' humor, blinding them from seeing these core characteristics of giftedness.

One of the first signs of giftedness is strong verbal skill. However, if the student does not speak Standard English (e.g., speaks Black English Vernacular or Ebonics) or has limited English proficiency, the teacher may not recognize the student's strong verbal skills. A third example relates to independence, which is another characteristic of giftedness. Racial and ethnic minority students who have communal values, such as interdependence and cooperation, may be social and prefer to work in groups rather than individually and competitively (Boykin, 1994; Ramírez & Castañeda, 1974; Shade, Kelly, & Oberg, 1997). Consequently, the teacher may not consider such students to be independent workers or thinkers.

Like tests, checklists can be problematic. In addition to referrals/nomination forms and checklists being "culture blind," they frequently focus on demonstrated ability and performance. As a result, they overlook students who are gifted but lack opportunities to demonstrate their intelligence and achievement. These "potentially gifted" students and/or gifted underachievers are those who live in poverty and/or are culturally different from mainstream students. A study by Smith, Constantino, and Krashen (1997) sheds light on this issue. These researchers compared the number of books in the homes and classrooms of three California communities. There was an average of 199 books in the homes of Beverly Hills children, four in the homes of Watts children, and 2.7 in the homes of Compton children.

In terms of classrooms, there was an average of 392 books in Beverly Hills classrooms, 54 in Watts classrooms, and 47 in Compton classrooms. Essentially, because of exposure to books and educational opportunities, children from Beverly Hills homes and schools are more likely to demonstrate their giftedness (e.g., have a large vocabulary, be able to read at an early age) than are children from the other homes and schools. Many children in Compton and

Watts are gifted but lack essential academic experiences and exposure to develop their abilities and potential.

In 1993, the U.S. Department of Education recognized that our schools are filled with potentially gifted students. To help educators improve the recruitment of diverse students into gifted education, the department issued the following definition of giftedness, one that relies heavily on the notion of talent development:

> Children and youth with outstanding talent perform or show the potential for performing at remarkably high levels of accomplishment when compared with others of their age, experience, or environment. These children and youth exhibit high performance capacity in intellectual, creative, and/or artistic areas, possess an unusual leadership capacity, or excel in specific academic fields. They require services or activities not ordinarily provided by the schools. Outstanding talents are present in children and youth from all cultural groups, across all economic strata, and in all areas of human endeavor. (USDE, 1993, p. 3)

The percentage of school districts adopting this definition or some version of it is unknown. The ramification of not adopting the federal definition, or some version of it, is clear: continued underrepresentation of students from racial, ethnic, and language minorities in gifted education.

Identification/Assessment Issues and Barriers

Monolithic definitions of *giftedness* pose serious barriers to recruiting diverse students into gifted education. Monolithic definitions ignore human differences in general and cultural diversity in particular. They ignore the fact that what is valued as giftedness in one culture may not be valued in another. For example, most European Americans highly value cognitive and academic ability over spatial, musical, interpersonal, and other abilities (Gardner, 1993) and tend to value academic knowledge and skills over tacit or practical knowledge and skills (Sternberg, 1985). Conversely, navigational skills or hunting skills may be prized in another culture. These differences raise this question: If a student is not gifted in the ways that are valued by my culture, is the student gifted? Based on current practice, most culturally diverse students are not likely to be perceived as gifted.

Perceptions and definitions also influence the instruments or tests selected to assess giftedness. Dozens of intelligence and achievement tests exist. What determines which instrument a school district selects? If we value verbal skills, we will select an instrument that assesses verbal skills. If we value logic and/or problem-solving skills, we will select an instrument that assesses these skills. If we value creativity, the instrument we select will assess creativity. We are not likely to choose an instrument that measures a construct or skill that we do not value.

Many schools use intelligence and achievement tests—more than other types of tests—to assess giftedness. Test scores play a dominant role in identification and placement decisions. For example, a study by VanTassel-Baska, Patton, and Prillaman (1989) revealed that 88.5 percent of states rely primarily on standardized, norm-referenced tests to identify gifted students, including those from economically and culturally diverse groups. More than

90 percent of school districts use scores from these types of tests for labeling and placement (Colangelo & Davis, 2002; Davis & Rimm, 1997). These tests measure verbal skills, abstract thinking, math skills, and other skills considered indicative of giftedness (or intelligence or achievement) by educators. Likewise, they ignore skills and abilities that may be also valued by other groups (e.g., creativity, interpersonal skills, group problem-solving skills, navigational skills, and musical skills). Consequently, racial and ethnic minority students are more likely than others to display characteristics that place them at a disadvantage in testing situations (Helms, 1992; Office for Civil Rights, 2000). Monolithic definitions result in the adoption of unidimensional, ethnocentric tests that contribute significantly to racially homogeneous gifted education programs. These tests are more effective at identifying giftedness among middle-class White students than among racial and ethnic minority students, particularly if these students are from low-socioeconomic-status backgrounds.

An additional concern related to tests is the extensive use of cutoff scores, referred to earlier. The most frequently used cutoff score for placement in gifted education is an IQ score of 130 or above, two standard deviations above the average IQ of 100 (Colangelo & Davis, 2002). Decades of data indicate that groups such as African Americans, Puerto Rican Americans, and Native Americans, even at the highest economic levels, have mean tested IQ scores lower than White students. For the most part, the average tested IQ of African Americans is 83 to 87, compared to 97 to 100 for White students, on traditional intelligence tests (see Helms, 1992; Kaufman, 1994). The same holds for children who live in poverty, regardless of racial background. Their average IQ is about 85. I have consulted with several psychologists who believe that because the "average" IQ score of African Americans is about 85, giftedness would mean an IQ of 115 or higher among this population. Sadly, those holding racist ideologies will attribute these differences to genetics and argue that giftedness (or intelligence) is primarily inherited. This position implies that the environment is less important than heredity in the development of talents and abilities. Such a view is counterproductive in education, which is supposed to build on and improve the skills and abilities of students.

Conversely, those who recognize the influence of the environment and culture on performance attribute these different scores primarily to social, environmental, and cultural factors. For instance, it has been demonstrated in numerous studies on "environmental racism" that poverty, exposure to lead, malnutrition, and poor educational experiences negatively affect test performance (Baugh, 1991; Bullard, 1993; Bullard, 1994; Bryant & Mohai, 1992; Ford, 2004; Grossman, 1991). Thus, cutoff scores cannot be selected arbitrarily and in a culture-blind fashion. If adopted at all, cutoff scores should be used with caution and should take into consideration the different mean scores of the various racial, ethnic, cultural, and language groups.

A final issue related to testing is interpreting results (see Kaufman, 1994). When other information is considered, it is possible to select and use a test that effectively assesses the strengths of racial, ethnic, and language minority students. However, perceptions can prevent a teacher, counselor, or psychologist from interpreting the results in a culturally fair way. What if a teacher, counselor, or psychologist interpreting the test results holds negative stereotypes about African Americans? What if they hold stereotypes about groups who have limited English proficiency? What if a student from these two groups receives a very high IQ or achievement test score? How would this affect the psychologist's, teacher's, and counselor's interpretation of the results? Test interpretation is heavily subjective, and interpretations are influenced by the quantity and quality of training to work with diverse cultural, ethnic, and language groups. Results from a "good" test can be poorly interpreted if the interpreter has little understanding of how culture influences test performance (Ford, 2004).

In a collaborative effort, the American Educational Research Association (AERA), the American Psychological Association (APA), and the National Council on Measurement in Education (NCME) (1999) addressed the myriad problems of interpreting test scores. They noted the harmful effects of misinterpreting test results, especially with racial and ethnic minority groups: "The ultimate responsibility for appropriate test use and interpretation lies predominantly with the test user. In assuming this responsibility, the user must become knowledgeable about a test's appropriate uses and the populations for which it is appropriate" (p. 112). They advise, as do others (e.g., National Association for Gifted Children, 1997), that test users collect extensive data on students to complement test results and use a comprehensive approach in the assessment process (Armour-Thomas, 1992; Helms, 1992). Test users are encouraged to consider the validity of a given instrument or procedure as well as the cultural characteristics of the student when interpreting results (Office of Ethnic Minority Affairs, 1993; extensive information on equity and testing can be found at the National Center for Fair and Open Testing Web site: www.fairtest.org).

In sum, the data collected on all students should be *multidimensional*—a variety of information collected from multiple sources. For example, data are needed from school personnel, family members, and community members. Data on intelligence, achievement, creativity, motivation, interests, and learning styles are essential when making decisions about students. In this era of high-stakes testing, educators should err on the side of having "too much" information rather than too little to make informed, educationally sound decisions. The data collected should also be *multimodal*, that is, collected in a variety of ways. Information should be collected verbally (interviews, conversations) and nonverbally (e.g., observations, writing, performances), and both subjective and objective information should be gathered. Furthermore, if the student speaks a first language other than English, educators should use an interpreter and use instruments translated into that student's primary or preferred language. Essentially, assessment should be made with the students' best interests in mind, and the principle of "do no harm" should prevail. As noted by Sandoval, Frisby, Geisinger, Scheuneman, and Grenier (1998): "In any testing situation, but particularly high stakes assessments, examinees must have an opportunity to demonstrate the competencies, knowledge, or attributes being measured" (p. 183). Few equitable opportunities exist when assessments are unidimensional, unimodal, and ethnocentric (color blind or culture blind) (Ford, Moore, & Milner, 2005). How can we make responsible and defensible decisions about culturally diverse students when assessments and interpretation of test results ignore or trivialize the impact of culture? After screening, the next step is placement considerations. Like screening, placement considerations are complex and riddled with potential problems.

Placement Issues and Barriers

Giftedness is often equated with achievement or productivity. To most educators and laypersons alike, the notion of a "gifted underachiever" may seem paradoxical. However, any educator who has taught students identified as gifted knows that gifted students can and do underachieve; some are unmotivated and uninterested in school, some are procrastinators, and others do not complete assignments or do just enough to get by. In my work with gifted African American students, I have observed about 80 percent of them underachieving (Ford, 1996). Other researchers believe that at least 20 percent of gifted students underachieve, especially gifted females (Reis & Callahan, 1989; Rimm, 1995; Silverman, 1993).

One problem associated with placement, therefore, is the belief that gifted students should receive gifted education services *if* they are high achievers, hard workers, and motivated. That is, achievement must be manifested (e.g., high grade point average [GPA] or high achievement test scores). Gifted underachievers are not likely to be referred for or placed in gifted education. If placement occurs, it is often provisional for this group. For example, several school districts will remove students from a gifted program if their GPA falls below a designated level, they fail a course, or they have poor attendance that is unexcused. This situation of students meeting gifted education criteria (e.g., high test scores) but underachieving often arises when testing has been unidimensional and unimodal: Educators have focused solely on determining the students' IQ scores and with a narrow range of instruments. Conversely, if intelligence *and* achievement data were collected during screening, educators would know whether the student is (1) gifted and achieving or (2) gifted and underachieving, and they could make placement decisions based on these data. For example, they could place gifted underachievers in gifted education classes and provide them with a tutor, study skills, language skills, or counseling (Ford, 1996). The objective would be to help gifted underachievers become achievers and experience success in gifted education classrooms.

Many racial, ethnic, and language minority groups are likely to be gifted underachievers or potentially gifted students (Ford, 1996). Some educators do not wish to place these students in gifted education programs and AP classes because they believe that the level and pace of the schoolwork may frustrate these students. In theory, the issue of underachievers being overwhelmed in gifted education programs may be a valid concern, depending on why the students are underachieving. In practice, it has harmed gifted students who are members of racial, ethnic, and language minority groups.

Instead of supporting diverse students and helping them to overcome their weaknesses and achievement barriers, educators have often chosen the option of least resistance under the guise of altruism ("I don't want him to be frustrated." "She'll be unhappy." "He'll just fall further behind."). As we seek to prevent students from being frustrated, we should ask: What are we doing to help to alleviate their frustration? Tutoring, counseling, and other support systems (academic, vocational, social-emotional) are essential. When placement is combined with support, gifted underachieving students are more likely to be successful in gifted education and AP classes.

As described next, recruiting students from diverse groups into gifted education programs is one thing; retaining them is another. What policies, practices, procedures, philosophies, and supports should be in place for diverse students to experience success and remain in gifted education?

RECRUITMENT RECOMMENDATIONS

Recruiting students from diverse groups into gifted education is the first half of resolving their underrepresentation in gifted education. As described here, recruitment should include a talent-development philosophy, changes in standardized tests and assessment practices, culturally sensitive tests, multicultural assessment preparation for professionals, and the effective development of policies and procedures.

Talent Development Philosophy

Educators who support a talent-development philosophy and culturally sensitive definitions of giftedness are more likely than others to have supports in place to assist students from diverse groups. For example, school districts would begin screening and placing students in gifted education at the preschool and primary levels. Currently, most gifted education programs begin in grades 2–4, which may be too late for potentially gifted students and those beginning to show signs of underachievement, commonly referred to as the *second grade syndrome*. Abilities—gifts and talents—should be recognized and nurtured early (USDE, 1993), especially among students already at risk of being unrecognized as gifted.

Changes in Standardized Tests and Assessment Practices

Tests standardized on middle-class White populations are here to stay despite the reality that they are another form of discrimination favoring the privileged (Sowell, 1993). However, educators concerned about improving the test performance of diverse students on these instruments have a number of options to consider. First and foremost, they should never select, use, and interpret tests that lack validity for students from racial, ethnic, and language minorities (AERA et al., 1999). Second, they need to mesh the process of assessment with the cultural characteristics of the group being studied while recognizing that assessment is made culturally sensitive through a continuing and open-ended series of substantive and methodological insertions and adaptations (Suzuki & Ponterotto, 2008). In essence, equitable and culturally sensitive assessment necessitates a combination of changed attitudes, accumulation of more knowledge, thoughtful practice, and development of keen insight into the dynamics of human behavior (Heubert & Hauser, 1999; Kornhaber, 2004; Sandoval et al., 1998). Tests should never be given so much power that other data are disregarded—tests simply assist educators in making *conditional probability statements* on the basis of the particular test (Kaufman, 1994; Sandoval et al.).

Culturally Sensitive Tests

Tests vary in the amount of language used in the directions and in the items. When working with linguistically diverse groups, we must use caution when tests have a high linguistic and/or high cultural demand (Flanagan, Ortiz, & Alfonso, 2007). Much data indicate that the results from such tests may underestimate what students from racial, ethnic, and language minorities can do or misjudge behaviors to be abnormal and in need of intervention when, in reality, they are normal within a different cultural context (Dana, 1993; Mercer, 1973; Naglieri & Ford, 2005). To address these issues, educators will need to include more culturally sensitive tests, such as nonverbal tests, in screening and identification procedures (Ford, 2004; Naglieri & Ford, 2003, 2005; Sandoval et al., 1998). To date, the most promising instruments for assessing the strengths of African American students are such nonverbal tests of intelligence as the

Naglieri Non-Verbal Abilities Test and Raven's Matrix Analogies Tests, which are considered less culturally loaded than traditional tests (Flanagan et al., 2007; Kaufman, 1994; Saccuzzo, Johnson, & Guertin, 1994).

Contrary to popular misconceptions, nonverbal tests do not mean that students are nonverbal. Rather nonverbal tests measure abilities nonverbally; they rely less on language proficiency. Thus, the intelligence of students with limited English proficiency, bilingual students, and students who speak nonstandard English can be assessed with less reliance on language skills.

Relative to cultural loading, Jensen (1980) distinguished between culturally loaded and culturally reduced tests. Culturally reduced tests are often performance based and include abstract figural and nonverbal content; culturally loaded tests have printed instructions, require reading, have verbal content, and require written responses. Essentially, nonverbal tests decrease the confounding effects of language skills on test performance and consequently increase the chances of students from diverse groups being identified as gifted. Other testing accommodations in the best interest of diverse students include using tests that have been translated into different languages, using interpreters and translators when students are not proficient in English, and having educators who are bilingual and bicultural administer the tests.

Multicultural Assessment Preparation

Finally, on the issue of testing, multicultural assessment preparation is essential for any educator who administers, interprets, and uses results based on tests with diverse students (AERA et al., 1999). As stated earlier, the test results are only as good as the test-taking situation, including the qualifications and competencies of the educator administering the test. Comas-Diaz (1996) has developed a list of cultural assessment variables with which educators should be familiar when making comprehensive assessments and interpreting results. These cultural assessment variables include information about the individual's heritage, religion, history of immigration, child-rearing practices, language skills, gender roles, and views about assimilation and about authority figures and family structure. The more information, the better is the assessment.

Policies and Procedures

Students should be placed in gifted education based on multiple data, which are then used to create profiles of students' strengths and weaknesses. Consequently, recruitment becomes diagnostic and prescriptive with the idea and ideal that strengths are used to place students in gifted education, and weaknesses are remediated rather than used as an excuse to avoid placement.

If teacher referral is the first step in the screening and placement process, and diverse students are underreferred and underidentified, then teachers are serving as gatekeepers and schools should reevaluate this practice. To qualify as a valid referral source, teachers require preparation in at least three areas: (1) gifted education, (2) urban and multicultural education, and (3) multicultural assessment (Ford & Frazier Trotman, 2001; Ford, Grantham, & Whiting, 2008a, 2008b). Preparation in these areas prepares educators to be knowledgeable about gifted students from diverse groups as well as the limitations of testing them.

RETENTION RECOMMENDATIONS

Half of our efforts to desegregate gifted education should focus on recruitment and half on retention. This section centers almost extensively on how multicultural education can be used to retain diverse students in gifted education. Just as important, teachers require substantive preparation in multicultural education to ensure that classrooms are culturally responsive and responsible (Ford & Harris, 1999; Ford & Frazier Trotman, 2001).

Multicultural Instruction

Boykin (1994), Saracho and Gerstl (1992), and Shade et al. (1997) are just a few of the scholars who have presented convincing research supporting the notion that culture influences learning styles and thinking styles. Due to space limitations, only Boykin's work will be discussed in this chapter. Before doing so, we want to add a word of caution. As noted by Irvine and York (2001), we must never adhere so strongly to generalizations or frameworks that they become stereotypes. Irvine and York point out that "negative teacher expectations can be fueled if teachers incorporate generalized and decontextualized observations about children of color without knowledge of the limitations of learning-styles labels" (p. 492). This model is presented with the understanding that although each of us belongs to several groups, we are nonetheless individuals first and foremost.

In his Afrocentric model, Boykin (1994) identified nine cultural styles commonly found among African Americans: spirituality, harmony, oral tradition, affective orientation, communalism, verve, movement, social time perspective, and expressive individualism. *Movement* and *verve* refer to African Americans being tactile and kinesthetic learners who show a preference for being involved in learning experiences. They are active learners who are engaged when they are physically and psychologically involved. Otherwise, they may be easily distracted and go off task. *Harmony* refers to an ability to read the environment well and to read nonverbal behaviors proficiently. Thus, students who feel unwelcome in their classes may become unmotivated and uninterested in learning. *Communalism* refers to a cooperative, interdependent style of living and learning in which competition—especially with friends—is devalued. Students with this learning preference may be unmotivated in highly individualistic and competitive classrooms, preferring instead to learn in groups.

Harmony, affective orientation, and communalism may explain why an increasing number of African American students—especially middle school and high school students—are choosing not to be in gifted programs. They recognize that such programs are primarily composed of White students and express concerns about alienation and isolation (Ford, 1996; Ford et al., 2008a). Furthermore, communalism may result in some African American students shunning participation in gifted programs and equating high achievement with "acting White" (Fordham, 1988; Fordham & Ogbu, 1986). Educators who take the time to get to know racial, ethnic, and language minority students and their families can avoid what I refer to as "drive-by teaching"—driving into minority communities, teaching students who are strangers, working with families without building relationships and respect, and driving out of the community immediately after school. Drive-by teaching is counterproductive to students and the educational process in general. It does not give educators time to get to know and understand their students and fails to give students opportunities to get to know their teachers in meaningful ways.

Teachers should learn to modify their teaching styles to accommodate different learning styles. For example, to accommodate students' preference for communalism, teachers can use cooperative learning strategies and place students in groups (Cohen & Lotan, 2004). To accommodate the oral tradition as well as verve and movement, teachers can give students opportunities to write and perform skits, to make oral presentations, and to participate in debates. More examples of ways in which teachers can use culturally responsive teaching activities are described by Ford (1998), Gay (2000), Lee (1993, 2007), and Shade et al. (1997).

Multicultural Gifted Curriculum

In the area of retention, curricular considerations are also critical. How to teach and what to teach gifted students have been discussed extensively by other scholars (Maker & Nielson, 2009; Tomlinson, 2001; VanTassel-Baska & Stambaugh, 2006). These strategies, such as curriculum compacting, independent study, acceleration, and grade skipping will not be discussed here because of space limitations. While these strategies are certainly appropriate for gifted students from diverse groups, an equally important but overlooked retention recommendation is the need to create culturally responsive and responsible learning environments (Gay, 2000) and to ensure that the curriculum for gifted students is multicultural. Ford and Harris (1999) have created a framework that uses Bloom's (1956) taxonomy and Banks' (2008) multicultural education model to assist educators in developing learning experiences that are multicultural and challenging. The result is a 24-cell matrix. The model is presented in Table 15.2. Four of the 24 levels in the model are described here (for a more complete discussion of the model, see Ford & Harris, 1998; Ford & Milner, 2005).

At the *knowledge–contributions* level, students are provided information and facts about cultural heroes, holidays, events, and artifacts. For example, students might be taught about Martin Luther King, Jr., and then asked to recall three facts about him on a test. They might be introduced to Cinco de Mayo and be required to recite the year when it became a holiday.

At the *comprehension–transformation* level, students are required to explain what they have been taught—but from the perspective of another group or individual. For instance, students might be asked to explain the events that led to slavery in the United States and then to discuss how enslaved persons might have felt about being held captive. They might discuss the Trail of Tears from the perspective of a Native American child living when this tragic event occurred.

At the *analysis–social action* level, students are asked to analyze an event from more than one point of view. Students might be asked to compare and contrast events during slavery with events associated with infractions of child labor laws today. Following these comparisons, students could be asked to develop a social action plan for eliminating illegal child labor.

At the *evaluation–social action* level, students might be asked to conduct a survey about prejudice in their local stores or businesses. This information could be given to store owners along with a plan of action for change, such as developing a diversity-training program.

Multicultural education can engage students and give them opportunities to identify with, connect with, and relate to the curriculum. It consists of deliberate, ongoing, planned,

Table 15.2   Ford-Harris Multicultural Gifted Education Framework—Description of Levels

	Knowledge	Comprehension	Application	Analysis	Synthesis	Evaluation
Contributions	Students are taught and know facts about cultural artifacts, events, groups, and other cultural elements.	Students show an understanding of information about cultural artifacts, groups, etc.	Students are asked to and can apply information learned about cultural artifacts, events, etc.	Students are taught to and can analyze (e.g., compare and contrast) information about cultural artifacts, groups, etc.	Students are required to and can create a new product from the information on cultural artifacts, groups, etc.	Students are taught to and can evaluate facts and information based on cultural artifacts, groups, etc
Additive	Students are taught and know concepts and themes about cultural groups.	Students are taught and can understand cultural concepts and themes.	Students are required to and can apply information learned about cultural concepts and themes.	Students are taught to and can analyze important cultural concepts and themes.	Students are asked to and can synthesize important information on cultural concepts and themes.	Students are taught to and can critique cultural concepts and themes
Transformation	Students are given information on important cultural elements, groups, etc., and can understand this information from different perspectives.	Students are taught to understand and can demonstrate an understanding of important cultural concepts and themes from different perspectives.	Students are asked to and can apply their understanding of important concepts and themes from different perspectives.	Students are taught to and can examine important cultural concepts and themes from more than one perspective.	Students are required to and can create a product based on their new perspective or the perspective of another group.	Students are taught to and can evaluate or judge important cultural concepts and themes from different viewpoints (e.g., minority group).
Social action	Based on information about cultural artifacts, etc., students make recommendations for social action.	Based on their understanding of important concepts and themes, students make recommendations for social action.	Students are asked to and can apply their understanding of important social and cultural issues; they make recommendations for and take action on these issues.	Students are required to and can analyze social and cultural issues from different perspectives; they take action on these issues.	Students create a plan of action to address a social and cultural issue; they seek important social change.	Students critique important social and cultural issues, and seek to make national and/or international change.

Note: Actions taken on the social action level can range from immediate and small scale (e.g., classroom and school level) to moderate scale (e.g., community or regional level) to large scale (state, national, and international levels). Likewise, students can make recommendations for action or actually take social action.

Source: Ford D. Y., & Harris, J. J., III. (1999). *Multicultural gifted education.* New York: Teachers College Press. Adapted from Banks, Chapter 10, this volume; and Bloom, B. S. (Ed.). (1956). *Taxonomy of educational objectives: The classification of educational goals.* New York: McKay.

and systematic opportunities to avoid drive-by teaching—to make learning meaningful and relevant to students and to give minority students mirrors in order to see themselves reflected in the curriculum. Multicultural gifted education challenges students culturally, affectively, academically, and cognitively.

Multicultural Counseling

Ford (1998), Fordham (1988), and Fordham and Ogbu (1986) have conducted research examining the concerns that high-achieving, gifted African American students have about being academically successful. A common finding is that many of these students are accused of "acting White" by other African American students because of their academic success (Ford et al., 2008a). Such accusations can be frustrating, overwhelming, and unmotivating for students. Should an antiachievement ethic be present in schools, educators should provide students—the accused and the accusers—with social-emotional and psychological supports. The students accused of acting White will need assistance with coping skills, conflict resolution skills, and anger management. The accusers will need assistance examining the negative implications—the self-defeating thoughts and behaviors—of an antiachievement ethic. Peer-group counseling is one potentially effective method for addressing these issues (Whiting, 2006).

Skills-Based Supports

Retention efforts must also address and rectify skill deficits. As stated earlier, many diverse students are gifted but need support to maintain an acceptable level of achievement. Supportive systems include test-taking skills, study skills, time-management skills, and organizational skills.

Ongoing Professional Development in Multicultural Education and Counseling

In order to implement the preceding recommendations, educators should participate in ongoing and formal preparation in multicultural education and counseling. Whether in the form of courses or workshops, such preparation should focus on educators becoming culturally competent in the following areas:

1. Understanding cultural diversity and its impact on (a) teaching, (b) learning, and (c) assessment
2. Understanding the impact of biases and stereotypes on (a) teaching, (b) learning, and (c) assessment (e.g., referrals, testing, expectations)
3. Working effectively and proactively with (a) students from racial, ethnic, and language minorities, (b) their families, and (c) their community
4. Creating multicultural (a) curricula and (b) instruction
5. Creating culturally responsive (a) learning and (b) assessment environments

SUMMARY AND CONCLUSIONS

Gifted students are gifted 24 hours of the day. Racial and ethnic minority students are culturally diverse 24 hours of the day.

In 1954, the U.S. Supreme Court ruled deliberate (*de jure*) school segregation unconstitutional. More recently, we have such legislation as No Child Left Behind targeting the pervasive achievement gap, yet *de facto* segregation persists in schools and in gifted education programs. Educators should focus extensively, consistently, and systematically on the many factors that contribute to and exacerbate the underrepresentation of students from racial, ethnic, and language minorities in gifted education. We have argued that a deficit orientation among educators, based primarily on a lack of understanding of culture, permeates all areas of the recruitment and retention of certain diverse students in gifted education programs and AP classes.

Deficit thinking has no place in education. Instead, educators should acknowledge the realities of the diversity in the world, in the United States, and in schools and seek to acquire and use the resources and preparation needed to become culturally responsive and responsible professionals. Culturally competent educators are advocates for students from diverse racial, ethnic, cultural, and language groups. The multicultural philosophy and preparation of educators will guide their referrals, instrument selection, test interpretation, and placement decisions—all of which are essential for recruiting and retaining diverse students into gifted education programs.

Questions and Activities

1. Why, according to the author, are racial and ethnic minority students and low-income students underrepresented in school programs for gifted students, including AP classes?
2. What does the author mean by "deficit thinking," and how might such thinking among educators affect the education of gifted minority students? In her view, how does deficit thinking contribute to the underrepresentation of minority students in programs for gifted students?
3. Why are many racial and ethnic minority and low-income students likely to be gifted underachievers? Describe some specific actions that teachers can take to identify these students and to provide them the support they need to achieve at higher levels.
4. The authors describe some ways in which culture influences learning and thinking. How might theories about culture and learning, such as those by Boykin (1994) and Shade and her colleagues (1997), help teachers to better meet the needs of gifted minority students? Do these theories have drawbacks and limitations? If so, what are they?
5. Visit a school in your community and interview teachers to determine (a) the criteria used to identify students for gifted programs, (b) the percentage of students from racial and ethnic and language minority students who are in gifted programs in the school, and (c) the steps that are taken by the school to recruit and retain students from low-income and minority groups into programs for gifted students, including AP classes.

References

American Educational Research Association (AERA), American Psychological Association (APA), & National Council on Measurement in Education (NCME). (1999). *Standards for educational and psychological testing*. Washington, DC: Author.

Armour-Thomas, E. (1992). Intellectual assessment of children from culturally diverse backgrounds. *School Psychology Review, 21*(4), 552–565.

Artiles, A. J., Trent, S. C., & Palmer, J. D. (2004). Culturally diverse students in special education: Legacies and prospects. In J. A. Banks & C. A. M. Banks (Eds.), *Handbook of research on multicultural education* (2nd ed., pp. 716–735). San Francisco: Jossey-Bass.

Banks, J. A. (2008). *An introduction to multicultural education* (4th ed.). Boston: Allyn & Bacon.

Baugh, J. A. (1991). African Americans and the environment: A review essay. *Policy Studies Journal, 19*(2), 182–191.

Bloom, B. S. (Ed.). (1956). *Taxonomy of educational objectives: The classification of educational goals*. New York: McKay.

Boykin, A. W. (1994). Afrocultural expression and its implications for schooling. In E. R. Hollins, J. E. King, & W. C. Hayman (Eds.), *Teaching diverse populations: Formulating a knowledge base* (pp. 243–273). Albany: State University of New York Press.

Bullard, R. D. (Ed.). (1993). *Confronting environmental racism: Voices from the grassroots*. Boston: South End Press.

Bullard, R. D. (1994). Overcoming racism in environmental decision making. *Environment, 36*(4), 10–20, 39–44.

Byrant, B. I., & Mohai, P. (Eds.). (1992). *Race and the incidence of environmental hazards: A time for discourse*. Boulder, CO: Westview.

Cohen, E. G., & Lotan, R. A. (2004). Equity in heterogeneous classrooms. In J. A. Banks & C. A. M. Banks (Eds.), *Handbook of research on multicultural education* (2nd ed., pp. 736–750). San Francisco: Jossey-Bass.

Colangelo, N., & Davis, G. A. (2002). *Handbook of gifted education* (3rd ed.). Boston: Allyn & Bacon.

College Board. (2008). *The 4th annual AP report to the nation*. Washington, DC: Author.

Comas-Diaz, L. (1996). Cultural considerations in diagnosis. In E. W. Kaslow (Ed.), *Handbook on relational diagnosis and dysfunctional family patterns* (pp. 152–168). New York: Guilford Press.

Dana, R. H. (1993). *Multicultural assessment perspectives for professional psychology*. Boston: Allyn & Bacon.

Davis, G. A., & Rimm, S. B. (1997). *Education of the gifted and talented* (4th ed.). Boston: Allyn & Bacon.

Donovan, M. S., & Cross, C. T. (Eds.). (2002). *Minority students in special and gifted education*. Washington, DC: National Academy Press.

Elementary and Secondary School Civil Rights Survey. (1998, 2000, 2002, 2004). Retrieved January 26, 2009, from http://ocrdata.ed.gov/ocr2002rv30/wdsdata.html

Flanagan, D. P., Ortiz, S. O., & Alfonso, V. C. (2007). *Essentials of cross-battery assessment* (2nd ed.). Boston: Allyn and Bacon.

Ford, D. Y. (1996). *Reversing underachievement among gifted Black students: Promising practices and programs.* New York: Teachers College Press.

Ford, D. Y. (1998). The underrepresentation of minority students in gifted education: Problems and promises in recruitment and retention. *Journal of Special Education, 32*(1), 4–14.

Ford, D. Y. (2004). *Intelligence testing and cultural diversity: Concerns, cautions, and considerations.* Storrs: University of Connecticut National Research Center on the Gifted and Talented.

Ford, D. Y., & Frazier Trotman, M. (2001). Teachers of gifted students: Suggested multicultural characteristics and competencies. *Roeper Review, 23*(4), 235–239.

Ford, D. Y., Grantham, T. C., & Whiting, G. W. (2008a). Another look at the achievement gap: Learning from the experiences of gifted Black students. *Urban Education, 43*(2), 216–239.

Ford, D. Y., Grantham, T. C., & Whiting, G. W. (2008b). Culturally and linguistically diverse students in gifted education: Recruitment and retention issues. *Exceptional Children, 74*(3), 289–308.

Ford, D. Y., & Harris, J. J., III. (1999). *Multicultural gifted education.* New York: Teachers College Press.

Ford, D. Y., Harris, J. J., III, Tyson, C. A., & Frazier Trotman, M. (2002). Beyond deficit thinking: Providing access for gifted African American students. *Roeper Review, 24*(2), 52–58.

Ford, D. Y., & Milner, H. R. (2005). *Teaching culturally diverse gifted students.* Waco, TX: Prufrock Press.

Ford, D. Y., Moore, J. L., III, & Milner, H. R. (2005). Beyond cultureblindness: A model of culture with implications for gifted education. *Roeper Review, 27*(2), 97–103.

Fordham, S. (1988). Racelessness as a factor in Black students' school success: Pragmatic strategy or Pyrrhic victory? *Harvard Educational Review, 58*(1), 54–84.

Fordham, S., & Ogbu, J. (1986). Black students' school success: Coping with the "burden of 'acting White.'" *Urban Review, 18*(3), 176–206.

Frasier, M. M., Martin, D., Garcia, J., Finley, V. S., Frank, E., Krisel, S., & King, L. L. (1995). *A new window for looking at gifted children.* Storrs: University of Connecticut National Research Center on the Gifted and Talented.

Gallagher, J. (2004). *Public policy in gifted education.* Thousand Oaks, CA: Corwin Press and National Association for Gifted Children.

Gardner, H. (1993). *Frames of mind: The theory of multiple intelligences* (2nd ed.). New York: Basic Books.

Gay, G. (2000). *Culturally responsive teaching: Theory, research, and practice.* New York: Teachers College Press.

Gould, S. J. (1996). *The mismeasure of man* (rev. and expanded ed.). New York: Norton.

Grossman, K. (1991). Environmental racism. *Crisis, 98*(4), 14–17, 31–32.

Harris, J. J., III, Brown, E. L., Ford, D. Y., & Richardson, J. W. (2004). African Americans and multicultural education: A proposed remedy for disproportionate special education placement and underinclusion in gifted education. *Education and Urban Society, 36*(3), 304–341.

Helms, J. E. (1992). Why is there no study of cultural equivalence in standardized cognitive ability testing? *American Psychologist, 47*(9), 1083–1101.

Herrnstein, R. J., & Murray, C. (1994). *The bell curve: Intelligence and class structure in American life.* New York: Free Press.

Heubert, J. P., & Hauser, R. M. (Eds.). (1999). *High stakes: Testing for tracking, promotion, and graduation.* Washington, DC: National Academy Press.

Irvine, J. J., & York, D. E. (2001). Learning styles and culturally diverse students: A literature review. In J. A. Banks & C. A. M. Banks (Eds.), *Handbook of research on multicultural education* (pp. 484–497). San Francisco: Jossey-Bass.

Jensen, A. R. (1980). *Bias in mental testing*. New York: Free Press.

Kaufman, A. S. (1994). *Intelligent testing with the WISC-III*. New York: Wiley.

Kitano, M. K., & DiJosia, M. (2002). Are Asian and Pacific Americans overrepresented in programs for the gifted? *Roeper Review, 24*(2), 76–80.

Kornhaber, M. (2004). Assessment, standards, and equity. In J. A. Banks & C. A. M. Banks (Eds.), *Handbook of research on multicultural education* (2nd ed., pp. 91–109). San Francisco: Jossey-Bass.

Lee, C. D. (1993). *Signifying as a scaffold for literary interpretation: The pedagogical implications of an African American discourse genre*. Urbana, IL: National Council of Teachers of English.

Lee, C. D. (2007). *Culture, literacy, and learning: Taking bloom in the midst of the whirlwind*. New York: Teachers College Press.

Majors, R., & Billson, J. M. (1992). *Cool pose: The dilemmas of Black manhood in America*. New York: Touchstone.

Maker, C. J., & Nielson, A. B. (2009). *Curriculum development and teaching strategies for gifted learners* (3rd ed.). Austin, TX: PRO-ED.

Menchaca, M. (1997). Early racist discourses: The roots of deficit thinking. In R. Valencia (Ed.), *The evolution of deficit thinking: Educational thought and practice* (pp. 13–40). New York: Falmer.

Mercer, J. R. (1973). *Labeling the mentally retarded: Clinical and social system perspectives on mental retardation*. Berkeley: University of California Press.

Naglieri, J. A., & Ford, D. Y. (2003). Addressing underrepresentation of gifted minority children using the Naglieri Nonverbal Ability Test (NNAT). *Gifted Child Quarterly, 47*(2), 155–160.

Naglieri, J. A., & Ford, D. Y. (2005). Increasing minority children's representation in gifted classes using the NNAT: A response to Lohman. *Gifted Child Quarterly, 49*(1), 29–36.

National Association for Gifted Children. (1997). *Position paper on testing*. Washington, DC: Author.

National Association for Gifted Children. (2002). Does the No Child Left Behind Act "do" anything for gifted students? Retrieved March 2, 2006, from http://www.nagc.org/index.aspx?id=999

Office of Ethnic Minority Affairs. (1993). Guidelines for providers of psychological services to ethnic, linguistic, and culturally diverse populations. *American Psychologist, 48*(1), 45–48.

Office for Civil Rights. (1998). *Elementary and secondary schools civil rights survey*. Retrieved November 24, 2008, from http://ocrdata.ed.gov/ocr2002rv30/

Office for Civil Rights. (2000a). *Elementary and secondary schools civil rights survey*. Retrieved November 24, 2008, from http://ocrdata.ed.gov/ocr2002rv30/

Office for Civil Rights. (2000b). *The use of tests as part of high-stakes decision-making for students: A resource guide for educators and policy-makers*. Washington, DC: Author.

Office for Civil Rights. (2002). *Elementary and secondary schools civil rights survey*. Retrieved November 24, 2008, from http://ocrdata.ed.gov/ocr2002rv30/

Office for Civil Rights. (2004). *Elementary and secondary schools civil rights survey*. Retrieved November 24, 2008, from http://ocrdata.ed.gov/ocr2002rv30/

Pang, V. O., Kiang, P. N., & Pak, Y. K. (2004). Asian Pacific American students: Challenging a biased educational system. In J. A. Banks & C. A. M. Banks (Eds.), *Handbook of research on multicultural education* (2nd ed., pp. 542–563). San Francisco: Jossey-Bass.

Pfeiffer, S. I. (2003). Challenges and opportunities for students who are gifted: What the experts say. *Gifted Child Quarterly, 47*(2), 161–169.

Ramírez, M., III, & Castañeda, A. (1974). *Cultural democracy, bicognitive development, and education.* New York: Academic Press.

Reis, S. M., & Callahan, C. M. (1989). Gifted females: They've come a long way—or have they? *Journal for the Education of the Gifted, 12*(2), 99–117.

Rimm, S. B. (1995). *Why bright kids get poor grades: And what you can do about it.* New York: Crown.

Saccuzzo, D. P., Johnson, N. E., & Guertin, T. L. (1994). *Identifying underrepresented disadvantaged gifted and talented children: A multifaceted approach* (Vols. 1 & 2). San Diego, CA: San Diego State University.

Sandoval, J., Frisby, C. L., Geisinger, K. F., Scheuneman, J. D., & Grenier, J. R. (1998). *Test interpretation and diversity: Achieving equity in assessment.* Washington, DC: American Psychological Association.

Sapon-Shevon, M. (1996). Beyond gifted education: Building a shared agenda for school reform. *Journal for the Education of the Gifted, 19*(2), 194–214.

Saracho, O. N., & Gerstl, C. K. (1992). Learning differences among at-risk minority students. In H. C. Waxman, J. Walker de Felix, J. E. Anderson, & H. P. Baptiste (Eds.), *Students at risk in at-risk schools: Improving environments for learning* (pp. 105–135). Newbury Park, CA: Corwin.

Shade, B. J., Kelly, C., & Oberg, M. (1997). *Creating culturally responsive classrooms.* Washington, DC: American Psychological Association.

Silverman, L. K. (1993). *Counseling the gifted and talented.* Denver, CO: Love.

Smith, C., Constantino, R., & Krashen, S. (1997). Differences in print environment for children in Beverly Hills, Compton, and Watts. *Emergency Librarian, 24*(4), 8–9.

Sowell, T. (1993). *Inside American education: The decline, the deception, the dogmas.* New York: Free Press.

Sternberg, R. J. (1985). *Beyond IQ: A triarchic theory of human intelligence.* New York: Cambridge University Press.

Storti, C. (1989). *The art of crossing cultures.* Yarmouth, ME: Intercultural Press.

Suzuki, L. A., & Ponterotto, J. G. (Eds.). (2008). *Handbook of multicultural assessment: Clinical, psychological, and educational applications* (3rd ed.). San Francisco: Jossey-Bass.

Tomlinson, C. A. (2001). *How to differentiate instruction in mixed-ability classrooms* (2nd ed.). Alexandria, VA: Association for Supervision and Curriculum Development.

U.S. Department of Education (USDE). (1993). *National excellence: A case for developing America's talent.* Washington, DC: Author.

VanTassel-Baska, J., Patton, J., & Prillaman, D. (1989). Disadvantaged gifted learners at-risk for educational attention. *Focus on Exceptional Children, 22*(3), 1–16.

VanTassel-Baska, J., & Stambaugh, T. (2006). *Comprehensive curriculum for gifted learners* (3rd ed.). Boston: Allyn and Bacon.

Whiting, G. (2006). Promoting a scholar identity in African American males: Recommendations for gifted education. *Gifted Education Press Quarterly, 20*(3), 1–6.

Students benefit when parents and community leaders work together for school reform.

School Reform

Reforming schools so that all students have an equal opportunity to succeed requires a new vision by educators who are willing to advocate for and participate in change. The two chapters in Part VI discuss effective ways to conceptualize and implement school reform within a multicultural framework. In Chapter 16, Nieto and Bode present and analyze five conditions that will promote student achievement within a multicultural perspective. According to Nieto and Bode, schools should (1) be antiracist and antibiased, (2) reflect an understanding and acceptance of all students as having talents and strengths that can enhance their education, (3) be considered within the parameters of critical pedagogy, (4) involve those people most intimately connected with teaching and learning, and (5) be based on high expectations and rigorous standards for all learners.

Cherry A. McGee Banks, in Chapter 17, discusses ways to involve parents in schools. She argues that parent involvement is an important factor in school reform and student achievement and that parents can be a cogent force in school reform. Parents, perhaps more than any other group, can mobilize the community to support school reform. Parents have first-hand knowledge about the school's effectiveness and can be vocal advocates for change. As consumers of educational services, parents can raise questions that are difficult for professional educators and administrators to raise, such as "What is the proportion of males in special education classes?" and "What is the ethnic breakdown of students enrolled in higher-level math and science classes?"

Banks argues that parents are more willing to work for school reform when they are involved in schools. They are more likely to become involved in schools when parent involvement opportunities reflect their varied interests, skills, and motivations. Banks suggests ways to expand traditional ideas about parent involvement and to increase the number and kinds of parents involved in schools.

CHAPTER 16

School Reform
and Student Learning:
A Multicultural Perspective

Sonia Nieto and Patty Bode

Learning is at the heart of schooling. If this is the case, then it makes sense that student learning be a major focus of school reform efforts. This means that educational policies and practices need to be viewed in terms of how they affect the learning and academic achievement of students. But some school policies, especially as espoused in the reform movement that began with the publication of *A Nation at Risk* (National Commission on Excellence in Education, 1983) and that are now institutionalized through the No Child Left Behind Act (2001), pay scant attention to whether and to what extent students actually learn. These reform efforts often end up punishing schools, teachers, districts, and ultimately students who have not measured up to norms of success predetermined by politicians, policy makers, and others who know little about schools. Longer school days and years, strict retention policies, placement of schools "on probation," state takeovers, privatization, more high-stakes testing, and less attention to pedagogy and curricula have been the result (Abernathy, 2007; Berliner, 2005; Meier & Wood, 2004; Rothstein, 2008). Such studies point out that students who are most at risk of receiving an inadequate education are often the ones most jeopardized by such reform efforts. Darling-Hammond (2006) points out that:

> Current conceptions of accountability hold children accountable to the
> government for achieving specific levels of test score performance, but
> they do not hold government accountable to the students, their families,
> or their schools for providing the basic foundation for learning. (p. 22)

This chapter asserts that student learning can be positively influenced by changes in school policies and practices that affirm students' identities and that are part of systemic school reform measures. Two related assumptions that undergird this assertion are (1) that students, families, and teachers bring strengths and talents to teaching and learning and (2) that a comprehensive and critical approach to multicultural education can provide an important framework for rethinking school reform. Given the social nature of schooling, it is impossible to ascribe a fixed causal relationship between student learning and schooling. Many complex forces influence student learning, including personal, psychological, social, cultural, community, and institutional factors (Nieto & Bode, 2008). That is, we cannot simply say that eliminating tracking will help all students succeed or that native-language instruction will guarantee success for all language-minority students. Neither can we state unequivocally that culturally responsive pedagogy is always the answer. Although these changes may in fact substantially improve educational outcomes for many more students than are now achieving academic success, taken in isolation, they may fail to reflect the complex nature of student learning.

In what follows, we explore the meaning of school reform with a multicultural perspective and consider implications for student learning. We begin by defining school reform with a multicultural perspective, including how a school's policies and practices implicitly illustrate beliefs about who deserves the benefits of a high-quality education. That is, certain school policies and practices may exacerbate the pervasive structural inequalities that exist in society. We then describe a set of five interrelated conditions for successful school reform within a multicultural perspective. These conditions are intimately interconnected, but for the purpose of expediency, we explain the five conditions separately with implications for increasing student achievement.

SCHOOL REFORM WITH A MULTICULTURAL PERSPECTIVE

Many people assume that multicultural education consists of little more than isolated lessons in sensitivity training or prejudice reduction or separate units about cultural artifacts or ethnic holidays. To some it might mean education geared for urban schools or, more specifically, for African American students. If conceptualized in this limited way, multicultural education will have little influence on student learning.

When conceptualized as broad-based school reform, however, multicultural education can have a major influence on how and to what extent students learn. To approach school reform with a multicultural perspective, we need to begin with an understanding of multicultural education within its *sociopolitical context* (Nieto & Bode, 2008). A sociopolitical context underscores that education is part and parcel of larger societal and political forces, such as inequality based on stratification due to race, social class, gender, and other differences. Given this perspective, decisions concerning such practices as ability tracking, high-stakes testing, native-language instruction, retention, curriculum reform, and pedagogy are all influenced by broader social policies.

As Freire (1985) states, every educational decision, whether made at the classroom, city, state, or national level, is imbedded within a particular ideological framework. Such decisions can be as simple as whether a classroom should be arranged in rows with all students facing the teacher, in tables with groups of students to encourage cooperative work, or in a variety of ways depending on the task at hand. Alternatively, these decisions can be as far reaching as eliminating tracking in an entire school system, teaching language-minority students by using both their native language and English, or by using English only. Within each educational decision are assumptions about the nature of learning, about what particular students are capable of achieving, about whose language has value, and about who should be at the center of the educational process. As stated more extensively elsewhere, Nieto (1992) defined multicultural education within a sociopolitical context, and continues (Nieto & Bode, 2008) to assert it as:

> ... a process of comprehensive school reform and basic education for all students. It challenges and rejects racism and other forms of discrimination in schools and society and accepts and affirms the pluralism (ethnic, racial, linguistic, religious, economic, and gender, among others) that students, their communities, and teachers reflect. Multicultural education permeates the schools' curriculum and instructional strategies as well as the interactions among teachers, students, and families, and the very way that schools conceptualize the nature of teaching and learning. Because it uses critical pedagogy as its underlying philosophy and focuses on knowledge, reflection, and action (*praxis*) as the basis for social change, multicultural education promotes democratic principles of social justice. (p. 44)

This definition of multicultural education assumes a comprehensive school reform effort rather than superficial additions to the curriculum or one-shot treatments about diversity, such as workshops for teachers or assembly programs for students. As such, we use this definition as a lens through which to view conditions for systemic school reform that can improve the learning of all students.

CONDITIONS FOR SYSTEMIC SCHOOL REFORM WITH A MULTICULTURAL PERSPECTIVE

Failure to learn does not develop out of thin air; it is scrupulously created through policies, practices, attitudes, and beliefs. In a very concrete sense, the results of educational inequality explain by example what a society believes its young people are capable of achieving and what they deserve. For instance, offering only low-level courses in schools serving culturally diverse and poor youngsters is a clear message that the students are not expected to achieve to high levels; in like manner, considering students to be "at risk" simply because of their ethnicity, native language, family characteristics, or social class is another clear sign that some students have been defined by conventional wisdom as uneducable based simply on their identity. Although it is true that conditions such as poverty and attendant hardships such as poor health and nutrition may create obstacles to learning, they should not be viewed as insurmountable obstacles because we have substantive evidence that some students *can* achieve despite such roadblocks. More students achieve to high levels, however, when these obstacles are removed.

As a result, we cannot think about education reform without taking into account both micro- and macrolevel issues that may affect student learning. Microlevel issues include the cultures, languages, and experiences of students and their families and how these are considered in determining school policies and practices (Cummins, 2000; Nieto, 1999). Macrolevel issues include the racial stratification that helps maintain inequality and the resources and access to learning that schools provide or deny (Kozol, 2005; Orfield, 2001; Rothstein, 2004; Spring, 2007). Ladson-Billings (2006b) has argued that the focus on school performance gaps is misplaced and that what must be considered are the historical, economic, sociopolitical, and moral components of racial stratification that have accumulated over time, amounting to what she has dubbed "the education debt" (p. 3).

In addition, how students and their families view their status in schools and society must be considered. Recent research focuses on students' perceptions of opportunity structures as well as their personal assertions of identity. Conchas (2006) points out that linking academic rigor with strong collaborative relationships among students and teachers plays a significant, positive role in high achievement for some youths from economically strapped communities. Yet he maintains that transforming students' perceptions of the opportunity structure is tied to the larger social and economic inequality and "its devastating impact on the perceptions of racial minority youth concerning social mobility" (p. 123). Carter (2005) notes the complex ways in which youths take up, express, and border-cross cultural identities in relation to schooling. She calls for teachers, parents, and other adults in the community to become "multicultural navigators" (p. 137), that is, to help demonstrate to students how to use both dominant and nondominant cultural capital and develop adeptness at moving though a range of sociocultural settings. To ensure that all students succeed academically, Carter argues, multicultural navigators are needed to increase students' investment in their education.

Conditions such as inequitable school financing (National Center for Education Statistics, 2008), unrepresentative school governance (Meier & Stewart, 1991), and large class size (Biddle & Berliner, 2002; Muennig & Woolf, 2007) may play powerful roles in promoting student underachievement. For example, inequities in school financing have remained quite stable since Kozol's (1991) landmark study of almost two decades ago (National Center for Educational Statistics). Yet reform strategies such as longer school days, more rigorous graduation standards, and increased standardized testing often do not take such issues into account. The evidence is growing, for example, that school size and class size make a difference in student learning and that these may also influence students' feelings of belonging and, thus, their engagement with learning (Carter, 2005; Yosso, 2006). In fact, equalizing just two conditions of schooling—funding and class size—would probably result in an immediate and dramatic improvement in learning for students who have not received the benefits of these two conditions.

School reform strategies that do not acknowledge such macrolevel disparities are bound to be inadequate because they assume that schools provide all students with a level playing field (Grant-Thomas & Orfield, 2008; Rothstein, 2004). The conditions described later, while acknowledging these disparities, nevertheless provide hope for school systems in which such changes as equitable funding or small class size may not occur in the near future. Rather than wait for these changes to happen, schools and teachers can begin to improve the possibility for successful student learning by attending to a number of conditions. Five such conditions are described here, which, along with changes in funding and resource allocation, would help create schools where all students have a better chance to learn (these conditions are described in greater detail in Nieto, 2010).

School Reform Should Be Antiracist and Antibias

An antiracist and antibias perspective is at the core of multicultural education. This is crucial because too often people believe that multicultural education automatically takes care of racism, but this is far from the reality. In fact, multicultural education without an explicit antiracist focus may perpetuate the worst kinds of stereotypes if it focuses only on superficial aspects of culture and the addition of ethnic tidbits to the curriculum.

Addressing racism is critical, yet if not rooted in theory and in student experience, educators might make erroneous assumptions about students' racial affiliations and other dimensions of multiple identities. We have written elsewhere with colleagues (Nieto, Bode, Kang, & Raible, 2008) drawing from Dolby (2000) and other critical and postmodern perspectives, to address the hybrid nature of contemporary U.S. society. Specifically, we ask how multicultural education might transcend typically essentialist notions of race and other identities to promote a more nuanced, critical understanding of multicultural perspectives. Postmodern frameworks on identity insist that identities and cultures are not static, but they shift and evolve in context, so then curriculum and instruction also must. Yet racism remains a stark reality and needs to be addressed by multicultural education even while contemporary discourse of identities calls into question the notion of race.

Being antiracist means paying attention to all areas in which some students may be favored over others, including the curriculum and pedagogy, sorting policies, and teachers' interactions and relationships with students and their communities. Schools committed to multicultural education with an antiracist perspective need to examine closely both school policies and the attitudes and behaviors of their staff to determine how these might be complicit in causing academic failure. The kind of expectations that teachers and schools have for students (Conchas, 2006; Nieto, 2002–2003; Noguera, 2003), whether native language use is permitted or punished (Cummins, 2000; Gebhard, Austin, Nieto, & Willett, 2002), how sorting takes place (Oakes, 2005), and how classroom organization, pedagogy, and curriculum may influence student learning (Bennett deMarrais & LeCompte, 1999) all need to be considered.

To become antiracist, schools also need to examine how the curriculum may perpetuate negative, distorted, or incomplete images of some groups while exalting others as the makers of all history. Unfortunately, many textbooks, children's books, software, audiovisual media, and web media are still replete with racist and sexist images and with demeaning portrayals of people from low-income communities. Although the situation is improving and the stereotypes that exist are not as blatant as they once were, there are still many inaccuracies and negative portrayals (Botelho & Rudman, 2009; Clawson, 2002; Loewen, 2007, 2008; Willis, 1998).

The images generated by the media and the competing political parties throughout the U.S. presidential campaign of 2008 brought forth multiple examples of how the general public either perpetuated and embraced or refuted and rejected racism and sexism. This makes a compelling case for developing a more critically literate public through multicultural education. Most of the women and men presented as heroes or heroines in the standard curriculum—whether from dominant or nondominant cultures—are "safe"; that is, they do not pose a challenge to the status quo. Other people who have fought for social justice are omitted, presented as bizarre or insane, or made safe by downplaying their contributions. A now-classic article by Kozol (1975) graphically documents how schools bleed the life and soul out of even the most impassioned and courageous heroes, such as Helen Keller and Martin Luther King, Jr., in the process making them boring and less-than-believable caricatures. More recently, a powerful book by Kohl (2005) demonstrates how Rosa Parks, the mother of the Civil Rights Movement, was made palatable to the mainstream by portraying her not as a staunch civil rights crusader who consciously battled racist segregation but as a tired woman who simply did not want to give up her seat on the bus. These examples are misleading or even racist representations of reality.

Through this kind of "safe" curriculum, students from dominant groups learn that they are the norm, and consequently they often assume that anyone different from them is culturally or intellectually disadvantaged. On the other hand, students from subordinated cultures may internalize the message that their cultures, families, languages, and experiences have low status, and they learn to feel inferior. The result may be what Claude Steele (1999) has called "stereotype threat" (p. 44). Steele describes stereotype threat as the impact that devaluation in schools and society may have on African Americans, other people of color, and women to underperform academically (Aronson & Steele, 2005). All students suffer as a result of these messages, but students from dominated groups are the most negatively affected.

The issue of institutional power is also at play here. The conventional notion of racism is that it is an *individual* bias toward members of other groups. This perception conveniently skirts the issue of how institutions themselves, which are much more powerful than individuals, develop harmful policies and practices that victimize American Indians, African Americans, Asians, Latinos, low-income European Americans, females, gays, lesbians, transgender people, and others from dominated groups. The major difference between *individual racism* and *institutional racism and bias* is the wielding of power because it is primarily through the power of the people who control institutions such as schools that oppressive policies and practices are reinforced and legitimated (Tatum, 2003, 2007; Weinberg, 1996). That is, when racism is understood as a systemic problem, not just as an individual dislike for a particular group of people, we can better understand its negative and destructive effects.

We do not wish to minimize the powerful effect of individual prejudice and discrimination, which can be personally very painful, nor do we suggest that individual discrimination occurs only in one direction, for example, from Whites to African Americans. No group monopolizes prejudice and discrimination; they occur in all directions and even within groups. But interethnic hostility, personal prejudices, and individual biases, while certainly hurtful, do not have the long-range and life-limiting effects on entire groups of people that institutional racism and bias have.

Testing practices, for example, may be institutionally discriminatory because they label students from culturally and socially dominated groups as inferior as a result of their performance on these tests (McNeil, 2000; Nichols & Berliner, 2005). Rather than critically examining the tests themselves, the underlying purpose of such tests, or their damaging effects, the students themselves are often blamed (Orfield & Kornhaber, 2001). In addition, the fact that textbook companies and other companies that develop tests earn huge profits from test construction and dissemination is often unmentioned, yet it, too, is a reality (Miner, 2004).

An antiracist perspective is apparent in schools when students are permitted, and even encouraged, to speak about their experiences with racism and other biases. Many White teachers feel great discomfort when racism is discussed in the classroom. They are uncomfortable for several reasons: their lack of experience in confronting such a potentially explosive issue, the conspiracy of silence about racism (as if not speaking about it will make it disappear), the guilt they may feel being a member of the group that has benefited from racism, the generally accepted assumption that we live in a color-blind society, or a combination of these reasons (Howard, 2006; Sleeter, 1994; Tatum, 2007). According to Pollock (2004), while seemingly color blind, this discourse is in fact highly racialized because the deletion of race in both classroom practice and policy talk is a deliberate and race-conscious act. Referring to this practice as "colormuteness," Pollock argues that it is an active struggle to mask the perceived or possible relevance of race. She also suggests that true color blindness is an impossibility in a nation as racialized as the United States. In her edited compilation, *Everyday Antiracism*, Pollock (2008) advances insights from dozens of educators to make the struggle around issues of race and racism more visible and audible.

When students are given time and support for expressing their views, the result can be compelling because their experiences are legitimated and used in the service of their learning. For example, teachers have written eloquently about the impact of addressing issues of racism and discrimination in the classroom (Landsman, 2001; Levin, 2001). Van Ausdale and Feagin (2001) provide compelling evidence of preschoolers' racialized views, actions, and language with a focus on the role of the teacher in antiracist education. Michie (2005) documented how five teachers in Chicago public schools supported students' learning through a rigorous academic program with a social justice focus. These researchers found that, rather than shying away from such topics, teachers who directly confront issues of bias can help students become more engaged, critical, and reflective learners.

In our research on students' concerns about their education, they mentioned racism and other examples of discrimination on the part of fellow students and teachers (Nieto & Bode, 2008). Rashaud, an African American high school student in Georgia, said, "Being an African American student, to me, really it's kinda' tense. People are already judging you when you're African American" (p. 102). Nadia, a Syrian student in a Midwest college town told us:

> [A]fter September 11th it was a little shaky, and I didn't want to tell
> people that I was Arabic because you got the weird looks ... they said,
> "Are you ... you kind of look Afghani?" That's when it's a bit of a
> burden, just when you get singled out. People look at you different
> when they find out you're Arabic, especially now. (p. 346)

Other students also talked about discrimination on the part of teachers. Christina, a recent immigrant from Kenya who was a novice learner of technology, mentioned how teachers expected her to be computer literate and to "get a move on" with her computer assignments. Likewise, she reacted with astonished humor when the track coach in her school assumed she would be a strong runner simply because she was from Kenya although she had never been on a track team. Nini, who describes herself as racially and ethnically mixed, gave an account of the competing expectations from peers in segregated White and Black racial groups, as well as confronting low expectations from teachers who assume, "Oh she's Black ... she's not going to achieve well" (p. 284). Eugene, who was adopted by two gay dads, shared the perspective of growing up in a loving, secure family while also feeling the pressure to keep his family "in the closet":

> One time in Spanish class we were doing "family words." My teacher
> was talking to everyone about their mother and their father and I did
> not want to get called on.... [A]nother time we had to do a family tree
> ... I only put in one of my parents. (p. 399)

As these examples demonstrate, an antiracist and antibias perspective is essential in schools if all students are to be given equitable environments for learning. An antiracist perspective is a vital lens through which to analyze a school's policies and practices, including the curriculum, pedagogy, testing and tracking, discipline, faculty hiring, student retention, and attitudes about and interactions with families.

School Reform Should Reflect an Understanding and Acceptance of All Students as Having Talents and Strengths That Can Enhance Their Education

Many educators believe that students from culturally subordinated groups have few experiential or cultural strengths that can benefit their education. A classic example comes from Ryan (1972), who coined the expression "blaming the victim" for the tendency to place responsibility on students and their families for their failure to achieve in school. These students, generally low-income children of all groups and children of color specifically, are often considered deficient or "culturally deprived," a patronizing term popularized in the 1960s (Reissman, 1962). But Ryan turned the perspective of "cultural deprivation" on its head when he wrote:

> We are dealing, it would seem, not so much with culturally deprived
> children as with culturally depriving schools. And the task to be
> accomplished is not to revise, amend, and repair deficient children, but
> to alter and transform the atmosphere and operations of the schools to
> which we commit these children. (p. 61)

Students might be thought of as culturally deprived simply because they speak a language other than English as their native language or because they have just one parent or live in poverty. Sometimes they are labeled in this way just because of their race or ethnicity. These notions of "the culture of poverty" were developed by Lewis (1965) and Harrington (1971/1997) decades ago. Ladson-Billings (2006a) notes that the way the concept of "culture" is used by some teachers and students in preservice teacher education can exacerbate the problem and perpetuate stereotypes. Teachers muse that "maybe it is part of their culture" for groups of students to be noisy or for parents to be absent from open house night. Ladson-Billings points out that a growing number of teachers use "culture" as a catch basin for all manner of behaviors and characteristics when discussing students who are not White, not English-speaking, or not native-born U.S. citizens. A growing body of research points to the most detrimental results of this deficit view in what has come to be called to "the school to prison pipeline" (Edelman, 2007; Noguera, 2003).

Given such dire results, it is urgent to begin with a more positive and, in the end, more realistic and hopeful view of students and their families. School reform measures based on the assumption that children of all families bring cultural and community strengths to their education would go a long way toward providing more powerful learning environments for a higher number of youngsters. The research of Gonzalez, Moll, and Amanti (2005) on incorporating "funds of knowledge" into the curriculum—that is, using the experiences and skills of all families to encourage student learning—is a more promising and productive way of approaching families than is the viewpoint that they have only deficits that must be repaired.

If we begin with the premise that children and their families have substantial talents that can inform student learning, a number of implications for improving schools follow. Instead of placing the blame for failure to learn solely on students, teachers need to become aware of how their own biases can act as barriers to student learning. Teachers also need to consider how their students best learn and how their own pedagogical practices need to change as a result. This implies that teachers need to learn culturally responsive ways of teaching all of their students (Gay, 2004; Irvine, 2003; Ladson-Billings, 2001, 2006a).

Teachers also need to consider how the native language of students influences their academic achievement. For this to happen, they need to dispel some of the conventional myths surrounding native-language use (Crawford, 2008). For instance, it is common practice in schools to try to convince parents whose native language is other than English that they should speak only English with their children. This recommendation makes little sense for at least three reasons. First, these parents often speak little English themselves, and their children are thus provided with less than adequate models of the language. Second, this practice often results in cutting off, rather than stimulating, communication between parents and children. Third, if young people are encouraged to learn English at the expense of their native language rather than in conjunction with it, they may lose meaningful connections that help maintain close and loving relations with family members (Beykont, 2000).

A more reasonable recommendation, and one that would honor the contributions parents can make to their children's education, is to encourage rather than discourage them to speak their native language with their children, to speak it often, and to use it consistently. In schools, this means that students would not be punished for speaking their native languages; rather, they would be encouraged to do so, and to do so in the service of their learning (Reyes & Halcón, 2001; Zentella, 2005). A rich communicative legacy, both in school and at home, could be the result.

Another example of failing to use student and community strengths can be found in the curriculum. A perspective that affirms the talents and experiences of students and their families can expand the people and roles included in the curriculum. We have written elsewhere (Nieto & Bode, 2008) about a curriculum in which first-grade teachers Susie Secco and Gina Simm endeavor to make *all* families visible by honoring the diversity of their lived experiences through a classroom activity about *Family Responsibilities*. Here we provide a glimpse into the work of these teachers:

> Each first grader conducts a family survey, by interviewing the adults at
> home with questions such as: What responsibilities do you have while I
> am at school? What jobs do you do either at home or away from home?
> These interview techniques make space for a range of replies to be
> respected as opposed to a more narrow question that children hear
> frequently "where do your parents work?" The first graders learn more
> about what their caregivers are doing, they learn more about the

assortment of possibilities of adult responsibilities and the teachers and classmates gain an intimate view into the complex workings of each student's family. The assignment reaps replies from the adults such as: caring for younger children or elders, searching for employment, cleaning or fixing up the home, volunteer work, going to school, resting to go to the night shift at work and much more. The students also hear about a variety of places that people call "work": the office, the school, the fire station, the bakery, the construction site, the chemistry lab, the home, the sandwich shop, the docks, the houses that need cleaning, the hospital, grandma's house, the cafeteria, the bus garage, the vending cart, the highway toll booth, the hotel and more. In addition to the academic and research skills gained by six-year-olds, the end result is that each family's *contributions* are visible and honored in the classroom. This is only one of many activities in the Family Diversity Curriculum designed by Secco and Simm to investigate their four "big ideas" (Wiggins & McTighe, 2005) that include: 1) *There are all kinds of families*, 2) *Families have wants and needs*, 3) *Family responsibilities*, and 4) *Experiencing change is common to all families*. (pp. 387–392)

A further consideration concerning the talents and strengths of students and their families is what Cummins (1996) has called the "relations of power" in schools. In proposing a shift from "coercive" to "collaborative" relations of power, Cummins argues that traditional teacher-centered transmission models can limit the potential for learning, especially among students from communities whose cultures and languages are devalued by the dominant canon. In a powerful study of urban high school students becoming critical researchers, Morrell (2008) documented how students' experiences, knowledge, and enthusiasm can help engage them in robust learning. He concluded that a significant outcome of the study was students' recognition that youth and urban issues were worthy of serious study and that research can have a social impact. These findings suggest that using students as collaborators in developing the curriculum can help promote learning. By encouraging collaborative relations of power, schools can begin to recognize other sources of legitimate knowledge that have been overlooked.

School Reform Should Be Considered Within the Parameters of Critical Pedagogy

According to Banks (2009), the main goal of a multicultural curriculum is to help students develop decision-making and social action skills. Consequently, when students learn to view situations and events from a variety of viewpoints, critical thinking, reflection, and action are promoted. Critical pedagogy is an approach through which students and teachers are encouraged to view what they learn in a critical light, or, in the words of Freire, by learning to read both "the word and the world" (1970, p. 69). According to Freire, the opposite of a critical or empowering approach is "banking education," where students learn to regurgitate and passively accept the knowledge they are given (p. 53). A critical education, on the other hand, expects that students will seek their own answers, be curious, and be questioning.

Shor's (1992) pioneering analysis concerning critical pedagogy is instructive. He begins with the assumption that because no curriculum can be truly neutral, it is the responsibility of schools to present students with the broad range of information they will need to learn to read and write critically and in the service of social justice. Thus, critical pedagogy is not simply the transfer of knowledge from teacher to students even though it may be knowledge that has heretofore not been made available to them. A critical perspective does not simply operate on the principle of substituting one truth for another; instead, students are encouraged to reflect on multiple and contradictory perspectives in order to understand reality more fully. This is essential at the K–12 level as well as in teacher education (Shor & Pari, 1999, 2000). For instance, learning about the internment of Americans of Japanese descent and Japanese residents in the United States during World War II is not in itself critical pedagogy; it becomes so only when students analyze different viewpoints and use them to understand the inconsistencies they uncover. They can then begin to understand the role played by racist hysteria, economic exploitation, and propaganda as catalysts for the internment, and they can judge this incident through the stated ideals of our nation.

Without a critical perspective, reality is often presented to students as if it were static, finished, and flat; underlying conflicts, problems, and inherent contradictions are omitted. As we have seen, textbooks in all subject areas generally exclude information about unpopular perspectives or the perspectives of disempowered groups in society. Few of the books to which students have access present the viewpoints of people who have built our country, from enslaved Africans to immigrant labor to other working-class people even though they have been the backbone of society (Bigelow, 2008; Zinn, 2005; Takaki, 2008).

Using critical pedagogy as a basis for school reform renders very different policies for schools than do traditional models of school reform. Even more important than just increasing curricular options, critical pedagogy helps to expand teachers' and schools' perspectives about students' knowledge and intellectual capabilities. The use of critical pedagogy helps students become agents of their own learning so they can use what they learn in productive and critical ways. The knowledge they learn can be used to explore the reasons for certain conditions in their lives and to design strategies for changing them.

Examples can be found in a range of approaches to critical pedagogy, especially when adapting curriculum for the multicultural K–12 classroom that we have described elsewhere (Nieto & Bode, 2008). An abbreviated summary of one of the case studies of curriculum follows.

Studying Specific Cultures and Geographic Regions: A Study of Cambodia and the Cambodian American Experience

A team of seventh-grade teachers was concerned about the academic achievement of their Cambodian and Cambodian American students, so they planned a curriculum that aimed to expand the academic prowess of all students while affirming the identities of a specific group. The teachers drew from students' questions, curiosities, concerns, and even from their prejudices. They developed "big ideas," learning objectives, assessments, and activities for a curriculum that was engaging and rigorous for students of all learning approaches, ethnicities, languages, and racial identities (Wiggins & McTighe, 2005; Sleeter, 2005). Students engaged in literature research, community action, math and science analysis, artistic production, and more.

They enlisted religious leaders from the local Buddhist temple, elders from the community, high school students, and veterans from the Vietnam War in their classrooms.

Authentic learning was reported from students of Cambodian and non-Cambodian heritages. After the class attended a dance performance, a seventh-grade boy, Eric, stated, "I wish I was a Cambodian dancer. Those guys can break dance mad-cool and then they know their culture, too. I wish I had something like that." The teachers noted that they had never before heard a European American student express appreciation (and even envy) of Cambodian cultural experiences. One Cambodian student, Prasour, wrote: "I liked this part of school when we studied my own culture. I thought it was awesome. The kids who aren't Cambodian thought it was awesome. It just makes you feel awesome to be Cambodian." (Nieto & Bode, 2008, p. 377)

While feeling "awesome" is a beneficial by-product of critical pedagogy and certainly lends to attachment to and engagement with school, it is not its primary goal. Critical pedagogy listens and responds to students' needs, questions, and knowledge to cultivate critical judgment and decision-making skills they will need if they are to become productive members of a democratic society. Other accounts of critical pedagogy in action are contained in publications by Rethinking Schools (Bigelow, Christensen, Karp, Miner, & Peterson, 1994; Bigelow, Harvey, Karp, & Miller, 2001) and Teaching for Change (Lee, Menkart, Okazawa-Rey, 2007; Menkart, Murray, & View, 2004). Book-length accounts of critical pedagogy (Cowhey, 2006; Vasquez, 2004) provide compelling examples of the positive and empowering influence that teachers' guidance can have on student learning.

The People Most Intimately Connected with Teaching and Learning (Teachers, Families, and Students) Need to Be Meaningfully Involved in School Reform

Research on involvement by families, students, and teachers has consistently indicated that democratic participation by people closest to learners can dramatically improve student learning. This is especially true in urban schools and in schools that serve low-income, African American, Latino, and immigrant students (Epstein, 2001; Henderson, Mapp, Johnson, & Davies, 2006; Olsen, 2008), yet these are the people most often excluded from discussions and implementation of school reform measures.

Cummins (1996) reviewed programs that included student empowerment as a goal and concluded that students who are encouraged to develop a positive cultural identity through interactions with their teachers experience a sense of control over their own lives and develop the confidence and motivation to succeed academically. School reform measures that stress the meaningful involvement of teachers, families, and students look quite different from traditional approaches. These measure begin with the assumption that these groups have substantial and insightful perspectives about student learning. Rather than thinking of ways to bypass their ideas, school reformers actively seek the involvement of students, families, and teachers in developing, for instance, disciplinary policies, curriculum development, and decisions concerning tracking and the use of tests. Similarly, allowing time in the curriculum for students to engage in critical discussions about issues such as whose language is valued in the school can help to affirm the legitimacy of the discourse of all students.

At the same time, these kinds of discussions also acknowledge the need to learn and become comfortable with the discourse of the larger society (Delpit 2006; Delpit & Dowdy, 2008). In addition, involving families in curriculum development enriches the curriculum, affirms what families have to offer, and helps students overcome the shame they may feel about their cultures, languages, and values, an all-too-common attitude for students from culturally subordinated groups (Nieto & Bode, 2008; Olsen, 2008).

School Reform Needs to Be Based on High Expectations and Rigorous Standards for All Learners

Many students come to school with experiences and conditions, including speaking a language other than English or simply belonging to a particular racial or ethnic group, that some teachers and schools consider obstacles that place them at risk for learning. But beginning with this perspective leaves teachers and schools with little hope. Rather than viewing language and cultural differences as impediments to learning, they can be viewed as resources that students bring to their education. In this way, instead of using these differences as a rationalization for low expectations of what students are capable of learning, they can be used to promote student learning. In addition, in our society, we have generally expected schools to provide an equal and equitable education for all students, not just for those who have no problems in their lives or who fit the image of successful students due to race, class, or language ability. The promise of an equal education for all students of all backgrounds in the United States has yet to be realized as is evident from a number of classic critiques of the myth of our schools as "the great equalizer" (Mann, 1848/1903), a charge countered by Bowles & Gintis (1976), Katz (1975), and Spring (1989). Nevertheless, the ideal of equitable educational opportunity is worth defending and vigorously putting into practice.

Far too many students cope on a daily basis with complex and difficult problems, including poverty, violence, racism, abuse, families in distress, and lack of health care and proper housing. While it is undeniably true that many students face unimaginably difficult problems, the school cannot be expected to solve them all. To address this reality, the Economic Policy Institute convened a task force in 2006 to consider the broader context of the No Child Left Behind Act to inform the nation's approach to education and youth development policy. A group of educational researchers drafted the statement *A Broader, Bolder Approach to Education* to inform legislators and the general public that for "school improvement to be fully effective, [it] must be complemented by a broader definition of schooling and by improvements in the social and economic circumstances of disadvantaged youth" (Ladd, Noguera & Payzant, 2006, para. 2). This point has been taken up by Geoffrey Canada, president of the Harlem Children's Zone (HCZ), which is "an innovative and unique community-based organization, offering education, social-service and community-building programs to children and families" (HCZ, n.d.). HCZ, which is funded primarily by private donations, and has flooded the neighborhood with social, medical, and educational services that are available for free to the 10,000 children and their families who live within the 100 blocks of the zone with the specific intent of raising academic achievement for every child. Canada's reluctance to wait for governmental funding for comprehensive reform led him to integrate private funding with public programs. HCZ's rates of success have been a model to public social service and public school reformers throughout the nation who point out what the possibilities can be to government officials who have the will and the resources to back such programs (Tough, 2008).

In the absence of the will and the resources to back comprehensive social programs, overwhelming social and economic circumstances cannot be overlooked. At the same time, however, we cannot dismiss the heroic efforts of many teachers and schools that, with limited financial and other material resources, teach students who live in dire circumstances under what can best be described as challenging conditions (Ayers, Ladson-Billings, Michie, & Noguera, 2008). Nevertheless, the difficult conditions in which some students live need not be viewed as insurmountable barriers to their academic achievement. It is too often the case that society's low expectations of students, based on these situations, pose even greater obstacles to their learning.

If we are serious about giving all students more options in life, particularly students from communities denied the necessary resources with which to access these options, then we need to begin with the assumption that these students are academically capable, both individually and as a group. Too many students have been dismissed as uneducable simply because they were not born with the material resources or family conditions considered essential for learning. The conventional attitude that students who do not arrive at school with such benefits are incapable of learning is further promoted by assertions of race-based genetic inferiority, an assumption that is unfortunately still too prevalent (Herrnstein & Murray, 1994; Murray, 2008).

Numerous examples of dramatic success in the face of adversity are powerful reminders that great potential exists in all students. Consider, for example, the case of Garfield High School in East Los Angeles, California. There the mostly Mexican American students taught by Jaime Escalante, the protagonist of the popular film *Stand and Deliver*, were tremendously successful in learning advanced mathematics (Menéndez, 1988). In fact, when they took the advanced placement (AP) calculus test, they did so well that the test makers assumed they had cheated. As a result, they had to take it a second time, and this time their performance was even better.

The success of the Algebra Project is another example (Moses & Cobb, 2002). This project has expanded throughout the country from Cambridge, Massachusetts, to Jackson, Mississippi, and New Orleans, Louisiana, to young people who had previously been denied access to algebra because they were thought to be incapable of benefiting from it yet became high achievers in math. When they went on to high school, 39 percent of the first graduating class of the project were placed in honors geometry or honors algebra classes; in fact, none of the graduates was placed in a low-level math course. The Algebra Project continues to spread to other school systems throughout the United States.

Although students' identities are often perceived to be handicaps to learning by an assimilationist society that encourages cultural and linguistic homogeneity, numerous success stories of students who use their cultural values and traditions as strengths have been reported in the educational research literature (Carter, 2005; Conchas, 2006; Lomawaima, 2004; McCarty, 2002; Nieto & Bode, 2008; Zentella, 2005). This result leads us to the inevitable conclusion that before fixing what they may consider to be problems in students, schools and society need to change their own perceptions of students and view them as capable learners.

CONCLUSION

There is no simple formula for increasing student learning. A step-by-step blueprint for school reform is both unrealistic and inappropriate because each school differs from all others in its basic structure, goals, and human dimensions. Moreover, inequitable conditions such as school funding and the distribution of resources for learning also help explain why some students are successful but others are not. In spite of these challenges, certain conditions can dramatically improve the learning of many students who are currently marginalized from the center of learning because of school policies and practices based on deficit models. If we begin with the assumptions that students cannot achieve at high levels, that their backgrounds are riddled with deficiencies, and that multicultural education is a frill that cannot help them to learn, we will end up with school reform strategies that have little hope for success.

This chapter presented and analyzed five conditions to promote student achievement within a multicultural perspective:

1. School reform should be antiracist and antibiased.
2. School reform should reflect an understanding and acceptance of all students as having talents and strengths that can enhance their education.
3. School reform should be considered within the parameters of critical pedagogy.
4. The people most intimately connected with teaching and learning (teachers, parents, and students themselves) need to be meaningfully involved in school reform.
5. School reform needs to be based on high expectations and rigorous standards for all learners.

This chapter is based on two related assumptions: (1) that students, families, and teachers bring strengths and talents to teaching and learning and (2) that a comprehensive and critical approach to multicultural education can provide an important framework for rethinking school reform. Given these assumptions, we have a much more promising scenario for effective learning and for the possibility that schools can become places of hope and affirmation for students of all backgrounds and situations.

Questions and Activities

1. What do the authors mean by "culturally responsive education?" Why do they think it is important? According to the authors, is culturally responsive education sufficient to guarantee academic success for students of color and low-income students? Why or why not?
2. What does it mean to say that multicultural education takes place within a sociopolitical context? What social, political, and economic factors must be considered when multicultural education is being implemented? How can a consideration of sociopolitical factors help multicultural school reform to be more effective?
3. What five conditions do the authors believe are needed to improve students' academic achievement? How are these factors interrelated?

4. How do the authors distinguish *individual* and *institutional racism?* Why do they think this distinction is important? Give examples of each type of racism from your personal experiences and observations.

5. What is an antiracist perspective? Why do the authors believe that an antiracist perspective is essential for the implementation of multicultural education? Give specific examples of antiracist teaching and educational practices with which you are familiar.

6. The authors briefly describe the concept of incorporating community knowledge into the curriculum advanced by Gonzalez, Moll, and Amanti (2005). How does this concept help teachers to implement "culturally responsive" teaching?

7. What is critical pedagogy? How, according to the authors, can it be used to enrich and strengthen multicultural education?

8. What positive contributions can parents and students make to create an effective multicultural school? Give specific examples.

References

Abernathy, S. (2007). *No Child Left Behind and the public schools*. Ann Arbor: University of Michigan Press.

Aronson, J., & Steele, C. M. (2005). Stereotypes and the fragility of academic competence, motivation, and self-concept. In A. J. Elliott & C. S. Dweck (Eds.), *Handbook of competence and motivation* (pp. 436–456). New York: Guilford Press.

Ayers, W., Ladson-Billings, G., Michie, G., & Noguera, P. (Eds.). (2008). *City kids, city schools: More reports from the front row*. New York: New Press.

Banks, J. A. (2009). *Teaching strategies for ethnic studies* (8th ed.). Boston: Allyn & Bacon.

Bennett deMarrais, K., & LeCompte, M. G. (1999). *The way schools work: A sociological analysis of education* (3rd ed.). New York: Longman.

Berliner, D. C. (2005). Our impoverished view of educational reform. *Teachers College Record, 108*(6), 949–995.

Beykont, Z. F. (Ed.). (2000). *Lifting every voice: Pedagogy and politics of bilingual education*. Cambridge, MA: Harvard Educational Publishing Group.

Biddle, B. J., & Berliner, D. C. (2002). What research says about small classes and their effects. San Francisco: WestEd. *Policy Perspectives* [Online]. Retrieved August 15, 2008, from http://www.wested.org/online_pubs/small_classes.pdf

Bigelow, B. (2008). *A people's history for the classroom*. Milwaukee, WI: Rethinking Schools. Also available from http://www.zinnedproject.org/

Bigelow, B., Christensen, L., Karp, S., Miner, B., & Peterson, B. (Eds.). (1994). *Rethinking our classrooms: Teaching for equity and justice* (Vol. 1). Milwaukee, WI: Rethinking Schools.

Bigelow, B., Harvey, B., Karp, S., & Miller, L. (Eds.). (2001). *Rethinking our classrooms: Teaching for equity and justice* (Vol. 2). Milwaukee, WI: Rethinking Schools.

Botelho, M. J., & Rudman, M. K. (2009). *Critical multicultural analysis of children's literature: Mirrors, windows, and doors*. New York: Routledge.

Bowles, S., & Gintis, H. (1976). *Schooling in capitalist America: Educational reform and the contradictions of economic life*. New York: Basic Books.

Carter, P. I. (2005). *Keepin' it real: School success beyond Black and White*. New York: Oxford University Press.

Clawson, R. A. (2002). Poor people, Black faces: The portrayal of poverty in economics textbooks. *Journal of Black Studies, 32*(3), 352–362.

Conchas, G. Q. (2006). *The color of success: Race and high achieving urban youth*. New York: Teachers College Press.

Cowhey, M. (2006). *Black ants and Buddhists: Thinking critically and teaching differently in the primary grades*. Portland, ME: Stenhouse.

Crawford, J. (2008). *Advocating for English learners: Selected essays*. Buffalo, NY: Multilingual Matters.

Cummins, J. (1996). *Negotiating identities: Education for empowerment in a diverse society*. Ontario: California Association for Bilingual Education.

Cummins, J. (2000). *Language, power, and pedagogy: Bilingual children in the crossfire*. Buffalo, NY: Multilingual Matters.

Darling-Hammond, L. (2006). Securing the right to learn: Policy and practice for powerful teaching and learning. *Educational Researcher, 35*(7), 13–24.

Delpit, L. (2006). *Other people's children: Cultural conflict in the classroom* (2nd ed.). New York: New Press.

Delpit, L., & Dowdy, J. K. (Eds.). (2008). *The skin that we speak: Thoughts on language and culture in the classroom* (3rd ed.). New York: New Press.

Dolby, N. (2000). Changing selves: Multicultural education and the challenge of new identities. *Teachers College Record, 102*(5), 898–912.

Edelman, M. W. (2007). The cradle to prison pipeline: An American health crisis. *Preventing Chronic Disease, 4*(3), A43.

Epstein, J. L. (2001). *School, family, and community partnerships: Preparing educators and improving schools*. Boulder, CO: Westview.

Freire, P. (1970). *Pedagogy of the oppressed*. New York: Seabury.

Freire, P. (1985). *The politics of education: Culture, power, and liberation*. South Hadley, MA: Bergin & Garvey.

Gay, G. (2004). Beyond *Brown*: Promoting equality through multicultural education. *Journal of Curriculum and Supervision, 19*(3), 193–216.

Gebhard, M., Austin, T., Nieto, S., & Willett, J. (2002). "You can't step on someone else's words": Preparing all teachers to teach language minority students. In Z. F. Beykont (Ed.), *The power of culture: Teaching across language difference* (pp. 219–243). Cambridge, MA: Harvard Educational Publishing Group.

Gonzalez, N., Moll, L. C., & Amanti, C. (Eds.). (2005). *Funds of knowledge: Theorizing practices in households and classrooms*. Mahwah, NJ: Lawrence Erlbaum.

Grant-Thomas, A., & Orfield, G. (Eds.). (2008). *Twenty-first century color lines: Multiracial change in contemporary America*. Philadelphia: Temple University Press.

Harlem Children's Zone (HCZ). (n.d.). *Mission statement*. Retrieved September 9, 2008, from http://www.hcz.org/

Harrington, M. (1997). *The other America: Poverty in the United States*. New York: Scribner. (Original work published 1971)

Henderson, A. T., Mapp, K., Johnson, V., & Davies, D. (2006). *Beyond the bake sale: The essential guide to family-school partnerships*. New York: New Press.

Herrnstein, R. J., & Murray, C. (1994). *The bell curve: Intelligence and class structure in American life*. New York: Free Press.

Howard, G. (2006). *We can't teach what we don't know: White teachers, multiracial schools* (2nd ed.). New York: Teachers College Press.

Irvine, J. J. (2003). *Educating teachers for diversity: Seeing with a cultural eye*. New York: Teachers College Press.

Katz, M. B. (1975). *Class, bureaucracy, and the schools: The illusion of educational change in America*. New York: Praeger.

Kohl, H. (2005). *She would not be moved: How we tell the story of Rosa Parks and the Montgomery Bus Boycott*. New York: New Press.

Kozol, J. (1975, December). Great men and women (tailored for school use). *Learning Magazine, 4*(4), 16–20.

Kozol, J. (1991). *Savage inequalities: Children in America's schools*. New York: Crown.

Kozol, J. (2005). *The shame of the nation: The restoration of apartheid schooling in America*. New York: Crown.

Ladd, H., Noguera, P., & Payzant, T. (2006). *A broader, bolder approach to education*. Retrieved September 1, 2008, from http://www.boldapproach.org/

Ladson-Billings, G. (2001). *Crossing over to Canaan: The journey of new teachers in diverse classrooms*. San Francisco: Jossey-Bass.

Ladson-Billings, G. (2006a). It's not the culture of poverty, it's the poverty of culture: The problem with teacher education. *Anthropology and Education Quarterly, 37*(2), 104–109.

Ladson-Billings, G. (2006b). From the achievement gap to the education debt: Understanding achievement in U.S. schools. *Educational Researcher, 35*(7), 3–12.

Landsman, J. (2001). *A White teacher talks about race*. Lanham, MD: Scarecrow.

Lee, E., Menkart, D., & Okazawa-Rey, M. (2007). *Beyond heroes and holidays: A practical guide to k–12 anti-racist, multicultural education and staff development*. Washington, DC: Teaching for Change.

Levin, M. (2001). *Teach me! Kids will learn when oppression is the lesson*. Lanham, MD: Rowman & Littlefield.

Lewis, O. (1965). *La vida: A Puerto Rican family in the culture of poverty—San Juan and New York*. New York: Random House.

Loewen, J. W. (2007). *Lies across America: What our historic sites got wrong*. New York: Touchstone/Simon & Schuster.

Loewen, J. W. (2008). *Lies my teacher told me: Everything your American history textbook got wrong* (rev. ed.). New York: Free Press.

Lomawaima, K. T. (2004). Educating Native Americans. In J. A. Banks & C. A. M. Banks (Eds.), *Handbook of research on multicultural education* (2nd ed., pp. 441–461). San Francisco: Jossey-Bass.

Mann, H. (1903). *Twelfth annual report to the Massachusetts State Board of Education, 1848.* Boston: Directors of the Old South Work. (Original work published 1848)

McCarty, T. L. (2002). *A place to be Navajo: Rough Rock and the struggle for self-determination in indigenous schooling.* Mahwah, NJ: Lawrence Erlbaum.

McNeil, L. (2000). *Contradictions of school reform: Educational costs of standardized testing.* New York: Routledge.

Meier, D., & Wood, G. (Eds.). (2004). *Many children left behind: How the No Child Left Behind Act is damaging our children and our schools.* Boston: Beacon Press.

Meier, K. J., & Stewart, J., Jr. (1991). *The politics of Hispanic education: Un paso pa'lante y dos pátras.* Albany: State University of New York Press.

Menéndez, R. (Writer/Director). (1988). *Stand and deliver* [Motion picture]. United States: Warner Bros.

Menkart, D., Murray, A. D., & View, J. (2004). *Putting the movement back into civil rights teaching.* Washington, DC: Teaching for Change and the Poverty and Race Research Action Council (PRRAC).

Michie, G. (2005). *See you when we get there: Teaching for change in urban schools.* New York: Teachers College Press.

Miner, B. (2004). Testing companies mine for gold. *Rethinking Schools, 19*(2), 5–7.

Morrell, E. (2008). *Critical literacy and urban youth: Pedagogies of access, dissent, and liberation.* New York: Routledge.

Moses, R. P., & Cobb, C. E., Jr. (2002). *Radical equations: Math literacy and civil rights.* Boston: Beacon.

Muennig, P., & Woolf, S. H. (2007). Health and economic benefits of reducing the number of students per classroom in US primary schools. *American Journal of Public Health, 97*(11), 2020–2027.

Murray, C. (2008). *Real education: Four simple truths for bringing America's schools back to reality.* New York: Random House/Crown Forum.

National Center for Education Statistics. (2008). *Revenues and expenditures for public elementary and secondary school districts: School year 2005–06* (Fiscal Year 2006). *First Look: CES 2008–345.* Retrieved September 10, 2008, from http://nces.ed.gov/pubsearch/pubsinfo.asp?pubid=2008345

National Commission on Excellence in Education. (1983). *A nation at risk: The imperative for educational reform.* Washington, DC: Author.

Nichols, S., & Berliner, D. C. (2005). *The inevitable corruption of indicators and educators through high-stakes testing.* Tempe: Educational Policy Studies Laboratory, Educational Policy Research Unit, Arizona State University.

Nieto, S. (1992). *Affirming diversity: The sociopolitical context of multicultural education.* New York: Longman.

Nieto, S. (2010). *The light in their eyes: Creating multicultural learning communities* (2nd ed.). New York: Teachers College Press.

Nieto, S. (2002–2003). Profoundly multicultural questions. *Educational Leadership, 60*(4), 6–10.

Nieto, S., & Bode, P. (2008). *Affirming diversity: The sociopolitical context of multicultural education* (5th ed.). Boston: Allyn & Bacon.

Nieto, S., Bode, P., Kang, E., & Raible, J. (2008). Identity, community and diversity: Retheorizing multicultural curriculum for the postmodern era. In F. M. Connelly, M. F. He, & J. Phillion (Eds.), *The Sage handbook of curriculum and instruction* (pp. 176–197). Thousand Oaks, CA: Sage.

No Child Left Behind Act (NCLB), 107th Cong., 1st sess. HR 1, P.L. 107-110. (2001).

Noguera, P. (2003). Schools, prisons, and social implications of punishment: Rethinking disciplinary practices. *Theory into Practice, 42*(4), 341–350.

Oakes, J. (2005). *Keeping track: How schools structure inequality* (2nd ed.). New Haven, CT: Yale University Press.

Olsen, L. (2008). *Made in America: Immigrant students in our public schools* (10th anniv. ed.). New York: New Press.

Orfield, G. (2001). *Schools more separate: Consequences of a decade of resegregation.* Cambridge, MA: Harvard Civil Rights Project.

Orfield, G., & Kornhaber, M. L. (Eds.). (2001). *Raising standards or raising barriers? Inequality and high-stakes testing in public education.* New York: Century Foundation Press.

Pollock, M. (2004). *Colormute: Race talk dilemmas in an American school.* Princeton, NJ: Princeton University Press.

Pollock, M. (Ed.). (2008). *Everyday antiracism: Getting real about race in school.* New York: New Press.

Reissman, F. (1962). *The culturally deprived child.* New York: Harper & Row.

Reyes, M. d. l. L., & Halcón, J. J. (Eds.) (2001). *The best for our children: Critical perspectives on literacy for Latino students.* New York: Teachers College Press.

Rothstein, R. (2004). *Class and schools: Using social, economic, and educational reform to close the Black–White achievement gap.* New York: Teachers College Press.

Rothstein, R. (2008). Leaving "No Child Left Behind" behind: Our No. 1 education program is incoherent, unworkable, and doomed. But the next president still can have a huge impact on improving American schooling. *American Prospect, 19*(1), 50–54.

Ryan, W. (1972). *Blaming the victim.* New York: Vintage.

Shor, I. (1992). *Empowering education: Critical teaching for social change.* Chicago: University of Chicago Press.

Shor, I., & Pari, C. (Eds.). (1999). *Education is politics: Critical teaching across differences, K-12.* Portsmouth, NH: Boynton/Cook.

Shor, I., & Pari, C. (Eds.). (2000). *Education is politics: Critical teaching across differences, postsecondary.* Portsmouth, NH: Boynton/Cook.

Sleeter, C. E. (1994). White racism. *Multicultural Education, 1*(4), 5–8, 39.

Sleeter, C. E. (2005). *Un-standardizing curriculum: Multicultural education in the standards-based classroom.* New York: Teachers College Press.

Spring, J. H. (1989). *The sorting machine revisited: National educational policy since 1945.* White Plains, NY: Longman.

Spring, J. (2007). *Deculturalization and the struggle for equality: A brief history of the education of dominated cultures in the United States* (5th ed). New York: McGraw-Hill.

Steele, C. M. (1999). Thin ice: "Stereotype threat" and Black college students. *Atlantic Monthly, 284*(2), 44–54.

Takaki, R. (2008). *A different mirror: A history of multicultural America.* Boston: Back Bay Books.

Tatum, B. D. (2003). *"Why are all the Black kids sitting together in the cafeteria?" and other conversations about race* (rev. ed.). New York: Basic Books.

Tatum, B. D. (2007). *Can we talk about race? And other conversations in an era of school resegregation*. Boston: Beacon.

Tough, P. (2008). *Whatever it takes: Geoffrey Canada's quest to change Harlem and America*. New York: Houghton Mifflin.

Van Ausdale, D., & Feagin, J. R. (2001). *The first r: How children learn race and racism*. New York: Rowman & Littlefield.

Vasquez, V. M. (2004). *Negotiating critical literacies with young children*. Mahwah, NJ: Lawrence Erlbaum.

Weinberg, M. (1996). *Racism in contemporary America*. Westport, CT: Greenwood.

Wiggins, G., & McTighe, J. (2005). *Understanding by design* (2nd ed). Alexandria, VA: Association for Supervision and Curriculum Development.

Willis, A. (Ed.). (1998). *Teaching and using multicultural literature in grades 9–12: Moving beyond the canon*. Norwood, MA: Christopher-Gordon.

Yosso, T. (2006). *Critical race counterstories along the Chicana/Chicano pipeline*. New York: Routledge.

Zentella, A. C. (2005). *Building on strengths: Language and literacy in Latino families and communities*. New York: Teachers College Press.

Zinn, H. (2005). *A people's history of the United States: 1492–present* (rev. ed.). New York: Harper Perennial.

CHAPTER 17

Communities, Families, and Educators Working Together for School Improvement

Cherry A. McGee Banks

It was almost time for her ninth-grade general science class to begin and Miss Horton faced a dilemma—one that frequently confronts teachers who are teaching controversial issues. All week the students had discussed the scientific method and how it relates to evolution. The discussions had gone well, and today the students would consider the evidence for evolution by identifying different types of fossils and investigating how they were formed.

Miss Horton had just finished organizing the science lab when Mrs. Mann knocked on her door and asked to talk with her. Mrs. Mann was Joyce Mann's mother. Joyce was an average student who was always well behaved and pleasant but never seemed to get excited about class activities or any of the topics they discussed. This was the first time Miss Horton had spoken with Mrs. Mann, and she was happy to see her. She welcomed her into her classroom and asked her to take a seat by her desk. Mrs. Mann got directly to the reason for her visit. She was concerned about the evolution unit. Mrs. Mann explained that they were a Christian family and as such believed in creationism. She was concerned that Miss Horton's lessons about Darwinian evolution were undermining what they were teaching Joyce about intelligent design, a concept that explains that an intelligent cause—not natural selection—best explains certain features of the universe and living things. The Manns do not believe that an undirected process such as natural selection as explained by Darwin in the *Origin of Species* (1859) can account for the diverse physical and biological systems observed in the universe. At the end of the conversation, Mrs. Mann gave Miss Horton a copy of *Intelligent Design: The Bridge Between Science & Theology*, by William A. Dembski (1999), and encouraged her to read it.

What would you do if you were Miss Horton? This is how Miss Horton responded. She thanked Mrs. Mann for the book and for taking the time to talk to her. Then she shared some of the key points she covered in the science curriculum and explained that evolution was part of the approved district curriculum for ninth-grade general science. Miss Horton wanted

417

Mrs. Mann to understand that while she respected her opinion and appreciated her concern for her daughter, she did not plan to teach a unit on intelligent design. She encouraged Mrs. Mann to stay in communication with her and to visit her classroom whenever she would like to do so. Mrs. Mann was not completely satisfied with the outcome of the meeting, but she left the meeting knowing that Miss Horton was a competent and caring teacher who was open to listen to her concerns. For now, she planned to visit the class on a regular basis and stay in touch with Miss Horton. Miss Horton understood that while it was important for parents and teachers to have open lines of communication, good communication does not necessarily eliminate tensions between home and school. To make sure that she was following school protocol, Miss Horton discussed Mrs. Mann's visit with her principal. As a result of their conversation, she knew that her principal supported her actions and was prepared to talk with Mrs. Mann should she decide to contact him.

The diversity of parent and community groups with their different concerns and issues illustrates one of the important complexities of parent and community involvement in schools (De Carvalho, 2001). This complexity—which may be reflected in different interaction styles, expectations, and concerns—complicates but does not negate the need for parent and community involvement in schools (DeSteno, 2000). Educators lose an important voice for school improvement when parents and community groups are not involved in schools. They can give teachers unique and important views of their students as well as help the school garner resources that are available in the community. After Mrs. Mann's visit, Miss Horton had some additional information about Joyce and some possible reasons for her lack of excitement about the science curriculum. As a result of Mrs. Mann's visit, Miss Horton started thinking about invisible barriers, such as values and beliefs, that may limit students' full access to the curriculum. Mrs. Mann's visit helped Miss Horton become more sensitive and aware of the range of student diversity in her classroom. By showing respect and appreciation for the concerns of a parent, Miss Horton will hopefully have an ally as she learns to work more effectively with her students.

In a comprehensive review of research on parent involvement, Henderson and Berla (2002) found compelling evidence that parent involvement improves student achievement. Parent involvement is also associated with improvements in students' attendance and social behavior. However, to capitalize on the benefits of parent and community involvement, involvement strategies must be broadly conceptualized. Parents should be given an opportunity to contribute to school improvement by working in different settings and at different levels of the educational process (Henderson, Mapp, Johnson, & Davies, 2006; Hidalgo, Sau-Fong, & Epstein, 2004). For example, some parents may want to focus their energies on working with their own children at home. Other parents may want to work on decision-making committees. Still others may be able to provide in-class assistance to teachers. Epstein (2008) and her colleagues have identified six different types of involvement: (1) parenting, (2) communicating, (3) volunteering, (4) learning at home, (5) decision making, and (6) collaborating with the community. Though very different, each type of involvement provides opportunities for parents to have a positive influence on their students' school experience.

Other family members and community groups as well as parents can also work with teachers to reform schools. Many tasks involved in restructuring schools, such as setting goals and allocating resources, are best achieved through a collaborative problem-solving structure that includes parents, educators, and family and community members (Ouimette, Feldman, & Tung, 2006). Family and community members can form what Goodlad (1984) calls "the necessary coalition of contributing groups" (p. 293). Educational reform needs their support, influence, and activism. Schools are highly dependent on and vulnerable to citizens who can support or impede change. Family members and community leaders can validate the need for educational reform and can provide an appropriate forum for exploring the importance of education. They can also extend the discussion on school improvement issues beyond formal educational networks and can help generate support for schools in the community at large. Family members and community leaders can help provide the rationale, motivation, and social action necessary for educational reform.

REASONS THAT PARENT AND FAMILY INVOLVEMENT IN SCHOOLS IS IMPORTANT

Parent involvement is important because it acknowledges the importance of parents in the lives of their children, recognizes the diversity of values and perspectives within the community, provides a vehicle for building a collaborative problem-solving structure, and increases the opportunity for all students to learn in school. Parents, however, are not the only adults who support and contribute to the care of children. When parents struggle with poverty, incarceration, substance abuse, mental illness, and other challenges, grandparents and other relatives often become the children's primary caregivers (McCallion, Janicki, & Kolomer, 2004). In 2007, 4,013,000 children under 18 lived with their grandparents. In some cases, the child's mother or father also lived with the grandparent. However, neither a mother nor father was present in 32.5 percent of these families. From 1970 to 2006, there was a 55 percent increase in the number of grandchildren living in grandparent-headed households and a 73 percent increase in cases where neither parent was present in the household (U.S. Census Bureau, 2007). This suggests that parent involvement programs should be conceptualized broadly enough to include grandparents and other family members.

Parent and family involvement in schools benefits not only students and teachers but also parents and family members (Center for Mental Health in Schools at UCLA, 2007). When parents help their children at home, the children perform better in school (Aikens, 2002). Parent involvement allows parents and teachers to reinforce skills and provides an environment that has consistent learning expectations and standards. Parents benefit because through their involvement with the school, they become more knowledgeable about their child's school, its policies, and the school staff. Perhaps most important, parent involvement provides an opportunity for parents and children to spend time together. During that time, parents can communicate a high value for education, the importance of effort in achievement, and positive regard for their children.

Parents and family members are often children's first and most important teachers. Students come to school with knowledge, values, and beliefs they have learned from their parents and in their communities. Parents directly or indirectly help shape their children's value system, orientation toward learning, and view of the world (Caspe, Lopez, & Wolos, 2006/2007). Most parents want their children to succeed in school. Schools can capitalize on the high value most parents place on education by working to create a school environment that respects the students' home and community (Hidalgo et al., 2004). When schools are in conflict with their students' home and community, they can alienate students from their families and communities.

To create harmonious relations among the school, home, and community, parents need information about the school. They need to know what the school expects their children to learn, how they will be taught, and the required books and materials their children will use in school. Most important, parents need to know how teachers assess students and how they can support their children's achievement. Teachers need to understand their students' community and home life. Teachers also need to know about their students' parents, homes, and communities. It would be helpful for teachers to have a clear understanding of the educational expectations parents have for their children, the languages spoken at home, the family's values and norms, and how children are taught in their homes and communities. Teachers and principals who know parents treat them with greater respect and show more positive attitudes toward their children (Berger, 2008). Teachers generally see involved parents as concerned individuals who support the school. Parents who are not involved in schools are frequently seen as parents who do not value education.

HISTORICAL OVERVIEW

While parent involvement in education is not new, its importance and purpose have varied over time. In the early part of the nation's history, families were often solely responsible for educating children. Children learned values and skills by working with their families in their communities.

When formal systems of education were established, parents continued to influence their children's education. During the colonial period, schools were viewed as an extension of the home. The school reinforced parental and community values and expectations. Teachers generally came from the community and often personally knew their students' parents and shared their values.

At the beginning of the 20th century, when large numbers of immigrants came to the United States, schools became a major vehicle for assimilating immigrant children into U.S. society (Banks, 2008). In general, immigrant parents were not welcomed in schools. Children of immigrants were taught that their parents' ways of speaking, behaving, and thinking were inferior to those of mainstream Americans. In his study of the sociology of teaching, Waller (1932/1965) concluded that parents and teachers lived in a state of mutual distrust and even hostility. There were, however, some notable exceptions.

One such exception was Benjamin Franklin High School (BFHS) in East Harlem, New York. Leonard Covello, principal at BFHS, instituted a program of intergroup education there in the 1930s. Parents were welcome at Franklin, and teachers encouraged students to appreciate their parents' language, values, and customs. Community groups were also actively involved at BFHS. Covello saw parent and community involvement as a way to promote democratic values, reduce prejudice, and increase cross-cultural understanding and appreciation (Banks, 2005).

As society changed and education became more removed from the direct influence of parents, responsibility for transmitting knowledge from generation to generation was transferred from the home and community to the school. Formal education was seen as a job for trained professionals. Schools became autonomous institutions staffed by people who were often strangers in their students' home communities. Teachers did not necessarily live in their students' neighborhoods, know their students' parents, or share their values.

Schools were given more and more duties that traditionally had been the responsibility of the home and community. Schools operated under the assumption that they were *in loco parentis*, and educators were asked to assume the role of both teacher and substitute parent.

In a pluralist society, what the school teaches as well as whom and how the school teaches can create tensions between parents and schools. Issues ranging from what the school teaches about the role of women in our society to mainstreaming students with disabilities point to the need for teachers, parents, and community leaders to work together. However, parents, community leaders, and teachers do not always agree on meaningful ways to cooperate and partner in the educational process (Anderson, 2006).

THE CHANGING FACE OF THE FAMILY

Parent/family diversity mirrors student diversity. As the student population becomes more diverse, parent/family diversity also increases. Involving parents in schools means that teachers have to be prepared to work with a range of parents, including single parents, parents with special needs, low-income parents, parents with disabilities, same-sex parents, and parents who do not speak English as their first language. Working with parents from diverse backgrounds requires sensitivity to and an understanding of their circumstances and worldviews (Amatea, Smith-Adcock, & Villares, 2006; Chavkin & Gonzalez, 1995; Kagan, 1995; Pena, 2000; Schneider & Coleman, 1993).

It is especially important that teachers understand and be sensitive to the changing nature of the ethnic and racial makeup of their students and their students' parents. The ethnic landscape of U.S. schools includes an increasing number of Arab, Jewish, Eastern European, and African students (McFalls, 2007). One of the most significant changes in U.S. immigration in the early 21st century is the increase in immigrants of African descent from African and Caribbean nations. Today African immigrants constitute 6 percent of all the immigrants to the United States and almost 5 percent of the African American community. It is important to remember, however, that African immigrants are not all members of the same race. A small percentage of immigrants from East Africa are of Asian origin, and a number of immigrants from South Africa are white (Dodson & Diouf, 2005). In addition, ethnic identity has primacy over racial identity for many African immigrants. For example, some immigrants of African descent would identify themselves as Cubans, Dominicans, Nigerians, Kenyans, Haitians, or Puerto Ricans, not as Blacks or Whites. Their phenotype, however, might conflict with physical characteristics that traditionally are used to identify races in the United States. For example, a Cuban American with brown skin may consider himself White because phenotype is not the only factor that is used to identify race in most Caribbean nations. This can be confusing for Americans who historically have equated race and phenotype.

However, even in the United States, the lines between racial groups are becoming blurred. A growing number of students and parents are members of more than one racial group. Even though marriage between people from different races is still an exception rather than the rule, more and more people are marrying interracially. Typically, interracial marriages are between a White person and a person from a minority racial group. It does not typically involve two people from minority racial groups (Lee & Edmonston, 2005). In 2007, more than 4.8 million people identified with two or more races (U.S. Census Bureau, 2007). While this is a relatively small percentage of the U.S. population, the percentage of people who are multiracial is more salient when geographic regions and subgroups within the population are examined. For example, children are more likely to be multiracial than adults, and racial groups that have small populations tend to include higher percentages of multiracial people. Additionally, urban areas tend to have higher rates of interracial marriage than rural areas. California, Nevada, Alaska, and Oklahoma have the highest percentage of interracial marriages in the United States. Between 10.0 and 29.3 percent of the married couples in those states are interracial (Lee & Edmonston). Among all racial groups, Whites and Blacks have the lowest rate of interracial marriage and American Indians, Hawaiians, and multiracial individuals have the highest. With respect to gender, interracial marriage is about equal for all racial groups except African Americans and Asians. African American men are more likely to intermarry than African American women, and Asian women are more likely to intermarry than Asian men (Lee & Edmonston). The increase in interracial children, foreign-born children—usually Asian—who are adopted by American families—usually White—and immigrant children who do not use their phenotype to define their race, highlight the importance of teachers not making assumptions about the racial and ethnic background of their students and their parents but allowing them to define their own identity.

Diversity in parent and community groups can be a tremendous asset to the school. However, it can also be a source of potential conflict and tension. Some parents are particularly difficult to involve in their children's education. They resist becoming involved for several reasons (Harry, 1992; Walker, 1996). In a national survey, parents indicated that a lack of time was the primary reason they were not involved in their children's schools (Clark, 1995). The pressures of earning a living and taking care of a home and children can result in a great deal of stress. At the end of the day, some parents just want to rest. Other parents do not believe they have the necessary educational background to be involved in their children's school. They feel intimidated by educators and believe that education should be left to teachers. Still others feel alienated from their children's schools because of negative experiences they had in school or because they believe the school does not support their values (Berger, 2008; Clark, 1995; Rasinski, 1989).

Three groups of parents are frequently underrepresented in school activities: parents with special needs, single parents, and low-income parents. These are not the only groups that are underrepresented in school activities; however, their experiences and needs illustrate particular problem areas. The specific groups of parents discussed should not be viewed as an indication that only parents from these groups are difficult to involve in schools or that all parents from these groups resist participation in schools. Parents from all groups share many of the concerns discussed next.

Parents with Special Needs

Parents with special needs include a wide range of individuals. They are found in all ethnic, racial, and income groups. Chronically unemployed parents, parents with long-term illnesses, abusive parents, and parents with substance abuse problems are examples of parents with special needs. As you can see from the list, the concerns are varied, and in some cases they can overlap. Each requires specific responses. For example, abusive parents require special attention from the school. Most schools have policies on how to treat suspected cases of child neglect and abuse. Teachers should be aware of those policies, which should be written and available to all school personnel. All states require schools to report suspected cases of child abuse.

Although parents with special needs frequently have serious problems that the school cannot address, teachers should not ignore the importance of understanding their students' home environments. Knowing the difficulties students are coping with at home can help teachers create school environments that are supportive (Swadener & Niles, 1991). Schools can help compensate for the difficult circumstances students experience at home. The school, for some students, is the only place during the day where they are nurtured.

Working with special-needs families requires district or building support in identifying places for family referrals and support for students and teachers. Some schools hire outreach community service workers to provide these kinds of services. Although some special-needs parents may resist the school's help, they need to know that their problems can negatively affect their children's success in school. Referring these parents to places where they can receive help can show students who are in difficult home environments that they are not alone. Most parents want to feel that they are valued and adequate human beings and that they can help their children succeed. When they are willing to be involved in school, they do not want to be humiliated (Berger, 2008).

Some parents with special needs will be able to be actively involved in schools, but many will be unable to sustain ongoing involvement. An important goal for working with parents with special needs is to keep lines of communication open. To the extent possible, try to get to know the parents. Do not accept a stereotypical view of them without ever talking to them. Encourage parents to become involved whenever and however they are able to participate. Your goal should be to develop a clear understanding of your student's home environment so that you can provide appropriate intervention at school.

Members of the community who are involved in school may be willing to serve as intermediaries between the school and uninvolved parents and in some cases as surrogate parents. In an ethnography of an inner-city neighborhood, Shariff (1988) found that adults shared goods and services and provided support for each other. Educators can build on the sense of extended family and fictive kinship that may exist in some neighborhoods to connect with community support groups for students whose parents cannot be involved in school. Civic and social community groups, such as The Links, Inc., and the Boys and Girls Clubs, can also provide support for students who do not have the support they need at home.

Working with students whose parents have special needs is complicated and challenging. However, regardless of the circumstances students confront at home, teachers have a responsibility to help them perform at their highest level at school. Schools with large numbers of parents with special needs require experienced and highly qualified teachers who have district and school support to help them meet the additional challenges that they will face. Traditionally, however, these schools have many teachers who are relatively new to the field and are not certified in the areas in which they teach (Darling-Hammond, 2004).

Single Parents

One of the most significant social changes in the United States in the last 30 years is the increase in the percentage of children living with one parent. In 2005, 73.5 million children under eighteen lived in households headed by a single parent. Women head most single-parent families (U.S. Census, 2005). Approximately 4 or 5 percent of the children living with one parent lived with their father. The number of single-parent families is particularly significant in the African American community. In 2005, about half of Black children lived with a single mother compared to 10 percent of Asian children who lived with a single mother. Among Hispanic children, 25 percent lived with a single mother (U.S. Census). Gender is an important factor in single-parent homes because women tend to earn less than men. In 2004, 39 percent of children living with a single father lived in households with an annual income below $30,000 compared to 62 percent of children living with a single mother. Of children in two-parent families, 14 percent lived in households with incomes below $30,000 (U.S. Census).

Single-parent families have many of the same hopes, joys, and concerns about their children's education as do two-parent families. However, because these parents have a lower rate of attendance at school functions, they are frequently viewed as not supporting their children's education. When teachers respond sensitively to their needs and limitations, they can be enthusiastic partners with teachers. Four suggestions for working with single parents follow. Many of these suggestions apply to other groups of parents as well.

1. Provide flexible times for conferences, such as early mornings, evenings, and weekends.
2. Provide baby-sitting service when activities are held at the school.
3. Work out procedures for acknowledging and communicating with noncustodial parents. For instance, under what circumstances are noncustodial parents informed about their children's grades, school behavior, or attendance? Problems can occur when information is inappropriately given to or withheld from a noncustodial parent.
4. Use the parent's correct surname. Students will sometimes have different names from their parents.

Low-Income Parents

The number of people living below the poverty line slightly decreased from 2006 to 2007. Even so, the poverty rate in the United States was 13 percent in 2007, with more than 38 million people living in poverty (Bishaw & Semega, 2008). The poverty level is an official governmental estimate of the income necessary to maintain a minimally acceptable standard of living. Poverty rates vary by family type. In 2007, households headed by single women had the highest poverty rate at 28.3 percent, compared to a rate of 4.9 percent for married couples (U.S. Census, 2007).

Even though the number of individuals of color in the highest income brackets has more than doubled since 1980, race continues to be a salient factor in poverty. The poverty rate in 2007 was 9.0 percent for non-Hispanic Whites, 24.7 percent for African Americans, 25.3 percent for American Indians and Native Alaskan Natives, 10.6 percent for Asians, and 15.7 percent for Native Hawaiians and Other Pacific Islanders. Most minorities earn less than Whites. However, Asian males earn more than all other groups. In 2007, their median income was $51,174 compared to $50,139 for non-Hispanic White males, $29,239 for Hispanic males, $35,652 for African American males, $34,833 for American Indian and Alaskan Native males, and $36,624 for Native Hawaiian and Other Pacific Islander males. Women in each group earned less than their male counterparts (Bishaw & Semega, 2008).

Low-income parents are often among the strongest supporters of education because they often see it as a means to a better life for their children. However, their definition and understanding of "support for education" may be different from that of the school staff. Additionally, they are often limited in their ability to buy materials and to make financial commitments that can enable their children to participate in activities such as field trips or extracurricular programs. Schools can provide workbooks and other study materials for use at home as well as transportation for school activities and conferences. The school can also support low-income parents by establishing community service programs. For example, students can help clean up neighborhoods and distribute information on available social services. The school can provide desk space for voter registration and other services.

Perhaps the most important way for schools to work with low-income parents is to recognize that they can contribute a great deal to their children's education. Even though their contributions may not be in the manner traditionally associated with parent involvement, they can be very beneficial to teachers and students. The positive values and attitudes parents communicate to their children and their strong desire for their children to get a good education in order to have a better chance in life than they had are important forms of support for the school.

TEACHER CONCERNS WITH PARENT AND FAMILY INVOLVEMENT

Even though teachers often say they want to involve parents, they may be suspicious of parents and are not sure what parents expect from them. Some teachers think parents may disrupt their routine, may not have the necessary skills to work with students, may be inconvenient to have in the classroom, and may be interested only in helping their own child, not the total class. Even teachers who would like to involve parents may not be sure that they have the time, skill, or knowledge to involve parents in the school. Many teachers believe that they already have too much to do and that working with parents would make their already overburdened jobs impossible.

Many of these concerns derive from a limited view of the possibilities for parent involvement. Frequently, when parents and teachers think of parent involvement, they think it means doing something for the school generally at the school or having the school teach parents how to become better parents. In today's ever-changing society, a traditional view of parent involvement inhibits rather than encourages parents and teachers to work together. Traditional ideas about parent involvement have a built-in gender and social-class bias and can be a barrier to many men and low-income parents. Moreover, the ideas tend to focus on parents, not on community groups. With a national focus on education, more and more community groups are interested in working with schools. It is not uncommon for schools to have corporate or community sponsors. While these are generally supportive and cooperative relationships, they are typically linked to the school district or school, not to specific classrooms. Administrators will need to think carefully about how to involve classroom teachers with these groups.

When parent involvement is viewed as a means of getting support for the school, parents are encouraged to bake cookies, raise money, or work at the school as unpaid classroom, playground, library, or office helpers. This form of parent involvement is generally directed to mothers who do not work outside the home. However, the number of mothers available for this form of involvement is decreasing. In 2007, 71 percent of mothers with children under eighteen years old were either working or looking for work outside the home (U.S. Bureau of Labor Statistics, 2008).

The parent-as-helper idea is geared toward parents who have the skills, time, and resources to become school helpers. While this is a role that many educated, middle-class parents eagerly embrace, not all parents want to or feel they can or should do things for the school. Whether parents are willing to come to school depends largely on their attitudes toward school. These attitudes result in part from the parents' own school experiences.

Cultural perspectives also play an important role in the traditional approach to parent involvement. To be effective, strategies for parent and community involvement should reflect what Bullivant (1993) calls the core of the social group's cultural program, which consists of the knowledge and conceptions embodied in the group's behaviors and artifacts and the values the group subscribed to. When teachers do not understand a group's cultural program, they may conceptualize parent involvement as a means to help deficient parents become better parents (Linn, 1990). This view of parent involvement is often directed toward culturally different and low-income parents (Jennings, 1990). Teachers are presented as more skilled in parenting than parents. Instead of helping parents and teachers work cooperatively, this attitude can create barriers by suggesting that parents are the cause of their children's failure in school. Parents and teachers may even become rivals for the child's affection (Lightfoot, 1978). Involvement efforts based on "the parent in need of parenting skills" assume that there is one appropriate way to parent and that parents want to learn it. Both "the parent as helper" and "the parent in need of parenting skills" are conceptualizations derived from questionable assumptions about the character of contemporary parents and reflect a limited cultural perspective.

STEPS TO INCREASE PARENT AND FAMILY INVOLVEMENT

Teachers are a key ingredient in parent and family involvement. They play multiple roles, including facilitator, communicator, and resource developer. Their success in implementing an effective parent/community involvement program is linked to their skill in communicating and working with parents and community groups. Teacher attitudes are also very important. Parents are supportive of the teachers they believe like their children and want their children to succeed. Teachers who have a negative attitude toward students will likely have a similar attitude toward the students' parents. Teachers tend to relate to their students as representatives of their parents' perceived status in society. Teachers use such characteristics as class, race, gender, and ethnicity to determine students' prescribed social category. Being aware of this tendency can help teachers guard against it.

You can take five steps to increase parent/community involvement in your classroom: (1) establish two-way communication, (2) enlist support from staff and students, (3) enlist support from the community, (4) develop resource materials for home use, and (5) broaden the activities included in parent involvement.

Establish Two-Way Communication Between the School and the Home

Establishing two-way communication between the school and the home is an important step in involving parents (Decker & Majerczyk, 2000). Most parents are willing to become involved in their children's education if they understand what you are trying to accomplish and how they can help. Teachers should be prepared to engage in outreach to parents, not to wait for them to become involved. Actively solicit information from parents on their thoughts about classroom goals and activities. When you talk with parents and community members, be an active listener. Listen for their feelings as well as for specific information. Listed next are seven ways you can establish and maintain two-way communication with parents and community members.

1. If possible, have an open-door policy in your classroom. Let parents know they are welcome to assist in your classroom. When parents visit, make sure they have something to do.

2. Send home written information about school assignments and goals so that parents are aware of what is going on in the classroom. Encourage parents to send notes to you if they have questions or concerns.

3. Talk to parents by phone. Let them know when they can reach you by phone. Call parents periodically and let them know when things are going well. Have something specific to talk about. Leave some time for the parent to ask questions or make comments.

4. Report problems to parents, such as failing grades and behavior problems, before it is too late for them to take remedial action. Let parents know what improvements you expect from their children and how they can help.

5. Get to know your students' community. Take time to shop in their neighborhoods. Visit community centers and attend religious services. Let parents know when you will be in the community and that you are interested in talking to them.

6. If you teach in an elementary school, try to have at least two in-person conferences a year with parents. When possible, include the student in at least part of the conference. Be prepared to explain your curriculum to parents and have books and materials that students use available for them to examine. Let the parents know in specific terms how their children are doing in class. Find out how parents feel about their children's levels of achievement, and let them know what you think about their children's achievement levels. Give the parents some suggestions on what their children can do to improve and how they can help.

7. Solicit information from parents about their views on education. Identify their educational goals for their children, ways they would like to support their children's education, and their concerns about the school. There are a number of ways to get information from parents, including sending a questionnaire home and asking parents to complete it and return it to you, conducting a telephone survey, and asking your students to interview their parents. Do not forget high-tech solutions for staying in touch with parents. These include school Web pages, homework hotlines, e-mail correspondence, videotaped events, and televised meetings. Be sure to work with local libraries to make sure that parents who do not own computers will be able to use computers in the library to access the information.

Enlist Support from Other Staff Members and Students

Teachers need support from staff, students, the principal, and district-level administrators to design, implement, and enhance their parent-involvement activities (Kirschenbaum, 2001). Teachers generally have some flexibility in their classrooms but are not always able to determine other important factors that influence their ability to have a strong parent-involvement program. For example, when teachers are consulted about the type and amount of supplies purchased for their classroom, they should be able to decide whether they want to have enough supplies to be able to send paper, pencils, and other materials home for parents to use with their children. If the school cannot provide extra supplies for teachers to send home with students, community groups may be able to provide them. Also, if teachers are allowed to modify their schedules, they can find free time to telephone parents, write notes, and hold morning or evening conferences with parents. Additionally, school climate influences parent involvement. Parents will not have positive feelings about schools where they do not believe they are welcome. School climate, however, is not determined by the teacher alone. A broad range of individuals, including students, teachers, the principal, and the school secretary, influence it. The support of all of these individuals is necessary to create a positive school environment.

Your students can help solicit support for parent and community involvement from school staff and other students. Take your class on a tour of the school. Ask the students to think about how their parents would feel if they came to the school. Two obvious questions for students are these: Is there a place for visitors to sit? Are there signs welcoming visitors and inviting them to the school office? Ask your students to list things they could do to make the school a friendlier place for parents.

Invite your principal to come to your classroom and discuss the list with your students. Divide the class into small groups and have them discuss how they would like their parents to become involved in their education. Ask them to talk to their parents and get their views. Have each group write a report on how parents can be involved in their children's education. Each group could make presentations to students in the other classrooms in the building on how they would like to increase parent involvement in their school. They could also publish a newsletter on parent involvement in schools. The newsletter could be sent to the students, parents, and other schools in the district.

If funds or other forms of support are needed from the district office for parent-involvement activities, have the students draw up a petition requesting funding and solicit signatures from teachers, students, and parents. When all of the signatures have been gathered, they can be delivered to an appropriate district administrator. The petition could also be used to inform community groups about school issues and solicit their support.

Building principals and district administrators can give teachers the support they need to do the following:

1. Help create and maintain a climate for positive parent/community involvement. This can include supporting flexible hours for teachers who need to be out of the classroom to develop materials or to work with parents. Teachers can be given time out of the classroom without negatively affecting students. Time can be gleaned from the secondary teacher's schedule by combining homerooms one day a week, by team-teaching a class, or by combining different sections of a class for activities such

as chapter tests. At the elementary school level, team teaching, released time during periods when students are normally out of the classroom for specialized subjects such as music and art, or having the principal substitute in the classroom are ways to provide flexible hours for teachers.

2. Set up a parent room. It could be used for a number of functions, including serving as a community drop-in center where parents could meet other parents for a cup of coffee or as a place for parents to work on school activities without infringing on the teachers' lounge. It could also be used as a waiting room for parents who need to see a student or a member of the school staff.

3. Host parent nights during which parents can learn more about the school, the curriculum, and the staff.

4. Send a personal note to students and to their parents when students make the honor roll or do something else noteworthy. Some schools give parents bumper stickers for their cars announcing their student's achievements.

5. Develop and distribute a handbook that contains the names and phone numbers of students, PTA or other parent-group contacts, and staff. Be sure to get permission before publishing phone numbers, addresses, and other personal information.

6. Ask the school secretary to make sure visitors are welcomed when they come to the school and that they are given directions as needed.

7. Encourage students to greet visitors and help them find their way around the building.

Enlist Support from the Community

To enlist support from the community, you need to know something about the people, organizations, and issues in it. The following are some questions you should be able to answer:

1. Are there any drama, musical, dance, or art groups in the community?

2. Is there a senior-citizen group, a public library, or a cooperative extension service in the community?

3. Are employment services such as the state employment security department available in the community?

4. Are civil rights organizations such as the Urban League, Anti-Defamation League (ADL), or National Association for the Advancement of Colored People (NAACP) active in the community?

5. What is the procedure for referring people to the Salvation Army, Goodwill, or the state department of public assistance for emergency assistance for housing, food, and clothing?

6. Does the community have a mental health center, family counseling center, or crisis clinic?

7. Are programs and activities for youth—such as Boys and Girls Clubs, Campfire U.S.A., Boy Scouts, Girl Scouts, YMCA, and YWCA—available for your students?

As you learn about the community, you can begin to develop a list of community resources and contacts that can provide support to families, work with your students, and provide locations for students to perform community service projects. Collecting information about your students' community and developing community contacts should be viewed as a long-term project. You can collect information as your schedule permits and organize it in a notebook. This process can be shortened if several teachers work together. Each teacher could concentrate on a different part of the community and share information and contacts.

Community groups can provide support in several ways. They can develop big sister and big brother programs for students, provide quiet places for students to study after school and on weekends, donate educational supplies, help raise funds for field trips, set up mentor programs, and tutor students. Community-based institutions and groups can also provide opportunities for students to participate in community-based learning programs. These learning programs provide an opportunity for students to move beyond the textbook and experience real life. They give students an opportunity to see how knowledge is integrated when it is applied to the real world. It puts students in touch with a variety of people and lets them see how people cope with their environments. Community-based learning also enhances career development. It can help students learn about themselves, gain confidence, and better understand their strengths and weaknesses. Students can learn to plan, make decisions, negotiate, and evaluate their plans. Here are some examples of community work students can do:

- Paint an apartment for an ill neighbor
- Clean alleys and backyards for the elderly
- Write letters for people who are ill
- Read to people who are unable to read
- Prepare an empty lot as a play area for young children
- Plant a vegetable garden for the needy
- Collect and recycle newspapers
- Serve on a community council

Develop Learning Resources for Parents to Use at Home

Parents can use at home many of the learning materials teachers use with students at school to help students improve their skills. The materials should be in a format suitable for students to take home and should provide clear directions for at-home completion. Parents could let the teacher know how they liked the material by writing a note, giving their child a verbal message for the teacher, or by calling the school. Clark (1995) has written a series of math home-involvement activities for kindergarten through eighth grade. The activities are included in booklets and are designed to help students increase their math skills. Teachers can create similar math home-involvement activities that parents can use with their students to reinforce the skills their children learn at school. These kinds of materials are convenient for both parents and teachers to use.

It is important for teachers to have resources available for parents to use. This lets parents know that they can help increase their children's learning and that teachers want their help.

Simply telling parents they should work with their children is not sufficient. Parents need specific suggestions. Once parents get an idea of what you want them to do, some will develop their own materials. Other parents will be able to purchase materials or check them out from the library. You can suggest specific books, games, and other materials for parents to purchase and let them know where these learning materials are available. Some parents, however, will not have the financial resources, time, or educational background to develop or purchase learning materials. With help from your principal or from community groups, you can set up a learning center for parents. The learning center could contain paper, pencils, books, games, a portable typewriter, a portable computer, and other appropriate resources. The learning center could also have audiocassettes on such topics as instructional techniques, classroom rules, educational goals for the year, and readings from books. Parents and students could check materials out of the learning center for use at home.

Broaden the Conception of Parent and Community Involvement

Many barriers to parent/community involvement can be eliminated by broadly conceptualizing it. Parents can play many roles, depending on their interests, skills, and resources. It is important to have a variety of roles for parents so that more of them will have an opportunity to be involved in the school. It is also important to make sure that some roles can be performed at home as well as at school. Following are four ways parents and community members can be involved in schools. Some of the roles can be implemented by the classroom teacher. Others need support and resources from building principals or central office administrators.

Parents Working with Their Own Children

Working with their own children is one of the most important roles parents can play in the educational process. Parents can help their children develop a positive self-concept and a positive attitude toward school as well as a better understanding of how their effort affects achievement. Most parents want their children to do well in school and are willing to do whatever they can to help them succeed. Teachers can increase the support they receive from their students' homes by giving parents a better understanding of what is going on in the classroom, by letting parents know what is expected in the classroom, and by suggesting ways in which they can support their children's learning. Teachers can work with parents to support the educational process in these three ways:

1. Involve parents in monitoring homework by asking them to sign homework papers.
2. Ask parents to sign a certificate congratulating students for good attendance.
3. Give students extra points if their parents do things such as sign their report card, attend conferences, or read to them.

Some parents want a more active partnership with the school. These parents want to help teach their children. The following are three ways you can help parents work with their children to increase their learning:

1. Encourage parents to share hobbies and games, discuss news and television programs, and talk about school problems and events with their children.

2. Send information home on the importance of reading to children and include a reading list. A one-page sheet could be sent home stating, "One of the best ways to help children become better readers is to read to them. Reading aloud is most helpful when you discuss the stories, learn to identify letters and words, and talk about the meaning of the words. Encourage leisure reading. Reading achievement is related to the amount of reading kids do. It increases vocabulary and reading fluency." Then list several books available from the school library for students to check out and take home.

3. Supply parents with materials they can use to work with their children on skill development. Students can help make math games, crossword puzzles, and other materials that parents can use with them at home. Parents should also be encouraged to take their children to the local library where they can get their own library card.

Professional Support Person for Instruction

Many parents and community members have skills that can be shared with the school. They are willing to work with students as well as teachers. These people are often ignored in parent and community-involvement programs. A parent or community member who is a college professor could be asked to talk to teachers about a topic that interests the professor or to participate in an in-service workshop. A bilingual parent or community member could be asked to help tutor foreign-language students or to share books or magazines written in the person's language with the class. Parents who enjoy reading or art could be asked to help staff a humanities enrichment course before or after school or to recommend materials for such a course. Parents and community members who perform these kinds of duties could also serve as role models for your students and demonstrate the importance of education in the community. Review this list and think of how you could involve parents and community members in your classroom. Parents and community members can do the following:

- Serve as instructional assistants
- Use carpentry skills to build things for the school
- Tutor during school hours or after school
- Develop or identify student materials or community resources
- Share their expertise with students or staff
- Expand enrichment programs offered before, after, or during school, such as a program on great books or art appreciation
- Sew costumes for school plays
- Videotape or photograph school plays or activities
- Type and edit a newsletter

General Volunteers

Some parents are willing to volunteer their time, but they do not want to do a job that requires specific skills. When thinking of activities for general volunteers, be sure to include activities that can be performed at school as well as ones that can be performed at home. Some possible activities include these:

- Working on the playground as a support person
- Working in the classroom as a support person
- Working at home preparing cutouts and other materials that will be used in class
- Telephoning other parents to schedule conferences

Decision Makers

Some parents are interested in participating in decision making in the school. They want to help set school policy, select curriculum materials, review budgets, or interview prospective staff members. Roles for these parents and community members include school board, committee, and site council members. Serving on a site council is an excellent way for parents to participate in decision making. Site councils are designed to increase parent involvement in schools, empower classroom teachers, and allow decisions to be made at the school level.

The Comer (1995) model is an effective way to involve parents, classroom teachers, and other educators in decision making. Comer (1997) believes schools can be more effective when they are restructured in ways that encourage and support cooperation among parents and educators. Comer did much of his pioneering work on parent involvement and restructuring schools in Prince George's County, Maryland, where he implemented two committees: the School Planning and Management Team (SPMT) and the Student Staff Services Team (SSST).

The SPMT included the school principal, classroom teachers, parents, and support staff. Consensus was used to reach decisions. The committee also had a no-fault policy, which encouraged parents not to blame the school and educators not to blame parents. The SPMT provided a structure for parents and educators to create a common vision for their school, reduce fragmentation, and develop activities, curriculum, and in-service programs. It also developed a comprehensive school plan, designed a schoolwide calendar of events, and monitored and evaluated student progress. The SPMT met at least once a month. Its subcommittees met more frequently.

The second committee that Comer implemented was the SSST, which included the school principal, guidance counselor, classroom teachers, and support staff, including psychologists, health aides, and other appropriate personnel. Teachers and parents were encouraged to join this group if they had concerns they believed should be addressed. The SSST brought school personnel together to discuss individual student concerns. It also brought coherence and order to the services that students receive.

SUMMARY

Parent and community involvement is a dynamic process that encourages, supports, and provides opportunities for teachers, parents, and community members to work together to improve student learning. Parent and community involvement is also an important component of school reform and multicultural education. Parents and community groups help provide the rationale, motivation, and social action necessary for educational reform.

Everyone can benefit from parent/community involvement. Students tend to perform better in school and have more people supporting their learning. Parents know more about what is going on at school, have more opportunities to communicate with their children's teachers, and are able to help their children increase their learning. Teachers gain a partner in education. Teachers learn more about their students through their parent and community contacts and are able to use that information to help increase their students' performance.

Even though research has consistently demonstrated that students have an advantage in school when their parents support and encourage educational activities, not all parents know how they can support their children's education or feel they have the time, energy, or other resources to be involved in schools. Some parents have a particularly difficult time supporting their children's education. Three such groups are parents who have low incomes, single parents, and parents with special needs. Parents from these groups are often dismissed as unsupportive of education. However, they want their children to do well in school and are willing to work with the school when the school reaches out to them and responds to their needs.

To establish an effective parent/community involvement program, teachers should establish two-way communication with parents and community groups, enlist support from the community, and have resources available for parents to use in working with their children. Expanding how parent/community involvement is conceptualized can increase the number of parents and community members able to participate. Parents can play many roles. Ways to involve parents and community members include having parents work with their own children, parents and community members share their professional skills with the school, parents and community groups volunteer in the school, and parents and community members work with educators to make decisions about school reform.

Questions and Activities

1. Compare the role of parents in schools during the colonial period and now. Identify and discuss changes that have occurred and changes you would like to see occur in parent involvement.
2. Consider this statement: Regardless of the circumstances students experience at home, teachers have a responsibility to help them perform at their highest level at school. Do you agree? Why or why not?

3. Interview a parent of a bilingual, ethnic minority, religious minority, or low-income student to learn more about the parent's views on schools and the educational goals for the child. This information cannot be generalized to all members of these groups, but it can be an important departure point for learning more about diverse groups within our society.

4. Consider this statement: All parents want their children to succeed in school. Do you agree? Why or why not?

5. Interview a classroom teacher and an administrator to determine the views each has on parent/community involvement.

6. Write a brief paper about your personal views on the benefits and drawbacks of parent/community involvement.

7. Form a group with two other members of your class or workshop. One person in the group will be a teacher, the second a parent, and the third an observer. The teacher and the parent will role-play a teacher-parent conference. Afterward, discuss how it felt to be a parent and a teacher. What can be done to make the parent and teacher feel more comfortable? Was the information shared at the conference helpful? The observer can share his or her view of the parent and teacher interaction. Then change roles and repeat the process.

References

Aikens, A. M. (2002). Parental involvement: The key to academic success. *Dissertation Abstracts International, 63*(6), 2105. (UMI No. 3056043)

Amatea, E. S., Smith-Adcock, S., & Villares, E. (2006). From family deficit to family strength: Viewing families' contributions to children's learning from a family resilience perspective. *Professional School Counseling, 9*(3), 177–189.

Anderson, J. J. (2006). Bearing olive branches: A case for school-based and home educator dialogue. *Phi Delta Kappan, 87*(6), 468–472.

Banks, C. A. M. (2005). *Improving multicultural education: Lessons from the intergroup education movement.* New York: Teachers College Press.

Banks, J. A. (2008). *Teaching strategies for ethnic studies* (8th ed.). Boston: Allyn & Bacon.

Berger, E. H. (2008). *Parents as partners in education: Families and schools working together* (7th ed.). Upper Saddle River, NJ: Prentice Hall.

Bishaw, A., & Semega, J. (2008). *American Community Survey reports ACS-09: Income, earnings, and poverty data from the 2007 American Community Survey.* Washington, DC: U.S. Government Printing Office.

Bullivant, B. M. (1993). Culture: Its nature and meaning for educators. In J. A. Banks & C. A. M. Banks (Eds.), *Multicultural education: Issues and perspectives* (2nd ed., pp. 29–47). Boston: Allyn & Bacon.

Caspe, M., Lopez, M. E., & Wolos, C. (2006/2007). Family involvement in elementary school children's education. *Family Involvement Makes a Difference, 2.* Retrieved January 24, 2009, from http://www.hfrp.org/content/download/1182/48686/file/elementary.pdf

Center for Mental Health in Schools at UCLA. (2007, August). *Parent and home involvement in schools.* Los Angeles, CA: Author.

Chavkin, N. F., & Gonzalez, D. L. (1995). *Forging partnerships between Mexican American parents and the schools.* Charleston, WV: Clearinghouse on Rural Education and Small Schools. (ERIC Document Reproduction Service No. ED388489)

Clark, C. S. (1995). Parents and schools: Will more parental involvement help students? *CQ Researcher, 5*(3), 51–69.

Comer, J. P. (1995). *School power: Implications of an intervention project.* New York: Free Press.

Comer, J. P. (1997). *Waiting for a miracle: Why schools can't solve our problems—and how we can.* New York: Dutton.

Darling-Hammond, L. (2004). What happens to a dream deferred? The continuing quest for equal educational opportunity. In J. A. Banks & C. A. M. Banks (Eds.), *Handbook of research on multicultural education* (2nd ed., pp. 607–630). San Francisco: Jossey-Bass.

Darwin, C. (1859). *On the origin of species by means of natural selection, or the preservation of favored races in the struggle for life.* London: John Murray.

De Carvalho, M. E. P. (2001). *Rethinking family–school relations: A critique of parental involvement in schooling.* Mahwah, NJ: Lawrence Erlbaum.

Decker, J., & Majerczyk, D. (2000). *Increasing parent involvement through effective home/school communication.* Chicago: Saint Xavier University. (ERIC Document Reproduction Service No. ED 439790)

Dembski, W. A. (1999). *Intelligent design: The bridge between science & theology.* Downers Grove, IL: InterVarsity Press.

DeSteno, N. (2000). Parent involvement in the classroom: The fine line. *Young Children, 55*(3), 13–17.

Dodson, H., & Diouf, S.A. (2005). *In motion: The African-American migration experience.* New York: National Geographic.

Epstein. J. L., Sanders, M. G., Simon, B. S., Salinas, K. C., Jansorn, N. R., & Van Voorhis, F. L. (2008). *School, family, and community partnerships: Your handbook for action* (3rd ed.). Thousand Oaks, CA: Corwin Press.

Goodlad, J. I. (1984). *A place called school: Prospects for the future.* New York: McGraw-Hill.

Harry, B. (1992). Restructuring the participation of African-American parents in special education. *Exceptional Children, 59*(2), 123–131.

Henderson, A.T., Mapp, K.L., Johnson, V. R., & Davies, D. (2006). *Beyond the bake sale: The essential guide to family-school partnerships.* New York: New Press.

Henderson, A. T., & Berla, N. (Eds.). (2002). *A new wave of evidence: The impact of school, family, and community connections on student achievement.* Austin, TX: National Center for Family & Community Connections with Schools.

Hidalgo, N. M., Sau-Fong, S., & Epstein, J. L. (2004). Research on families, schools, and communities: A multicultural perspective. In J. A. Banks & C. A. M. Banks (Eds.), *Handbook of research on multicultural education* (2nd ed., pp. 631–655). San Francisco: Jossey-Bass.

Jennings, L. (1990). Parents as partners: Reaching out to families to help students learn. *Education Week, 9*(40), 23–32.

Kagan, S. L. (1995, December). *Meeting family and community needs: The three C's of early childhood education*. Paper presented at the Australia and New Zealand Conference on the First Years of School, Tasmania, Australia.

Kirschenbaum, H. (2001). Educating professionals for school, family, and community partnerships. In D. B. Hiatt-Michael (Ed.), *Promising practices for family involvement in schools* (pp. 185–189). Greenwich, CT: Information Age.

Lee, S. M., & Edmonston, B. (2005). New marriages, new families: U.S. racial and Hispanic intermarriage. *Population Bulletin*, 60(2). Washington, DC: Population Reference Bureau.

Lightfoot, S. L. (1978). *Worlds apart: Relationships between families and schools*. New York: Basic Books.

Linn, E. (1990). Parent involvement programs: A review of selected models. *Equity Coalition, 1*(2), 10–15.

McCallion, P., Janicki, M. P., & Kolomer, S. R. (2004). Controlled evaluation of support groups for grandparent caregivers of children with developmental disabilities and delays. *American Journal on Mental Retardation, 109*(5), 352–361.

McFalls, J. A., Jr. (2007). Population: A lively introduction (5th ed.). *Population Reference Bulletin, 62*(1), 1–33.

Ouimette, M. Y., Feldman, J., & Tung, R. (2006). Collaborating for high school student success: A case study of parent engagement at Boston Arts Academy. *School Community Journal, 16*(2), 91–114.

Pena, D. C. (2000). Parent involvement: Influencing factors and implications. *Journal of Educational Research, 94*(1), 42–54.

Rasinski, T. V. (1989). Reading and the empowerment of parents. *Reading Teacher, 43*(3), 226–231.

Schneider, B. L., & Coleman, J. S. (Eds.). (1993). *Parents, their children, and schools*. Boulder, CO: Westview.

Shariff, J. W. (1988). Free enterprise and the ghetto family. In J. S. Wurzel (Ed.), *Toward multiculturalism: A reader in multicultural education* (pp. 30–54). Yarmouth, ME: Intercultural Press.

Swadener, B. B., & Niles, K. (1991). Children and families "at promise": Making home–school–community connections. *Democracy and Education, 5*(3), 13–18.

U.S. Bureau of Labor Statistics. (2008). *Economics news release: Employment characteristics of families summary*. Retrieved December 10, 2008, from http://www.bls.gov/news.release/famee.nr0.htm

U.S. Census Bureau, (2005). *Current population survey, annual social and economic supplement, 1970, 1980, 1990, 2000, 2005*. Washington, DC: U.S. Government Printing Office. Retrieved January 34, 2009, from www.census.gov/apsd/techdoc/cps/cpsmar05.pdf

U.S. Census Bureau. (2007). *Current population survey: March and annual social and economic supplements, 2007 and earlier*. Washington, DC: U.S. Government Printing Office. Retrieved January 25, 2009, from www.census.gov/population/socdemo/hh-fam/ms2.csv

Walker, V. S. (1996). *Their highest potential: An African American school community in the segregated South*. Chapel Hill: University of North Carolina Press.

Waller, W. (1965). *The sociology of teaching*. New York: John Wiley. (Original work published 1932)

Internet Resources for Information on Parent Involvement

Center on School, Family, and Community Partnerships: http://www.csos.jhu.edu/P2000/center.htm

National Coalition for Parent Involvement in Education: http://www.ncpie.org/

National Parent Information Network: http://www.npin.org/

Parents as Teachers National Center: http://www.parentsasteachers.org/

Partnership for Family Involvement in Education: http://www.ed.gov/pubs/whoweare/index.html

APPENDIX

Multicultural Resources

Issues and Concepts

Banks, C. A. M. (2005). *Improving multicultural education: Lessons from the intergroup education movement*. New York: Teachers College Press.

Banks, J. A. (2007). *Educating citizens in a multicultural society* (2nd ed.). New York: Teachers College Press.

Banks, J. A. (2006). *Cultural diversity and education: Foundations, curriculum, and teaching* (5th ed.). Boston: Allyn and Bacon.

Banks, J. A. (2006). *Race, culture, and education: The selected works of James A. Banks*. London and New York: Routledge.

Banks, J. A. (2009). *Teaching strategies for ethnic studies* (8th ed.). Boston: Allyn and Bacon.

Banks, J. A. (Ed.). (2009). *The Routledge international companion to multicultural education*. New York and London: Routledge.

Banks, J. A., Au, K., Ball, A. F., et al. (2007). *Learning in and out of school in diverse environments: Life-long, life-wide, life-deep*. Seattle: LIFE Center and the Center for Multicultural Education, University of Washington.

Banks, J. A., & Banks, C. A. M. (Eds.). (2004). *Handbook of research on multicultural education* (2nd ed.). San Francisco: Jossey-Bass.

Cornbleth, C. (2008). *Diversity and the new teacher: Learning from experience in urban schools*. New York: Teachers College Press.

Derman-Sparks, L., Ramsey, P. G., & Edwards, J. O. (2006). *What if all the kids are White? Anti-bias multicultural education with young children and families*. New York: Teachers College Press.

Green, R. L. (Ed.) (2009). *Expectations in education: Readings on high expectations, effective teaching, and student achievement*. Columbus, OH: SRA/McGraw-Hill.

Howard, G. (2006). *We can't teach what we don't know: White teachers, multiracial schools* (2nd ed.). New York: Teachers College Press.

Johnson, L., & Joshee, R. (Eds.). (2007). *Multicultural education policies in Canada and the United States*. Vancouver, BC: University of British Columbia Press.

Pollock, M. (Ed.). (2008). *Everyday racism: Getting real about race in school*. New York: New Press.

Schniedewind, N., & Davidson, E. (2006). *Open minds to equality: A sourcebook of learning activities to affirm diversity and promote equality* (3rd ed.). Milwaukee, WI: Rethinking Schools.

Sleeter, C. E. (Ed.). (2007). *Facing accountability in education: Democracy and equity at risk*. New York: Teachers College Press.

Wagner, U., Tropp, R., Finchilescu, G. & Tredoux, C. (Eds.). (2008). *Improving intergroup relations: Building on the legacy of Thomas F. Pettigrew*. Malden, MA: Blackwell.

Social Class

Howard, A. (2008). *Learning privilege: Lessons of power and identity in affluent schooling*. New York: Routledge.

Kincheloe, J. L., & Steinberg, S. R. (2007). *Cutting class: Socioeconomic status and education*. Lanham, MD: Rowman & Littlefield.

Lareau, A. (2008). *Social class: How does it work?* New York: Russell Sage Foundation.

Ornstein, A. C. (2007). *Class counts: Education, inequality, and the shrinking middle class*. Lanham, MD: Rowman & Littlefield.

Preston, J. (2007). *Whiteness and class in education*. Dordrecht, Netherlands: Springer.

Sacks, P. (2007). *Tearing down the gates: Confronting the class divide in American education*. Berkeley: University of California Press.

Scott, A., & Freeman-Moir, J. (2007). *The lost dream of equality: Critical essays on education and social class*. Rotterdam, Netherlands: Sense.

Stevens, M. L. (2007). *Creating a class: College admissions and the education of elites*. Cambridge, MA: Harvard University Press.

Religion

Alba, R., Raboteau, A., & DeWind, J. (Eds.). (2008). *Immigration and religion in America: Comparative and historical perspectives*. New York: New York University Press.

Barnes, I. (2007). *World religions*. London: Cartographica Press.

Hefner, R. W., & Qasim, M. (2007). *Schooling Islam: The culture and politics of modern Muslim education*. Princeton, NJ: Princeton University Press.

Hollinger, D. A. (2006). *Cosmopolitanism and solidarity: Studies in ethnoracial, religious, and professional affiliation in the United States*. Madison: University of Wisconsin Press.

Kunzan, R. (2006). *Grappling with the good: Talking about religion and morality in public schools*. Albany: State University of New York Press.

Merry, M. S. (2007). *Culture, identity, and Islamic schooling: A philosophical approach*. New York: Pelgrave Macmillan.

Prothero, S. R. (2007). *Religious literacy: What every American needs to know—and doesn't*. San Francisco: HarperSanFrancisco.

Salili, F., & Hoosain, R. (2006). *Religion in multicultural education*. Greenwich, CT: Information Age.

Stern, J. (2007). *Schools and religions: Imagining the real*. New York: Continuum.

Thomas, R. M. (2008). *God in the classroom: Religion and America's public schools*. Lanham, MD: Rowman & Littlefield.

Trent, M. A. (2007). *Religion, culture, curriculum, and diversity in 21st century America*. Lanham, MD: University Press of America.

Gender

Allan, E. J. (2008). *Policy discourses, gender, and education: Constructing women's status*. New York: Routledge.

Cole, M. (2006). *Education, equality and human rights: Issues of gender, 'race', sexuality, disability and social class*. London and New York: Routledge.

Davison, K. G. (2007). *Negotiating masculinities and bodies in schools: The implications of gender theory for the education of boys*. New York: Edwin Mellen Press.

Dillabough, J., & McLeod, J. (2008). *Troubling gender in education*. London: Routledge.

Forde, C. (2007). *Feminist utopianism and education: Educating for the good society*. Rotterdam, Netherlands: Sense.

Fuller, C. (2009). *Sociology, gender and educational aspirations: Girls and their ambitions*. New York: Continuum.

Gurian, M., & Stevens, K. (2007). *The minds of boys: Saving our sons from falling behind in school and life*. Hoboken, NJ: Wiley.

James, A. N. (2007). *Teaching the male brain: How boys think, feel, and learn in school*. Thousand Oaks, CA: Corwin Press.

Jones, L., & Barron, I. (2007). *Research and gender*. London and New York: Continuum.

Klein, S. S. (Ed.). (2007). *Handbook for achieving gender equity through education*. Mahwah, NJ: Lawrence Erlbaum.

Mirza, H. S. (2009). *Race, gender and educational desire: Why Black women succeed and fail*. London and New York: Routledge.

Moss, G. (2007). *Literacy and gender: Researching texts, contexts and readers*. London and New York: Routledge.

Noguera, P. A. (2008). *The trouble with Black boys: And other reflections on race, equity, and the future of public education*. San Francisco: Jossey-Bass.

Nouraie-Simone, F. (Ed.) (2005). *On shifting ground: Muslim women in the global era*. New York: Feminist Press.

Pinker, S. (2008). *The sexual paradox: Men, women and the real gender gap*. New York: Scribner.

Rasmussen, M. L. (2006). *Becoming subjects: Sexualities and secondary schooling*. New York: Routledge.

Sadker, D. M., & Silber, E. S. (2007). *Gender in the classroom: Foundations, skills, methods, and strategies across the curriculum*. Mahwah, NJ: Lawrence Erlbaum.

Skelton, C., Francis, B., & Smulyan, L. (Eds.). (2006). *The Sage handbook of gender and education*. Thousand Oaks, CA: Sage.

Unterhalter, E. (2007). *Gender, schooling and global social justice*. London & New York: Routledge.

Sexual and Gender Minorities

Casper, V., & Schultz, S. B. (1999). *Gay parents, straight schools: Building communication and trust*. New York: Teachers College Press.

Driver, S. (Ed.). (2008). *Queer youth cultures*. Albany: State University of New York Press.

Gray, M. L. (1999). *In your face: Stories from the lives of queer youth*. New York: Harrington Park Press.

Kumashiro, K. (2002). *Troubling education: Queer activism and antioppressive education*. New York: Routledge.

MacGillivray, I. K. (2004). *Sexual orientation and school policy: A practical guide for teachers, administrators, and community activists*. Lanham, MD: Rowan & Littlefield.

Mayo, C. (2007). *Disputing the subject of sex: Sexuality and public school controversies*. Lanham, MD: Rowman and Littlefield.

Pasco, C. J. (2007). *Dude, you're a fag: Masculinity and sexuality in high school*. Berkeley: University of California Press.

Rodriguez, N. M., & Pinar, W. F. (Eds.). (2007). *Queering straight teachers: Discourse and identity in education*. New York: Peter Lang.

Race, Ethnicity, and Language

Alim, H. S., & Baugh, J. (2007). *Talkin Black talk: Language, education, and social change*. New York: Teachers College Press.

Brisk, M. (2006). *Bilingual education: From compensatory to quality schooling*. Mahwah, NJ: Lawrence Erlbaum.

Clewell, B. C., Campbell, P. B., & Perlman, L. (2007). *Good schools in poor neighborhoods: Defying demographics, achieving success*. Washington, DC: Urban Institute Press.

Collins, P. H. (2009). *Another kind of public education: Race, schools, the media, and democratic possibilities*. Boston: Beacon Press.

Conchas, G. Q. (2006). *The color of success: Race and high-achieving urban youth*. New York: Teachers College Press.

Everett, A. (Ed.). (2008). *Learning race and ethnicity: Young and digital media*. London: MIT Press.

Gandara, P., & Contreras, F. (2009). *The Latino education crisis: The consequences of failed social policies*. Cambridge, MA: Harvard University Press.

Genishi, C., & Goodwin, A. L. (Eds.). (2008). *Diversities in early childhood education: Rethinking and doing*. New York and London: Routledge.

Gillborn, D. (2008). *Racism and education: Coincidence or conspiracy?* London and New York: Routledge.

Kubota, R. (2009). *Race, culture, and identities in second language education: Exploring critically engaged practice*. New York: Routledge.

Ladson-Billing, G. (2009). *The dreamkeepers: Successful teachers of African American children* (2nd ed.). San Francisco: Jossey-Bass.

Landsman, J., & Lewis, C. W. (2006). *White teachers, diverse classrooms: A guide to building inclusive schools, promoting high expectations, and eliminating racism*. Sterling, VA: Stylus.

Lee, C. D. (2006). *Culture, literacy and learning: Taking bloom in the midst of the whirlwind*. New York: Teachers College Press.

Leonardo, Z. (2009). *Race, Whiteness, and education*. New York: Routledge.

Marx. S. (2006). *Revealing the invisible: Confronting passive racism in teacher education*. New York: Routledge.

Nasir, N. S., & Cobb, P. (Eds.). (2007). *Improving access to mathematics: Diversity and equity in the classroom*. New York: Teachers College Press.

Noguera, P. A., & Wing, J. Y. (Eds.). (2008). *Unfinished business: Closing the racial achievement gap on our schools*. San Francisco: Jossey-Bass.

Ovando, C. J., Combs, M. C., & Collier, V. P. (2006). *Bilingual and ESL classrooms: Teaching in multicultural contexts* (4th ed.). Boston: McGraw-Hill.

Payne, C. M., & Strickland, C. S. (2008). *Teach freedom: Education for liberation in the African-American tradition*. New York: Teachers College Press.

Pollock, M. (2008). *Because of race: How Americans debate harm and opportunity in our schools*. Princeton, NJ: Princeton University Press.

Ross, E. W., & Pang, V. O. Eds. (2006). *Race, ethnicity and education 4 Vols*. Wesport, CT: Praeger.

Suárez-Orozco, C, Suárez-Orozco, M. M., & Todorova, I. (2008). *Learning a new land: Immigrant students in American society*. Cambridge, MA: Harvard University Press.

Tatum, B. D. (2007). *Can we talk about race? And other conversations in an era of school resegregation*. Boston: Beacon Press.

Teel, K. M., & Obidah, J. E. (2008). *Building racial and cultural competence in the classroom: Strategies from urban educators*. New York: Teachers College Press.

Williams, H. A. (2007). *Self-taught: African American education in slavery and freedom*. Chapel Hill: University of North Carolina Press.

Exceptionality

Florian, L. (Ed.). (2007). *The Sage handbook of special education*. Thousand Oaks, CA: Sage.

Gallagher, J. J. (2006). *Driving change in special education*. Baltimore: Brookes.

Harry, B., & Klingner, J. K. (2006). *Why are so many minority students in special education? Understanding race and disability in schools*. New York: Teachers College Press.

Harry, B., Klingner, J. K., Cramer, E. P., & Sturges, K. M. (2007). *Case studies of minority student placement in special education*. New York: Teachers College Press.

Jimenez, T. C., & Graf, V. L. (2008). *Education for all: Critical issues in the education of children and youth with disabilities*. San Francisco: Jossey-Bass.

Osgood, R. L. (2008). *The history of special education: A struggle for equality in American public schools*. Westport, CT: Praeger.

Sapon-Shevin, M. (2007). *Widening the circle: The power of inclusive classrooms*. Boston: Beacon Press.

Wallace, B., & Eriksson, G. I. (2006). *Diversity in gifted education: International perspectives on global issues*. New York: Routledge.

Turnbull, A. (2007). *Exceptional lives: Special education in today's schools*. Upper Saddle River, NJ: Prentice Hall.

Ysseldyke, J. E., & Algozzine, R. (2006). *Effective assessment for students with special needs: A practical guide for every teacher*. Thousand Oaks, CA: Corwin Press.

School Reform

Au, K. (2006). *Multicultural issues and literacy achievement*. Mahwah, NJ: Earlbaum.

Aladjem, D. K., & Borman, K. M. (2006). *Examining comprehensive school reform*. Washington, DC: Urban Institute Press.

Clarke, S. E. (2006). *Multiethnic moments: The politics of urban education reform*. Philadelphia: Temple University Press.

Cohen, J. E., Bloom, D. E., & Malin, M. B. (2006). *Educating all children: A global agenda*. Cambridge, MA: American Academy of Arts and Sciences and MIT Press.

Conchas, G. Q., & Rodríguez, L. F. (2008). *Small schools and urban youth: Using the power of school culture to engage students*. Thousand Oaks, CA: Corwin Press.

Cuban, L. (2008). *Frogs into princes: Writings on school reform*. New York: Teachers College Press.

Irons, E. J., & Harris, S. (2007). *The challenges of No Child Left Behind: Understanding the issues of excellence, accountability, and choice*. Lanham, MD: Rowman & Littlefield.

Kaestle, C. F., & Lodewick, A. E. (2007). *To educate a nation: Federal and national strategies of school reform*. Lawrence: University Press of Kansas.

Lortie, D. C. (2009). *School principal: Managing in public*. Chicago: University of Chicago Press.

Nitta, K. (2008). *The politics of structural education reform*. New York: Routledge.

Segall, W. E. (2006). *School reform in a global society*. Lanham, MD: Rowman & Littlefield.

Sizemore, B. A. (2008). *Walking in circles: The Black struggle for school reform*. Chicago: Third World Press.

Thompson, G. L. (2007). *Up where we belong: Helping African Americans and Latino students rise in school and in life*. San Francisco: Jossey-Bass.

Vernez, G., Karam, R., & Mariano, L. (2006). *Evaluating comprehensive school reform models at scale: Focus on implementation*. Santa Monica, CA: Rand Corporation.

Glossary

African Americans U.S. residents and citizens who have an African biological and cultural heritage and identity. This term is used synonymously and interchangeably with Blacks and Black Americans to describe both a racial and a cultural group. African Americans are projected to increase from 41.1 million, or 14 percent of the population, in 2008 to 65.7 million, or 15 percent in 2050 (U.S. Census Bureau, 2008). An excellent one-volume encyclopedia on African Americans is *Africana: The Encyclopedia of the African and African American Experience* (Appiah & Gates, 1999).

Afrocentric curriculum A curriculum approach in which concepts, issues, problems, and phenomena are viewed from the perspectives of Africans and African Americans. This curriculum is based on the assumption that students learn best when they view situations and events from their own cultural perspectives (Asante, 1998).

American Indians See *Native Americans and Alaska Natives*.

Anglo Americans Americans whose biological and cultural heritage originated in England or Americans with other biological and cultural heritages who have assimilated into the dominant or mainstream culture in the United States. This term is often used to describe the mainstream U.S. culture or to describe most White Americans. The non-Hispanic, single-race White population is projected to be only slightly larger in 2050 (203.3 million) than in 2008 (199.8 million). In fact, this group is projected to lose population in the 2030s and 2040s and comprise 50 percent of the total population in 2042, down from 66 percent in 2008 (U.S. Census Bureau, 2008).

Antiracist education A term used in the United Kingdom and Canada to describe a process used by teachers and other educators to eliminate institutionalized racism from the schools and society and to help individuals to develop nonracist attitudes. When antiracist educational reform is implemented, curriculum materials, grouping practices, hiring policies, teacher attitudes and expectations, and school policy and practices are examined and steps are taken to eliminate racism from these school variables. A related educational reform movement in the United States that focuses more on individuals than on institutions is known as *prejudice reduction* (Stephan & Vogt, 2004).

Asian Americans Americans who have a biological and cultural heritage that originated on the continent of Asia. The largest groups of Asian Americans in the United States in 2007 were (in descending order) Chinese, Filipinos, Asian Indians, Vietnamese, Koreans, and Japanese. Other groups included Laotians, Thai, Hmong, Taiwanese, Cambodians, Pakistanis, and Indonesians. The Asian American population is projected to increase from 15.5 million in 2008 to 40.6 million by 2050. Its share of the nation's population is expected to increase from 5.1 percent to 9.2 percent (U.S. Census Bureau, 2008).

Cultural assimilation A phenomenon that takes place when one ethnic or cultural group acquires the behavior, values, perspectives, ethos, and characteristics of

444

another ethnic group and sheds its own cultural characteristics. (For a further discussion of assimilation of ethnic groups in the United States since the 1960s, see Alba & Nee, 2003).

Culture The ideations, symbols, behaviors, values, and beliefs that are shared by a human group. Culture can also be defined as a group's program for survival and adaptation to its environment. Pluralistic nation-states such as the United States, Canada, and Australia are made up of an overarching culture, called a *macroculture*, which all individuals and groups within the nation share. These nation-states also have many smaller cultures, called *microcultures*, that differ in many ways from the macroculture or that contain cultural components manifested differently than in the macroculture. (See Chapters 1 and 2 for further discussions of culture.)

Disability The physical or mental characteristics of an individual that prevent or limit that person from performing specific tasks.

Discrimination The differential treatment of individuals or groups based on categories such as race, ethnicity, gender, sexual orientation, social class, or exceptionality.

Ethnic group A microcultural group or collectivity that shares a common history and culture, values, behaviors, and other characteristics that cause members of the group to have a shared identity. A sense of peoplehood is one of the most important characteristics of an ethnic group, which also shares economic and political interests. Cultural characteristics rather than biological traits are the essential attributes of an ethnic group. An ethnic group is not the same as a racial group. Some ethnic groups, such as Puerto Ricans in the United States, are made up of individuals who belong to several different racial groups. White Anglo-Saxon Protestants, Italian Americans, and Irish Americans are examples of ethnic groups. Individual members of an ethnic group vary considerably in the extent to which they identify with the group. Some individuals have a very strong identification with their particular ethnic group whereas other members of the group have a very weak identification with it.

Ethnic minority group An ethnic group with several distinguishing characteristics. An ethnic minority group has distinguishing cultural characteristics, racial characteristics, or both, which enable members of other groups to identify its members easily. Some ethnic minority groups, such as Jewish Americans, have unique cultural characteristics. African Americans have unique cultural and physical characteristics. The unique attributes of ethnic minority groups make them convenient targets of racism and discrimination. Ethnic minority groups are usually a numerical minority within their societies. However, the Blacks in South Africa, who are a numerical majority in their nation-state, were often considered a sociological minority group by social scientists because they had little political power until the constitution of the Republic of South Africa was established in 1996 (Moodley & Adam, 2004).

Ethnic studies The scientific and humanistic analysis of behavior influenced by variables related to ethnicity and ethnic group membership. This term is often used to refer to special school, university, and college courses and programs that focus on specific racial and ethnic groups. However, any aspects of a course or program that includes a study of variables related to ethnicity can accurately be referred to as ethnic studies. In other words, ethnic studies can be integrated within the boundaries of mainstream courses and curricula.

Eurocentric curriculum A curriculum in which concepts, events, and situations are viewed primarily from the perspectives of European nations and cultures and in which Western civilization is emphasized. This approach is based on the assumption that Europeans have made the most important contributions to the development of the United States and the world. Curriculum theorists who endorse this approach are referred to as *Eurocentrists* or *Western traditionalists*.

European Americans *See Anglo Americans*.

Exceptional Term used to describe students who have learning or behavioral characteristics that differ substantially from those of most other students and that require special attention in instruction. Students who are intellectually gifted or talented as well as those who have disabilities are considered exceptional.

Gender A category consisting of behaviors that result from the social, cultural, and psychological factors associated with masculinity and femininity within a society. Appropriate male and female roles result from the socialization of the individual within a group.

Gender identity An individual's view of the gender to which the person belongs and his or her shared sense of group attachment to other males or females.

Global education A curriculum reform movement concerned with issues and problems related to the survival of human beings in the world community. International studies is a part of global education, but the focus of global education is the interdependence of human beings and their common fate regardless of the national boundaries within which they live. Many teachers confuse global education and international studies with ethnic studies, which deal with ethnic groups within a particular national boundary, such as the United States, Canada, or Australia.

Handicapism The unequal treatment of people who are disabled and the related attitudes and beliefs that reinforce and justify discrimination against people with disabilities. The term *handicapped* is considered negative by some people who prefer the term *disabled*. "People with disabilities" is considered a more sensitive phrase than "disabled people" because the word *people* is used first and given emphasis.

Hispanic Americans Americans who share a culture, heritage, and language that originated in Spain. Most of the Hispanics living in the United States have cultural origins in Latin America. Many Hispanics in the United States prefer to use the word *Latino* rather than *Hispanic*, as do the editors of this book. However, the U.S. Census uses the term *Hispanic*. Most Hispanics in the United States speak Spanish and are *mestizos*, persons of mixed biological heritage. Most Hispanics in the United States have an Indian as well as a Spanish heritage, and many also have an African biological and cultural heritage.

Hispanics are the fastest-growing ethnic group of color in the United States. The Hispanic population is projected to nearly triple, from 46.7 million in 2008 to 132.8 in 2050. The Hispanic percentage of the nation's total population is projected by the U. S. Census to double, from 15 to 30 percent. Thus, nearly one in three U.S. residents would be Hispanic (U.S. Census Bureau, 2008). The largest groups of Hispanics in the United States are Mexican Americans (Chicanos), Puerto Ricans, and Cubans. In 2007, there were 29.2 million Mexican Americans, 4.1 million Puerto Ricans in the mainland United States, 1.6 million Cubans, and 10.5 million Hispanics from other nations, notably Central and South America (U.S. Census Bureau, 2007).

It is misleading to view Hispanics as one ethnic group. Some Hispanics believe that the word *Hispanics* can help to unify the various Latino groups and thus increase their political power. The primary identity of most Hispanics in the United States, however, is with their particular group, such as Mexican American, Puerto Rican American, or Cuban American.

Mainstream American A U.S. citizen who shares most of the characteristics of the dominant ethnic and cultural group in the nation. Such an individual is usually White Anglo-Saxon Protestant and belongs to the middle class or a higher social-class status.

Mainstream-centric curriculum A curriculum that presents events, concepts, issues, and problems primarily or exclusively from the points of view and perspectives of the mainstream society and the dominant ethnic and cultural group in the United States: White Anglo-Saxon Protestants. The mainstream-centric curriculum is also usually presented from the perspectives of Anglo males.

Mainstreaming The process that involves placing students with disabilities into the regular classroom for instruction. They might be integrated into the regular classroom for part or all of the school day. This practice was initiated in response to Public Law 94–142 (passed by Congress in 1975), which requires that students with disabilities be educated in the least restricted environment.

Multicultural education A reform movement designed to change the total educational environment so that students from diverse racial and ethnic groups, students of both genders, exceptional students, and students from each social-class group will experience equal educational opportunities in schools, colleges, and universities. A major assumption of multicultural education is that some students—because of their particular racial, ethnic, gender, and cultural characteristics—have a better chance of succeeding in educational institutions as they are currently structured than do students who belong to other groups or who have different cultural and gender characteristics. See Chapter 1 in the *Handbook for Research on Multicultural Education* (Banks & Banks, 2004) for further discussion of multicultural education.

Multiculturalism A philosophical position and movement that assumes that the gender, ethnic, racial, and cultural diversity of a pluralistic society should be reflected in all of the institutionalized structures of educational institutions, including the staff, the norms and values, the curriculum, and the student body.

Native Americans and Alaska Natives U.S. citizens who trace their biological and cultural heritage to the original inhabitants in the land that now makes up the United States. The term *Native American* is sometimes used synonymously with American Indian. In 2007, seven of the ten largest tribes—the Cherokee, Navajo, Choctaw, Sioux, Chippewa, Apache, and Blackfoot—each had a population of more than 100,000 persons. The two largest American Indian tribes were the Cherokee (961,855) and the Navajo (337,262). Eskimos (50,396) constituted the largest group of Alaska Natives (U.S. Census Bureau, 2007). Native Americans and Alaska Natives are projected to increase from 4.9 million in 2008 to 8.6 million by 2050 (from 1.6 to 2.0 percent) of the total population (U.S. Census Bureau, 2008).

Native Hawaiians and Other Pacific Islanders U.S. citizens who self-identify as having Native Hawaiian and/or Pacific Islander descent. This group comprises Polynesians (257,770, including Native Hawaiians, Samoans, and Tongans), Micronesians (123,214, including Guamanians or Chamorros), Melanesians (23,334, including Fijians), and other Pacific Islanders (27,357). This population is projected to more than double, from 1.1 million in 2008 to 2.6 million by 2050 (U.S. Census Bureau, 2008).

People of color Groups in the United States and other nations who have experienced discrimination historically because of their unique biological characteristics that enabled potential discriminators to identify them easily. African Americans, Asian Americans, and Hispanics in the United States are among the groups referred to as *people of color*. Most members of these groups still experience forms of discrimination today.

The U.S. Census (2007) projects that ethnic minorities will increase from one-third of the nation's population in 2006 to 50 percent in 2042 (cited in Roberts, 2008). Ethnic minorities made up 100 million of the total U.S. population of just over 300 million in 2006. By 2023, more than half of all children are projected to be children of color (U.S. Census Bureau, 2008).

Positionality An idea that emerged out of feminist scholarship stating that variables such as an individual's gender, class, and race are markers of that individual's relational position within a social and economic context and influence the knowledge that the person produces. Consequently, valid knowledge requires an acknowledgment of the knower's position within a specific context (See Chapter 7).

Prejudice A set of rigid and unfavorable attitudes toward a particular individual or group that is formed without consideration of facts. Prejudice is a set of attitudes that often leads to *discrimination*, the differential treatment of particular individuals and groups.

Race A term that refers to the attempt by physical anthropologists to divide human groups according to their physical traits and characteristics. This has proven to be very difficult because human groups in modern societies are highly mixed physically. Consequently, different and often conflicting race typologies exist. An excellent book on the social construction of race that gives a historical perspective on it is *Whiteness of a Different Color: European Immigrants and the Alchemy of Race* (Jacobson, 1999).

Racism A belief that human groups can be validly grouped according to their biological traits and that these identifiable groups inherit certain mental, personality, and cultural characteristics that determine their behavior. Racism, however, is not merely a set of beliefs but is practiced when a group has the power to enforce laws, institutions, and norms based on its beliefs, which oppress and dehumanize another group. Two informative references on racism are *Racism: A Short History* (Fredrickson, 2002) and *Two-Faced Racism: Whites in the Backstage and Frontstage* (Picca & Feagin, 2007).

Religion A set of beliefs and values, especially about explanations that concern the cause and nature of the universe, to which an individual or group has a strong loyalty and attachment. A religion usually has a moral code, rituals, and institutions that reinforce and propagate its beliefs.

Sex The biological factors that distinguish males and females, such as chromosomal, hormonal, anatomical, and physiological characteristics.

Sexism Social, political, and economic structures that advantage one sex group over the other. Stereotypes and misconceptions about the biological characteristics of each sex group reinforce and support sex discrimination. In most societies, women have been the major victims of sexism. However, males are also victimized by sexist beliefs and practices.

Social class A collectivity of people who have a similar socioeconomic status based on such criteria as income, occupation, education, values, behaviors, and life chances. Lower class, working class, middle class, and upper class are common designations of social class in the United States.

References

Alba, R. D., & Nee, V. (2003). *Remaking the American mainstream: Assimilation and contemporary immigration*. Cambridge, MA: Harvard University Press.

Appiah, K. A., & Gates, H. L., Jr. (Eds.). (1999). *Africana: The encyclopedia of the African and African American experience*. New York: Perseus.

Asante, M. K. (1998). *The Afrocentric idea* (rev. ed.). Philadelphia: Temple University Press.

Banks, J. A., & Banks, C. A. M. (Eds.). (2004). *Handbook of research on multicultural education* (2nd ed.). San Francisco: Jossey-Bass.

Fredrickson, G. M. (2002). *Racism: A short history*. Princeton, NJ: Princeton University Press.

Jacobson, M. F. (1999). *Whiteness of a different color: European immigrants and the alchemy of race*. Cambridge, MA: Harvard University Press.

Moodley, K. A., & Adam, H. (2004). Citizenship education and political literacy in South Africa. In J. A. Banks (Ed.), *Diversity and citizenship education: Global perspectives* (pp. 159–183). San Francisco: Jossey-Bass.

Picca, L. H., & Feagin, J. (2007). *Two-faced racism: Whites in the backstage and frontstage*. New York: Routledge.

Roberts, S. (2008, August 14). A generation away, minorities may become the majority in U.S. *New York Times*, A1, A18.

Stephan, W., & Vogt, W. P. (Eds.). (2004). *Education programs for improving intergroup relations: Theory, research, and practice*. New York: Teachers College Press.

U.S. Census Bureau. (2007). *2007 American Community Survey*. Retrieved October 20, 2008, from http://factfinder.census.gov/servlet/IPGeoSearch ByListServlet?ds_name = ACS_2007_1YR_G00_& _lang = en&_ts = 242586192888

U.S. Census Bureau. (2008). *An older and more diverse nation by midcentury*. Retrieved October 20, 2008, from http://www.census.gov/Press-Release/www/ releases/archives/population/012496.html

Contributors

Cherry A. McGee Banks is professor of education at the University of Washington, Bothell. Her publications include *Improving Multicultural Education: Lessons from the Intergroup Education Movement*. Professor Banks has served on several national committees and boards and is currently chair of the AERA Books Editorial Board.

James A. Banks is the Kerry and Linda Killinger Professor of Diversity Studies and founding director of the Center for Multicultural Education at the University of Washington, Seattle. His research focuses on multicultural education and diversity and citizenship education in a global context.

Jill Bevan-Brown is an associate professor of inclusive education at Massey University College of Education, New Zealand. Of Maori heritage, she has a particular interest in the special education needs of Maori children and has concentrated her writing and research on their education.

Sara Bicard is assistant professor of special education at the University of Memphis and director of the Restructuring for Inclusive School Environments Project. Her research interests include reading instruction and materials for students with reading difficulties, active student responding, and inclusive practices.

Patty Bode is the director of art education at Tufts University in affiliation with the School of the Museum of Fine Arts, Boston. Her research focuses on multicultural education, urban art education, and the role of visual culture in K–12 art rooms.

Frederick Erickson is the George F. Kneller Professor of Anthropology of Education at the University of California, Los Angeles. His study and teaching focus on culture in education, video-based research on social interaction as a learning environment, and methods of qualitative data collection, analysis, and reporting.

Donna Y. Ford is professor in the special education program at Vanderbilt University. She has written numerous articles and four books on multicultural education and gifted education. Her work focuses on recruiting and retaining culturally diverse students in gifted education, creating culturally responsive learning environments, and improving student achievement.

Carl A. Grant is Hoefs-Bascom Professor of Teacher Education in the Department of Curriculum and Instruction at the University Wisconsin–Madison. His research focuses on multicultural education, teacher preparation, and urban schools in the global context.

Annette Henry is professor of multicultural education at the University of Washington, Tacoma. Her scholarship examines the practices of Black women teachers in the United States and Canada, as well as race, language, gender, and culture in sociocultural contexts of teaching and learning.

William L. Heward is professor emeritus of special education at The Ohio State University. His research focuses on increasing the effectiveness of group instruction, improving the academic success of students with disabilities in general education classrooms,

449

and promoting the generalization and maintenance of newly learned skills.

Charles H. Lippy is the LeRoy A. Martin Distinguished Professor of Religious Studies Emeritus at the University of Tennessee at Chattanooga. His interests in American religious life range widely with emphasis on current issues. He is coeditor of the forthcoming four-volume *Encyclopedia of Religion in America*.

Cris Mayo is associate professor in gender and women's studies and educational policy studies at the University of Illinois at Urbana-Champaign. Her publications in queer studies and philosophy of education include *Disputing the Subject of Sex: Sexuality and Public School Controversies*.

Luanna H. Meyer is director of the Jessie Hetherington Centre for Educational Research and professor of education (research) at Victoria University in Wellington, New Zealand. Her major research interests are inclusive education, student motivation, global mindedness, culturally responsive teaching, and positive interventions for challenging behavior.

Sonia Nieto is professor emerita of language, literacy, and culture at the University of Massachusetts, Amherst. She has written widely on multicultural education, teacher education, and the education of students with culturally and linguistically diverse backgrounds. She has taught at all levels and has received many awards for her research, advocacy, and service.

Hyun-Sook Park is professor of special education in the Connie L. Lurie College of Education at San Jose State University in California. Her major research interests are social relationships of students with disabilities, transition from school to work, global mindedness, special education for culturally and linguistically diverse students, and research methods.

Caroline Hodges Persell is professor of sociology at New York University. She is conducting research with Jean Yeung on racial disparities in educational achievement and is the author of many scholarly articles. Her books include *Preparing for Power: America's Elite Boarding Schools* (with Peter W. Cookson, Jr.) and *Education and Inequality*.

David Sadker is professor emeritus at American University and adjunct professor at the University of Arizona. He is the coauthor of seven books, including *Teach-*

ers, Schools, and Society and *Still Failing at Fairness*. He invites readers interested in gender issues, scholarships, and teacher awards to visit www.sadker.org.

Catherine Savage is senior lecturer in the School of Educational Psychology and Pedagogy at Victoria University of Wellington, New Zealand. Her research focuses on behavioral support and intervention in schools.

Janet Ward Schofield is professor of psychology and senior scientist at the University of Pittsburgh's Learning Research and Development Center. Her research focuses, which includes four books, on school desegregation, intergroup relations, and school technology use. She has served on the American Psychological Association (APA) Council of Representatives and National Academy of Sciences boards and committees.

Christine E. Sleeter is professor emerita of teacher education and multicultural education at California State University, Monterey Bay. Her research and writing focus on multicultural education and antiracist teacher education. Her most recent books include *Un-Standardizing Curriculum* and *Doing Multicultural Education for Achievement and Equity* (with Carl A. Grant).

Tom Stritikus is associate dean for academic programs and associate professor in the College of Education at the University of Washington, Seattle. His research examines the political, social, and cultural contexts that shape the education of culturally and linguistically diverse students. His work has been published in leading education journals.

Mary Kay Thompson Tetreault is provost emerita at Portland State University. Her most recent book (with Frances Maher) is *Privilege and Diversity in the Academy*. She is also the author (with Frances Maher) of *The Feminist Classroom* (2nd ed.).

Manka Varghese is assistant professor of language, literacy, and culture at the University of Washington, Seattle. Her research specialization is linguistic minority education in the United States with an emphasis on teacher education and development.

Karen Zittleman has taught in elementary and middle schools and at American University. She is the coauthor of *Teachers, Schools, and Society* and *Still Failing at Fairness*. Her academic interests focus on educational equity, teacher preparation, and contemplative education.

Photo Credits

Part I

Dynamic Graphics, Inc.
Mel Yates/PhotoDisc/Getty Images
PhotoDisc, Inc./Getty Images

Part II

Corbis Digital Stock
Creatas

Part III

PhotoDisc, Inc./Getty Images
PhotoDisc, Inc./Getty Images
Digital Vision
Dynamic Graphics, Inc.

Part IV

PhotoDisc, Inc./Getty Images
PhotoDisc, Inc./Getty Images
Dynamic Graphics, Inc.

Part V

Creatas
PhotoDisc, Inc./Getty Images
Richard T. Nowitz/Photo Researchers, Inc.

Part VI

Digital Vision
Purestock
Dynamic Graphics, Inc.

Index

Linguistic diversity, 286. *See also* Language
  diversity
  bilingual debate, 295–96
  dialect variation, 289–90
  indigenous languages, 289–90
  instructional programs, 294–95
  programmatic responses to, 294–97
  reality of, 296–97
  successful educational practice and, 296
Links, Inc., 423
Literacy, critical, 192
Little Richard, 235
Longue durée, 167
Lorde, Audre, 219
Lord's Prayer, 120
Low-income families, 5, 61, 86, 90, 91, 239,
  424–25
  statistics, 424–25
Lutherans, 111, 112, 114

Macroculture
  defined, 7
  microculture *versus,* 7–8
Magical consciousness, 68
Mainstream-centric curriculum, 233–36
Mainstreaming, 7, 331
  culture of, 347–48
  inclusion *versus,* 357
Maintenance bilingual education (MBE), 294
Male-defined curriculum, 159, 160–61
Males
  crime and, 148
  in crisis, 147–49
  sexism and, 140
  substance abuse and, 148
Management of ambition, 86
Mandarin, 290
Manifest curriculum, 23
Manifest Destiny, 10
Marriage, ending in divorce, 18
*Martin Luther King Junior Elementary School
  Children v. Ann Arbor School
  District,* 292
Mass movement, of people, 287
Mastery, 160, 171
Mathematics
  females and, 197
  tracking in, 94
Mayhew, Jonathan, 114
McClintoch, Barbara, 175
McCollum v. Board of Education, 120
McGowan v. Maryland, 118–19
McGuffey Readers, 113
Meaning, negotiation of, 300
Mennonites, 119
Mental retardation
  inappropriate labeling of students, 12–13,
    19

mild, 344
  as socially determined status, 13, 19
Meritocracy, 297
Methodists, 112, 115
Microcultures
  defined, 7
  family, 44
  macroculture *versus,* 7–8
  school as social system and, 25
  in United States, 11–13
Middle class, IQ scores of, 86, 89, 95
Middle-class students, educational structures
  for, 87–88
Mild mental retardation, 344
Miller, William, 117
Miner, Myrtilla, 138
Miner Normal School for Colored Girls, 138
Minersville School District v. Gobitis, 119
Minimal group paradigm, 4
Minority group, 184
Misdiagnosis, avoiding, 346–47
The Mismeasure of Man (Gould), 20, 89
Misogyny, 164
Model minority, 188, 347
Momaday, N. Scott, 244
Monroe, Marilyn, 234
Moral analysis, 246
Mormons, 116
Morphology, 298
Morrison, Toni, 244
Morton, Samuel, 375
Mount Holyoke, 138
Movement, 383
Multicultural assessment preparation, 382
Multicultural content
  guidelines for teaching, 249–52
  integration of, 249
Multicultural counseling, 386
Multicultural curriculum
  additive approach, 240–42
  contributions approach, 237–40
  efforts to establish, 236–37
  heroes/heroines, 238, 240
  institutionalization of, 237
  levels of integration of content, 237–49
  mixing and blending approaches, 248–49
  social action approach, 245–47
  transformation approach, 242–44
Multicultural curriculum reform
  approaches to, 233–56
  mainstream-centric curriculum, 233–36
  public sites and popular history, 235–36
Multicultural education, 66–67
  additive approach to, 240–42
  approaches to, 62–69
  as broad concept, 7
  conceptualizing, 1
  as counter-hegemonic, 46
  defined, 3

development of, 7
dimensions of, 20–22
gender minorities in, 209–30
heroes/heroines in, 238, 240
historical development, 6–7
human relations approach to teaching, 64
implementing by considering school as
  social system, 22–25, 23–25
as international reform movement, 5
LGBTQ issues and, 210–11
major goal of, 13
nature of, 3–4
need for school reform, 392–438
in New York City, 214
professional development in, 386
sample approach, 69–76
sexual minorities in, 209–30
single-group studies approach to
  teaching, 65–66
skills-based supports, 386
social justice approach to teaching, 245–47
sociopolitical definition of, 396
without stereotyping, 43
transformation approach to
  teaching, 242–44
Multicultural gifted curriculum, 384–86
  analysis-social action level, 384
  comprehension-transformation level, 384
  evaluation-social action level, 384
  Ford-Harris model, 385
  knowledge-contributions level, 384
Multicultural instruction, 383–84
Multiculturalism, LGBTQ movements
  and, 211–14
Multicultural issues, in special
  education, 343–68
Multicultural pedagogy, 46–47
Multicultural perspective
  conditions for systemic school reform
    with, 397–408
  of school reform, 396–97
Multicultural social justice education, 67–69
Multidimensionality, of data, 379
Multimodal data, 379
Music, African American, 244
Muslim Americans, 125. *See also* Arab
  Americans
Muslims, 125
Myrdal, Gunnar, 10–11

Naglieri Non-Verbal Abilities Test, 382
Naïve consciousness, 68
National Assessment of Educational Progress
  (NAEP), 148
National Association for the Advancement of
  Colored People (NAACP), 76, 429
National Council of Teachers of English, 143
National Council on Measurement in
  Education (NCME), 379